From Convent
to Concert Hall

From Convent to Concert Hall

A Guide to Women Composers

Edited by
SYLVIA GLICKMAN
and
MARTHA FURMAN SCHLEIFER

GREENWOOD PRESS
Westport, Connecticut • London

Library of Congress Cataloging-in-Publication Data

From convent to concert hall: a guide to women composers / edited by
Sylvia Glickman and Martha Furman Schleifer.
    p. cm.
  Includes bibliographical references (p.), discographies, and index.
  ISBN 1-57356-411-7 (alk. paper)
  1. Women composers. I. Glickman, Sylvia. II. Schleifer, Martha
Furman.
ML82.F76 2003
780'.92'2—dc21   2002035224

[B]

British Library Cataloguing in Publication Data is available.

Library of Congress Catalog Card Number: 2002035224
ISBN: 1-57356-411-7

First published in 2003

Greenwood Press, 88 Post Road West, Westport, CT 06881
An imprint of Greenwood Publishing Group, Inc.
www.greenwood.com

Printed in the United States of America

The paper used in this book complies with the
Permanent Paper Standard issued by the National
Information Standards Organization (Z39.48-1984).

10 9 8 7 6 5 4 3 2 1

Contents

Acknowledgments

We want to thank Donna Sanzone, formerly of the Oryx Press, for suggesting we write this book, and Anne Thompson, for shepherding its move to Greenwood Press. We are most appreciative of the continuing support of our families, especially our husbands, Dr. Harvey Glickman and Dr. Charles Schleifer.

Sylvia Glickman and
Martha Furman Schleifer

1

Introduction

Sylvia Glickman

> Even now at the start of the 21st century, decades after the
> dawn of the contemporary feminist movement saw a rise in
> women's orchestras and gender-based musicological studies
> and long after the inclusion of a single piece by a female
> composer on a concert program has ceased to be remarkable,
> a whole concert of music by women, performed by women,
> still feels unusual. It remains an exception to the classical
> music norm, which is a concert of music written entirely by
> men. — *Anne Midgette (2002)**

This volume brings together narratives of bold, independent women
who used their musical talent to forge a path through music history, a
path that has only recently been identified. Often supported by a mere
handful of contemporaries, women composers of the past battled prevailing cultural biases against recognition and were well-nigh ignored
by succeeding generations. However, buoyed by new scholarship and
today's social movement toward equality, the recognition of their creativity throughout history is emerging. The works of women composers
are now published and performed with a growing regularity, a trend set
in motion toward the end of the twentieth century.

From Convent to Concert Hall: A Guide to Women Composers leads the
reader through the study of a representative group of over 150 important women composers writing in the Western Art Music tradition from
the ninth century to the present. A guide to their lives and work, the
book can serve as a text for a "Women in Music 101" course; or the general reader may follow it simply as a tale of discovery. It integrates information culled from a wide variety of sources, and is designed as a loom
upon which to weave a pattern of information around biographies of selected composers, genres and styles of their music within a historical
perspective. The crescendo of women's opportunities and activities is reflected in the increased numbers of composers as the centuries progress.
Composers have been selected for discussion in depth using a variety of

criteria: available information and music (chapters two and three); large, representative output of major genres and styles of the period (chapter four); importance in musical life as both composers and performers (chapter five); significant attention earned via receipt of prizes and awards, and work in a broad range of styles including experimental genres and unusual performances (chapter six). The chapters are arranged chronologically by century, rather than by the period nomenclature found in typical music histories. Chapters 2–6 include bibliography, discography, and lists of selected modern editions of scores. A general bibliography and glossary are provided at the end of the book.

These women, chosen by the contributing authors and the editors, are the most important women composers of their times. Others are cited in the broader lists in the accompanying appendices, and in time lines within each chapter. These contain information about contemporaneous people and events in history and politics, science and education, the arts and literature, and music. Three appendices group composers a) by country and b) by century, and c) offer suggestions for a course syllabus.

Chapter 2: The Middle Ages and the Renaissance

This chapter examines the lives and work of the earliest women composers, describing significant creativity and achievement in both sacred and secular realms. Women who entered convents were educated and supported for life. Through participation in singing the daily Mass, nuns absorbed the traditional repertory that often inspired their own religious compositions. Secular women included the *trobairitz*, writers of poetry who sometimes composed music to accompany it. Despite the fact that the creative output of women of this time was largely undocumented, many composers inspired enough support from an inner circle of their contemporaries to ensure that their music survived, either as manuscripts or in early printed editions. It is these documents that have enabled us to rediscover the works of women, including the ninth-century Kassia, the now famous twelfth-century polymath Hildegard von Bingen, and the mysterious Aleotti/Aleotta duo.

Chapter 3: The Seventeenth Century

The music of this century began to take on a different look and sound. Marked by a blossoming of women musicians as both composers and performers (especially singers), earlier polyphony gave way to accompanied monody, and the rise of opera and oratorio presented opportunities for dramatic performances. Other new forms of the period included the cantata and purely instrumental suites and sonatas. Many nuns continued to write music, members of the well-educated nobility sang and played instruments for which they composed, and talented daughters of prominent male composers benefited from their fathers' teaching.

Fortunately, a great deal of music by women of this period was published and has survived, for few manuscript sources are known for them. The prolific Venetian Barbara

Strozzi published eight volumes of music containing over one hundred works of impressive quality and high emotional impact. Isabella Leonarda, the most widely published female of the century, produced a prodigious body of work published in twenty volumes containing over two hundred compositions, including the earliest trio sonatas (for two violins and continuo) published by a woman to have been preserved.

Chapter 4: The Eighteenth Century

The composers described in this chapter were all from the secular world and represent major genres and styles of composition which women employed in eighteenth-century Italy, France, the German-speaking lands, England, and North America. The rise of the bourgeoisie, industrialization, and the availability of music education, instruments, and educational musical materials created a rich musical life for amateur musicians. Professional women performed and composed for their own instruments before broadening their writing to include other genres. Chosen for inclusion by the quality of the available music, the importance of the composer in the musical life of her time, and the intrinsic interest of the details of her life and work to modern-day readers, these women wrote lieder, sonatas, variations sets, dances, chamber music, and concerti. The wide variety of women includes violinist Maddalena Lombardini Sirmen, Maria Theresia von Paradis, the blind prodigy performer and composer, and Josepha Barbara von Auernhammer, a pianist/composer/teacher who, unusual for this period, kept her maiden name after marriage.

Chapter 5: The Nineteenth Century

The expanding opportunities of the nineteenth century allowed an unprecedented number of women to achieve varying degrees of success as composers; therefore the selection in this chapter is representative rather than exhaustive. The availability of affordable instruments, especially the development of the modern piano, led to an era of amateur music-making in the home—a piano in every parlor—which increased the consumer base for teaching materials, and engaged larger, educated audiences for concert music.

Fanny Mendelssohn Hensel and Clara Wieck Schumann were the best-known female composers of the era, and their compositions continue to enjoy acclaim today. In addition, the choices they were forced to make by their differing status in society make them intriguing case studies. Other women of note were the political revolutionary Johanna Kinkel, the women's rights activist Ethel Smyth, and the first group of women composers in America, including Amy Marcy Cheney Beach, known as the "Dean of American Women Composers" during her lifetime.

Chapter 6: The Twentieth Century

Hundreds of women have worked as composers in the twentieth century. Selections here were made with two canonic principles in mind: first, an introduction to the most well-known figures (e.g.: prize-winners Zwilich, Tower, Ran and Wagner), and second, an inclusiveness that displays a breadth of style. As with male composers of the twentieth century, this was a period of vast experimentation, coupled with developments and advances of the discipline. The goal of including at least one composer of note from each of the major schools, genres, and "isms" of twentieth-century classical music and its closest neighbors produces chapter subtitles ranging from "The Last of the Pre-moderns" and "Romantic Nationalism," to "Sound Installation," "Performance Art," and "Postmodernism." Composer names intermingle the more familiar: Laurie Anderson, Violet Archer, Lili Boulanger and Ruth Crawford Seeger, with the lesser known Lucia Dlugoszewski, Violeta Dinescu, Adriana Hölszky and Julia Perry. The extended boundaries of producing sound and listening with technology via the computer, electro-acoustic compositions and sound installations have also expanded performance sites to include informal and unusual places.

A portrait of a civilization is painted with many brushes—depicting its history, geography, politics, sciences, religions, and arts. When a significant portion of the population is omitted, a skewed picture emerges. Women composers have been absent from survey books about music until recently; where they are included, their numbers and information about them remain scanty. Despite the recent expansion of attention in journals, dissertations, conferences, performances, dictionaries, encyclopedias, general books, and biographies, women musicians, especially composers, remain distinctly marginal.

This problem not only is found in the discipline of music but is part of a broader global realization. Historian Bernard Lewis quotes the Ottoman Turkish writer Namîk Kemal in 1867 on the subject of women's rights in the Middle East:

> Our women…constitute half and perhaps more than half of our species. Preventing them from contributing to the sustenance and improvement of others by means of their efforts infringes the basic rules of cooperation to such a degree that our national society is stricken like a human body that is paralyzed on one side.

Women were denied public musical education equal to that for men until the twentieth century; opportunities for hearing their own music were also restricted; their works were rarely acknowledged or anthologized. Despite this, more than 6,000 women who composed music since the ninth century have now been identified. Their music has withstood the test of time, and is now in the process of rediscovery.

Setting the Scene

In 1895 American pianist/composer Florence Sutro described searching music stores to find books on women composers. Most salesmen smiled and gently explained that there were no such books because there were no such people. In 1917 an anonymous article entitled "Why Women Cannot Compose" appeared in New Haven, Connecticut, under the auspices of the Yale Publication Association. The title is explained by remarks in the text, such as "lack of native ability," "musical talent is hereditary and is usually inherited by boys," and "women are not listed in *Grove's Dictionary of Music and Musicians*, and that proves that they are of no significance."

Over a half century ago, Sophie Drinker published *Music and Women, the Story of Women in Their Relation to Music* (1948). She could find no music composed by women for her women's chorus in Philadelphia to sing in the late 1920s, but she discovered a book by George Upton entitled *Women in Music* (1880). However, it depicted females only as friends, relatives, and inspirers of famous male musicians. Drinker spent twenty more years in research. She produced a pathbreaking volume, an anthropological, socio-logical, and psychological study that begins with rock paintings and legends about mu-sical acts of goddesses and other feminine spirits and continues through the nuns of the Middle Ages, twelfth- and thirteenth-century troubadours (*trobairitz*), through nineteenth-century prima donnas, to composers in the first half of the twentieth cen-tury. Drinker concludes that "women's silence in musical expression is...due to his-torical causes that have brought about a non-permissive environment for the woman musician."

Three inquiries in recent years pose pertinent questions. In the earliest one in 1987, Diane Jezic and Daniel Binder queried, "...Benign Neglect of Women Composers?" A survey of fourteen music appreciation texts published between 1979 and 1985 shows that 28 percent cited no women composers, over 50 percent named only one or none, and only five of the fourteen texts included names of three or more women composers. Mixing pop music women with classical composers, one finds three citations each for Joni Mitchell, Thea Musgrave, and Clara Schumann; Joan Baez, Carole King, Amy Beach, Miriam Gideon, and Pauline Oliveros receive two citations each; and single mentions show up for Hildegard von Bingen, Germaine Tailleferre, Francesca Caccini, Ruth Crawford, Elisabeth-Claude Jacquet de la Guerre, Janis Joplin, and Judy Collins. Where Clara Schumann is mentioned, it is only as the wife of Robert, as a wonderful pianist, and as an inspiration for Brahms.

In reviewing forty-seven music history textbooks published between 1947 and 1985, Jezic and Binder found that twelve did not include a single woman composer, seventeen named one or two, and twelve texts included one or more paragraphs on women composers, limited to American or twentieth-century women. Behind the sheer statistics, the texts project the "great man/great works" view. One great genius followed another, all of them male, writing music "typical" of the period. In fact, however, many of the composers were cited because their music was unusual. Jezic and Binder assert that the omission of women extends to editors and publishers as well.

In the second inquiry Georgia Peeples and Jennifer Holz revisited the textbook scene with "Where Are We Now?" (2001). Limiting their research to the Classic-Romantic period (1750–1900), they examined four music history texts and three music appreciation texts. The small numbers of women composers whom they found and the minimal growth in their inclusion during fourteen years of feminist musical activity reflect a bleak picture. While Grout and Palisca's sixth edition of *History of Western Music*

(2001) contains fourteen women in music from the Classic-Romantic period, only five are composers. (Donald J. Grout's prominent *History of Western Music*, first published in the 1960s, did not contain a single woman composer in its original edition. The 1980 edition contained two women composers, and the 1996 edition included a total of thirteen women in all centuries, twelve from the Classic-Romantic period.) Reinhard G. Pauly's *Music in the Classic Period* increased its mention of women from six in the 1965 edition to nineteen (including six composers) in the 2000 edition. In Rey M. Longyear's *Nineteenth-Century Romanticism in Music* (1969) citations of women increased from three to eleven in 1988 (eight composers).

Peeples and Holz's inspection of music appreciation texts reveals that Joseph Machlis and Kristine Forney's eighth edition of *Enjoyment of Music* (1999) names eighteen women (ten composers); Roger Kamien's seventh edition of *Music: An Appreciation* expanded from two women earlier to five (three composers) and cites several other women as talented wives of male composers. Joseph and Vivian Kerman's fourth edition of *Listen* contains five women (three composers). In contrast, a poster entitled "Notable Women Composers," prepared by the Hildegard Publishing Company in 1994, offers 391 names, including ninety-four women born between 1750 and 1900.

Not all editors and publishers have continued to ignore women. Macmillan/Norton issued *The New Grove Dictionary of Women Composers* in 1994. G. K. Hall is in the process of issuing *Women Composers: Music Through the Ages*, a multivolume anthology of music and articles. Several new publishing companies are dedicated to advancing the work of women composers by focusing solely on their music. These books and publications, however, are completely devoted to women and are, for the most part, authored by women. Their aim is to draw attention to the woman composer's existence and excellence so that the music becomes mainstreamed (i.e., printed and performed without reference to gender). Even today this remains an uphill battle. The Philadelphia Orchestra recently devoted an entire season to "twentieth-century music" to celebrate its own centenary. Not a single work by a woman composer appeared on the repertoire list, although this orchestra does sometimes program music by women.

In the third inquiry, "Eve…Blowing in Our Ears?…" (2001), Suzanne G. Cusick questions twentieth-century music scholarship on women. She describes her journey through eighty-five years of the *Musical Quarterly* (first edition 1915), and reports that articles on women rarely appeared. When they did, the women were described as doomed to "categorical failure to achieve excellence in music" or, in the case of Pauline Garcia-Viardot and Clara Wieck Schumann, portrayed as "musical humans understood as interesting associates of canonic male composers, but not as figures to be studied in their own right." Cusick ascribes the new scholarship (mostly by women) to the recrudescence of feminism in the 1970s and the establishment of new organizations, new books, and new networking.

A survey of 195 American and foreign competitions in instrumental and vocal performance, conducting, and composition (Glickman 1991) investigated the proportion of participating women, the numbers of women winners, and a comparison of these numbers with those of male participants. The results demonstrate that women consistently placed behind men in all competitions, except in competitions for sopranos. When year-by-year findings were analyzed with reference to concurrent political activity in the women's movement (e.g., the founding of the National Organization for Women [NOW], the passage of Title IX legislation, and efforts to pass the Equal Rights Amendment [ERA] in the 1970s and 1980s), remarkably, women's accomplishment in musical competitions improved; they won more prizes. When the ERA was defeated in 1982, women's achievements declined to a level only slightly above that in 1967.

The latest edition of *The New Grove Dictionary of Music and Musicians* appeared in 2001, both in print and on-line. Of the 12,191 musicians listed in this multivolume reference, 578 (less than 5 percent) are women.

Historical Perspective

We now have found music by women composers dating back to the ninth century. Christine Ammer (1980) describes the proper climate for a creative artist's production and participation in society: access to education, financial stability, time, encouragement, acceptance by society, and survival of the creation. To these, we add talent. Exploring the lives of women composers through these elements demonstrates that:

- talent is, in all cases, a given;
- access to education has varied through the ages, and today in the West it is equal to that for men;
- financial stability for women composers is attained in a variety of ways;
- time to create is dependent on a woman's domestic and financial position;
- encouragement by an inner circle is necessary for initial support and continuing psychological strength;
- acceptance by society permits performances, publication, inclusion in histories, and competition honors;
- survival of the music depends on all of the above, especially publication.

Talent

Talent may be inherited but is not reserved only for male descendants. For example, composers Francesca and Settimia Caccini (sixteenth century) were the daughters of composer Giulio Caccini; eighteenth-century Clara Wieck Schumann's father was a musician, as were both parents of Anna Bon. Fanny Mendelssohn Hensel (nineteenth century) and her brother Felix shared a genetic heritage. Examples of mother–daughter composer families include Julianne Benda Reichardt and Louise Reichardt (eighteenth century), Pauline Garcia-Viardot and Louise Héritte-Viardot (nineteenth century), and Elizabeth Maconchy and her daughter Nicola Lefanu (twentieth century). Other female connections are seen in the Lebrun-Danzi-Dülcken women, the Krumpholtz family, and the Dussek-Corri-Bulkley-Cianchettini family (all eighteenth to nineteenth century).

Access to Education

The earliest music education of women occurred in convents and courts and later in conservatories called *ospedali*. The latter institutions hired male teachers, such as the composer Antonio Vivaldi, who instructed and composed several hundred instrumental concerti for the resident women. In the seventeenth century education for women continued in the *ospedali*; boys were trained in choir schools associated with churches. In the eighteenth century the availability of music education, instruments, and didactic materials enabled women to study music in the secular world, but they were not permitted to study theory or composition. Members of royalty, the aristocracy, and the wealthy studied with professional musicians. Women, who often studied music for an "accomplishment," were encouraged primarily to sing or play the piano but not instruments that were deemed "unladylike." As the number of conservatories increased throughout Europe and America during the early and mid-nineteenth century, some accepted women students, but only as instrumentalists. Where some women had earlier studied composition privately with male teachers, by the end of the century they were finally permitted to receive comprehensive musical education (including theory and composition). The breakdown of all barriers to women in conservatories occurred in the twentieth century.

Financial Stability

Before the seventeenth century women musicians either remained in the convent or achieved financial stability as performers, through family or patronage support, or as members of the aristocracy or the moneyed classes. The seventeenth century saw the rise of professional musicians: singers and instrumentalists, teachers, and publishers. The nobility maintained orchestras and singers at court, thereby creating jobs. In the eighteenth and nineteenth centuries women performed, composed, and taught privately. Some were still hired as court musicians (although the eighteenth-century Emilie Zumsteeg was not allowed to follow her father's position at the Württenberg court because of her gender).

Today women perform (as soloists, chamber musicians, orchestral musicians), compose, teach, research, edit, write, are music librarians, and publish music. In *Unsung* (1980), Christine Ammer stated that "today women students outnumber men in most conservatories. In America, more women than men teachers are trained; fewer are employed; more are part-time than full-time, and those employed are at lower rank. When over 50 percent of all American women are now in the work-force, surely something other than lack of ability must be keeping them out" (echoes of Sophie Drinker). Complete equality remains elusive.

Although women make up the majority of instrumental students in most conservatories in the United States today, they do not win the majority of orchestra jobs. Auditions are frequently held behind screens, and women applicants wear soft footwear to hide feminine footsteps. In unscreened finals when they are "unmasked," few are hired for first desk positions. The picture is even more unwelcoming in Europe, where some orchestras do not even allow women to audition (Osborne 1996). Universities now employ women; however, recent College Music Society studies report that women are still hired preponderantly at lower levels in higher education, and few have the opportunity to become mentors to younger women.

Time to Create

In *Silences* (1979) Tillie Olsen sadly opens an essay with the words, "As I stand here ironing." Describing the problems of those "non-privileged" people (read "women") who are driven to create but are frustrated by lack of time, quiet space, financial freedom, and encouragement and are thwarted by society's indifference or neglect, Olsen describes the plight of frustrated women writers (read "composers" as well). She describes three categories of women who in the past were able to find time to fulfill musical or artistic creativity:

1. those who never married or married late,
2. married women with no children, and
3. those with children who had households with servants.

Many composers had children but stopped writing when they were born (e.g., Ruth Crawford Seeger) or supported them with performing fees (e.g., Clara Schumann and Maria Szymanowska). The question of time to create involves much more than putting notes on paper; it requires musical gestation time as well.

Encouragement

Because women historically have been inhibited by a combination of the ambivalence of society and their own internal conflicts, encouragement by an inner circle (family or contemporaneous musicians) plays a crucial role in their lives. Female composers often drew strength from supportive, musical fathers and other important musical mentors, and mother–daughter and sister pairings are found throughout history. Some women feel that professional success, which enhances a man's identity, is a threat to their own identity. The need to develop the mastery and assertion necessary for artistic creation conflicts with their contrary wish for the security and protection that feeds their sense of femininity.

Clara Schumann wrote in her diary on November 26, 1839, "a woman must not wish to compose—there never was one able to do it. Am I intended to be the one? It would be arrogant to believe that....May Robert always create: that must always make me happy" (Reich 1985).

Amy Beach, in an interview in *Étude* magazine, said, "activities I love are writing, [studying] the piano, and [I am] very interested in housekeeping" (Armstrong 1904).

Barbara Kolb distinguishes the activities thus: "composing a piece of music is very feminine. It is sensitive, emotional, contemplative. By comparison, doing house work is positively masculine" (1975).

And Thea Musgrave avers, as quoted by Kyle Gann (1997), "Music is a human art, not a sexual one. Sex is no more important than eye color."

Acceptance

Women composers of the earliest extant music were rarely acknowledged in early society; chant composers were often "anonymous." Music by nuns was sometimes preserved by their church or convent, enabling us to find the works of Kassia (ninth century) and Hildegard (twelfth century) in the twentieth century. Other pieces by women were included in rare anthologies, and a few nuns, like Vizzana and Assandra (both sixteenth century), saw their music published during their lifetime. In the seventeenth century women wrote music for the choirs they directed, for the opera houses in which they sang, for the court appointments they held, and for the appearances they made as instrumentalists (e.g., de la Guerre, seventeenth century).

The expanded opportunities for women in eighteenth-century musical life included lavish performances at court, musical salons in the homes of the wealthy, and the emergence of public concerts. They composed for soloists and small ensembles and often were the performers of their own works. In rare circumstances some were fortunate in acquiring the patronage of a famed musician (e.g., Auernhammer and Mozart in the eighteenth century), a poet (e.g., Martines and Metastasio in the eighteenth century), or a royal personage (e.g., Paradis and Empress Maria Theresa in the eighteenth century).

The woman composer who was easily accepted by society and by other musicians in the early nineteenth century was exceptional. Nineteenth-century society was ambivalent; composing was deemed a "masculine," unladylike activity. German conductor and pianist Hans von Bülow stated that "reproductive genius can be admitted to the pretty sex, but productive genius unconditionally cannot." While this era of progress accepted new aesthetic ideals, genres, forms, and styles, and women composed program music and character pieces as men did, it was as performers that women made their musical mark in this century. Virtuoso traveling singers and pianists were acclaimed and, as in the previous century, often played their own compositions. It was still unusual for a woman to hear her large compositions performed.

In the twentieth century, acceptance began to grow—slowly. William Schuman won the first Pulitzer Prize awarded for musical composition in 1943. Forty years later, in 1983, Ellen Taaffe Zwilich won the first Pulitzer Prize in composition awarded to a woman. It took only eight years for another woman, Shulamit Ran, to win and eight more years for Melinda Wagner to receive a Pulitzer Prize in 1999. Works by women composers were programmed more frequently in the last quarter of the century, but mostly by groups devoted to promoting this repertoire. Programming by major large music organizations is still infrequent. Publication opportunities for women by mainstream publishers have improved, sometimes inspired by the activities of other publishers who primarily are devoted to promoting women. Inclusion in mainstream histories and competition opportunities, as previously seen, still leaves much room for improvement.

Survival of the Music

For any historical period, survival of music depends on publication (print and recording) so that it will endure and be (re-) discovered and circulated. Publication depends on acceptance by at least one element of society—the publisher (who must believe in the product). Unless an inner circle of encouragement supports a composer, there will be no product. Unless the composer has time to create (and time to think and even to try and fail), there will be nothing to encourage. Time depends on financial stability; the composer needs access to education, and for the education to be meaningful, there needs to be a talent to be fed. We have come full circle.

> The eye delights in new sensation. Not so the ear, which seeks patterns and is grateful for repetition. If in hearing a new piece the ear does not recognize a familiar structure or pattern, the listener is prevented from participating and responding and so is unable to find the significance or meaning of the whole....Only as the patterns and relationships become familiar does the music itself become evocative and significant. This is why most people go to concerts to hear a beautiful performance of music that they know. (Janet Baker-Carr in Ammer, 2001)

And this is why music by women must be programmed and reprogrammed until its very familiarity supports its journey to equality.

* Bibliography for this chapter is incorporated into the General Bibliography.

2

The Middle Ages and the Renaissance

Martha Furman Schleifer

Introduction

> [T]he women should keep silence in the churches. For they are not permitted to speak, but should be subordinate, as even the law says. If there is anything they desire to know, let them ask their husbands at home. For it is shameful for a woman to speak in church. — *I. Corinthians 14: 34–35*

Written around the year 54 by Saint Paul, these sentences prohibited women from singing in church for many centuries. Cloistered nuns circumvented this restriction not only by singing but also by composing sacred music. Women also composed secular works and supported the arts during the Middle Ages and the Renaissance.

The Middle Ages, also known as the Dark Ages, extended from the collapse of the Roman Empire (ca. 450) to the beginning of the Renaissance (ca. 1450). The Roman Catholic Church, where most composers and musicians were trained and employed and their music preserved, dominated this period. Plainchant, the official music of the church, enhanced the sacred texts used in various church services. The chants commonly were unaccompanied, monophonic, without fixed meter or rhythm, based on medieval modes, and varied from simple recitations to complex songs depending on their function and place in services. The music is also known as Gregorian chant in honor of Pope Gregory I (ca. 540–604), who is credited with assembling and organizing the chants.

Chant composers were often anonymous, and some scholars argue that "anonymous" may have been a woman. Some of these women, however, were recognized during their lifetimes. Kassia, a Byzantine nun discussed later in this chapter, composed the earliest extant music by an identifiable woman. Hildegard von Bingen, a German nun who wrote music based on her own texts, is also discussed in depth, along with other composers of sacred music.

During the Middle Ages some noblewomen were tutored at home or in monastic schools. Their education generally included music. As kings and their courts solidified their political power, noblemen and noblewomen became patrons of the arts. Many secular court songs written by troubadours, *trouvères*, and minnesingers have been found. However, music by only one woman troubadour, the Comtessa de Dia, has survived, and few women *trouvères* have been identified.

During the Renaissance (ca. 1450–1600) the motet was the sacred genre most commonly written by nun composers. It is generally an unaccompanied choral composition based on a sacred Latin text, for four to six or more voice parts, alternating homophonic and polyphonic passages.

The madrigal, originating in Italy in the 1520s, became so popular between 1530 and 1600 that about 2,000 collections were published. The madrigal eventually broadened in concept and style, and by the late sixteenth century it was the dominant genre of secular music. A musical setting of a single-stanza poem using a free rhyme scheme, it was intended for a group of solo singers—amateur or professional—in four to six parts. Madrigals are usually unaccompanied, shifting in texture from polyphonic to homophonic, and include many experimental techniques such as chromaticism, dissonance, and word-painting. Some are complex, and others are simpler in texture. Composers of the time endeavored to create sensitive, intensely expressive musical settings of carefully selected words by well-known poets of the day.

Greek and Roman literature dominated learning during this period, and, according to Karin Pendle: "The Renaissance Man was to be not a specialist but a generalist, one who had absorbed the best ideas of classical civilization in order to enhance his own humanity....The humanistic view of life...was shared largely by the monied, the titled, the male." Another scholar, Joan Kelly, writes

> that there was no "renaissance" for women—at least not during the Renaissance. There was, on the contrary, a marked restriction of the scope and powers of women....Renaissance ideas on love and manners, more classical than medieval, and almost exclusively a male product, expressed this new subordination of women to the interests of husbands and male-dominated kin groups and served to justify the removal of women from an "unladylike" position of power....Noblewomen...were increasingly removed from public concerns—economic, political, and cultural...the noblewoman [was molded] into an aesthetic object: decorous, chaste, and...dependent.

Two important religious movements, the Reformation and Counter-Reformation, occurred during the Renaissance. The Reformation began in 1517, when Martin Luther protested certain practices of the Roman Catholic Church. Before this, Europe was dominated by the Catholic Church. Afterward, many Protestant churches vied for the allegiance of worshipers. The Reformation engendered the Counter-Reformation movement and its resulting reforms within the Catholic Church, developed during the meetings of the Council of Trent.

Prior to the Council of Trent (held between 1545 and 1563) religious communities for women could be open or cloistered; women chose whether or not to take vows. The work of the council attempted to counteract effects of the Protestant Reformation and to redefine Catholic beliefs. As Katherine Gill writes, "At the end of the sixteenth century, in the wake of the Council of Trent, 'open monasteries' were subjects of hot debate at the papal court....Pius V [reigned 1566–1572] more or less ended [the debate] with the bull *Circa Pastoralis* which decreed universal imposition of *clausura* [enclosure] on women's [religious] communities." Nuns became unseen, veiled and cloistered. As Craig A. Monson writes in *Disembodied Voices*, "the nun becomes an invisible voice...the invisible singer."

Rules instituted in Italy ca. 1580 and enforced for the next 150 years were intended to keep groups of singing nuns hidden. Within the inner choir, a section physically screened from the central part of the church, soloists were permitted to sing religious music accompanied by the organ. The rule of *clausura* was eventually applied to convent organs also, requiring that the instruments facing the main sections of churches be removed. A variety of schemes, such as building a large instrument that could be heard in the outer church, adding extra instruments that would sound through the grillwork, using the Baroque art of monody (singing by a single accompanied voice), and *concertato* (contrast of the hidden nuns with secular musicians in the outer church) were used by the musical and resourceful nuns to circumvent the restrictions imposed on them.

Outside music teachers were forbidden to enter the convents, and the Council of Trent even argued against the use of polyphonic music, because the complex multiple melodic lines often rendered the text difficult to understand; it finally decided that such music could be used in church if texts were not obscured. However, since polyphony was also considered sensuous and stimulating to women, only plainchant was permitted in the convents. Despite these limitations, music flourished in some convents, possibly because the local authorities not only permitted but also even encouraged it.

Most nun composers wrote a small amount of music, often before taking their final vows, and then disappeared from the musical scene. Limitations placed on the nuns and the need for permission to publish from the convent, the order, and the bishop presented additional obstacles to their creativity.

In Venice four foundations called *ospedali* were established in which women were trained as musicians. The Ospedale degl'Incurabili (Hospice for the Chronically Ill) was founded by 1522. It initially took in syphilitics, then orphans and reformed prostitutes, and finally it became a boarding school for young girls of poor, noble and citizen classes. The Ospedale della Pietà (House of Mercy) was founded by 1336 to care for abandoned infants, who could remain there for their lifetime. The Ospedale di Santa Maria dei Dereletti ai Santi Giovanni e Paolo (St. Mary's Home for Waifs Annexed to the Ospedale di Santi Giovanni e Paolo) was founded in 1528 as a collection point for street children, according to Jane Baldauf-Berdes. The Ospedale di San Lazaro e dei Mendicanti

(Home of Saint Lazare and the Mendicants (beggars) was founded by 1182 (then re-structured in 1595) as a refuge for Crusaders. A leper colony in the thirteenth century, toward the end of the sixteenth century it became a welfare foundation. The *ospedali* had separate children's departments and established schools mainly for the teaching of re-ligion, but also for other subjects, including music. (More information concerning these institutions is included in Chapters 3 and 4.)

This chapter presents the stories of the nun composers, secular composers, and no-blewomen who composed and sponsored and encouraged music as patrons of the arts.

Composers of the Middle Ages

Nuns

The life of **Kassia (ca. 810–before 867)** exemplifies the indomitable character, inner strength, and independence of women composers throughout history. Born about 810 in the Byzantine-Greek Empire, she is the most prominent woman composer and poet from the Byzantine Era whose music has been preserved. However, as Diane Tou-liatos states:

> Kassia is by no means the only medieval [from the Middle Ages] Greek woman composer. Following a legacy of Greek women composers from Antiquity (for example, Pythia of Delphi; Telesilla of Argos; Sappho of Lesbos; Polygnota, daughter of Socrates of Thebes; and the daughter of Aristocrates of Cyme), she is joined by a sisterhood of other Byzantine women composers such as Martha, mother of Symeon the Stylite; Theodosia; Thekla; Kouvouklisena; Palae-ologina; and the daughter of Ioannes Kladas [name unknown]. Of these women composers, music has been preserved from Byzantine times for only Kassia and the daughter of Ioannes Kladas.

Kassia was well educated in Greek classical literature and the Bible, as was cus-tomary for young women from aristocratic families. She was considered the most likely choice to be the bride of Emperor Theophilos (r. 830–842), not only because of her ex-ceptional intellect but also for her great beauty. According to Byzantine tradition, the empress was selected in a "brideshow," an event where potential brides, young women who met the highest standards of physical attractiveness and intelligence, were dis-played before the ruler, who signified his choice by presenting a golden apple to one of the women. Theophilos was especially interested in Kassia and commented to her that a woman was the "source of all man's tribulation" (referring to Eve). Kassia retorted (alluding to the Virgin Mary), "And from a woman sprang the course of man's regen-eration." In the patriarchal society of the Middle Ages, where the sins of Eve were con-sidered transferred to all women, even an aristocratic woman was expected to be obedient and remain silent. Kassia's witty response was considered insulting, and the offended emperor did not select her to be his wife.

While this story gives insight into Kassia's strong and independent personality, another example of her unconventional behavior was her decision to join a large group of women and clergymen who risked imprisonment and even martyrdom in defense of the Orthodox tradition of worshiping religious icons in the church, a practice vigorously opposed by the imperial court. Kassia was persecuted and whipped for her active participation. Her rejection by the emperor made marriage an unlikely possibility, and Kassia, a very devout Christian, chose to become a nun. Founding her own cloistered convent around 843, she remained as abbess of the strict order until she died.

Kassia was a gifted poet who produced 261 secular verses, many dealing with moral issues. She was even better known for her sacred poems on topics such as the Virgin Mary, various saints, and Christian martyrs, including a number of women. Kassia set her own poems (and those of others) as monophonic chants sung primarily during the morning and evening services at the convent. The exact number of her chants is not known, but twenty-three works are accepted as genuine, and twenty-six others are possibly hers. Most of her music is in the category of *sticheron*, long verses chanted in various parts of the morning and evening offices. *The Fallen Woman*, Kassia's most admired hymn, is considered a masterpiece. Written about Mary Magdalene, it is printed in many books of Greek poetry and is still sung during the morning Office of Holy Wednesday in the Orthodox Church. More recent composers have also been attracted to this hymn, making their own arrangements and sometimes adding harmonizing voice parts.

Unlike the music of most of her male contemporaries, Kassia's works have survived. Although manuscripts from her own era are not extant, her chants are preserved in documents dating back to the eleventh century and housed in a monastery outside Athens. The manuscripts were discovered and transcribed into modern notation by Diane Touliatos. Their originality and beauty, their strong affirmation of faith and expression of human emotions, and their imaginative coordination of the music with the text contributed to Kassia's fame after her death. Kassia's name, her hymns, and even her picture appear in a number of religious documents and in the historical chronicles of the Byzantine Empire. Although not the only Byzantine woman to compose chants and write religious poetry, she is the only one to have had her work accepted by the church and included in both past and current liturgical volumes of the Eastern Orthodox Church.

Composer, poet, visionary, and healer, the politically astute Benedictine nun **Hildegard von Bingen (1098–1179)** was born in the German village of Bermersheim. The daughter of Hildebert von Bermersheim and his wife, Machtild, Hildegard's extraordinary accomplishments in male-dominated Germany in the twelfth century world were astounding. The tenth child from a family of minor nobility, the sickly Hildegard was given as a tithe to the religious community at Disibodenberg at the age of eight. Jutta von Spanheim, a noblewoman who had become a recluse, cared for Hildegard's special spiritual needs. Hildegard began to have visions as a very young child: "In the third year of my life I saw so great a brightness that my soul trembled; yet because of my infant condition I could express nothing of it. But in my eighth year I was of-

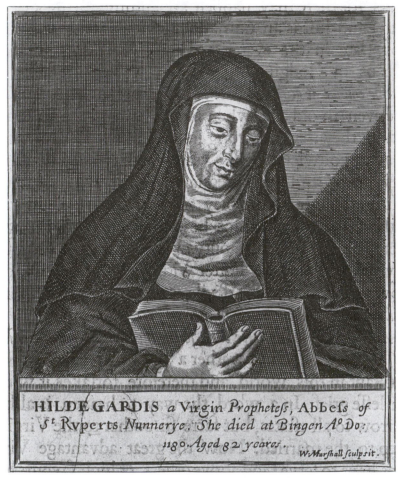

Hildegard von Bingen.
Hulton|Archive by Getty Images.

fered to God, given over to a spiritual way of life" (translated from Peter Dronke in *Women Writers* by Marianne Richert Pfau in "Hildegard von Bingen"). There is speculation that some of Hildegard's lifelong physical ailments were caused by migraine headaches. In a letter written at the age of seventy-five she described what she called the *umbra viventis lucis* (the reflection of the Living Light): "From my early childhood...I have always seen this vision in my soul...I see [visions] wide awake, day and night. And I am constantly fettered by sickness and often in the grip of pain so intense that it threatens to kill me" (Dronke).

Hildegard took vows as a nun in 1112. She studied first with Jutta and then with Volmar of Disibodenberg, the confessor to the women in the convent. Normally, as *magistra* (mistress or teacher), Jutta would have taught Hildegard to read basic Latin in order to chant the Psalter. However, Hildegard claimed that she had

scarcely any knowledge of letters, as an uneducated woman [Jutta] had taught her...; the main purpose of her...self-deprecation, however, was not to belittle herself or comment on the faults of her early training but to emphasize that the source of her revelations was divine, not human. Without this indispensable claim to prophesy, her career as a writer and preacher would have been unthinkable. (Newman in *Voice of the Living Light*)

Initially, Hildegard shared her visions only with Jutta. When Jutta died in 1136, Hildegard, then in her late thirties, was elected *magistra* of the order and soon confided in Volmar:

> I was forced by a great pressure of pains to manifest what I had seen and heard. But I was much afraid... I indicated this to a monk who was my *magister*.... Astonished, he bade me write these things down secretly, till he could see what they were and what their source might be. Then, realizing that they came from God, he indicated this to me, with great eagerness. (Dronke/Pfau)

Volmar remained Hildegard's secretary and friend until he died in 1173. The monk Gottfried then began writing the *Vita Sanctae Hildegardis* (Life of St. Hildegard), a biography interspersed with autobiographical sections, assuming that her community would propose her as a saint. Gottfried died before Hildegard, and the monk Theodoric of Echternach was commissioned to finish the *Vita* several years later. Newman notes in *Voice of the Living Light* that Theodoric

> made an extraordinary choice: he decided to fill book 2 of the *Vita* with memoirs that Hildegard herself had dictated to help her earlier biographer, interspersing his own awed if sometimes uncomprehending comments.... [and he] tried to fit her life into the stereotyped pattern of female sanctity fashionable in his own age.

(*Vita* is the primary source of information concerning Hildegard's life, particularly the period 1141–1155, when, at the age of forty-three, she received the divine command to prophesy and record her visions. Other sources include her letters, prefaces to her books, and documents concerning her monasteries.)

In 1141 Hildegard started her first book, *Scito vias Domini*, called *Scivias* (Know the Ways of the Lord), after receiving a vision from God commanding, "Write what you see and hear! Tell people how to enter the kingdom of salvation" (Fox, *Hildegard von Bingen's Mystical Visions*). Although unfinished, the book received support from Pope Eugenius III, whose declaration in 1147 that Hildegard's visions were not heretical brought her more fame, disciples, and independence. Hildegard stated:

> With joy [Eugenius] had [my visions] read out in [the] presence of many people and read them for himself, and with great trust in God's grace, sending me his blessing... bade me commit whatever I saw or heard in my vision to writing. (Dronke, *Women Writers*)

As Hildegard's fame as a visionary spread, more women joined her order. In 1148 she asked permission to move her followers from Disibodenberg to Rupertsberg, a location that she claimed had been revealed to her in a vision. When Kuno, the abbot of

Disibodenberg, refused consent for the move, Hildegard became very ill, recovering only after the abbot capitulated. John Van Engen writes: "For the monks [the move] meant potentially the loss of a visionary of growing fame, of recluses with strong ties to the local nobility, and of the material gifts [dowries, including cash and land] they had brought to the house." The community finally relocated in 1155, thereby gaining financial and political independence. In 1158, at the age of sixty, Hildegard made the first of four preaching tours; three by boat along the Main, Moselle, and Rhine Rivers and the fourth by land into Swabia, a medieval duchy in southwestern Germany. Around 1165 Hildegard founded a daughterhouse (a companion convent) across the Rhine River at Eibingen, where her order remains today.

Hildegard's literary works include three books containing her visions: *Scivias*, completed in 1151; *Liber vitae meritorum* (Book of Life's Merits), written between 1158 and 1163; and *De Operatione Dei* (Book of Divine Works), completed about 1173–1174. The preface to her *Liber vitae meritorum* lists a previous book entitled *Subtilitates diversarum naturarum creaturarum* (Subtleties of the Different Natures of Creatures). Although this book has not survived, two other medical texts have: *Physica* or *Liber simplicis medicinae* (Book of Simple Medicine) and *Liber compositae medicinae* (Book of Compound Medicine), also called *Causae et curae* (Causes and Cures). Hildegard's simple cures were remedies that employed a single ingredient; her compounds employed many ingredients, some difficult to find. Other books include *The Life of St. Rupert, The Life of St. Disibod*, and *Subtleties*. She also developed her own language called *Lingua ignota* (Unknown Language), containing almost 1,000 imaginary nouns and a secret alphabet. Hildegard may also have been an illustrator. Madeline Caviness contends "Perhaps the strongest argument for Hildegard's direct involvement in the designs that appeared in finished form in the Rupertsberg *Scivias* manuscript is based on features that have long been recognized as reflections of the visual disturbances typically associated with migraine attacks."

Hildegard wrote over 300 letters: to church officials including popes, cardinals, and bishops; to abbesses of other religious communities; to simple monks and nuns; and to men and women at all levels of secular society. Her correspondence included references to religious issues, politics, and personal matters. She gave advice, acted as a mediator, and reminded those in power of their responsibilities to humans and God. "It is a testament to Hildegard's importance as a public figure both that her letters were preserved, copied, collected, and revised and that the range of her correspondence is so vast…no women and few men had the number or scope of Hildegard's correspondence," writes Joan Ferrante.

All of Hildegard's music is contained in the *Symphonia armonie celestium revelationum* (Symphony of the Harmony of Celestial Revelations) and in the morality play *Ordo Virtutum*. She penned both the words and melodies, unusual in this period, during which new words were often set to existing melodies, or existing words were sung with new melodies. Hildegard's music was almost certainly written for use in her Benedictine convent, at which there were eight daily offices (also called hours) or prayer services (different from the Mass). Each office included Psalms, canticles, antiphons, responsories, hymns, lesson readings, and prayers.

Her powerful music is remarkable in light of her claim that she never studied musical notation or any form of singing. The *Symphonia* contains over seventy settings of her own poetry, described by Marianne Richert Pfau as "groupings that reflect the heavenly and ecclesiastical hierarchy, from the divine to the mundane, ranging from the persons of the Trinity at one end of the spectrum to widows and innocents at the other." Forty-three works are antiphons, usually sung before and after a psalm suited to the theme or feast of each day. Eighteen pieces are responsories, sung most often at the matins service (held during the night, usually between midnight and dawn). Fourteen are longer pieces—sequences, hymns, and three unclassified songs.

Hildegard's music is atypical of her time: the melodic range of her chants is often two octaves, sometimes more. She wrote wide melodic leaps and repeated motives with clever variation. Her antiphons are more complex and her responsories often longer and more ornate than those of her contemporaries. Her music is unpredictable; set to her own poetry, it is rich in unusual, elaborate imagery and without regular meter or form.

Hildegard's *Ordo Virtutum*, the earliest known morality play, is "unique because it is the only medieval music drama for which both the composer of the music and author of the text is known. Moreover...the only medieval music drama by a woman composer [that] possesses such power and beauty that it may be claimed as the most original of its time" (Davidson). Alternating solo and choral material, she writes both syllabic and melismatic melodies. A short version of the *Ordo Virtutum* text is found in *Scivias*, and a version with music appears in the *Riesencodex* manuscript, following the *Symphonia*. In mystical language the play presents a battle for the soul (Anima), between the Devil (the only significant male role) and the Virtues, represented by women.

In spite of her lifelong health problems and the burden of administering her convents, Hildegard remained productive until her death, continuing her intellectual work, teaching, preaching, effecting church reforms, and prophesying. She died in 1179. Her incredible accomplishments are summarized in Barbara Newman's *Voice of the Living Light*:

> Hildegard was the only woman of her age to be accepted as an authoritative voice on Christian doctrine; the first woman who received express permission from a pope to write theological books; the only medieval woman who preached openly, before mixed audiences of clergy and laity, with full approval of church authorities; the author of the first known morality play [*Ordo Virtutum*] and the only twelfth-century playwright who is not anonymous; the only composer of her era (not to mention the only medieval woman) known both by name and by a large corpus of surviving music; the first scientific writer to discuss sexuality and gynecology from a female perspective; and the first...whose official biography includes a first-person memoir.

Pope Gregory IX began official canonization proceedings for Hildegard von Bingen in 1227, almost fifty years after her death. Most of the witnesses who had known her were dead, however, and an official decree of sainthood was never achieved, although in 1940 a feast day in her honor in German dioceses was approved.

Herrad of Landsperg (?–1195) was the abbess of Hohenburg in Alsace from 1167 to 1195. Her illustrated manuscript *Hortus deliciarum* (Garden of Delight), described as a "compendium of contemporary knowledge" by Anne Bagnall Yardley, (*Women Composers: Music Through the Ages, vol. 1*) contained musical settings of Herrad's poems addressed to her nuns as well as the writings of others. Only two songs survive from the *Hortus deliciarum* because the original manuscript was destroyed in a fire in 1870. **Mechtild von Magdeburg (1212–1282)** and **Gertrude the Great (1256–1302)**, at the Cistercian convent of Helfta in Saxony, were other medieval nuns credited with composing; however, none of their music is extant. The Flemish **Hadewijch of Brabant (fl. 1230–1260/1265)**, a member of the Beguines, also composed music. (The Beguines, a group of religious women established in the twelfth century, took no vows and were not subject to the rules of any order. They devoted themselves to charitable works.) **Adelheid of Landau (fl.? 1300s)** was another composer mentioned by Yardley.

Saint Birgitta of Sweden (ca. 1303–1373) established the Brigittine Order of the Holy Savior at Vadstena, Sweden, sometime before 1348. "The Brigittine Order centered upon women and devotion, its sisters carrying out the mandated chanted Brigittine Offices day and night; their devotional music was transmitted across space and time," writes Sister Julia Bolton Holloway. Birgitta claimed that her writings and music were dictated to her by an angel on the orders of Christ, after which she wrote them in Swedish. Holloway concludes that "[Birgitta] is less an actual composer of music than she is the instigator of a body of sacred music to be sung and transmitted by women."

Suster Bertken (1426/1427–1514) was born Bertha Jacobs in Utrecht and entered a cloister there in 1456 or 1457. Her works were published in two small books that include eight sacred songs printed without melodic notation. However, Song No. 5, *Die werelt hielt mi in hair gewout* (The World Held Me in Its Power), is contained in the *Utrecht Liederbuch* ca. 1500, where the melody of the first verse is notated.

"Undoubtedly the earliest extant keyboard composition by a woman composer is the organ setting of *Conditor Alme* by the Spanish nun **Gracia Baptista (fl. 1557),**" writes Calvert Johnson. Nothing is known about Baptista except that she was a nun whose music was so highly respected that it was included in one of the first printed collections of Spanish keyboard music—Luys Venegas de Henestrosa's *Libro de Cifra Nueva para tecla, harpa, y vihuela*, published in 1557. Baptista's work for organ is based on a plainchant hymn still in use today.

"Throughout the Middle Ages, the nunnery offered women the opportunity to sing, arrange, and compose music for the worship of God," writes Yardley in her article "Ful weel she soong...." She quotes Bishop Gray, who described the requirements for a nun entering the Benedictine Abbey at Elstow, England, in 1432:

> We enjoin and command that from now on you admit no one as a nun of the said monastery unless...taught in singing and reading and the necessary things in this part, or it is probable that in the near future she may easily be instructed

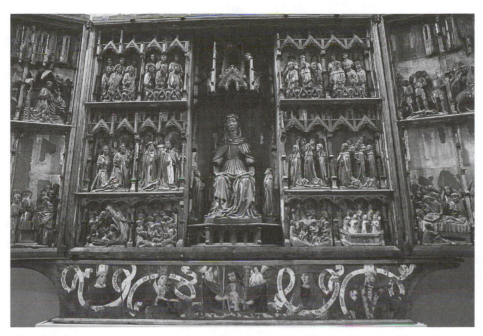

A carved thirteenth-century altarpiece at a church in Vadstena, Sweden, honors St. Birgitta.
© Patrick Ward/CORBIS.

and will be able to manage such things as the burdens of the choir and the other things connected with religion.

However idealistic this requirement, nuns did spend much of their time singing prayers, and, "while it is virtually impossible to establish with certainty the gender of an anonymous composer [there is] the likelihood that at least some anonymous composers of medieval chant were women." She has also identified several chants from English convents that appear in manuscripts used only by women, leading her to "support the conclusion that Anonymous might well have been a woman" (Yardley, *Women Composers: Music Through the ages*, vol. 1).

Troubadours and Trouvères

Meg Bogin identifies fifteen aristocratic women poets as troubadours; three others remain anonymous. (Women troubadours are also called *trobairitz*.) Troubadours were poet-musicians of southern France in the twelfth and thirteenth centuries; they were the first to establish a tradition of songs in the vernacular, usually concerning chivalrous love. The movement later spread to northern France, where the musicians were called *trouvères*. In *Songs of the Women Troubadours*, Matilda Tomaryn Bruckner writes that thirteen *trobairitz* are named in short *vidas* (biographies) or *razos* (commentaries). She continues: "The trobairitz give...testimony of the ways aristocratic women in Southern France were able to participate fully in the game and life of poetry, not only as pa-

trons and objects of song but as poets singing and reshaping the art of the troubadours....Each biography locates the lady in a place, gives her a lover (often named) and
sometimes a husband." According to Maria V. Coldwell, "about 2600 poems by 450
troubadours have been preserved...[and] fewer than 300 melodies by about 40 troubadours have survived." *A chantar m'er* by Comtessa de Dia is the only song by a woman
for which music is extant.

Melodies for troubadour poetry were either originally composed or borrowed, possible because many poems used the same basic structures and rhyme schemes. The *canso*
(love song) in AAB form is most characteristic. Another pattern is the *tenso*, a dialogue
or debate in which lovers disagree or argue, often written by two troubadours. While
all the songs are monophonic, an improvised instrumental accompaniment may have
been added during performance; this is suggested by early pictures showing a singer
holding an instrument or being assisted by an instrumentalist. The songs (*chansons*) are
preserved in manuscript anthologies called *chansonniers*. The musical notation, *neumes*,
is the same as that found in early chants where pitches were indicated without rhythm.

Chansons were written on a variety of topics, but the favorite was courtly love. Typically, a male troubadour addressed his poem to an unknown or even fictitious noblewoman whom he proclaimed to love with great passion. Much of the poem was devoted
to his lament that this beautiful and virtuous woman did not return his love. The love,
with some exceptions, was probably platonic, with the poetry serving as a vehicle for
demonstrating the troubadour's literary skill in devising clever rhyme schemes, puns,
ambiguities, and other poetic techniques.

Women's poems were similar to those of the male troubadours, but with the genders reversed: the woman's love was for the unattainable or faithless nobleman. In general, *trobairitz* poetry was more straightforward in style than that of male troubadours
and lacked the clever word devices previously mentioned. Female poets rarely ideal-
ized the man's character, and his good looks were not excessively extolled. Bruckner
writes that one "might expect the cultural model of the passive woman to make it difficult for the lady to speak out, in fact very few trobairitz mention such constraint."

Coldwell concludes: "These songs are not 'woman's songs' in the literary sense, but
'songs by women'; they represent a broad spectrum of courtly love poetry. Just as men
could write woman's songs, women could write in the elevated aristocratic style generally associated with men."

The Comtessa de Dia is an example of an unusual twelfth-century noblewoman bold
enough to contribute to the arts of her time. No biographical information about the
comtessa (countess) is available other than that she lived in the late twelfth century in
the Provence region of southern France. Some sources give her Christian name as Beatriz,
the wife of Guilhem de Poitiers, but recent scholars have questioned this designation.

The comtessa was a woman troubadour who wrote lyrical love poetry in Old Occi-
tan, or *langue d'oc*, a regional language quite different from modern French, during the
twelfth and thirteenth centuries. Her song *A chantar m'er* has five seven-line stanzas,
each sung to the same music, plus a final stanza of two lines. The simple melody moves
mainly by step within the range of an octave and relies on a standard structural pattern

based on two different melodies (A and B). The A melody is used for the first two lines of poetry and is repeated for lines three and four. The B melody is used for lines five and six. The second part of the A melody is repeated for the concluding line of poetry. This *trobairitz* song is available in a number of sources and has been recorded.

The opening and closing verses of Comtessa de Dia's *A chantar m'er* read:

I

I must sing of what I'd rather not,
I'm so angry about him whose friend I am,
For I love him more than anything;
mercy and courtliness don't help me
with him, nor does my beauty, or my rank, or my mind;
for I am every bit as betrayed and wronged
as I'd deserve to be if I were ugly.

V

My rank and lineage should be of help
to me, and my beauty and, still more, my true heart;
this song, let it be my messenger;
therefore, I send it to you, out in your estate,
and I would like to know, my fine, fair friend,
why you are so fierce and cruel to me.
I can't tell if it's from pride or malice.

VI

I especially want you, messenger, to tell him
That too much pride brings harm to many persons.

(Translation from *Songs of the Women Troubadours*)

Biographical facts about the troubadours are often difficult to establish; however, *vidas* and *razos* inform us that **Tibors (n.d.)**, a lady of Provence, was either a sister of troubadour Raimbaut d'Orange or possibly his mother and was the wife of the troubadour patron Bertrand de Baux.

Meg Bogin quotes the *vida* of **Azalais de Porcairagues (n.d.)**:

Azalais de Porcairagues was from the region of Montpellier, a noble and accomplished lady. And she fell in love with Ein Gui Guerrejat, who was the brother of En Guilhem de Montpellier. And she knew how to write poems, and she composed many good *chansons* in his honor.

The *trobairitz* **Garsenda (b. ca. 1170?)**, author of one extant poem, is mentioned in the *vidas* of two male troubadours who professed love for her. She played a role in the power struggle between two important and powerful families of southern France: the Forcalquiers, her birth family, and the Aragon family of her husband, Alphonse II of

Provence. **Maria de Ventadorn (b. ca. 1165?)**, an important patron of troubadours and daughter of a viscount, married Ebles V de Ventadorn, a viscount from a family of troubadours. Bogin writes:

> The *razo* paints the picture of a perfect literary hostess....It is easy to imagine periods of great activity in Maria's eagle-nest *chateau*—banquets, song fests, costuming and dances—but it should be remembered that the isolated castle must have passed many a bleak month unvisited, with only such entertainments as the members of the court could themselves provide. Perhaps it was in "dry spells" such as these that a patron would find herself...a poet....We have no trace of her after her husband became a monk.

Trouvères were poet-musicians in northern France in the late twelfth century, similar to the troubadours in the south. Their music is also preserved in *chansonniers*. Over 4,000 poems, about 1,400 with melodies, are extant. A majority of these are love songs in strophic form with an AAB rhyme scheme.

Few women *trouvères* have been identified. One seven-line verse of *Mout m'abelist quant je voi revenir* (It Pleases Me Much When I See), the only *chanson* with extant music by a woman, is attributed to **Dame Maroie de Dregnau de Lille**, who flourished in the thirteenth century. Three Old French *jeu-partis* (debate songs) with music by women have survived, including *Je vous pri Dame Maroie* (I Beg You Lady Maroie), coauthored by Dame Maroie and **Dame Margot**, another *trouvère*. There are two different, unrelated melodies for the song.

Blanche of Castile (?–1252), a *trouvère*, was the granddaughter of Eleanor of Aquitaine (?1122–1204). A patron of music, Eleanor became the wife of Louis VII, king of France, divorced him in 1152, and then married Henry II of England, bringing her inheritance—Aquitaine—with her. The poet/composer **Marie de France** (twelfth century) was associated with the English court of Eleanor and Henry. Eleanor supported troubadours at her court in France and then in England, as did her daughter Marie, countess of Champagne. Eleanor brought her granddaughter, Blanche, from Spain to marry the heir to the French throne, the future Louis VIII (1187–1226). Blanche became very powerful as regent for her son Louis IX (1214–1270) after Louis VIII died; she was his adviser, regent again in 1248 when he went on a Crusade, then coregent (1250) with her son Alphonse until her death.

The Renaissance

Nuns

One composer or two? The unsolved biographical mystery of **Vittoria Aleotti/ Raphaela Aleotta (ca. 1574?–1646?)** continues to puzzle musicologists. Karin Pendle writes: "Some scholars maintain that the two women were in fact one person, and that Vittoria simply took the name Rafaella [*sic*] upon entering Ferrara's San Vito convent, while others maintain that they are two separate persons." Thomasin LaMay includes expanded information concerning both (?) composers in "Vittoria Aleotti/ Raphaela Aleotti" (*Women Composers: Music Through the Ages*), citing evidence from birth certificates and wills. I refer here to Vittoria as the composer of madrigals and Raphaela as the composer of motets.

Vittoria's madrigals display two unusual characteristics: she uses harmony and dissonance that do not always fit the text, and major cadences occur in unexpected places. A single madrigal by Vittoria appeared in a 1591 anthology of works by composers of Ferrara called *Il giardino de'musici ferraresi* (A Garden of Music from Ferrara).

In the introduction to Vittoria's madrigal collection, *Ghirlanda de madrigali a quarto voci* (Garland of Madrigals for Four Voices) (1593), her father, Giovanni Battista Aleotti, described the musical talents of his five daughters. As the oldest had decided to be a nun, he hired a music teacher for her and wrote: "It happened while she was learning, my second daughter and her sister Vittoria (a child of four years going on five) were always present." Vittoria was so talented that she was given her own lessons and at the age of six or seven became a resident at the convent of San Vito in order to continue her musical studies. Vittoria "does not care for things of this world, so she entrusted me with this matter [the dedication to the work]." Giovanni continued: "I saw how much she was working in the Theory of Music, so I arranged to have some madrigals [poems] of the very illustrious and very excellent cavaliere Guarini, in which all the good and honest qualities are apparent, which she set to music." Her collection of madrigals was presented to Count Zaffo, who published them in 1593.

Only four of the eighteen poems can be absolutely attributed to Guarini, although he may have written others. The first and last pieces are set to religious texts that may have been supplied by Vittoria herself. LaMay writes:

> The framing of the volume by two quasi-religious madrigals was clearly an important decision. The two madrigals may have served as a form of apology for the fact that a woman was composing in a medium usually reserved for men. But the inclusion of such texts may also have afforded Vittoria…an opportunity to diverge from standard madrigal texts which were about women but not from a woman's point of view.…her settings of the texts imply that she was not always comfortable with traditional love sentiments. Perhaps she also resented the presumptions of her father, who appears to have been over-bearing in pressing her to compose these pieces.

Her father added to the introduction that at the age of fourteen "she wisely decided to remain there [San Vito] and dedicate herself to the service of God." Nothing more is known about Vittoria after she joined the convent.

A volume of sacred motets by Raphaela Aleotta, *Sacrae cantiones quinque, septem, octo, et decem vocibus decantande* (Sacred Songs of Praise for Five, Seven, Eight, and Ten Voices), also dated 1593, is the earliest published collection of sacred music by a woman composer.

The nuns at San Vito, trained and directed by Raphaela, played a variety of musical instruments, sang, and gave public performances. After a visit to the convent Hercole Bottrigari wrote:

It appeared to me that the persons who ordinarily participated in this concert were not human, bodily creatures, but were truly angelic spirits. Nor must you imagine that I refer to the beauty of face and richness of garments and clothing, for you would err greatly, since one sees only the most modest grace and pleasing dress and humble deportment in them....[no] other musician living or man, has had any part either in their work or in advising them; and so it is all the more marvelous, even stupendous, to everyone who delights in music.

Raphaela's *Sacrae cantiones* contains eighteen motets, thirteen for five voices, two each for seven and eight voices, and one for ten voices. One of the five-voice motets and the final piece for ten voices were composed by her teacher, Ercole Pasquini (ca. 1550–between 1608 and 1619). Raphaela's motets "are beautifully crafted works that are vocally fluid, textually clear, and expressive. The shifting textures...are...reminiscent of the *Ghirlanda*, however, there is no sense that the music contradicts the text," according to LaMay. Raphaela uses a wider range of tonal centers than many of her contemporaries. LaMay concludes:

Raphaela Aleotta's abilities as composer, performer, and director at S. Vito are undisputed. Since she functioned both privately within the convent, where most women musicians were trained, and publicly in the training of young children, she may have been one of the most influential musicians of her time. Unbound by court strictures and not interested in a job as court composer, she was able to visualize and actualize her own career, an option not often available to either male or female composers....What remains evident is that both collections are the works of a talented musician: Raphaela claimed her voice and operated comfortably in her musical environment, while Vittoria was less at ease with madrigal texts and made no effort to claim them as her voice.

Sulpitia Lodovica Cesis (1577–after 1619), a nun at the Agostinian convent of San Geminiano in Modena, Italy, city of her birth, published a single volume of music at the age of forty-two. She was mentioned in a traveler's account of 1596 as a performer and composer. Candace Smith quotes from it: "The nuns there are versed in all sorts of musical instruments...[including] Sister Sulpitia, daughter of the most illustrious Signor Count Cesis, who plays the lute excellently...they performed a motet of hers which was highly praised."

Cesis' *Motetti spirituali* (Spiritual Motets), preserved in eight partbooks, contains twenty-three motets for various numbers of voices; two include specific instruments, unusual in this period. In the twelve-part motet *Parvulus filius*, Cesis indicates string instruments for the third tenor and the bass in the first chorus; more surprising are the two trombones for the third tenor and bass part of the second chorus. In *Hodie gloriosus* for eight voices, viols and trombone are also indicated. Although Faustina Borghi, a famous organist, was in residence at the convent, Cesis included no continuo part. Since the music was written to be sung by females (nuns), the organ may either have substituted for tenor and bass voices or realized the accompaniment indicated by the bass line.

Although Cesis' motets were published in 1619, they resemble the earlier polychoral compositions of sixteenth-century Venice written by Andrea Gabrieli (1510–1586).

Lucrezia Orsina Vizzana (1590–1662) has the distinction of being the only nun from Bologna, Italy, whose music was published, according to Craig Monson. Vizzana was born into an upper-class family on July 3, 1590. After the death of her mother in 1598, the eight-year-old child entered the convent of Santa Cristina della Fondazza of the Camaldolese Order, taking her vows several years later. Two of her sisters and three of her aunts were also members of Santa Cristina, a beautifully decorated convent favored by wealthy families, especially those whose daughters were interested in the arts. While Vizzana was there, the Santa Cristina Church was completely rebuilt in the ornate Italian Baroque style; the nuns and their families provided much of the funding.

Santa Cristina was noted for its fine singers, organists, and instrumentalists. The talented young Vizzana was fortunate that so many accomplished musicians were available to teach and inspire her, including her aunt, Camilla Bombacci, an excellent organist. Nothing is known of Vizzana's ability as a performer, but she was a highly skilled composer. A collection of twenty of her motets, *Componimenti Musicali* (Musical Compositions), was published in Venice in 1623 and dedicated to the nuns of the convent. A few are brilliant works, probably intended for religious festivals, but many are more personal reflections about penitence, virtue, and Jesus.

Despite limitations on outside contacts decreed by the archbishop of Bologna, Vizzana was well aware of the current trends in music composition practiced by contemporary composers of sacred music. While motets of this period were usually unaccompanied choral compositions, Vizzana's motets were primarily written for one or two solo voices with basso continuo accompaniment in the modern style of monody. By the second decade of the seventeenth century basso continuo, playing the chords indicated by figures under the bass notes (also called realizing the figured bass part) arose. The motets are distinctive for striking interpretations of text, including the use of ornamented melodies to stress significant words and wide leaps and dissonances to emphasize dramatic ideas. The intensity of expression in some of her works is more closely allied with the early seventeenth-century Italian madrigals and arias of composers such as Claudio Monteverdi (1567–1643) than with the conservative sacred music of the period.

About the time Vizzana published *Componimenti Musicali*, Santa Cristina was in turmoil because of complaints by three of the resident nuns to church authorities that the convent was spiritually lax. After an investigation, Santa Cristina was punished by removal from the Camaldolese Order and placed under the direct supervision of the archbishop of Bologna. The nuns fought back for more than twenty-five years, defying both church orders and the pope, who threatened them with excommunication. The unrest and conflict had a crushing effect on Vizzana, who, according to her father confessor, was "driven literally mad." She is not known to have published any music after 1623, although she lived for almost forty more years.

Caterina Assandra (early 1590s–1620) was the second Italian nun to publish an entire collection of music. *Motetti a due, & tre voci per cantar nell'organo con il basso continuo*, op. 2 (Motets for Two and Three Voices with Basso Continuo) is the earliest extant volume of her own compositions. Assandra, who had adopted the religious name Agata, dedicated it to the newly elected bishop of her hometown of Pavia in 1609, writing in the dedication that she was "about to serve God in the Monastery of Saint Agatha of Lomello" (Bowers, *Women Composers: Music Through the Ages*, vol. 1). Op. 2 contains eighteen compositions. Two works by Don Benedetto Rè (n.d.; also known as Benedetto or Benedicto Regio), *Maestro di Cappella* at the cathedral and her "Maestro di contraponto" (teacher of counterpoint), are printed at the end of the volume. He published both her eight-voice *Salve Regina* in 1611 and her *Audite verbum Domini* for four voices and organ in 1618, in volumes of his own music. Composer Giovanni Paola Cima (ca. 1570–?) dedicated a collection of keyboard works to her in 1606.

Claudia Sessa, a nun in Milan at the convent of Santa Maria Annunciata, was a singer-composer. In *Women Composers: Music Through the Ages*, vol. 1, Candace Smith quotes a description written in 1619 extolling her as "the best musician of the time"; however, only two songs in the monodic tradition of northern Italy (solo voice with continuo) are extant. They are included in a Venetian collection published in 1613 based on the features of Christ's face and set to music by different composers. Sessa's works describe Christ's eyes (*Occhi io vissi di voi* [I Lived through Your Eyes]) and ears (*Vattene pur lasciva orecchia humana* [Go Away, Lascivious Human Ears]).

Secular Composers and Patrons

Paula Higgins asks:

> Since there is abundant evidence that women in convents and monasteries, as well as aristocratic women, did compose monophonic music up to ca. 1300 and polyphonic music from 1566 on, often against considerable odds, what would have stopped them from doing so during the intervening years? (Higgins 1991)

"If large quantities of their compositions have not survived, one reason must be that they were partially or totally improvised and never committed to paper," responds Donna G. Cardamone (*Women Composers: Music Through the Ages*, vol. 1). By the fifteenth century a noblewoman's education included learning to dance gracefully, to read music, to improvise songs, and to sing and play quiet instruments.

The first woman composer to have a complete volume of her music published (in 1568), **Maddalena Casulana (ca. 1540–ca. 1590)** was born in Italy, probably in a village not far from Siena. Information about her early years is not available, but her later accomplishments as a composer, singer, and lutenist are evidence of her musical training. Casulana specialized in Italian madrigals, a well-established genre by the time that she began composing. Like many unknown musicians, she tried to attract the attention of wealthy sponsors by publishing a few of her early works in anthologies that featured compositions by more prominent composers, including Orlando di Lasso (1532–1594), Cipriano de Rore (1515/1516–1565), and Andrea Gabrieli (ca. 1510–1586). Four of Casulana's madrigals were printed in a volume called *Il Desiderio* I (Desire) (1566), and an additional one appeared in *Il Desiderio III* (1567).

The following year *Primo libro de madrigali* (First Book of Madrigals), a collection of twenty-one madrigals, exclusively her own music, was published. Printed in Venice, the center for music publishing at the time and the place where many of the new compositional styles developed, the collection was dedicated to the duchess of Bracciano, Isabella de' Medici Orsini, a patron of the arts and a talented amateur poet and musician. Casulana's remarkable dedication states that "the foolish error of men, who so greatly believe themselves to be the masters of high intellectual gifts that cannot, it seems to them, be equally common among women." This (Lerner, *Women Composers: Music Through the Ages,* vol. 1) collection, popular enough to warrant reprinting, established Casulana's reputation as a serious and talented composer.

Casulana was a pioneer among successful women composers. Although developing a career was difficult for a woman, Casulana was fortunate that northern Italy, particularly Venice, displayed a more liberal attitude toward providing artistic venues for women. She was able to seek opportunities as a performer and composer at the courts, in the salons sponsored by wealthy patrons, and at the intellectual academies organized to study, discuss, and perform poetry and music. Although the academies did not allow women to become members, their participation was encouraged.

Casulana dedicated her second volume of madrigals (1570) to Antonio Londonio, an important government official in Milan and a devoted supporter of music. Her name on the title page of the third volume of madrigals, "Maddalena Mezari detta Casulana Vicentina," indicates that by then she was married to someone named Mezari and living in Vicenza in northeast Italy. Published in 1583, it was dedicated to Count Mario Bevilacqua, a major patron of the arts and the sponsor of a prestigious cultural academy in Verona. In the dedication, Casulana states that she lived at the home of an aristocratic family in that city; she probably attended and performed at the academy.

In addition to her activities as a singer and composer, Casulana was a respected teacher. Although teaching in music schools other than convents was a career still closed to women, a few well-known women taught privately. One of Casulana's pupils, Antonio Molino (a wealthy Venetian merchant), published his own book of madrigals (1568). In his dedication to Casulana he praised her ability in glowing terms. Philippe de Monte (1521–1603) also dedicated a collection of madrigals to Casulana in 1582.

Casulana's madrigals were similar to those of her contemporaries, and she embraced the various trends that were popular during the second half of the century. With few exceptions, her works were written for four or five voices and were based on the poetry of favored writers such as Francesco Petrarch, Jacopo Sannazaro, and Torquato Tasso. She often selected pastoral texts about the beauties of the countryside and love among the shepherds and shepherdesses. Her madrigals are noted for their imaginative use of colorful harmonic effects, chromaticism, and word-painting. One of the most famous composers of the sixteenth century, di Lasso, selected one of her works to be performed in Munich as part of the elaborate wedding celebration that he planned for Archduke Wilhelm V of Bavaria and Renée of Lorraine in 1568. In a field dominated by men, Casulana was counted among the leading composers of her time, regardless of gender.

Some noblewomen, including **Margaret of Austria (1480–1530)**, were music patrons (usually of secular music) and owned and collected volumes of manuscripts and printed music. Margaret was born in Brussels, then capital of The Netherlands. "Her national sympathies were Burgundian, although her title was Austrian and her tastes and education French," writes Martin Picker (Women composers: *Music Through the Ages*, vol. 1). He translates from Jean Lemaire de Belges, a contemporary observer:

> She is excellently skilled in vocal and instrumental music, in painting and rhetoric, in the French as well as the Spanish language; moreover she likes erudite, wise men. She supports clever minds, expert in many fields, and frequently she reads lofty books, of which she has a great number in her rich ample library, concerning all manner of things worth knowing. Yet not content merely to read, she has taken pen in hand and described elegantly in prose as well as in French verse her misfortunes and her admirable life.

Picker continues about her song *Se je souspire/Ecce iterum* (Thus I Sigh/Behold, Again): "In view of the personal character of the text and its idiosyncratic musical style, Margaret may well have been its composer, or at least a collaborator in its musical conception."

Ferrara's renown as a center for the arts began around 1480, when Ercole d'Este became duke. His daughter Isabella d'Este (1474–1539), married Francesco II Gonzaga, in 1490 and was the marchessa of Mantua for almost fifty years. Well educated at her father's court, her voluminous correspondence attests to her patronage of the arts. Musicians, including singers and string and keyboard players, were in her personal service and paid from her own household funds. Her patronage was a single-minded one, concentrating only on the *frottola*, a type of secular song that preceded the madrigal. "There is no trace in her correspondence of interest in…anything other than secular and devotional vocal music with texts in the Italian vernacular," writes Prizer in "Games of Venus: Secular Vocal Music in the Late Quattrocento and Early Cinquecento," *Journal of Musicology*, 9 (1991).

Isabella d'Este's sister-in-law, Lucrezia Borgia (1480–1519) married Alfonso d'Este, duke of Ferrara, in 1501. Although both were noblewomen and patrons of the arts, Borgia's background differed significantly from d'Este's; they were rivals rather than friends. Borgia was the illegitimate daughter of the Spanish cardinal Rodrigo Borgia (later Pope Alexander VI) and his mistress, Vanozza Catenei. Lucrezia Borgia was married three times in her family's quest for greater status and political alliances: first, at the age of only thirteen years, to Giovanni Sforza of the Milanese family, a marriage declared void on the grounds of nonconsummation by her father in 1497; second, at the

Margaret of Austria.
Erich Lessing/Art Resource, New York.

age of eighteen to Alfonso d'Aragona of the Neapolitan family, whom Borgia's brother, Cesare, had murdered in 1500; and finally, at the age of twenty-one, to Alfonso d'Este, duke of Ferrara. An amateur musician and poet, she loved to entertain lavishly, always with music. Prizer writes that hers was "a complete, self-contained court including all the main elements of her husband's court, with the sole exception of military retainers. Unlike…the previous generation of Italian noblewomen, she also maintained a self-sufficient [though smaller than her husband's] corps of musicians." (*Rediscovering the Muses: Women's Musical Traditions*)

Only one song has been attributed to **Anne Boleyn** (?1502/1507–1536), the second wife of Henry VIII of England. Although Boleyn's authorship of *O Deathe, Rock Me Asleepe* has not been fully authenticated, her noblewoman's education would have enabled her to write music and poetry. The court of Henry VIII "had one of the most impressive musical establishments of the world: at the end of his reign he had 60 musicians

Anne Boleyn.
© Archivo Iconografico, S.A./CORBIS.

on his payroll in addition to those in the Chapel Royal," writes Edith Borroff. Elizabeth I (1533–1603), the daughter of Anne Boleyn and Henry VIII, became queen of England in 1558. The years of her reign, a time of great achievements for the country, are considered a golden age. Elizabeth inherited her father's interests in music and art, and her court was a center for musicians, literary figures and scholars.

The extremely wealthy and politically shrewd Medici family, rulers of Florence from about 1435 to 1737, patronized music and musicians. Musical chapels were instituted under the first Cosimo (1389–1464). His sons, Piero (1416–1469) and Giovanni (1421–1463), both friends of the great composer Guillaume Dufay (ca. 1400–1474), recruited musicians for the new chapels. The family's music patronage reached its height under the Medici Pope Leo X (r. 1513–1521), a well-trained musician. Some women of the Medici family were composers as well as patrons of music. Catherine de' Medici (1519–1589), wife of King Henry II of France and the mother of three French

Portrait of Isabella de' Medici by Agnolo Bronzino.
© North Carolina Museum of Art/CORBIS.

kings, was a patron of the arts, according to Pendle, and was responsible for introducing Italian ballet into France. **Isabella de' Medici Orsini (1542–1576)** was the dedicatee of Maddalena Casulana's first book of madrigals. Isabella, daughter of the Florentine grand duke Cosimo de' Medici (1519–1574), was called "a perfect musician, a very good singer, poetess, and *improvisatrice* by nature" (quotes Cardamone), and one song, *Lieta vivo e contenta dapoi ch'il mio bel sole* (I Live Happy and Content as Long as My Handsome Sun [Shows me his bright rays]), is attributed to her. Her husband, Paolo Giordano Orsini, duke of Bracciano, murdered Isabella in 1576. Their daughter **Leonora de' Medici Orsini (?1560–1634)** moved to Rome by 1588, where she established a group of women singers similar to the *concerto delle donne* in Ferrara discussed later. In 1592 she married Alessandro Sforza and continued her activities as a music patron and, according to Candace Smith, "as an occasional performer at court." Orsini's only known composition is a song with lute accompaniment, *Per pianto la mia carne* (My Flesh Melts in Weeping), found in the same manuscript that includes the work by her mother, Isabella. After separating from her husband, Leonora Orsini founded the convent of Santa Chiara delle Cappuccine in Santa Fiore.

In 1580 at the court of Ferrara, the first group of three professional women singers (later joined by a fourth), called *concerto delle donne*, was formed. They were called upon regularly to provide musical entertainment for the duke and to impress visitors from outside the duchy. Although listed in the court rolls as ladies-in-waiting to the duchess, not as musicians, "the ladies owed their positions in court primarily to their gifts as musicians, that their positions were of great honor and prestige, and that the question was a novel and delicate one, whether or not the members of the *concerto* were in fact serving as musicians," writes Anthony Newcomb. Similar groups soon formed in Florence, Rome, and Mantua. The *concerto* in Florence was dissolved by Ferdinand I de' Medici (1549–1609) shortly after his accession as grand duke of Tuscany in 1588. However, it was unofficially re-formed in 1590 by Maria de' Medici (1573–1642) and Leonora de' Medici Orsini. The first extant opera, *Euridici* by Jacopo Peri (1561–1633), was commissioned for the wedding celebration of Maria de' Medici to Henry IV of France in 1600. After Henry was murdered, Maria became regent for her son Louis XIII from 1610 to 1617. Maria's positions as queen and regent afforded her continued opportunities as a patron of music.

The only known work of **Paola Massarenghi** (1565–?), *Quando spiega l'insegn'al sommo padre* (When One Unfurls the Insignia of the Highest Father), appeared in 1585. This madrigal was included in F. Arcangelo Gherardini's *Il primo libro de' madrigali a cinque voci* (The First Book of Madrigals for Five Voices), in which all other works were his. Although Massarenghi's text is set in a battlefield, a decidedly unfeminine locale, the music is serene. Little is known of her life; she may have lived in the Ferrara area, home of the *concerto delle donne* and the musically renowned convent of San Vito.

Italian composer **Cesarina Ricci** (ca. 1573–?), born in Cingoli, flourished in 1597. Her twenty madrigals were published in Venice in 1597. Nothing else is known about her life.

Timeline for the Middle Ages and the Renaissance

Date	History/Politics	Science/Education	The Arts/ Literature	Music
395	Separation of Eastern and Western Roman Empires			
413	Establishment of the seven liberal arts			
458		Lokavibhaga demonstrates the concept of zero (Sanskrit)		
500				Boethius (480–524): *De institutione musica*
529	Benedictine Order founded			
590	Pope Gregory the Great elected (ca. 540–604)			
691	Dome of the Rock built in Jerusalem			
700		Introduction of the stirrup in early 8th c. enabled development of the armored knight (Frankish lands)	Chao Luan-luan, poet (fl. 8th c.)	
778	Huneberc of Heidenheim, nun (fl. 778–786)			
793		Chinese invent paper		
800	Charlemagne (742–814), crowned 800		Qernertoq, female Eskimo poet (fl. 9th c.)	
810				**Kassia** (ca. 810–+/- 867)
871	Alfred the Great (849–899), crowned king of England			
935			Roswitha of Gandersheim, first female German playwright and poet (935–1000)	
962	Otto the Great (912–973) crowned first emperor of the Holy Roman Empire			
995				Guido d'Arezzo (ca. 991–after 1033)
1000			*Beowulf* heroic poem in Old English	Wallada al-Mustakfi, troubadour (fl. 1000–1035)
1027			Omar Khayyam (1027–1123)	
1075			Judah Halevi (1075–1141)	

Date	History/Politics	Science/Education	The Arts/ Literature	Music
1083			Anna Comnena, first female Byzantine historian (1083–1153)	
1098			Héloise, writer (letters of Abelard and Héloise) (1098?–1164)	Hildegard von Bingen (1098–1179)
1119		Bologna University founded Paris University founded		
1122	Eleanor of Aquitaine (ca. 1122–1204)			
1125				Beginning of *troubadour* and *trouvère* music in France
1130			Lady Horikawa, Japanese poet (fl. 1130–1165)	
1140				Almucs de Castelnau, troubadour (1140–?)
1145	Chartres Cathedral begun			
1150				Bernart de Ventadorn, troubadour (ca. 1150–1180)
1160		Oxford University founded		Comtessa Beatriz de Dia (fl. 12th c.) Marie de France (12th c.)
1165				Maria de Ventadorn (b. ca. 1165) Herrad of Landsperg (fl. 1167–1195) Garsenda (b. ca. 1170)
1189	Richard the Lionhearted (1157–99) crowned king of England			
1209	St. Francis of Assisi (1182–1226) founds Franciscan Order			
1212				Mechtild von Magdeburg (1212–1282)
1215	Magna Carta			
1225	St. Thomas Aquinas (1225–1274)	Roger Bacon (ca. 1220–1292)		
1230				Hadewijch of Brabant (fl. 1230–1260/1265)
1245				Adam de la Halle (ca. 1245–1300)
1254		Marco Polo (1254–1324)		
1256				Gertrude the Great (1256–1302)

Date	History/Politics	Science/Education	The Arts/Literature	Music
1265			Dante Alighieri (1265–1321)	
1291				Philip de Vitry (1291–1361)
1300				Guillaume de Machaut (ca. 1300–1377)
1303				**St. Birgitta of Sweden (ca. 1303–1373)**
1304			Francesco Petrarch (1304–1374)	**Adelheid von Landau (fl. ? 1300s)**
1313			Giovanni Boccacio (1313–1375)	
1337	Outbreak of the Hundred Years' War			
1340			Geoffrey Chaucer (ca. 1340–1400)	
1342			Juliana of Norwich, writer and mystic (1342–1417/23)	
1362			*Piers Plowman*, poem by William Langland	
1386			Donatello (ca. 1386–1466)	
1390			Jan van Eyck (ca. 1390–1441)	John Dunstable (ca. 1390–1453)
1396		Johann Gutenberg, inventor of printing press (ca. 1396–1468)		
1400			Fra Angelico (ca. 1400–1455)	Guillaume Dufay (ca. 1400–1474) Gilles Binchois (ca. 1400–1460) **Dame Maroie de Dregnau de Lille (fl. 13th c.)**
1410				Johannes Ockeghem (ca. 1410–1497)
1412	Joan of Arc (ca. 1412–1431)			
1425			Lucrezia de'Medici, Italian poet (1425–1482)	
1426				**Suster Bertken (1426/1427–1514)**
1431	Joan of Arc burned at the stake at Rouen			
1450	ca. 1450: Beginning of the Renaissance		Hieronymus Bosch (ca. 1450–1516)	Josquin des Prés (ca. 1450–1521) Jacob Obrecht (ca. 1450–1505)
1452	Columbus (1452–1506)		Leonardo da Vinci (1452–1519)	
1456		The Gutenberg Bible appears		
1466		Erasmus (1466–1536)		

Date	History/Politics	Science/Education	The Arts/ Literature	Music
1469	Niccolò Machiavelli (1469–1527)	Vasco da Gama (ca. 1469–1524)		
1473		Copernicus (1473–1543)		
1474	Isabella d'Este (1474–1539)			
1475			Michaelangelo (1475–1564)	
1480	Lucrezia Borgia, Italian nobility (1480–1519)			**Margaret of Austria** (1480–1530)
1483	Martin Luther (1483–1546)			
1490			Vittoria Colonna (1490–1547)	John Taverner (ca. 1490–1545) Adrian Willaert (ca. 1490–1562)
1491	Henry VIII (1491–1547)			
1492	Columbus discovers America		Marguerite de Navarre (1492–1549)	
1495			François Rabelais (1493/1495–1553)	
1498				Ottaviano dei Petrucci granted license to print music
1500	Charles V crowned	Black lead pencils appear in England		
1502	Anne Boleyn, English queen (?1502/1507–1536)			
1503		Nostradamus (1503–1566)		
1505				Thomas Tallis (ca. 1505–1585)
1509	John Calvin (1509–1564)			
1510				Andrea Gabrieli (ca. 1510–1586)
1517	Martin Luther issues 95 Theses			
1519	Catherine de'Medici (1519–1589)			
1520s				Origin of the madrigal in Italy
1524			Hans Holbein the Elder (d. 1524)	
1525				Giovanni Pierluigi da Palestrina (1525–1594)
1530	Ivan the Terrible (1530–1584)			
1532				Orlando di Lasso (1532–1594)

Date	History/Politics	Science/Education	The Arts/Literature	Music
1533	Queen Elizabeth I, English queen (1533–1603)			Claudio Merulo (1533–1604)
1540		Sir Francis Drake (1540–1596)		**Madalena Casulana (ca. 1540–ca. 1590)**
1541			El Greco (1541–1614)	
1542	Mary of Scots, English queen and poet (1542–1587)			**Isabella de'Medici Orsini (1542–1576)**
1543				William Byrd (1543–1623)
1545	Council of Trent (1545–1563)			
1547			Miguel de Cervantes (1547–1616)	
1550				Guilio Caccini (ca. 1550–1618)
1553				Giovanni Gabrieli (ca. 1553–1612)
1557				**Gracia Baptista (fl. 1557)**
1560				H. Praetorius (1560–1629) Jacopo Peri (1561–1633) **Leonora Orsini (?1560–1634)** Leonora de'Medici Orsini (?1560–1634)
1561		Francis Bacon (1561–1620)		Carlo Gesualdo (ca. 1561–1613) Jacopo Peri (1561–1633)
1562				John Dowland (1562–1626) Jan Sweelinck (1562–1621)
1564		Galilei-Galileo (1564–1642)	William Shakespeare (1564–1616) Christopher Marlowe (1564–1593)	
1565			Marie le Jars de Gournay (1565–1645) (*The Equality of Men and Women—1622*)	Giles Farnaby (ca. 1565–1640) **Paola Massarenghi (1565–?)**
1567				Claudio Monteverdi (1567–1643)
1570				**Claudia Sessa (ca. 1570–1613/19)**
1571		Johannes Kepler (1571–1630)		Michael Praetorius (1571–1621)
1572			John Donne (1572–1631) Ben Jonson (1572–1637)	

Date	History/Politics	Science/Education	The Arts/Literature	Music
1573			Michelangelo da Caravaggio (1573–1610) Inigo Jones (1573–1652)	Cesarina Ricci (ca. 1573–?)
1574				Vittoria Aleotti/Raphaela Aleotta (ca. 1574–?1646)
1577			Peter Paul Rubens (1577–1640)	Sulpitia Lodovica Cesis (1577–after 1619)
1581		Clausura imposed ca. 1580	Frans Hals (ca. 1581–1666)	
1582		Gregorian calendar created		
1583				Girolamo Frescobaldi (1583–1643) Orlando Gibbons (1583–1625) Giulio Strozzi (1583–1652)
1585	Cardinal Richelieu (1585–1642)			Heinrich Schütz (1585–1672)
1586				Johann Schein (1586–1630)
1587				Francesca Caccini (1587–1645)[1] Samuel Scheidt (1587–1654)
1588		Thomas Hobbes (1588–1679)		
1590s				Caterina Assandra (early 1590s–1620)
1590				Lucrezia Orsina Vizzana (1590–1662) Alba Trissina (ca. 1590 after 1638)[2]
1591				Settimia Caccini (1591–ca. 1660)[3]
1594				Tarquinio Merula (ca. 1594–1665)
1596		René Descartes (1596–1650)		
1597			Rachel Speght, feminist poet (1597–post-1621)	Peri: *Dafne* (first known extant opera)

1 See Chapter 3 for more information on F. Caccini.
2 See Chapter 3 for more information on Trissina/Trissini.
3 See Chapter 3 for more information on S. Caccini.

Bibliography

Vittoria Aleotti/Raphaela Aleotta

Bottrigari, Hercole. *Il Desiderio*. Translated by Carol MacClintock. N.p.: American Institute of Musicology, 1962.

Carruthers-Clement, Ann. "The Madrigals and Motets of Vittoria/Raphaela Aleotti." Ph.D. diss., Kent State University, 1982.

Cavicchi, Adriano. "Vittoria Aleotti. Raphaella Aleotti." In *The New Grove Dictionary of Music and Musicians*, edited by Stanley Sadie. London: Macmillan, 1980.

Caviochi, Adriano, and Suzanne G. Cusick. "Aleotti, Rafaella." In *The New Grove Dictionary of Women Composers*, edited by Julie Anne Sadie and Rhian Samuel. London: Macmillan Press Limited, 1994.

———. "Aleotti, Vittoria." In *The New Grove Dictionary of Women Composers*, edited by Julie Anne Sadie and Rhian Samuel. London: Macmillan Press Limited, 1994.

Cook, Susan, and Thomasin K. LaMay. *Virtuose in Italy 1600–1640: A Reference Guide*. New York and London: Garland Publishing, Inc., 1984.

LaMay, Thomasin. "Vittoria Aleotti/Raphaela Aleotti." In *Women Composers: Music Through the Ages*. vol. 1, edited by Sylvia Glickman and Martha Furman Schleifer. New York: G. K. Hall, 1996.

Anonymous

Yardley, Anne Bagnall. "Ful weel she soong the service dyvyne." In *Women Making Music: The Western Art Tradition, 1150–1950*, edited by Jane Bowers and Judith Tick. Urbana and Chicago: University of Illinois Press, 1987.

———. "Was Anonymous a Woman?" in *Women Composers: Music Through the Ages*, vol. 1, edited by Sylvia Glickman and Martha Furman Schleifer. New York: G. K. Hall, 1996.

Caterina Assandra

Bowers, Jane. "Caterina Assandra." In *Women Composers: Music Through the Ages*, vol. 1, edited by Sylvia Glickman and Martha Furman Schleifer. New York: G. K. Hall, 1996.

Kendrick, Robert L. "Assandra, Caterina." In *The New Grove Dictionary of Music and Musician*, 2d ed. London New York: Macmillan, 2001.

Monson, Craig A. "Disembodied Voices: Music in the Nunneries of Bologna in the Midst of the Counter-Reformation." In *The Crannied Wall: Women, Religion, and the Arts in Early Modern Europe*, edited by Craig A. Monson. Ann Arbor: University of Michigan Press, 1992.

Roche, Jerome. "Caterina Assandra." In *The New Grove Dictionary of Women Composers*, edited by Julie Anne Sadie and Rhian Samuel. London: Macmillan, 1994.

Gracia Baptista

Johnson, Calvert. "Gracia Baptista." In *Women Composers: Music Through the Ages*, vol. 1, edited by Sylvia Glickman and Martha Furman Schleifer. New York: G. K. Hall, 1996.

Suster Bertken

Hospenthal, Christina. "Suster Bertken (1426/27–1514)." In *Women Composers: Music Through the Ages*, vol. 1, edited by Sylvia Glickman and Martha Furman Schleifer. New York: G. K. Hall, 1996.

Saint Birgitta of Sweden

Berquist, Lars. *Saint Birgitta*. Sweden: Lars Berquist and the Swedish Institute, 1996.

Holloway, Julia Bolton. "Saint Birgitta of Sweden and Brigittine Music." In *Women Composers: Music Through the Ages*, vol. 1, edited by Sylvia Glickman and Martha Furman Schleifer. New York: G. K. Hall, 1996.

Sancta Birgitta. *Saint Bride and Her Book: Birgitta of Sweden's Revelations*. Edited by Julia Bolton Holloway. Newburyport, Mass.: Focus, 1992; Cambridge: Boydell and Brewer, 2000.

Anne Boleyn

Borroff, Edith. "Anne Boleyn (1507–1536)." In *Historical Anthology of Music by Women*, edited by James R. Briscoe. Bloomington and Indianapolis: Indiana University Press, 1987.

Milsom, John. "Boleyn, Anne." In *The New Grove Dictionary of Women Composers*, edited by Julie Anne Sadie and Rhian Samuel. London: Macmillan, 1994.

Maddalena Casulana

Bowers, Jane. "The Emergence of Women Composers in Italy 1566–1700." In *Women Making Music: The Western Art Tradition 1150–1950*, edited by Jane Bowers and Judith Tick. Chicago: University of Illinois Press, 1986.

Lerner, Ellen D. "Madalena [*sic*] Casulana." In *Women Composers: Music Through the Ages*, vol. 1, edited by Sylvia Glickman and Martha Furman Schleifer. New York: G. K. Hall, 1996.

Newcomb, Anthony. "Courtesans, Muses, or Musicians? Professional Women Musicians in Sixteenth-Century Italy." In *Women Making Music: The Western Art Tradition, 1150–1950*, edited by Jane Bowers and Judith Tick. Urbana and Chicago: University of Illinois Press, 1987.

Sulpitia Lodovica Cesis

Cook, Susan, and Thomasin K. LaMay. *Virtuose in Italy 1600–1640: A Reference Guide*. New York and London: Garland Publishing, Inc., 1984.

Smith, Candace. "Sulpitia Cesis." In *Women Composers: Music Through the Ages*, vol. 1, edited by Sylvia Glickman and Martha Furman Schleifer. New York: G. K. Hall, 1996.

The Comtessa de Dia, Troubadours and *Trouvères*

Bogin, Meg. *The Women Troubadours*. New York: W. W. Norton & Company, 1980.

Cheyette, Fredric, and Margaret Switten. "Women in Troubadour Songs: Of the Comtessa and the Vilana." *Women and Music: A Journal of Gender and Culture* 2 (1998): 26–45.

Coldwell, Maria V. "*Jougleresses* and *Trobairitz*: Secular Musicians in Medieval France." In *Women Making Music: The Western Art Tradition, 1150–1950*, edited by Jane Bowers and Judith Tick. Urbana and Chicago: University of Illinois Press, 1987.

Edwards, J. Michelle. "Women in Music to ca. 1450." In *Women in Music: A History*, 2d ed., edited by Karin Pendle. Bloomington and Indianapolis: Indiana University Press, 2001.

Paden, William D. *The Voice of the Trobairitz: Perspectives on the Women Troubadours*. Philadelphia: University of Pennsylvania Press, 1989.

Phan, Chantal. "The Comtessa de Dia (fl. 12th c.) and the Trobairitz." In *Women Composers: Music Through the Ages*, vol. 1, edited by Sylvia Glickman and Martha Furman Schleifer. New York: G. K. Hall, 1996.

Songs of the Women Troubadours. Edited and translated by Matilda Tomaryn Bruckner, Laurie Shepard, and Sarah White. New York and London: Garland Publishing, Inc. 1995.

Hildegard von Bingen

Bent, Ian D. "Hildegard of Bingen." In *The New Grove Dictionary of Women Composers*, edited by Julie Anne Sadie and Rhian Samuel. London: Macmillan Press Limited, 1994.

Bobko, Jane, ed. *Vision: The Life and Music of Hildegard von Bingen*. New York: Penguin Studio Books, 1995.

Caviness, Madeline. "Artist: 'To See, Hear, and Know All at Once.'" In *Voice of the Living Light: Hildegard of Bingen and Her World*, edited by Barbara Newman. Berkeley and Los Angeles: University of California Press, 1998.

Davidson, Audrey Ekdahl, ed. *The* Ordo Virtutum *of Hildegard of Bingen: Critical Studies*. Early Drama, Art and Music Monograph Series 8. Kalamazoo, MI: Medieval Institute Publications, 1992.

Dronke, Peter. *Poetic Individuality in the Middle Ages: New Departures in Poetry 1000–1150*. Oxford: Clarendon Press, 1970.

———.*Women Writers of the Middle Ages: A Critical Study of Texts from Perpetua (d. 203) to Marguerite Porete (d. 1310)*. Cambridge: Cambridge University Press, 1984.

Engen, John Van. "Abbess: 'Mother and Teacher.'" In *Voice of the Living Light: Hildegard of Bingen and Her World*, edited by Barbara Newman. Berkeley and Los Angeles: University of California Press, 1998.

Ferrante, Joan. "Correspondent: 'Blessed Is the Speech.'" In *Voice of the Living Light: Hildegard of Bingen and Her World*, edited by Barbara Newman. Berkeley and Los Angeles: University of California Press, 1998.

Flanagan, Sabina. *Hildegard of Bingen, 1098–1179: A Visionary Life*. London and New York: Routledge, 1989.

Fox, Matthew. *Hildegard von Bingen's Mystical Visions*. Santa Fe, NM: Bear & Company Publishing, 1986.

Hildegard of Bingen. *Scivias*. Translated by Columbia Hart and Jane Bishop. New York: Paulist Classics of Western Spirituality, 1990.

Hildegard's Healing Plants. Translated by Bruce W. Hozeski. Boston: Beacon Press, 2001.

Maddocks, Fiona. *Hildegard of Bingen: The Woman of Her Age*. New York: Doubleday, 2001.

Newman, Barbara. "Sibyl of the Rhine: Hildegard's Life and Times." In *Voice of the Living Light: Hildegard of Bingen and Her World*, Newman, Berkeley and Los Angeles: University of California Press, 1998.

Pfau, Marianne Richert. "Hildegard von Bingen." In *Women Composers: Music Through the Ages*, vol. 1, edited by Sylvia Glickman and Martha Furman Schleifer. New York: G. K. Hall, 1996.

Kassia

The Oxford Dictionary of Byzantium, s.v. "Kassia." New York: Oxford University Press, 1991.

Topping, Eva Catafygioty. "Kassiane the Nun and the Sinful Woman." *The Greek Orthodox Theological Review* 26, no. 3 (1981): 201–9.

Touliatos, Diane. "Kassia." In *Women Composers: Music Through the Ages*, vol. 1, edited by Sylvia Glickman and Martha Furman Schleifer. New York: G. K. Hall, 1996.

———. "The Traditional Role of Greek Women in Music from Antiquity to the End of the Byzantine Empire." In *Rediscovering the Muses: Women's Musical Traditions*, edited by Kimberly Marshall. Boston: Northeastern University Press, 1993.

Touliatos-Banker, D. "Medieval Women Composers in Byzantium and the West." *Proceedings of the VIth International Congress of Musicology "Musica Antiqua Europae Orientalis."* Bydgoszcz, Poland, 1982, pp. 687–712.

———. "Women Composers of Medieval Byzantine Chant." *College Music Symposium* 24, no. 1 (Spring 1984): 62–80.

Margaret of Austria

Hare, Christopher. *The High and Puissant Princess Marguerite of Austria*. London: Harper, 1907.

Iongh, Jane de. *Margaret of Austria, Regent of the Netherlands*. Translated by M. D. Herter Norton. New York: W. W. Norton, 1953.

Picker, Martin. *The Chanson Albums of Marguerite of Austria*. MSS 228 and 11239, Bibliothèque Royale de Belgique, Brussels. Berkeley: University of California Press, 1965.

———. "Margaret of Austria." In *Women Composers: Music Through the Ages*, vol. 1, edited by Sylvia Glickman and Martha Furman Schleifer. New York: G. K. Hall, 1996.

Paola Massarenghi

Kendrick, Robert. "Paola Massarenghi." In *Women Composers: Music Through the Ages*, vol. 1, edited by Sylvia Glickman and Martha Furman Schleifer. New York: G. K. Hall, 1996.

Isabella de' Medici Orsini

Cardamone, Donna G. "Lifting the Protective Veil of Anonymity: Women as Composer-Performers, ca. 1300–1566." In *Women Composers: Music Through the Ages*, vol. 1, edited by Sylvia Glickman and Martha Furman Schleifer. New York: G. K. Hall, 1996.
Smith, Candace. "Leonora Orsini." In *Women Composers: Music Through the Ages*, vol. 1, edited by Sylvia Glickman and Martha Furman Schleifer. New York: G. K. Hall, 1996.

Leonora Orsini

Newcomb, Anthony. *The Madrigal at Ferrara, 1579–1597*. Princeton, NJ: Princeton University Press, 1980.
Smith, Candace. "Leonora Orsini." In *Women Composers: Music Through the Ages*, vol. 1, edited by Sylvia Glickman and Martha Furman Schleifer. New York: G. K. Hall, 1996.

Renaissance Patrons of Music

Pendle, Karin. "Musical Women in Early Modern Europe." In *Women and Music, a History*, 2d ed., edited by Karin Pendle. Bloomington: Indiana University Press, 2001.
Prizer, William F. "Games of Venus: Secular Vocal Music in the Late Quattrocento and Early Cinquecento." *Journal of Musicology* 9 (1991): 3–4.
Prizer, William F. "Renaissance Women as Patrons of Music: The North-Italian Courts." In *Rediscovering the Muses: Women's Musical Traditions*, edited by Kimberly Marshall. Boston: Northeastern University Press, 1993.

Cesarina Ricci

Bridges, Thomas W. "Ricci, Cesarina." In *The New Grove Dictionary of Women Composers*, edited by Julie Anne Sadie and Rhian Samuel. London: Macmillan Press Limited, 1994.

Claudia Sessa

Kendrick, Robert L. "Sessa, Claudia." In *The New Grove Dictionary of Women Composers*, edited by Julie Anne Sadie and Rhian Samuel. London: Macmillan Press Limited, 1994.
Smith, Candace. "Claudia Sessa." In *Women Composers: Music Through the Ages*, vol. 1, edited by Sylvia Glickman and Martha Furman Schleifer. New York: G. K. Hall, 1996.

Lucrezia Vizzana

Monson, Craig. *Disembodied Voices: Music and Culture in an Early Modern Italian Convent*. Berkeley: University of California Press, 1995.
———. "The Making of Lucrezia Orsina Vizzana's *Componimenti Musicali* (1623)." In *Creative Women in Medieval Early Modern Italy*, edited by E. Ann Matter and John Coakley. Philadelphia: University of Pennsylvania Press, 1994.
———. "Vizzana, Lucrezia Orsina." In *The New Grove Dictionary of Women Composers*, edited by Julie Anne Sadie and Rhian Samuel. London: Macmillan Press Limited, 1994.
Roche, Jerome. "Orsina, Lucretia." In *The New Grove Dictionary of Music and Musicians*, edited by Stanley Sadie. London: Macmillan Press Limited, 1980.

Selected Discography

Vittoria Aleotti/Raphaela Aleotta

Vittoria Aleotti, Baciai per haver vita. Maenniskors motete, with the Gothenburg chamber choir "Kammarkoeren A Cappella" Vittoria Aleotti/Raffaela Aleotta (ca. 1574–1646). Fusion records CD 117 (1995).

Caterina Assandra

Ave verum corpus and *Ego flos campi*. On *Go Tell It on the Mountain*. Calvert Johnson, organ. Ithaca, NY: Calcante Recordings, CAL CD/CS 006 (1994).

Jubilate Deo (1609). On *Women's Voices: Five Centuries of Song*. Neva Pilgrim, soprano; Edward Smith, harpsichord; Steven Heyman, piano. Leonarda Records, LE 338 (1997).

Rosa Mistica: musiche di monache lombarde del Seicento (Music of the Lombard Nuns of the seventeenth century). Works by Isabella Leonarda, Maria Xaveria Peruchona, Caterina Assandra, Chiara Margarita Cozzolani, Rosa Giacinta Badalla, Bianca Maria Meda, Claudia Sessa, and Claudia Francesca Rusca. Cappella Artemisia TACTUS TC 600003 (Allegro Imports) (1999).

Gracia Baptista

Go Tell It on the Mountain. Calvert Johnson, organist. Ithaca, NY: Calcante Recordings, CD CAL-006 (1993).

MUSICA DE LA PUEBLA DE LOS ANGELES: Music by Women of the Mexican, Cuban, and European Baroque. Teodora Gines. Son de La Ma Teodora. Ars Femina Ensemble. Music by Teodora Gines, Maria Paterina, Gracia Baptista, Sor Juana Ines De la Cruz, Anna Ovena Hoijer, Lucrezia Vizana, Chiara Margarita Cozzolani, Maria Joachina Rodrigues, Maria Xavera Peruchona, and Guadalupe Ortiz. NANNERL 004 (1996). (Order from ARS FEMINA.)

Women Composers for Organ Music Spanning Five Centuries. Barbara Harbach, organist. Jaffrey, NH: Gasparo Records GSCD 294 (1993).

Saint Birgitta of Sweden

Hildegard of Bingen and Birgitta von Schweden. Hildegard of Bingen, 8 songs; 5 songs from Birgitta's *Cantus Sororum*. Les Flamboyants, Miriam Andersen, Kelly Landerkin, and Marilla Vargas; with Susanne Ansong, fiddle; Michael Form, recorder. BaumKlang RK 9802 (1997).

Anne Boleyn

Historical Anthology of Music by Women. Isabella Leonarda, *Messe e motetti*, op. 18; *Messa*, no. 1 (*Kyrie*); with music by Anne Boleyn, Maddalena Casulana, Francesca Caccini, Anna Amalia Princess of Prussia, Elisabeth-Claude Jacquet de la Guerre, Maria Grimani, and others. Compiled by James R. Briscoe, Indiana University Press, ISBN: 0-253-31268-X (1991). (Cassette)

The Pleasures and Follies of Love. Koch International Classics 7527 (2001).

Maddalena Casulana

Historical Anthology of Music by Women. Isabella Leonarda, *Messe e motetti*, op. 18; *Messa*, no. 1 (*Kyrie*); with music by Anne Boleyn, Maddalena Casulana, Francesca Caccini, Anna Amalia Princess of Prussia, Elisabeth-Claude Jacquet de la Guerre, Maria Grimani, and others. Compiled by James R. Briscoe, Indiana University Press, ISBN: 0-253-31268-X (1991). (Cassette)

Dia, Comtessa de Troubadours and *Trouvères*

Bella Domna, the Medieval Woman: Lover, Poet, Patroness, Saint. Comtessa de Dia, *A chantar m'er de so qu'ien non volria.* Mara Kiek, voice. Sinfonye, Stevie Wishart, dir. HYPERION CDA 66283 (1988).

Cansós de Trobairitz: Songs of the Women Troubadours (c1200). Comtessa de Dia, *A Chantar; Estat ai en greu cossirier; Ab joi et ab joven m'apais.* Hespèrion XX, Jordi Savall, dir.; Montserrat Figueras and Pilar Figueras, sopranos; Josep Benet, tenor. EMI Records, new release on Virgin veritas VER S 61310 2 (1996).

La Chanson d'ami: chansons de femme, XII-XIII Centuries. Maroie de Dregnau de Lille, *Mout m'abellist quant je voi revenir* (with cover of a painting of "Marie de France at Her Writing Desk"). Perceval Ensemble, Guy Robert, director; Katia Caré, voice. ARION 68290 (1995).

A Chantar: Lieder der frauen-minne: Songs of Courtly Love in the Middle Ages. Comtessa de Dia, *A Chantar.* Estampie Münchner Ensemble für frühe Musik. CHRISTOPHORUS digital 74583 (1994).

The Medieval Lady. Comtessa de Dia, *A Chantar.* Elizabethan Conversation ensemble, Susan Sandman, Derwood Crocker, Andrea Folan, guest soprano. With music by the Maroie de Dregnau de Lille, Queen Blanche, Hildegard of Bingen, Anne Boleyn, Mary Harvey, et al. Leonarda 338 (1997).

The Sweet Look and the Loving Manner, Troubairitz Love Lyrics and Chansons De Femme. Comtessa de Dia, Estampie on *A chantar m'er*, instrumental realization arranged by Wishart; *Estat ai en greu cossirier* (I Have Been in Great Perplexity). Sinfonye, Stevie Wishart, dir. Voice, medieval fiddle, oud, bendir, hurdy-gurdy. HYPERION CDA66625 (1993).

The Unicorn: Medieval French Songs. Marie de France, *Issi Avint Qu'un Cers Beveit* (A Thirsty Deer Was Standing By) and *D'Un Gupil Dit* ("A Fox They Say"). Set to music by anonymous. Anne Azema, voice, with Cheryl Ann Fulton, harps; Shira Kammen, vielle, rebec, harp; Jesse Lepkoff, flute. Erato 4509-94830-2 (1994).

Herrad of Landsperg

Hortus Deliciarum. Music from Herrad of Landsperg's "Garden of Delights," with music also by Hildegard of Bingen (1098–1179). DISCANTUS, all-woman vocal ensemble, Brigitte Lesne, dir. OPUS 111, OPS 30-220 (1998).

Hildegard von Bingen

Celestial Light. Chants by Hildegard with new settings of Hildegard's texts by Robert Kyr. TAPESTRY. TELARC CD-80456 (1997).

Celestial Stairs. 15 works. Ensemble fur Fruhe Musik Augsburg. Christophorus CH77205 (1997).

Early Music. 0 Virtus Sapientie, with music by Kassia, other early music composers, and contemporary composers writing in early music styles. Kronos Quartet. LACHRYME ANTIQUA Nonesuch 79457-2 (1997).

11 Songs by ALBA. Agnethe Christensen, alto; Poul Hoxbro, Pipe-&-psaltery, tar, triangle; Helen Davies, harp; and members of the vocal ensemble CON FUOCO. Class CD 198 (1998).

11,000 Virgins: Chants for the Feast of St. Ursula. ANONYMOUS 4, Ruth Cunningham, Marsha Genensky, Susan Hellauer, Johanna Maria Rose. Harmonia Mundi. USA 907200 (1997).

Feminea Forma Maria. 12 Marian songs from the Dendermonde Codex: *Ave Maria; 0 clarissima gemma; 0 Splendidissima Hodie aperuit; Quia ergo femina; Cum processit; Cum erubuerint; 0 frondens virga; 0 quam magnum; Ave generosa; 0 virga ac diadema; 0 tu suavissima virga.* Ensemble Mediatrix, by Johannes Berchman Goschi, dir. CALIG 50 982 (1996).

Hesperus: "Chants of Hildegard of Bingen." Rosa Lamoreaux, soprano, with Tina Chancery, vielle, kamenj, lyra, viola da gamba, recorder; Scott Reiss, recorders, hammered dulcimer. KOCH 3-7443-2 (1998).

Hildegard of Bingen and Birgitta von Schweden. Hildegard of Bingen, 8 songs; 5 songs from Birgitta's *Cantus Sororum.* Les Flamboyants, Miriam Andersen, Kelly Landerkin, and Marilla Vargas; with Susanne Ansong, fiddle; Michael Form, recorder. BaumKlang RK 9802 (1997).

Hildegard von Bingen und Ihre Zeit. CRISTOPHORUS 74584 (1994).

Monk and the Abbess. O quam mirabilis; O Ecclesia; O Clarissima Mater; O Tu Illustrata. Musica Sacra, Richard Westenburg; with Judith Malafronte, mezzo-soprano: Music by Catalyst 09026-68329-2 (1996).

O Nobilissima Viriditas. 16 songs. Catherine Schroeder, voice; accompanied by Catherine Sergent, soprano, Deya Marshall, cloches; Emmanuel Bonnardot, viele; and Stephane Gallet, ney. Champeaux recordings CSM 0006 (1996).

Ordo Virtutum. Cologne Sequentia Ensemble for Medieval Music. RCA, 77394 (1998).

Ordo Virtutum. Ensemble for MUSIK DES MITTLELATTERS, Stefan Morent, dir., Jill Feldman, Cornelia Melian, Monika Mauch, Sterling Jones, Andrea von Ramm, vocals. Bayer Records, BR 100 249 (1998).

Ordo Virtutum. Bmg/Deutsche Harmonia mundi 77394 (1998).

SAINTS: Hildegard of Bingen. SEQUENTIA, works from Hildegard of Bingen's Symphoniae, focusing on Christian saints. Deutsche Harmonia Mundi, 05472 77378-2 (1998).

Symphony of the Harmony of Celestial Revelations: The Complete Hildegard von Bingen, Volume I (other volumes to follow). SINFONYE, by Stevie Wishart, dir., and realizations with members of the Oxford Girls Choir. CELESTIAL HARMONIES, 13127-2 (1996).

O Vis Aeternitatis: Vesper in Der Abtei St. Hildegard. 12 works. Schola der Benediktinerinnenabtei St. Hildegard Eibingen, by Johannes Berchmans Goschl and Sr. Christiane Rath, osb. dir. ARS MUSIC, AM 1203-2 (1997).

Kassia

Ancient Greek Women's Laments. Two ancient Greek songs concerning women's laments, performed utilizing ancient Greek music styles and instruments. Pandourion Records, PRCD 1001 (1995).

Early Music. Hildegard of Bingen, *O Virtus Sapientie*, with music by Kassia, other early music composers, and contemporary composers writing in early music styles. Kronos Quartet. LACHRYME ANTIQUA Nonesuch 79457-2 (1997).

Fallen Women/Arab & Byzantine Chant/Women as Composers and Performers of Medieval Chant. Kassia, *The Fallen Woman; Augustus*; includes early Christian women's chants in the Middle Eastern Churches, works by Kassia, Hildegard of Bingen, and music from the Codex las Huelgas. SARBAND and Osnabrueck Jugendchor. JARO 4210-2/(1998).

Margaret of Austria

Danses de la Renaissance. 4 dances: *L'esperance de bourbon; Sans faire; La danse de cleves; Filles a marier*. Clemencic Consort, Rene Clemencic, dir. Instruments include renaissance trombone, harp, flute a bec, viols, lute, fiddle, drum, with Zeger Vandersteene, Hans Breitschopf, countre-tenors and Kurt Spanier, tenor. Also dances by Moderne, Susato, Gervaise, Phalese, Franck, Hassler, Attaingnant, Demantius, Machaut, and Dufay. Harmonia Mundi HMC 90610 (1986).

Claudia Sessa

Rosa Mistica: musiche di monache lombarde del Seicento (Music of the Lombard Nuns of the Seventeenth Century). Works by Isabella Leonarda, Maria Xaveria Peruchona, Caterina Assandra, Chiara Margarita Cozzolani, Rosa Giacinta Badalla, Bianca Maria Meda, Claudia Sessa, and Claudia Francesca Rusca. Cappella Artemisia TACTUS TC 600003 (Allegro Imports) (1999).

Lucrezia Vizzana

Canti nel chiostro: musiche nei monasteri femminili del '600 a Bologna. Lucrezia Orsina Vizzana, *O invictissima* (1623); *Ave Stella* (1623); *Protector noster* (1623). Cappella Artemisia, Candace Smith, dir. TACTUS TC600001 (1994).

Componinenti Musicali. Lucretia Orsina Vizzana, 20 extant motets. Musica Secreta (Deborah Roberts, Tessa Bonner, Mary Nichols), with John Toll, organist; David Miller, chitarrone; Catherine King, mez. LINN Records, CKD 071 (1998).

Selected List of Works—Modern Editions

Vittoria Aleotti/Raphaela Aleotta

Cinque madrigali a 4 voci miste, premessa e trascrizione di Giuliana Gialdroni (Aleotti, Vittoria). Roma: Pro Musica Studium, 1986.

Ghirlanda de madrigali a quarto voci. Edited by C. Ann Carruthers; Introduction by C. Ann Carruthers; revised and expanded by Thomas W. Bridges and Massimo Ossi. New York: Broude Brothers, 1994.

Sacrae cantiones. Angelus ad pastores ait. Edited by Ann Carruthers-Clement (Aleotta, Raphaela). New York: Broude Brothers, 1983.

Sacrae cantiones. Ascendens Christus in altum. Edited by Ann Carruthers-Clement (Aleotta, Raphaela). New York: Broude Brothers, 1983.

T'amo Mia Vita (Aleotti); *Io V'amo Vito Mia* (Aleotti); *Exurgat Deus* (Alleota); *Ego Flos Campi* (Alleota). In "Vittoria Aleotti/Raphaela Aleotta," by Thomasin LaMay. In *Women Composers: Music Through the Ages*, vol. 1, edited by Sylvia Glickman and Martha Furman Schleifer. New York: G. K. Hall, 1996. Bryn Mawr, PA: Hildegard Publishing Company (G. K. Hall reprint), 1998.

Caterina Assandra

Ave verum corpus; Ego flos campi. In *Organ Music by Women Composers before 1800*, edited by Calvert Johnson. Pullman, WA: Vivace Press, 1993.

Duo Seraphim (from op. 2). In *Two Sacred Works for Three Treble Voices*, edited by Barbara Garvey Jackson. Fayetteville, AK: ClarNan Editions, 1990.

Jubilate Deo (from op. 2). In *The Monody*, edited by Karl Gustav Fellerer and translated by Robert Kolben. Cologne: Arno Volk Verlag, 1968.

O dulcis amor Jesu. In "Caterina Assandra," by Jane Bowers. In *Women Composers: Music Through the Ages*, vol. 1, edited by Sylvia Glickman and Martha Furman Schleifer. New York: G. K. Hall, 1996.

O dulcis amor Jesu. In *Three Choral Works from the 16th Century*. Bryn Mawr, PA: Hildegard Publishing Company (G. K. Hall reprint), 1996.

Gracia Baptista

Conditor Alme. In "Gracia Baptista," by Calvert Johnson. In *Women Composers: Music Through the Ages*, vol. 1, edited by Sylvia Glickman and Martha Furman Schleifer. New York: G. K. Hall, 1996.

Johnson, Calvert. *Organ Music by Women Composers before 1800*. Pullman, WA: Vivace Press, 1993.

La Música en la Corte de Carlos V, 2d ed. rev., 2 vols. (vol. 1 text, vol. 2 music) Anglés, Higinio. Monumentos de la Música Española II. Barcelona: Consejo Superior de Investigaciones Científicas; Instituto Español de Musicología, 1965.

Reprint: Venegas de Henestrosa, Luys. *Libro de Cifra Nueva*, 4 vols. (music only, without text), Higinio Anglés, ed. Boca Raton, FL: Masters Music, n.d.

Suster Bertken

Die werelt hielt mi in hair gewout. In "Suster Bertken," by Christina Hospenthal. In *Women Composers: Music Through the Ages*, vol. 1, edited by Sylvia Glickman and Martha Furman Schleifer. New York: G. K. Hall, 1996.

Anne Boleyn

O Deathe, Rock Me Asleepe, for voice and keyboard or lute (attributed; 1536). In *Anne Boleyn* by Edith Boroff. In *Historical Anthology of Music by Women*, edited by James R. Briscoe. Bloomington and Indianapolis: Indiana University Press, 1987.

Maddalena Casulana

Madrigal VI (1570). In *Maddalena Casulana* by Beatrice Pescerelli. In *Historical Anthology of Music by Women*, edited by James R. Briscoe. Bloomington and Indianapolis: Indiana University Press, 1987.

Se scior se ved'il laccio a cui dianz'io. In "Madalena [*sic*] Casulana," by Ellen D. Lerner. In *Women Composers: Music Through the Ages*, vol. 1, edited by Sylvia Glickman and Martha Furman Schleifer. New York: G. K. Hall, 1996.

Se scior se ved'il laccio. Bryn Mawr, PA: Hildegard Publishing Company (G. K. Hall reprint), 1998.

Sulpitia Cesis

Maria Magdalena et altera Maria; Stabat Mater; Il mio piu vago Sole; Io Son ferito sì; Cantate Domino; Parvulus Filius. In "Sulpitia Cesis," by Candace Smith. In *Women Composers: Music Through the Ages*, vol. 1, edited by Sylvia Glickman and Martha Furman Schleifer. New York: G. K. Hall, 1996.

Maria Magdalena; Parvulus Filius. Bryn Mawr, PA: Hildegard Publishing Company (G. K. Hall reprint), 1998.

Three Motets for 4, 5, and 8 voices. Edited by Candace Smith. Bryn Mawr, PA: Hildegard Publishing Company, 1998.

Comtessa de Dia

A Chantar, troubadour song. In *Countess of Dia*, by Beverly J. Evans. In *Historical Anthology of Music by Women*, edited by James R. Briscoe. Bloomington and Indianapolis: Indiana University Press, 1987.

A chantar m'er. In "The Comtessa de Dia (fl. 12th c.) and the Trobairitz," by Chantal Phan. In *Women Composers: Music Through the Ages*, vol. 1, edited by Sylvia Glickman and Martha Furman Schleifer. New York: G. K. Hall, 1996.

Hildegard von Bingen

De Sancta Marta (chant sequence); *In Evangelium* (chant antiphon); *Kyrie* (Mass ordinary chant). In *Hildegard von Bingen*, by Barbara Jean Jeskalian. In *Historical Anthology of Music by Women*, edited by James R. Briscoe. Bloomington and Indianapolis: Indiana University Press, 1987.

Five songs from the *Symphonia: Vos flores rosarum; O Clarissima Mater; O lucidissima aostolorum turba; Cum vox sanguinis; O Ecclesia*. In "Hildegard von Bingen," by Marianne R. Pfau. In *Women Composers: Music Through the Ages*, vol. 1, edited by Sylvia Glickman and Martha Furman Schleifer. New York: G. K. Hall, 1996.

Flos campi: no. 38, Gaudete, O socii: no. 80, Procession: *In principio: no. 87* from the *Ordo Virtutum*. In "The *Ordo Virtutum*" by Audrey Davidson. In *Women Composers: Music Through the Ages*, vol. 1, edited by Sylvia Glickman and Martha Furman Schleifer. New York: G. K. Hall, 1996.

Hildegard von Bingen: Lieder. Edited by Prudentia Barth, OSB, M. Immaculata Ritscher, OSB, and Joseph Schmidt-Goerg. Salzburg: Otto Müller Verlag, 1969.

Hildegard von Bingen: Symphonia armonie celestium revelationum. Vols. 1–8. *The Trinity-Father and Son*. Vol. 1 (*O vis eternitatis; O virtus Sapientie; O quam mirabilis; O pastor animarum; O cruor sanguinis; O magne pater; O eterne Deus*). *The Blessed Virgin Mary*. Vol. 2 (*Ave Maria; O clarissma mater; O splendidissima gemma; Hodie aperuit; Quia ergo femina; Cum processit; Cum erubuerint; O frondens virga; O quam magnum miraculum; Ave generosa; O virga mediatrix; O viridissima virga; O virga ac diadema; O tu suavissima; O quam preciosa; O tu illustrata*). *The Holy Spirit*. Vol. 3 (*Spiritus sanctus vivificans; Karitas habundat; Laus trinitati; O ignee spiritus; O ignis spiritus paracliti*). *The Celestial Hierarchy*. Vol. 4 (*O gloriosissimi lux vivens angeli; O vos angeli; O spectabilis viri; O vos felices radices; O cohors milicie; O lucidissima apostolorum; O speculum columbe; O dulcis electe; O victoriosissimi; Vos flores rosarum; O vos imitatores; O successores*). *The Patron Saints*. Vol. 5 *O mirum admirandum; O viriditas digiti Dei; O felix anima; O beata infantia; O presul; O felix apparicio pparicio, O beatissime Ruperte; Quia felix puericia; O Ierusalem; Mathias sanctus; O Bonifaci, O Euchari columba; O Euchari in leta via; Columba aspexit*). *Women—Virgins, Widows, Innocents*. Vol. 6 (*O pulcre facies; O nobilissima viriditas; O dulcissime amator; O Pater omnium; Rex noster promptus). Saint Ursula and 11,000 Virgins.* Vol. 7 (*Spiritui sancto; O rubor sanguinis; Favus distillans; Antiphons for Matins: Studium divinitatis, Unde quocumque, De-patria, Deus enim in prima, Aer enim volat, Et ideo puelle, Deus enim rorem, Sed diabolus, O Ecclesia; Cum vox sanguinis. The Church.* Vol. 8 (*O virgo Ecclesia; Nunc gaudeant; O orzchis Ecclesia; O chorus-cans*). Edited and translated by Marianne Richert Pfau. Bryn Mawr, PA: Hildegard Publishing Company, 1997.

Ordo Virtutum. Edited by Audrey Davidson. Bryn Mawr, PA: Hildegard Publishing Company, 2002.

Songs of the Living Light (14 antiphons and responsories from Scivias III, vision 13). Edited by Marianne Pfau. Bryn Mawr, PA: Hildegard Publishing Company, 1995.

Kassia

Augustus, the Monarch; The Fallen Woman. Edited by Diane Touliatos-Banker. In *Historical Anthology of Music by Women*, edited by James Briscoe. Bloomington and Indianapolis: Indiana University Press, 1987.

Edessa Rejoices; The Five-Stringed Lute and Fivefold Lamp; Above the Teachings of the Greeks; Now the Voice of Isaiah the Prophet; Let Us Praise Peter and Paul. In "Kassia," by Diane Touliatos. In *Women Composers: Music Through the Ages*, vol. 1, edited by Sylvia Glickman and Martha Furman Schleifer. New York: G. K. Hall, 1996.

13 antiphons: (We Praise Your Great Mercy, Oh Christ; Leaving the Wealth of Her Family; Christ, the Power of Your Cross; Christina, the Martyr, Holding the Cross; Christ, the King of Glory; Hymn to the Pious Pelagia: Wherever Sin Has Become Excessive; The Fallen Woman: Lord, the Woman Fallen into Many Sins; Augustus, the Monarch; Let Us Praise Peter and Paul; Now the Voice of Isaiah the Prophet; The Five-Stringed Lute and Fivefold Lamp Above the Teachings of the Greeks; Edessa Rejoices). Modern transcriptions by Diane Touliatos. Bryn Mawr, PA: Hildegard Publishing Company, 2000.

Margaret of Austria

The Chanson Albums of Marguerite of Austria. MSS 228 and 11239, Bibliothèque Royale de Belgique, Brussels. Berkeley: University of California Press, 1965.

Se je souspire/Ecce iterum. In "Margaret of Austria," by Martin Picker. In *Women Composers: Music Through the Ages*, vol. 1, edited by Sylvia Glickman and Martha Furman Schleifer. New York: G. K. Hall, 1996.

Se je souspire/Ecce iterum. In *Three Choral Works of the 16th Century.* Bryn Mawr, PA: Hildegard Publishing Company (G. K. Hall reprint), 1996.

Paola Massarenghi

Quando spiega. In "Paola Massarenghi," by Thomasin LaMay. In *Women Composers: Music Through the Ages*, vol. 1, edited by Sylvia Glickman and Martha Furman Schleifer. New York: G. K. Hall, 1996.

Quando spiega. In *Three Choral Works of the 16th Century.* Bryn Mawr, PA: Hildegard Publishing Company, 1996.

Isabella de' Medici Orsini

Lieta vivo e contenta dapoi ch'il mio bel sole. In "Lifting the Protective Veil of Anonymity: Women as Composer-Performers ca. 1300–1566," by Donna G. Cardamone. In *Women Composers: Music Through the Ages*, vol. 1, edited by Sylvia Glickman and Martha Furman Schleifer. New York: G. K. Hall, 1996.

Leonora Orsini

Per pianto la mia carne. In "Leonora Orsini," by Candace Smith. In *Women Composers: Music Through the Ages*, vol. 1, edited by Sylvia Glickman and Martha Furman Schleifer. New York: G. K. Hall, 1996. Bryn Mawr, PA: Hildegard Publishing Company (G. K. Hall reprint), 1998.

Claudia Sessa

Vattene pur lasciva orecchia umana; Occhi io vissi di voi. In "Claudia Sessa," by Candace Smith. In *Women Composers: Music Through the Ages*, vol. 1, edited by Sylvia Glickman and Martha Furman Schleifer. New York: G. K. Hall, 1996. Bryn Mawr, PA: Hildegard Publishing Company (G. K. Hall reprint), 1998.

Lucrezia Orsina Vizzana

Domine Dominus noster. Bryn Mawr, PA: Hildegard Publishing Company, 1998.

Five Arias: Sonet vox tua in auribus cordis mei; Usquequo oblivisceris me in finem; O magnum mysterium; Ornaverunt faciem templi; O invictissima Christi martyr. Bryn Mawr, PA: Hildegard Publishing Company (G. K. Hall reprint), 1998.

Protector noster. Bryn Mawr, PA: Hildegard Publishing Company (G. K. Hall reprint), 1998.

Sonet vox tua in auribus cordis mei; Usquequo oblivisceris me in finem; O magnum mysterium; Ornaverunt faciem templi; O invictissima Christi martyr; Domine Dominus noster, quam admirabile; Protector noster. In "Donna Lucrezia Orsina Vizzana" by Craig A. Monson. In *Women Composers: Music Through the Ages*, vol. 1, edited by Sylvia Glickman and Martha Furman Schleifer. New York: G. K. Hall, 1996.

3
The Seventeenth Century

Barbara Garvey Jackson

Introduction

Roles of Women in the Seventeenth Century

There was the new female career as a professional singer, at first attached to courts, but later also in the new public opera houses. Women also composed operas, although more often for court performances than for the public stage. Women composed and published sacred music, although with many restrictions. The Venetian ospedali (or conservatories) cared for orphaned or abandoned girls and trained the most talented in music, originally to encourage almsgiving by the public who heard the musical performances. In the seventeenth century there were four such institutions in Venice, and the performances given by the girls were among the most splendid in Europe. The conservatories also made possible a new career for women, for after following a ten-year course of study, some of the girls became teachers at the institution—a career which did not involve joining a religious order. Aristocratic ladies, particularly those in German lands, often received splendid musical educations and some became composers.

Women and Church Music

By the latter part of the sixteenth century, dynastic families of court and operatic musicians arose in which both male and female members of the family were professional musicians. Many male church musicians, Catholic as well as Protestant, were no longer required to be celibate, and dynasties like the Bachs in Lutheran Germany and the Couperins in Catholic France transmitted both their talent and good training to their daughters as well as to their sons. The children had access to music training, professional careers, and in some cases church employment. Even in

Protestant churches the rule of all-male choirs was retained, just as it was in Catholic practice, still true in later centuries. For example, the choir of the Lutheran St. Thomas Church
in Leipzig trained boys in the associated school to sing treble parts in church music, and
the Anglican choirs in England followed a similar pattern. To this day there are many all-
male choirs, with old establishments like the Vienna Boys' Choir still training boys as
treble singers. Among the Protestants, women could only sing hymns in church as members of the congregation—Lutheran chorales and Calvinist psalms. The one exception was
the singing of nuns' choirs in convents—available only to Catholic women.

In seventeenth-century Italy, the practice in convents was a mixed picture. After the
Council of Trent had established rules for the Counter-Reformation of the Catholic
church in the mid-sixteenth century, there had been much debate about the role of music,
including whether polyphonic music should be allowed in the church at all. The council finally decided that sacred texts could be set to music and even acknowledged that
they could be spiritually uplifting. Therefore, drastic changes were not required in
church music performed or composed by males in churches or in monasteries.

However, in the convents it was a very different matter. Many members of the council
were terrified of corruption through the wiles of women and were convinced that "reform"
of the convents was necessary. Lurid descriptions of abuses abound in the literature, most of
which were unsubstantiated gossip and fantasy. Nevertheless, to avoid the stimulation of
any sort of appetite through the "sensuous art" of polyphony, the council prescribed only
plainsong (Gregorian chant) for convents, with absolutely no polyphonic music and no outside musicians or teachers. The local authorities would sometimes relent and allow some
music with just one voice and organ. This appears to be restrictive, but in fact, perhaps un-
wittingly, the clergy was prescribing the new (and fashionable) musical texture of soloist
with organ continuo. Also, by allowing a type of music that focused on a soloist, the
anonymity of the singers was lost, and some of the nun soloists became quite famous.

All convents were ultimately under the control of male ecclesiastics, so if music
flourished in a particular convent, it was possible only because the local authorities permitted it. In actual practice, many not only permitted but even encouraged music making by nuns, and more than half the music published by women in northern Italy in
the seventeenth century was by nuns. Milan, Bologna, and Novara were the sites of famous seventeenth-century musical convents, as Ferrara had been in the sixteenth century. Male composers also wrote music specifically for the use of nuns.

Among the obstacles faced by all nuns after the Council of Trent was the enforce-
ment of *clausura*, the strict enclosure of the nuns within the convent, with no contact
with the outside world except to a limited degree by family members. Some nuns complained to their families that not even doctors could see them. Supposedly, nun musicians would have had no contact with new developments in music after they were
professed as nuns. The music that they wrote, however, clearly indicates that this was
not an effective ban and that they were often well aware of current musical developments. The music that male composers wrote for them was one possible route by which
they learned what was going on in the outside musical world; another was the recent
training and musical contacts of newly professed nuns.

Italian patrician families tended to preserve family estates for their male heirs by sending most of their daughters to convents, often encouraging renunciation of family inheritance rights by the nuns. (Between 1600 and 1650 it has been shown that in Milan about 75 percent of noble daughters were nuns.) A dowry was required for convent entrance, but it was not as large as a marriage dowry. Some convents even exempted needed talented musicians from part of the dowry requirement. This meant that there were large populations in the convents and that many of the women were well educated in the arts. Although some girls may have been there against their will, most were truly religious and may have preferred a nun's life to an arranged marriage. Many who entered the convents in the early part of this period did not expect to be put in enclosure, however, and music became their great solace.

Even with enclosure, families often sent supposedly forbidden musical instruments to their relatives, as seen in convent property lists, gift lists, and wills. In some controversies between nuns and church authorities, the families outside the walls were involved in the fray, usually supporting the nuns. The aristocratic backgrounds of the young girls, which had given them opportunities for training and contact with new musical trends before entering the convent, were reinforced when gifts of printed music also found their way within.

Education

By the sixteenth century, treble voice ranges had become an essential part of polyphonic (multivoiced) musical style. Boys trained in choir schools sang soprano and alto parts, and the male falsetto voice was also used, especially for alto parts. In Italy the practice arose of prolonging the high voices of talented boys by castration, and the use of the resulting high voice (castrato) persisted through the nineteenth century. This made trained soprano and alto voices available for choirs without resorting to what was regarded as the far more scandalous mixing of male and female voices and the equally undesirable use of female voices in church music. *Castrati* had become common in church singing in previous centuries, but in the seventeenth century the developing world of opera also realized the potential usefulness of the strong, male treble voices.

The Venetian *ospedali*, or conservatories, in which musical training was originally established encouraged almsgiving by the public who attended musical performances there, cared for many in need and continued to train orphaned or abandoned girls (often illegitimate children) in music. They were called *ospedali* because of their rescuing mission. By the seventeenth century there were still four in operation in Venice, the ospedali della Pietà, dei Mendicanti, degl' Incurabili, and dei Derelitti or l'Ospedaletto; the musical performances given by the residents were among the most splendid in Europe. The money to run these establishments came from public and private funds, gondola fees, the sale of indulgences, and alms collections. The alms collections were especially important in providing dowries for the girls so that they could later have respectable marriages. Girolamo Miani, the founder of l'Ospedaletto (later, Saint Emiliani), believed that the poor should be educated, including training in the arts, and there, the students also performed the chants for the daily services. Although the institutions served

Print of Santi Giovanni e Paolo in Venice by Giovanni Battista Borghesi, the Ospedale Mendicanti.
© Historical Picture Archive/CORBIS.

The doorway of the Incurabili Hospital in Venice, Italy.
© Philippa Lewis; Edifice/CORBIS.

many clients, it was the girls who received musical training. By 1600 there were about forty in a special program at l'Ospedaletto learning music.

The other three *ospedali* also offered excellent musical education for talented young women, and each had its own female choir and orchestra. Their concerts of oratorios and other choral and instrumental music were open to the public. The greatest teachers available were hired for them; for example, Antonio Vivaldi (1678–1741) taught at the Pietà beginning in 1703 and wrote most of his more than 400 concertos for these students. They were taught all instruments, including the wind instruments like the bassoon (which females never played in the outside world), and as a result there is a great repertory of music written for them.

The Music

Interesting questions arise about the performance of some of the music written by the convent composers. Much of the repertory is for solo voice with continuo, and one would expect that soprano or alto voices would be the only ones used. In the solo works by Isabella Leonarda, however, several of those for a soprano are marked as also possible for a tenor, and of her ninety-seven pieces for solo voice fourteen are for bass, not likely to be resident in the convent. Many of the published works which are for three or more voice parts, call for tenor and bass singers. Although there are records of nuns with quite low voices, and the tenor ranges were high enough that altos could sing those parts, the problem of the bass parts remains. There are several potential explanations. Possibly the music was first written for female voices and, when published, adapted to more general use—for boys and adult males—since on no account did the Catholic church tolerate mixing voices of men and women (certainly not officially). Or perhaps the first form of the music was the composer's true conception of the piece, which was then altered by various means to fit an all-female group of singers. When sung in the convents, all the parts could be transposed up so that the lowest written parts were possible for the women to sing. It is known that such transpositions did occur, and some successful modern recordings demonstrate that this solution can work. The third possibility is that bass instruments played the bass parts. The mystery remains.

At this time a truly new musical technique called figured bass was becoming widespread. It comprised a written-out bass line with numerals beneath the notes to indicate the chords to be played. This bass line plus chords, referred to as a continuo part, was used in choral music, solo song, and orchestral and chamber music of the period. Normally, the continuo part was shared by two people; one played the single notes of the bass line on a cello or viola da gamba and occasionally on the bassoon or trombone, and the other player combined the bass line and appropriate chords on an organ, harpsichord, or lute. This practice, developed in the late sixteenth century, may have originated to provide organists with a system for playing chords to accompany a choral piece from a bass partbook (full scores were not yet the usual practice), but it clearly also made for the new polarity in musical texture—a solid bass line with chords on the low side and a treble part or parts above.

By the seventeenth century composers were exploring new ways of using older musical forms while also developing new forms. The general term "monody" (e.g., a solo singer supported by a continuo part in a single piece or in a section of an opera) covers many kinds of accompanied Italian solo songs. "Aria" or "madrigal" might be terms that the composers used, but, for example, the "madrigals" of Giulio Caccini (ca. 1550–1618) are for solo high voice rather than the many-voiced madrigals of the Renaissance. In sacred music, the word "motet" still meant a musical setting of a text that was not part of the prescribed liturgy of the Mass, but the musical style was now usually for soloists or groups of soloists accompanied by continuo, as opposed to the many-voiced a cappella, Renaissance-style motet. Caccini, a singer-composer and the father of composers Francesca and Settimia Caccini, promoted this emphasis on solo singing. He was a member of the Florentine Camerata, a group that experimented with new styles of singing and composition. Caccini, in the preface to *Nuove Musiche* (1602), says that he set text so that the singer "almost spoke in tones," discreetly supported by a continuo played by a lute or similar instrument. His aims were to "move the affect of the soul" with an emotional style of singing that let the words "speak" through their musical setting and to "delight the senses" with many spectacular, improvised ornaments, for which he wrote out examples in his published collections. He took credit for originating these new styles, as well as for the invention of opera (although his contemporaries were also working along similar lines, and two other Florentine composers had already written operas).

Opera, the new genre of the century, became so influential that even works written for the church eventually became operatic in style. The early Florentine operas of Giulio Caccini and his friend Jacopo Peri (1561–1633) used recitative, a single sung line reflecting the rhythm of the text, accompanied by a bass line and chords (continuo). Brief melodic sections appeared at moments of intense feeling, and short choral or dance passages were interspersed in the course of the opera. Eventually, the more lyric sections were extended and became further developed into arias (songs). In the second half of the century the da capo aria arose; this consisted of a musical and textual section (A), a second contrasting section (B), and the return of the first part (A).

At first opera was court entertainment only, and the singers were salaried members of the court musical staff, as seen in the career of Francesca Caccini. Public performance of opera began in 1637 in Venice. Opera houses had their own orchestras, normally strings and continuo, and in the interest of economy the earlier use of a chorus was abandoned. For solo roles, however, the star singers of the day were increasingly sought after. Among the composers of the new type of opera were Claudio Monteverdi (1567–1643) and Pier Francesco Cavalli (1602–1676), who was the teacher of Barbara Strozzi and Antonia Bembo. Librettists included Giulio Strozzi (1583–1652), composer Barbara Strozzi's adoptive father. Opera spread rapidly from Italy to the rest of Europe, and the first Italian opera performed outside Italy was by Francesca Caccini.

With the growth of opera came the rise of professional singers outside the church. Many women are known to have been opera singers, although they did have competition for some high-voice roles from a surprising quarter—the castrati who sang the treble parts of church music. The world of opera began to realize the advantages of the male treble voice. Well trained and powerful, the high soprano range in a male body was discovered to be useful on the stage, and for those who became stars the career was far more lucrative than singing in the church. Castrati sang many sorts of operatic roles. Commonly, the hero was a male soprano, and the heroine was a female soprano. Tenors generally sang the roles of fathers, and basses were villains. There was an astonishing mixture of genders among the singers and the characters on the opera stage just as in Elizabethan spoken drama by William Shakespeare and others, in which boys played women's roles. This practice lent itself to the many disguise plots used in both spoken and sung drama. Despite competition from castrati, women opera singers had spectacular careers.

The oratorio was a dramatic form of music that was performed in seasons when the opera houses were closed—an approved form of spiritual recreation for times like Lent. Performed in prayer halls called "Oratories," these works were usually unstaged and based on contemplative, serious texts, often from the Old Testament. They used no scenery, costumes, or ballet but shared musical forms with opera, including the overture, arias, recitatives, and orchestral accompaniments. The Italian Camilla de Rossi wrote oratorios based on the model of Alessandro Scarlatti (1660–1725), one of the earliest oratorio composers.

In church music of this century the older polyphonic, choral, a cappella motet was replaced by either the solo motet or motets for two or three voices, in which singers were accompanied by a continuo part. These motets, sometimes substituting for the prescribed texts in services or for portions of the official liturgy, were often designated as suitable for a particular saint's day or an occasion such as the Nativity or the Resurrection. Sacred dialogues were a popular form of religious motet at this time. They commonly involved two or more voices or groups of voices, sung by soloists or choruses. Texts were either in question-and-answer form between the groups or set a dramatic scene between named characters. There were also some secular motets composed in the seventeenth century. The madrigal of this period was for solo high voice rather than the multivoiced madrigals of the Renaissance.

Another genre of vocal chamber music was the cantata, developed in Italy about 1630 and adopted by French composers as the seventeenth century ended. Originally conceived as a solo song, the genre became more and more sharply sectional in structure. Later in the century, Italian cantatas were based mostly on secular subjects and alternated recitatives and arias. French cantatas (in which arias are called *airs*) were often based on Greek mythology. Usually for just one solo singer, they are scored for harpsichord and stringed instrument continuo, sometimes with one or two treble instruments, and do not contain the choruses associated with the eighteenth-century German cantatas of J. S. Bach. The French Elisabeth-Claude Jacquet de la Guerre was in the first generation of composers using the new cantata form.

Two forms of purely instrumental music developed in this period. French harpsichord music included a series of short movements (*pièces*), each with two repeated sections. The music is heavily ornamented with short formulas, indicated by special signs (*agréments*). The *pièces*, usually dance forms all in the same key, were grouped together in suites. The sonata, an Italian multimovement work for a solo keyboard instrument or another melodic instrument and continuo, was imported into France in the latter

Jacquet de la Guerre.
Private Collection, London.

part of the century. François Couperin (1668–1733), regarded today as the best-known composer of his age, wrote sonatas that combined French and Italian characteristics and was followed by many other French composers, including de la Guerre.

Nuns

Italy

> All the works of this illustrious and incomparable Isabella Leonarda are so beautiful, so gracious, and at the same time so learned and wise that my great regret is not having all of them.—*Sebastian de Brossard (1724)*

Of all the women composing in the seventeenth century, **Isabella Leonarda** (1620–1704) has left the largest body of work: twenty published volumes, of which opp. 1, 2, 5, and 9 have, unfortunately, been lost. The extant volumes contain almost 200 individual sacred compositions and one set of sonatas for stringed instruments (eleven trio sonatas and one sonata for solo violin and organ).

She seems to have been destined for the church, as were many in her family. Her brothers included two officials in the cathedral in Novara, and at least one of her sisters joined the Ursuline Order of the Collegio di Santa Orsola (Congregation of Saint Ursula), as did Leonarda. She entered at the age of sixteen and two years later was described by the convent inspectors as having skills in singing, composing music, writing, and arithmetic. Her family was noteworthy for its financial support of the Collegio.

Leonarda probably studied organ with the novice-mistress Elisabeth Casata and may have also studied with Gasparo Casati (ca. 1610–1641), the *maestro di cappella* (music director) at the Cathedral in Novara and probably related to Casata. (Stewart Carter suggests that Leonarda also played the violin.) Casata's publication of 1640, *Terzo libro di sacri concerti* (Third Book of Sacred Concerti), included two sacred dialogues by Leonarda along with his own compositions. It was a common practice for teachers to include a few works by their students along with their own music, a way of displaying both the good student and the music as products of the master.

Leonarda's compositions often include two violin parts as well as an organ continuo, indicating that some of the sisters played instruments as well as sang. She wrote one volume of trio sonatas for two violins and continuo (op. 16, published in 1693), the first extant set by a woman. The last sonata of the set is for solo violin with organ. These may have been used as part of the church services or played in some nonservice setting. Italian devotional or secular music was sometimes performed in the nuns' parlors, where they visited with family members and, if enclosure was not too strict, their friends.

Although Leonarda's first two sacred dialogues were published by her teacher when she was twenty years old, her next surviving publication, the *Sacri concenti*, op. 3 (Sacred Pieces) of 1670, was not written until she was fifty. Thereafter her works appeared at frequent intervals until her last volume in 1700. She had apparently published two other volumes during the thirty years between 1640 and op. 3, but the gap is lengthy. It is likely that she was writing during this period and simply selected manuscripts from her compositions to form the groups of twelve pieces that commonly created a set for Baroque composers. She was busy with her various convent duties as *mater et cancellieria* (mother and clerk); *magistra musicae* (music teacher) in 1658; *madre* (mother) in 1676; *superiora* (mother superior?) in 1686; *madre vicaria* (provincial governor?) in 1693 and 1696; and *consigliera* (counselor) in 1700. However, she remarks in one preface that she had not neglected her duties but had taken the time to write music during the hours reserved for sleep.

Leonarda's works include four Masses: all set for four voices, two violins, and organ continuo. In the *Mass*, op. 4, the violins are optional, and in the three Masses op. 18, the continuo line is reinforced by violone or theorbo. She often inserts instrumental interludes between sections of the Masses. She sets the texts quite expressively, dwelling musically on the meaning of words or phrases. The common practice in northern Italy during the later seventeenth century was to set only three of the five sections of the Ordinary of the Mass polyphonically—those portions in which the text is the same every time Mass is said or sung. Leonarda set only the Kyrie, Gloria, and Credo.

Leonarda also wrote eleven sets of motets. Her motet *Ave suavis dilectio*, op. 6, is an extensive work for communion. The text, which may be by the composer herself, begins:

> Hail, sweet delight,
> Hail, full of grace.
> O feeding food,
> O vast table,
> To drink of you is to live,
> To feed on you is to be born.

It is in seven sections, each set with expressive content that reflects the text. At the section beginning "Salve" (save) there are long melismas (many notes for a single syllable) for the ecstatic contemplation of salvation. The closing section is a typical seventeenth-century poetic irony, set to the pastoral rhythms of a *siciliano* (a lulling, gently rocking dance of the late seventeenth century):

> O for mortals a death which lives,
> For the truly faithful, o such a fate.

Alba Trissina [Trissini] (ca. 1590–after 1638) published only four pieces of music; they are in the collection by her teacher Leone Leoni (fl. 1580–1620) entitled *Sacri fiori, libro quarto de motetti a 1–4* (Holy Flowers, Book Four of Motets for 1–4 voices) (1622). In his preface he praised her decision to be a nun and her beautiful voice and "graceful singing and playing." A choirmaster in Vicenza, his style was much influenced by sixteenth-century Venetian composers. Trissina was a nun at the rich and prestigious convent Santa Maria in Aracoeli in Vicenza; she served as abbess there for two years (1636–1638), but nothing else is known of her.

The convent of Santa Radegonda in Milan was notable for its glorious music throughout most of the seventeenth century. When Archbishop Federico Borromeo (in office 1595–1631) was the prelate in charge of the Milan diocese, he was a strong supporter of sacred music in the convents. He gave the nuns gifts of lutes and printed music, believing that music enhanced the devotional experience of the liturgy and was a "modest and holy recreation." Borromeo wrote to one nun that "singing sacred and wholly spiritual things…is divine praise." In this nourishing atmosphere **Chiara Margarita Cozzolani (1602–ca. 1677)** took her vows as a Benedictine nun, entering her novitiate in 1619 and taking her final vows in 1620.

There had been a long tradition in the Cozzolani family for girls to enter this monastery—at least five Cozzolanis were there during the seventeenth century—and Margarita (who took the name Chiara on entering) was following her older sister into the order. Music at Santa Radegonda appears to have been a normal part of their education. The convent had not one but two choirs, two nuns as *maestrae di cappella*, and music was also performed in the external parlor where nuns visited with family members. When the Grand Duke Cosimo III de' Medici visited in 1664, he was delighted to report that among the more than 100 nuns in the institution, 50 were "singers and instrumentalists of utter perfection."

In this favorable environment, Cozzolani became known in the convent as a singer, and when she was about thirty-seven, she began to publish her work. Her first opus, *Primavera dei fiori musicali* (Springtime of Musical Blossoms) appeared in 1640 but is now lost—it was last known to be in Berlin in the mid-nineteenth century. In 1642 she published a volume of *Concerti sacri* (from two to four voices with continuo) and in 1648 a book of solo motets (for which the continuo part has unfortunately been lost). Her last published volume (1650) contained Vesper Psalms, Magnificats, motets, and dialogues for as many as eight voices, often accompanied by two violins and continuo.

Cozzolani included four sacred dialogue motets in each of her two surviving volumes (1642 and 1650). In *O caeli cives* the two tenor parts ask questions about Saint Catherine and are answered by three soprano angel parts. The motet concludes with all singing "alleluia," together, with a common ending for a dialogue.

Cozzolani's *Magnificat* for eight voices and organ continuo (1650) has two bass parts, both quite low (one goes to D below the bass clef staff), beyond the range of even a woman's very low voice. The work alternates between pairs of similar voices and *tutti* passages and was clearly conceived as employing (forbidden) male voices. It is also remarkable in deliberately employing the voices in such a way as to focus on the particular qualities of color of each voice range.

Robert Kendrick points out that secular arias in Italian for voice and continuo by Cozzolani and her sister-nun, Rosa Badalla, indicate that in Milan at least, there was secular music inside the convent walls. Cozzolani's song was lost during World War II, and Badalla's was not published and survives only in manuscript.

Only a single surviving volume of music, often published in their youth, represents most nun composers. Unpublished music from the convents has seldom survived, perhaps due in part to destruction when many of the convents were dissolved in the late eighteenth century. We do not know whether they indeed wrote no other music, or whether it seemed to them unwise to publish more. Prohibitions against music-making in the convents seemed to be directed at performances inside the walls and not against publishing, but official disapproval could have been expressed in many ways.

Maria Xaveria Peruchona (ca. 1652–after 1709) published her only known works in 1675, *Sacri concerti de motetti a una, due, tre, e quattro voci, parte con violini, e parte senza* (Sacred Concertos of Motets for One, Two, Three and Four Voices, part with violins and part without). About twenty-three years old at the time, she states in the preface that these are her first works. The volume includes a lovely Christmas cantata (motet), *Ad gaudia, ad jubila* (To Joy, to Songs of Joy) for soprano, two violins, and continuo, and *Regina Caeli* (Queen of Heaven—her only setting of a Latin liturgical text) for soprano, alto, and tenor. Peruchona, an Ursuline nun at the Collegio di Sant' Orsola in Galliate, a town quite near Novara, studied with Francesco Beria (n.d.) and Antonio Grosso (n.d.), and as she was from Novara, she may have known and perhaps also studied with Isabella Leonarda.

Seventeenth-century religious expression could be very intense, even erotic. There is no doubt that many texts written for or by the nuns expressed a truly passionate religious feeling, as in this passage from a motet text set by Peruchona:

Dissolve, now my eyes, run with tears.
Into my heart, into my breast, come sorrowfully.
Strike rapidly this life, this breast, strike rapidly.
Chosen Jesus, whom I cultivated in my heart,
Spouse God, whom I wanted alone,
He whom I love, He whom I chose, lost,
for which now I live, while I always sigh.
Wherefore at last I do not breath[e], while I always sigh.

She may have written this text herself; no author has been identified.

Maria Francesca Nascinbeni (1658–?) was from Ancona and studied there with the Augustinian monk Scipione Lazzarini (n.d.). In his own collection of *Motetti a due, e tre voci* (Motets for Two and Three Voices) (1674) Lazzarini included her three-voice piece *Sitientes venite* ([Ye Who] Are Thirsty), a motet for two sopranos and bass with continuo. It is a long sectional motet intended for the Feast of Corpus Christi, a very important feast in the seventeenth century because it emphasized the Doctrine of Transubstantiation (transformation of bread and wine to the flesh and blood of Jesus). This was important to the Counter-Reformation Catholic church, as opposed to the Protestant rejection of that doctrine. Later that year, Nascinbeni published a complete volume of her own works, *Canzoni e madrigali morali e spirituali* (Moral and Spiritual Canzonas and Madrigals), all based on Italian spiritual madrigal texts. It is not certain that Nascinbeni became a nun, but the religious nature of the works suggests that possibility.

Rosa Giacinta Badalla (ca. 1660–ca. 1715), like Cozzolani, was a nun composer in Santa Radegonda in Milan. She took her vows about 1678, just after the death of Cozzolani, and published a collection of twelve *Motetti a voce sola* (Motets for Solo Voice) in 1684, when, according to the preface, she was just over twenty years old. Although she is thought to have come from Bergamo, nothing is known of her life or her role in the convent—not even her voice range. If her music was written for herself, however, she had a high soprano range and great vocal agility. The solo motet *Pane angelico* (Angelic Bread) for soprano goes up to high C, two octaves above middle C, in ornate, melismatic passages on the words "jubilate" (rejoice) and "alleluia." The motet, labeled "For the Feast of Corpus Christi," celebrates the doctrine of the Real Presence of Christ in the bread and wine of the Mass. Kendrick suggests that evidence of the period indicates that the Elevation of the Host (lifting up the wafer of bread by the priest at Mass) might have been the time when such a motet was sung. Two secular cantatas have survived in manuscript: *Vuò cercando* (I Seek) for alto voice, in an eighteenth-century manuscript collection written out by an English collector, and *Camillio Tellier* (for bass voice, two trumpets, and organ) in a manuscript dated 1697 and now in the Bibliothèque Nationale in Paris.

Bianca Maria Meda (ca. 1665–after 1700) was a Benedictine nun at San Martino del Leano in Pavia, just south of Milan. Her only published volume was *Motetti a uno,* *due, tre, quattro voci, con violini, e senza* (Motets for One, Two, Three, or Four Voices, with violins and without); nothing further is known of her life. Her writing style displays vocal virtuosity.

Oratorio Composers in Vienna

A group of four composers living in Vienna at the opening of the eighteenth century includes an Austrian nun and three Italian women who appear not to have been in religious orders. They all composed oratorios for the Viennese Imperial Court, which were performed by the outstanding singers there at important times like Holy Week. The oratorios are large works in the formal scheme used by Alessandro Scarlatti after 1700. They are all in two acts, each introduced by a single or multimovement *sinfonia* (instrumental piece). The pattern in each act is a succession of da capo arias alternating with recitative. Occasionally, there are duets. The surviving oratorios of this group are for soloists without choruses. When the term "coro" is used in these scores, it indicates an ensemble of soloists, not a chorus. Many arias are accompanied only by continuo, but others are with string orchestra or other groups of instruments.

The Austrian nun was Marianne von Raschenau; the others were Italians for whom no biographical information is known: Caterina Benedicta Grazianini, Camilla de Rossi (Romana), and Maria Margherita Grimani. None of these composers' names appear on any court pay list, and their presence in any other aspect of Viennese life is not documented. Yet their music is all extremely well crafted, full of intense feeling, and completely performable for today's audience. The works stand up well beside those of their distinguished contemporaries.

Marianne von Raschenau (fl. 1690s–1703) was the *Chormeisterin* (choir director) at the convent of Saint Jakob auf der Hülben in Vienna. Her oratorio *Le sacre visioni di Santa Teresa* (The Sacred Vision of Saint Teresa) and a secular stage work were performed during the reign of Leopold I (d. 1705), but only the printed libretti have survived.

Two oratorios by **Caterini Benedicta Grazianini [Gratianini] (fl. early eighteenth century)** have survived in manuscript. Her works were heard during the reign of Joseph I (r. 1705–1711). The manuscripts spell her name differently: she is "Caterina Benedetta Gratianini" in the score for *Santa Teresa* and "Caterina Benedicta Grazianini" in *San Gemigniano vescovo e protettore di Modena* (Saint Gemigniano, Bishop and Protector of Modena). The second oratorio, dated 1705, was "sung before the Highness of Brunswick and Modena…and wondrously received," according to a note on the score. Such a local topic suggests that it was either composed for a special visit of dignitaries from Modena to Vienna or perhaps had been written earlier in Modena, possibly the composer's home.

The greatest amount of extant music from this group is by **Camilla de Rossi (fl. 1707–1709)**, whose name is followed on her scores by "Romana," indicating that she was from Rome. She was active in Vienna during the reign of Joseph I (1678–1711). She wrote four oratorios that have survived and one secular cantata for soprano and alto soloists and string orchestra for which the score is now in Dresden. *Il Sacrifizio di Abramo* (Abraham's Sacrifice), written for performance in Holy Week in 1708, uses string orchestra and two chalumeaux (predecessors of the clarinet, which had been introduced into the Vienna opera just one year earlier). De Rossi often uses instrumental color for characterization; the lute accompanies the innocent Issaco in *Il Sacrifizio,* and trumpets are used for the villain in *Santa Beatrice d'Este* (1707). Like Grazianini's *San Gemigniano*, this has a very localized subject: an uncanonized, but saintly, woman of the d'Este family in Modena. Again, it seems that this may have been performed for visiting Modenese nobility. Rossi's other oratorios are *San Alessio* (1710) and *Il figliuol prodigo* (The Prodigal Son) (1709), for which she also wrote the libretti. The cast lists for performances appear on the manuscripts of several of her works.

Maria Margherita Grimani (fl. 1715–1718) composed two oratorios and one opera, *Pallade e Marte*. The opera, written for the emperor's name day, is inscribed "Bologna, April 5, 1713." It is not known whether Grimani was in Bologna at the time or had been born there. Her most likely place of origin, however, was Venice, where the extremely important Grimani family lived. Pietro Grimani was the Venetian ambassador who negotiated the alliance between Venice and Emperor Charles VI against the Turks in 1713, the year both *Pallade e Marte* and Grimani's oratorio *La visitazione di Elisabetta* (The Visitation of St. Elizabeth) were performed. Her other oratorio, *La decollazione di S Giovanni Battista* (The Beheading of St. John the Baptist), was performed in 1715.

Secular Composers

Italy

Francesca Caccini (1587–1645) was a splendid singer and a prolific composer. The first woman composer of opera, she also wrote music for ballet. Caccini, educated by her father, is a woman who developed professionally within a musical family where she had access to training in singing, guitar, harp, keyboard and composition, as well as enough literary knowledge to compose poetry in Italian and Latin.

As the seventeenth century opened, members of the Caccini family in Florence were at the forefront of new trends of solo song and dramatic representation in music. The patriarch of the family was the singer-composer Giulio Romolo Caccini, also called "Romano" (from Rome). He had worked in various northern Italian courts before coming under the patronage of a nobleman named Giovanni de' Bardi in Florence. There, Giulio joined the Florentine Camerata, a group that was speculating on, and experimenting with, new styles of singing and composition. He also trained his family members to sing in the new, emotive style.

Giulio's first wife, Lucia di Filippo Gagnolanti, was a singer; their two daughters, Francesca and Settimia, were involved from childhood in the musical activities of their father and his circle. He was proud of having taught his "new style of singing" to his daughters, his second wife, Margherita di Agostino Benevoli della Scala, and his illegitimate son Pompeo. Margherita may have studied previously with Vittoria Archilei (1582–1620), a spectacular virtuoso soprano who, with her singer-composer husband

(Antonio Archilei), also worked in the Florentine court. The Caccini family performed to great acclaim as a group called the Donne di Giulio Romano (ladies of Giulio Romano [Caccini]), both in Florence and on a lengthy tour to Paris, Modena, Milan, Turin, and Lyons. Francesca's singing was so splendid that she was offered a job at the court of Maria de' Medici, queen of France; she was unable to accept because Grand Duke Ferdinand I of Florence refused to release her from his service.

Francesca Caccini became permanently attached to the Florentine court and in 1607 married court singer Giovanni Battista Signorini (d. 1626). That year she had a great success with *La stiava* (the music is lost), composed for the Carnival season entertainment. In 1611, she performed chamber music in Florence with a group that she apparently had organized herself, "La sig.a Francesca e le sue figliuole" (Signorina Francesca and Her Female Students), an indication that she was both singing and teaching at the court. By the 1620s, she had earned the nickname "La Cecchina" (the songbird) and was the most highly paid musician in the court, regularly writing music for important court festivities. Her duties also included singing for the Office of Holy Week services at a time when women were officially not supposed to sing in church. She also taught music (including composition) to members of the court (both noblewomen and serving women) and to at least one nun.

While little is known of her husband's career, it is possible that Caccini may have sung duets with him. The couple did tour Genoa, Savona, and Milan in 1617. They had one daughter, Margherita (b. 1622), who was also trained as a singer and performed with her mother. When Margherita was a teenager, however, Francesca refused to let her perform on stage in a *commedia*, lest it jeopardize her chances for marriage or placement in a convent. Although her own professional activities had brought Caccini affluence and a socially prominent position, she apparently felt that her daughter's position could still be endangered by stage appearances. Margherita eventually became a nun.

After Signorini's death in 1626, Caccini married Tomaso Raffaelli (d. 1629), a music-loving aristocrat, and entered service as a singer with a banking heir in Lucca. Raffaelli was a member of an Accademia in Lucca for which his wife probably composed. He died only three years later, leaving her with their infant son Tomaso (b. 1628). Because the town of Lucca was then under quarantine for plague, Caccini remained there until 1633. She then reentered the service of the Medici family in Florence, where she remained until her retirement in 1641. It is thought that she died in 1645, the year that Tomaso became the ward of his uncle.

Of Caccini's fifteen known dramatic works, only one, *La liberazione di Ruggiero dall' isola d'Alcina* (The Liberation of Ruggiero from the Island of Alcina), has survived. Based on Ariosto's epic poem *Orlando Furioso*, it is a story of the struggle of a good sorceress and the evil Alcina for power over the young knight Ruggiero. Daring tonal excursions and relationships, in contrast to the simpler recitative of the good character Ruggiero, represent Alcina. Recent studies have pointed out that the tonal contrasts in the work even reflect gender: Alcina sings in flat keys, Ruggiero and other males in sharp keys, and the good sorceress, mostly in C major (the key with neither sharps nor flats). Antonio Vivaldi and George Frederick Handel (1685–1759) also used the poem for operas.

Caccini's *La liberazione* was first performed at the Villa Poggio Imperiale in Florence in 1625 for the visiting Polish prince Wladislaw. He was so taken with the work that he presented it in Warsaw three years later, where it became the first Italian opera to be performed outside Italy. It was published in Florence in 1625. Caccini's other extant publication, *Il primo libro delle musiche* (The First Book of Music) (1618), is a collection of thirty-two solo songs and four duets for soprano and bass and includes monodies identified by terms such as madrigal, aria, and *canzonetta*. There are several sacred arias in *Il primo libro*, and some of the texts may have been hers. It is a splendid collection of the major types of solo song of her day. Although many of her works have been lost, her one remaining opera and *Il primo libro delle musiche* give a glowing view of Caccini's mastery of a wide variety of forms.

Settimia Caccini (1591–ca. 1660), the younger sister of Francesca, also studied with their father, Giulio Caccini. In 1600, when she was just nine years old, she and her sister performed in his opera *Il rapimento di Cefalo* at the famous festivities for the marriage of Maria de' Medici and Henri IV of France.

Settimia married Alessandro Ghivizzani (b. ca. 1572), a singer in the Medici service, in 1609. They soon left Florence, without permission from the court, to go to Ghivizzani's native city, Lucca, and from 1613 to 1620 they were working at the Gonzaga court in Mantua, where she became one of the most highly paid musicians. In 1622 they were in Parma, where Settimia sang in two works by Monteverdi. After her husband died in 1632, she returned to Florence. The name "Settimia Ghivizzani" is found in court account books as a musician; she was probably the daughter of Settimia and Alessandro.

Settimia Caccini published no music, but eight strophic songs (in which each stanza of a poem is set to the same music) survive in manuscript. They are quite melodic but omit any of the written-out ornamentation found in her sister Francesca's works. It is possible that if she had prepared them for publication, more of the ornaments used in performance might have been preserved. Settimia Caccini writes melismas, which sometimes express the meaning of the text, although they often fit some of the stanzas of the poem better than others. For example, in *Cantan gl'augelli* (The Lovebirds Sing) she begins with the line "the lovebirds sing" and on the word for "birds" has a melismatic passage. This fits well on the word "breast" in the next stanza, which begins "In your lovely breast," but in the last stanza the same music is awkwardly employed on "hours" in the line "the hours pass." She particularly enjoyed using a long-held note in the voice while the bass moved (examples are found in the same song), and she wrote interesting rhythmic and metric changes. It is not known if Settimia Caccini wrote any dramatic works.

The singer-composer **Francesca Campana (ca. 1605/1610–1665)** was reputed to be one of the two best female singers in Rome. She married into the famous Rossi family; her husband, Giovan Carlo (1617–?), was the youngest brother of the more famous Luigi Rossi (1597–1653). Thomasin LaMay speculates that Campana probably wrote a great deal more music than she published. Campana's one volume of music, *Arie a una, due, e tre voci* (Arias for One, Two and Three Voices) (1629), was followed by two works in the collection *Risonante sfere* (Resounding Sphere), published the same year by Giovanni Battista Robletti (fl. 1609–1650), a major Roman printer in the first half of the seventeenth century. Her three-voiced madrigal *Occhi belli, occhi amati* (Beautiful Eyes, Beloved Eyes) from Robletti's collection is a Renaissance-style madrigal with no accompanying continuo part, while *Semplicetto augellin* (Naive Little Bird), from the *Arie* volume is an up-to-date solo madrigal in which the virtuosity no doubt reflects the singing abilities of the composer. The bass line is a continuo part but lacks chord symbol figures; the realization of the harmonies is left to the performer.

One secular song by **Lucia Quinciani (fl. 1611)** was included in the second edition (1611) of a collection of *Affetti amorosi* (Amorous Feelings) by Marc' Antonio Negri (?–1624), her teacher. Almost every word of her piece involves text-painting, or melodic patterns that depict the language of the text; she uses descending phrases to depict *inferno* (Hell) and chromaticism for *lagrimosi* (tearful). Throughout there is emphasis on arousing intense emotions (affects) through the music, a strong characteristic of the period. Unfortunately, no other music by Quinciani has survived, and absolutely nothing is known of her life.

If one is not born into a musician's family, the next best way to gain access to a musical education is to be a member of a wealthy family. **Barbara Strozzi (ca. 1619–ca. 1664)** is one of the few musicians of any age to establish her professional persona by publishing her own music. The (illegitimate) daughter of Giulio Strozzi (1583–1652), a wealthy, socially prominent lover of the arts, and his longtime servant Isabella Garzoni, she was subsequently adopted by Giulio. While Barbara and her mother were both named inheritors in his early will of 1628, in his final will, Barbara Strozzi was his principal heir. She showed early musical promise and studied with the opera composer Pier Francesco Cavalli, the teacher also of Antonia Bembo. Two volumes of solo songs were dedicated to Barbara Strozzi by Nicolò Fontei (in 1635 and 1636), a friend and composer, who set the songs to texts by her father.

Giulio was active in the literary Academia degli Incogniti, which was frequented by several librettists of Venetian opera. In 1637 he founded his own group, the Academia degli Unisoni, which met at his house and included music among its activities. Although she was not a member of the all-male group, Barbara Strozzi acted as hostess, often sang at their meetings, and sometimes even suggested subjects for their learned debates. Among the many testimonials to her brilliance as an artist the poet Fontei called her "la virtuossima Cantatrice" (the most virtuoso singer) in his *Bizzarie Poetiche* (1635). Unfortunately, the views of the members of the group were regarded as quite libertine, and Strozzi was subjected to insulting gossip, much of which probably had little foundation in her own behavior but reflected the public view of her father's circle of friends.

Strozzi never married, but she did bear four children (all born in the early 1640s). Ellen Rosand speculates that the father of at least three of the children was a friend of Giulio's named Giovanni Paolo Vidman. Her daughters Isabella and Laura entered the convent of San Sepolcro, and one son, Massimo, became a monk in the Servite Order at the monastery of San Stefano in Belluno. Nothing is known about her other son. The religious vocations of the three children suggest that Strozzi was sufficiently comfortable financially or had enough support from her lover(s) to be able to pay dowries to the convent for the nuns.

Strozzi never performed in public and did not write operas, although Cavalli, her teacher, was the leading opera composer in Venice at the time, and her father's friends included many librettists. Giulio also wrote libretti, and Cavalli set at least one of them. Strozzi's first publication was a book of madrigals on texts by her father. In her second published volume (appearing shortly before his death) Strozzi did set some texts drawn from two of her father's opera libretti. Her other publications appeared after his death. Although Giulio left her his estate, she needed additional support. Beginning in 1644, she published a series of volumes of her music, all dedicated to persons of great importance who were probably her patrons: Ferdinand II of Austria and Eleanora of Mantua (op. 2, 1651), Anne of Austria, archduchess of Innsbruck (op. 5, 1655), Nicolò Sagredo, later doge of Venice (op. 7, 1659), and Sophie Elizabeth, duchess of Brunswick and Lüneburg (op. 8, 1664) (see later).

Unlike Isabella Leonarda's, none of Strozzi's patrons were church officials, but she did write one volume of sacred works, the *Sacri musicale affetti*, Book One (Sacred Musical Feelings), which she apparently intended to follow with another volume of religious music. Her works also include the three-voice motet *Quis dabit mihi*, included in Bartolomeo Marcesso's 1656 collection entitled *Sacra corona, motetti a due e tre voci di diversi eccelentissimi autori moderni* (Sacred Crown, Motets in Two and Three Voices by Various Most Excellent Modern Authors).

All told, Strozzi composed and published over 100 pieces in eight volumes, making her one of the most productive composers of secular vocal chamber music of her time. Early publication copies of all but the works in op. 4 have survived, but no manuscripts are extant. Modern editions have started to appear, and many fine modern recordings of her music are now available.

France

In 1937, the French musicologist Yvonne Rokseth (1890–1948) discovered six large, gorgeously bound manuscript volumes of music in the French National Library. They were all by one previously unknown composer, **Antonia Bembo (ca. 1643–ca. 1715)**, birth name Padoani. She had, for mysterious reasons, been abandoned "by the one who brought her" to Paris, as she indicates in the autobiographical preface to her manuscripts. At the time, all that could be learned about the composer from the preface was that she was grateful to King Louis XIV, who had granted her a pension so that she could live in the refuge of a religious community. Recently, Claire Fontijn and Marinella Laini have unearthed a wealth of information about Bembo. Through their efforts, we now know that she was the daughter of the physician Giacomo Padoani and his wife, Diana Paresco, that she was born about 1643, probably in Venice, and that she died in Paris about 1720. While in Italy, she had studied music with the famous opera composer Pier Francesco Cavalli, teacher also of Barbara Strozzi.

Although a commoner by birth, Bembo married a young nobleman, Lorenzo Bembo, with whom she had three children. It appears that Lorenzo was a spendthrift and that the marriage was not happy. Antonia left the family sometime before 1676 and went to Paris, where she sang for Louis XIV. It seems clear that she intended to stay away from Venice, for although she left her two sons with their father, she placed her daughter at the convent of San Bernardo of Murano. She also left her jewels there, many of which were sold in 1685 to pay her daughter's convent bills; Claire Fonijn suggests the father was "unwilling or unable to pay." After her arrival in Paris and in need of assistance, Bembo was granted a pension by the king. She lived in the parish of Notre Dame de Bonne Nouvelle at the Petite Union Chrètienne de Dames de Saint Chaumont, home also of other pensioned ladies.

As one examines her music, written over a period of years, the merging of her Italian training with the new music that she was hearing in France becomes evident. François Couperin (1668–1733) called this melding of the two national tastes "les goûts reunis" (the reunited tastes). Bembo's first large volume contains forty-one works: arias, cantatas, motets, and a *serenata*, most for soprano and basso continuo. She states that she is a singer and sets Italian, French, and Latin texts with vocal virtuosity, expressive dissonance, and a sensitivity to languages. Her next book contains some religious choral music: a small *Te Deum* (a sacred text of thanksgiving beginning, "We praise thee God") to celebrate the birth of the first duke of Brittany in 1704. It also includes an *Italian Serenata* (little diversion). Her third volume includes another *Te Deum* for five voices and orchestra, a setting of the Nineteenth Psalm for three voice parts, and an instrumental trio of two violins and basso continuo.

Bembo's largest work, the opera *Hercole amante* (Hercules in Love), occupies two volumes of manuscript. This is quite a mysterious work; the text had been set by Cavalli in 1662 to celebrate the wedding of the king, and it is not known why Bembo chose to set the same libretto again in 1707. Certainly, it was not normal practice to reuse such an old libretto for a work in a new and different style, and there is no record that it was ever performed at the time. (It was performed in Boston in the twentieth century.) Since no one at the time undertook to write an opera without a commission or a planned performance, the rationale for its composition is also a mystery. The setting is not in the style of her teacher but is more like those of opera composers of the latter seventeenth century, for example, Andrè Campra (1660–1744) and Jean-Baptiste Lully (1632–1687), another Italian (from Florence) then in Paris, who was the absolute monarch of seventeenth-century French opera. Bembo's opera emulates the French style by using a chorus and the dances so loved there. The only opportunity in Europe to hear men and women sing in mixed choruses was in French opera at that time; choruses no longer appeared in Italian public opera, in part for reasons of economy.

Bembo's last book, *Les sept Pseaumes de David* (The Seven Psalms of David) (after 1707), shows her complete command of setting French texts, using French paraphrases of seven penitential Psalms from *Essay de pseaumes* (1694) by Elisabeth Sophie Chéron (1648–1711). Chéron was herself an interesting figure, famous as a painter, engraver, poet, and musician. Raised a Huguenot, she became Catholic in order to continue working as a portraitist under royal patronage; she was also a poet member of the French Académie. It had become very fashionable for Parisians to read the Psalms in French, and Chéron's paraphrases found an especially responsive reception in the court.

Bembo's great contemporary Elisabeth-Claude Jacquet de la Guerre was well known in Paris while Bembo lived there, but there is no indication that they knew each other or each other's works.

> Madame de la Guerre had a very great genius for composition, and excelled in vocal music the same as in instrumental; as she has made known by several works in all kinds of music that one has of her compositions....One can say that never had a person of her sex had such talents as she for the composition of music, and for the admirable way she performed it at the harpsichord and on the organ. *Titon du Tillet, Le Parnasse Francaise (1732)*

Elisabeth-Claude Jacquet de la Guerre (1665–1729) was a stunning child prodigy, called "the marvel of our century" in the *Mercure de France*. Shortly after her death, Titon du Tillet gave her the preceding tribute in his account of the great French musicians whom he believed had earned a place on Mount Parnassus. Like many successful women musicians of the seventeenth and eighteenth centuries, la Guerre was born into a musical family from whom she received her earliest musical instruction. Her father, Claude Jacquet (d. 1702), was the organist at Saint-Louis-en-Ile and a well-known organ builder. Her mother, Anne de la Touche, was related to the musical Daquin family. Other relatives included instrument builders, painters, a lutenist, and several organists.

Elisabeth-Claude's playing, at the age of five, led King Louis XIV to praise her and tell her that she "should cultivate the marvelous talent Nature had given her." From childhood until her marriage, she played and sang at the royal court. In 1673, she entered the service of Mme. de Montespan, the king's mistress, and received her general education together with their eight children, under the supervision of Mme. de Maintenon (who became Louis' wife after the queen's death). Her book of secular cantatas on subjects of Greek mythology, published that year, was dedicated to the elector of Bavaria, Maximilian II Emanuel.

In 1684 Elisabeth-Claude married Marin de la Guerre (d. 1704), an organist first at the Jesuit Church on the Rue Saint-Antoine and later at Saint-Séverin and the Sainte-Chapelle. His father, Michel de la Guerre, had, in 1655, written the first theater work set entirely to music. It seemed destined that Marin and Elisabeth-Claude would continue their musical dynasties, for according to Titon du Tillet, their son was also precociously gifted in music. However, he died at the age of ten; soon thereafter Elisabeth-Claude lost her father, and two years later, her husband.

When she left the court to marry, la Guerre was given a pension by King Louis XIV and permission to dedicate her works to him. Until 1715, the year of his death, all her music was dedicated to him. Although she had frequently improvised in public, July 1, 1685, marked her formal debut as a composer with a short opera (now lost). The king then asked her to write a short stage work for the marriage of Mlle. de Nantes, one of his daughters by his mistress, Mme. de Montespan. Although la Guerre noted in her dedication to her 1687 volume of harpsichord pieces that she had composed three new operas, they were unfortunately not named there, and none appear to have survived. La Guerre also composed a ballet *Jeux à l'honneur de la victoire* (A Play in Honor of the Victory) in about 1691 (now lost). Her one surviving opera, *Céphale et Procris, a tragédie en musique*, was performed at the Académie Royale de Musique in 1694 and published that same year. These dramatic works established her position as the first woman in France to write for the musical stage.

By this time, la Guerre was renowned throughout Paris for her harpsichord playing and teaching. Her two books of music for the instrument—*Les pièces de clavessin...premier livre* (Harpsichord Pieces...First Book) (1687) and a subsequent volume (1707)—contain suites of short dance movements called *pièces*, each in two repeated sections.

La Guerre also wrote sonatas that reflected the combination of French and Italian characteristics popularized by François Couperin. Sébastien de Brossard, a music scholar and author of the first music dictionary in French, was so delighted with la Guerre's sonatas that in 1695 he made copies for himself of the six sonatas for one violin and continuo and the two sonatas for violin, viola da gamba, and organ continuo. With these works, unpublished during her lifetime, la Guerre became the first woman composer of French sonatas.

La Guerre published two books of six cantatas each in 1708 and 1711, *Cantates françoises sur des sujets tirez de l'Écriture* (French Cantatas on Subjects Drawn from Scripture). Based on stories from the Bible they are unlike most of the other cantatas by other French composers. She was the first composer to publish sacred cantatas in France. Most are for a single voice with continuo, with other instruments sometimes used in interludes. The singer usually alternates roles between that of narrator (singing récitatif the French equivalent of recitative) and a participant in the drama (singing da capo airs) and concludes with a moral commentary. One of her sacred cantatas is entitled *Le Passage de la Mer Rouge* (The Crossing of the Red Sea). Here, the short *Prélude* is scored for violin and continuo and is followed by a récitatif in which the narrator describes the plight of the Israelites. Although the cantata is written for soprano, the singer assumes the masculine role of Moses in the air that follows. La Guerre published three cantatas on mythological subjects in 1715. Her last known work, a *Te Deum* to celebrate the recovery of Louis XV from smallpox in 1721, has been lost. Many of her cantatas are now available in modern recordings, and her instrumental music is in the standard repertory for modern harpsichordists today.

German Noblewomen

One of Europe's grimmest wars erupted in the German lands during the seventeenth century. The Thirty Years' War (1618–1648) began as a religious struggle among German principalities but ultimately involved a chaotic mix of motives, becoming a civil war in which many countries participated. [Only those born in the latter half of the century grew up in relative peace.]

Many aristocratic noblewomen received excellent training in music during this century, but few were known to be composers. **Sophie Elisabeth, duchess of Brunswick**

Elizabeth Sophie Marie Von Herzogin, Duchess of Brunswick-Lüneburg.
Hulton|Archive by Getty Images.

and Lüneburg (1613–1676), was a principal figure. Although she (and her family) spent much of her early life in exile, she did receive a fine education in languages, music, and literature. In 1635 she married Duke August the Younger of Brunswick and Lüneberg, and although they lived temporarily in Brunswick instead of Wolfenbüttel, the capital, August established an orchestra, and the court celebrated various festivities. Sophie Elisabeth composed music for two plays and was engaged in the musical life of the court in many ways. During the disruptions of the war Heinrich Schütz (1585–1672), the greatest composer of the age in German lands and *Kapellmeister* (music director) at Dresden, lived in Brunswick. Sophie Elisabeth showed him some of her works, and he gave her suggestions for improvement. She turned to him again for advice when the court orchestra was reorganized in 1655. Her later compositions were deeply religious in nature and may have been influenced by some of Schütz's music. Although both Sophie Elisabeth and Schütz lived through the entire Thirty Years' War, they were still able to be productive when it finally ended. The next century was to see many cultivated German princesses and duchesses who were composers, such as Anna Amalia of Prussia, Anna Amalia of Saxe-Weimar, and Maria Antonia Walpurgis.

Cities in which Italian women musicians of the seventeenth century lived.
Barbara Garvey Jackson.

Secular musicians
Bologna? Maria Margherita Grimani
    (worked in Vienna)
Florence. Vittoria Archilei
Francesca Caccini
Settimia Caccini
Lucca. Settimia Caccini

Mantua. Adriana Basile
Rome. Camilla de Rossi (worked
    in Vienna)

Francesca Campana
Venice. Barbara Strozzi Anna Maria
    della Pietà
Verona or Venice? Lucia Quinciana

Nuns
Ancona. Maria Francesca Nascinbeni
    (may have become a nun)
Bologna. Lucretia Vizana

Milan. Chiara Margharita Cozzolani
    Rosa Giacinto Badalla
    Claudia Rusca
Modena. Sulpitia Lodovica Cesis
Novara. Isabella Leonarda Maria
    Xaveria Peruchona (born in
    Novara, in convent in nearby
    Galliate)

Pavia. Bianca Maria Meda

Vicenza. Alba Trissina

Timeline for the Seventeenth Century

Date	History/Politics	Science/Education	The Arts/Literature	Music
1600				Jacopo Peri: *Euridice* Giulio Caccini: *Euridice*
1602	Priscilla Alden, Pilgrim (?1602–pre-1687) Dutch East India Company founded			**Chiara Margarita Cozzolani (1602–ca. 1677)** Pier Francesco Cavalli (1602–1676)
1605				**Francesca Campana (ca. 1605/1610–1665)** Giacomo Carissimi (1605–1674)
1606			Rembrandt van Rijn (1606–1669)	
1607	Founding of Jamestown Colony			Claudio Monteverdi: *Orfeo*
1608		Telescope invented by Hans Lippershey	John Milton (1608–1674)	
1610	Louis XIII crowned		King James version of the Bible	
1611				**Lucia Quinciani (fl. 1611)**
1613				**Sophie Elisabeth, duchess of Brunswick and Lüneburg (1613–1676)**
1618	Start of Thirty Years' War			
1619				**Barbara Strozzi (ca. 1619–ca. 1664)**
1620	Mayflower arrives at Plymouth Rock			**Isabella Leonarda (1620–1704)**
1622			Molière (1622–1673)	**Alba Trissina (fl. 1622)**
1623		Blaise Pascal (1623–1662) Invention of the slide rule		**Lucrezia Orsina (1623–?)**
1626	Manhattan Island bought by Peter Minuit			L. Couperin (ca. 1626–1661)
1632		John Locke (1632–1704) Sir Christopher Wren (1632–1723)	Jan Vermeer (1632–1675)	Jean-Baptiste Lully (1632–1687) G. Vitali (1632–1692)
1636		Harvard College founded		
1637				Dietrich Buxtehude (ca. 1637–1707)
1638	Louis XIV (1638–1715)			
1639			Jean Baptiste Racine (1639–1699)	
1640			Aphra Behn (1640–1689) novelist	Bay Psalm Book printed

Date	History/Politics	Science/Education	The Arts/ Literature	Music
1642		Isaac Newton (1642–1727)		J. Christoph Bach (1642–1703)
1643				**Antonia Bembo (ca. 1643–1715)**
1644				Heinrich Ignaz Franz von Biber (1644–1704)
1646		G. W. Leibniz (1646–1716)	Glückel of Hameln, writer and diarist (1646–1724)	
1647		Maria Sibylla Merian (1647–1717) Scientific Illustrator		
1648			Elisabeth Sophie Chéron (1648–1711) painter, engraver, poet and musician	
1651				D. Gabrieli (1651–1690)
1652				**Maria Xaveria Peruchona (ca. 1652–after 1709)**
1653				Arcangelo Corelli (1653–1713) Johann Pachelbel (1653–1706)
1656				Marin Marais (1656–1728)
1657				**Maria Francesca Nascinbeni (1657/8–?)**
1659				Henry Purcell (ca. 1659–1695)
1660				**Rosa Giacinta Badalla (ca. 1660–ca. 1715)** Johann Joseph Fux (1660–1741) Johann Kuhnau (1660–1722) Alessandro Scarlatti (1660–1725)
1665				**Elisabeth Jacquet de la Guerre (1665–1729) Bianca Maria Meda (ca. 1665–after 1700)**
1666			Mary Astell (1666–1731) feminist writer	
1667			Jonathan Swift (1667–1745)	
1668				François Couperin (1668–1733)
1669				Allesandro Marcello (1669–1747)
1670			William Congreve (1670–1729)	

Date	History/Politics	Science/Education	The Arts/ Literature	Music
1671				Tomaso Albinoni (1671–1751)
1672	Peter the Great (1672–1725)			
1674/5		Microscope invented by A. van Leeuwenhock	Rosalba Carriera (1675–1757) portraitist	
1678				Antonio Vivaldi (1678–1741)
1681				George Phillip Telemann (1681–1767)
1682				Jean François Dandrieu (ca. 1682–1738)
1683				Johann Christian Gottlieb Graupner (1683–1760) Jean-Philippe Rameau (1683–1764)
1685			John Gay (1685–1732)	Johann Sebastian Bach (1685–1750) George Frederick Handel (1685–1759) Domenico Scarlatti (1685–1757)
1686				Benedetto Marcello (1686–1739)
1687				Francesco Geminiani (1687–1762)
1688			Alexander Pope (1688–1744)	Karl Fasch (1688–1758)
1689				Joseph Bodin de Boismortier (1689–1775)
1690				**Marianne von Raschenau (fl. 1690s–1703)**
1692	Salem witch trials			Giuseppe Tartini (1692–1770)
1694			Voltaire (1694–1778)	
1695				Pietro Locatelli (1695–1764) Giovanni Sammartini (1695–1750)
1697				Jean-Marie Leclair (1697–1764) Johann Joachim Quantz (1697–1773)
1699				Johann Adolph Hasse (1699–1783)

Bibliography

Vittoria Archilei

Hitchcock, H. Wiley, and Tim Carter. "Archilei, [née Concarini], Vittoria ["La Romanina"]." In *The New Grove Dictionary of Music and Musicians*, 2d ed. 2001.

Rosa Giacinta Badalla

Kendrick, Robert. "Rosa Giacinta Badalla." In *Women Composers: Music Through the Ages*, vol. 2, edited by Sylvia Glickman and Martha Furman Schleifer. New York: G. K. Hall, 1996.

Antonia Bembo

Fontijn, Claire A. "Antonia Bembo." In *Women Composers: Music Through the Ages*, vol. 2, edited by Sylvia Glickman and Martha Furman Schleifer. New York: G. K. Hall, 1996.

———. "Antonia Bembo: 'Les goût réunis,' Royal Patronage and the Role of the Woman Composer during the Reign of Louis XIV." Ph.D. diss., Duke University, 1994.

Fontijn, Claire A., and Marinella Laini. "Antonia Bembo." In *The New Grove Dictionary of Music and Musicians*, 2d ed. 2001. London and New York: Macmillan Press.

Laini, Marinella. "Le 'Produzioni armoniche' di Antonia Bembo." Ph.D. diss., University of Pavia, 1987.

Rokseth, Yvonne. "Antonia Bembo, Composer to Louis XIV." *Musical Quarterly* 23 (1937): 147–69.

Francesca Caccini and Settimia Caccini

Caccini, Francesca. *La Liberzaione di Ruggiero.* Edited by Doris Silbert, Northampton, MA: Smith College, 1945.

Carter, Tim, and H. Wiley Hitchcock (1); Suzanne G. Cusik (2); Susan Parisi (3). "Giulio Romolo Caccini" (1); "Francesca Caccini" (2); Settimia Caccini" (3). In *The New Grove Dictionary of Music and Musicians*, 2d ed. 2001. London and New York: Macmillan Press.

Cunningham, Caroline. "Francesca Caccini." In *Women Composers: Music Through the Ages*, vol. 1, edited by Sylvia Glickman and Martha Furman Schleifer. New York: G. K. Hall, 1996.

Raney, Carolyn. "Francesca Caccini." In *Historical Anthology of Music by Women*, edited by James R. Briscoe. Bloomington: Indiana University Press, 1987.

———. "Francesca Caccini, Musician to the Medici and Her Primo Libro (1619)." Ph.D. diss., New York University, 1971.

Smith, Candace. "Settimia Caccini." In *Women Composers: Music Through the Ages*, vol. 1, edited by Sylvia Glickman and Martha Furman Schleifer. New York: G. K. Hall, 1996.

Francesca Campana

LaMay, Thomasin. "Francesca Campana." In *Women Composers: Music Through the Ages*, vol. 2, edited by Sylvia Glickman and Martha Furman Schleifer. New York: G. K. Hall, 1996.

Whenham, John. "Campana, Francesca." In *The New Grove Dictionary of Women Composers*. London: Macmillan Press, 1994.

Chiara Margarita Cozzolani

Kendrick, Robert L. "Chiara Margarita Cozzolani." In *Women Composers: Music Through the Ages*, vol. 2, edited by Sylvia Glickman and Martha Furman Schleifer. New York: G. K. Hall, 1996.

———. "Cozzolani, Chiara Margarita." In *The New Grove Dictionary of Women Composers*. London: Macmillan Press, 1994.

———. "Cozzolani, Chiara Margarita." In *The New Grove Dictionary of Music and Musicians*, 2d ed. 2001. London and New York: Macmillan Press.

Camilla de Rossi

Jackson, Barbara Garvey. "Oratorios by Command of the Emperor: The Music of Camilla de Rossi." *Current Musicology*, no. 42 (1986): 7–19.

———. "Rossi, Camilla de." In *The New Grove Dictionary of Music and Musicians*, 2d ed. 2001. London and New York: Macmillan Press.

Caterina Benedetta Gratianini (also spelled Grazianini, Caterina Benedicta)

Cusick, Suzanne G. "Grazianini, Caterina Benedicta." In *The New Grove Dictionary of Women Composers*. London: Macmillan Press, 1994.

Jackson, Barbara Garvey. "Caterina Benedetta Gratianini." In *Women Composers: Music Through the Ages*, vol. 2, edited by Sylvia Glickman and Martha Furman Schleifer. New York: G. K. Hall, 1996.

Maria Margherita Grimani

Cusick, Suzanne G., and Rudolf Klein. "Grimani, Maria Margherita." In *The New Grove Dictionary of Women Composers*. London: Macmillan Press, 1994.

Jackson, Barbara Garvey. "Maria Margherita Grimani." In *Women Composers: Music Through the Ages*, vol. 2, edited by Sylvia Glickman and Martha Furman Schleifer. New York: G. K. Hall, 1996.

Isabella Leonarda

Carter, Stewart. "Isabella Leonarda." In *Women Composers: Music Through the Ages*, vol. 2, edited by Sylvia Glickman and Martha Furman Schleifer. New York: G. K. Hall, 1996.

———. "Isabella Leonarda [Leonardi, Anna Isabella]." In *The New Grove Dictionary of Music and Musicians*, 2d ed. 2001. London and New York: Macmillan Press.

———. "The Music of Isabella Leonarda (1620–1704)." Ph.D. diss., Stanford University, 1981.

Elisabeth-Claude Jacquet de la Guerre

Bates, Carol Henry. "Elizabeth-Claude Jacquet de la Guerre. Biography and Overview of [Instrumental] Works." In *Women Composers: Music Through the Ages*, vol. 1, edited by Sylvia Glickman and Martha Furman Schleifer. New York: G. K. Hall, 1996.

———. "Elizabeth Jacquet de La Guerre: A New Source of Seventeenth-Century French Harpsichord Music." *RMFC* 22 (1984), 7–49.

———. "The Instrumental Music of Elizabeth-Claude Jacquet de La Guerre." Ph.D. diss., Indiana University, 1978.

Borroff, Edith. *An Introduction to Elisabeth-Claude Jacquet de La Guerre*. Brooklyn, NY: The Institute of Mediaeval Music, 1966.

Cessac, Catherine. "Elizabeth Jacquet de la Guerre (1665–1729): claveciniste et compositeur." Ph.D. diss., University of Paris, Sorbonne, 1993.

———. "Jacquet de La Guerre, Elisabeth." In *The New Grove Dictionary of Music and Musicians*, 2d ed. 2001. London and New York: Macmillan Press.

Griffiths, Wanda R. "Jacquet de la Guerre's *Cephale et Procris:* Style and Performance" D.M.A. diss., University of North Carolina at Greensboro, 1992.

Guthrie, Diane Upchurch. "Elizabeth-Claude Jacquet de la Guerre. [Cantatas]." In *Women Composers: Music Through the Ages*, vol. 1, edited by Martha Furman Schleifer and Sylvia Glickman. New York: G. K. Hall, 1996.

Rose, Adrian. "Élizabeth-Claude Jacquet de la Guerre and the Secular *cantate Françoise*." *Early Music* 13, no. 4 (1985): 529–41.

Titon du Tillet, Évrard. *La Parnasse françois*. Paris: Jean-Baptiste Coignard Fils, 1732.

Bianca Maria Meda

Kendrick, Robert. "Bianca Maria Meda" "Isabella Leonarda." In *Women Composers: Music Through the Ages*, vol. 2, edited by Sylvia Glickman and Martha Furman Schleifer. New York: G. K. Hall, 1996.

Maria Francesca Nascinbeni

Jackson, Barbara Garvey. "Maria Francesca Nascinbeni." In *Women Composers: Music Through the Ages*, vol. 2, edited by Sylvia Glickman and Martha Furman Schleifer. New York: G. K. Hall, 1996.

Maria Xaveria Peruchona

Bowers, Jane. "Maria Xaveria Peruchona." In *Women Composers: Music Through the Ages*, vol. 2, edited by Sylvia Glickman and Martha Furman Schleifer. New York: G. K. Hall, 1996.

Lucia Quinciani

Bridges, Thomas W. "Quinciani, Lucia." In *The New Grove Dictionary of Women Composers*. London: Macmillan Press, 1994.

Smith, Candace. "Lucia Quinciani." In *Women Composers: Music Through the Ages*, vol. 1, edited by Sylvia Glickman and Martha Furman Schleifer. New York: G. K. Hall, 1996.

Marianne von Raschenau

Cusick, Suzanne G. "Raschenau, Maria Anna de." In *The New Grove Dictionary of Women Composers*. London: Macmillan Press, 1994.

Jackson, Barbara Garvey. "Caterina Benedetta Gratianini." In *Women Composers: Music Through the Ages*, vol. 2, edited by Sylvia Glickman and Martha Furman Schleifer. New York: G. K. Hall, 1996.

———. "Musical Women of the 17th and 18th Centuries." In *Women and Music: A History*. Bloomington: Indiana University Press, 1991.

Sophie Elisabeth

Geck, Karl Wilhelm. "Sophie Elisabeth, Duchess of Brunswick and Lüneburg." In *Women Composers: Music Through the Ages*, vol. 2, edited by Sylvia Glickman and Martha Furman Schleifer. New York: G. K. Hall, 1996.

Barbara Strozzi

Rosand, Ellen. "Barbara Strozzi, *virtuosissima cantatrice:* The Composer's Voice." *Journal of the American Musicological Society*, 31 (1978): 241–81.

Rosand, Ellen, with Beth L. Glixon. "Strozzi, Barbara." In *The New Grove Dictionary of Music and Musicians*, 2d ed. 2001. London and New York: Macmillan.

Wong, Randall. "Barbara Strozzi." In *Women Composers: Music Through the Ages*, vol. 2, edited by Sylvia Glickman and Martha Furman Schleifer. New York: G. K. Hall, 1996.

———. "Barbara Strozzi's 'Arie,' op. 8 (1664): An Edition and Commentary." Ph.D. diss., Stanford University, 1992.

Alba Trissina

Kendrick, Robert. "Alba Trissina." In *Women Composers: Music Through the Ages*, vol. 1, edited by Sylvia Glickman and Martha Furman Schleifer. New York: G. K. Hall, 1996.

Venetian Musicians in the Ospedali

Baldauf-Berdes, Jane L. *Women Musicians of Venice: Musical Foundations, 1525–1855*. Oxford: Oxford University Press, 1995.

Discography

Bembo, Antonia

Lamento della Vergine, cantata for soprano & continuo (from *Produzioni Armoniche*). In *Donne Barocche: Women Composers from the Baroque Period*. Opus III #30341 (2002).

Francesca Caccini

Coro delle piante incantate, Aria per pastore; Madrigal per fine di tutta la festa from *La Liberazione di Ruggiero dall'Isola d'Alcina*. In *Full Well She Sang: Women's Music from the Middle Ages and Renaissance*. Toronto Consort, SRI Classics SRI 005 (1991).

La Liberazione di Ruggiero dall'Isola d'Alcina. Masato Makino, Fusako Yamuchi, Tomoko Tanaka. Kunitachi College of Music Research. FOCD 3261/2 (2 CDs) (1989).

La Liberazione di Ruggiero dall'Isola d'Alcina. Ars Femina Ensemble. Nannerl Records NR-ARS003 (1993).

Maria, dolce Maria. In *Women's Voices: Five Centuries of Song*. Neva Pilgrim, soprano; Edward Smith, harpsichord. Leonarda LE338 (1997).

O che nuovo stupor from *Il Primo libro* (1610). In *Strana Armonia d'Amore*, vol. 1. Ensemble Concerto, Roberto Gini, dir. Stradivarius DULCIMER STR 33406 (1995).

Chiara Margarita Cozzolani

Laudate Domino. In *Musica de la Puebla de Los Angeles: Music by Women of the Mexican, Cuban, and European Baroque*. Ars Femina Ensemble. Nannerl Records 004 (1996).

Vespri Natalizi (1650). Cappella Artemisia, directed by Candace Smith. Edition and performance decisions prepared by and with Robert L. Kendrick. Tactus TC 600301 (1997).

Camilla de Rossi

Il Sacrifizio di Abramo. Weser-Renaissance, Manfred Cordes, dir. Classic Produktion Osnabrück cpo 999 371-2 (1996).

Oratorio "San Alessio." Graham Pushee, countertenor; Rosa Dominguez, Agnieszka Kowakzyk, sopranos; William Lombardi, tenor. Ensemble Musica Fiorita, Daniela Doki, harpsichord and director. Pan Classics 510 136 (2002).

Sinfonia [to Part II] from *Il Sacrifizio di Abramo*. In *Baroquen* [sic] *Treasures*, Bay Area Women's Philharmonic, JoAnn Falletta, lutenist and conductor. Newport Classics (1990); rereleased (ca. 1998).

Maria Margherita Grimani

Sinfonie [sic] to *Pallade e Marte* (1713). New England Women's Symphony, Concertmaster, Jean Lamon. Galaxia Women's Enterprises, 1980. Reissued in *Historical Anthology of Music by Women*, edited by James R. Briscoe. Bloomington and Indianapolis: Indiana University Press, 1991.

Isabella Leonarda

Isabella Leonarda: The Muse of Novara. [*Sonatas* 1, 10, and 12 from op. 16, *Messa Prima* from Opus 18; *Ave Suavis Dilectio*] Ars Femina Ensemble. Nannerl Records 005 (1999).

Messa Prima, from op. 18; *Ave suavis dilectio*. In *Baroque for the Mass: Ursuline Composers of the 17th Century*. *Messa Prima* by the University of Arkansas Schola Cantorum, Jack Groh, conductor (rerelease of Leonarda LP recording of 1982). *Ave suavis dilectio* by St. Ursula Ensemble: Andrea Folan, soprano; Brian Brooks and Deborah Howell, violins; Rob Haskins, continuo. Leonarda LE 346 (1998).

Sonatas 2 and 12, from op. 16; *Alta dei ciel regina; Veni amor, veni Jesu* from op. 15. In *Kurtisane und Nonne*. Rosina Sommerschmidt, soprano, Sephira-Ensemble Stuttgart. Bayer CD 100078/79 (1990).

Sonata Duodecima, from op. 16. In *In stil moderna*. Ingrid Matthews, violin; Byron Schenkman, harpsichord. Wildboar WLBR 9512 (1995).

Elisabeth-Claude Jacquet de la Guerre

The Complete Harpsichord Suites. Carole Cerasi, harpsichord (played on 1633 Ruckers, rebuilt in 1763). Metronome MET CD 1026 (1998).

Jonas. In *Baroque Treasures*. Judith Nelson, soprano; Bay Area Women's Philharmonic, JoAnn Falletta, conductor. Newport Classics (1990).

L'isle de Delos and *Jonas* [cantatas], with Suite de clavecin No. 3. L'ensemble de Idées heureuses, Isabelle Desrochers, soprano; Geneviève Soly, harpsichord. ATMA S.R.I. Classics ACD 2-2191 (2000).

Piano Compositions by Women Composers. Monica Pons, pianist. La Ma de Guido DISC 037.

Pièces de Clavecin (1687). Szilvia Elik, harpsichord. Hungaroton HCD 31729 (1998).

Les Pièces de Clavecin. Includes *Suites I, II* and *III* from Book I (1687) and *Suite I* from Book II (1707). Blandine Verlet, harpsichord. AUVIDIS E8644 (1998).

Sonates a un e deux violons avec viole ou violoncelle obliges. Frederic Martin and Odile Edouard, violins; Christine Plubeau, viola da gamba; David Simpson, violoncello; Eric Bellocq, theorbo and guitar; Noelle Spieth, harpsichord and organ. Ensemble Variations, ACCORD 20-782 (1997).

Sonates pour le Viollon (1707), with *Chaconne: L'Inconstante* (1687) Ingrid Matthews, baroque violin; Byron Schenkman, harpsichord; Margriet Tindemans, viola da gamba. WILDBOAR WLBR 9601 (1996).

Suzanne, Judith, Esther, Rachel and *Jephté*. In *Cantata Bibliques* [5 cantatas on women's stories from Scripture]. Isabelle Poulenard and Sophie Boulin, sopranos; Ensemble Instrumentaux, Guy Robert and Georges Guillard, dirs. Arion ARN 268012 (1986).

Nuns, Various

Rosa Mistica: musiche di monache lombarde del Seicento (Music of Lombard Nuns of the 17th century). Works by Isabella Leonarda, Maria Xaveria Peruchona, Caterina Assandra, Chiara Margarita Cozzolani, Rosa Giacenta Badalla, Bianca Maria Meda, Claudia Sessa, and Claudia Francesca Rusca. Cappella Artemisia. Tactus TC600003—Allegro Imports (1999).

Maria Xaveria Peruchona

Ad gaudia, ad iubila; Solvite, Solvite; Regina Cæli. Baroque for the Mass: Ursuline Composers of the 17th Century. Andrea Folan, soprano; Roya Bauman, alto; Kirk Dougherty, tenor, Brian Brooks and Deborah Howell, violins; Rob Haskins, continuo. Leonarda LE 346 (1998).

Barbara Strozzi

Amor dormiglione; Chiamata a nuovi amori; Spesso per entro al petto. In *Women's Voices: Five Centuries of Song*. Neva Pilgrim, soprano; Edward Smith, harpsichord. Leonarda 338 (1997).

L'astratto. In *The Orpheus Circle*. Emma Kirby, soprano; Anthony Rooley, lute. Musica Oscura CD 0988 (1994).

Barbara Strozzi: Arie, Cantate & Lamenti. Ensemble Incantato: Mona Spägle, soprano. CPO 999 533–2 (1998).

Barbara Strozzi, La Virtuosissima Cantatrice: The Vocal Music of Barbara Strozzi. Musica Secreta, Deborah Roberts and Suzie le Blanc sopranos; Mary Nichols, alto; Kasia Elsner, theorbo; John Toll, harpsichord. Amon-Ra Records CD-SAR 61 (1994).

Cantates. [11 arias, cantatas, and lamenti] Susanne Rydén, Ensemble Musica Fiorita. Harmonia Mundi HMC 905249 (2000).

Diporti di Euterpe: overo Cantate & Ariette a voce Sola: Opera Settima (Venezia 1659). Emanuela Galli, soprano, with Ensemble Galilei, Paul Beier, dir. Stradivarius DULCIMER STR 33487 (1998).

Lagrime mie. In *Musica Dolce*. Julianne Baird, soprano; Colin Tilney, harpsichord. Dorian DOR 90123 (1992).

Lagrime mie; Non occore; Tradimento, tradimento!; Lilla dici; Miei pensieri; Luci belle; Soccorete luci avare; Apresso a i molli argenti; Serenata: Hor che Apollo. In *Kurtisane und Nonne*. Rosina Sommerschmidt, soprano, Sephira-Ensemble Stuttgart. Bayer CD 100078/79 (1990).

Lamenti Barocchi. Soloists of the Cappella Musicale di S. Petronio, Sergio Vartolo, director. In vol. 1, *Le tre Grazie a Venere*; in vol. 2, *Merci di voi*; in vol. 3., *Lamento del Marchese Cinq-Mars*. Naxos 8.553318-20 (1995, 1996).

A New Sappho: Barbara Strozzi and Nicolo Fontei [8 duets]. Favella Lyrica ensemble. Koch 3-7491-2HI (2000).

Il primo libro de madrigali (1644). La Veneziana ensemble. Cantus C 9612 (1998).

From *Sacri Musicali Affetti*, libro 1, op. 5 (Venice 1655). Christina Kiehr, soprano; Christina Pluhar, arpa tripla and tiorba; Sylvie Moquet, viola da gamba and violoncino; Matthias Spaeter, archiliuto, and chitarrone; Jean-Marc Aymes, organo and clavicembalo. Harmonia Mundi ED 13048 (1995).

To the Unknown Goddess: A Portrait of Barbara Strozzi. [17 songs] Catherine Bott, soprano; Paula Chateuaneuf, chitarrone and baroque guitar; Timothy Roberts, harpsichord; Frances Kelly, harp. Carlton Classics 30366 00412 (1996).

Selected Modern Editions

General

Women Composers: Music Through the Ages, vols. 1 and 2, Edited by Sylvia Glickman and Martha Furman Schleifer. New York: G. K. Hall, 1996.

Rosa Giacinta Badalla

Camillo Tellier (1697). Cantata for baritone, 2 trumpets, and organ/violoncello. Louisville, KY: Ars Femina, n.d.

Pane angelico, Vuò cercando. In "Rosa Giacinta Badalla," by Robert L. Kendrick. In *Women Composers: Music Through the Ages*, vol. 2, edited by Sylvia Glickman and Martha Furman Schleifer. New York: G. K. Hall, 1996; Bryn Mawr, PA: Hildegard Publishing Company, 1998 (G. K. Hall reprint).

Antonia Bembo

Amor mio, Tota pulcra es; Ha, que l'absence est un cruel martire. In "Antonia Bembo," by Claire A. Fontijn. In *Women Composers: Music Through the Ages*, vol. 2, edited by Sylvia Glickman and Martha Furman Schleifer. New York: G. K. Hall, 1996; Bryn Mawr, PA: Hildegard Publishing Company, 1998 (G. K. Hall reprint).

In amor ci vuol ardir, from *Produzioni Armoniche* on a text by Aurelia Fedeli. In *Italian Arias of the Baroque and Classical Eras*, edited by John Glenn Paton. Van Nuys, CA: Alfred, 1994.

Per il Natale. Cantata for soprano, 2 treble instruments, and continuo. Edited by Claire A. Fontijn. Fayetteville, AR: ClarNan Editions, 1999.

Francesca Caccini

Canzonettas, edited by Barbara Starapoli. Bryn Mawr, P.A. Hildegard Publishing Company, 2000.

Dove io credea le mie speranze vere. In *L'Arte Musicale in Italia: Secolo XVII*, vol. 5, edited and arranged by Luigi Torchi. Milan: 1898–1907; reprint, Milan: Ricordi, 1968.

Laudate Dominum; Maria dolce Maria. From *Il Primo Libro* and *Aria of the Shepherd* from *La Liberazione di Ruggiero*. In "Francesca Caccini," by Carolyn Raney. In *Historical Anthology of Music by Women*, edited by James R. Briscoe. Bloomington and Indianapolis: Indiana University Press, 1987.

La Liberzaione di Ruggiero. Edited by Doris Silbert. Northampton, MA: Smith College, 1945.

Sonetto spirituali; Madrigale: Nel cammino; Aria romanesca; Motetto: Regina caeli; Himno: Jesu corona Virginum; Madrigale a due voci: Io mi distruggo: Aria: La pastorella mia; Canzonetta: Chi desia di saper. In "Francesca Caccini," by Caroline Cunningham. In *Women Composers: Music Through the Ages*, vol. 2, edited by Sylvia Glickman and Martha Furman Schleifer. New York: G. K. Hall, 1996; Bryn Mawr, PA: Hildegard Publishing Company, 1998 (G. K. Hall reprint).

Settimia Caccini

Già sperai; Core di questo core; Cantan gl'augelli; Due luci ridenti. In "Settimia Caccini," by Candace Smith. In *Women Composers: Music Through the Ages*, vol. 2, edited by Sylvia Glickman and Martha Furman Schleifer. New York: G. K. Hall, 1996; Bryn Mawr, PA: Hildegard Publishing Company, 1998 (G. K. Hall reprint).

Chiara Margarita Cozzolani

Magnificat (1650). Edited by Barbara Garvey Jackson. Fayetteville, AR: ClarNan Editions, 1998.

O dulcis Jesu; O caeli cives. In "Chiara Margarita Cozzolani," by Robert L. Kendrick. In *Women Composers: Music Through the Ages*, vol. 2, edited by Sylvia Glickman and Martha Furman Schleifer. New York: G. K. Hall, 1996; Bryn Mawr, PA: Hildegard Publishing Company, 1998 (G. K. Hall reprint).

Caterina Benedetta Gratianini

Il ancor ti resta in petto, from *Santa Teresa; A veder si raro oggetto*, from *S. Gemigniano Vescovo, e Protettore di Modena*. In *Arias from Oratorios by Women Composers of the Eighteenth Century*, vol. 3. Fayetteville, AR: ClarNan Editions, 1990.

In questo chiaro: Dia lode il grato Core, from *S. Gemigniano; Tutti pace, frena il pianto* from *S. Teresa*. In *Arias from Oratorios by Women Composers of the Eighteenth Century*, vol. 4. Fayetteville, AR: ClarNan Editions, 1992.

Non timor d'aspri tormenti; Deh! Lascia à quest' alma, from *S. Teresa*. Edited by Barbara Garvey Jackson. In *Arias from Oratorios by Women Composers of the Eighteenth Century*, vol. 5. Fayetteville, AR: ClarNan Editions, 1996.

Sinfonias to Part I and Part II of *Santa Teresa*. In "Caterina Benedetta Gratianini," by Barbara Garvey Jackson. In *Women Composers: Music Through the Ages*, vol. 2, edited by Sylvia Glickman and Martha Furman Schleifer. New York: G. K. Hall, 1996.

Maria Margherita Grimani

I fulmini d'un Dio; Cari lacci...Ogni aspetto...Son lieto; S'hò fra nodi il piede avvinto. From *La decollazione de San Giovanni Battista*, edited by Barbara Garvey Jackson. In *Arias from Oratorios by Women Composers of the Eighteenth Century*, vol. 7. Fayetteville, AR: ClarNan Editions, 1999.

La decollazione de San Giovanni Battista. Scene between Erode and Salome. In "Maria Margherita Grimani," by Barbara Garvey Jackson. In *Women Composers: Music Through the Ages*, vol. 2, edited by Sylvia Glickman and Martha Furman Schleifer. New York: G. K. Hall, 1996.

L'esser fida; A un core innocente, from *La decollazione de San Giovanni Battista*. Edited by Barbara Garvey Jackson. In *Arias from Oratorios by Women Composers of the Eighteenth Century*, vol. 1. Fayetteville, AR: ClarNan Editions, 1987.

Ogni Colle from *La visitazione di Santa Elisabetta*. Louisville, KY: Editions Ars Femina, 1992.

Sinfonia from *Pallade e Marte*. In "Maria Margherita Grimani," by Barbara Garvey Jackson. In *Historical Anthology of Music by Women*, edited by James R. Briscoe. Bloomington and Indianapolis: Indiana University Press, 1987.

Sinfonia to *La decollazione di San Giovanni Battista*. Louisville, KY: Editions Ars Femina, 1992.

Sinfonia to *La visitazione di Santa Elisabetta*. Louisville, KY: Editions Ars Femina, 1992.

Isabella Leonarda

Ave Regina coelorum, from op. 10. Edited by Stewart Carter. In *Nine Centuries of Music by Women* (series). New York: Broude Brothers, 1980.

Ave suavis dilectio, from op. 6 (1676). Edited by Barbara Garvey Jackson. Fayetteville, AR: ClarNan Editions, 1996.

Messa Prima, from op. 18 (1696). Edited by Barbara Garvey Jackson. Fayetteville AR: ClarNan Editions, 1981, 2d ed. 1988.

Quam dulcis es, from op. 13 (1687). Edited by Barbara Garvey Jackson. Fayetteville AR: ClarNan Editions, 1984.

Selected Compositions. Edited by Stewart Carter. *Recent Researches in Music of the Baroque Era*, no. 59. Madison, WI: A-R Editions, 1988.

Sonata duodecima, from op. 16 (1693). Edited by Barbara Garvey Jackson. Ottawa: Dovehouse, 1983.

Spes mondane, from op. 6 (1676); *Surge virgo*, from op. 10 (1684). In "Isabella Leonarda," by Stewart Carter. In *Women Composers: Music Through the Ages*, vol. 2, edited by Sylvia Glickman and Martha Furman Schleifer. New York: G. K. Hall, 1996; Bryn Mawr, PA: Hildegard Publishing Company, 1998 (G. K. Hall reprint).

Elisabeth-Claude Jacquet de la Guerre

Cephale et Procris. Edited by Wanda R. Griffiths. *Recent Researches in Music of the Baroque Era*, no. 88. Madison, WI: A-R Editions, 1998.

Deux sonates pour violon seul (1707) *avec viola de gambe obligèe et continuo*. Edited by Renée Viollier. Geneva, Switzerland: Sociéte des emissions de radio-Geneve [195-?].

Esther from *Cantates françoises sur des sujets tirez de l'Écriture*. Kassel: Furore, 1998.

Instrumental music, complete. In "The Instrumental Music of Elizabeth-Claude Jacquet de La Guerre," by Bates, Carol Henry. Ph.D. diss., Indiana University, 1978.

Judith from *Cantates françoises sur des sujets tirez de l'Écriture*. Kassel: Furore, 1995.

Le Passage de la Mer Rouge, from *Cantates françoises sur des sujets tirez de l'Écriture*. Edited by Diane Guthrie. In "Elisabeth-Claude Jacquet de La Guerre," by Diane Guthrie. In *Women Composers: Music Through the Ages*, vol. 2, edited by Sylvia Glickman and Martha Furman Schleifer. New York: G. K. Hall, 1996.

Pièces de Clavecin. Edited by Carol Henry Bates. *Le pupitre* no. 66. Paris: Heugel, 1986.

Pièces de Clavecin qui peuvent se Jouer sur le Viollon (1707). Edited by Paul Brunold (1938), revised by Thurston Dart (1965). Les Remparts, Monaco: Éditions de l'Oiseau-lyre, by J. B. Hanson, 1965.

Sarabande et gigue, from *Pièces de Clavecin qui peuvent se Jouer sur le Viollon* (1707). In *Les Maîtres français du clavecin des XVIIe et XVIIIe siècles*, edited by Paul Brunold. Paris: Sénart, 1921.

Semelé, Cantate avec Simphonie (ca. 1715). Edited by Susan Erickson and Robert Bloch. In *Historical Anthology of Music by Women*, edited by James R. Briscoe. Bloomington and Indianapolis: University of Indiana Press, 1987.

Sonata No. 1 in G for 2 Violins (Oboes/Flutes) and Basso Continuo. Edited by Robert Block. *Music for Chamber Ensemble* (N.M. 243). London: Nova Music, 1985.

Sonata for violin & continuo, No. 2 in D Major. Edited by Edith Borroff. Pittsburgh: University of Pittsburgh Press, 1961.

Susannah, from *Cantates françoises sur des sujets tirez de l'Écriture*. Edited by Valerie Macintosh. Bryn Mawr, PA: Hildegard Publishing Company, 1995.

Trio Sonatas for 2 violins, viola da gamba and continuo (2 vols.). Edited by Carol Henry Bates. Kassel: Furore, 1996.

Raccomodement comique de Pierrot et de Nicole. Edited by Carolyn Raney. Nine Centuries of Music by Women (series). New York: Broude Brothers, 1978.

Bianca Maria Meda

Cari Musici. In "Bianca Maria Meda" by Robert L. Kendrick. In *Women Composers: Music Through the Ages*, vol. 2, edited by Sylvia Glickman and Martha Furman Schleifer. New York: G. K. Hall, 1996; Bryn Mawr, PA: Hildegard Publishing Company, 1998 (G. K. Hall reprint).

Maria Francesca Nascinbeni

Non tema nò di morte, from *Canzoni e madrigali morali e spirituali* (1674). In *Two Sacred Works for Three Treble Voices*, edited by Barbara Garvey Jackson. Fayetteville AR: ClarNan Editions, 1990.

Sitientes venite, Communion motet for the Feast of the Most Blessed Sacrament, from Lazzarini, Scipione, *Motetti a due e tre voci* (1674). Edited by Barbara Garvey Jackson. Fayetteville: ClarNan Editions, 1995.

Una fiamma rovente à due Canti, from *Canzoni e madrigali morali e spirituali* (1674). In "Maria Francesca Nascinbeni" by Barbara Garvey Jackson. In *Women Composers: Music Through the Ages*, vol. 2, edited by Sylvia Glickman and Martha Furman Schleifer. New York: G. K. Hall, 1996.

Maria Xaveria Peruchona

Ad gaudia, ad iubila; A Christmas cantata from *Sacri concerti de motetti a una, due, tre, e quattro voci* (1675). Edited by Barbara Garvey Jackson. In *Three Sacred Works for Soprano, Two Violins, and Organ Continuo*. Fayetteville: ClarNan Editions, 1996.

Quid pavemus sorores (Della Madonna). In "Maria Xaveria Peruchona" by Jane Bowers. In *Women Composers: Music Through the Ages*, vol. 2, edited by Sylvia Glickman and Martha Furman Schleifer. New York: G. K. Hall, 1996; Bryn Mawr, PA: Hildegard Publishing Company, 1998 (G. K. Hall reprint).

Regina Cœli (for soprano, alto, tenor, and organ continuo), from *Sacri concerti de motetti a una, due, tre, e quattro voci* (1675). Edited by Barbara Garvey Jackson. Fayetteville: ClarNan Editions, 1999.

Solvite, solvite (motet for soprano, 2 violins and continuo), from *Sacri concerti de motetti a una, due, tre, e quattro voci* (1675). Edited by Barbara Garvey Jackson. Fayetteville: ClarNan Editions, 1999.

Lucia Quinciani

Udite lagrimosi spirti. Edited by Candace Smith. In *Women Composers Through the Ages*, vol. 1, edited by Sylvia Glickman and Martha Furman Schleifer. New York: G. K. Hall, 1996. Bryn Mawr, PA: Hildegard Publishing Company, 1998.

Camilla de Rossi

Abramo nell' addormentarsti; *Morirai, Figlio, adorato*, from *Il Sacrifizio di Abramo*; *Cangia pur la rozza veste*, from *Il figliuol prodigo*. Edited by Barbara Garvey Jackson. In *Arias from Oratorios by Women Composers of the Eighteenth Century*, vol. 5. Fayetteville, AR: ClarNan Editions, 1996.

Dal Sol ogn' Astro apprende; *Un sospiro*, from *Il Sacrifizio di Abramo*. Edited by Barbara Garvey Jackson. In *Arias from Oratorios by Women Composers of the Eighteenth Century*, vol. 7. Fayetteville, AR: ClarNan Editions, 1999.

Dori e Fileno. Edited by Barbara Garvey Jackson. Fayetteville, AR: ClarNan Editions, 1984.

Il figliuol prodigo, Scene 1. In "Camilla de Rossi, Romana" by Barbara Garvey Jackson. In *Women Composers: Music Through the Ages*, vol. 2, 356–65, edited by Sylvia Glickman and Martha Furman Schleifer. New York: G. K. Hall, 1996.

Il Sacrifizio di Abramo. Edited by Barbara Garvey Jackson. Fayetteville, AR: ClarNan Editions, 1984.

Quanto, quanto mi consola, from *Santa Beatrice d'Este*; *Strali, fulmini, tempeste, procelle*, from *Il Sacrifizio di Abramo*; *Cielo, pietoso Cielo*, from *S. Alessio*. Edited by Barbara Garvey Jackson. In *Arias from Oratorios by Women Composers of the Eighteenth Century*, vol. 1. Fayetteville, AR: ClarNan Editions, 1987.

Quella nave, che riposa, from *Il figliuol prodigo*. Edited by Barbara Garvey Jackson. In *Arias from Oratorios by Women Composers of the Eighteenth Century*, vol. 4. Fayetteville, AR: ClarNan Editions, 1992.

Rompe il morso; *Lascia, o Figlio, il tuo dolore*, from *Il figliuol prodigo*; *Sono il fasto, e la bellezza*, from *Santa Beatrice d'Este*. Edited by Barbara Garvey Jackson. In *Arias from Oratorios by Women Composers of the Eighteenth Century*, vol. 3. Fayetteville, AR: ClarNan Editions, 1990.

Santa Beatrice d'Este. Edited by Barbara Garvey Jackson. Fayetteville, AR: ClarNan Editions, 1984; with revised preface and translation, 1993.

Seven Sinfonias (1707–1710) for Strings and Continuo. Edited by Barbara Garvey Jackson. In *Arias and Sinfonias from Oratorios by Women Composers of the Eighteenth Century*, vol. 6. Fayetteville, AR: ClarNan Editions, 1996.

Sonori concenti, from *S. Alessio*; and *Qui dove il Po…Poiche parmi di sentire*, from *Santa Beatrice d'Este*. Edited by Barbara Garvey Jackson. In *Arias from Oratorios by Women Composers of the Eighteenth Century*, vol. 2. Fayetteville, AR: ClarNan Editions, 1990.

Barbara Strozzi

Arie, op. 8 (1664). Edited by Randall Wong. In "Barbara Strozzi's 'Arie,' op. 8 (1664): An Edition and Commentary." Ph.D. diss., Stanford University, 1992.

Con le belle non ci vuol fretta, from *Il primo libro de' madrigali*. Edited by Carolyn Raney. In Nine Centuries of Music by Women (series). New York: Broude Brothers, 1978.

Consiglio amoroso, from *Il primo libro de' madrigali*. Edited by Carolyn Raney. In Nine Centuries of Music by Women (series). New York: Broude Brothers, 1978.

Five Madrigals for 2–5 accompanied Voices. Edited by Andrew Kosciesza. Bryn Mawr, PA: Hildegard Publishing Company, 1996.

Lagrime miei, from *Diporti di Euterpe op. 7*. Edited by Carol MacClintock. In *The Solo Song, 1580–1730: A Norton Music Anthology*. New York: Norton, 1973.

L'Astratto; Hor che Apollo. In "Barbara Strozzi" by Randall Wong. In *Women Composers: Music Through the Ages*, vol. 1, edited by Sylvia Glickman and Martha Furman Schleifer. New York: G. K. Hall, 1996; Bryn Mawr, PA: Hildegard Publishing Company, 1998 (G. K. Hall reprint).

Mercé di voi, mia fortunata stella; Quante volte ti bacio; Che dolce udire; Anima del mio core, from *Il Primo Libro de Madrigali*. Edited by Elke Masche Blankenburg. Kassel: Furore-Edition, 1993.

Spesso per entro al petto, from *Cantate, ariette e duetti*, op. 2. Edited by Knud Jeppesen. In *La Flora*, vol. 2. Copenhagen/Frankfurt: Hansen, 1949.

Alba Trissina

Vulnerasti cor meum, from Leone Leoni; *Sacri fiori, libro quarto* (1622). In "Alba Trissina" by Robert L. Kendrick. In *Women Composers: Music Through the Ages*, vol. 2, edited by Sylvia Glickman and Martha Furman Schleifer. New York: G. K. Hall, 1996; Bryn Mawr, PA: Hildegard Publishing Company, 1998 (G. K. Hall reprint).

4
The Eighteenth Century

Valerie Woodring Goertzen

Introduction

In eighteenth-century Europe, industrialization and changes in the social, economic, and political order led to expanded opportunities for women in musical life. In lavish performances at court, music in the salons of aristocratic and wealthy families, concerts open to paying audiences, and the growing culture of music in middle-class homes, women played important roles as patrons, performers, composers, teachers, instrument builders, and music publishers. The ideals of the Enlightenment emphasizing reason, order and naturalness inspired the growth of new musical styles, and genres such as the keyboard sonata and lied, in which women excelled.

In the second half of the century, nearly every important European court employed women as performers and teachers. The Imperial Court in Vienna, the courts of Frederick the Great and his nephew, Frederick William II at Potsdam, near Berlin, the courts of Louis XV and Louis XVI in Paris, and the courts of Peter the Great and Catherine the Great in St. Petersburg were the grandest musical centers. Smaller ones, also important, included those at Weimar and Milan and the Esterházy palace at Eisenstadt. Several royal women composed and performed and used their positions of influence to further the careers of other women.

In Paris, Vienna, Berlin, and other centers, aristocratic and upper-middle-class women hosted musical gatherings in their homes. These fashionable salons served as forums where local and foreign artists and intellectuals gathered to enjoy and perform music and engage in conversations about the arts, literature, philosophy, politics, and social causes. Visiting artists often made private appearances to build audiences before risking the expense and effort required to stage public concerts. Moreover, salons were the main venue for solo and chamber genres that were not normally featured in public or formal court concerts. Thus salon concerts featured some of the most accomplished artists and newest and most challenging works. The salons of composers Marianna Martines in Vienna, Maria Szymanowska in St. Petersburg, Madame de Brillon in Paris and Passy, Madame Louis in Paris, and Bettine von Arnim in Berlin were among the most prestigious in Europe.

Concerts in which performers and composers appeared before a paying public were an important innovation in eighteenth-century musical life. The Concert Spirituel in Paris (founded in 1725), the Grosse Konzerte in Leipzig (operating in 1743–1756 and 1763–1778—later called the Gewandhaus concerts), and the London concerts of Johann Christian Bach (1732–1795) and Carl Friedrich Abel (1723–1787) during 1765–1781 were among the most prominent series. Public concerts typically featured concertos, symphonies (sometimes single symphonic movements), overtures, opera arias, and other vocal works and, toward the end of the century, virtuoso works for piano or violin. Although women frequently appeared as soloists in these concerts, they were rarely hired as members of established performing groups.

Women's opportunities for involvement in music depended partly on their social class or station. Members of royalty, the aristocracy, and the wealthy upper middle class studied with the best musicians in Europe; some became skilled singers, instrumentalists, and composers. As a rule, however, their social status prevented them from embarking upon professional careers. Instead, they composed and performed for themselves and for family and friends and sometimes taught children in their own circles, although not for monetary compensation. Other women of the upper classes studied singing or an instrument primarily for social reasons: music, like needlework or dancing, was one of the "accomplishments" through which a woman could demonstrate good breeding, bring honor to her family, and enhance her marriage prospects. Women of lower status emulated this model, creating a market for teachers, instruction books, accessible music, affordable instruments, and journals covering musical events and topics.

Women were encouraged first and foremost to sing. In the courts and in the public sphere, they performed in fully staged opera. In the home and other private venues, they sang opera excerpts and more intimate songs, often accompanying themselves on a keyboard instrument, harp, or guitar. Eighteenth-century women also played harp and a variety of keyboard instruments as soloists. Importantly in this period, these instruments could be played while sitting "as a lady." When the piano replaced the harpsichord and clavichord and became the principal concert instrument during the last two decades of the century, women were among the star performers. Women typically did not play string, wind, or brass instruments because they required "distortion" of the face or body position. The violin virtuoso Maddalena Lombardini Sirmen, educated in one of the Venetian *ospedali* (see previous chapters), is an important exception. A few of the professional musicians and aristocratic amateurs surveyed in this chapter were child prodigies. But crucial to the development of all the composers discussed here were the support and guidance of musicians and influential sponsors who supervised their technical training and fostered their intellectual growth.

In the second quarter of the century, new styles and genres of music developed in response to Enlightenment ideals and to the growing public for music. Transparent textures, flexible dynamics, slow harmonic change, and architectural forms defined by long-range harmonic goals were fundamental to the Classical style that flourished in the second half of the century. Female singers and composers found opportunities in new genres of vocal music that emerged: the national varieties of comic opera, and the German lied. The lied developed in the Berlin area and became a principal outlet for the creative efforts of German-speaking composers in the second half of the eighteenth century. Early composers of lieder sought to emulate folk song through sensitive and natural presentations of text in strophic or through-composed settings. Later in the century (and continuing into the nineteenth), composers drew upon more complex harmonies and structures to express the imagery and emotion in the texts, giving the accompanying instrument (usually piano) a larger role in interpreting the drama. As the families and close friends of Louise Reichardt, Emilie Zumsteeg, and Bettine von Arnim included prominent poets and composers of lieder, it was natural for these women also to compose in the genre.

The keyboard sonata, with or without an accompanying instrument such as violin, and the keyboard concerto were among instrumental genres that emerged in the second quarter of the century; these served as the principal vehicles for harpsichord and (later) piano virtuosos, both male and female. The first movement (and sometimes other movements) of these and other multi-movement works followed a structure now termed "sonata form," which eighteenth-century writers understood as a kind of binary (two-part) form. The first section established a home key (tonic) and a contrasting key through the presentation of themes in those keys; in the second section, more distant keys were explored as the composer elaborated upon ideas from the themes, and then the tonic was reaffirmed as the themes returned, now all in the home key. This design became a hallmark of Western music.

Some eighteenth-century women ventured to compose in the large genres—orchestral overtures, operas, chamber works for several instruments, and works for chorus and orchestra—but this was not common. In general, women were not thought to need (or deserve) the thorough musical training considered essential for aspiring male composers. Moreover, women who wrote for large ensembles rarely had the opportunity to hear and receive feedback about their compositions. Given these hampering circumstances, the accomplishments of women who did create music for large ensembles are all the more remarkable.

Most of the women discussed here belonged to a class of professional musicians and artists that was a subset of the middle class. Some were part of extended families of musicians and were expected to study music and perhaps aspire to professional careers. Some women gave up their careers when they married, although this was far more common among women who did not have the support of musical families. Some married women toured jointly with their husbands and collaborated with them on publications; still others left their husbands and children home or left them altogether in favor of performing careers.

Composers throughout Europe and in North America shared the principal features of musical style in the eighteenth century. Nevertheless, because the contexts for musical activity and the compositional genres varied from one region to the next, the composers are grouped geographically. Within each group, individuals are discussed in roughly chronological order. The chapter includes composers from Italy, Austria, other German-speaking lands, France, Poland, England, and the American colonies and the United States.

Italy

Maddalena Laura Lombardini Sirmen (1745–1818), violinist, composer and singer, is the most famous of the musicians educated in the Venetian *ospedali* and enjoyed an international career. Born in Venice to Piero Lombardini and Gasparina Gambirasi, she auditioned at the age of seven and was accepted by the governors of the Mendicanti as an apprentice to the *coro* (music school or conservatory), one of four girls chosen from a group of thirty applicants. For the next fourteen years she was part of the musical life of this institution and of the city of Venice.

Teaching girls to sing and play instruments was seen as a means of edifying them spiritually, while also creating a resource for the city's musical life and attracting potential benefactors to the four Venetian *ospedali*. Students received instruction in music fundamentals, sight-singing, solmization, ear-training, performance practice, foreign languages, and counterpoint. They were introduced to the instruments owned by the *coro* and were given private lessons on at least two of them; a course in vocal training was also offered. The *ospedali* hired outside (male) musicians as teachers, ensuring that their students were apprised of current developments in the European musical mainstream. Upon completion of their course of study, students became teachers. Each was required to remain an additional ten years to perform with the group and to instruct at least two younger students. With this obligation fulfilled and with the permission of the governors, the woman could then choose to leave and marry or to stay on as a permanent resident, performing and teaching and sometimes accepting external students for financial remuneration. She could eventually retire within the *ospedale*. In this way, some musicians of the *cori* were able to achieve greater personal and financial independence than was generally possible for women in the society.

As the reputations of the *cori* increased, noble and wealthy middle-class families from Venice and the European courts sought music education in these institutions for their daughters. External students paid tuition as well as board if they lived on the premises, creating an additional source of revenue for the *ospedali*. In this century, all *ospedali* except the heavily populated Pietà actively recruited talented singers and instrumentalists from Italy and other parts of Europe; some older women were also accepted. Among *figlie del coro* (daughters of the *coro*) who became composers were Vincenta da Ponte (fl. second half of the eighteenth century), Teresa Orsini (1788–1829), Michielina (fl. ca. 1701–1744), Santa (fl. ca. 1725–1750), and Agata (fl. ca. 1800), all educated at the Pietá. The *ospedali* served many of the functions of modern-day music schools, and their high level of musicianship and professionalism helped to make them a star attraction for visitors. In August 1770, after Lombardini had left the Mendicanti, music historian Charles Burney wrote of his visit to that institution:

> This evening, in order to make myself more fully acquainted with the nature of the conservatories, and to finish my musical enquiries here, I obtained permission to be admitted into the music school of the Mendicanti (of which Signor Bartoni is *maestro*), and was favored with a concert, which was wholly performed on my account, and lasted two hours, by the best vocal and instrumental performers of this hospital: it was really curious to see, as well as to hear every part of this excellent concert, performed by female violins, hautbois, tenors, bas[s]es, harpsichords, French horns, and even double bas[s]es....
>
> The singing was really excellent in different styles; Laura Risegari and Giacoma Frari had very powerful voices, capable of filling a large theater; these sung bravura songs, and capital scenes selected from Italian operas; and Francesca Tomj, sister of the Abate of that name, and Antonia Lucuvich...whose voices were more delicate, confined themselves chiefly to pathetic songs, of taste and expression. The whole was judiciously mixed; no two airs of the same kind followed each other, and there seemed to be great decorum and good discipline observed in every particular; for these admirable performers, who are of different ages, all behaved with great propriety, and seemed to be well educated. (Neuls-Bates 1996)

By the age of fourteen Lombardini was teaching violin at the Mendicanti and was also a featured performer. The Abbé Jérôme Richard wrote of a girl who was probably Lombardini:

> I saw there a young girl of, at most, twelve or thirteen years of age perform some solo sonatas for the violin to general applause; they must have had confidence in her talent to display it in public on one of the solemn feastdays before a large assembly. Only in Venice can one see these musical prodigies. (Baldauf-Berdes 1993)

Lombardini's musical gifts attracted the attentions of Giuseppe Tartini (1692–1770), then the most famous violin teacher in Europe. His 1760 letter to her concerning the use of the bow and the left hand, the handling of dynamics, and instructions for practicing was later translated into several languages and circulated widely. The Mendicanti sponsored Lombardini's travel to Padua to study with Tartini on three different occasions in the early 1760s; she studied violin performance, ornamentation and embellishment, and composition.

The governors expected and hoped that Lombardini would remain at the Mendicanti as a permanent resident and teacher. However, she wished for a more public life as a performer and apparently wanted to ensure that she would not lose her unusually large marriage dowry. In 1766 she enlisted Tartini's help in finding a husband and the following year was granted permission to marry violinist Lodovico Maria Gaspar Sirmen di Ravenna (1738–1812). As a former *ospedale* musician, Maddalena Lombardini Sirmen (hereafter called Sirmen) was barred from performing in Venice. Instead, the couple embarked on a tour that took them to Faenza, Turin, and Paris. Sirmen was hailed as Tartini's "authentic and worthy descendant," a characterization that was all the more remarkable because the violin was not generally considered a woman's instrument. *L'Avant-coureur* reported on her performance at the Concert Spirituel in Paris in August 1768:

> Her violin is the lyre of Orpheus in the hands of a goddess. The beauty of tone, the expression, the style, and the facility of her playing combine to qualify her among the best virtuosi. (Baldauf-Berdes 1993)

Mme Bérault published a set of six string quartets under the names "Lodovico and Maddalena Laura Syrmen" in Paris; however, stylistic features of the quartets indicate that they are Maddalena Sirmen's work alone. These are the first published string quartets by a woman composer.

The couple traveled to London in 1770, where Sirmen performed her concertos and other works in the prestigious Bach-Abel concert series, at King's Theatre and at Covent Garden (between the acts of operas), and elsewhere. In addition, she sang operatic roles at King's Theatre and in the Marylebone Gardens. By the early 1770s Lodovico had returned to Ravenna with the couple's daughter, Alessandra, to pursue his own career as a composer, teacher, performer, and instrument maker. Don Giuseppe Terzi, a priest from the Mendicanti who had been with Sirmen since her departure from the *ospedale*, stayed on as her traveling companion and remained with her the rest of her life. She toured in Italy and France and was employed as a very highly paid singer in Dresden in 1779. In 1783 she was appointed principal singer at the Imperial Theater in St. Petersburg, where Lodovico joined her for about a year, assuming the position of concertmaster. She performed as both singer and violinist there and in other Russian cities.

When Sirmen returned to Paris in 1785, she found the musical fashions changed since her last visit in 1768–1769. Her playing was compared unfavorably with that of younger violinists, such as Giovanni Battista Viotti (1755–1824), who were now emphasizing speed, technical prowess, and bravura tone. A review in the *Mercure de France* of May 7, 1785, proved damaging to her reputation:

> This reviewer believes Mme Sirmen would do well to change her playing style so that it conforms to what is fashionable today. If she does, then we do not doubt that she will again receive the same enthusiastic applause that she did previously. (Arnold and Eive 1998)

Although Sirmen's works were still popular enough in the mid-1780s to warrant the publication of new editions, her career as a ranking violinist was essentially over.

In 1789 the Venetian Senators recalled Sirmen to Venice from a post in Naples; her activities in Venice are not known. Her will of 1798 left generous amounts to her family and friends and to the poor, as well as money for Masses for her soul. However, a codicil of 1806 and her final will of 1817 indicate that she had little left at the end of her life. She died of a heart condition on May 18, 1818.

Sirmen's international status as a performer was mirrored in her published music, which appeared in Vienna, London, Paris, Leipzig, Brussels, St. Petersburg, Amsterdam, and other European cities. She composed at least twenty-six works, primarily for stringed instruments: string trios, violin duos, string quartets, six violin concertos, and a sonata for violin and cello obbligato. Many of these are available in modern editions, and a few have been recorded. Tomaso Giordani (ca. 1730–1806) transcribed the violin concertos for harpsichord—both as concertos and solos—in the early 1770s; these were published in several editions. Leopold Mozart (1719–1787), father of Wolfgang Amadeus Mozart (1756–1791), was one of many who played her works and praised them.

The violin concertos, probably composed in the 1760s, are in the style of the early Classical concerto, with three movements in the familiar fast-slow-fast design. The solo parts are demanding, but Sirmen's focus is on expression rather than virtuosity for its own sake. Most of her chamber works (usually in two movements), were probably intended for performance in church and at the Mendicanti. In these works, one observes a number of frequently used melodic ideas that can be considered "signature motives" of the composer. The six *String Quartets*, op. 3, show the influence of the quartets of Franz Josef Haydn (1732–1809) and are among Sirmen's most progressive works. Within each work, the movements are related by shared melodic motives and the harmony is enriched by pungent chords and brief excursions to unexpected keys.

The Italian composer and harpsichordist **Anna Bon (1739/1740–after 1767 [Anna Lucia Boni** and **Anna Bon di Venezia])** was born into a professional life in music and came to be associated with some of the most illustrious artistic centers in Europe. Her father, Girolamo Boni (fl. 1730–1762), was an artist, stage designer, librettist, and composer, and her mother, Rosa Ruvinetti (fl. 1730–1762), a fine opera singer. At the time of her birth they were on leave from the service of the St. Petersburg court, but it is not certain whether Anna was born in Russia or in Girolamo's home of Venice or elsewhere. In March 1743 the four-year-old Anna Bon was admitted as a boarding student to the famed Venetian music school of the Ospedale della Pietà, where she began to develop her skills as a singer, harpsichordist, and composer. (The alliance with this city was clearly important to Anna Bon, for in her published works she always appended the words "di Venezia" to her name.) It is not known precisely when she rejoined her parents in their itinerant life. In 1746 her parents began a two-year stay in Dresden at the court of Elector Frederick August II and his wife, Archduchess Maria Josepha of Austria, and participated in lavish theatrical performances there. Following this they served as musicians at the court of Frederick the Great in Potsdam, one of the principal centers of musical life in Europe at the time, and visited other cities.

In 1755 the family was employed in Bayreuth at the court of Margrave Friedrich of Brandenburg Culmbach. The margrave's wife, Wilhelmine (1709–1785), sister of Frederick the Great, was herself a composer of operas and instrumental music and an enthusiastic patron of opera. (A new opera house was built at their court in 1748.) Anna Bon's position there was that of chamber musician. While in Bayreuth, she published three collections through the prestigious Nuremberg firm of Balthasar Schmid's widow, which also published music by Johann Sebastian Bach (1685–1750) and Georg Philipp Telemann (1681–1767). Bon's first collection, *Six Sonatas for Flute and Basso Continuo* (op. 1, 1756), was published when she was sixteen and dedicated to Margrave Friedrich, a flutist. Her next published opus was *Six Harpsichord Sonatas* (1757), which she dedicated to another member of the German royalty, Princess Ernestine Auguste Sophie of Sachsen-Weimar. Her third and last publication was *Six Divertimenti for Two Flutes and Basso Continuo* (op. 3, ca. 1759), dedicated to Carl Theodor of Mannheim, elector of Bavaria, also a flutist. Modern editions and recordings of all of these works are available. After Margravine Wilhelmine's death in 1758, the Bons may have lost their positions, for in the following year they made appearances at Pressburg (now Bratislava) and at Eisenstadt, where Anna Bon performed also as a singer.

In 1759 Girolamo Boni formed a touring opera company with his wife and daughter as leading singers; it specialized in presenting Italian comic operas. The company was so successful in its performances at the court of Prince Esterházy in Eisenstadt, Austria, that they were hired on a full-time basis. Arriving one year after Haydn was engaged as assistant music director in 1762, the company remained at the court for several years. From Girolamo Boni and his company Haydn learned much about the Italian comic opera repertory and was inspired to compose his first Italian opera (*La marchesa Nespola*), which the troupe performed at the court.

It is known that Anna Boni married a singer named Mongeri and was living with him in Hildburghausen in 1767, but there is no further information about her life or music except for the claim that she composed a Mass, parts of which survive, and an opera, now lost. She is mentioned in three late-eighteenth- and early-nineteenth-century music reference books in discussions of "sonata" and "trio."

Boni's compositions combine the Baroque practice of spinning out motivic ideas with the architectural features of pre-Classical *galant* style. Her harpsichord sonatas are each in three movements with a fast-slow-fast tempo scheme; two of the finales are minuets. Her *Divertimenti*, op. 3, are written in Baroque trio texture for two flutes and basso continuo, but are also playable by other treble instruments. Boni's music has endured and is still performed today. All of her compositions were published in twentieth-century editions and have been recorded in recent years.

Two other Italian composers are especially worthy of mention here. **Maria Teresa Agnesi** [also d'Agnesi] (1720–1795) of Milan is the only Italian woman known to have composed in the genre of *opera seria*. She was supported by the patronage of Empress Maria Theresa and of Maria Antonia Walpurgis, electress of Saxony. **Maria Rosa Coccia** (1759–1833), while a child, impressed Pietro Metastasio (1698–1782), Padre Martini (1706–1784), and the famous castrato Farinelli with her compositions. Like Marianna Martines, Coccia was admitted to the exclusive Accademia Filarmonica of Bologna. However, her creative work in music seems not to have continued in adulthood.

Austria

Empress Maria Theresa's reign from 1740 to 1780, the last fifteen years of which she shared with her son, Joseph II (1741–1790), was a golden age for music in Vienna. Sacred music composed on a grand scale flourished in cathedrals, churches, and private chapels. There were enthusiastic audiences for Italian *opera seria*, for French *opéra comique*, and, during the reign (1780–1790) of Joseph II after his mother's death, for German opera and Italian *opera buffa*. During a few days in Advent and for the entire season of Lent, when opera was forbidden, the court theater (Burgtheater) was made available for public concerts. Far more important to Viennese musical life, however, was music making in the salons of wealthy aristocratic and upper-middle-class patrons. Many noble homes had orchestras and other performing ensembles at their disposal, making possible the performance of symphonies, concertos, oratorios, and chamber music, as well as solo vocal and instrumental pieces. Music was also an established part of life in the home, in public places, and in outdoor entertainments. This rich musical culture drew talented young composers to the city from all over Europe, including Christoph Willibald Gluck (1714–1787) in 1736 and in 1754, Mozart in 1781, and Ludwig van Beethoven (1770–1827) in 1792, while also supporting the development of two of the most gifted female composers and performers of the century.

Marianna [von] Martines (1744–1812 [née Anna Katharina, also Martinez]) one of the most accomplished and prolific female composers of the century, was among the small number of women who composed grand-scale music—masses, oratorios, sacred choral works, and secular cantatas. The fortunate circumstances of her life allowed her to develop her talents to a high level and to be in contact with many distinguished artists of her time.

Martines' father, Nicolò, of Spanish descent, moved to Vienna from Naples to become master of ceremonies in the papal embassy to the Imperial Court. Little is known about her mother, Maria Theresia. In 1730 Pietro Metastasio, a friend of Nicolò's in Naples, was appointed Imperial court poet. From that time until his death in 1782, he lived with the Martines family on the third floor of the Michaelerhaus, an apartment building adjacent to the Michaelerkirche (the court chapel), just outside the Imperial palace. Metastasio assumed the supervision of the education of Marianna and her five siblings. Recognizing her unusual musical talent, he arranged for her to have harpsichord lessons with the young Haydn, then living in an attic apartment in the same building, in exchange for his meals. Martines also studied singing with Nicola Porpora (1686–1768), counterpoint and composition with the court composer Giuseppe Bonno (1711–1788), and composition with Johann Adolph Hasse (1699–1783).

By the 1760s Martines was writing large-scale sacred works. One of her Masses was performed in the Michaelerkirche in 1761. When her father died three years later, Metastasio stepped in to assist the careers of the children. Although it was not appropriate for a woman of Martines' social status to become a professional musician, Metastasio worked to build her reputation internationally (although Martines herself probably never traveled far from Vienna). In 1772 she met Charles Burney, who reported:

> Sunday 6th. The discourse [with Metastasio and others] then became general and miscellaneous, till the arrival of a young lady, who was received by the whole company with great respect. She was well dressed, and had a very elegant

Portrait of Marianna Martines.
© Archivo Iconografico, S.A./CORBIS.

appearance.... After the high encomiums bestowed by the Abbate Taruffi on the talents of this young lady, I was very desirous of hearing and conversing with her; and Metastasio was soon so obliging as to propose her sitting down to the harpsichord, which she immediately did, in a graceful manner.... Her performance indeed surpassed all that I had been made to expect. She sung [*sic*] two airs of her own composition, to words of Metastasio, which she accompanied on the harpsichord, in a very judicious and masterly manner.... Her voice and manner of singing, both delighted and astonished me! I can readily subscribe to what Metastasio says, that it is a style of singing which no longer subsists elsewhere, as it requires too much pains and patience for modern professors.... Let me only add, that in the *portamento*, and divisions of tones and semitones into infinitely minute parts, and yet always stopping in the exact fundamental, Signora Martinez was more perfect than any singer I had ever heard: her cadences too, of this kind, were very learned, and truly pathetic and pleasing.

After these two songs, she played a very difficult lesson, of her own compo-sition, on the harpsichord, with great rapidity and precision. She has composed a *Miserere*, in four parts, with several psalms, in eight parts, and is a most excel-lent contrapuntalist. (Neuls-Bates 1996)

In 1773 at the age of twenty-nine Martines applied to Metastasio's friend Padre Mar-tini for membership in the Accademia Filarmonica of Bologna and was the first woman granted this celebrated honor. In the same year she struck up a friendship with Mozart, then in his late teens. He composed some of his four-hand sonatas to perform with her, and the Piano Concerto in D Major K. 175 was probably also written for her.

Marianna Martines and her sister Antonia cared for Metastasio in his later years, and he bequeathed his sizable estate to the family. Marianna received his harpsichord and clavichords, his musical papers, and a sum of 20,000 florins, which provided her an annual income of 1,000 florins per year (nearly twice the amount that Haydn was paid at Esterhàza). With this income and her family inheritance, she was able to main-tain a large house, where she held salons attended by Haydn and Mozart. She also trained a number of outstanding artists in a singing school in her home and continued to com-pose well into the 1780s.

Martines wrote over 200 works in nearly every genre except opera. Among her com-positions are four Masses, several oratorios, motets and other sacred works, thirty-five secular cantatas and arias (perhaps for her own performance at court), one overture (sin-fonia), three keyboard concertos, and three keyboard sonatas (see the catalog of works in Godt 1995). Only a few of the approximately seventy works that survive were pub-lished. Her keyboard works are in early Classical style, with rococo embellishments of melodies, clear harmonic structures, and binary or small sonata forms. They contain lighthearted finales, and slow movements in the *empfindsamer Stil* that was then fash-ionable. As models she cited the works of Johann Adolph Hasse (1699–1783), Nic-colò Jomelli (1714–1774), Baldassare Galuppi (1706–1785), and George Frideric Handel (1685–1759).

Martines died of tuberculosis in 1812 at age sixty-eight. During her lifetime, music in Vienna had undergone dramatic changes of style. Yet she essentially held to the style that she had mastered as a young woman. In the first decade of the nineteenth century her compositions were deemed old-fashioned when compared with the transformations of musical language in the hands of Beethoven and others. A set of memoirs published in 1844 by Caroline Pichler, a rival *salonière* in the 1780s and part of the middle-class circle around Franz Schubert (1797–1828) in the teens and twenties, was harshly crit-ical of Martines and effectively tarnished her reputation. A more objective view of her accomplishments and historical position emerged in the 1980s and 1990s.

Maria Theresia von Paradis (1759–1824), born in Vienna, was hailed as a fine pianist and singer with an extraordinary memory. Blind from early childhood, she was the beneficiary of an influential sponsor who oversaw her musical training and assisted her career. Her father, Josef von Paradis, was imperial secretary and court councilor to Empress Maria Theresa and named his daughter after his employer. When her remarkable musical talent became evident, the empress took charge of her education and granted her a stipend. Paradis studied the piano with Leopold Kozeluch (1747–1818), singing and composition with Antonio Salieri (1750–1825), singing with Vincenzo Righini (1756–1812), and theory and composition with Abbé George Joseph Vogler (1749–1814). By age sixteen she had built such a fine reputation as a performer that Salieri had dedicated an organ concerto to her; both Mozart and Haydn composed piano concertos for her.

In 1783 Paradis embarked on a three-year tour with her mother, Maria Levassori della Motta, accompanied by librettist Johann Riedlinger, a family friend. They visited the Mozarts in Salzburg, and Paradis played concerts in several German and Swiss cities. In the spring of 1784 she began a series of at least fourteen concerts in Paris. The *Mercure de France* of April 24, 1784, reflected on her performance at the Concert Spirituel:

> Mademoiselle Paradis is the one artist whom our nation is not able to praise too highly. This gifted keyboard player is truly astonishing. Blind since the age of two, she has reached an unbelievable level of perfection in the knowledge of her instrument....The lack of one faculty [surely] affects the sensitivity of the others....More faultless, more precise, more polished playing is not known. (Neuls-Bates 1996)

While in Paris, Paradis also helped Valentin Haüy develop a curriculum for the first school for the blind, which he opened there in 1785. The teaching at the school drew on methods that had been used in Paradis' own education.

From Paris, the travelers went to London, where Paradis played for King George III and accompanied the Prince of Wales, a cellist and later King George IV, on the piano. Her public concerts there were less successful than those in Paris, and the English climate may have aggravated a respiratory condition. She returned to Vienna early in 1786 after concertizing in Brussels, Amsterdam, Berlin, and Hamburg—where she met Carl Phillip Emmanuel Bach (1714–1788).

During her extended tour of Europe, Paradis began to compose piano music and songs, apparently for use in her concerts. A collection entitled *Zwölf Lieder auf ihrer Reise in Musik gesetzt* (Twelve Lieder Set to Music on Her Trip) is the most substantial of these early works. She also composed two piano concertos and a piano trio (all now lost), two piano fantasies, a sonata for violin and piano, and a toccata in A major. (The famous *Sicilienne*, originally for violin and piano, is apparently spurious.)

After 1789 Paradis focused her efforts increasingly on composition, producing at least five operas and three cantatas as well as a second collection of lieder. She traveled to Prague in 1797 to conduct the premiere of *Rinaldo und Alcina* (now lost), based on a libretto by the blind author Ludwig von Baczko; it was not successful. After this she devoted herself mainly to teaching until her death on February 1, 1824. Among her few late works is a *Fantaisie pour le Piano-Forte in G Major*, published in 1807 and dedicated to Abbé Vogler. Its bold modulations and unusual key relationships reflect Vogler's teaching. This work is available in a modern edition.

Paradis composed with the help of a wooden pegboard devised by her friend Riedlinger, after which a copyist would transcribe the composition in conventional notation. One of these "Kompositionstafeln," on which pegs of different shapes represent a variety of note values, is on display in the Music Instrument Collection of the Kunsthistorisches Museum in Vienna.

Josepha Barbara von Auernhammer (1758–1820 [also Josephine Auernhammer or Aurnhammer]), was a talented pianist who had the good fortune to study with Mozart. He helped to promote her career, dedicated works to her, and performed duo piano music with her in concerts.

Born in Vienna, the daughter of economic councillor Johann Michael von Auernhammer, Josepha studied piano with Georg Friedrich Richter (n.d.) and Kozeluch. When Mozart arrived in Vienna in March 1781, he began teaching her. She made such excellent progress under his tutelage that Mozart asked her to join him in performing his own concertos and sonatas for two pianos; they played several concerts together between 1781 and 1785. Mozart dedicated six sonatas for piano and violin to her, and she supervised the printing of these and a few of his other publications.

Auernhammer had a romantic interest in Mozart and pursued him, but he did not reciprocate her affection. In letters to his father in 1781 and 1782, he complained at length about her "frightful" appearance and flirtatious behavior. He was, however, concerned for her welfare. After the death of her father, Mozart found room, board, and a position for her at the home of one of his patrons, Baroness von Waldstädten; he also performed with her in two of her concerts.

In 1786 Auernhammer married magistrate Johann Bessenig (1751–1837) retaining her maiden name professionally. She had become a respected piano teacher and performed regularly in Vienna, on occasion with her daughter pianist, singer, teacher and composer Marianna Auenheim. In the early nineteenth century, her playing came to be viewed as too technical and lacking in expressiveness. She retired from the stage in 1813, and died on January 30, 1820, in Vienna.

All of Auernhammer's works are for solo piano, with the exception of a group of six lieder and a sonata for violin and piano. Most of her piano compositions are sets of variations, a genre also prominent in the piano music of Mozart, Haydn, Beethoven, Schubert, and countless other composers of the time. Such pieces were either based on original melodies or on familiar tunes such as folk tunes or operatic arias, which underwent a series of melodic, rhythmic, and harmonic transformations; brilliant passagework that displayed the pianist's technical skill was also a hallmark of the genre. Auernhammer's *Six Variations on the Aria "Der Vogelfänger bin ich ja"* from Mozart's opera *Die Zauberflöte* (The Magic Flute) is based on Papageno's comic aria, a favorite with the operagoing public and a frequent subject for variation sets. Auernhammer's set was published in 1792, shortly after Mozart's death in 1791, no doubt a tribute to her teacher's memory.

A *Sonata for Harpsichord in E-flat Major*, published around 1781, is the single known work by **Marianna von Auenbrugger (d. 1786 [also d'Auenbrugg])**, daughter of prominent Austrian physician Leopold von Auenbrugger. The sonata is available in modern editions and in several recordings. In a letter to the publisher Artaria, Haydn wrote with admiration about Marianna and her sister Katharina, commending their manner of playing and their genuine insight into music.

Other German-Speaking Lands

A gifted singer and actress, **Corona Elisabeth Wilhelmine Schröter (1751–1802)** made important contributions to the development of German musical drama and to the lied, while enjoying an unusually high degree of personal and financial independence. She, her sister, and two brothers studied music with their father, oboist Friedrich Schröter (1724–1811), and toured with him as child prodigies. In 1764 Corona Schröter moved to Leipzig, where she studied voice and piano with Johann Adam Hiller (1728–1804). She and another of Hiller's students, **Gertrud Schmeling (later, Madame Mara, 1749–1833)**, became rival sopranos in Leipzig through their performances in Johann Adam Hiller's (1728–1804) Grosse Konzerte series. Whereas Schmeling was known for her virtuosity, Schröter, who seems to have damaged her voice during her training and performances as a child, was known for her expression. As a star in the public subscription series, Schröter was paid handsomely, earning many times a court musician's annual salary. Nearly all of Hiller's musical-dramatic works (*Singspiele*) date from this period of association with her. Schröter also became friends with Johann Wolfgang von Goethe (1749–1832) and Johann Friedrich Reichardt (1752–1814) during this period.

When Goethe moved to the court at Weimar in 1775, he arranged for Schröter's appointment there; she was given a yearly income (guaranteed for life) equal to that which she had received in Leipzig. Although Schröter's official position was as court singer, she was occupied mainly at the court's Privattheater, taking leading roles in at least eighteen productions, including several of Goethe's early dramas. In *Iphigenie auf Tauris* (1779) as well as in several other works, she played opposite Goethe himself. Duchess Anna Amalia (see later) composed music for Goethe's *Erwin und Elmire* (1776), in which Schröter sang the female lead. In the somewhat insular environment of Weimar, where class and gender roles were fairly flexible, Schröter found the freedom to develop her gifts as an actor and as a painter, fields not fully open to respectable women in the more public environment of Leipzig. Goethe acknowledged the importance of her contributions to drama, as well as her impact on his own works while in Weimar. Schröter completed an autobiography that she gave to Goethe in 1778; it is lost.

In 1783 a professional company replaced the court theater in Weimar. Schröter, still in the post of court singer, continued to perform in other venues and taught singing and acting. She wrote poetry, composed, published some of her music, and presented herself publicly as a portrait painter. She enjoyed a friendship with Friedrich Schiller (1759–1805) starting in 1787 and set several of his poems as lieder.

While in Leipzig and Weimar, Schröter lived with her friend Wilhelmine Probst and supported herself financially. She had close working relationships with several men;

both Goethe and Duke Karl August had a romantic interest in her. Around 1801 she moved to the mountain town of Ilmenau in the hope of helping a lung condition, but her health deteriorated, and she died there on August 23, 1802. At the time of her death, she was extremely wealthy.

Schröter's principal compositions are two books of lieder and incidental music (mainly songs) for Goethe's *Singspiel* entitled *Die Fischerin* (The Fisherwoman). Fewer than a dozen of her songs are available in modern editions or on recordings. Music for two other dramas and a collection of 360 arias and duets are lost, as are her lieder set to poems of Schiller. Her *Funf und zwanzig Lieder in Musik gezetzt* (Twenty-five Lieder Set to Music) of 1786 and *Gesaenge mit Begleitung des Fortepiano* ([16] Songs with Piano Accompaniment) of 1794 are among the earliest large collections of lieder published by a woman. The songs in *Funf und zwanzig Lieder*, more than half of which set poems from *Volkslieder* (1779) by Johann Gottfried von Herder (1744–1803), are generally less complex than those in *Gesaenge*. Her later collections of lieder contain more elaborate songs, some of them with French or Italian text. Schröter's music for *Die Fischerin* (1782) includes the earliest musical setting of Goethe's familiar text, Erlkönig (Erlking), here presented as a simple strophic ballad.

It is sobering to note that even the independent and successful Corona Schröter, in many ways not bound by expectations for women of her time, felt the need (or obligation) to announce an upcoming publication of her lieder with the following notice in *Cramer's Magazin der Musik* in 1785:

> I have had to overcome much hesitation before I seriously made the decision to publish a collection of short poems that I have provided with melodies. A certain feeling toward propriety and morality is stamped upon our sex, which does not allow us to appear alone in public, nor without an escort. Thus how can I present this, my musical work, to the public with anything other than timidity? The work of any lady…can indeed arouse a degree of pity in the eyes of some experts. (Citron 1986)

Schröter's contemporaries included several women composers connected through birth or related by marriage. **Franziska Danzi Lebrun** (1756–1791) enjoyed an operatic career at the Mannheim court and at the King's Theatre in London. Her sister-in-law, **Maria Margarethe Marchand Danzi** (1768–1800), published two sets of sonatas and was known for her singing roles in Mozart operas, and her daughter **Sophie Lebrun Dülcken {Dülken}** (1781–1863) made a career as a pianist and composed sonatas and concertos. **Sophia Maria Fritscher** Westenholz (1759–1838), whom Johann Friedrich Reichardt described as one of Europe's leading musicians, performed as a singer, pianist, and on the glass harmonica. She served as piano teacher to the princesses at the Schwerin court and composed lieder, sonatas, and other works for keyboard.

The next two generations of women composers in Germany particularly excelled in the genre of the lied. **Louise** (also **Luise**) **Reichardt** (1779–1826) was the first daughter of singer, keyboardist, and composer **Juliane Benda Reichardt** (1752–1783 [also **Bernhardine**]) and Johann Friedrich Reichardt, a violinist, composer, writer, and Kapellmeister to Frederick the Great. Juliane, who composed about thirty lieder and two keyboard sonatas, was a member of a large family of professional musicians and participated in concerts in Berlin both before and after her marriage. When Juliane died shortly after the birth of her third child, Louise was just four years old. Louise received some musical training from her father, and her education was greatly enriched by her later association with guests who visited her Berlin home and, later, her family's estate in Giebichenstein, near Halle. At Giebichenstein, which Goethe referred to as "the sheltering place of Romanticism," Louise Reichardt developed friendships with many of the leading German Romantic philosophers and writers.

In 1809 Reichardt moved to Hamburg, where she established herself as a singing teacher and composer; apart from a trip to England in 1819 and a few visits to Berlin and Giebichenstein, she remained there the rest of her life. She directed several women's choruses and studied music with Johannes Friedrich Clasing (n.d.), with whom she founded the Hamburg Gesangverein (Singing Society) in 1819. For this organization Reichardt made German translations of texts of Handel's oratorios and works of Johann Adolph Hasse and Johann Gottlieb Graun (1703–1771) and prepared the chorus for performances. She did not seek public acclaim; her male associates conducted the performances.

Between 1806 and her death, Louise Reichardt published more than ninety compositions for solo voice with piano or guitar accompaniment and for a cappella choral groups. Her music is found in anthologies, school music books, and hymnals. The majority of her works are German songs set to texts by Clemens Brentano, Johann Gottfried von Herder, Achim von Arnim, Ludwig Tieck, and the Grimm brothers. She was among the first to set folk poems from the Arnim and Brentano collection *Des Knaben Wunderhorn* (From the Youth's Magic Horn, 1805–1808), as she was familiar with the contents before the work's publication. Many of Reichardt's German songs resemble folk settings with their lyrical, singable melodies, strophic forms, and accompaniments that support the voice while remaining in the background. *Herbstlied* (on a text by Arnim) and *Schäfers Klagelied* (on a text by Goethe) are examples that are available in modern editions. In fact, some of her songs became accepted as folk songs. Her brother-in-law, Henrich Steffens, commented in 1843:

> Many of her compositions found general acceptance because of their characteristic depth and became more popular than [Johann Friedrich] Reichardt's; true folksongs, one often heard them sung on the streets by servant girls and peasant maidens....Even now they are hardly forgotten. (Reich 1981)

In addition, there are nine songs on Italian texts by Metastasio that Reichardt composed for her voice students. These have more florid melodies; some constitute small da capo arias. More than forty of the solo songs and a handful of sacred choral pieces for women's voices are available in modern editions; just over a dozen songs have been recorded.

Catharina Elisabetha Ludovica Magdalena ("Bettine") Brentano von Arnim (1785–1859) was born into the influential Brentano family and met the major intel-

Bettine Von Arnim.
Hulton|Archive by Getty Images.

lectual, musical, and political figures of the day in her home. Born in Frankfurt to the wealthy Italian businessman Peter Anton Brentano and a French mother, Maximiliane Laroche (daughter of the author Sophie Laroche), she was sent to the Ursuline Convent School in Fritzlar after her mother died in 1793. She studied piano, voice, theory, and composition as a girl and is described as having a passionate and rich alto voice and skill at vocal improvisation. From 1810 to 1812 she sang with the Berlin Singakademie under the direction of Karl Friedrich Zelter (1758–1832).

Among strong influences on Bettine in early adulthood were her brother Clemens, a poet, and the writer Karoline von Günderrode. She also developed close friendships with Goethe's mother, Elisabeth, with Goethe himself (from 1807), and with Beethoven (from 1810). (Although she has frequently been suggested as the possible intended recipient of Beethoven's letters to his "Immortal Beloved," discovered unsent after his death, it is now believed that the letters were to Bettine's sister-in-law, Antonie, the wife of Franz Brentano.) Her correspondence with these individuals served as the basis for several of her novels.

Bettine married Achim von Arnim in 1811; during the next sixteen years, the couple had seven children who survived childhood. They started out at Achim's country home in Wiepersdorf, about 100 kilometers south of Berlin. However, as country life did not suit Bettine, she and the children lived mainly in Berlin from 1818 onward. After Achim's death in 1831, she devoted herself to writing and spoke out about social and political issues, among them the plight of Poland in 1848. She also hosted a salon that was a center of literary and musical life in Berlin. Her circle included Franz Liszt (1811–1886), Giacomo Meyerbeer (1791–1864), Robert (1810–1856) and Clara Schumann (1819–1896), Joseph Joachim (1831–1907), and Johannes Brahms (1833–1897). She died in Berlin on January 20, 1859, after a protracted illness.

Arnim's oeuvre consists of an overture to Goethe's *Faust* (now lost) and around fifty complete or partially finished songs; fewer than a dozen were published during her lifetime. Her earliest published songs were included with literary works of her husband in 1810 and 1812, over the signature "Beans Beor." Her difficulty with written musical notation and the rules of harmony forced her to rely on other musicians to help her notate her compositions.

Arnim's lieder, which set texts by her husband, her brother Clemens, Goethe, and others, employ strophic forms and folklike melodies. The irregular phrase structures, unusual harmonies, and breathless melodies of some songs call to mind the descriptions of Arnim's improvisatory manner of singing. In the late nineteenth century, Max Friedlaender revised and expanded Arnim's songs to conform to the late Romantic style. However, some newer editions revert to the primary sources.

Emilie Zumsteeg (1796–1857), a composer of lieder, piano pieces and choral music who held "Sunday Musicales" in her home, was a vital presence in the musical life of Stuttgart in the first half of the nineteenth century. She was the youngest of seven children born to Johann Rudolf Zumsteeg (1760–1802), a court musician and well-known composer of lieder and *Singspiele*, and Luise Andreae (n.d.), daughter of a prominent physician in Stuttgart. When Emilie's father died in 1802, her mother opened a music shop where Emilie also worked to help support the family. Zumsteeg showed musical talent at an early age, studying the piano and composition.

Although Zumsteeg, as a woman, could not follow in her father's footsteps in positions at the Württemberg court, she became thoroughly enmeshed in the musical life of Stuttgart and earned respect as a teacher, performer, and composer. She taught piano and voice at the Katharinenstift, an academy for young women, and added long teaching hours to accommodate the many who sought her instruction privately. She was a founder of the Verein für Klassische Kirchenmusik (Society for Classical Church Music) and worked with its conductor, Peter Josef von Lindpainter (1791–1856), as a coach and assistant. This group performed oratorios and other sacred works of Bach, Handel, Haydn, and Felix Mendelssohn (1809–1847), including the first Stuttgart performance of Handel's *Messiah* in 1826.

After the death of her mother, Zumsteeg inaugurated the "Sunday Musicales" in her home, where local and visiting artists performed. In 1841 the city council recognized her contributions by awarding her a certificate of appreciation and a yearly stipend.

Zumsteeg wrote over 100 compositions, including about sixty lieder for voice with piano or guitar, a handful of short pieces for piano, and a substantial body of choral music for women's, men's, and mixed voices. Her choral works were performed at court and civic ceremonies, among them the commemoration for Friedrich Schiller in 1829. Zumsteeg lived in Stuttgart all her life and never toured as a concert artist; consequently, she did not earn the international recognition of many of her contemporaries. Nevertheless, her works were highly praised in the German-speaking lands during her lifetime and later in the century. She published her music with Schott in Mainz, with Simrock in Bonn and Cologne, and with her brother, Gustav Zumsteeg, in Stuttgart. Several of her compositions were reviewed favorably in German music periodicals. Zumsteeg's obituary in the *Schwäbische Merkur* reported:

> Many, unbelievably many, must thank her for their knowledge of music, and what is more, their ability to enjoy the most beautiful in this Art with a refined understanding.... Emilie Zumsteeg has earned a place of honor in the history of our time. (Summerville 1998)

Zumsteeg's lieder are her best-known works. They are settings of poems treating the Romantic subjects of nature, love, and longing and sometimes have a religious cast to them. She was strongly influenced by her father's sensitive handling of text and vivid depiction of mood in his own lieder. She composed both strophic and through-composed songs, in which the piano takes an interpretive role. Roughly two dozen of Zumsteeg's lieder and at least one choral work are available in modern editions published in the 1990s; very few have been recorded.

Other women from the German courts who composed include **Anna Amalia, princess of Prussia (1723–1787)**, youngest sister of Frederick the Great, who began to study composition seriously in her forties after the death of her music-hating father, Frederick William I. She composed contrapuntal music in the style of J. S. Bach and other old masters but is best known as a patron of the arts. Her magnificent library (the "Amalien-Bibliothek," now in the Deutsche Staatsbibliothek in Berlin) includes her collection of scores by eminent seventeenth- and eighteenth-century composers. Her niece, **Anna Amalia, duchess of Saxe-Weimar (1739–1807)**, presided over the court at Weimar from 1758 to 1775 and composed and supported contemporary music. **Maria Antonia Walpurgis, electress of Saxony (1724–1780)**, performed at the Dresden court as a singer and keyboard player and composed operas, including *Talestri, regina delle amazoni* (Talestri, Queen of the Amazons) (1760).

France

Salons devoted to artistic and intellectual pursuits and to entertainment were a vital part of musical life in Paris in the second half of the eighteenth century. Because the French deemed it unseemly for an aristocrat to perform before a paying audience, these salons served as the principal outlet for upper-class musicians, both male and female. Devoted primarily to music (as opposed to conversation or spoken drama), they featured resident ensembles, performances by local amateurs (including members of the French court), and visiting professional artists. The quality of performance in these concerts

Duchess Anna Amalia of Brunswick-Wolfenbuttel (1723–1787).
Hulton|Archive by Getty Images.

was equal to, or higher than, that of public concerts, which were managed by the bourgeoisie. Salons were the only venue where some of the smaller chamber genres could be
heard. They also offered an opportunity for trial performances of large works such as
operas and orchestral compositions that were to be presented publicly in the future.

Salon concerts were not open to a paying public; attendance was by invitation only.
In this environment, musicians built a market for their published works and secured
students and future performing engagements. Women exerted considerable influence
in this milieu as hostesses, organizers, composers, performers, and arbiters of taste. The
Revolution of 1789 curtailed these salons nearly completely, as many of the aristocracy
were in exile or otherwise unable to participate. Private concerts were obliged to rely
more heavily on professional performers, and full-scale productions of opera and orchestral works were consigned to the public arena.

Anne-Louise Boyvin d'Hardancourt Brillon de Jouy (1744–1824), harpsichordist, pianist, composer, and close friend of Benjamin Franklin (1706–1790), was
one of the most celebrated personalities in the salon society of prerevolutionary Paris.

Anna Amalia, Princess of Prussia (1739–1807).
Hulton|Archive by Getty Images.

She was born in that city and had made a name for herself by the age of twenty-one.
Her father, Louis-Claude Boyvin d'Hardancourt, a wealthy, lower-level aristocrat,
served as financial officer to the crown. Johann Schobert (1735–1767), who may have
been her teacher, dedicated his set of *Trio Sonatas*, op. 6, to her, and Luigi Boccherini
(1743–1805) dedicated sonatas to her. Anne-Louise d'Hardancourt married a wealthy
financier, Jacques Brillon, in the early 1760s; the couple had two daughters, Cunégonde
and Aldegonde. The Brillons established salons in their homes in the Marais district of
Paris and at their estate in Passy overlooking the city. Brillon performed on harpsichord and piano at these, also taking part in discussions of art, theology, and politics.
When the seventy-one-year-old Benjamin Franklin took up residence in Passy as the
American Revolutionary government's diplomatic representative to France, the Brillons invited him to join in their semiweekly concerts. Franklin and Brillon at first
shared an amorous relationship, but in time this was redefined as one of father and

daughter. During the eight years that Franklin lived in Passy, he frequently performed at Brillon's salons (which he referred to as his "opera"), playing on his invention, the glass harmonica, while also establishing nonmusical, political contacts.

After a year in Nice to recover from what apparently was a bout of chronic depression in 1781–1782, Brillon and her family purchased the Hotel de Mailly, a Paris landmark built in the sixteenth century. Before long the Brillons, their daughters, and their husbands were all in residence, entertaining and conducting business there. Just before the Revolution, Brillon suffered personal and financial losses with the death of her husband and the departure of Franklin for America. During the Revolution the family managed to hold on to some of their properties and immense fortune through shrewd financial maneuvers. Personal information about Brillon's later years is sketchy. By 1808 she was living at the family estate in Villers-sur-Mer and was still active in Parisian musical life, though probably no longer composing. She died at Villers on December 5, 1824, shortly before her eightieth birthday.

An account by Charles Burney provides a glimpse into Brillon's performance in her salon in 1770:

> After coffee we went into the music room where I found an English piano forte which Mr. [Johann Christian] Bach had sent her. She played a great deal and I found she had not acquired her reputation in music without meriting it. She plays with great ease, taste and feeling—is an excellent sightswoman, of which I was convinced by her executing some of my own music. She likewise composes and she was so obliging as to play several of her own pieces both on the harpsichord and piano forte accompanied with the violin by M. Pagin....I could not persuade Madame B. to play the piano forte with the stops on [i.e., with the dampers down] *c'est sec* [that is dry], she said—but with them off unless in arpeggios, nothing is distinct—'tis like the sound of bells, continual and confluent. (Gustafson 1998)

Among the first in Paris to own a piano, Brillon obtained an English instrument from J. C. Bach. It was a square model (perhaps by Zumpe) on which the dampers were controlled by two hand stops, one for the lower half of the keyboard and one for the upper half. This mechanism did not allow the frequent clearing of the pedal that was possible on later English pianos or on the German pianos with knee levers in the 1770s and 1780s. Pianos were uncommon in France through the 1770s and did not rival the harpsichord in number and popularity until two decades later.

Brillon was a prolific composer. Eighty-eight works survive, nearly all of them involving keyboard instruments and all probably composed between 1775 and 1785. A large collection of her pieces is in the American Philosophical Society Library in Philadelphia. Her two trios for English piano, German piano, and harpsichord are the only known pieces for that combination of instruments. Since all three instruments were in the Brillon home, the trios may have been composed for her and her two daughters to play together. There are also sonatas for keyboard and violin, as well as vocal *romances* and *canzonettas*. The *Marche des insurgents* for strings, winds, horns, and timpani, a celebration of the American victory at Saratoga, New York, in 1777, was composed early in her association with Benjamin Franklin. She was fascinated with the piano and came to prefer it to the harpsichord for her own performances. Nevertheless, she and other composers of the 1770s and 1780s generally did not compose differently for the two instruments. The piano was new and unproven, and a sense of idiomatic style and technique had not yet developed.

Brillon's keyboard works are in the Italian sonata style that was fashionable in Paris in the 1770s and 1780s. The aim of simplicity and charm was accomplished by use of a melody in the right hand, accompanied by figuration in the middle register of the keyboard and a simple harmonic structure. Brillon's songs are strophic with figural accompaniments and sometimes contain surprising harmonic twists. Five of her songs, the *Marche des insurgents* (arranged for brass quintet), a duo for harp and violin, and a *Sonata in B-flat for Violin and Keyboard* (from her *Troisième Recueil de Sonates*, ca. 1775–1783) are available in modern editions and await recording.

Brillon's contemporary, **Marie-Emmanuelle Bayon Louis (1746–1825)**, opera composer and friend of the encyclopedist Denis Diderot, was born in Marcei, Orne. Although little is known about her early life, the dedication in her opus one sonatas, thanking the family of Madame la Marquise de Langeron for the many kindnesses "heaped on me since my tenderest infancy," suggests that she probably had noble patrons or sponsors. Bayon maintained social and political connections with members of the aristocracy throughout her life. In 1767 she was a member of the prestigious salon of Madame de Genlis (Stéphanie Félicité du Crest, 1746–1830), a gifted harpist and author of a method book for the instrument, and performed there as harpsichordist, pianist, and actor-singer. In the same year she began a friendship with Diderot and his daughter, Angélique (later Madame de Vandeul), who studied harpsichord with her.

Bayon's marriage in 1770 to the prominent architect Victor Louis gave her an entrée into the world of opera. Victor Louis had important connections in the theater and had been the scenic designer for at least one production at the Comédie Italienne. The couple moved to Bordeaux in the early 1770s for Victor Louis to design and supervise the construction of the Grand-Théâtre; the Louis salon became a center of musical life in that city. In 1774 their daughter, Marie-Hélène-Victoire, was born. Also during this time, Louis composed her two-act *opéra comique, Fleur d'épine* (May Flower), on a libretto by Claude-Henri Fusée, abbé de Voisenon. The opera received twelve performances in the 1776–1777 season and was so popular that several publishers issued arrangements of excerpts from the work. The full score, published by Huguet in Paris in 1776, contains an Italian-style overture and twenty numbers, including eleven arias, two duets, two trios, ensemble finales for each act, two small chorus numbers, and an instrumental fanfare. The overture and several of the vocal numbers are available in modern editions.

Once the Grand-Théâtre was completed in 1780, the Louis family returned to Paris, where they hosted an exclusive salon involving prominent literary and artistic figures of the day. Victor Louis died in 1800; his largest project, the Théâtre National, was completed in 1793. Louis, whose health had deteriorated, remained in Paris; she died in Aubervoye, Eure, on March 19, 1825.

Madame Louis was described as a "woman of boundless wit and great beauty." Like Madame Brillon, she was credited with promoting the fortepiano in France through her performances. The *Six Sonates pour le clavecin ou le piano forte* [1769] (Six Sonatas for the Harpsichord or Pianoforte) is her only surviving instrumental work and is available in a modern facsimile edition. This publication is one of the earliest to identify the piano as an alternative to harpsichord on the title page; several of the movements indicate dynamics. Numbers IV through VI have accompaniment parts for violin that are integral to their design: melodic ideas pass back and forth between the violin and piano. Also noted on the title page is the availability of the sonatas from Madame Louis at her home or from the music shops in the city. The sonatas were also known in Germany and in England, where Queen Charlotte, wife of George III, owned a copy of them.

Unlike her two countrywomen, singer, actor, and composer **Amélie-Julie Candeille** (1767–1834) had a public career in the French theater. Her father, the composer and singer Pierre Joseph Candeille (1744–1827), groomed her from childhood for the operatic stage, by far the most illustrious and lucrative form of musical entertainment in Paris at the time. At the age of fifteen she sang the title role in Gluck's *Iphigénie en Aulide*. However, her voice was described as too small for opera, and her shy personality also drew criticism. In the next few years, she appeared as a pianist at several concerts of the Concert Spirituel, performing a concerto by Muzio Clementi (1752–1832) and one of her own compositions. She made her debut as an actor at the Comédie Française in 1785 and played tragic and comic roles there on a regular basis during the next five years.

In 1792 Candeille joined the Théâtre Français, which gave her the opportunity to combine all her musical talents plus that of author. For this company she composed a three-act opéra comique, *Catherine, ou La belle fermière* (Catherine, or the Beautiful Farmer's Wife) to her own libretto. She sang and accompanied herself on both the piano and harp in the first performances of the work. *Catherine* enjoyed considerable popularity: it was performed more than 150 times in Paris, Brussels, Lille, Amsterdam (in a Dutch translation), and elsewhere over the next thirty-five years, and numerous arrangements of the airs with harp or piano accompaniment were published. One review of the premiere praised Candeille's performance in these words:

> Beauty, talent, wit: she does not lose any of her advantages, but manages to develop all of them—the characterization, the actress, and the author are intermingled endlessly in the animated applause which she receives. Men would love this piece as they would love a charming woman, and women would be pleased with it out of love for themselves. (Johnson 1998)

Writers described Candeille as extremely hardworking, talented, beautiful, and compassionate but also criticized her sharply for her vanity. In the intrigues of the postrevolutionary Parisian operatic world, there was ample opportunity to attack her character and her theater productions. She also incurred difficulties with her employers. In 1796 a theater company in Belgium sued her for failing to fulfill the terms of her contract, with the result that she was forbidden to perform on stage for the next five years. Although she produced several other works for the stage, none enjoyed the success of *Catherine*.

Candeille married military doctor Louis-Nicolas Delaroche in 1794, but they divorced three years later. Her second husband, a wealthy Belgian businessman named Jean Simons (d. 1821), lost his fortune in the wake of Napoleon's reforms and suffered a mental breakdown. Candeille (who always used her own surname publicly) returned to Paris in 1802, giving lessons and publishing music in order to support her husband, as well as her father, whose pension had been revoked under Napoleon's rule. She also wrote essays, memoirs, and several historical novels and composed a two-act *opéra comique* entitled *Ida, ou L'orpheline de Berlin* (Ida, or the Orphan of Berlin) based on an episode in the life of playwright Stéphanie de Genlis. Candeille fled to England during Napoleon's last "Hundred Days" and performed there; she returned to Paris in 1816, when Louis XVIII granted her a pension for her performances in the theater and her contributions as an author. (Her father's pension was also restored.) In 1822 she married the painter Hilaire-Henri Périé de Senovert; they settled in Nîmes. After her husband's death in 1833, Candeille returned to Paris where she died of a stroke on February 4 of the following year.

Catherine, ou La belle fermière tells the story of a woman who moves to a farm after the death of her husband, who had treated her poorly and left her destitute. Catherine's father-in-law, making amends for her suffering at the hands of his son, encourages her to marry a rich young man with whom she has fallen in love. The opera exemplifies characteristics of the *opéra comique*, a genre that was well established by 1792, and provided a bit of needed comic relief during Napoleon's Reign of Terror. The plot is set in humble surroundings and revolves around hidden identities, leveling the differences among social classes. The airs feature beautiful melodies supported discreetly by the orchestra. The overture provides a preview of themes heard in the body of the work.

Among Candeille's other compositions are a keyboard concerto, piano sonatas with and without violin accompaniment, duos for two pianos, fantasies and variations for piano, and songs with French texts. The concerto and selections from *Catherine* are available in modern editions; the concerto and her first sonata have been recorded.

Among other important musical figures in eighteenth-century France was the composer and singer **Henriette Adélaïde Villard de Beaumesnil** (1748–1813), who sang Iphigenia in Gluck's *Iphigénie en Tauride* and also played leading roles in comic opera. Composer and **Hélène de Nervo de Montgeroult** (1764–1836), holds a place in the history of piano pedagogy through teaching at the Conservatoire in Paris and the publication of one of the earliest instruction books for the piano in the mid-1790s. The Alsatian composer and pianist **Marie Kiené Bigot** (1786–1820) numbered Felix Mendelssohn among her piano students.

Poland

The first Polish woman to gain recognition as a composer and concert artist was **Maria Agate Wolowska Szymanowska** (1789–1831), born in Warsaw to middle-class Jewish parents. Franciszek Wolowski, a wealthy brewery owner, and Barbara

Lanckorónska Wolowska were not musicians themselves, but as their household became a center of cultural and intellectual life in Warsaw, their daughter had the advantage of being exposed to a range of musicians, writers, and intellectuals at an early age. She displayed musical talent as a young child and began to study piano around the age of eight, then later studied theory. Maria Wolowska performed in concerts of the Warsaw Society of Musical Amateurs, some of which were held in her home, and heard many visiting artists who concertized in Warsaw on their way to the Russian court. In 1809 she gave concerts in Paris, where she began an important friendship with Luigi Cherubini (1760–1843). By the time she was in her early twenties Wolowska was considered to be one of Europe's outstanding pianists.

Upon her return to Poland, Wolowska married Józef Szymanowski, a member of the landed gentry. The couple had three children (including twins) in the first two years of their marriage. Józef did not share or fully support his wife's public life, and after ten years they divorced, leaving Maria Szymanowska to support herself and her children through teaching and composing. Breitkopf und Härtel published seven volumes of her music in 1820, and her works were also taken on by publishers in Paris, Warsaw, St. Petersburg, Moscow, Kiev, and Odessa. From 1818 on, Szymanowska toured in Poland and abroad with great financial success.

Szymanowska was appointed "first pianist to the Grand Czars" in 1822, becoming the first female professional musician to serve as pianist to the Russian court. She also participated in concerts of the [Russian] Society of Musical Amateurs, which was under the patronage of the Romanovs. For the next five years Szymanowska toured most of the Western European countries, earning great praise for her singing tone and brilliant technique. Late in 1827 she returned to Russia and spent time in Moscow with the poets Adam Michiewicz and Aleksandr Pushkin and the Irish composer John Field (1782–1837), with whom she enjoyed a long professional association. She settled permanently in St. Petersburg the following year. During her absence, Nicholas I had become czar (after the assassination of his brother Alexander I); his marriage to the daughter of the Prussian king brought with it a shifting of musical allegiances. Szymanowska's character pieces in genres associated with the French were now criticized as outmoded, as was her improvisatory style of composition. Nevertheless, she managed to live independently and very comfortably, teaching piano at court, composing, and taking part in the vibrant salon life of the city. Her own salon, which she maintained until her sudden death from cholera in 1831, was a rich center for Russian and foreign artists and for gatherings of the Polish expatriate community.

Characteristic of Szymanowska's music are her *sostenuto cantabile* style, in which she imitated the lyrical, ornamental style of Italian opera singers, and her reliance on Polish folk music. Her more than 100 compositions include mazurkas and polonaises, as well as concert études, nocturnes, and dances for piano. These provided repertoire for her concerts, and some of the less challenging works were appropriate for the large amateur and student market. Szymanowska's *Nocturne* in A-flat Major (ca. 1826) one of her most popular compositions during her lifetime, and the *Nocturne* in B-flat Major (ca. 1828–1831) but published posthumously in 1852, grew out of her association in the 1820s with the genre's inventor, John Field. She also composed chamber music, including a *divertissement* for piano and violin and a serenade for piano and cello, and songs with Polish, French, and Italian texts. As one would expect, the piano plays a strong interpretive role in her songs. A few French songs, the two chamber pieces mentioned, and many of the piano pieces are available in modern editions; a number of the piano pieces and a few songs have been recorded.

Szymanowska was a generation older than Frédéric Chopin (1810–1849), her prominent countryman. Both were inspired by nationalistic fervor and Romantic ideals of expression to explore possibilities of sonority and technique on the developing piano. Szymanowska's *sostenuto cantabile* style, which left its imprint on the works of Robert and Clara Schumann, among others, became one of the hallmarks of Romantic music.

Great Britain

In London, public concerts flourished as early as the 1670s. The Bach-Abel concerts (1765–1781) and the rival Professional Concerts, as well as the concerts of Johann Peter Salomon (responsible for bringing Haydn to London in 1791), were among prominent venues for local and visiting artists. By the late eighteenth century, London had two opera houses: Covent Garden and Drury Lane; oratorio series; the Concerts of Antient [sic] Music (founded and organized in 1776 by members of the aristocracy to perform music more than twenty years old); nightly concerts in the pleasure gardens during the summer months; and a host of benefit concerts by local and visiting artists and groups. Music also flourished in private salon concerts.

England's lively commercial market and advanced technology supported the early establishment of music publishers and instrument manufacturers. Instructional materials and thousands of pieces of music for voice, keyboard, harp, and other instruments were published in London in the eighteenth and nineteenth centuries for amateur use. English pianos by John Broadwood and by Robert Stodart were known for their brilliant and powerful sound, produced as early as 1772 through triple stringing and the use of iron braces to withstand the extra tension. English pianos also featured a sustaining pedal that controlled the dampers (as opposed to hand stops or knee levers on continental instruments). For several decades these features were only on English pianos. From the 1770s to the early 1800s, some of the best pianists in Europe flocked to London, forming a loose-knit cosmopolitan group known as the London Pianoforte School. Among the principal figures were Italian Muzio Clementi, his pupils Johann Baptist Cramer (1771–1858) and John Field, Bohemian Jan Ladislav Dussek (1760–1812), the Germans Daniel Steibelt (1765–1823) and August Alexander Klengel (1783–1852), and, in the nineteenth century, the Englishman William Sterndale Bennett (1816–1875). These composers, several of whom were also involved in music publishing, had a great impact on the development of piano technique and musical style.

In a letter of 1761, **Elisabetta (Elisabeth) de Gambarini (1731–1765)** claimed that she was "born in London, [could] speak English, French, Italian, and German," and had "composed many pieces of music, particularly an ode on his Majesty's birthday" (Asti 1998). Her parents were Charles Gambarini, an Italian who held the post of counselor to the Landgrave of Hessen-Kassel, and his wife, teacher of music to children of the aristocracy. Gambarini's *Lessons for Harpsichord*, op. 2, gives her birth date as September 7, 1731, but it is possible that this claim follows the long-standing custom of shaving a year or two off the age of a precocious young musician. Gambarini performed as a soprano soloist beginning as a young woman; during her career she sang roles in Handel's *Occasional Oratorio* and *Judas Maccabaeus* and possibly in *Samson* and *Messiah*. A benefit concert that she presented in 1761 included an ode of her own composition as well as a cantata by Francesco Geminiani (1687–1762), who may have been her teacher. There are accounts of her playing the organ and conducting performances of her own music.

Gambarini's works include two collections of harpsichord pieces published around 1748. These are available in modern editions and have been recorded. *Six Sets of Lessons for the Harpsichord*, op. 1, was printed in London and sold at her home in Argyle's Building. She dedicated the collection to the Lady Viscountess Howe of the Kingdom of Ireland and included in it a list of more than 200 subscribers, including the Princess of Wales and George Frideric Handel. Each of the "lessons," called "sonata" within the collection, consists of two or three short, lighthearted movements of contrasting character and tempo, usually in a two-voice texture. Among these are binary dance movements and variations.

The *Lessons for the Harpsichord, Intermix'd with Italian and English Songs*, op. 2, is dedicated to the Prince of Wales and includes a list of distinguished subscribers as well as a portrait of the seventeen-year-old Gambarini composing at her writing table. The volume contains two variation sets, several English or Italian songs with keyboard accompaniment and basso continuo figures, and a selection of one-movement pieces. An organ concerto, odes for chorus, and a *pastorella* for two violins and basso continuo are also attributed to Gambarini.

Gambarini married a Mr. Chazal (n.d.), probably near the end of her short life. She died in London on February 9, 1765, at the age of thirty-three.

Maria Hester Reynolds Park (1760–1813), harpsichordist, composer and singer, has been confused in the literature with a later English singer, composer, and pianist named **Maria F. Parke (1772/1773–1822)**. Maria Hester Reynolds participated in musical activities in Oxford in the 1770s; by 1785 she had moved to London, marrying antiquarian and writer Thomas Park in about 1790. She published her early works under the name "Maria Hester Reynolds" and, after her marriage, signed her name "Maria Hester Park" or "M. H. Park." Her works include sonatas for harpsichord or piano, a concerto for keyboard and strings, and a set of glees; she may also have composed a divertimento for piano with violin accompaniment. Park taught music to members of the nobility in London, including among her pupils the duchess of Devonshire (**Georgiana Cavendish**, 1757–1806, later a composer) and the duchess' daughters.

Anne-Marie Steckler Krumpholtz (ca. 1755–1813 [Madame Krumpholz]), born in Metz, France, is believed to have been the daughter of harp maker Christian

Steckler. She studied harp with Johann Baptiste Krumpholtz (1747–1790) in Metz and married him in 1783. Both musicians appeared many times in the Concert Spirituel in Paris in the late 1770s and 1780s, where Anne-Marie Krumpholtz performed music by her husband and others.

About 1788 Krumpholtz is said to have run off to England with a younger man. (Her husband did not drown himself in the Seine as has been claimed but continued to teach and compose.) She enjoyed an illustrious career as a harpist in London for the next fifteen years, giving benefit concerts and appearing regularly in the Salomon concerts along with Haydn, Jan Ladislav Dussek, Sophia Corri Dussek, and Gertrud Schmeling-Mara. In 1802 the *Allgemeine musikalische Zeitung* of Leipzig described her as "without a doubt the foremost harp player in the world," indicating that her fame had spread well beyond the borders of Great Britain. A journal entry by Mrs. Papendiek, employed at the English court, gives an idea of Krumpholtz's appearance and conveys the importance of harp playing as an emblem of grace and refinement in a woman in fashionable English society:

> Solomon's [*sic*] benefit we attended with our Windsor party, where he introduced Madame Krumpholtus [*sic*], a German [*sic*] whose harp playing was in every respect perfect.... What rendered her performance more interesting was that she was a most elegant little woman, not handsome, but so beautifully formed, and her taste so exquisite that she was consulted by the nobility about their superior dresses for drawing-rooms, balls, routs, &c. Her harp was made a proper size for her, as she was too small to use a full-sized one with comfort and grace. (Rempel 1998)

In the mid-1790s, Krumpholtz withdrew from public performance for two years but returned for another year in response to appeals in the press. From 1797 until her death of a stroke on November 15, 1813, she was recognized as a composer and arranger of pieces for the harp. Krumpholtz was among the first to compose music that was idiomatic for the harp and distinct from keyboard music. She wrote variation sets on familiar tunes and other accessible pieces for the growing market of middle-class women who sought to emulate the performances of herself, Sophia Dussek, and other well-known artists. Several of these pieces were reprinted many times. Krumpholtz's daughter, **Fanny Krumpholtz Pittar (ca. 1785–after 1815)**, was also a composer of works for harp and piano. The composer V. Krumpholtz may well have been the younger daughter of Anne-Marie Krumpholtz.

Sophia Giustina Corri Dussek (1775–ca. 1847) was a member of a prominent musical family in London in the late eighteenth and early nineteenth centuries. Her father, Italian-born Domenico Corri (1746–1825), had immigrated to Scotland in 1771 and established a music publishing company there; he was also a composer and teacher. Her mother, named Bachelli (n.d.), was one of Corri's singing pupils. Sophia Corri, born in Edinburgh, studied piano with her father as a child; she and her four brothers all pursued musical careers.

The family moved to London in 1788, where Corri studied singing. She made her first appearance in the Salomon Concerts in April 1791 and presented a benefit concert in June in which both she and Haydn performed. She continued to perform into the early 1800s in London and concertized in other English cities as well as in Edinburgh and Dublin.

In 1792 Corri married the Czech Jan Ladislav Dussek, one of the most gifted of the pianists and composers who flocked to London around the turn of the century. (Dussek was associated with the aristocracy in Paris and fled at the time of the French Revolution.) From 1794 to 1799 Sophia Dussek's father and her husband were business partners in a firm known as Corri, Dussek & Company, publishing music by composers including Haydn, Ignaz Pleyel (1757–1831), Jan Ladislav, and Sophia Dussek. Although the Dusseks performed together, the marriage was not a happy one. When the publishing company went bankrupt in 1799, her husband fled the country, leaving her father in jail. After Jan Ladislav's death in 1812, Sophia Dussek married the violist John Alvis Moralt, and the couple established a music school in Paddington. Sophia Dussek's daughter, **Olivia Dussek Bulckley {Buckley or Bulkley}** (1791/ 1801–1847), was a composer, pianist, and harpist and is said to have served as organist of Kensington Parish Church for a number of years. **Veronika Rosalia Dussek Cianchettini (1769–1833)**, teacher, performer, and composer, was a sister of Jan Ladislav Dussek.

Although Sophia Dussek was a singer, she composed little or no vocal music. Her works include several sonatas for harp and several for keyboard with or without accompaniment for flute or violin, thirty-five variation sets for harp, and one duet for harp and piano. The three *Sonatas* for Harp, op. 2, were attributed incorrectly to Jan Ladislav Dussek for many years. However, the title page of the Corri, Dussek & Company edition describes the sonatas as "by Madame Dussek."

Dussek's music displays her interest in harmony and sonority and leans toward figurative melodic motives rather than extended melodies. Her *Sonata for Pianoforte or Harpsichord with an Accompaniment for Violin or German Flute*, op. 1 (published ca. 1793) contains some striking chord progressions in the final movement. Typical for accompanied sonatas of the time, however, the violin/flute part here is subordinate, with only modest demands on the player. The *Sonata in C Minor for Harp*, op. 2, no. 3 (published in the late 1790s) is a much stronger work and features a plaintive, lyrical slow movement and a playful rondo finale; it has been recorded several times. Book 5 of the six books of *Favorite Airs Arranged for Harp* contains variation sets on familiar Scottish folk melodies: *Lewie Gordon, Thy Fatal Shafts*, and *Queen Mary's Lamentation*. These are straightforward, sensitive variations in which the melody, always clearly apparent, is embedded in changing figuration while the structure and harmonic pattern remain constant. There was an enthusiastic market for works of this kind among amateur players of the harp and keyboard instruments.

Other English composers for keyboard instruments include Maria Young Barthélemon (ca. 1749–1799) and her daughter, Cecilia Maria Barthélemon (1769/1770–after 1840), **Jane Mary Guest Miles (ca. 1765–ca. 1830)** and organist **Ann Valentine (1762–1842)**.

The American Colonies and the United States

In the American colonies, both men and women participated in singing schools in Boston (the first founded in the 1720s), Philadelphia, Charleston, and other cities on the eastern seaboard. American singing schools, like their British counterparts, were social occasions as well as opportunities for people to master the principles of sight-singing and learn music for worship. Under the direction of itinerant teachers, participants sang from printed tune books containing harmonizations of psalm and hymn tunes, as well as "fuging tunes" in which the voices enter imitatively in the second half of the tune. Although most of the repertoire of American psalmody was the work of men, women also contributed some hymn texts and melodies to published tune books.

A more cosmopolitan musical culture modeled on that of Europe coexisted for several decades with this musical tradition, gradually overtaking it after the Revolutionary War. English ballad operas and public concerts featuring songs and short instrumental pieces became part of the musical life of major cities as early as the 1730s. The market for secular music suitable for amateur use in the home grew steadily, fueled by a lively sheet music industry from the 1770s and by the establishment of American builders of harpsichords, pianos, and other instruments. French opera came to New Orleans in the 1790s, and Italian opera to New York in 1825. Women of wealthy and eventually also middle-class families, engaged in music as an "accomplishment," singing and playing keyboard instruments, guitar, and harp. Also, women composers and performers from Europe visited America as members of opera companies or touring families of musicians, and some moved permanently to the new land.

Mary Ann Matthews Wrighten Pownall (1751–1796) was born in London and immigrated to the United States after the Revolutionary War. As Mrs. Wrighten she was a popular singer and actor in the pleasure gardens of London and at Drury Lane Theatre, where she played the role of Lucy Lockit in *The Beggar's Opera* by John Gay. Her husband, James Wrighten, worked as a prompter in the theater.

Around 1786 this singer-actor embarked on a second phase of her career when she traveled to America with her second husband, Mr. Pownall. She joined the Old American Theater Company in Boston and traveled with the troupe to New York, Philadelphia, Charleston, and other cities on the eastern seaboard. She also performed as an independent artist in subscription concerts and in her own benefit concerts. Her repertory included English theater songs, as well as arias from operas and oratorios. Eventually, her children moved from England and performed with her. She died during a concert tour in Charleston on August 11, 1796, reputedly of a broken heart after the elopement of one of her daughters.

Mary Ann Wrighten wrote songs for her own performance and for amateur use in London and continued to do so as Mrs. Pownall in the United States. She collaborated with the English American composer James Hewitt (1770–1827) on a set of *Six Songs for Harpsichord* in 1794 and published other songs the following year. These are among the earliest songs published by a woman in the United States. In the style of English theater and popular songs, some are humorous and flirtatious, and others sentimental.

Several, including *Kisses Sued For* on a text by Shakespeare, published in New York in 1795, belong to the category of Scottish ballad-style songs that were fashionable in England and America around the turn of the nineteenth century.

American composer and author **Maria Eicher (1710–1784)** head of the sisterhood of Pennsylvania's Ephrata Cloister, composed hymns in German for the use of this communal society founded in 1732 by Conrad Beissel. The music at Ephrata, composed by community members and sung in harmony was famous in the colonies and in Europe for its beautiful, unearthly sound.

As opportunities for women in music expanded in the eighteenth century, women took part in a variety of important ways. Continuing the practice of the previous century, they excelled especially as vocalists and keyboardists; some became concert violinists and harpists. Women composed music for their own performance, for the use of other concert artists (both male and female), and for the growing market of amateurs and students. They served as teachers, sponsors, advisors, and role models.

Several women surveyed in this chapter hosted salons or regular concert series in their homes. Far from being on the periphery, these gatherings were at the heart of musical developments in Paris, Vienna, Berlin, Stuttgart, and St. Petersburg. Salons served as meeting grounds for the most progressive musical ideas and personalities and therefore played a role in the shaping of musical taste, in addition to providing creative and social outlets for women and men of the aristocracy and upper middle class.

The expectations placed on women in eighteenth-century society made it difficult for many to realize their potential as musicians. Women rarely received strong encouragement or substantial training in their youth, and most did not have sufficient opportunities for travel, for personal interaction with other composers and performers, or to hear their compositions performed before audiences and critics. These factors had a tremendous impact on women's views of their ability to become composers.

Today, newly published scores of women's music of the eighteenth century include a multitude of fine additions to the repertoire for solo voice, choral groups, keyboards, and chamber ensembles; many other works await publication and recording. As more music by women becomes known we will continue to refine our understanding of genres, regional styles, and styles of individual composers, while further exploring the intersection of gender, social roles, education, and creativity.

Timeline for the Eighteenth Century

Date	History/Politics	Science/Education	The Arts/Literature	Music
1701		Yale College founded University of Venice founded		**Caterina Benedicta Gratianini (fl. early 18th century)**
1706	Benjamin Franklin (1706–1790)			Baldassare Galuppi (1706–1785)
1708				**Camilla de Rossi (fl. 1708–1709)**
1709				Bartolomeo Cristofori: invention of the pianoforte **Wilhelmine, Margravine of Bayreuth (1709–1785)**
1710				Thomas Augustine Arne (1710–1778) **Maria Eicher (1710–1784) Giovanni Battista Pergolesi (1710–36)**
1711		David Hume (1711–1776)		William Boyce (1711–1779)
1712	Frederick the Great, king of Prussia (1712–1786)		Cotton Mather (1663–1728) begins *Curiosa Americana*	Frederick II (1712–1786) Jean-Jacques Rousseau (1712–1778)
1713		Denis Diderot (1713–1784)		**Maria Margherita Grimani (fl. 1713–1718)**
1714				Christoph Willibald Gluck (1714–1787) C.P.E. Bach (1714–1788)
1715	Reign of Louis XV begins		Opéra Comique founded	**Caterina Bendetta Gratianini (fl. 1715)** Georg Christoph Wagenseil (1715–1777)
1717	Maria Teresa (1717–1780)	Lady Mary Wortley Montagu introduces smallpox vaccinations		Johann Stamitz (1717–1757)
1719				Leopold Mozart (1719–1787)
1720				**Maria Teresa Agnesi (1720–1795)**
1721			Jeanne-Antoinette Poisson de Pompadour, patron of arts and literature (1721–1764)	Johann Kirnberger (1721–1783)
1723		Adam Smith (1723–1790)		**Anna Amalia, Princess of Prussia (1723–1787)** Carl Friedrich Abel (1723–1787)
1724		Immanuel Kant (1724–1804)		**Maria Antonia Walpurgis (1724–1780) Electress of Saxony**

Date	History/Politics	Science/Education	The Arts/Literature	Music
1725		St. Petersburg Academy of Science founded		
1729				Antonio Soler (1729–1783)
1731	Martha Washington, First Lady (1731–1802)	Erasmus Darwin (1731–1802)		**Elisabetta de Gambarini (1731–1765)** Christian Cannabich (1731–1798)
1732	George Washington (1732–1799)			Franz Joseph Haydn (1732–1809) Johann Christoph Friedrich Bach (1732–1795)
1733		Franz Anton Mesmer (1733–1815)		
1735				Johann Christian Bach (1735–1782)
1736		Manufacture of glass begins in Venice		
1737				Michael Haydn (1737–1806)
1739				**Anna Amalia, duchess of Saxe-Weimar (1739–1807) Anna Bon (1739/40–after 1767)** Karl Ditters von Dittersdorf (1739–99)
1740	Reign of Maria Teresa (1740–1780)	Berlin Academy of Science founded		Giovanni Paisiello (1740–1816)
1741				Andre Grétry (1741–1813)
1742		Invention of the centigrade thermometer (A. Celsius)		**Anne Home Hunter (1742–1821)**
1743	Thomas Jefferson (1743–1826)			Luigi Boccherini (1743–1805)
1744	Abigail Adams, First Lady and feminist (1744–1818)			**Anne-Louise d'Hardancourt Brillon de Jouy (1744–1824) Marianna Martines (1744–1812)**
1745		Benjamin Rush (1745–1813)		**Maddelena Lombardini Sirmen (1745–1818)** Carl Stamitz (1745–1801)
1746		College of New Jersey founded (became Princeton University in 1896)	Francisco Goya (1746–1828)	**Marie-Emmanuelle Bayon Louis (1746–1825)** William Billings (1746–1800)
1748				**Henriette Adélaïde Villard de Beaumesnil (1748–1813)**
1749		Philadelphia Academy founded (became University of Pennsylvania in 1791)	Johann Wolfgang von Goethe (1749–1832)	**Maria Young Barthélemon (1749–1799) Gertrude Schmeling Mara (1749–1833)** Domenico Cimarosa (1749–1810)

Date	History/Politics	Science/Education	The Arts/ Literature	Music
1750				**Elizabeth von Hagen (1750–1809/10)**
1751				**Corona Schröter (1751–1802)**
				Mary Ann Wrighten Pownall (1751–1796)
1752		Benjamin Franklin discovers electricity		Muzio Clementi (1752–1832)
				Juliane Benda Reichardt (1752–1783)
1755	Marie Antoinette (1755–1793)		Elisabeth Vigée-Lebrun, painter (1755–1842)	**Anne-Marie Steckler Krumpholtz (ca. 1755–1813)**
				Giovanni Battista Viotti (1755–1824)
1756				Wolfgang Amadeus Mozart (1756–1791)
				Franziska Danzi Lebrun (1756–1791)
1757			William Blake (1757–1827)	**Georgiana Cavendish (1757–1806)**
				Ignace Joseph Pleyel (1757–1831)
1758				**Josepha Barbara von Auernhammer (1758–1820)**
				Henriette Abrams (ca. 1758–ca. 1822)
				Carl Friedrich Zelter (1758–1832)
1759			Mary Wollstone-craft (1759–1797): *Vindication of the Rights of Woman*	**Maria Rosa Coccia (1759–1833)**
				Maria Cosway (1759/60–1838)
				Maria Theresia von
			Frederich Schiller (1759–1805)	**Paradis (1759–1824)**
				Sophia Maria Fritscher Westenholz (1759–1838)
1760				**Jane Savage (ca. 1760–1830)**
				Luigi Cherubini (1760–1842)
				Jan Ladislav Dussek (1760–1812)
				Maria Hester Reynolds Park (1760–1813)
1762				**Ann Valentine (1762–1842)**
1763				Franz Danzi (1763–1826)
				Etienne-Nicolas Méhul (1763–1817)
1764				**Helene de Nervo de Montgeroult (1764–1836)**
1765				**Jane Mary Guest (ca. 1765–1830)**
				Daniel Steibelt (1765–1823)

Date	History/Politics	The Arts/ Science/Education	Literature	Music
1766			Mme de Staël, novelist and feminist (1766–1817)	Samuel Wesley (1766–1837)
1767				**Amélie-Julie Candeille (1767–1834)**
1768		Jean Baptiste Fourier (1768–1830), mathematician		**Maria Margarethe Marchand Danzi (1768–1800)**
1769	Napoleon (1769–1821)			**Cecilia Maria Barthélemon 1769/1770–after 1840**
1770		G.W.F. Hegel (1770–1831)	William Wordsworth (1770–1850)	Ludwig van Beethoven (1770–1827) Anton Reicha (1770–1836)
1771		*Encyclopedia Britannica* first edition, 1771		
1772			Samuel Coleridge (1772–1834)	Maria F. Parke (1772/1773–1822)
1773	Boston Tea Party Prince Metternicht (1773–1859)	First cast-iron bridge built in Shropshire		
1775	American Revolution begins	André Ampere (1775–1836), physicist Invention of the steam engine	Jane Austen, novelist (1775–1817) J.M.W. Turner (1775–1851)	**Sophia Corri Dussek (1775–1847)**
1776	Declaration of Independence			
1778			La Scala opens in Milan, Italy	Johann Nepomuk Hummel (1778–1837) Fernando Sor (1778–1839)
1779				**Veronika Dussek Cianchettini (1779–1833) Louise Reichardt (1779–1826)**
1781				Anton Phillip Heinrich (1781–1861) **Sophie Lebrun Dülken (1781–1863)**
1782			Stendahl (pseud. of Marie Henri Bayle) (1782–1842)	John Field (1782–1837) Niccoló Paganini (1782–1840)
1783	End of American Revolution			August Alexander Klengel (1783–1852)
1784				Louis Spohr (1784–1859)
1785			Jakob Grimm (1785–1863)	**Bettine Brentano von Arnim (1785–1859) Fanny Krumpholtz Pittar (ca. 1785–after 1815)**
1786				**Marie Kiené de Morognes Bigot (1786–1820)** Daniel Friedrich Kuhlau (1786–1832)

Date	History/Politics	Science/Education	The Arts/Literature	Music
1786				**Marianna von Auenbrugger (d. 1786)** Carl Maria von Weber (1786–1826)
1788	American Constitution ratified		Friedrich Rückert (1788–1866) Joseph von Eichendorff (1788–1857) Lord Byron (1788–1824)	
1789	French Revolution (1789–1795)		James Fenimore Cooper (1789–1851)	**Maria Agate Szymanowska (1789–1831)**
1791		University of Pennsylvania founded Samuel Morse (1791–1872)		Carl Czerny (1791–1857) Giacomo Meyerbeer (1791–1864) **Olivia Dussek Bulckley (1791–1847)**
1792			Percy Bysshe Shelley (1792–1822)	Giochino Rossini (1792–1868)
1793	Lucretia Coffin Mott (1793–1880)	Invention of the cotton gin (Eli Whitney)		
1794		First telegraph Paris–Lille		Ignaz Moscheles (1794–1870)
1795		Conservatoire National in Paris founded	John Keats (1795–1821)	**Margaret Essex (fl. 1795–1802)**
1796		Vaccinations introduced in England by Dr. Edward Jenner	Jean Baptiste Camille Corot, (1796–1875)	**Emilie Zumsteeg (1796–1857)** **Hélène Liebmann (1796–1819)**
1797			Heinrich Heine (1797–1856)	Franz Schubert (1797–1828) Gaetano Donizetti (1797–1848)
1798		Lithography invented		
1799		Rosetta Stone found in Egypt Egyptian Institute founded in Cairo	Alexander Pushkin (1799–1837) Honoré de Balzac (1799–1850)	Jacques-François Halévy (1799–1862)

Bibliography

Maria Teresa Agnesi

Britton, Carolyn, and Robert L. Kendrick. "Maria Teresa Agnesi." In *Women Composers: Music Through the Ages*, vol. 3, edited by Sylvia Glickman and Martha Furman Schleifer. New York: G. K. Hall, 1998.

———. "Maria Teresa Agnesi." In *Women Composers: Music Through the Ages*, vol. 4, edited by Sylvia Glickman and Martha Furman Schleifer. New York: G. K. Hall, 1998.

deJong, Carolyn. "The Life and Keyboard Music of Maria Teresa Agnesi." D.M.A. thesis, University of Minnesota, 1979.

Hansell, Sven, and Robert L. Kendrick. "Agnesi, Maria Teresa." In *The Norton/Grove Dictionary of Women Composers*, edited by Julie Anne Sadie and Rhian Samuel. New York: W. W. Norton, 1994.

Kendrick, Robert L. *Maria Teresa Agnesi: An Introduction to Her Works*. Forthcoming.

Anna Amalia, Duchess of Saxe-Weimar

Abert, Anna Amalie "Anna Amalia [Amalie] (ii), Duchess of Saxe-Weimar." In *The Norton/Grove Dictionary of Women Composers*, edited by Julie Anne Sadie and Rhian Samuel. New York: W. W. Norton, 1994.

Anna Amalia, Princess of Prussia

Helm, Eugene. "Anna Amalia (i), Princess of Prussia." In *The Norton/Grove Dictionary of Women Composers*, edited by Julie Anne Sadie and Rhian Samuel. New York: W. W. Norton, 1994.

Bettine Brentano von Arnim

Citron, Marcia J. "Brentano [von Arnim], Bettina [Elisabeth]." In *The Norton/Grove Dictionary of Women Composers*, edited by Julie Anne Sadie and Rhian Samuel. New York: W. W. Norton, 1994.

Lemke, Ann Willison. "Bettine's Song: The Musical Voice of Bettine von Arnim, née Brentano, 1785–1859." Ph.D. diss., Indiana University, 1998.

———. "Bettine von Arnim." In *Women Composers: Music Through the Ages*, vol. 4, edited by Sylvia Glickman and Martha Furman Schleifer. New York: G. K. Hall, 1998.

Waldstein, Edith. *Bettine von Arnim and the Politics of Romantic Conversation*. Studies in German Literature, Linguistics, and Culture 33. Columbia, SC: Camden House, 1988.

Willison, Ann. "Bettina Brentano-von Arnim: The Unknown Musician." In *Bettina Brentano-von Arnim: Gender and Politics*, edited by Elke Frederiksen and Katherine Goodman. Detroit: Wayne State University Press, 1995.

Marianna d'Auenbrugg

Glickman, Sylvia. "Auenbrugger [D'Auenbrugg], Marianna von." In *The Norton/Grove Dictionary of Women Composers*, edited by Julie Anne Sadie and Rhian Samuel. New York: W. W. Norton, 1994.

———. "Marianna d'Auenbrugg." In *Women Composers: Music Through the Ages*, vol. 3, edited by Sylvia Glickman and Martha Furman Schleifer. New York: G. K. Hall, 1998.

Josepha Barbara von Auernhammer

Marciano, Rosario, and Jorge Sanchez-Chiong. "Auernhammer, Josepha Barbara von." In *The Norton/Grove Dictionary of Women Composers*, edited by Julie Anne Sadie and Rhian Samuel. New York: W. W. Norton, 1994.

Meyer, Eve R. "Josepha Barbara von Auernhammer." In *Women Composers: Music Through the Ages*, vol. 3, edited by Sylvia Glickman and Martha Furman Schleifer. New York: G. K. Hall, 1998.

Cecilia Maria Barthélemon

Baldwin, Olive, and Thelma Wilson. "Barthélemon, Cecilia Maria." In *The Norton/Grove Dictionary of Women Composers*, edited by Julie Anne Sadie and Rhian Samuel. New York: W. W. Norton, 1994.

Hayes, Deborah. "Cecilia Maria Barthélemon." In *Women Composers: Music Through the Ages*, vol. 3, edited by Sylvia Glickman and Martha Furman Schleifer. New York: G. K. Hall, 1998.

Maria Young Barthélemon

Baldwin, Olive, and Thelma Wilson. "Barthélemon [née Young], Maria [Polly; Mary]." In *The Norton/Grove Dictionary of Women Composers*, edited by Julie Anne Sadie and Rhian Samuel. New York: W. W. Norton, 1994.

Hayes, Deborah. "Maria Barthélemon." In *Women Composers: Music Through the Ages*, edited by Sylvia Glickman and Martha Furman Schleifer, vol. 5. New York: G. K. Hall, 1998.

Henriette Adélaïde Villard de Beaumesnil

Cook, Elisabeth. "Beaumesnil, Henriette Adélaïde Villard de." In *The Norton/Grove Dictionary of Women Composers*, edited by Julie Anne Sadie and Rhian Samuel. New York: W. W. Norton, 1994.

Kaufman, Deborah. "Henriette-Adelaïde de Villars." In *Women Composers: Music Through the Ages*, vol. 4, edited by Sylvia Glickman and Martha Furman Schleifer. New York: G. K. Hall, 1998.

Marie Kiené Bigot

Lee, Soon-bok. "Marianne Martines, Marie Bigot, and Maria Szymanowska: An Examination of Selected Keyboard Works in Historical Perspective." D.M.A. thesis, University of Washington, 1994.

Macdonald, Hugh. "Bigot (de Morogues) [née Kiené], Marie." In *The Norton/Grove Dictionary of Women Composers*, edited by Julie Anne Sadie and Rhian Samuel. New York: W. W. Norton, 1994.

Anna Bon di Venezia

Berdes, Jane L. "Boni [Bon, Bonn], Anna Lucia." In *The Norton/Grove Dictionary of Women Composers*, edited by Julie Anne Sadie and Rhian Samuel. New York: W. W. Norton, 1994.

Fortino, Sally. "Anna Bon." In *Women Composers: Music Through the Ages*, edited by Sylvia Glickman and Martha Furman Schleifer, vol. 3. New York: G. K. Hall, 1998.

Mathiesen, Penelope. "Winds of Yore—Women Woodwind Composers of the 18th Century: Anna Bon di Venezia." *Continuo: An Early Music Magazine* 15, no. 2 (April 1991): 9–11.

Minkin, Marina. "Anna Bon di Venezia: Life and Works, with a Discussion of the Bon Family of Musicians." D.M.A. thesis, Boston University, 1998.

Anne-Louise Boyvin d'Hardancourt Brillon de Jouy

Gustafson, Bruce. "Brillon de Jouy, Anne Louise Boyvin d'Hardancourt." In *The Norton/Grove Dictionary of Women Composers*, edited by Julie Anne Sadie and Rhian Samuel. New York: W. W. Norton, 1994.

———. "Madame Brillon." In *Women Composers: Music Through the Ages*, vol. 5, edited by Sylvia Glickman and Martha Furman Schleifer. New York: G. K. Hall, 1998.

———. Madame Brillon et son salon. *Revue de Musicologie* 85 (1999): 297–332.

———. "The Music of Madame Brillon: A Unified Collection from Benjamin Franklin's Circle." *Notes* 43 (March 1987): 522–43.

Gustafson, Bruce, and David Fuller. *A Catalogue of French Harpsichord Music, 1699–1780*. London: Clarendon Press, 1990.

Van Buren, Cheryl. "The Music of Mme Brillon (1744–1824) in the American Philosophical Society Archives, Philadelphia." *Music Research Forum* 7 (1992): 1–13.

Viano, Richard J. "By Invitation Only: Private Concerts in France during the Second Half of the Eighteenth Century." *Recherches sur la musique française classique* 27 (1991–1992): 131–62.

Olivia Dussek Buckley (or Bulkley)

Craw, Howard Allen, and Bonnie Shaljean. "Olivia Buckley [née Dussek]." In *The Norton/Grove Dictionary of Women Composers*, edited by Julie Anne Sadie and Rhian Samuel. New York: W. W. Norton, 1994.

Rempel, Ursula M. "Olivia Dussek Bulkley." In *Women Composers: Music Through the Ages*, vol. 3, edited by Sylvia Glickman and Martha Furman Schleifer. New York: G. K. Hall, 1998.

Amélie-Julie Candeille

Dwyer, Helen, and Barry Dwyer. "Candeille, Amélie Julie." In *Index Biographique Français*. London: K. G. Saur, 1993.

Fend, Michael. "Candeille, (Amélie) [Emilie] Julie [Simons, Julie]." In *The New Grove Dictionary of Opera*, edited by Stanley Sadie. London: Macmillan Press Ltd., 1992.

Johnson, Calvert. "Amélie-Julie Candeille." In *Women Composers: Music Through the Ages*, vol. 4, edited by Sylvia Glickman and Martha Furman Schleifer. New York: G. K. Hall, 1998.

———. "Amélie-Julie Candeille." In *Women Composers: Music Through the Ages*, vol. 5, edited by Sylvia Glickman and Martha Furman Schleifer. New York: G. K. Hall, 1998.

———. "Amélie-Julie Candeille: (1767–1834). I-II." *Women of Note Quarterly* 7, nos. 3–4 (August–November 1999): 12–25 and 10–27.

Kennedy, Emmet, Marie-Laurence Netter, James P. McGregor, and Mark V. Olsen. *Theatre, Opera, and Audiences in Revolutionary Paris: Analysis and Repertoire*. Westport, CT: Greenwood Press, 1996.

Neuls-Bates, Carol, ed. *Women in Music: An Anthology of Source Readings from the Middle Ages to the Present*. Rev. ed. Boston: Northeastern University Press, 1996.

Rushton, Julian, and Julie Anne Sadie. "Candeille, (Amélie) [Emilie] Julie [Simons, Julie]." In *The Norton/Grove Dictionary of Women Composers*, edited by Julie Anne Sadie and Rhian Samuel. New York: W. W. Norton, 1994.

Sadie, Julie Anne. "Musiciennes of the Ancien Régime." In *Women Making Music*, edited by Jane Bowers and Judith Tick, 191–223. Urbana and Chicago: University of Illinois Press, 1986.

Georgiana Cavendish, Duchess of Devonshire

Jackson, Barbara Garvey. "Duchess of Devonshire [Georgiana Cavendish]." In *Women Composers: Music Through the Ages*, vol. 4, edited by Sylvia Glickman and Martha Furman Schleifer. New York: G. K. Hall, 1998.

Veronika Dussek Cianchettini

Craw, Howard Allen, and Bonnie Shaljean. "Katerina Veronika Anna Dusíkova [Veronika Rosalia Dussek; Veronika Elisabeta Dusíkova; Veronica Cianchettini]." In *The Norton/Grove Dictionary of Women Composers*, edited by Julie Anne Sadie and Rhian Samuel. New York: W. W. Norton, 1994.

Rempel, Ursula M., and Sarah Mahler Hughes. "Veronica Cianchettini." In *Women Composers: Music Through the Ages*, vol. 3, edited by Sylvia Glickman and Martha Furman Schleifer. New York: G. K. Hall, 1998.

Maria Rosa Coccia

Burton, Anthony. "Coccia, Maria Rosa." In *The Norton/Grove Dictionary of Women Composers*, edited by Julie Anne Sadie and Rhian Samuel. New York: W. W. Norton, 1994.

Maria Margarethe Marchand Danzi

Cunningham, Caroline. "Maria Margarethe Marchand Danzi." In *Women Composers: Music Through the Ages*, vol. 5, edited by Sylvia Glickman and Martha Furman Schleifer. New York: G. K. Hall, 1998.

Höft, Brigitte. "Danzi [née Marchand], (Maria) Margarethe." In *The Norton/Grove Dictionary of Women Composers*, edited by Julie Anne Sadie and Rhian Samuel. New York: W. W. Norton, 1994.

Sophie Lebrun Dülken

Münster, Robert. "Lebrun [Dülken], Sophie." In *The Norton/Grove Dictionary of Women Composers*, edited by Julie Anne Sadie and Rhian Samuel. New York: W. W. Norton, 1994.

Sophia Giustina Corri Dussek

Craw, Howard Allen, Barbara Garvey Jackson, and Bonnie Shaljean. "Sophia (Giustina) Dussek." In *The Norton/Grove Dictionary of Women Composers*, edited by Julie Anne Sadie and Rhian Samuel. New York: W. W. Norton, 1994.

Rempel, Ursula M. "Sophia Dussek." In *Women Composers: Music Through the Ages*, edited by Sylvia Glickman and Martha Furman Schleifer, vol. 3. New York: G. K. Hall, 1998.

Rensch, Roslyn. *Harps and Harpists*. Bloomington: Indiana University Press, 1989.

Temperley, Nicholas. General Introduction to *The London Pianoforte School*. 20 vols. New York: Garland, 1987.

Weidensaul, Jane B. "Notes on Jan Ladislav Dussek and Mrs. Dussek (Sophia Corri): A Review of Contemporary Sources." *American Harp Journal* 14, no. 2 (Winter 1993): 3–5.

Maria Eicher

Seachrist, Denise A. "Maria Eicher." In *Women Composers: Music Through the Ages*, vol. 4, edited by Sylvia Glickman and Martha Furman Schleifer. New York: G. K. Hall, 1998.

Elisabetta de Gambarini

Asti, Martha Secrest. "Elisabetta de Gambarini." In *Women Composers: Music Through the Ages*, vol. 3, edited by Sylvia Glickman and Martha Furman Schleifer. New York: G. K. Hall, 1998.

Dean, Winton. "Gambarini, Elisabetta de." In *The Norton/Grove Dictionary of Women Composers*, edited by Julie Anne Sadie and Rhian Samuel. New York: W. W. Norton, 1994.

Peterson, Anne Wallace. "Elisabetta de Gambarini: A Composer and Performer of the Middle Eighteenth Century." M.A. thesis, Lone Mountain College, 1978.

Jane Mary Guest

Bowers, Jane. "Jane Mary Guest (Mrs. Miles)." In *Women Composers: Music Through the Ages*, vol. 5, edited by Sylvia Glickman and Martha Furman Schleifer. New York: G. K. Hall, 1998.

Kidd, Ronald R. "Guest [Miles], Jane Mary." In *The Norton/Grove Dictionary of Women Composers*, edited by Julie Anne Sadie and Rhian Samuel. New York: W. W. Norton, 1994.

Raessler, Daniel M. "Jane Mary Guest (Mrs. Miles)." In *Women Composers: Music Through the Ages*, vol. 3, edited by Sylvia Glickman and Martha Furman Schleifer. New York: G. K. Hall, 1998.

Anne-Marie Steckler Krumpholtz

Jackson, Barbara Garvey, and Ursula M. Rempel. "Krumpholtz [née Steckler or Stekler], Anne-Marie." In *The Norton/Grove Dictionary of Women Composers*, edited by Julie Anne Sadie and Rhian Samuel. New York: W. W. Norton, 1994.

Papendiek, Charlotte Louise Henrietta. *Court and Private Life in the Time of Queen Charlotte, Being the Journals of Mrs. Papendiek, Assistant Keeper of the Wardrobe and Reader to Her Majesty*. London: Bentley and Son, 1887.

Rempel, Ursula M. "Fanny Krumpholtz and Her Milieu." *American Harp Journal* 5, no. 4 (1976): 11–15.

———. "Madame Krumpholtz." In *Women Composers: Music Through the Ages*, vol. 3, edited by Sylvia Glickman and Martha Furman Schleifer. New York: G. K. Hall, 1998.

———. "The Perils of Secondary Sources: An Annotated Bibliography of Encyclopedia and Dictionary Sources Relating to Harpist Members of the Krumpholtz Family." *American Harp Journal* 7, no. 3. (1980): 25–30.

Rensch, Roslyn. *Harps and Harpists*. Bloomington: Indiana University Press, 1989.

Franziska Danzi Lebrun

Cunningham, Caroline. "Francesca Lebrun." In *Women Composers: Music Through the Ages*, vol. 5, edited by Sylvia Glickman and Martha Furman Schleifer. New York: G. K. Hall, 1998.

Höft, Brigitte. "Lebrun [née Danzi], Franziska [Francesca] (Dorothea)." In *The Norton/Grove Dictionary of Women Composers*, edited by Julie Anne Sadie and Rhian Samuel. New York: W. W. Norton, 1994.

Hélène Riese Liebmann

Meyer, Eve R. "Hélène Riese Liebmann." In *Women Composers: Music Through the Ages*, vol. 3, edited by Sylvia Glickman and Martha Furman Schleifer. New York: G. K. Hall, 1998.

Reich, Nancy B. "Liebmann [née Riese], Helene." In *The Norton/Grove Dictionary of Women Composers*, edited by Julie Anne Sadie and Rhian Samuel. New York: W. W. Norton, 1994.

Marie Emmanuelle Bayon Louis

Gustafson, Bruce, and David Fuller. *A Catalogue of French Harpsichord Music, 1699–1780*. London: Clarendon Press, 1990.

Hayes, Deborah. "Bayon, Marie Emmanuelle." In *The Norton/Grove Dictionary of Women Composers*, edited by Julie Anne Sadie and Rhian Samuel. New York: W. W. Norton, 1994.

———. "Madame Louis." In *Women Composers: Music Through the Ages*, vol. 4, edited by Sylvia Glickman and Martha Furman Schleifer. New York: G. K. Hall, 1998.

———. "Madame Louis." In *Women Composers: Music Through the Ages*, vol. 5, edited by Sylvia Glickman and Martha Furman Schleifer. New York: G. K. Hall, 1998.

———. "Marie-Emmanuelle Bayon, Later Madame Louis, and Music in Late Eighteenth-Century France." *College Music Symposium* 30 (1990): 14–33.

Sadie, Julie Anne. "Musiciennes of the Ancien Régime." In *Women Making Music*, edited by Jane Bowers and Judith Tick, 191–223. Urbana and Chicago: University of Illinois Press, 1986.

Viano, Richard J. "By Invitation Only: Private Concerts in France during the Second Half of the Eighteenth Century." *Recherches sur la musique française classique* 27 (1991–1992): 131–62.

Gertrud Schmeling Mara

Jackson, Barbara Garvey. "Madame Mara." In *Women Composers: Music Through the Ages*, vol. 4, edited by Sylvia Glickman and Martha Furman Schleifer. New York: G. K. Hall, 1998.

Rosselli, John. "Mara [née Schmeling], Gertrud Elisabeth." *The New Grove Dictionary of Opera*. London: Macmillan, 1994.

Marianna Martines

Bean, Shirley. "Marianna Martines." In *Women Composers: Music Through the Ages*, vol. 4, edited by Sylvia Glickman and Martha Furman Schleifer. New York: G. K. Hall, 1998.

Brown, A. Peter. "Mariana Martines' Autobiography as a New Source for Haydn's Biography during the 1750s." *Haydn-Studien* 7 (1986): 68–70.

Clark, Hallie Kathleen. "Progressive and Conservative Elements in Marianna Martines' Quarta Messa (1765)." M. Mus. thesis, Northern Arizona University, 1998.

Fremar, Karen. "The Life and Selected Works of Marianna Martines (1744–1812)." Ph.D. diss., University of Kansas, 1983.

Godt, Irving. "Marianna in Italy: The International Reputation of Mariana Martines (1744–1812). *Journal of Musicology* 13 (Fall 1995): 538–61.

———. "Marianna in Vienna: A Martines Chronology." *Journal of Musicology* 16 (Winter 1998): 136–58.

Gordy, Laura. "Women Creating Music 1750–1850: Marianne Martinez, Maria Theresia von Paradis, Fanny Mendelssohn Hensel, and Clara Wieck Schumann." D.M.A. thesis, University of Alabama, 1987.

Lee, Soon-bok. "Marianne Martines, Marie Bigot, and Maria Szymanowska: An Examination of Selected Keyboard Works in Historical Perspective." D.M.A. thesis, University of Washington, 1994.

Neuls-Bates, Carol, ed. *Women in Music: An Anthology of Source Readings from the Middle Ages to the Present*. Rev. ed. Boston: Northeastern University Press, 1996.

Nopp, Regina. *Frau und Musik: Komponistinnen zur Zeit der Wiener Klassik*. Linz: R. Trauner, 1996.

Sperber, Roswitha, ed. *Women Composers in Germany*. Translated by Timothy Nevill. Bonn: Inter Nationes, 1996. With a compact disc containing the opening chorus from *In exitu Israel* by Martines.

Stevenson, R. "Marianna Martines=Martínez (1744–1812): Pupil of Haydn and Friend of Mozart." *Inter-American Music Review* 11 (1990–1991): 25–44.

Wessely, Helene. "Martínez, Marianne [Anna Katharina] von." In *The Norton/Grove Dictionary of Women Composers*, edited by Julie Anne Sadie and Rhian Samuel. New York: W. W. Norton, 1994.

Hélène de Nervo de Montgeroult

Johnson, Calvert. "Hélène Montgeroult." In *Women Composers: Music Through the Ages*, vol. 5, edited by Sylvia Glickman and Martha Furman Schleifer. New York: G. K. Hall, 1998.

Sadie, Julie Anne. "Montgeroult, Hélène de Nervo de [Countess de Charnay]." In *The Norton/Grove Dictionary of Women Composers*, edited by Julie Anne Sadie and Rhian Samuel. New York: W. W. Norton, 1994.

Maria Theresia von Paradis

Burney, Charles. "An Account of Mademoiselle Theresa Paradis of Vienna." *London Magazine* (1785): 30.

Gordy, Laura. "Women Creating Music 1750–1850: Marianne Martinez, Maria Theresia von Paradis, Fanny Mendelssohn Hensel, and Clara Wieck Schumann." D.M.A. thesis, University of Alabama, 1987.

Matsushita, Hidemi. "Maria Theresia von Paradis." In *Women Composers: Music Through the Ages*, vol. 3, edited by Sylvia Glickman and Martha Furman Schleifer. New York: G. K. Hall, 1998.

———. "The Musical Career and Compositions of Maria Theresia von Paradis 1758–1824." Ph.D. diss., Brigham Young University, 1989.

———. "Paradis [Paradies], Maria Theresia von." In *The Norton/Grove Dictionary of Women Composers*, edited by Julie Anne Sadie and Rhian Samuel. New York: W. W. Norton, 1994.

Neuls-Bates, Carol, ed. *Women in Music: An Anthology of Source Readings from the Middle Ages to the Present*. Rev. ed. Boston: Northeastern University Press, 1996.

Ullrich, Hermann. "Maria Theresia Paradis and Mozart." *Music and Letters* 27 (October 1946): 224–33.

———. "Maria Theresia Paradis in London." *Music and Letters* 43 (1962): 16–24.

———. "Maria Theresia Paradis: Werkverzeichnis." *Beiträge zur Musikwissenschaft* 5 (1963): 117–54.

Maria Hester Reynolds Park

Baldwin, Olive, and Thelma Wisdom. "Park [née Reynolds], Maria Hester." In *The Norton/Grove Dictionary of Women Composers*, edited by Julie Anne Sadie and Rhian Samuel. New York: W. W. Norton, 1994.

Hayes, Deborah. "M. H. Park." In *Women Composers: Music Through the Ages*, vol. 5, edited by Sylvia Glickman and Martha Furman Schleifer. New York: G. K. Hall, 1998.

Maria F. Parke

Baldwin, Olive, and Thelma Wilson. "Parke, Maria F." In *The Norton/Grove Dictionary of Women Composers*, edited by Julie Anne Sadie and Rhian Samuel. New York: W. W. Norton, 1994.

Fanny Krumpholtz Pittar

Jackson, Barbara Garvey, and Ursula M. Rempel. "Pittar [née Krumpholtz], Fanny." In *The Norton/Grove Dictionary of Women Composers*, edited by Julie Anne Sadie and Rhian Samuel. New York: W. W. Norton, 1994.

Rempel, Ursula M. "Fanny Krumpholtz Pittar." In *Women Composers: Music Through the Ages*, vol. 3, edited by Sylvia Glickman and Martha Furman Schleifer. New York: G. K. Hall, 1998.

———. "The Perils of Secondary Sources: An Annotated Bibliography of Encyclopedia and Dictionary Sources Relating to Harpist Members of the Krumpholtz Family." *American Harp Journal* 7, no. 3 (1980): 25–30.

Mary Ann Wrighten Pownall

Goldberg, Loretta. "Pownall, Mary Ann." In *The Norton/Grove Dictionary of Women Composers*, edited by Julie Anne Sadie and Rhian Samuel. New York: W. W. Norton, 1994.

Jackson, Barbara Garvey. "Mary Ann Wrighten Pownall." In *Women Composers: Music Through the Ages*, vol. 4, edited by Sylvia Glickman and Martha Furman Schleifer. New York: G. K. Hall, 1998.

Sonneck, Oscar G. *Early Concert-Life in America (1731–1800)*. New York: Musurgia, 1949.

Juliane Benda Reichardt

Reich, Nancy B. "Juliane Reichardt." In *Women Composers: Music Through the Ages*, vol. 3, edited by Sylvia Glickman and Martha Furman Schleifer. New York: G. K. Hall, 1998.

———. "Reichardt [née Benda], (Bernhardine) Juliane." In *The Norton/Grove Dictionary of Women Composers*, edited by Julie Anne Sadie and Rhian Samuel. New York: W. W. Norton, 1994.

Louise Reichardt

Reich, Nancy B. "Louise Reichardt." In *Ars Musica, Musica Scientia: Festschrift Heinrich Hüschen*, edited by Detlef Alterburg, 369–77. Cologne: Gitarre and Laute Verlagsgesellschaft, 1980.

———. "Louise Reichardt." In *Women Composers: Music Through the Ages*, vol. 4, edited by Sylvia Glickman and Martha Furman Schleifer. New York: G. K. Hall, 1998.

———. "Reichardt, Louise." In *The Norton/Grove Dictionary of Women Composers*, edited by Julie Anne Sadie and Rhian Samuel. New York: W. W. Norton, 1994.

Corona Elisabeth Wilhelmine Schröter

Bauman, Thomas. *North German Opera in the Age of Goethe*. Cambridge: Cambridge University Press, 1985.

Beutler, Ernst. "Corona Schröter." In *Essays um Goethe*, edited by Christian Beutler, 459–501. Zurich and Munich: Artemis Verlag, 1980.

Citron, Marcia J. "Corona Schröter: Singer, Composer, Actress." *Music and Letters* 61 (1980): 15–27.

Kidd, Ronald R. "Schröter, Corona Elisabeth Wilhelmine." In *The Norton/Grove Dictionary of Women Composers*, edited by Julie Anne Sadie and Rhian Samuel. New York: W. W. Norton, 1994.

Neuls-Bates, Carol, ed. *Women in Music: An Anthology of Source Readings from the Middle Ages to the Present*. Rev. ed. Boston: Northeastern University Press, 1996.

Randall, Annie Janeiro. "Corona Schröter." In *Women Composers: Music Through the Ages*, vol. 4, edited by Sylvia Glickman and Martha Furman Schleifer. New York: G. K. Hall, 1998.

———. "Music and Drama in Weimar 1776–1782: A Social-Historical Perspective." Ph.D. diss., College-Conservatory of Music, University of Cincinnati, 1995.

———. "The Mysterious Disappearance of Corona Schröter's Autobiography." *Journal of Musicological Research* 14 (1994): 1–15.

Maddalena Lombardini Sirmen

Arnold, Denis. "Music at the Mendicanti in the Eighteenth Century." *Music and Letters* 65 (1984): 345–56.

Arnold, Elsie, and Gloria Eive. "Maddalena Lombardini Sirmen." In *Women Composers: Music Through the Ages*, vol. 5, edited by Sylvia Glickman and Martha Furman Schleifer. New York: G. K. Hall, 1998.

Baldauf-Berdes, Jane L. *Women Musicians of Venice: Musical Foundations, 1525–1855*. Rev. ed. Oxford: Clarendon Press, 1993.

Berdes, Jane. "Lombardini Sirmen [Syrmen, Sijrmen, Seriman, Ceriman], Maddalena Laura." In *The Norton/Grove Dictionary of Women Composers*, edited by Julie Anne Sadie and Rhian Samuel. New York: W. W. Norton, 1994.

McVeigh, Simon. *Concert Life in London from Mozart to Haydn*. Cambridge: Cambridge University Press, 1993.

———. *The Violinist in London's Concert Life 1750–1784: Felice Giardini and His Contemporaries*. New York: Garland, 1989.

Neuls-Bates, Carol, ed. *Women in Music: An Anthology of Source Readings from the Middle Ages to the Present*. Rev. ed. Boston: Northeastern University Press, 1996.

Roth, Jan Traci. "The Six Violin Concertos of Maddalena Laura Lombardini-Sirmen: An Introduction and Analysis." M. Mus. thesis, Kansas State University, 1990.

White, Chappell. *From Vivaldi to Viotti: A History of the Early Classical Violin Concerto*. Philadelphia: Gordon and Breach, 1992.

Maria Agate Wolowska Szymanowska

Cypin, Gennadij. "Chopin and the Russian Piano Tradition." Translated by Beatrice L. Frank. *Journal of the American Liszt Society* 38 (July–December 1995): 67–82.

Glickman, Sylvia. "Szymanowska [née Wolowska], Maria Agate." In *The Norton/Grove Dictionary of Women Composers*, edited by Julie Anne Sadie and Rhian Samuel. New York: W. W. Norton, 1994.

Harley, Maria Anna. "Maria Szymanowska." In *Women Composers: Music Through the Ages*, vol. 4, edited by Sylvia Glickman and Martha Furman Schleifer. New York: G. K. Hall, 1998.

Karlowicz, Sarah Hanks. "Maria Szymanowska." In *Women Composers: Music Through the Ages*, vol. 5, edited by Sylvia Glickman and Martha Furman Schleifer. New York: G. K. Hall, 1998.

Lee, Soon-bok. "Marianne Martines, Marie Bigot, and Maria Szymanowska: An Examination of Selected Keyboard Works in Historical Perspective." D.M.A. thesis, University of Washington, 1994.

Swartz, Anne. "Maria Szymanowska." In *Women Composers: Music Through the Ages*, vol. 3, edited by Sylvia Glickman and Martha Furman Schleifer. New York: G. K. Hall, 1998.

———. "Maria Szymanowska and the Salon Music of the Early Nineteenth Century." *The Polish Review* 30, no. 1 (1985): 43–58.

———. "Maria Szymanowska: Contemporary Accounts from Moscow and St. Petersburg." *New Journal for Music* 1, no. 1 (Summer 1990): 38–64.

———. "Szymanowska: The Virtuoso-Composer in Transition." *New Journal for Music* 1, no. 3 (Winter 1991): 17–31.

Temperley, Nicholas. General Introduction to *The London Pianoforte School*. 20 vols. New York: Garland, 1987.

———. "John Field and the First Nocturne." *Music and Letters* 56, nos. 3–4 (July–October 1975): 335–40.

Ann Valentine

Hayes, Deborah. "Ann Valentine." In *Women Composers: Music Through the Ages*, vol. 3, edited by Sylvia Glickman and Martha Furman Schleifer. New York: G. K. Hall, 1998.

Sadie, Julie Anne. "Valentine, Ann." In *The Norton/Grove Dictionary of Women Composers*, edited by Julie Anne Sadie and Rhian Samuel. New York: W. W. Norton, 1994.

Maria Antonia Walpurgis, Electress of Saxony

Allroggen, Gerhard. "Maria Antonia Walpurgis, Electress of Saxony." In *The Norton/Grove Dictionary of Women Composers*, edited by Julie Anne Sadie and Rhian Samuel. New York: W. W. Norton, 1994.

Fankhauser, Jill Munroe. "Talestri, Regina Delle Amazzoni: An Opera Seria by Maria Antonia Walpurgis." M.Mus. thesis, College-Conservatory of Music, University of Cincinnati, 1998.

McLamore, Alyson. "Princess Royal of Saxony, Maria Antonia Walpurgis." In *Women Composers: Music Through the Ages*, vol. 5, edited by Sylvia Glickman and Martha Furman Schleifer. New York: G. K. Hall, 1998.

Sophia Maria Fritscher Westenholz

Härtwig, Dieter. "Westernholz [née Fritscher], (Eleonore) Sophia Maria." In *The Norton/Grove Dictionary of Women Composers*, edited by Julie Anne Sadie and Rhian Samuel. New York: W. W. Norton, 1994.

Shafer, Sharon Guertin. "Sophia Westenholz." In *Women Composers: Music Through the Ages*, vol. 4, edited by Sylvia Glickman and Martha Furman Schleifer. New York: G. K. Hall, 1998.

Emilie Zumsteeg

Citron, Marcia J. "Zumsteeg, Emilie." In *The Norton/Grove Dictionary of Women Composers*, edited by Julie Anne Sadie and Rhian Samuel. New York: W. W. Norton, 1994.

Rebmann, Martina. "'Wie Deine Kunst, so edel war Dein Leben': Ein Werkverzeichnis der Stuttgarter Komponistin Emilie Zumsteeg." *Musik in Baden-Württemberg* 2 (1995): 51–74.

Summerville, Suzanne. "Emilie Zumsteeg." In *Women Composers: Music Through the Ages*, vol. 4, edited by Sylvia Glickman and Martha Furman Schleifer. New York: G. K. Hall, 1998.

Discography

Anna Amalia, Duchess of Saxe-Weimar

Goethe-Lieder. Auf dem Land und in der Stadt. Dietrich Fischer-Dieskau, baritone, and Karl Engel, piano. Orfeo D'Or#389951 (1995).

Lieder by Women Composers from the Classical Period to Modern Times, vol. 1. *Sie scheinen zu spielen*. Yoshie Tanaka and Yasuko Mitsui. Musical Heritage Society 512350 (1989).

Lieder von Komponistinnen des 18. und 19. Jahrhunderts. Sieh mich, Heil'ger, wie ich bin (from *Erwin und Elmire*). Elisabeth Scholl, soprano, and Burkhard Schäffer, piano. Salto Records International SAL 7007 (1999).

Rosario Marciano Plays Tailleferre, Chaminade, Anna Amalia, Duchess of Saxe-Weimar. Concerto for 12 Instruments and Cembalo obbligato; Divertimento for Piano and Strings. Rosario Marciano, piano; Orchestra of Radio Luxembourg, conducted by Louis de Fromant; Vienna Chamber Orchestra, conducted by Kurt Rapf. Turnabout TV 34754 (1980).

Songs of the Classical Age. Auf dem Land und in der Stadt. Patrice Michaels Bedi, soprano, and David Schrader, piano. Cedille Records CDR 90000 049 (1999).

Women's Voices: Five Centuries of Song. Ihr solltet geniessen, from *Erwin und Elmire.* Neva Pilgrim, soprano; Edward Smith, harpsichord; Steven Heyman, piano. Leonarda LE 338 (1996).

Anna Amalia, Princess of Prussia

Music by Women Composers. Adagio from *Sonata in F.* Kristan Aspen, flute; Janna MacAnslan, guitar. Musica Femina (1984). 1 sound cassette.

Bettine Brentano von Arnim

Lieder by Women Composers from the Classical Period to Modern Times, vol. 1. *O schaud're nicht* from *Faust.* Yoshie Tanaka and Yasuko Mitsui. Musical Heritage Society 512350 (1989).

Lieder und Texte. Romanze; Mondenschein; O schaudre nicht; Ein Stern der Lieb' am Himmelslauf; Zu dir, mein Herzenssehnen; Der Himmel ist oft hell; Ach neige, du Schmerzenreiche; Lass los von der Welt; An Luna; Die dunkle Nacht; Romanze; Hafis; Wanderers Nachtlied; Suleika. Renate Brosch, soprano; Karl-Friedrich Schäfer, piano. Salto Records International SAL 7008 (1999).

Lieder von Komponistinnen des 18. und 19. Jahrhunderts. Ach neige, du Schmerzenreiche. Elisabeth Scholl, soprano; Burkhard Schäffer, piano. Salto Records International SAL 7007 (1999).

Marianna d'Auenbrugg

18th Century Women Composers: Music for Harpsichord, vol. 1. *Rondo* from *Sonata in E-flat Major.* Barbara Harbach, harpsichord. Gasparo Records GSCD 272 (1995).

Frauenmusik für cembalo. Women Composers for the Harpsichord. Sonata in E-flat Major. Sally Fortino, harpsichord. Basel: K.e.n.wald Nr. 1 (1993).

Harpsichord Solos by 18th Century Women Composers. Rondo from *Sonata in E-flat Major.* Barbara Harbach, harpsichord. Kingdom KCLCD 2010 (1989).

Vienna: Two Centuries of Harpsichord Music (1600–1800). Sonata in E-flat Major. Barbara Baird, harpsichord. Don Ross Productions DRP 1011 (1995).

Josepha Barbara von Auernhammer

Wolfgang Amadeus Mozart, seine Freunde und Schüler. Sonata in A major. Consortium Classicum. Electrola EMI 1C 187-28 836/39 (1975).

Cecilia Maria Barthélemon

18th Century Women Composers: Music for Harpsichord, vol. 1. *Sonata in E Major, op. 1, no. 3.* Barbara Harbach, harpsichord. Gasparo Records GSCD 272 (1995).

18th Century Women Composers: Music for Harpsichord, vol. 2. *Sonata op. 3 in G Major.* Barbara Harbach, harpsichord. Gasparo Records GSCD 281 (1993).

Harpsichord Solos by 18th Century Women Composers. Sonata in E Minor, op. 1, no. 3. Barbara Harbach, harpsichord. Kingdom KCLCD 2010 (1989).

Hofkomponistinnen in Europa/Women Composers at the Courts of Europe. Vol. 1. *Sonata II for Flute, Cello, and Harpsichord in F Major, op. 1, no. 2.* Irene Schmidt, Baroque flute; Jaroslav Sveceny, violin; Wladimir Kissen, cello; Fine Zimmermann, harpsichord. Cybele UBC 1801 (1998).

Maria Young Barthélemon

"Non tacete" I'll Not Be Silent! Se pieta da voi non trovo. Ars Femina Ensemble. Nannerl Recordings NRARS002 (1991).

Marie Kiené Bigot

Music by Maria Hester Park, Marie Bigot, and Fanny Mendelssohn Hensel. Etude in C minor; Etude in A minor. Betty Ann Miller, piano. Centaur#2320 (1997).

Anna Bon di Venezia

The Baroque Flute: Italienische Flötensonaten. Sonata da camera, op. 1, no. 5 in G Minor. Hans-Joachim Fuss, Baroque flute; René Schiffer, violoncello; Nicolau de Figueiredo, harpsichord. Discover DICD 920256 (1995).

Flute Sonatas, op. 1. Six Sonatas for Flute and Basso Continuo, op. 1. Sabine Dreier, Baroque flute, and Irene Hegen, square piano. CPO 999 181-2 (1992).

Frauenmusik für cembalo. Women Composers for the Harpsichord. Sonata II in B-flat major. Sally Fortino, harpsichord. Basel: K.e.n.wald Nr. 1 (1993).

Il Grande Barocco Italiano—Bon: 6 Sonatas {Sonatas for Flute and Basso Continuo, op. 1}. Claudio Ferrarini, flute; Andrea Corsi, bassoon; Francesco Tasini, harpsichord. Mondo Musica MM 96006 (1997).

Hofkomponistinnen in Europa/Women Composers at the Courts of Europe. Vol. 1. *Divertimento "Trio III" for Flute, Violin, Cello, and Harpsichord in D Major, op. 3, no. 3*. Irene Schmidt, Baroque flute; Jaroslav Sveceny, violin; Wladimir Kissen, cello; Fine Zimmermann, harpsichord. Cybele UBC 1801 (1998).

Sechs Sonaten für Flote & Cembalo. Sonatas for Flute and Piano, op. 1: no. 1 in C Major, no. 2 in F Major, no. 3 in B-flat Major, no. 4 in D Major, no. 5 in G Minor, no. 6 in G Major. Christiane Meininger, flute; Traud Kloft, harpsichord. Bayer Records CD 100057 (1994).

6 Flute Trios, op. 3. Sabine Dreier and Peter Spohr, flutes; Rhoda Patrick, bassoon; Tatjana Geiger, harpsichord. Editorial de Musica Española EMEC (Spain) #23 (1998).

Sonata Veneziane del '700. Sonata for Flute and Basso Continuo, op. 1, no. 4. Stefano Bet, flute; Francisco Cera, harpsichord. Tactus (Italy) 700002 (1999).

Amélie-Julie Candeille

Mostly Romantic Music by Women Composers. Sonata no. 1. Selma Epstein, piano. Chromattica (1987). 1 sound cassette.

Piano Concerto, op. 2. Jennifer Paul, harpsichord. Bay Area Women's Philharmonic; JoAnn Falletta, conductor. San Francisco, November 21, 1991.

Women Composers: An International Sampler. Grande Sonata no. 1. Selma Epstein, piano. Chromattica (1988). 1 sound cassette.

Sophia Giustina Corri Dussek

Arpeggio. Sonata in C major (formerly attributed to J. L. Dussek). Nicole Mastero, harp. Erasmus WVH 073 (1993).

L'autre jour—Harp Music of the 18th and 19th Centuries. Sonata for Harp, op. 2, no. 3 in C Minor. Laura Zaerr, single-action pedal harp. Pandourion PRD 1002 (1995).

Great Works for the Harp. Sonata in C minor, op. 2, no. 3 (formerly attributed to J. L. Dussek). Willy Postma, harp. Victoria (Norway) (1996).

North Pacific Music Library Sampler 1988–89. Sonata in C minor. Laura Zaerr, celtic harp. North Pacific Music (1999).

Récital de harpe. Sonata pour harpe (formerly attributed to J. L. Dussek). Isabelle Moretti, harp. Harmonia Mundi France (1997).

Elisabetta de Gambarini

18th Century Women Composers: Music for Harpsichord, vol. 1. *Tambourin, Cariglion, Allegro, and Variations on "Lover, Go and Calm Thy Sighs" from op. 2*. Barbara Harbach, harpsichord. Gasparo Records GSCD 272 (1995).

Gambarini: Lessons for the Harpsichord. Six Sets of Lessons for the Harpsichord, op. 1; Pieces for Harpsichord, op. 2. Paule van Parys, harpsichord. Pavane ADW 7395 (1998).

Harpsichord Solos by 18th Century Women Composers. Pieces for the Harpsichord, op. 2. Barbara Harbach, harpsichord. Kingdom KCLCD 2010 (1989).

Franziska Danzi Lebrun

Hofkomponistinnen in Europa/Women Composers at the Courts of Europe. Vol. 1. *Sonata II for Violin and Harpsichord in E-flat Major, op. 1, no. 2.* Irene Schmidt, Baroque flute; Jaroslav Sveceny, violin; Wladimir Kissen, cello; Fine Zimmermann, harpsichord. Cybele UBC 1801 (1998).

Hélène Liebmann

Grande sonate pour pianoforte et violoncello… oeuvre XI. Camilla de Souza, cello; Heike Dörr, piano. Sacral SACD 9016-3 (1992).

Hofkomponistinnen in Europa/Women Composers at the Courts of Europe. Vol. 1. *Grande Sonata for Cello and Harpsichord in B-flat Major, op. 10; Grand Trio for Violin, Cello, and Harpsichord in A Major, op. 11.* Irene Schmidt, Baroque flute; Jaroslav Sveceny, violin; Wladimir Kissen, cello; Fine Zimmermann, harpsichord. Cybele UBC 1801 (1998).

Kennst du das Land (Performed on Cello). Camilla de Souza, cello; Igo Beketov, piano. GEMA (1996). Recording available from SALTO-Musikverstand, Kassel.

Lieder von Komponistinnen des 18. und 19. Jahrhunderts. Mignon, op. 4. Elisabeth Scholl, soprano; Burkhard Schäffer, piano. Salto Records International SAL 7007 (1999).

Marie Emmanuelle Bayon Louis

Frauenmusik für cembalo. Women Composers for the Harpsichord. Sonata I in F Major. Sally Fortino, harpsichord. Basel: K.e.n.wald Nr. 1 (1993).

Marianna Martines

Baroquen Treasures. Sinfonia in C. Bay Area Women's Philharmonic, JoAnn Falletta, conductor; Terrie Baune, violin. Newport Classic, 1990. 1 sound cassette.

18th Century Women Composers: Music for Harpsichord, vol. 1. *Sonata in E Major; Sonata in A Major.* Barbara Harbach, harpsichord. Gasparo Records GSCD 272 (1995).

Frauenmusik für cembalo. Women Composers for the Harpsichord. Sonata da cembalo G Major. Sally Fortino, harpsichord. Basel: K.e.n.wald Nr. 1 (1993).

Great Women Composers. Sonata in A Major; Sonata in E Major. Compiled by Gail Smith. Creative Keyboard Publications MB 96008CD (1997).

Harpsichord Solos by 18th Century Women Composers. Sonata in E Major; Sonata in A Major. Barbara Harbach, harpsichord. Kingdom KCLCD 2010 (1989).

Historical Anthology of Music by Women. Sonata in A major, mvt. I. Compiled by James R. Briscoe. Bloomington and Indianapolis: Indiana University Press (1987).

"Non tacete" I'll Not Be Silent! La tempesta. Ars Femina Ensemble. Nannerl Recordings NRARS002 (1991).

Vienna: Two Centuries of Harpsichord Music (1600–1800). Sonata in A Major. Barbara Baird, harpsichord. Don Ross Productions DRP 1011 (1995).

Women Composers and the Men in Their Lives. Sonata for Harpsichord in A Major. Leanne Rees, piano. Fleur de Son 57939 (2000).

Maria Theresia von Paradis

Historical Anthology of Music by Women. Morgenlied eines armen Mannes; Sicilienne (spurious). Compiled by James R. Briscoe. Bloomington and Indianapolis: Indiana University Press (1987).

Lieder by Women Composers from the Classical Period to Modern Times, vol. 1. *Endlich winkt der Freund der Müden; Es war einmal ein Gärtner; Ihr Lieben, die ich Schwermuthsvolle*. Yoshie Tanaka and Yasuko Mitsui. Musical Heritage Society 512350 (1989).

Songs of the Classical Age. *Morgenlied eines armen Mannes*, from *Lieder auf ihrer Reise in Musik gesetzt*. Patrice Michaels Bedi, soprano; David Schrader, piano. Cedille Records CDR 90000 049 (1999).

Women Composers: An International Sampler. *Fantaisie*. Selma Epstein, piano. Chromattica (1988). 1 sound cassette.

Women's Voices: Five Centuries of Song. *Gärtnerliedchen aus dem Siegwart*, from *Lieder auf ihrer Reise in Musik gesetzt*. Neva Pilgrim, soprano; Edward Smith, harpsichord; Steven Heyman, piano. Leonarda LE 338 (1996).

Maria Hester Reynolds Park

18th Century Women Composers: Music for Harpsichord, vol. 1. *Sonata for Keyboard, op. 4, no. 1 in F Major*. Barbara Harbach, harpsichord. Gasparo Records GSCD 272 (1995).

18th Century Women Composers: Music for Harpsichord, vol. 2. *Sonata for Keyboard in C Major, op. 7; Concerto for Keyboard and Strings in E-flat Major, op. 6*. Barbara Harbach, harpsichord. Gasparo Records GSCD 281 (1993).

Harpsichord Solos by 18th Century Women Composers. *Sonata in F major*. Barbara Harbach, harpsichord. Kingdom KCLCD 2010 (1989).

Music by Maria Hester Park, Marie Bigot, and Fanny Mendelssohn Hensel. *Sonata in F Major, op. 4, no. 1; Sonata in C major, op. 7*. Betty Ann Miller, piano. Centaur #2320 (1997).

Louise Reichardt

Lieder by Women Composers from the Classical Period to Modern Times, vol. 1. *Unruhiger Schlaf; Wassernoth; Daphne am Bach; Heimweh; Nach Sevilla!* Yoshie Tanaka and Yasuko Mitsui. Musical Heritage Society 512350 (1989).

Lieder von Komponistinnen des 18. und 19. Jahrhunderts. *Schäfers Klagelied*. Elisabeth Scholl, soprano; Burkhard Schäffer, piano. Salto Records International SAL 7007 (1999).

Musikalisches Biedermeier in Hamburg. *Heimweh; Betteley der Vögel; Unruhiger Schlaf; Die Blume der Blumen; Hier liegt ein Spielmann begraben*. Tuula Nienstedt, alto; Uwe Wegner, piano. Musica viva 30-1126 (1987).

Schubert, Reichardt, Mendelssohn-Hensel, Songs. *Tre Canzoni (Metastasio): Giusto Amor, Notturno, Vanne felice ri; Die Blume der Blumen; Hier liegt ein Spielmann begraben; Betteley der Vögel; Bergmannslied; Heimweh; Duettino*. Grayson Hirst, tenor; Michel Yuspeh, piano. Leonarda LPI 112 (1982).

Corona Elisabeth Wilhelmine Schröter

Lieder by Women Composers from the Classical Period to Modern Times, vol. 1. *Für Männer uns zu plagen* (from *Die Fischerin*); *Jugendlied*. Yoshie Tanaka and Yasuko Mitsui. Musical Heritage Society 512350 (1989).

Songs of the Classical Age. *Für Männer uns zu plagen*, from *Die Fischerin*. Patrice Michaels Bedi, soprano; David Schrader, piano. Cedille Records CDR 90000 049 (1999).

Maddalena Lombardini Sirmen

Baroquen Treasures. *Concerto no. 5 in B-flat for Violin*. Bay Area Women's Philharmonic, JoAnn Falletta, conductor; Terrie Baune, violin. Newport Classic, (1990). 1 sound cassette.

Sei Quartetti per Archi. 6 Quartets for Strings, op. 3. Accademia della Magnifica Comunità. Tactus (Italy) TC 731201 (1999).

The Six String Quartets. Allegri String Quartet. CALA CACD 1019 (1994).

String Quartets. *Quartetto no. 2 in B-flat Major; Quartetto no. 3 in G Minor*. Erato-Quartett. CPO 999 679-2 (1999).

Summershimmer. Concerto for Violin and Orchestra op. 3, no. 1, arranged for organ. Barbara Harbach, organ. Hester Park CD 7704 (1996).

Maria Agate Wolowska Szymanowska

Concerto Etudes and Toccatas by 19th and 20th Century Women Composers. Etudes. Christine Harnisch, piano. Aurophon AU 31473 (1991).

Great Women Composers. Nocturne. Compiled by Gail Smith. Creative Keyboard Publications MB 96008CD (1997).

Historical Anthology of Music by Women. Nocturne in B-flat Major. Compiled by James R. Briscoe. Bloomington and Indianapolis: Indiana University Press, 1987.

Klaviernacht. Piano Works by Women Composers. Waltz for Piano in E-flat Major; Waltz in A Major; Waltz in F Major. Eva Schieferstein, piano. Bayer Records BR 100255 (1996).

Lieder by Women Composers from the Classical Period to Modern Times, vol. 1. *Peine et plaisir; Le connais-tu?* Yoshie Tanaka and Yasuko Mitsui. Musical Heritage Society 512350 (1989).

Mostly Romantic Music by Women Composers. Le murmure. Selma Epstein, piano. Chromattica (1987). 1 sound cassette.

Rags and Riches: Ragtime and Classical Piano Music by Women. Nocturne in B-flat Major; Nocturne in A-flat Major; Mazurkas no. 19 in C Major, no. 8 in D Major, no. 1 in C Major, no. 2 in F Major, no. 3 in C Major, no. 13 in B-flat Major, no. 4 in F Major, no. 17 in C Major, no. 20 in F Major; Etudes no. 15 in C Major, no. 18 in E Major. Nancy Fierro, piano. Dorchester Classic CD DRC 1004 (1993).

Songs of the Classical Age. Ballade; Se spiegar. Patrice Michaels Bedi, soprano; David Schrader, piano. Cedille Records CDR 90000 049 (1999).

Women Composers. Nocturne in B-flat Major. Solveig Funseth, piano. Swedish Society Discotel SCD 1043 (1991).

Maria Antonia Walpurgis, Electress of Saxony

Lieder by Women Composers from the Classical Period to Modern Times, vol. 1. *Prendi l'ultimo addio*. Yoshie Tanaka and Yasuko Mitsui. Musical Heritage Society 512350 (1989).

Sophia Maria Fritscher Westenholz

Songs of the Classical Age. Morgenlied. Patrice Michaels Bedi, soprano; David Schrader, piano. Cedille Records CDR 90000 049 (1999).

Emilie Zumsteeg

Música, Femini Singular. Trennung ohne Abschied; Morgenfreude. Isabel Rosselló, soprano; Marta Pujol, piano. Editions Albert Moraleda REF 7478 (1997).

Schwäbische Romantik. Das Lied der Nebelhöhle. Ensemble La Violetta. Bayer Records 100 155 and 100 156 (1996).

Selected Modern Editions

Maria Teresa Agnesi

Concerto in F Major for Harpsichord, 2 Violins, and Bass. Louisville, KY: Ars Femina, 1993.

Non piangete, amati rai, Aria IV from *Arie con istromenti*. In "Maria Teresa Agnesi" by Carolyn Britton and Robert L. Kendrick. In *Women Composers: Music Through the Ages*, vol. 4, edited by Sylvia Glickman and Martha Furman Schleifer. New York: G. K. Hall, 1998; Bryn Mawr, PA: Hildegard Publishing Company, 1998.

Sonata in F for Keyboard. Louisville, KY: Ars Femina, 1993.

Sonata in G. In "Maria Teresa Agnesi" by Carolyn Britton and Robert L. Kendrick. In *Women Composers: Music Through the Ages*, vol. 3, edited by Sylvia Glickman and Martha Furman Schleifer. New York: G. K. Hall, 1998; Bryn Mawr, PA: Hildegard Publishing Company, 1998 (G. K. Hall reprint).

Sonata in G Major; Allegro ou presto. In *Two Pieces for Solo Piano or Harpsichord*, edited by Barbara Harbach. Pullman, WA: Vivace Press, 1996.

Anna Amalia, Duchess of Saxe-Weimar

Auf dem Land und in der Stadt (from *Erwin und Elmire*). In *Frauen Komponieren: 25 Lieder für Singstimme und Klavier*, edited by Eva Rieger and Käte Walter. Mainz and New York: Schott, 1992.

Auf dem Land und in der Stadt. In *Goethe in Lied: Kompositionen seiner Zeitgenossen für Singstimme und Klavier*. Kassel: Bärenreiter, 1949.

Divertimento B-Dur, für Klarinette, Viola, Violoncello und Klavier. Edited by Horst Heussner. Vienna: Doblinger, 1997.

Erwin und Elmire. Edited by Max Friedlaender. Leipzig: C.F.W. Siegel, 1921.

Quartet for Clarinet {Violin}, Viola, Cello, and Pianoforte. Louisville, KY: Ars Femina, 1995.

Sieh mich, Heil'ger, wie ich bin (from *Erwin und Elmire*). In *Von Goethe inspiriert*, edited by Ann Willison Lemke. Kassel: Furore, 1999.

Das Veilchen; Auf dem Land und in der Stadt; Sie scheinen zu spielen; Sieh mich, Heil'ger, wie ich bin. In *Gedichte von Goethe in Compositionen seiner Zeitgenossen*, edited by Max Friedlaender. Weimar: Goethe-Gesellschaft, 1896 and 1916. Reprint Hildesheim: Olms, 1975.

Anna Amalia, Princess of Prussia

Adagio, from *Sonata in F major for Flute and Continuo.* In *Historical Anthology of Music by Women*, edited by James R. Briscoe. Bloomington and Indianapolis: Indiana University Press, 1987.

Trio Sonata for Two Violins and Continuo. Louisville, KY: Ars Femina, 1993.

Bettine Brentano von Arnim

An Luna; Ach neige, du Schmerzenreiche (from *Faust*). In *Von Goethe inspiriert*, edited by Ann Willison Lemke. Kassel: Furore, 1999.

Ach neige, du Schmerzenreiche (from *Faust*); *O schaudre nicht* (from *Faust*); *Herbstgefühl; Wanderers Nachtlied; Suleika; An Luna.* In *Goethe-Vertonungen für Singstimme und Klavier*, edited by Renate Moering and Reinhard Schmiedel. Kassel: Furore, 1999.

Aus Faust; Ein Stern der Lieb' am Himmelslauf; Vision des heiligen Johannes vom Kreuz; Hafis; Wandrers Nachtlied. In *Five Lieder*, edited by Shoshana Shay. Bryn Mawr, PA: Hildegard Publishing Company, 1994.

Lieder und Duette für Singstimme und Klavier: Handschriften, Drucke, Bearbeitungen. Edited by Renate Moering. Kassel: Furore, 1996.

O schaudre nicht (from *Faust*). In *Gedichte von Goethe in Compositionen seiner Zeitgenossen*, edited by Max Friedlaender. Weimar: Verlag der Goethe-Gesellschaft, 1896.

O schaudre nicht (from *Faust*); *Ein Stern der Lieb' am Himmelslauf; Abendstille öffnet Thüren; Weihe an Hellas.* In "Bettine von Arnim" by Ann Willison Lemke. In *Women Composers: Music Through the Ages*, vol. 4, edited by Sylvia Glickman and Martha Furman Schleifer. New York: G. K. Hall, 1998.

O schaudre nicht (from *Faust*); *Ein Stern der Lieb' am Himmelslauf; Abendstille öffnet Thüren; Weihe an Hellas.* In *Four Lieder*. Bryn Mawr, PA: Hildegard Publishing Company, 1998 (G. K. Hall reprint).

Marianna von Auenbrugger

Largo, from *Sonata per il clavicembalo o forte piano.* In "Marianna d'Auenbrugg" by Sylvia Glickman. In *Women Composers: Music Through the Ages*, vol. 3, edited by Sylvia Glickman and Martha Furman Schleifer. New York: G. K. Hall, 1998.

Rondo allegro, from *Sonata in E-flat Major*. In *Women Composers for Harpsichord*, edited by Barbara Harbach. Bryn Mawr, PA: Elkan-Vogel, 1986.

Rondo, from *Sonata in E-flat Major*. In *At the Piano with Women Composers*, edited by Maurice Hinson. 2d ed. Van Nuys, CA: Alfred, 1995.

Sonata per il clavicembalo o forte piano. Edited by Sylvia Glickman. Bryn Mawr, PA: Hildegard Publishing Company, 1990.

Josepha Barbara von Auernhammer

Sechs Variationen über ein ungarisches Thema. Edited by Rosario Marciano. Kassel: Furore, 1998.

Six Variations on "Der Vogelfänger bin ich ja" from Wolfgang Amadeus Mozart's Die Zauberflöte. In "Josepha Barbara von Auernhammer" by Eve R. Meyer. In *Women Composers: Music Through the Ages*, vol. 3, edited by Sylvia Glickman and Martha Furman Schleifer. New York: G. K. Hall, 1998; Bryn Mawr, PA: Hildegard Publishing Company, 1998 (G. K. Hall reprint).

Cecilia Maria Barthélemon

The Capture of the Cape of Good Hope for the Piano Forte or Harpsichord, Concluding with a Song & Chorus. In "Cecilia Maria Barthélemon" by Deborah Hayes. In *Women Composers: Music Through the Ages*, vol. 3, edited by Sylvia Glickman and Martha Furman Schleifer. New York: G. K. Hall, 1998; Bryn Mawr, PA: Hildegard Publishing Company, 1998 (G. K. Hall reprint).

Four Accompanied Keyboard Sonatas for the Piano Forte or Harpsichord. Edited by Calvert Johnson. Fayetteville, AR: ClarNan, 1993.

Sonatas, op. 1, no. 1 in C Major; op. 1, no. 3 in E Major; op. 3 in G Major. In *Three Sonatas for Piano*, edited by Barbara Harbach. Pullman, WA: Vivace Press, 1995.

Sonata op. 3 for the Pianoforte or Harpsichord. In *Four Keyboard Sonatas by Early English Women Composers*, edited by Sally Fortino. Bryn Mawr, PA: Hildegard Publishing Company, 1996.

Maria Young Barthélemon

Fra un dolce deliro. In *Treasury of Art Songs by Women before 1800*, edited by Caterini Galli. Louisville, KY: Ars Femina, 1997.

Six Sonatas for Piano and Violin. Introduction by Sylvia Glickman. Bryn Mawr, PA: Hildegard Publishing Company, 2000.

Sonata III for the Harpsichord or Piano Forte with an Accompanyment for a Violin. In "Maria Barthélemon" by Deborah Hayes. In *Women Composers: Music Through the Ages*, vol. 5, edited by Sylvia Glickman and Martha Furman Schleifer. New York: G. K. Hall, 1998; Bryn Mawr, PA: Hildegard Publishing Company, 1998 (G. K. Hall reprint).

Sonata no. 4. In *Three Marias: Three Eighteenth Century Sonatas*, edited by Susan Eileen Pickett. Bryn Mawr, PA: Hildegard Publishing Company, 1997.

Henriette Adelaïde Villard de Beaumesnil

Vainement je voudrais feindre, from *Tibulle et Délie*. In "Henriette-Adelaïde de Villars" by Deborah Kaufman. In *Women Composers: Music Through the Ages*, vol. 4, edited by Sylvia Glickman and Martha Furman Schleifer. New York: G. K. Hall, 1998.

Marie Kiené Bigot

Sonata, piano op. 1, B-flat major; Suite d'études. Edited by Calvert Johnson. Pullman, WA: Vivace Press, 1992.

Anna Bon di Venezia

Die Cembalo Musik der Anna Bon de Venezia: Sechs Sonaten, {op. 2}. Edited by Traud Kloft. Facsimile of 1757 edition. Düsseldorf: Edition Donna, 1990.

Six Divertimenti op. III for 2 Flutes and Basso Continuo. Edited by Sally Fortino. Bryn Mawr, PA: Hildegard Publishing Company, 1993.

Six Sonatas for Harpsichord or Piano. Edited by Barbara Harbach. Pullman, WA: Vivace Press, 1995.

Six Sonatas for Keyboard, op. II. Edited by Jane Schatkin Hettrick. Bryn Mawr, PA: Hildegard Publishing Company, 1997.

VI Sonate da camera per il flauto traversiere e violoncello o cembalo {1756}. Edited by Barbara Garvey Jackson. Fayetteville, AR: ClarNan, 1989.

Sonata II in B-flat major {op. 2, no. 2}. In "Anna Bon" by Sally Fortino. In *Women Composers: Music Through the Ages*, vol. 3, edited by Sylvia Glickman and Martha Furman Schleifer. New York: G. K. Hall, 1998.

Anne-Louise Boyvin d'Hardancourt Brillon de Jouy

Canzonnetta: Grâce a tant de tromper rien; Romance: Sur le bord d'une onde; Romance: Au fond d'une heureuse vallée; O nuit, que tu me semble belle; Heureux qui voit chaque matin (with horn). In *Songs of Anne-Louise Brillon de Jouy and Maria Cosway.* Lieder and Other Songs by Women of the Classic Era 3. Fayetteville, AR: ClarNan, 1994.

Madame Brillon: Multiple Keyboard Works. Edited by Bruce Gustafson. Madison, WI: A-R Editions, forthcoming.

Marche des insurgents. Edited and arranged for brass quintet by Daniel Nightingale. Bryn Mawr, PA: Hildegard Publishing Company, 1992.

2nd Duo de harpe et piano, sol mineur {after 1783}. Edited by Barbara Garvey Jackson. Fayetteville, AR: ClarNan, 1993.

Sonata VII. In "Madame Brillon" by Bruce Gustafson. In *Women Composers: Music Through the Ages*, vol. 5, edited by Sylvia Glickman and Martha Furman Schleifer. New York: G. K. Hall, 1998; Bryn Mawr, PA: Hildegard Publishing Company, 1998 (G. K. Hall reprint).

Olivia Dussek Buckley (or Bulkley)

Fantasia for the Piano Forte. In "Olivia Dussek Bulkley" by Ursula M. Rempel. In *Women Composers: Music Through the Ages*, vol. 3, edited by Sylvia Glickman and Martha Furman Schleifer. New York: G. K. Hall, 1998; Bryn Mawr, PA: Hildegard Publishing Company, 1998 (G. K. Hall reprint).

Amélie-Julie Candeille

Concerto pour le Forte Piano ou Clavecin {op. 2}; Ouverture from Catherine, ou la Belle Fermière; March, act 3, scene 7 from *Catherine, ou la Belle Fermière*. In "Amélie-Julie Candeille" by Calvert Johnson. In *Women Composers: Music Through the Ages*, vol. 5, edited by Sylvia Glickman and Martha Furman Schleifer. New York: G. K. Hall, 1998; Bryn Mawr, PA: Hildegard Publishing Company, 1998.

Fille, avec ses quinze ans, act 1, scene 11 finale; *Au tems orageux des folies*, act 2, scene 3; *Ah, mon Dieu! qu'est-c'qu'on dira*, act 3, scene 10 finale; from *Catherine, ou la Belle Fermière*. In "Amélie-Julie Candeille" by Calvert Johnson. In *Women Composers: Music Through the Ages*, vol. 4, edited by Sylvia Glickman and Martha Furman Schleifer. New York: G. K. Hall, 1998.

Ouverture from Catherine, ou la Belle Fermière. Bryn Mawr, PA: Hildegard Publishing Company, 1998 (G. K. Hall reprint).

Three Arias from Catherine, ou la Belle Fermière for voice and piano. Edited by Calvert Johnson. Bryn Mawr, PA: Hildegard Publishing Company, 2000.

Georgiana Cavendish, Duchess of Devonshire

I Have a Silent Sorrow Here. In "Duchess of Devonshire [Georgiana Cavendish]" by Barbara Garvey Jackson. In *Women Composers: Music Through the Ages*, vol. 4, edited by Martha Furman Schleifer and Sylvia Glickman. New York: G. K. Hall, 1998.

Veronika Dussek Cianchettini

Andantino cantabile, from *Sonata, op. 4, no. 2*. In "Veronica Cianchettini" by Ursula M. Rempel and Sarah Mahler Hughes. In *Women Composers: Music Through the Ages*, vol. 3, edited by Sylvia Glickman and Martha Furman Schleifer. New York: G. K. Hall, 1998.

Piano Sonata, Op. 8 and Variations on a Roman Air. Edited by Sarah Mahler Hughes. Fayetteville, AR: ClarNan, 1999.

Sonata in F Major for the Piano Forte with or without Additional Keys. In *Four Keyboard Sonatas by Early English Women Composers*, edited by Sally Fortino. Bryn Mawr, PA: Hildegard Publishing Company, 1996.

Two Sonatas for the Pianoforte, with an Accompaniment for Violin and Cello, op. 4. Edited by Sylvia Glickman. Bryn Mawr, PA: Hildegard Publishing Company, 2000.

Maria Rosa Coccia

Dixit Dominus Domino meo. Edited by Irene Hegen. Kassel: Furore, 1997.

Sophia Giustina Corri Dussek

A Sonata for the Piano Forte; Three Favorite Airs Arranged for the Harp (Book 5). In "Sophia Dussek" by Ursula M. Rempel. In *Women Composers: Music Through the Ages*, vol. 3, edited by Sylvia Glickman and Martha Furman Schleifer. New York: G. K. Hall, 1998.

A Sonata for the Piano Forte. Bryn Mawr, PA: Hildegard Publishing Company, 1998 (G. K. Hall reprint).

Sonata No. 1 in B-flat for the Harp, op. 2, no. 1. Formerly attributed to J. L. Dussek. New York: Lyra Music Co., 1978.

Sonata opus 1 for the Piano Forte or Harpsichord with an Accompaniment for Violin or German Flute. Edited by Sally Fortino. Bryn Mawr, PA: Hildegard Publishing Company, 1995.

Sonata, op. 2 no. 3. Formerly attributed to J. L. Dussek. Edited by Nicanor Zabaleta. London and New York: Schott, 1954.

Three Favorite Airs Arranged for the Harp: Lewie Gordon, Thy Fatal Shaft, Queen Mary's Lamentation. Bryn Mawr, PA: Hildegard Publishing Company, 1998 (G. K. Hall reprint).

Maria Margarethe Marchand Danzi

Sonata op. 1, no. 1. In *Three Marias: Three Eighteenth Century Sonatas*, edited by Susan Eileen Pickett. Bryn Mawr, PA: Hildegard Publishing Company, 1997.

Sonata I in E Major for Violin and Piano. Edited by Barbara Harbach. Pullman, WA: Vivace Press, 1996.

Sonata II in B-flat Major for Violin and Piano. Edited by Barbara Harbach. Pullman, WA: Vivace Press, 1996.

Sonata terza pour le pianoforte with violin obbligato. In "Maria Margarethe Marchand Danzi" by Caroline Cunningham. In *Women Composers: Music Through the Ages*, vol. 5, edited by Sylvia Glickman and Martha Furman Schleifer. New York: G. K. Hall, 1998; Bryn Mawr, PA: Hildegard Publishing Company, 1998 (G. K. Hall reprint).

Sonata III in E Major for Violin and Piano. Edited by Barbara Harbach. Pullman, WA: Vivace Press, 1996.

Maria Eicher

O Tauben Einfalt! In "Maria Eicher" by Denise A. Seachrist. In *Women Composers: Music Through the Ages*, vol. 4, edited by Sylvia Glickman and Martha Furman Schleifer. New York, NY. G. K. Hall, 1998.

Elisabetta de Gambarini

Gigue; Tambourin. In *At the Piano with Women Composers*, edited by Maurice Hinson, 2d ed. Van Nuys, CA: Alfred, 1995.

Harpsichord Sonata, op. 2 no. 1. Louisville, KY: Ars Femina, n.d.

Lessons for Harpsichord, opus I and opus II. Edited by Martha Secrest Asti. Bryn Mawr, PA: Hildegard Publishing Company, 1995.

Lover, Go Calm Thy Sighs {Aria, Gavotte, Variations on the Foregoing Song, Giga}, from *Lessons for Harpsichord, op. 2*. In *Eighteenth Century Women Composers for the Harpsichord or Piano*, vol. 1, edited by Barbara Harbach. Pullman, WA: Vivace Press, 1992.

Lover Go and Calm Thy Sighs. In *Treasury of Art Songs by Women before 1800*, edited by Caterini Galli. Louisville, KY: Ars Femina, 1997.

Six lessons for the Harpsichord, Sonata 1. In "Elisabetta de Gambarini" by Martha Secrest Asti. In *Women Composers: Music Through the Ages*, vol. 3, edited by Sylvia Glickman and Martha Furman Schleifer. New York: G. K. Hall, 1998.

Six Sonatas for Harpsichord or Piano. Edited by Barbara Harbach. Pullman, WA: Vivace Press, 1994.

Three Selections from Lessons for the Harpsichord: Minuet, Tambourin, Allegro. In *Women Composers for Harpsichord*, edited by Barbara Harbach. Bryn Mawr, PA: Elkan-Vogel, 1986.

Jane Mary Guest

Adagio, from *Sonata for the Piano Forte with an Accompaniment for the Violin (ad libitum); Divertimento for the Piano Forte, in Which Is Introduced the Favorite Round "Hark the Bonny Christ Church Bells."* In "Jane Mary Guest (Mrs. Miles)" by Daniel M. Raessler. In *Women Composers: Music Through the Ages*, vol. 3, edited by Sylvia Glickman and Martha Furman Schleifer. New York: G. K. Hall, 1998.

Divertimento for the Piano Forte, in Which Is Introduced the Favorite Round "Hark the Bonny Christ Church Bells." Bryn Mawr, PA: Hildegard Publishing Company, 1998 (G. K. Hall reprint).

Sonata in D Major, op. 1, no. 2 for Violin or Flute and Harpsichord or Piano. In "Jane Mary Guest (Mrs. Miles)" by Jane Bowers. In *Women Composers: Music Through the Ages*, vol. 5, edited by Sylvia Glickman and Martha Furman Schleifer. New York: G. K. Hall, 1998; Bryn Mawr, PA: Hildegard Publishing Company, 1998 (G. K. Hall reprint).

Anne-Marie Steckler Krumpholtz

A Favorite Piemontois Air, with Variations by Dalvimare; Lison Dormoit, with an Introduction & Variations Arranged for the Harp; The Favorite Air of Pray Goody Arranged for the Harp. In "Madame Krumpholtz" by Ursula M. Rempel. In *Women Composers: Music Through the Ages*, vol. 3, edited by Sylvia Glickman and Martha Furman Schleifer. New York: G. K. Hall, 1998.

Three Pieces for Harp. Bryn Mawr, PA: Hildegard Publishing Company, 1998 (G. K. Hall reprint).

Franziska Danzi Lebrun

Six Sonatas for the Harpsichord or Piano-Forte. In *Keyboard Sonatas of Francesca Lebrun and Marie-Emmanuelle Bayon*, edited by Deborah Hayes. Women Composer Series, 23. New York: Da Capo, 1990.

Sonata for Violin and Piano, op. 3, no. 1. In *Frauen Komponieren: 13 Stücke für Violine und Klavier*. Mainz: Schott, 1994.

Sonata VI with violin obbligato. In "Francesca Lebrun" by Caroline Cunningham. In *Women Composers: Music Through the Ages*, vol. 5, edited by Sylvia Glickman and Martha Furman Schleifer. New York: G. K. Hall, 1998. Bryn Mawr, PA: Hildegard Publishing Company, 1998 (G. K. Hall reprint).

Hélène Liebmann

Grande sonate {B-flat major} pour le piano-forte et violoncelle...oeuvre XI. Edited by Nona Pyron. London: Grancino Editions, 1982.

Grande sonate for the Pianoforte, op. 15. In "Hélène Riese Liebmann" by Eve R. Meyer. In *Women Composers:*

Music Through the Ages, vol. 3, edited by Sylvia Glickman and Martha Furman Schleifer. New York: G. K. Hall, 1998. Bryn Mawr, PA: Hildegard Publishing Company, 1998 (G. K. Hall reprint).

Kennst du das Land, op. 4. In *Lieder by Women Composers of the Classic Era*, vol. 1, edited by Barbara Garvey Jackson. Fayetteville, AR: ClarNan, 1987.

Mignon, from *Wilhelm Meister*. In *Von Goethe inspiriert*, edited by Ann Willison Lemke. Kassel: Furore, 1999.

Marie Emmanuelle Bayon Louis

Overture to Fleur d'épine. In "Madame Louis" by Deborah Hayes. In *Women Composers: Music Through the Ages*, vol. 5, edited by Sylvia Glickman and Martha Furman Schleifer. New York: G. K. Hall, 1998.

Quand on est tendre, act 1, scene 2; *À l'amour tout est possible*, act 1, scene 3; *On ne doit compter*, act 1, scene 4; *C'est l'etat de notre coeur*, act 1, scene 6; *Écho que Fleur d'épine est belle*, act 2, scene 6; *Au bord d'une onde pure*, act 2, scene 6; from *Fleur d'épine*. In "Madame Louis" by Deborah Hayes. In *Women Composers: Music Through the Ages*, vol. 4, edited by Sylvia Glickman and Martha Furman Schleifer. New York: G. K. Hall, 1998.

Six sonates pour le clavecin ou le piano forte, dont trois avec accompagnement de violon obligé, oeuvre I. In *Keyboard Sonatas of Francesca Lebrun and Marie-Emmanuelle Bayon*, edited by Deborah Hayes. Women Composer Series 23. New York: Da Capo, 1990.

Gertrud Schmeling Mara

Caro, l'affanno mio; Say Can You Deny Me. In *Eighteenth Century Theater Songs and Concert Arias Composed by Women*, vol. 1, edited by Barbara Garvey Jackson. Fayetteville, AR: ClarNan, 1995.

Say Can You Deny Me. In "Madame Mara" by Barbara Garvey Jackson. In *Women Composers: Music Through the Ages*, vol. 4, edited by Sylvia Glickman and Martha Furman Schleifer. New York: G. K. Hall, 1998.

Marianna Martines

Alfin fra le tempeste, from *La Tempestà*. In "Marianna Martines" by Shirley Bean. In *Women Composers: Music Through the Ages*, vol. 4, edited by Sylvia Glickman and Martha Furman Schleifer. New York: G. K. Hall, 1998.

Allegro, from *Sonata in E major*. In *Women Composers for Harpsichord*, edited by Barbara Harbach. Bryn Mawr, PA: Elkan-Vogel, 1986.

Allegro, from *Sonata in A major*. In *Historical Anthology of Music by Women*, edited by James R. Briscoe. Bloomington and Indianapolis: Indiana University Press, 1987.

Concerto for Piano and Orchestra in A Major. Edited by Rosario Marciano. Kassel: Furore Editions, 1996.

Dixit Dominus. Edited by Irving Godt. Recent Researches in Music of the Classical Era, 48. Madison, WI: A-R Editions, 1997.

In exitu Israel de Agypto. Edited by Conrad Misch. Kassel: Furore, 1993.

Mass No. 1 in C Major for Strings, 2 Oboes, 2 Trumpets, Timpani, SATB, and Organ Continuo. Edited by Shirley Bean. Fayetteville, AR: ClarNan, 1998. [Movements also available separately.]

Miserere for SATB Chorus and Continuo. Edited by Shirley Bean. Fayetteville, AR: ClarNan, 1996.

Per pietà bell' idol mio; Se per tutti ordisce amore, from the *First Mass*. In *Two Arias for Soprano*, edited by Shirley Bean. Fayetteville, AR: Clar Nan, 1996.

Quarta Messa. Edited by Conrad Misch. Kassel: Furore, 1993.

Salmo 51 (revised version), for SATB Chorus, Organ, and String Orchestra. Louisville, KY: Ars Femina, n.d.

Sinfonia in C. Kansas City, MO: Fremar, n.d.

Sonata No. 3 in A major, mvt. I. In *Frauen Komponieren: 22 Klavierstücke des 18–20. Jahrhunderts*, edited by Eva Rieger and Käte Walter. Mainz: Schott, 1985.

Sonata no. 3 in A major. In *Eighteenth Century Women Composers for the Harpsichord or Piano*, vol. 2, edited by Barbara Harbach. Pullman, WA: Vivace Press, 1992.

Sonata in A major; Sonata in E major. In *Die Cembalo Musik der Maria Anna Martinez*, edited by Traud Kloft. Düsseldorf: Frauenmusikvertrieb, 1990.

Sonata in A Major; Sonata in E Major. In *Great Women Composers*, edited by Gail Smith. Pacific, MO: Creative Keyboard, 1996. [CD accompanies the score.]

Sonata in E major. In *At the Piano with Women Composers*, edited by Maurice Hinson, 2d ed. Van Nuys, CA: Alfred, 1995.

Sonata in E Major; Sonata in A Major; Sonata in G Major. In *Three Sonatas for Keyboard*, edited by Shirley Bean. Bryn Mawr, PA: Hildegard Publishing Company, 1994.

Hélène de Nervo de Montgeroult

Sonate pour le Pianoforte avec l'Accompagnement d'un Violon, op. 2, no. 3. In "Hélène Montgeroult" by Calvert Johnson. In *Women Composers: Music Through the Ages*, vol. 5, edited by Sylvia Glickman and Martha Furman Schleifer. New York: G. K. Hall, 1998. Bryn Mawr, PA: Hildegard Publishing Company, 1998 (G. K. Hall reprint).

Maria Theresia von Paradis

Auf die Damen. In *Lieder and Other Songs by Women Composers of the Classical Era*, vol. 4, edited by Barbara Garvey Jackson and Hidemi Matsushita. Fayetteville, AR: ClarNan, 1997.

Da eben seinen Lauf vollbracht (from *Zwölf Lieder*). In *Lieder by Women Composers of the Classic Era*, vol. 1, edited by Barbara Garvey Jackson. Fayetteville, AR: ClarNan, 1987.

Fantasie pour le pianoforte. In "Maria Theresia von Paradis" by Hidemi Matsushita. In *Women Composers: Music Through the Ages*, vol. 3, edited by Sylvia Glickman and Martha Furman Schleifer. New York: G. K. Hall, 1998; Bryn Mawr, PA: Hildegard Publishing Company, 1998 (G. K. Hall reprint).

Lenore, Ballad for Voice and Piano. Edited by Hidemi Matsushita. Fayetteville, AR: ClarNan, 1989.

Morgenlied eines armen Mannes. In *Historical Anthology of Music by Women*, edited by James R. Briscoe. Bloomington and Indianapolis: Indiana University Press, 1987.

Der Schulkandidat, Overture. Edited by Hidemi Matsushita. Fayetteville, AR: ClarNan, 1992.

String Quartet in D Major. Louisville, KY: Ars Femina, 1991.

Zwölf Lieder auf ihrer Reise in Musik gesetzt: 1784–86. In *Lieder by Women Composers of the Classic Era*, vol. 2, edited by Hidemi Matsushita. Fayetteville, AR: ClarNan, 1989.

Maria Hester Reynolds Park

Concerto for the Piano Forte or Harpsichord in E-flat Major. Edited by Barbara Harbach. Pullman, WA: Vivace Press, 1993. Arranged for solo keyboard.

A Divertimento for the Piano Forte. In "M. H. Park" by Deborah Hayes. In *Women Composers: Music Through the Ages*, vol. 5, edited by Sylvia Glickman and Martha Furman Schleifer New York: G. K. Hall, 1998; Bryn Mawr, PA: Hildegard Publishing Company, 1998 (G. K. Hall reprint).

Six Sonatas for Violin and Keyboard. Edited by Barbara Govatos. Bryn Mawr: Hildegard Publishing Company, 1995.

Sonata I in F Major, op. 4; Sonata in C Major, op. 7. In *Eighteenth Century Women Composers for the Harpsichord or Piano*, vol. 1, edited by Barbara Harbach. Pullman, WA: Vivace Press, 1992.

Sonata II, from *Two Sonatas for the Pianoforte or Harpsichord, op. 4*. In *Four Keyboard Sonatas by Early English Women Composers*, edited by Sally Fortino. Bryn Mawr, PA: Hildegard Publishing Company, 1996.

Sonata op. 13, no. 2. In *Three Marias: Three Eighteenth Century Sonatas*, edited by Susan Eileen Pickett. Bryn Mawr, PA: Hildegard Publishing Company, 1997.

Fanny Krumpholtz Pittar

"Dedans mon petit reduit," Air, Arranged with Variations for the Harp; A Military Divertimento for the Harp or Piano Forte. In "Fanny Krumpholtz Pittar" by Ursula M. Rempel. In *Women Composers: Music Through the Ages*, vol. 3, edited by Sylvia Glickman and Martha Furman Schleifer. New York: G. K. Hall, 1998; Bryn Mawr, PA: Hildegard Publishing Company, 1998 (G. K. Hall reprint).

Mary Ann Wrighten Pownall

Kisses Sued For; Kiss Me Now or Never. In "Mary Ann Wrighten Pownall" by Barbara Garvey Jackson. In *Women Composers: Music Through the Ages*, vol. 4, edited by Sylvia Glickman and Martha Furman Schleifer. New York: G. K. Hall, 1998.

Juliane Benda Reichardt

Claviersonata. In "Juliane Reichardt" by Nancy B. Reich. In *Women Composers: Music Through the Ages*, vol. 3, edited by Sylvia Glickman and Martha Furman Schleifer. New York: G. K. Hall, 1998; Bryn Mawr, PA: Hildegard Publishing Company, 1998 (G. K. Hall reprint).

Liedeines Mädchens; Liebe; An den Mond; Klage bei Hölty's Grabe. In *Lieder and Other Songs by Women Composers of the Classical Era*, vol. 4, edited by Barbara Garvey Jackson and Hidemi Matsushita. Fayetteville, AR: ClarNan, 1997.

Louise Reichardt

Die Blume der Blumen; Genoveva; Hinüber wall'ich. In *Frauen Komponieren: 25 Lieder für Singstimme und Klavier*, edited by Eva Rieger and Käte Walter. Mainz and New York: Schott, 1992.

Dem Herrn; Buss-Lied; Morgenlied; Fürbitte für Sterbende; Weihnachtslied; Tiefe Andacht. In *Sechs geistliche Lieder*, edited by Carolyn Raney. New York: Broude Brothers, 1979.

Frühlingsblumen; Wachtelwacht; Betteley der Voegel; Kaeuzlein; Hier liegt ein Spielmann begraben; Aus Ariels Offenbarungen; Ida; Kriegslied des Mays; Ein recht Gemüth; Unruhiger Schlaf; Nach Sevilla; Für die Laute componirt; Der Spinnerin Nachtlied; Durch den Wald; Duettino; Die Blume der Blumen; Der Sänger geht; Sehnsucht nach dem Vaterlande; Bergmannslied; Er besucht den Klostergarten; An Maria; Frühlingslied; Geistliches Lied; Aus Hymnen an die Nacht; Durch die bunten Rosenhecken; Poesie; Liebe; Aus Genoveva; Erinnrung am Bach; Stille der Andacht; Heimweh; Das Mädchen am Ufer; An den Erlöser; Poesia; Notturno; Poesia; Sei Canzoni di Metastasio. In *Songs*, compiled and with an introduction by Nancy Reich. Women Composer Series 7. New York: Da Capo, 1981.

Hoffnung. In *Fifty-six Songs You Love to Sing*. New York: G. Schirmer, 1937.

In the Time of Roses. In *Fifty-six Famous Songs the World Over*. New York: Remick, 1952.

Schäfers Klaglied. In *Von Goethe inspiriert*, edited by Ann Willison Lemke. Kassel: Furore, 1999.

Unruhiger Schlaf; Des Schäfers Klage; Herbstlied; Der Spinnerin Nachtlied; Se non piange un infelice. In "Louise Reichardt" by Nancy B. Reich. In *Women Composers: Music Through the Ages*, vol. 4, edited by Sylvia Glickman and Martha Furman Schleifer. New York: G. K. Hall, 1998; Reprint as *Five Lieder*. Bryn Mawr, PA: Hildegard Publishing Company, 1998 (G. K. Hall reprint).

Vanne felice rio; Giusto amor. In *A Collection of Art Songs by Women Composers*, edited by Ruth Drucker and Helen Strine. Fulton, MD: HERS, 1988.

Corona Elisabeth Wilhelmine Schröter

Erlkönig; Manchen langen Tag. In *Frauen Komponieren; 25 Lieder für Singstimme und Klavier*, edited by Eva Rieger and Käte Walter. Mainz and New York: Schott, 1992.

Erlkönig; O Mutter, guten Rat mir leiht. In *Von Goethe inspiriert*, edited by Ann Willison Lemke. Kassel: Furore, 1999.

Für Männer uns zu plagen (from *Die Fischerin*); *Das Mädchen am Ufer; An den Abendstern*. In "Corona Schröter" by Annie Janeiro Randall. In *Women Composers: Music Through the Ages*, vol. 4, edited by Sylvia Glickman and Martha Furman Schleifer. New York: G. K. Hall, 1998.

Für Männer uns zu plagen (from *Die Fischerin*); *Das Mädchen am Ufer; An den Abendstern*. In *Three Lieder*. Bryn Mawr, PA: Hildegard Publishing Company, 1998 (G. K. Hall reprint).

Jugendlied; Der Erlkönig (from *Die Fischerin*); *Mutter, guten Rat mir leiht* (from *Die Fischerin*). In *Gedichte von Goethe in Compositionen seiner Zeitgenossen*. Edited by Max Friedlaender. Weimar: Goethe-Gesellschaft, 1896 and 1916. Reprint Hildesheim: Olms, 1975.

Das Mädchen am Ufer; Anmunterung zur Freude; Die Liebe. In *Lieder and Other Songs by Women Composers of the Classical Era*, vol. 4, edited by Barbara Garvey Jackson and Hidemi Matsushita. Fayetteville, AR: ClarNan, 1997.

Die Wachtel; Das Mädchen am Ufer. In *Lieder by Women Composers of the Classical Era*, vol. 1, edited by Barbara Garvey Jackson. Fayetteville, AR: ClarNan, 1987.

Maddalena Lombardini Sirmen

Concerto I for Solo Organ. Edited by Barbara Harbach. Pullman, WA: Vivace Press, 1995.

Concerto I in B-flat Major; Concerto III in A Major; Concerto IV in B-flat Major (1773). In *Three Violin Concertos* [from op. 3], edited by Jane L. Berdes. Recent Researches in Music of the Classical Era 38. Madison, WI: A-R Editions, 1991.

Due terzetti per 2 violini e violoncello obbligato. Edited by Lauro Malusi. Padua: G. Zanibon, 1983.

Duo Sonata, op. 4, no. 1. In *Treasury of Music by Women before 1800: For Viola Ensembles*, edited by William Bauer. Louisville, KY: Editions Ars Femina, 1995.

Six Duos for Two Violins. Edited by Cora Cooper and Karen Clarke. Bryn Mawr, PA: Hildegard Publishing Company, 1994.

Sonatas pour deux violons, op. 4. Louisville, KY: Ars Femina, n.d.

String Quartet in E Major. Louisville, KY: Ars Femina, 1992.

String Quartets I-III. Edited by Sally Didrickson. Bryn Mawr, PA: Hildegard Publishing Company, 2003.

String quartets IV-VI. Edited by Sally Didrickson. Bryn Mawr, PA: Hildegard Publishing Company, 2003.

String Trio. Louisville, KY: Ars Femina, n.d.

Trio Sonatas for Two Violins and Cello Obbligato, op. 1. 2 vols. Edited by Ellen Grolman Schlegel. Bryn Mawr, PA: Hildegard Publishing Company, 1996, 1997.

Trio a due Violini e Basso. In "Maddalena Lombardini Sirmen" by Elsie Arnold and Gloria Eive. In *Women Composers: Music Through the Ages*, vol. 5, edited by Sylvia Glickman and Martha Furman Schleifer. New York: G. K. Hall, 1998.

Maria Agate Wolowska Szymanowska

Caprice sur la Romance de Joconde pour le Pianoforte. Bryn Mawr, PA: Hildegard Publishing Company, 1998 (G. K. Hall reprint).

Character Pieces. Bryn Mawr, PA: Hildegard Publishing Company, 1998 (G. K. Hall reprint).

Contradance in A-flat Major; Menuett in E Major; Polonez in F Minor; Etude in F Major; Etude in D Minor; Etude in C Major; Valse for Three Hands, nos. 1–4. In *Music for Piano*, edited by Sylvia Glickman. Bryn Mawr, PA: Hildegard Publishing Company, 1990.

Divertissement Pour le Pianoforte avec Accompagnement de Violon. Bryn Mawr, PA: Hildegard Publishing Company, 1988 (G. K. Hall reprint).

Divertissement Pour le Pianoforte avec Accompagnement de Violon; Sérénade pour le Pianoforte avec Accompagnement de Violoncelle. In "Maria Szymanowska" by Sarah Hanks Karlowicz. In *Women Composers: Music Through the Ages*, vol. 5, edited by Sylvia Glickman and Martha Furman Schleifer. New York: G. K. Hall, 1998.

Four Anglaises: Nos. 9, 10, 11, and 12. Bryn Mawr, PA: Hildegard Publishing Company, 1998 (G. K. Hall reprint).

Menuet, Polonaise and Trio. Bryn Mawr, PA: Hildegard Publishing Company, 1998 (G. K. Hall reprint).

Nocturne. In *Great Women Composers*, edited by Gail Smith. Pacific, MO: Creative Keyboard Publications, 1996. [CD accompanies the score.]

Nocturne in B-flat Major. In *At the Piano with Women Composers*, edited by Maurice Hinson. 2d ed. Van Nuys, CA: Alfred, 1995.

Nocturne in B-flat Major. In *Frauen Komponieren: 22 Klavierstücke des 18.-20. Jahrhunderts*, edited by Eva Rieger and Käte Walter. Mainz: Schott, 1985.

Nocturne in B-flat Major. In *Historical Anthology of Music by Women*, edited by James R. Briscoe. Bloomington and Indianapolis: Indiana University Press, 1987.

Peine et plaisir; Romance du Saule; Ballade; Romance à la nuit; Le connois-tu; Se spiegar. In "Maria Szymanowska" by Maria Anna Harley. In *Women Composers: Music Through the Ages*, vol. 4, edited by Sylvia Glickman and Martha Furman Schleifer. New York: G. K. Hall, 1998.

Piéc tánców na fortepian [5 dances for piano]. Edited by Regina Smendzianka. Kracow: Polskie Wydawnictwo Muzyczne, [1975].

Polonez in F Minor; Menuet in E Major; Le Murmure, Nocturne; Switezianka; Etude in E Major; Etude in E-flat Major; Etude in D Minor; Etude in E Major; Etude in C Major; Etude in E-flat Major. In *Maria Szymanowska 1789–1831, Album*, compiled by Józef Mirski [Mirscy] and M. Mirska. Kraków: Polskie Wydawnictwo Muzyczne, 1953.

Sérénade pour le Pianoforte avec Accompagnement de Violoncelle. Bryn Mawr, PA: Hildegard Publishing Company, 1988 (G. K. Hall reprint).

Six Romances: Peine et plaisir; Romance du Saule; Ballade; Romance à la nuit; Le connois-tu; Se spiegar. Bryn Mawr, PA: Hildegard Publishing Company, 1998 (G. K. Hall reprint).

Switezianka. In *Mickiewicz w piesni: na glos i fortepian* (Michewicz in Song, for Voice and Piano). Kraków Wydawnictwo Muzyczne, 1998.

Three Etudes from Vingt exercices et préludes pour le pianoforte; Menuet No. 2, from *Six Menuets pour le Pianoforte*; nine dances, from *Dix-huit danses de différent genres pour le piano-forte; Caprice sur la romance de Joconde pour le pianoforte.* In "Maria Szymanowska" by Anne Swartz. In *Women Composers: Music Through the Ages*, vol. 3, edited by Sylvia Glickman and Martha Furman Schleifer. New York: G. K. Hall, 1998.

Three Etudes: No. 6, No. 12, No. 17, from Vingt exercices et préludes pour le pianoforte Bryn Mawr, PA: Hildegard Publishing Company, 1998 (G. K. Hall reprint).

25 Mazurkas. Edited by Irena Poniatowska. Bryn Mawr, PA: Hildegard Publishing Company, 1993.

Valse No. 6, Valse for Three Hands, No. 7, and Valse No. 8. In *Three Valses.* Bryn Mawr, PA: Hildegard Publishing Company, 1998 (G. K. Hall reprint).

Vingt exercices et préludes (Nos. 1, 3, 8, 9, 12–15, 18); Danse polonaise; Dix-huit danses (Polonaise, Anglaises 1–2, Valses 1–3); Six Minuets (nos. 1 and 5); Le murmure; Nocturne; Fantaisie. In *Album per pianoforte*, edited by Maria Szmyd-Dormus. Kraków: Polskie Wydawnictwo Muzyczne, 1990.

Ann Valentine

Monny Musk, Arranged as a Rondo for the Piano Forte. In "Ann Valentine" by Deborah Hayes. In *Women Composers: Music Through the Ages*, vol. 3, edited by Sylvia Glickman and Martha Furman Schleifer. New York: G. K. Hall, 1998.

Ten Sonatas for the Piano Forte or Harpsichord with an Accompaniment for the Violin or German Flute, Op. 1. Edited by Calvert Johnson. Fayetteville, AR: ClarNan, 1994.

Maria Antonia Walpurgis, Electress of Saxony

Excerpts from *Il Trionfo della fedeltà and Talestri.* In *Musik am Sächsischen Hofe*, vol. 3, edited by Otto Schmid. Leipzig: Breitkopf and Härtel, 1919.

Overture IV from Talestri, regina delle amazoni, mvt. I. In "Princess Royal of Saxony, Maria Antonia Walpurgis" by Alyson McLamore. In *Women Composers: Music Through the Ages*, vol. 5, edited by Sylvia Glickman and Martha Furman Schleifer. New York: G. K. Hall, 1998.

Prendi l'ultimo addio, aria for soprano, string quartet, and basso continuo. Amsterdam: Broekmans and Van Poppel, 1977.

Sinfonia from The Queen of the Amazons (1762) for Strings, 2 Oboes, 2 Horns. Louisville, KY: Ars Femina, n.d.

Three Arias from Talestri for soprano and orchestra. Edited by Jill Fankhauser. Fayetteville, AR: ClarNan, forthcoming.

Triumphal March (On Themes from the Queen of the Amazons and the Triumph of Fidelity by Princess Maria Antonia Walpurgis of Saxony). Edited by Quinto Maganini. New York: Edition Musicus, 1962.

Sophia Maria Fritscher Westenholz

Die Erscheinung; Der Bund. In *Lieder by Women Composers of the Classic Era*, vol. 1, edited by Barbara Garvey Jackson. Fayetteville, AR: ClarNan, 1987.

Meine Wünsche; Das Glücke der Liebe; Das Grab; Lied des Liebe; Huldigung; Frühlingsreigen. In *Six Lieder*, edited by Barbara Garvey Jackson. Lieder by Women Composers of the Classical Era, vol. 5. Fayetteville, AR: ClarNan, 2000.

Trost der Hoffnung; Weine nicht es ist vergebens; Morgenlied. In "Sophia Westenholz" by Sharon Guertin Shafer. In *Women Composers: Music Through the Ages*, vol. 4, edited by Sylvia Glickman and Martha Furman Schleifer. New York: G. K. Hall, 1998; Bryn Mawr, PA: Hildegard Publishing Company, 1998 (G. K. Hall reprint).

Emilie Zumsteeg

Morgenfreunde, op. 4, no. 2; Trennung ohne Abschied. In *Frauen Komponieren: 25 Lieder für Singstimme und Klavier*, edited by Eva Rieger and Käte Walter. Mainz and New York: Schott, 1992.

Neun Lieder (without opus number); *Sechs Lieder, op. 5; Lieder, op. 6; Vier Lieder, op. 7; Lieder aus dem Buch ungedruckte Lieder; Einzelne Liedmanuskripte; Duette aus dem Buch ungedruckte Lieder.* In *Lieder und Duette für unterschiedliche Stimmlagen mit Begleitung des Klaviers*, edited by Martina Rebmann. Stuttgart: Carus-Verlag, 1998.

Sechs Lieder mit Begleitung des Pianoforte, op. 4. Mainz: B. Schott's Sohne, 1990.

Sehnsucht der Liebe; Schlafliedchen; Auf hoher Alp wohnt auch der liebe Gott; Ich denke Dein!; Das Epheublättchen. In "Emilie Zumsteeg" by Suzanne Summerville. In *Women Composers: Music Through the Ages*, vol. 4, edited by Sylvia Glickman and Martha Furman Schleifer. New York: G. K. Hall, 1998; Bryn Mawr, PA: Hildegard Publishing Company, 1998 (G. K. Hall reprint).

Songs for Voice and Piano, op. 4; Choral Song on Christmas Eve; Nine Songs for Voice and Piano; Five Songs for Voice with Guitar Accompaniment. Edited by Suzanne Summerville. Fairbanks, AK: Arts Venture, 1997.

5
The Nineteenth Century

E. Douglas Bomberger

Introduction

Persons living in the nineteenth century could rightfully claim that they lived in an era of progress. The century saw an unprecedented number of inventions that changed society radically, including the steam locomotive (1804), photography (1839), telegraph (1844), telephone (1876), phonograph (1877), incandescent light (1879), and the internal combustion engine (1885). The era also witnessed the Industrial Revolution, which modernized production methods and allowed these inventions to be manufactured cheaply and quickly. The notion of progress was fundamental to the important currents of thought in the nineteenth century. This forward-moving process also informed the thinking of Karl Marx, who believed that capitalism was a necessary evil that would eventually give way to the higher system of communism. Charles Darwin presented his theory of evolution in *Origin of Species* (1859) as an inevitable march toward higher life forms chosen through the process of "survival of the fittest."

Likewise in music, progress seemed to be the order of the day; new aesthetic ideals gave rise to new genres, forms, and styles. The Romantic era brought with it a new emphasis on emotion, personal expression, and spontaneity, as the balance and restraint of the Classical era were swept away in favor of passion. The new preference for program music displaced the absolute music that had been the norm in the Classical era. Rather than generic titles, many Romantic composers preferred to give their works descriptive titles that evoked a visual or literary image in the mind of the listener and provided a context for listening. Older genres like the symphony and sonata continued to be used by some composers, but they were challenged by a host of new genres that were less rigid in structure. In piano music, many pieces can be described generally as "character pieces," a term denoting a category of relatively short pieces with more or less evocative titles (nocturne, impromptu, intermezzo, song without words, etc.) or very specific programmatic titles, as in most of the piano works of Robert Schumann (1810–1856). In orchestral music, the overture was favored over the symphony or the suite, and the symphonic poem (a single-movement work with programmatic content) enjoyed widespread currency after 1850. Opera continued unabated, while chamber music went into serious decline along with the aristocratic patrons who had supported it in the eighteenth century. The solo art song with piano accompaniment, especially the German lied and French *mélodie*, enjoyed continued popularity.

Music benefited from technological progress as much as any sector of society. In the early nineteenth century, mechanical innovations produced improved brass and woodwind instruments, bringing them closer to string instrument flexibility and reliability. The second quarter of the century saw the development of the modern piano, as innovations such as the double-escapement action (Sébastien Erard, 1821), the iron frame (Alpheus Babcock, 1825), cross-stringing (Henri Pape, late 1820s, applied to the grand piano by Henry Steinway, 1859), and felt hammers (Pape, ca. 1830) turned the instrument into one of unprecedented power, speed, and responsiveness. The incorporation of new production techniques made the piano affordable for middle-class families and coincided with a boom in amateur music making. The invention of lithography (1798) and a process to produce paper from wood pulp (1863) laid the groundwork for a golden age in music publishing in the late nineteenth century that supported amateur music making as much as the affordable piano did.

The era also saw a surge of activism for women's rights. The Seneca Falls Convention of 1848 brought attention to the inequities that women suffered, and the second half of the century witnessed a steady crescendo of activity leading toward woman suffrage. New timesaving devices produced by the Industrial Revolution freed nineteenth-century women from many of the menial tasks that had occupied their female ancestors, while educational levels among women rose throughout the century. Woman suffrage after World War I became a reality because of the efforts of nineteenth-century activists, including Lucretia Mott, Elizabeth Cady Stanton, Lucy Stone, and Susan B. Anthony.

In the realm of music, women of the nineteenth century found expanding opportunities, which translated into increased visibility for women musicians. The age of the traveling virtuoso produced a small, but significant, number of female instrumental performers. In the mid-nineteenth century, pianists Clara Wieck Schumann and Marie Pleyel established new precedents for professional performers. They were followed in the second half of the century by Sophie Menter, Annette Essipoff, Teresa Carreño, Julie Rivé-King, Dory Petersen, Fannie Bloomfield Zeisler, Adele Aus der Ohe, and numerous less-famous pianists. Female violinists were a rarity in the nineteenth century, in large part because the instrument was still considered unladylike, but concert artists like the Italian sisters Teresa and Marie Milanollo and the American Maud Powell helped to pave the way for today's women violinists.

The new discipline of musicology, a field that was dominated mostly by German men, developed in this century. Despite the almost total exclusion of women, some female writers found a niche in the musicological world. Both Lina Ramann (1833–1912) and Marie Lipsius (who published under the pseudonym La Mara) received encouragement from Franz Liszt (1811–1886) and established their reputations with studies of this musician, then neglected by mainstream musicologists. Octavia Hensel (Mary Alice Ives Seymour) established herself with a biography of a similarly marginalized American composer, Louis Moreau Gottschalk (1829–1869), while Elise Polko wrote popular essays and books mixing musical fact and fiction. Other noteworthy female musicologists were Florence May and Marie Bobillier (who published under the pseudonym Michel Brenet).

George P. Upton's *Woman in Music* (1880), one of the first scholarly studies on women in music, is significant for discussing women only as performers and as muses to great men without ever mentioning women as composers. Two years later La Mara published an extensive study of twenty-four contemporary female musicians as volume five of her series *Musikalische Studienköpfe* (1882). Alfred Michaelis' *Frauen als schaffende Tonkünstler: ein biographisches Lexicon* (1888) contains separate entries for 147 women composers and a list of dozens of other names in an appendix. Otto Ebel's more extensive *Women Composers: A Biographical Handbook of Woman's Work in Music* appeared in 1902, and Arthur Elson's *Woman's Work in Music* was published a year later.

A primary factor in the expansion of musical opportunities for women was the growing number of conservatories in Europe and America. The Conservatoire National in Paris, founded in 1795, was the leader in musical education in France, accepting both men and (admittedly few) women from the beginning of its history. Conservatories were also founded in Würzburg (1804), Prague (1811), Graz (1815), Vienna (1817), Innsbruck (1818), and Brussels (1832), but the Leipzig Conservatory, founded by Felix Mendelssohn in 1843, provided the impetus for an unprecedented boom in schools for advanced musical training. Schools of music "sprouted like mushrooms" (Hugo Riemann's description) throughout Central Europe and, after the Civil War, in the United States as well. In many cases, American conservatories were modeled after specific European schools; thus, the Cincinnati Conservatory based its curriculum on that of the Stuttgart Conservatory, while the Oberlin Conservatory, founded by a graduate of the Leipzig Conservatory, was organized according to that model. Mendelssohn's goal of balancing practical musicianship with theoretical training in harmony, counterpoint, and history was the noble goal toward which these imitators aspired, despite a marked tendency to evolve into "virtuoso factories."

Among Mendelssohn's many innovations was the idea of equal (albeit separate) opportunities for female students. Although the world of professional music was almost exclusively male, the conservatories now offered women the chance to develop comparable skills by studying with many of the same teachers in segregated classes. During the first fifty years of the Leipzig Conservatory's existence (1843–1893), 45.7 percent of those admitted were women. Ethel Smyth, Helen Hopekirk, and other women studied composition at the conservatory with Carl Reinecke (1824–1910) and Salomon Jadassohn (1831–1902), though, as we shall see, these teachers received mixed reviews from their students. At many other conservatories, women students were actually in the majority. At the Hoch Conservatory in Frankfurt, founded in 1878 with Joachim Raff as director, 69.3 percent of the enrollees in the first ten years were women. Upon graduation these musicians faced limited opportunities in the professional realm, but their numbers caused a dramatic shift in the teaching profession, as female private teachers outnumbered men by the early years of the twentieth century.

In practice, women were initially forbidden to study such traditionally male subjects as composition and orchestration, but by the end of the century these strictures had been loosened at Leipzig and elsewhere. The changes were effected by a number of influential men who insisted that women deserved to study composition. The famous theorist Adolph Bernhard Marx (1795–1866) offered composition classes for women at the Berlin Conservatory in the early 1850s, justifying his position in an 1857 article in the *Berliner Musik-Zeitung Echo*, published after his resignation from the conservatory. His argument rested on his conviction that composition training was not merely for professional composers but was the best possible training for general musical understanding:

> Any man who wants to be a musician...will not neglect composition lessons; he would not be able to cope with his job, would not find himself satisfied with his artistic honor and securely placed, if he did not obtain the highest and securest training, the surest and overall most satisfactory elucidation for understanding, comprehension, and representation. With what right therefore do we deny to the other sex what is for us such a supremely venerable educational medium? (Quoted in Bomberger 1998)

A second prominent teacher who admitted women to his classes was Joachim Raff (1822–1882), director of the Hoch Conservatory in Frankfurt from its founding in 1879 to his death three years later. In his daughter Helene's biography, she described this as unusual for the time:

> Although he originally came from a circle where the women enjoyed minimal education and correspondingly little respect, the experience of his life had made him a champion of women. He advocated above all the view that any thinking being must be given the opportunity for development of her capabilities. "Let the people come!"—he admonished—"Oppress no one! Make no martyrs! Empty things and people will dispose of themselves." (Raff 1925)

The statements of Marx and Raff, along with the availability of composition classes for women at Frankfurt, Leipzig, and a few other conservatories, belie the general societal prejudice against the notion of women composers. For those who bothered to address this issue, the reason given for the lack of prominent female composers was a perceived difference in modes of thinking. Thus, for most nineteenth-century critics, women were seen as being incapable of the sort of abstract thought necessary to construct a large-scale composition. Although women were accepted as writers of songs (e.g., Carrie Jacobs-Bond and Lili`uokalani) and short piano works (e.g., Cécile Chaminade and Amy Beach), the notion of a woman composing large-scale works was more difficult for nineteenth-century audiences and critics to swallow. Nonetheless, by the 1890s, composers like Smyth, Beach, and Margaret Ruthven Lang were beginning to find performance opportunities for their orchestral works, an indication that nineteenth-century progress, though grudging, was also evident in the world of women's music.

The following biographies are arranged in groups by geography and topic rather than strictly by chronology, begining with Fanny Mendelssohn Hensel and Clara Schumann, two German contemporaries whose respective social stations determined their very different paths in life. Next, German composers from the midcentury are discussed: Johanna Kinkel, Josephine Lang, Emilie Mayer, Ingeborg von Bronsart, and Luise Adolpha Le Beau. French composers Louise Farrenc, Augusta Holmès, and Cécile Chaminade are considered next. The following composers were best known as piano virtuosos: Clara Kathleen Rogers, Marie Jaëll, Teresa Carreño, Helen Hopekirk, Sophie Menter, and Mary Wurm. Turning to England, the lives and works of Elizabeth Stirling and Ethel Smyth are examined. Two prolific songwriters, Liliʻuokalani and Carrie Jacobs-Bond are profiled before concluding with a group of Americans: Helen Hood, Eleanor Everest Freer, Amy Beach, Margaret Ruthven Lang, and Mabel Wheeler Daniels.

Two German Contemporaries

Fanny Hensel and Clara Schumann have been elevated to the status of cultural icons in Germany during the past several decades. Each was featured on a postage stamp in the 1980s, and a dreamy picture of the young Schumann graced the front of a currency bill until the advent of the Euro in 2002. Both women were accomplished musicians who were closely associated with famous early Romantic composers, but the similarity between them ends there. As commentators from their own day to ours have repeatedly stressed, these two composers followed very different career paths, largely because of the social conventions of nineteenth-century Germany.

Fanny Hensel (1805–1847 [née Fanny Caecilie Mendelssohn]) was born to wealth and privilege. The granddaughter of the famous Jewish Enlightenment philosopher Moses Mendelssohn and the daughter of Abraham Mendelssohn, a wealthy banker, she and her siblings enjoyed the best upbringing that money could buy. Prominent scholars and musicians gave them private instruction in their Berlin home, and they were challenged to work hard in order to develop their skills and intellect. Fanny and her three-and-one-half-year-younger brother Felix (1809–1847) were especially close, and it became evident that they shared an uncommon gift for music. Their respective gifts were cultivated through games and competition, as they alternately collaborated and tried to outdo one another in their chosen field. Each mastered the piano and began composing at a young age, dazzling family and friends. Their younger sister Rebekka later recalled what this meant for the family: "My older siblings stole my artistic fame. In any other family, I would have been much praised as a musician and perhaps even have directed a small circle. But next to Felix and Fanny, I could not have succeeded in attaining any such recognition" (Reich 1991).

Fanny Mendelssohn Hensel with her brother Felix Mendelssohn.
© Bettmann/CORBIS.

The family's attitude toward women was shaped both by the German bourgeois culture of the day and by their own special desire to fit in as acculturated Jews in a Protestant world. For Fanny and Felix, it meant that they could receive nearly equal training as children (although she was not allowed to study string instruments), but she was forbidden to pursue a public career. There is every indication that her musical gifts were as profound as his. However, she is known to have performed in public only once (at an 1838 charity benefit concert), and she did not publish her own works until the last year of her life. For a family like the Mendelssohns in early nineteenth-century Germany, a daughter's public activities in a sphere reserved for men could prove to be an acute embarrassment. Therefore, Fanny maintained a brilliant salon in her home, performing frequently with Berlin's best musicians, but she did not step outside the limits of acceptable female activity.

In 1829 Fanny (hereafter, Hensel) married Wilhelm Hensel, a painter at the Prussian court. He had a much more liberal attitude toward her musical career than did her father and brother, and at his urging she finally relented and published a few of her lieder and piano pieces in 1846. This new path was cut short almost as soon as it began, for she died unexpectedly from a stroke on May 14, 1847. Her brother's grief prompted him to publish several collections of her music posthumously, but his death, within six

Fanny Hensel.
The Granger Collection, New York.

months on November 4, 1847, left the vast majority of her works unpublished. These remained in the possession of the family for generations; many are now housed at the Preussicher Kulturbesitz (Berlin State Library—Prussian Cultural Heritage) and have recently become available to scholars.

Hensel's some 500 works cover a wide range of genres, dominated by lieder and piano pieces that demonstrate a facility at the piano and a familiarity with effective vocal writing, very similar to that of her brother. Her harmonic language, however, tends to be a bit more advanced than his. While Felix may be viewed as a conservative Romantic composer, Hensel's works show an adventurous attitude toward modulation and dissonance. Of the piano works, the most remarkable is a cycle of thirteen pieces entitled *Das Jahr*, a musical diary of a trip that the Hensels took to Italy in 1839–1840. This year was a high point in her life, as the escape from oppressive German restrictions provided freedom and artistic stimulation among a group of French musicians and painters in Rome. The cycle includes one short character piece for each of the twelve months of the year, ending with a setting of the traditional Protestant New Year's chorale, "Das alte Jahr vergangen ist."

Other principal areas of composition for Hensel were those that she presented in her salons: choral and chamber works. These include an oratorio, several cantatas, and a number of four-part choral works. Among her chamber works, the *Piano Trio*, op. 11 has been performed the most in recent years.

If **Clara Schumann** (1819–1896 [née Wieck]) faced restrictions in her creative activity, they were at first the result of being married to another musician and then to a self-imposed moratorium on composition after his death. Clara faced no parental opposition to her professional aspirations; in fact, her ambitious father destined her for a life in professional music before she was old enough to decide for herself.

Friedrich Wieck (1785–1873) was one of Germany's preeminent piano pedagogues, guiding the progress of an unusual number of important musicians, including Hans von Bülow (1830–1894) and Robert Schumann (1810–1856). His main attentions, though, were reserved for his son Alwin Wieck (1821–1885) and his daughters Clara and **Marie Wieck** (1832–1916). His methods were barbaric by twentieth-century standards: Schumann reported seeing Friedrich physically assault the young Alwin for playing poorly, while Clara's diaries show that she was subjected to psychological humiliation when her father felt that she was not doing her best. As adults, the children all earned respectable positions in music. Alwin played the violin in an orchestra in St. Petersburg and later taught piano in Dresden, publishing several books on his father's pedagogical principles. Marie appeared at one of her older sister's concerts at the age of eleven and was appointed court pianist to the prince of Hohenzollern in 1858. She taught in Dresden for most of her life and published lieder and piano compositions.

The star of the Wieck household was Clara, who was groomed from an early age for the career of concert pianist. In addition to cultivating her impeccable technique and musicianship, her father taught her the business side of a career by having her copy all his letters and accounts. She played at the prestigious Leipzig Gewandhaus at age nine, making her formal debut at eleven. She toured Germany and played in Paris during the year after her debut and continued to achieve success with concerts and tours throughout her teenage years. She took Vienna by storm at age eighteen, conquering the hearts of music lovers there as few of her male competitors ever had. In short, she fulfilled every ambition of her father's in establishing an unprecedented career as a female virtuoso.

Like all children, however, she eventually rebelled against her father's control. As a young teenager she had already begun to show the signs of willfulness that culminated in her love affair with Robert Schumann. Wieck was incensed at what he perceived as an inappropriate match, and indeed it is easy to understand his fear of losing his talented (and profitable) child to a poor and practically unknown composer and music critic. After an infamous court battle in 1840, the two received official permission to marry without her father's consent. The early years of their marriage were blissfully happy. They kept a joint marriage diary to express their feelings, settled into a domes-

Clara Schumann.

tic routine, and eventually produced eight children. They shared not only their home life but also their music—talking about musical ideas and working on projects together, for instance, their contrapuntal studies of 1845.

For Clara (hereafter, Schumann), the happiness of marriage was tempered by frustration. Her performances were scaled back despite the resulting loss of income, and her practice time was limited to hours when Robert would not be bothered. More serious were Robert's growing mental problems. A victim of bipolar disorder, his life consisted of increasingly manic highs followed by ever-deeper lows. In 1854 he attempted suicide and was committed to an asylum where he died in 1856. She was left with sole responsibility for their seven surviving children.

Schumann responded to this crisis by rekindling her performing career. Audiences soon re-embraced the beloved artist, and she continued to perform until 1891. She played at the Gewandhaus more times than any piano soloist of her era and made nineteen tours of the British Isles. Her concerts were characterized by a seriousness that led to her being described as a "priestess" of the piano. Biographer Nancy B. Reich has shown that her choice of repertoire (i.e., Beethoven piano sonatas) influenced the future direction of piano recitals by focusing attention on the composer as creator rather than the performer as virtuoso. Her playing was noteworthy for fidelity to the score and intelligent expression of the composer's intentions. In addition to playing works by Beethoven (1770–1827), Frédéric Chopin (1810–1849), Mendelssohn, and other older composers, she introduced the works of her husband to a sometimes-reluctant public through countless performances and the publication of a complete edition of his works.

In 1878 Schumann was appointed professor of piano at the newly founded Hoch Conservatory in Frankfurt. Director Joachim Raff, well known for his attempts to mediate between the progressive and conservative tendencies in late-nineteenth-century German music in his own compositions, hired a mix of teachers from both camps. Schumann's close ties to her half brother Woldemar Bargiel (1828–1897) and the composer Johannes Brahms (1833–1897) definitely placed her in the latter category, and the political atmosphere in this faculty was at times volatile. She attracted students from around the world and became known as one of Europe's leading teachers. The demand for her services was so great that she was able to establish a family tradition by hiring her daughters Marie and Eugenie as assistant teachers.

Schumann's activities as a composer were overshadowed both by her husband's composing career and by her own renown as a performer and teacher. Like many virtuosos of her day, she composed piano pieces for her own concerts, the first of which was a set of four polonaises dating from 1829 to 1830. Her compositions from the 1830s are in conventional forms, designed to demonstrate her own pianistic strengths more than her compositional inventiveness. She wrote a piano concerto in 1833–1835 for her own use as well. With marriage, she discovered new directions for her compositions, first in the area of lieder. She and Robert published a set of twelve songs together (his op. 37 and her op. 12), of which only a handwritten note in his copy of the score identifies hers, and she followed these with nearly fifty additional songs in the years afterward. She also produced a masterful *Piano Trio* in G minor, op. 17, in 1846, whose pathos reflects the stressful circumstances of her life at this time.

One of her most moving works is the set of variations on a theme of Robert Schumann, op. 20. She presented them to him on the last birthday that he would spend with his family, with the inscription, "To my beloved husband on June 8, 1853, this weak attempt once more from his old Clara." The variations are intricately constructed, employing canon and other contrapuntal devices, imaginative keyboard textures, and poignant melodies. The young Brahms also wrote a set of variations on the same theme that is more famous but in no way superior to Clara's.

After Robert's death, Clara stopped composing. Though she was known for her improvisations (several of which were written down late in her life), the only true composition from her last forty years was a march written for the 1879 wedding anniversary of some friends. Reich notes that she felt ambivalent about her own compositions, despite encouragement from her husband, and indeed the description of one of her best works as a "weak attempt" reflects this insecurity. An 1839 diary entry sums up her attitude toward composition: "I once thought that I possessed creative talent, but I have given up this idea; a woman must not desire to compose—not one has been able to do it, and why should I expect to? It would be arrogance, although, indeed, my father led me into it in earlier days" (Quoted in Reich 2001).

These brief descriptions of Schumann and Hensel demonstrate the social restrictions of the age. On the one hand, Hensel was kept from performing publicly and achieving her full potential because of middle-class expectations of a woman's role. However, in the privacy of her privileged home she enjoyed the leisure necessary to produce 500 compositions. Schumann was pushed into performance by her father, who helped her to reach professional heights never before attained by a woman and the envy of her male counterparts. But her familiarity with the competitive world of professional music made her all too conscious of the pitfalls that awaited an aspiring composer, while her rigorous practice schedule and the demands of domestic life left little time or solitude for the creative work of composing. Germany was still a very restrictive place for female musicians, and Hensel and Schumann were not alone in facing its challenges. Following are some female German composers who were lesser-known contemporaries.

Midcentury German Women

Johanna Kinkel (1810–1858 [Matthieux, née Mockel]), equally well known as musician and revolutionary, endured a turbulent personal life while balancing music and political activism. Johanna Mockel was born in Bonn, Germany, the daughter of a teacher at the local French lycée. Her early studies in music were with Franz Anton Ries (1775–1846), a childhood friend of Beethoven. In 1829 Ries entrusted her with the leadership of the Musikalische Liebhabergesellschaft, an amateur society. Johanna married book dealer Paul Matthieux in 1832 but left him after six months because of abuse. From 1836 to 1839 she lived in Berlin, where she studied composition with Carl Böhmer (1799–1884) and piano with Wilhelm Taubert (1811–1891). Matthieux (later, Kinkel) attracted the attention of Felix Mendelssohn and Robert Schumann with her lieder and stage works. Returning to Bonn in 1839, she resumed her earlier directorship of the Musikalische Liebhabergesellschaft and, together with theologian Gottfried Kinkel, founded a literary society, the Maikäferbund (Ladybug Society), in 1840. She married him in 1843 after converting to Protestantism. They had four children within the first six years of their marriage, during which time she balanced music teaching with increasing political activism. Gottfried was arrested and sentenced to life in prison in 1849 for his part in the failed revolutions, leaving her the sole support of their family. She engineered his escape from Berlin's Spandau Prison in November 1850 with the help of her friend Carl Schurz, after which the family fled to London. Shortly thereafter the zealous Gottfried traveled to America to raise funds for German revolutionaries, again leaving Johanna to support the family alone. By this time she had abandoned composition, finding that, in the words of Eva Weissweiler, "after a political catastrophe, composition was simply no longer possible" (Weissweiler 1981). The last years of her life were devoted to music teaching and advocacy of women's rights. She fell to her death from a window in her home on November 15, 1858.

Though not an exceptionally prolific composer, Kinkel has captivated the interest of recent German feminist writers because of her intense involvement with political issues of her day. The most significant of her compositions are the stage works—among them several operettas, *Die Landpartie* (The Picnic), *Die Assassinen* (The Assassins), and *Otto der Schütz* (Otto the Archer), and the choral works (including a *Vogelkantate* [bird cantata]) written for the Liebhabergesellschaft. She also wrote a significant number of lieder, including songs on revolutionary texts. Her *Acht Briefe an eine Freundin über das Clavierunterricht* (Eight Letters to a Female Friend on Piano Teaching, Stuttgart, 1852) elaborated her views on musical instruction for women.

In his 1888 biographical dictionary of women composers, Alfred Michaelis thought so highly of the music of **Josephine Lang (1815–1880)** that her entry is by far the longest. The introduction to it is nothing short of effusive:

> Lang, Josefine, born 14 March 1815 in Munich, died 2 December 1880 in Tübingen, was a genial song and piano composer of a highly poetic nature, who in this capacity deserves a place of honor among German women and is worthy of being known throughout the entire artistic-minded circles of our Fatherland. She was such an unusually situated and, because of her life's circumstances, was such an original artistic appearance, that we would search in vain for a counterpart in artistic history. No noble-minded person will read the life story of this noble, truly German woman without emotion, sympathy, enthusiasm, and admiration. In difficult buffets of fate, J.L. constantly proved herself to be a quiet, devout sufferer who always lifted herself up to the sublime muse, sought comfort here, and always found peace again after the rough storms of life. The holy gleam in her soul of a melodic source that never ran dry remained for her a true lodestar from the cradle to the grave. (Michaelis 1888)

Such praise reflects the author's view of ideal German womanhood as much as his admiration for his subject's musicianship, but he is one of many commentators who believe that Lang deserves a place beside her more famous contemporaries Schumann and Hensel.

Lang had the advantages of a very musical family. Her father, Theobald Lang, was a violinist in the court orchestra at Munich; her mother, Regina Hitzenberger, had been a singer with the court opera. Josephine began piano lessons at the age of five, and by eleven she was sufficiently proficient to make her debut in one of the Museum Concerts in Munich. In 1830 she met Felix Mendelssohn, who gave her lessons in composition during his visits to Munich. He wrote in glowing terms of her talent: "She is one of the sweetest creatures I ever saw…she has the gift for composing songs and singing them in a way I never heard before, causing me the most unalloyed musical delight I have ever experienced" (Mendelssohn *Letters*, 1945). Marcia J. Citron states that Mendelssohn urged her to study in Berlin, but her father decided against it. In 1835 she joined the court chapel as a singer, and in 1840 she was rewarded with the title of "Königliche

Hofsängerin" (Royal Court Singer). She continued to compose and was praised by Schumann as well as by Mendelssohn. In 1842 she married Christian Reinhold Köstlin, whose appointment as professor of jurisprudence at the University of Tübingen took her away from her hometown; the birth of six children limited her musical activities considerably. Upon his death in 1856, she returned to music to support her family. In addition to giving piano and voice lessons, she renewed her creative activities and looked for publishers for her earlier songs. She was eventually able to arrange for some publications with the help of Mendelssohn's friend Ferdinand Hiller (1811–1885). Breitkopf & Härtel published a posthumous collection of forty lieder in 1882.

Although Lang left a number of unpublished works for piano that found their way into print after her death, the most important part of her output consists of about 150 lieder. These reflect her personality closely; as she stated, "these Lieder are my diary." (Quoted in Michaelis 1888) Her contemporaries admired the quality of these songs. Schumann praised *Das Traumbild*, op. 28, no 1, in an 1837 review in the *Neue Zeitschrift für Musik*. Hiller wrote of her music that "it is sincere music, and its sincerity arises from a noble soul" (Quoted in Michaelis 1888).

Emilie Mayer (1821–1883) has been called "the most prolific German woman composer of the Romantic period" (Sadie, 1994), with compositions in nearly every genre of nineteenth-century music. However, the combination of a dearth of publications during her lifetime and a lack of performances after her death has left her voluminous legacy virtually unknown.

Mayer was born in Friedland, Mecklenburg, and began her early studies there with an organist by the name of Driver (n.d.). She later studied with the well-known song composer Carl Löwe (1796–1869) in Stettin before moving to Berlin in 1847. She found supportive teachers among Berlin's musical leaders, including Adolph Bernhard Marx for fugue and double counterpoint and Friedrich Wilhelm Wieprecht (1802–1872) for orchestration. Her first publication, *Three Songs*, op. 7, dates from 1849. She presented the first concert of her works to an invited audience in 1850, following this with numerous public and private concerts in the years after. In his *Dictionary of Musicians in Berlin*, Carl Ledebur noted that Mayer's works were also performed by other artists, including the Zimmermann Quartet and the Liebig Orchestra (which performed her *Symphony* in B minor at least eight times), and further summarized the reception of her works: "The unusual instance of a lady attempting the most difficult and lofty type of instrumental composition would have been sufficient to awaken interest in the music-loving public; the interest grew even more as her works were continually received with success on repeated hearings" (Ledebuhr 1861). She made successful tours to Vienna and Munich, and the 1855 performances in the latter city of an overture, a quintet, and a trio earned her the title of Honorary Member of the Philharmonic Society. Her successes continued in later life, the most important being the 1880 publication of her *Faust Overture*.

In addition to her musical activities, Mayer devoted considerable energy to creating sculptures out of white bread. These unusual pieces were widely acclaimed; the queen of Prussia gave her a gold medal for one of them, while the king of Saxony put another in his royal museum.

Mayer was extremely prolific, producing six symphonies, four overtures, a piano concerto, a *Singspiel* (*Die Fischerin* [The Fisherwoman], on a text by Goethe), nine violin sonatas, thirteen cello sonatas, seven string quartets, three string quintets, eleven piano trios, two piano quartets, numerous solo piano works, and approximately 200 songs for solo voice or vocal quartet. Most of these works remained unpublished at her death; the Preussicher Kulturbesitz in Berlin holds her musical manuscripts. Her early style has been described as Classical, after the pattern of W. A. Mozart (1756–1791) and Josef Haydn (1732–1809), while her later works are more akin to those of Mendelssohn and the early Romantics.

Ingeborg von Bronsart (1840–1913) was talented as both a pianist and a composer. Although her marriage cut short her career as a traveling virtuoso, it allowed her to devote more time to composition and assured her of lasting posterity. Ingeborg Starck was born in St. Petersburg, Russia, to Swedish parents. Her talents were recognized early and developed by studies with N. von Martinoff (n.d.), Constantin Decker (1810–1878), and Adolf Henselt (1814–1889) in her hometown. She made her debut as a pianist at age twelve and two years later performed Chopin's *Piano Concerto* in E minor in public by memory (an unusual feat at this time, as most pianists performed with scores).

In 1858 she traveled to Weimar, Germany, to apply for lessons with Franz Liszt. Otto Ebel relates that she surprised the experienced teacher on her first visit:

> By advice of Henselt, she journeyed to Weimar to become a pupil of Liszt. In offering her letters of introduction, she also submitted several of her compositions. Liszt, in looking them over, was somewhat skeptical as to their being all her own work, and to test her ability dictated to her the theme of a fugue. Ingeborg finished the same on the spot; and Liszt, after looking over the work, was highly pleased and jocularly remarked, "You do not look like it!" Ingeborg smilingly answered, "Well, I am glad I do not look like a Fugue." Such progress was made under Liszt's tuition that she was soon considered one of his most talented and favorite pupils. (Ebel 1902)

While in Weimar, she fell in love with one of her fellow students, Hans von Bronsart (1830–1913); they married in 1861. She had been touring successfully as a pianist since 1858 and continued her tours until 1867, when Hans took a position as director of the court theater in Hannover. At this point she discontinued her performing career and concentrated instead on composition. The couple stayed in Hannover for twenty years and returned to Weimar in 1867, where he served as director of the court theater until 1895. They retired to Munich in that year and died within a few months of each other in 1913.

Ingeborg von Bronsart's music covers a wide range of genres. Her early compositions were primarily solo piano works and a piano concerto (1863) for her own use. She later added a substantial number of chamber and vocal pieces. Her *Kaiser-Wilhelm-Marsch*, written during the patriotic year of 1871, was performed as part of the opening ceremony of the Women's Exhibit at the World's Columbian Exposition in Chicago in 1893. Despite these works, her fame among her contemporaries was primarily the result of her operatic works. *Jery und Bätely*, based on a libretto by Goethe, was premiered in Weimar in 1873. A *singspiel*, it enjoyed enviable popularity in the following years and was performed in theaters throughout Germany. Her opera *Hiarne* was successfully premiered in Berlin (1891) before an audience that included the kaiser. She continued to compose after her retirement to Munich, introducing the tragic opera *Die Sühne* (The Atonement) in Dessau (1909). An earlier opera, *Die Göttin von Sais* (The Goddess of Sais) was produced in Berlin (1867) but is now believed to be lost.

While the premise of this chapter is that the nineteenth century was generally an era of progress for women composers, the career of **Luise Adolpha Le Beau (1850–1927)** demonstrates that this progress was by no means universal. She earned widespread respect for her compositions from critics and musicians alike, but the discouragement that she faced throughout her career left her bitter and disappointed at the societal opposition to women composers in late-nineteenth-century Germany.

Le Beau was born in Rastatt and grew up in nearby Karlsruhe. Her parents encouraged her talent and interest in music, and she made her piano debut as soloist in the Mendelssohn *Piano Concerto* in G minor with the Baden Hofkapelle (court orchestra) at age eighteen. During the summer of 1873, she studied briefly with Clara Schumann and met Hans von Bülow, who encouraged her to study with Joseph Gabriel Rheinberger (1839–1901) in Munich. Well on his way to becoming one of Germany's most successful teachers of composition, Rheinberger boasted such students as Engelbert Humperdinck (1854–1921) and the Americans George Whitefield Chadwick (1854–1931) and Horatio Parker (1863–1919). He was so impressed by Le Beau's *Violin Sonata*, op. 10, that he broke two of his own rules: never to give private lessons and never to teach women. Le Beau recalled in her memoirs, published in 1910, "Professor Rheinberger often looked over my compositions; he found my violin sonata, op. 10, 'manly, not like one composed by a woman' and declared himself now ready to take me as a student, which was a great exception, since he never gave lessons to women" (Le Beau 1910). Accompanied by her recently retired father and mother, Le Beau lived in Munich from 1874 to 1885, continuing her studies with Rheinberger and earning a reputation through her publications and performances. Of particular note was first prize in an international composition contest held in Hamburg in 1882. The judges chose her *Four Pieces for Cello and Piano*, op. 24, in the anonymous competition and were surprised to learn that the winner was a woman.

After several years in Munich, Le Beau began to experience conflicts with Rheinberger and his wife that eventually led to the discontinuation of her lessons in 1880. In 1878 she had published an article in the *Allgemeine deutsche Musik-Zeitung* advocating increased educational opportunities for female musicians, in rebuttal of an earlier article by Eugen Lüning that claimed that female music students needed to be restricted because they were making too much headway in relation to their male counterparts. Possibly in response to her activism, Rheinberger called her a "liberated woman," and the two eventually became estranged, although she persisted in believing that it was because of her successes and his wife's jealousy.

Le Beau believed that opposition to her music in Munich was limiting her opportunities there; consequently, she moved first to Wiesbaden (where she lived from 1885 to 1890), then to Berlin (1890–1893), and finally to Baden-Baden, where she stayed until her death in 1927. Her memoirs chronicle the disappointments that she experienced in each place. In Wiesbaden, she was effectively shut out of local concert life when the management of the local theater orchestra changed hands in 1886. In Berlin she was considered for an honorific title but was denied because she was a woman. Repeated attempts to stage her opera *Hadumoth* in that city were unsuccessful; it finally received its premiere in Baden-Baden in 1894. Although she enjoyed the patronage of the grand duchess of Baden, she had difficulties arranging performances of her works there as well, especially of her second opera, *Der verzauberte Kalif* (The Enchanted Caliph). With each rebuff, she and her family became more embittered, and she responded by turning down even those opportunities that did come her way.

Le Beau's musical language was firmly established by the time she came to Rheinberger. As noted, he admired her "manly" style and helped her hone logical and classically oriented structural skills. Because her style did not incorporate the influences of Richard Wagner (1813–1883) that dominated late-nineteenth-century music, her works were somewhat dated by the 1890s. Nonetheless, Ebel wrote in 1902, "Lebeau [*sic*] is without doubt one of the most talented of female composers living. Her works, although not exceeding op. 40, show such sterling merit and great originality…that she must be accorded a place at the head of living women composers" (Ebel 1902). He believed that her chamber works were the most important part of her oeuvre. In addition to the violin sonata and the four pieces for cello, her works list includes two string quartets, a piano quartet, a piano trio, a cello sonata, a second violin sonata, and a number of smaller works for chamber combinations. In the larger genres, Le Beau wrote an oratorio, *Ruth*, op. 27, a *Concert Overture*, op. 23, a *Fantasy* for piano and orchestra, op. 25, a piano concerto, op. 37, a symphony, op. 41, and a symphonic poem, *Hohenbaden*, op. 43. The eminent Viennese critic Eduard Hanslick (1825–1904) was particularly complimentary of her choral works, and her opera *Hadumoth* was successfully mounted in Konstanz and Pforzheim, as well as in Baden-Baden. Perhaps more than any other composer of her era, Le Beau raises important issues of societal expectations and stereotypes regarding female composers. These issues permeate her own memoirs and are discussed at length by Judith E. Olson in a chapter on the composer in *Women Making Music*, edited by Jane Bowers and Judith Tick.

France

Turning to France, the careers of the following three composers, whose combined life spans cover nearly a century and a half, illustrate the highly centralized musical culture in that country. All three were closely related to the Conservatoire National, either as students or as teachers, and all made their careers in and around Paris. This pattern is repeated later in the chapter in the discussion of Marie Jaëll.

A birth relative or husband who advanced their careers aided a number of the women discussed throughout this book. **Louise Farrenc [née Dumont] (1804–1875)** had the good fortune to marry a music publisher who not only printed many of her own compositions but inspired a love of scholarship that resulted in a seminal edition of early keyboard works.

Farrenc came from a long line of visual artists, including both men and women who served the royal family of France. She showed early talent as a pianist and developed her skills through lessons with Ignaz Moscheles (1794–1870) and Johann Nepomuk Hummel (1778–1837). At age fifteen she began the study of composition with Anton Reicha (1709–1836) at the Conservatoire National. In 1821 she married Aristide Farrenc, flutist and music publisher, who encouraged her career in every way possible. In the words of biographer Bea Friedland: "The Farrenc union seems to have achieved a blend of mutuality and independence rare in the nineteenth century, and even now an ideal more pledged than realized. Theirs was a reciprocal influence, for they matured together musically and intellectually and the special strengths of each nourished the other" (Friedland 1999). Farrenc's earliest published works were issued by her husband's firm, although they were also printed in other European countries. Robert Schumann wrote a positive review of her *Air russe varié* in 1836 that helped spread her fame in Germany. In 1842 she was appointed professor of piano at the Conservatoire, where she taught for three decades. Her set of *Trente études dans tous le tons majeurs et mineurs*, op. 26 (*Thirty Études*, op. 26) was adopted as required material in the piano classes of the Conservatoire in 1845. She was granted the prestigious Prix Chartier by the Académie des Beaux Arts in 1861 (the first year that it was granted) and again in 1869.

In 1860 Aristide Farrenc announced an ambitious project entitled *Le trésor des pianistes* (The Pianists' Treasure), a series of volumes that would survey 300 years of keyboard music in newly edited scholarly editions. This monumental anthology was promoted through a series of concerts given by Louise to familiarize the public with the repertoire in preparation. When her husband died in 1865, only eight volumes had appeared; she continued the work alone, completing the twenty-three-volume series before her death in 1875. The project was so consuming that she, in essence, embarked on a third career as a musicologist after her previous successes as pianist and composer.

Farrenc was a close contemporary of Hector Berlioz (1803–1869), but her musical style was not nearly so radical as his, tending instead toward a conservative musical language that combined elements of the prevailing late Classical and early Romantic styles. Her best-known works were her piano pieces, which included numerous variation sets on popular melodies. Several of her chamber works were also successful, and her husband's firm published most of them. Friedland summarizes them by stating that "her most notable contribution is the corpus of chamber music, uniformly fine in craftsmanship and exceedingly tasteful and attractive, if a shade unadventurous." She wrote three symphonies and a pair of overtures that were performed in Paris and other cities but remained unpublished. The first and third symphonies are now available on compact disc.

The dramatic and at times bombastic works of **Augusta Holmès (1847–1903)** belie stereotypical views of both female passivity and French subtlety. Born in Paris to Irish parents, she was raised in Versailles, where she took her first lessons with cathedral organist Henri Lambert. She later studied instrumentation with Hyacinthe-Éléonore Klosé (1808–1880), clarinet professor at the Conservatoire National. In 1875 she joined the circle of César Franck's (1822–1890) pupils and may have studied with him. The principal influence on her works was Richard Wagner (1813–1883), whom she met in Switzerland and whose music she promoted in France. She was known as a lively and opinionated participant in the salons of Paris, and her beauty is said to have attracted numerous admirers, including the composer Camille Saint-Saëns (1835–1921), who proposed marriage to her, and the poet Catulle Mendés, with whom she reputedly had three children.

Her principal works are for large forces, following the example of Wagner. She wrote a number of "dramatic symphonies" with programmatic titles, as well as symphonic poems. As subject matter for these works she favored Greek mythology. She wrote four operas, *Héro et Léandre, Astarté, Lancelot du lac* (Lancelot of the Lake), and *La Montagne noir* (The Black Mountain), the last of which was performed at the Paris Opéra to negative reviews in 1895. Most historians state that the other three were never performed, but Arthur Pougin reports in the supplement to Fétis' *Biographical Dictionary* that he heard a production of *Héro et Léandre* at Châtelet in 1874. His assessment of the work demonstrates the reputation that Holmès had earned: "I attended the performance of this work, which seemed interesting to me and included several good qualities, in spite of the ultra-Wagnerian doctrines attributed to this author and which did not seem to me to appear in her score" (Fetis 1880). Contemporaries generally agreed that Holmès was more interesting as a conversationalist than as a composer, where the majority of her works were marred by bombastic orchestration and excessive drama. Her works cover a wide range, including choral works and over 100 solo songs.

Cécile Chaminade (1857–1944) was very different from Holmès, choosing to specialize in *mélodies* for voice and character pieces for piano. She achieved remarkable success during her lifetime, but as Marcia J. Citron has pointed out, the decline in her reputation during the later twentieth century was even more striking.

Chaminade was born in Paris and, after early lessons with her mother, studied privately with Antoine Marmontel (1816–1898), Benjamin Godard (1849–1895), and other members of the Conservatoire National faculty. She made her debut as a pianist at age eighteen, after which she toured Germany and England to much acclaim. She became a favorite of Queen Victoria during several visits. She was one of America's preferred composers around the turn of the century, thanks to her publications, and she finally toured the United States in 1908–1909. She was honored with numerous awards and medals, including the Jubilee Medal from Queen Victoria (1897) and admission to the French Legion of Honor (1913), the first time that such distinction was conferred on a female composer. She was admired by contemporary colleagues, including Ambroise Thomas, who commented that "this is not a woman who composes, but a composer who happens to be a woman" (Ledeen 1999).

Cécile Chaminade.

Several of Chaminade's early works were in larger genres, including a *Piano Trio* (1880), a *Suite for Orchestra* (1881), an opera entitled *La Sévillane* (The Girl of Seville) (1882), a dramatic symphony entitled *Les Amazones* (1888), and a symphonic ballet entitled *Callirhoë* (1888). Her fame, however, rested on her smaller works, including approximately 200 pieces for solo piano and 125 *mélodies* for solo voice. These were ideally suited for publication and popular consumption because they were genres considered within a woman's sphere. (In the late Victorian era women were still thought to be better suited to the small, light genres of salon music than to larger, more intellectually demanding compositions.) Chaminade's popularity as a composer of salon pieces reflects society's willingness to embrace tuneful compositions by a woman. The target audience for these pieces was primarily young women as well, which aided their popularity. Among the many pieces that gained a following among piano students, *Scarf Dance* (1888) was the most enduringly popular; it became a staple of piano teachers for nearly half a century. Chaminade's elegant, lyrical works for piano and voice were ideally suited to the Romantic era; however, their appeal faded as amateurs turned to jazz and other popular genres in the twentieth century. The only work that has maintained a place in the concert repertoire is the *Concertino* for flute and orchestra (1902).

Virtuoso Pianist/Composers

The Romantic era was the age of the virtuoso, as technological improvements to both the piano and the transportation systems made it practical for performers to travel widely and to find reliable pianos when they arrived at distant destinations. In addition, the growing middle class supported a corresponding growth in public concerts. The concert is in several ways the most democratic of musical events. First, the doors are open to anyone with the price of admission, which had seldom been true in the history of art music. Second, the virtuoso achieves success by pleasing his or her audience, and the most successful ones pander to public taste in the manner of a politician running for reelection. In the nineteenth century, the keys to success were dazzling virtuosity and moving expressiveness. Virtuosos also found that familiarity helped their appeal, hence the numerous paraphrases, variations, and other works based on popular tunes or operatic themes. As Europe and America swarmed with musicians vying for public attention, a number of women performers enjoyed successful careers; the following are some who also composed.

Clara Kathleen Rogers (1844–1931 [née Barnett]) was renowned as an opera singer before giving up her performing career to concentrate on teaching and composition. Born in Cheltenham, England, she received her early training from her musical parents, who prepared her to enter the Leipzig Conservatory at age twelve; there she focused on piano studies, performing Chopin's *Piano Concerto* in E minor upon graduation. After three years in Leipzig, she studied voice in Berlin and Italy. She made her Italian operatic debut in 1863 under the stage name "Clara Doria," toured successfully throughout Italy before returning to England, and then traveled to the United States in 1871, touring for two more years until she settled in Boston in 1873. After her marriage in 1878 to Henry M. Rogers of Boston, she remained in that city and gave up the operatic stage. Clara Rogers joined the faculty of the New England Conservatory of Music as a voice teacher in 1902 and published a number of books on vocal technique. Simultaneously with her career as a voice teacher, Rogers renewed a lifelong interest in composition. Because she had not been allowed to study composition at the Leipzig Conservatory, she was insecure about her writing; nevertheless, her excellent musicianship enabled her to produce works that were received enthusiastically by her Boston colleagues and published in substantial numbers by Arthur P. Schmidt. She was one of the featured composers in the concerts of Isabella Stewart Gardner's Boston Manuscript Club in 1888 and 1889, contributing several chamber works in those years. Her output eventually included around 100 songs, several piano works, two string quartets, and sonatas for both violin and cello.

Marie Trautmann Jaëll (1846–1925) was one of the important performing pianists of her day, but her work as a piano teacher and writer of books on piano technique was even more significant. Trautmann was a child prodigy who had the benefit of piano lessons with Ignaz Moscheles (1794–1870) and Henri Herz (1803–1888) as well as composition lessons with César Franck and Camille Saint-Saëns (1835–1921). She gave concerts in Germany, Switzerland, and France at the age of nine and won the first prize in piano at the Conservatoire National in Paris at the age of sixteen. In 1866 she married the pianist Alfred Jaëll (1832–1882), who was already a famous concert artist. He had toured the United States to great acclaim in the early 1850s and was known as much for his delicate touch as for his extremely rotund physical appearance. Pougin contrasted their respective styles of playing in the supplement to Fétis' *Biographical Dictionary*: "[H]er talent contrasts singularly with his, because the playing of Mme Jaëll shines above all by its ardor, power, and brilliance, while that of her husband distinguishes itself by a grace and an elegance that are almost feminine" (Fétis 1880).

Upon her husband's death in 1882, Jaëll traveled to Weimar and spent considerable time with Liszt, both there and in Budapest, during the final years of his life. He dedicated his *Mephisto Waltz*, no. 3 to her and composed a set of variations on one of her compositions. She did some secretarial work for him and performed often in his master classes. Her brilliant performances were coupled with a prodigious repertoire; she was reported to have played all of Liszt's major works for solo piano, all the Beethoven sonatas, all the major works of Schumann, and the complete Chopin *Études*.

The last thirty years of her life, from 1895 to 1925, were devoted almost entirely to teaching piano at the Conservatoire National and writing ten books on piano technique. Her goal was to describe and codify the revolutionary changes that had taken place during the nineteenth century, particularly the technical innovations of Liszt. Like many writers of her era, she emphasized relaxation and economy of motion. With Dr. Charles Féré she explored the notion that excessive practice was inefficient, recommending no more than two hours per day. She advocated stroking the key after contact in order to aid in continuity of melodic lines, an idea espoused by her most famous student, Albert Schweitzer. The most important aspect of her pedagogical system was the cultivation of a mental image of each sound before it is played, thereby connecting the physical mechanism with the sensation of tone.

Jaëll's activities as a composer were always secondary to her career as a pianist and piano teacher. Nonetheless, she produced two piano concertos, a string quartet, a violin sonata, a cello sonata, and several works for piano solo, among which the ten *Valses for Four Hands* (1877) were the most popular. Her most ambitious composition was the symphonic poem *Ossiane*, premiered in Paris in 1879. Pianist Alexandre Sorel has recorded a compact disc of her piano works on Solstice Records.

Sophie Menter (1846–1918), a leading pianist of the late nineteenth century, produced a small number of works for piano, despite what she described as a "miserable talent for composing" (Rieger in Sadie 1994). Born into a musical family in Munich, Menter studied with Siegmund Lebert (1822–1884) in Stuttgart from age seven to eight. She later studied with Joseph Gabriel Rheinberger (1839–1901) and others in Munich. Her brilliant professional debut took place at the Gewandhaus in Leipzig in 1867, after which she was counted as one of Germany's premier piano virtuosos. She refined her technique further during two years of study with Carl Tausig (1841–1871) and often played for Liszt in Weimar. The great pianist called her "my only legitimate piano daughter" (Sadie 1994) and furthered her career with his extensive connections; she, in turn, promoted his piano works through frequent performances. Her playing was remarkable for its speed, power, and brilliance, causing critic George Bernard Shaw to rate her as superior to Ignace Paderewski (1860–1941). (She became famous in later years for wearing large amounts of jewelry during her performances.) Her compositions, like those of most piano virtuosos of the day, consist almost exclusively of brilliant works for concert performance; it is an indication of contemporary lack of esteem for such pieces that neither Michaelis nor Ebel gives her an entry. The Leipzig firm of Forberg published a number of her pieces, three of which are reprinted in *Women Composers: Music Through the Ages*, vol. 6.

The fiery Venezuelan pianist **Teresa Carreño (1853–1917)** thrilled audiences with her virtuosity and reinforced stereotypes about Latin Americans during her extensive career. She was born in Caracas to an aristocratic family; her prodigious natural talent influenced her father to take the family to the United States in 1862. Her New York debut recital in Irving Hall a month before her ninth birthday was followed by four more recitals in New York. In January 1863, the nine-year-old wonder child played twelve recitals in Boston, creating great excitement among the public and prompting John Sullivan Dwight to caution against exploiting her talents at such a young age. She soon met and studied with Louis Moreau Gottschalk (1829–1869), whose style is reflected in her early compositions for piano. In 1866 she traveled to Europe, where she met Gioacchino Rossini (1792–1868), Liszt, Anton Rubinstein, and other famous musicians. She later reported that Rossini urged her to study singing. She made her operatic debut in 1872 in Edinburgh as the Queen in *Les Huguenots* by Giacomo Meyerbeer (1791–1864) and sang often in productions on both sides of the Atlantic in subsequent years. After years of pursuing varied opportunities in singing, conducting, (and child-raising), she returned to full-time piano performance with her Berlin debut on November 18, 1889.

Carreño was acclaimed as one of the great pianists of the age. In the words of Harold C. Schonberg, "Carreño had overpowering personality, overpowering talent, overpowering physical strength, overpowering technique. And on top of that she was one of the most beautiful women of her time, in an Amazonian sort of way. In short, she was overpowering in every direction, and there seemed nothing she could not do" (Schonberg 1987). She had large hands and thick fingers, which allowed her to perform technical feats normally reserved for men. Her temperament gave her interpretations an impetuosity that dazzled most listeners but offended more sensitive musicians like Edvard Grieg (1843–1907). Her virtuosity onstage was matched by a tempestuous private life; she was married four times, first to violinist Emile Sauret (1852–1920), then to baritone Giovanni Tagliapietra (1846–1921), then to pianist Eugen d'Albert (1864–1932), and finally to Tagliapietra's brother Arturo.

The majority of her compositions were the brilliant piano pieces written before her twentieth birthday. These reflect the influence of Gottschalk and other contemporary virtuosos—in fact her op. 1 was entitled *Gottschalk Waltz* (1863). A number of her works incorporate the sounds of her native Venezuela, and she wrote two choral compositions in Spanish, one a hymn to Simón Bolívar and the other a hymn to Antonio Guzmán Blanco. She wrote a string quartet and an incomplete string serenade during her brief marriage to d'Albert in the 1890s. A champion of several younger contemporary composers, she was especially helpful to Edward MacDowell (1860–1908) by including his works on her concerts. Both his second concerto and Amy Beach's concerto are dedicated to Carreño.

Helen Hopekirk (1856–1945) enjoyed the benefits of excellent training in both piano and composition, enabling her to pursue successful careers in both areas. She was born near Edinburgh, Scotland, where she gave her first piano recital at age eleven. She studied the instrument with George Lichtenstein (n.d.) and took composition lessons with A.C. Mackenzie (1847–1935). In the late 1870s she enrolled at the Leipzig Conservatory for two years, again pursuing studies in piano (Louis Maas) and composition (Carl Reinecke, Salomon Jadassohn, and Ernst Friedrich Richter [1808–1879]). Hopekirk made her piano debut at the Leipzig Gewandhaus in 1878 and at the Crystal Palace the following year, after which she toured as a virtuoso. After three years of concerts in the United States between 1883 and 1886 and a seemingly successful career, Hopekirk moved to Vienna in 1886 in order to study piano with Theodor Leschetizky (1830–1915) and composition with Karel Navrátil. Returning to the concert stage after eighteen months of study, she continued to tour under the management of her husband, William A. Wilson, whom she had married in 1882. When he was injured in a traffic accident in 1896, she sought other directions for her career and was pleased to accept an offer to teach at the New England Conservatory from her former Leipzig classmate George Whitefield Chadwick, now director of the conservatory. She taught there only from 1897 to 1901, preferring to teach privately thereafter, but she was an important part of Boston musical life both as a performer and as a composer. Hopekirk became a U.S. citizen in 1918 and spent most of the rest of her life there. She performed her final concert before a group of Boston piano teachers in 1939 and died six years later.

Hopekirk's works list includes numerous piano pieces and songs, as well as two piano concertos, a *Concertstück* for piano and orchestra, two violin sonatas, and two short orchestral compositions. The Boston Symphony Orchestra played all of the piano/orchestra works, while the Boston Pops concerts featured her works for orchestra. Many of her works have a strong Gaelic tinge, both in subject matter and in musical materials. Chief among them are her arrangements of seventy Scottish songs, published by Oliver Ditson in 1905.

Mary (Marie) Wurm (1860–1938) was an English pianist and composer who spent most of her career in Germany. Born in Southampton to a German musician, she showed early promise as a pianist, performing the Robert Schumann *Concerto* at the Crystal Palace in 1882. In 1884 she was awarded the prestigious Mendelssohn Scholarship to support her continuing musical education. After piano lessons at the Stuttgart Conservatory with Ludwig Stark (1831–1884) and Dionys Pruckner (1834–1896) she continued her studies with Clara Schumann in Frankfurt. Her composition teachers included Arthur Sullivan (1842–1900), Joachim Raff (1822–1882), and Carl Reinecke (1824–1910). She spent most of her career in Germany concertizing and teaching, first in Hannover, then in Berlin (from 1911) and in Munich (from 1925). In 1899 she or-

ganized and conducted a women's orchestra in Berlin. Her compositions were princi-
pally for piano, including a concerto in B minor, a piano sonata, and numerous solo
works. She also wrote a string quartet, a violin sonata, a cello sonata, and several works
for orchestra. She produced three operas, *Prinzess Lisa's Fee* (Lübeck, 1895), *Matsuyama
Kagami* (Hannover, 1904), and *Die Mitschuldigen* (Leipzig, 1923). Well over fifty of her
works were published by British and German publishing firms, and she also published
books on music, including *Das ABC der Musik* and *Praktische Vorschule zur Caland-Lehre*.
Though not one of the most famous composers of her day, Wurm was described in the
Frank/Altmann *Kurzgefasstes Tonkünstlerlexikon* as a "sehr geschätzte Pianistin u. tücht.
Komp" (very esteemed pianist and competent composer). (Frank and Altmann 1936)

England and the United States

The musical culture of nineteenth-century Britain and the United States was dominated by that of Germany. Many musicians from both countries traveled to Germany
for advanced training, and English-speaking composers often had a noticeable German
accent in their musical works.

The notion that some instruments were inappropriate for women to play persisted
throughout the nineteenth century, and so it is a surprise to find that **Elizabeth Stirling (1819–1895)** was a respected performer and composer on the organ at a time when
this was considered an instrument for male performers. Stirling was born in the London
suburb of Greenwich in the same year as both Clara Schumann and Queen Victoria. She
studied composition with George Alexander Macfarren (1813–1887), one of the leading British composers of the day, and organ with Edward Holmes (1797–1859) and
James Alexander Hamilton (1785–1845). She played a recital at age eighteen that was
remarkable both for its length of three hours and the difficulty of the repertoire by Bach
and other composers. She received her first professional appointment as organist of All
Saints, Poplar, at the age of twenty and became the organist at St. Andrew Undershaft
in 1858, where she remained for the rest of her career. She was admired as a recitalist
and was invited to perform at the 1862 International Exhibition at the Crystal Palace.
She published fifteen choral works, several songs, and a collection of *Six Pedal Fugues
and Eight Other Movements for Organ* (1857). Her organ works are noteworthy for their
difficult pedal parts, which were somewhat unusual at this time in England.

Dame Ethel Smyth (1858–1944) was not only one of England's most important
composers of the early twentieth century but also a significant author and activist for
women's rights. Taken all together, her three areas of activity add up to a profound influence on British cultural life.

Smyth's middle-class English childhood included music lessons, but she was not
satisfied with the accomplishments expected of a dilettante. After a protracted battle
with her parents, she was allowed to enroll at the Leipzig Conservatory in 1877, where
she studied piano with Louis Maas (1852–1919) and composition with Salomon Jadassohn and Carl Reinecke. This was one of the few institutions offering composition les-

Dame Ethel Smyth, ca. 1938.
© Hulton-Deutsch Collection/CORBIS.

sons for women at this time, but Smyth was less than pleased with her teachers. In her memoirs, written many years later, she left scathing portraits of both Jadassohn and Reinecke, painting them as inept and uninterested in their students' progress. She left the conservatory to study privately with Heinrich von Herzogenberg, conductor of the Leipzig Bach-Verein, and followed him to Berlin when he was appointed professor of composition at the Berlin Hochschule in 1885.

Smyth's earliest published compositions were two sets of lieder issued by the Leipzig firm Breitkopf & Härtel. The publisher was not encouraging about the prospects for women composers and Smyth was disappointed by the sales. Returning to London in 1888, she concentrated her efforts on orchestral works, premiering the *Serenade* and the overture *Antony and Cleopatra* in 1890. Her first major success came with the *Mass* in D, written in 1891 and premiered in London's Albert Hall on January 18, 1893. A sweeping work for chorus and orchestra, it inspired British musicologist Donald Tovey to compare it to Beethoven's *Missa Solemnis*. The dramatic qualities of this work made it clear that Smyth had potential as an operatic composer, and it was to this genre that she next turned her attention with great success.

There was a strong prejudice in the English-speaking world against indigenous opera; consequently, Smyth's most important works were written in other languages and premiered in other countries. *Fantasio* was premiered at Weimar in 1898, and *Der Wald* (The Forest) was staged at Berlin in 1902. The success of these works on the continent paved the way for their acceptance at home; *Der Wald* was premiered at Covent Garden in London three months after its Berlin premiere and at New York's Metropolitan Opera in 1903 (the first opera by a woman performed by that company). Her next—and most critically acclaimed—opera followed a similar peripatetic path. It was written in French with the title *Les Naufrageurs* but was premiered in Leipzig in 1906 as *Strandrecht* (Right of Salvage). It was finally translated into English as *The Wreckers*, premiered in a concert version in 1908, and staged in 1909. This opera is set in Cornwall and contains many evocative references to the sea. Her last three operas were premiered in England. The *Boatswain's Mate* (London, 1916) is a comic opera that recalls the ballad opera tradition. Its humor and light musical style made it her most popular opera with the public. *Fête galante* (Elegant Entertainment) (Birmingham, 1923) is a neo-classical work that uses dance forms from the past. Her final opera was *Entente cordiale* (Cordial Agreement) (London, 1925), subtitled a "postwar comedy."

Smyth's operas and other works earned her the admiration of the public and her musical colleagues. (Conductor Thomas Beecham called *The Wreckers* "one of the three or four English operas of real musical merit and vitality." [Sadie 1998]) She was given honorary doctorates by the University of Durham in 1910 and Oxford University in 1926 and was named a Dame of the British Empire in 1922.

From 1910 to 1912 Smyth devoted herself exclusively to the cause of woman suffrage. She worked closely with Emmeline Pankhurst, and each served two months in prison in 1912 for taking part in a coordinated act of civil disobedience. Her most important contribution to the movement was the song "The March of the Women," which served as the anthem of the suffragists.

During World War I, Smyth realized that she was gradually going deaf. In the remaining decades of her life, she wrote less music but began a fruitful career as an author. Her first book, the two-volume autobiography *Impressions That Remained* (1919), is a lively and entertaining account of her life and the people with whom she came into contact. She published eight additional books, many of which are substantially autobiographical.

Smyth's early style was heavily influenced by the music that she absorbed during her sojourn in Germany from 1877 to 1888. Many of her works betray this influence, even such mature works as *The Wreckers*. In later years, however, she came to believe that English composers were at their best in the lighter idioms, hence the ballad opera style of *The Boatswain's Mate*. The tension between these two stylistic tendencies is prevalent in her music.

Songwriters

For many, writing a popular song requires a different set of skills from those for composing art music, and many composers of the latter, in fact, have wished in vain that they could produce enough of the former to provide financial security. Lili'uokalani and Carrie Jacobs-Bond came from very different backgrounds, but each had the golden touch necessary to write popular songs.

Queen Lili'uokalani (1838–1917 [Lydia Kamaka'eha]) was a member of the *ali'i*, or ruling class, of the Kingdom of Hawai'i. Her brother, King David Kalakaua, named her heir to the throne in 1877, giving her the name Lili'uokalani. She ascended the throne in 1891 but was deposed in a coup by a group of American businessmen in 1893. She chose not to resist in order to avoid unnecessary suffering for her people and lived out her days under American rule after a year of imprisonment in 1895.

For Lili'uokalani, music was an essential part of life. She was skilled at sight-reading and played both keyboard and plucked string instruments. Her training was unusual in that she learned both ancient Hawaiian and Western musical styles. Many of her songs combine the Protestant hymn tradition with Hawaiian chant. Her first published song was "He Mele Lahui Hawai'i" (1866), which served as the Hawaiian national anthem until 1876. "Nani Na Pua" (1869) may have been her first Hawaiian song published in the continental United States. "Ke Aloha O Ka Haku" (published as "Lili'uokalani's Prayer") was written during her imprisonment and remains one of Hawai'i's favorite hymns. Without question, her most popular song was the perennial favorite "Aloha Oe," composed in 1878 and introduced during a visit to San Francisco by the Royal Hawaiian Band in 1883. Almost from the beginning, this song of farewell seemed to capture the spirit of her island kingdom; it remains a favorite of visitors and residents alike.

Carrie Jacobs-Bond (1862–1946), another songwriter, born in Wisconsin (USA), exhibited early skills in both painting and music, particularly in improvising songs to her own words. She had only minimal training but a distinctive compositional style. After the death of her second husband in 1895 she became frustrated with the difficulties that she faced in trying to find publishers for her songs. She consequently established her own publishing company with her son, known variously as Carrie Jacobs-Bond & Son and The Bond Shop. Most of her songs were published by this enterprise, including the most successful: "I Love You Truly" (1901) over one million copies, and "A Perfect Day" (1910), eight million copies of sheet music and five million records. Her distinctively appealing style of performing her own songs earned her an invitation to perform for Franklin D. Roosevelt at the White House. Like many writers of popular songs, she was viewed with suspicion by music critics who failed to grasp the intangible qualities that made them successful. Nicolas Slonimsky's assessment in *Baker's Biographical Dictionary* is typical: "Although deficient in musical training and technique, she succeeded in producing melodies with suitable accompaniment that became extremely popular."

Many American women in the nineteenth century, like women in Europe, treated music as a social ornament. They were encouraged to pursue the study of voice and piano

Lili'uokalani.
The Granger Collection, New York.

as dilettantes but faced opposition when stepping into the realm of professional music. Attitudes began to change during the last third of the century, however, as a small group of American women gained public attention as virtuosos, and increasing numbers of women went into music teaching as a profession. Following on the heels of these developments came a group of female composers who defied traditional stereotypes and created opportunities for themselves and their twentieth-century successors.

Helen Hood (1863–1949) was born during the Civil War and pursued a career in composition well into the 1930s. A native of the Boston area, she studied with Horatio Parker (1863–1919), John Knowles Paine (1839–1906), and George Whitefield Chadwick—three prominent members of the Second New England School. Piano studies in Berlin with Moritz Moszkowski (1854–1925) and Xaver Scharwenka (1850–1924) prepared her for a career as pianist and piano teacher in Boston, where she appeared several times with the Boston Symphony Orchestra. Hood was honored for her participation in the World's Columbian Exposition in Chicago in 1893. Her best-known works were her many songs, especially "The Robin," "Summer Song," and a set of six songs entitled *Song Etchings*, op. 8 (published in 1893). She also published chamber music, including two suites for violin and piano, opp. 6 and 10. Louis C. Elson repeated Ebel's opinion that her piano trio was her most important work in his influential book *The History of American Music*.

Eleanor Everest Freer (1864–1942) began her career as a singer and later devoted herself to composing a substantial amount of vocal music. She grew up in a musical home, where she played the piano and sang as a child. She studied in Paris from 1883 to 1886, taking voice lessons with Mathilde Marchesi (1821–1909) and composition lessons with Benjamin Godard. She taught voice at the National Conservatory of Music in New York from 1889 to 1891 but concentrated her energies on composition after her marriage in 1891. Freer was active in the Manuscript Society of New York and founded two societies in Chicago that merged in 1924 to become the American Opera Society. Her works are nearly all for voices, including over 150 songs and eleven operas, the first of which she wrote when she was nearly sixty years old. She had a particular fondness for Robert and Elizabeth Barrett Browning; she set forty-four of the latter's *Sonnets from the Portuguese* as a song cycle, op. 22, and composed an opera entitled *The Brownings Go to Italy*, op. 43.

The title of Adrienne Fried Block's biography, *Amy Beach, Passionate Victorian*, effectively captures the paradox of this prominent American composer. **Amy Beach (1867–1944)** appeared to be a model of Victorian propriety, but her music reveals a passionate inner life seemingly at odds with her staid exterior.

Many of the women in this book displayed early musical talent, but even in this company the young Amy Marcy Cheney was exceptional. She sang a large repertoire of songs at the age of two, could improvise an alto line to her mother's soprano, and demonstrated absolute pitch by crying whenever her mother sang a song to her in the "wrong" key. Like many other gifted musicians with perfect pitch, she associated colors with specific keys. Although she begged to play the piano, her mother delayed this pleasure until she was four years old. At this time she could reproduce what she had heard her mother play, leaving out the notes that her hands could not reach. Beach's first compositions were also produced at the age of four, when during a visit to the country she composed three waltzes in her head and played them on the piano after returning home.

Her parents chose to limit both the training and public performances of their talented daughter. Rather than send her abroad for study in an era when this was considered an essential prerequisite to a professional career in America, they kept her at home in Boston, where she studied piano with Ernst Perabo (1876–1882) and Carl Baermann (1882–1886). Her formal composition training was limited to one year of harmony and counterpoint with Junius Welch Hill (1881–1882). Later recognizing deficiencies in her background, Beach undertook disciplined study of orchestration and other compositional techniques by reading books on these subjects. Her performance opportunities were even more limited, as the talented girl was forced to wait until age sixteen to make her formal debut, playing the Moscheles *Piano Concerto* no. 2 on October 24, 1883.

Amy Marcy Cheney Beach.
© CORBIS.

Less than three months later she played her first solo recital in Chickering Hall. Within the next year and a half she played with the Boston Symphony Orchestra and with the Theodore Thomas Orchestra, showing a command of the technical and musical skills necessary for a major concert career.

On December 2, 1885, the eighteen-year-old Amy Cheney married Dr. Henry Harris Aubrey Beach, a prominent surgeon over twice her age. She moved into a fashionable home on Commonwealth Avenue and began a new life as Mrs. H.H.A. Beach. Her husband did not believe that a career of a professional virtuoso was appropriate for his wife, and she thus limited her performances to eagerly awaited annual charity recitals. She also agreed not to teach piano or to accept money for her performances. Instead, Dr. Beach encouraged her to cultivate her skills in composition, which had been a secondary interest to piano performance up to this time. Over the next twenty-five years, she produced a steady stream of works in Romantic style that earned her a reputation as one of America's most respected composers. Her *Mass* in E-flat major, op. 5 was written in 1890, the *Festival Jubilate*, op. 17 the following year, her *Gaelic Symphony* in E Minor, op. 32 in 1894–1896, the *Sonata* in A minor for piano and violin, op. 34 in 1896, her *Concerto* in C-sharp minor, op. 45 in 1899, and the thirty-minute set of *Variations on Balkan Themes* for piano, op. 60 in 1904. By far the majority of her works were for solo voice, solo piano, and chorus.

The peaceful life on Commonwealth Avenue ended with the deaths of her husband in 1910 and her mother in 1911. In the biography Block demonstrates that contrary to the traditional view that Beach was a wealthy widow, her husband left her more debts than anything else, and she found herself in need of increased income. At first she relied on her composing royalties, but in 1911 she renewed her career as a virtuoso by traveling to Europe for the first time. She stayed there from 1911 to 1914, establishing a reputation through her performances and compositions. When she was forced to return to the United States on the eve of World War I, she found that her European triumphs had paved the way for a successful career at home during the following decades. Although the hectic schedule of appearances limited her time for composition, she continued to produce significant works. She confided to John Tasker Howard something of her life as a composer/pianist:

> I have literally lived the life of two people, one a pianist, the other a writer. Anything more unlike than the state of mind demanded by these two professions I could not imagine! When I do one kind of work, I shut the other up in a closed room and lock the door, unless I happen to be composing for the piano, in which case there is a connecting link. One great advantage, however, in this kind of life, is that one never grows stale, but there is always a continual interest and freshness from the change back and forth. (Howard 1931)

Beach spent much of the rest of her life in New York in order to be close to the concert life and publishers there. Summers were divided between her home at Centerville on Cape Cod and the MacDowell Colony in Peterborough, New Hampshire. She died on December 27, 1944.

Beach's works had already begun to decline in popularity during her lifetime, perhaps because they seemed "dated" in the middle of the twentieth century. After her death, her works went out of print and were almost completely forgotten, with only a few persons who had known the dynamic woman attempting to keep her memory alive. The 1970s and 1980s saw a revival of interest in her music as recordings and scholarly studies began to appear. By the 1990s, there was a full-scale Beach renaissance under way with numerous recordings, a significant number of dissertations, and Block's biography reigniting interest in the forgotten composer. Beach's works have gradually been republished, and nearly all of them are now available.

Beach's music falls into distinct stylistic categories. The early works are very much in keeping with the prevailing Romantic style, featuring lush, virtuosic textures for piano and passionate melodic lines. Harmonically, she was more adventurous than her colleagues in the Second New England School, following the example of Brahms in undermining tonality through unconventional chord progressions. There is a high level of dissonance in these early works as well as a propensity for chromatic scales. The *Violin Sonata* is perhaps the masterpiece of this part of her repertoire. Its broad, sweeping lines mask a logical construction, while the energetic drive of the outer movements appealed to male violinists such as Eugene Ysaÿe. This work is one of only a handful by Romantic women composers that has been recorded multiple times by different artists, allowing for intelligent comparison among various interpretations. Shortly after the turn of the century, Beach began adding impressionistic techniques to her musical palette. She used more unresolved dissonances, atmospheric textures, and chords with added ninths or non-chord tones during this period. Two attractive pieces in this style are the piano pieces *A Hermit Thrush at Eve* and *A Hermit Thrush at Morn*, op. 92, nos. 1 and 2 (1921). Especially in the first piece, Beach uses harmonic planing to create her musical textures, introducing the song of the hermit thrush as a rude interruption. Her later works continue this harmonic experimentation, with a further reduction of texture away from the lush and virtuosic early style. The unusual *Quartet on Inuit Themes* of 1921 may be heard as a precursor to this late style, while *Three Pianoforte Pieces*, op. 128, and *Improvisations*, op. 148, are representative of her late works.

Margaret Ruthven Lang (1867–1972) has the distinction of being the longest-lived composer in this volume. Although she was alive through nearly three-quarters of the twentieth century, she is included in this Romantic chapter because her most important contributions occurred in this era. She was the daughter of Benjamin Johnson Lang (1837–1909), a conductor who played an important role in Boston's musical life in the second half of the nineteenth century. Her early studies were with him, Louis Schmidt (n.d.) in Boston, Franz Drechsler (n.d.), Ludwig Abel (1834–1895), and Victor Gluth (1852–1895) in Munich, and finally George Whitefield Chadwick in Boston. She was one of a number of composers who benefited from the American Composers' Concert movement in the 1880s and 1890s, which fostered performances of exclusively American works. Her first important exposure came when conductor Frank Van der Stucken featured her song "Ojalà" in American Composers' Concerts in Paris (July 12, 1889) and Washington (March 26, 1890). Her overture *Witichis*, op. 10 (now lost) was chosen for performance on an American Composers' Concert at the World's Columbian Exposition of 1893, and other works were featured in performances by the Manuscript Society of New York. Mrs. Gerrit Smith performed concerts devoted exclusively to Lang's works beginning in 1892.

It was in Boston that Lang was most performed and admired. Her music was featured regularly by the Boston Symphony Orchestra (noteworthy for ignoring women composers during this era) and by her father's Apollo Club and Cecilia Society. Her last published work appeared in 1919, but her songs and choral works continued to be appreciated for years afterward. Her harmonic language was not as complex as that of Beach, making her works more accessible to the average listener. Among many appealing works for vocal ensembles is *The Jumblies*, op. 5 (1890). For baritone solo, men's chorus, and two pianos, this creates a series of musical pastiches by setting limericks by Edward Lear in a variety of musical styles.

Like so many of the women in this book, **Mabel Wheeler Daniels (1878–1971)** grew up in an intensely musical family; both parents and grandparents were involved in the musical life of their native Massachusetts. After earning her B.A. from Radcliffe

College and studying with George Whitefield Chadwick, she moved to Munich in 1902, where she had the distinction of being the first woman accepted in Ludwig Thuille's class in score reading at the Akademie für Tonkunst. (An amusing account of this achievement is found in her 1905 memoir, *An American Girl in Munich*, and is reprinted in *Women in Music*, ed. Carol Neuls-Bates.) Daniels returned to Boston and taught briefly at Radcliffe College, the Bradford Academy, and Simmons College. From 1918 she was able to concentrate exclusively on composition with the financial support of her family. She was a Fellow of the MacDowell Colony for twenty-four years. Her earliest significant works were a number of operettas written for production at Radcliffe College. She continued to compose through the late 1950s.

In an article entitled "Passed Away is the Piano Girl" published in the book *Women Making Music* (1986) ed. Jane Bowers and Judith Tick, Tick points to the last three decades of the nineteenth century as a period of significant change for women musicians in the United States. She cites the growing percentage of female music teachers identified in census figures from 1870 to 1900, the rise of professional "lady orchestras," the change of rules allowing women to join the Musicians Union in 1904, and the increasing number of females composing in large genres as evidence of a new professionalism among women musicians. The situation for women composers had indeed been altered dramatically over the course of the nineteenth century as their opportunities and those of women performers gradually improved in this era. Although women still had to fight traditional stereotypes to gain acceptance for their music, the century had been one of unprecedented progress that would pave the way for a flood of twentieth-century innovators.

Timeline for the Nineteenth Century

Date	History/ Politics	Science/Education	The Arts/ Literature	Music
1801		First submarine produced		Vincenzo Bellini (1801–1835)
1802			Alexandre Dumas père (1802–1870) Victor Hugo (1802–1885)	
1803	Louisiana Purchase			Hector Berlioz (1803–1869)
1804	Benjamin Disraeli (1804–1884)	Steam locomotive invented Würzburg Conservatory founded	Nathaniel Hawthorne (1804–1864) George Sand (Amandine Aurore Lucie Dupin) writer (1804–1876)	**Louise Farrenc (1804–1875)** Mikhail Glinka (1804–1857) Johann Strauss (elder) (1804–1849)
1805				**Fanny Mendelssohn Hensel (1805–1847)**
1806			Elizabeth Barrett Browning, poet (1806–1861)	Jacobo Antonio de Arriaga (1806–1826)
1808				**Maria Felicia Malibran (1808–1836)**
1809	Abraham Lincoln (1809–1865)	Charles Darwin (1809–1882)	Edgar Allan Poe (1809–1849) Alfred, Lord Tennyson (1809–1892)	Felix Mendelssohn (1809–1847)
1810		Frederick Koenig invents an improved printing press	Ole Bull, violinist (1810–1880)	Frédéric Chopin (1810–1849) Robert Schumann (1810–1856) **Johanna Kinkel (1810–1858)**
1811		Prague Conservatory founded	Harriet Beecher Stowe (1811–1896)	Franz Liszt (1811–1886) **Marie Leopoldine Blahetka (1811–1887)**
1812	War of 1812		Charles Dickens (1812–1870) Robert Browning (1812–1889)	Friedrich von Flotow (1812–1883) Sigismond Thalberg (1812–1871)
1813				Charles-Henri Valentin Alkan (1813–1888) William Henry Fry (1813–1864) Giuseppe Verdi (1813–1901) Richard Wagner (1813–1883)
1814	Congress of Vienna			

Date	History/ Politics	Science/Education	The Arts/ Literature	Music
1815	Elizabeth Cady Stanton, newspaper editor and suffragist (1815–1902) Harriet Tubman, slave abolitionist (1815/1821?–1913)	Graz Conservatory founded	Invention of the metronome	**Josephine Karoline Lang (1815–1880)**
1816			Charlotte Brontë, novelist and poet (1816–1855)	
1817		Vienna Conservatory founded	Henry David Thoreau (1817–1862)	
1818		Innsbruck Conservatory founded	Emily Brontë (1818–1848)	Charles Gounod (1818–1893)
1819	Queen Victoria (1819–1901)		George Eliot (Mary Ann Evans), (1819–1880) Walt Whitman (1819–1892) Herman Melville (1819–1891)	**Clara Wieck Schumann (1819–1896) Elizabeth Stirling (1819–1895)** Franz von Suppé (1819–1895)
1820	Susan B. Anthony, educator and suffragist (1820–1906)	Florence Nightingale, nurse and writer (1820–1910)	Jenny Lind, opera singer (1820–1887)	Alexander Serov (1820–1871) Henri Vieuxtemps (1820–1881)
1821	Mary Baker Eddy, founder of Christian Science (1821–1910)	Elizabeth Blackwell, physician/writer (1821–1910) Clara Barton, nurse, writer, and Red Cross founder (1821–1912)	Charles Baudelaire (1821–1867) Gustave Flaubert (1821–1880) Feodor Dostoevsky (1821–1881)	**Pauline Viardot-Garcia (1821–1910) Emilie Mayer (1821–1883)**
1822		Louis Pasteur (1822–1895) Daguerre invents the diorama Gregor Mendel (1822–1884)		César Franck (1822–1890) **Faustina Hodges (1822–1895)** Joachim Raff (1822–1882)
1823	Monroe Doctrine			Edouard Lalo (1823–1892)
1824				**Jane Sloman (1824–?)** Anton Bruckner (1824–1896) Carl Reinecke (1824–1910) Bedrich Smetana (1824–1884)
1825				**Mary Ann Gabriel (1825–1877)** George Frederick Bristow (1825–1898) Johann Strauss (1825–1899)

Date	History/ Politics	Science/Education	The Arts/ Literature	Music
1826		University College, London, founded		
1827		Invention of the camera		Teresa Milanollo (1827–1902)
1828			Leo Tolstoy (1828–1910) Henrik Ibsen (1828–1906)	
1829		Louis Braille invents Braille printing Anton Rubinstein (1829–1894)		Louis Moreau Gottschalk (1829–1869)
1830		B. Thimonnier invents the sewing machine	Emily Dickinson (1830–1886)	**Maria Grandval (1830–1907)** Karl Goldmark (1830–1915) Hans von Bülow (1830–1894)
1831		Cyrus H. McCormick invents the reaper		Salomon Jadassohn (1831–1902)
1832		Samuel Morse invents the telegraph Brussels Conservatory founded	Louisa May Alcott (1832–1888) Lewis Carroll (Charles Lutwidge Dodgson) (1832–1898)	**Marie Milanollo (1832–1848)** **Marie Wieck (1832–1916)**
1833				**Lina Ramann (1833–1912)** Johannes Brahms (1833–1897) Alexander Borodin (1833–1887)
1834			Edgar Degas, painter (1834–1917)	
1835			Mark Twain (Samuel Langhorne Clemens) (1835–1910)	Cesar Cui (1835–1918) Camille Saint-Saëns (1835–1921) Henri Wieniawski (1835–1880)
1836				Leo Delibes (1836–1891)
1837	Queen Victoria starts her reign			**Marie Lipsius (1837–1927)** **Octavia Hensel (1837–1897)**
1838	Victoria Woodhull (1838–1927)	Samuel Morse invents Morse Code		Queen Lydia Kamekeha **Lili'uokalani, queen and songwriter (1838–1917)** **Thekla Badarzewska-Baranowska (1838–1861)** Georges Bizet (1838–1875) Max Bruch (1838–1920)

Date	History/ Politics	Science/Education	The Arts/ Literature	Music
1839		Louis Daguerre and J. N. Niepce invent Daguerreotype photography	New York Philharmonic founded Vienna Philharmonic founded	**Alice Mary Smith (1839–1884)** Modest Mussorgsky (1839–1881) Joseph Rheinberger (1839–1901)
1840			Pierre Auguste Renoir (1840–1919) Auguste Rodin (1840–1917) Claude Monet (1840–1926) Émile Zola (1840–1902) Thomas Hardy (1840–1928)	Peter Ilich Tchaikovsky (1840–1893) **Ingeborg von Bronsart (1840–1913)**
1841		Samuel Slocum patents the stapler The first university degrees granted to women in America	Berthe Morissot, painter (1841–1895)	Anton Dvorák (1841–1904) **Louise Heritte-Viardot (1841–1917)** Emmanuel Chabrier (1841–1894) Carl Tausig (1841–1871)
1842				Arrigo Boito (1842–1918) Edvard Grieg (1842–1907)
1843		Leipzig Conservatory founded	Henry James (1843–1916)	
1844		Telegraph invented	Sarah Bernhardt, actress (1844–1923) Mary Cassatt, painter (1844–1926)	Nikolai Rimsky-Korsakov (1844–1908) **Clara Kathleen Rogers (1844–1931)** Pablo de Sarasate (1844–1908)
1845				**Florence May (1845–1923) Agnes Zimmerman (1845–1925)** Gabriel Fauré (1845–1924)
1846	Carrie Nation, prohibitionist (1846–1911)			**Marie Trautmann Jaëll (1846–1925) Sophie Menter (1846–1918)**
1847		Alexander Graham Bell (1847–1922) Thomas Alva Edison (1847–1931)		**Agathe Ursula Backer-Grøndahl (1847–1907) Augusta Holmès (1847–1903)**
1848	First Women's Rights Convention Gold Rush—California		Karl Marx, *The Communist Manifesto*	Henri Duparc (1848–1933)
1850				**Luise Adolpha LeBeau (1850–1927) Emma Steiner (1850–1928)**

Date	History/ Politics	Science/Education	The Arts/ Literature	Music
1851			Kate Chopin, writer (1851–1904)	Annette Essipoff (1851–1914) **Mary Carmichael (1851–1935)**
1853			Vincent van Gogh (1853–1890) Lillie Langtry, actress (1853–1929)	**Teresa Carreño (1853–1917)**
1854		University College, Dublin, founded	Jennie Jerome Churchill, editor and playwright (mother of Winston Churchill) (1854–1921) Oscar Wilde (1854–1900)	George Whitefield Chadwick (1854–1931) Engelbert Humperdinck (1854–1921) Leo Janácek (1854–1928) John Philip Sousa (1854–1932)
1855				**Maude White (1855–1937)** **Rive-King, Julle (1855–1937)** Ernest Chausson (1855–1899)
1856		Sigmund Freud (1856–1939)	George Bernard Shaw (1856–1950)	**Helen Hopekirk (1856–1945)** Serge Taneyev (1856–1915)
1857			Fannie Farmer, cookbook author (1857–1903)	**Cécile Chaminade (1857–1944)** **Mary Wood (1857–1944)** Edward Elgar (1857–1934)
1858	Emmeline Pankhurst, suffragette (1858–1928) Carrie Chapman Catt, suffragist (1858–1947)	Max Planck (1858–1947)	Beatrice Potter Webb, author (1858–1943) Covent Garden Opera House opens	**Ethel Mary Smyth (1858–1944)** **Marie Bobillie (1858–1918)** **Mélanie (Mel) Bonis (1858–1937)** Ruggiero Leoncavallo (1859–1919) Giacomo Puccini (1858–1924) Eugene Ysäye (1858–1931)
1859		Pierre Curie (1859–1906)	Eleanora Duse, actress (1859–1924) Georges Seurat, painter (1859–1891)	Mikhail Ippolitiv-Ivanov (1859–1935)
1860	Jane Addams, social worker (1860–1935)	Invention of cork linoleum	Grandma Moses, painter (1860–1961)	Gustav Mahler (1860–1911)

Date	History/ Politics	Science/Education	The Arts/ Literature	Music
1860			Anton Chekhov, author (1860–1904)	Ignace Paderewski (1860–1941) **Mary (Marie) Wurm (1860–1938) Dory Petersen (1860–1902)** Hugo Wolf (1860–1903) Isaac Albéniz (1860–1909) Edward MacDowell (1860–1908)
1861	Civil War 1861–1865		Rabindranath Tagore, author (1861–1941) Ernestine Schumann-Heink, singer (1861–1936)	Anton Stepanovich Arensky (1861–1906) Charles Martin Loeffler (1861–1935)
1862	Brooklyn Bridge opened		Maurice Maeterlinck, writer (1862–1911) Edith Wharton, writer (1862–1937)	Claude Debussy (1862–1918) Frederick Delius (1862–1934) **Carrie Jacobs-Bond (1862–1946)**
1863	Emancipation Proclamation		Edvard Munch, painter (1863–1944)	**Helen Hood (1863–1949) Fannie Bloomfield Zeisler (1863–1927) Katharine Bainbridge (1863–1967) Anne Gilchrist (1863–1954)** Pietro Mascagni (1863–1945) Horatio Parker (1863–1919) Gabriel Pierné (1863–1937)
1864			Henri de Toulouse-Lautrec, painter (1864–1901) Elizabeth Coolidge, patron of the arts (1864–1953)	**Adele aus der Ohe (1864–1937) Eleanor Everest Freer (1864–1942)** Richard Strauss (1864–1949)
1865	Abraham Lincoln assassinated	Massachusetts Institute of Technology founded	Rudyard Kipling author (1865–1936) William Butler Yeats (1865–1929) Nellie Melba, singer (1865?–1931)	Paul Dukas (1865–1935) Alexander Glazunov (1865–1936) Jean Sibelius (1865–1957)
1866		Alfred Nobel invents dynamite	H.G. Wells, author (1866–1946)	**Clara Anna Korn (1866–1940)**

Date	History/ Politics	Science/Education	The Arts/ Literature	Music
1866				Henriette van den Boorn-Coclet (1866–1945) Ferruccio Busoni (1866–1924) Erik Satie (1866–1925)
1867		Marie Curie (1867–1934) Edith Hamilton, classical scholar (1867–1963)	Käthe Kollwitz, artist (1867–1945) Laura Ingalls Wilder, writer (1867–1957) Frank Lloyd Wright, architect (1867–1959)	**Amy Marcy Cheney Beach (1867–1944)** **Margaret Ruthven Lang (1867–1972)** Enrique Granados (1867–1916)
1868			Maud Powell, violinist (1868–1920)	Scott Joplin (1868–1917)
1869	Emma Goldman, political organizer (1869–1939)		Henri Matisse, artist (1869–1954)	Hans Pfitzner (1869–1949)
1870	Opening of the Suez Canal	Helena Rubinstein (1870–1965) Maria Montessori, teacher (1870–1952)		Franz Lehár (1870–1948) **Isabella Beaton (1870–1929)**
1871			Theodore Dreiser, writer (1871–1945) Marcel Proust, author (1871–1922) Georges Rouault, painter (1871–1958)	Alexander Zemlinsky (1871–1942)
1872			Maude Adams, actress (1872–1953) Piet Mondrian, painter (1872–1944)	Ralph Vaughan Williams (1872–1958)
1873			Willa Cather, journalist, poet, and novelist (1873–1947) Marie Dressler, actor (1873–1934) Colette, writer (1873–1954) Emily Post, etiquette writer (1873–1960)	**Mary Carr Moore (1873–1957)[1]** Joseph Jongen (1873–1953) Sergei Rachmaninoff (1873–1943) Max Reger (1873–1916)
1874			Gertrude Stein, writer (1874–1946)	Gustav Holst (1874–1934)

Date	History/ Politics	Science/Education	The Arts/ Literature	Music
1874				Charles Ives (1874–1954) Arnold Schoenberg (1874–1951) Josef Suk (1874–1935)
1875		Albert Schweitzer (1875–1965)	Rainer Maria Rilke, poet (1875–1926) Thomas Mann, author (1875–1955)	**Pearl Curran (1875–1941)** Samuel Taylor Coleridge (1875–1912) Reinhold Glière (1875–1956) Fritz Kreisler (1875–1962) Maurice Ravel (1875–1937)
1876		Invention of the telephone	Mary Roberts Rinehart, writer (1876–1958)	John Alden Carpenter (1876–1951) Carl Ruggles (1876–1971) Ermanno Wolf-Ferrari (1876–1948)
1877		Invention of the phonograph	Alice B. Toklas, cookbook writer (1877–1967) Mary Garden, opera singer (1877?–1967)	**Elisabeth Kuyper (1877–1953)** **Harriet Ware (1877–1962)** Ernst von Dohnanyi (1877–1960) **Mabel Wheeler Daniels (1877–1971)**
1878	Elizabeth Arden, businesswoman (1878–1966)		Carl Sandburg, poet (1878–1967) Isadora Duncan, dancer (1878–1927)	
1879		Albert Einstein (1879–1955) Invention of the incandescent lightbulb	Paul Klee (1879–1940) Ethel Barrymore, actress (1879–1959)	**Alma Schindler Mahler (1879–1964)** Wanda Landowska (1879–1959) **Johanna Senfter (1879–1961)** Frank Bridge (1879–1941) John Ireland (1879–1962) Ottorino Respighi (1879–1936)
1880	Jeanette Rankin, politician (1880–1973)	Helen Keller, lecturer and writer (1880–1968)	Ruth St. Denis, dancer and choreographer (1880–1968)	Ernest Bloch (1880–1959) **Irene Regine Wieniawski [Poldowski] (1880–1932)** **Florence Wickham (1880–1962)** **Ethel Barnes (1880–1948)** **Yulia Weissberg (1880–1942)** Nikolai Medtner (1880–1951)
1881		Alexander Fleming (1881–1955)	Pablo Picasso (1881–1973) Anna Pavlova, dancer (1881–1931)	**Gena Branscombe (1881–1977)** **Fannie Charles Dillon (1881–1947)**

Date	History/ Politics	Science/Education	The Arts/ Literature	Music
1881			Boston Symphony founded	Béla Bartók (1881–1945) George Enescu (1881–1955) Nicolas Miaskovsky (1881–1950)
1882	Franklin D. Roosevelt, U.S. president 1933–1945 (1882–1945) Sylvia Pankhurst, suffragist (1882–1960) Frances Perkins (1882–1965)		Virginia Woolf, writer (1882–1941) Georges Braque (1882–1963) James Joyce (1882–1941) Berlin Philharmonic founded	Igor Stravinsky (1882–1971) **Mary Howe (1882–1964)** Percy Grainger (1882–1961) Zoltan Kodaly (1882–1967) Gian Francesco Malipiero (1882–1973) Karol Szymanowski (1882–1937)
1883		Margaret Sanger, nurse and civil rights activist (1883–1966)	Franz Kafka (1883–1924) Metropolitan Opera House opened Amsterdam Concertgebouw founded Coco Chanel, designer (1883–1971)	**Adaline Shepherd (1883–1950)[2]** Arnold Bax (1883–1953) Alfredo Casella (1883–1947) Edgard Varèse (1883–1965) Anton Webern (1883–1945)
1884	Harry S Truman, U.S. president 1945–1953 (1884–1972) Eleanor Roosevelt (1884–1962)		Sara Teasdale, poet (1884–1933) Amadeo Modigliani, painter (1884–1920)	Charles Tomlinson Griffes (1884–1920)
1885		Karen Horney, psychiatrist and writer (1885–1952) Internal combustion engine invented Niels Bohr (1885–1962)	Elinor Wylie, poet (1885–1928) Isak Dinesen, writer (1885–1962) D. H. Lawrence, writer (1885–1930)	Alban Berg (1885–1935) Wallingford Riegger (1885–1961) **Adaline Shepherd (ca. 1885–1945)** Pejacevic, Dora (1885–1923)
1886	Statue of Liberty installed in New York Harbor		Oskar Kokoschka, painter (1886–1980) Hilda Doolittle, poet (1886–1961) Mary Wigman, dancer (1886–1973)	**Rebecca Clarke (1886–1979)** **Julia Neibergall (1886–1968)** **Fay Foster (1886–1960)** Marcel Dupré (1886–1971) Ethel Leginska (1886–1970) Charles Seeger (1886–1979)
1887		Julian Huxley (1887–1975)	Marc Chagall, artist (1887–1985)	**Marion Bauer (1887–1955)[3]**

Date	History/ Politics	Science/Education	The Arts/ Literature	Music
1887			Georgia O'Keeffe, artist (1887–1986)	**Nadia Boulanger (1887–1979)**[4]
			Edith Sitwell, poet (1887–1964)	Sigmund Romberg (1887–1951)
			Edna Ferber, novelist (1887–1968)	Lily Strickland (1887–1958)
				Heitor Villa-Lobos (1887–1959)
			Marianne Moore, poet (1887–1972)	**Florence Price (1887–1953)**[5]
1888	Eiffel Tower completed		Katherine Mansfield, writer (1888–1923)	**Ilse Fromm–Michaels (1888–1986)**
			Anita Loos, writer (1888–1981))	**Johanna Beyer (1888–1944**
			T. S. Eliot, poet (1888–1965)	**Lucile Crews (1888–1972)**
				May Aufderheide (1888–1972)[6]
			Eugene O'Neill, playwright (1888–1953)	**Emiliana Zubeldia (1888–1987)**
			Lotte Lehman, singer (1888–1976)	
1889			Charlie Chaplin, actor (1889–1977)	**Hanna Beekhuis (1889–1980)**
1890	Aimee Semple McPherson, evangelist (1890–1944)	Invention of the zipper	Katherine Anne Porter, writer (1890–1980)	**Marguerite Canal (1890–1978)**
				Jacques Ibert (1890–1962)
1891			Agatha Christie, writer (1891–1975)	**Frida Kern (1891–1988)**
			Zora Neale Hurston, folklorist and essayist (1891–1960)	Arthur Bliss (1891–1975)
				Serge Prokofiev (1891–1953)
			Grant Wood, artist (1891–1942)	
1892			Edna St. Vincent Millay, poet (1892–1950)	**Germaine Tailleferre (1892–1983)**[7]
			Vita Sackville-West, writer (1892–1962)	**Johanna Bordewijk-Roepman (1892–1971)**
				Ferde Grōfé (1892–1972)
			Pearl S. Buck, novelist (1892–1973)	Arthur Honegger (1892–1955)
				Darius Milhaud (1892–1974)
			Rebecca West, writer (1892–1983)	Bernard Wagenaar (1892–1971)
			Mary Pickford, actor (1892–1979)	

Date	History/ Politics	Science/Education	The Arts/ Literature	Music
1893	Madame Sun Yat-sen, political leader (1893–1981)		Dorothy Parker, writer (1893–1967) Sylvia Townsend Warner, writer (1893–1978) Mae West, actress (1893–1980) Joan Miró, artist (1893–1983)	Cole Porter (1893–1964) **Lili Boulanger (1893–1918)**[8] Federico Mompou (1893–1987)
1894			Martha Graham, dancer (1894–1991) Adela Rogers St. John, journalist (1894–1988)	**Elsa Respighi (1894–1996)** **Valley Weigl (1894–1982)** Walter Piston (1894–1976)
1895		Anna Freud (1895–1982)	Oscar Hammerstein, lyricist (1895–1960)	Paul Hindemith (1895–1963) **Maria Teresa Prieto (1895–1982)** Mario Castelnuovo-Tedesco (1895–1968) Carl Orff (1895–1982) William Grant Still (1895–1978) Dane Rudhyar (1895–1985)
1896			F. Scott Fitzgerald, writer (1896–1940)	**Lucie Vellère (1896–1966)** **Maria Bach (1896–1978)** **Elizabeth Gyring (1896–1970)** Roger Sessions (1896–1885) Virgil Thomson (1896–1988)
1897	Margaret Chase Smith, senator (1897–1995) Amelia Earhart, aviator, social worker, and activist (1897–1937)		Catherine Drinker Bowen, writer and historian (1897–1973) William Faulkner, writer (1897–1962)	**Margaret Sutherland (1897–1984)** Henry Cowell (1897–1965) Erich Korngold (1897–1957) Paul Ben-Haim (1897–1984)
1898	Golda Meir, prime minister/Israel (1898–1978) Spanish American War begun	Discovery of radium by the Curies. Invention of the typewriter Invention of the flashlight	Beatrice Lillie, actress (1898–1989) Judith Anderson, actor (1898–1992) Ariel Durant, historian (1898–1981) Henry Moore, sculptor (1898–1986)	**Stefanie Lachowska (1898–1966)** Hanns Eisler (1898–1962) George Gershwin (1898–1937)

Date	History/ Politics	Science/Education	The Arts/ Literature	Music
1898		Madame Chiang Kai-shek, educator, reformer, and sociologist (1898–?)	Federico Garciá Lorca, poet (1898–1936) Bertolt Brecht, playwright (1898–1956) Lotte Lenya, singer (1898–1981)	Roy Harris (1898–1979) Bessie Smith, singer (1898–?)
1899	First International Peace Conference at The Hague Boer War		Louise Nevelson, artist (1899–1988) Ernest Hemingway, writer (1899–1961) Vladimir Nabokov, writer (1899–1977)	Francis Poulenc (1899–1963) **Sophie-Carmen Eckhardt-Gramatté** (1899–1974) **Barbara Giuranna (1899–1999)** **Grete von Zieritz (b. 1899)** **Lorraine Finley (1899–1972)** Georges Auric (1899–1983) Carlos Chávez (1899–1978) Alexander Tcherepnin (1899–1977)

1 See Chapter 6 for more information on Moore.

2 See Chapter 6 for more information on Shepherd.

3 See Chapter 6 for more information on Bauer.

4 See Chapter 6 for more information on Boulanger.

5 See Chapter 6 for more information on Price.

6 See Chapter 6 for more information on Aufderheide.

7 See Chapter 6 for more information on Tailleferre.

8 See Chapter 6 for more information on Boulanger.

Bibliography

Amy Beach

Block, Adrienne Fried. *Amy Beach, Passionate Victorian: The Life and Work of an American Composer, 1867–1944.* New York and Oxford: Oxford University Press, 1998.

———. "Amy Marcy Cheney Beach." In *Women Composers: Music Through the Ages*, vol. 7, edited by Sylvia Glickman and Martha Furman Schleifer. New York: G. K. Hall, 2003.

Teresa Carreño

Mann, Brian. "Teresa Carreño." In *Women Composers: Music Through the Ages*, vol. 6, edited by Sylvia Glickman and Martha Furman Schleifer. New York: G. K. Hall, 1999.

Cécile Chaminade

Citron, Marcia J. *Cécile Chaminade: A Bio-Bibliography*. Westport, CT: Greenwood, 1988.

Ledeen, Lydia. "Cécile Louise Stephanie Chaminade." In *Women Composers: Music Through the Ages*, vol. 6, edited by Sylvia Glickman and Martha Furman Schleifer. New York: G. K. Hall, 1999.

Mabel Wheeler Daniels

Daniels, Mabel Wheeler. *An American Girl in Munich: Impressions of a Music Student*. Boston: Little, Brown, 1905.

Louise Farrenc

Farrenc, Louise. *Traité des abréviations (signes d'agrément et ornements) employés par les clavecinistes, XVIIe et XVIIIe siècles*. Paris: Leduc, [n.d.].

Friedland, Bea. "Louise Farrenc." In *Women Composers: Music Through the Ages*, vol. 6, edited by Sylvia Glickman and Martha Furman Schleifer. New York: G. K. Hall, 1999.

———. *Louise Farrenc, 1804–75: Composer, Performer, Scholar*. Ann Arbor, MI: UMI Research Press, 1981.

Le trésor des pianistes. 23 vols. Edited by Aristide and Louise Farrenc, with a new foreword by Bea Friedland. New York: Da Capo, 1977.

Eleanor Everest Freer

Eversole, Sylvia Miller. "Eleanor Everest Freer." Ph.D. diss., City University of New York, 1992. UMI 93-04,657.

———. "Eleanor Everest Freer." In *Women Composers: Music Through the Ages*, vol. 7, edited by Sylvia Glickman and Martha Furman Schleifer. New York: G. K. Hall, 2002.

Freer, Eleanor Everest. *Recollections and Reflections of an American Composer*. N.p., 1929.

Fanny Mendelssohn Hensel

Cai, Camilla. "Fanny Mendelssohn Hensel." In *Women Composers: Music Through the Ages*, vol. 6, edited by Sylvia Glickman and Martha Furman Schleifer. New York: G. K. Hall, 1999.

Citron, Marcia J., coll., ed., trans. *Letters from Fanny Hensel to Felix Mendelssohn*. Stuyvesant, NY: Pendragon Press, 1987.

Ochs, Ruth. "Fanny Mendelssohn Hensel." In *Women Composers: Music Through the Ages*, vol. 7, edited by Sylvia Glickman and Martha Furman Schleifer. New York: G. K. Hall, 2003.

Quin, Carol Lynelle. "Fanny Mendelssohn Hensel: Her Contributions to Nineteenth-century Musical Life." Ph.D. diss., University of Kentucky, 1981. UMI 81-29,758.

Reich, Nancy B. "The Power of Class: Fanny Hensel." In *Mendelssohn and His World*, edited by R. Larry Todd. Princeton, NJ: Princeton University Press, 1991, pp. 86–99.

Sirota, Victoria Ressmeyer. "The Life and Works of Fanny Mendelssohn Hensel." D.M.A. diss., Boston University, 1981. UMI 81-26,666.

Tillard, Françoise. *Fanny Mendelssohn*. Translated by Camille Naish. Portland, OR: Amadeus, 1996.

Wallace, Sean, and Ruth Ochs. "Fanny Mendelssohn Hensel." In *Women Composers: Music Through the Ages*, vol. 7, edited by Sylvia Glickman and Martha Furman Schleifer. New York: G. K. Hall, 2003.

Augusta Holmès

Barillon-Bauché, Paula. *Holmès et la femme compositeur*. Paris: Fischbacher, 1912.

Helen Hood

Fox, Pamela. "Helen Francis Hood." In *The Norton/Grove Dictionary of Women Composers*, edited by Julie Anne Sadie and Rhian Samuel. New York and London: W. W. Norton, 1995.

"Helen Hood." In *Women Composers: A Biographical Handbook of Woman's Work in Music*, by Otto Ebel. Brooklyn, NY: Chandler-Ebel Music Company, 1902.

Helen Hopekirk

Muller, Dana Gail. "Helen Hopekirk (1856–1945): Pianist, Composer, Pedagogue." Ph.D. diss., University of Hartford, 1995.

Schleifer, Martha Furman. "Helen Hopekirk." In *Women Composers: Music Through the Ages*, vol. 6, edited by Sylvia Glickman and Martha Furman Schleifer. New York: G. K. Hall, 1999.

Carrie Jacobs-Bond

Good, M. "Carrie Jacobs Bond: Her Life and Times." Thesis, Butler University, 1984.

Ingeborg von Bronsart

Asmus, W. "Ingeborg von Bronsart." *Neue Zeitschrift für Musik* 65 (1898): 193–95.

Deaville, James. "Ingeborg von Bronsart." In *Women Composers: Music Through the Ages*, vol. 7, edited by Sylvia Glickman and Martha Furman Schleifer. New York: G. K. Hall.

Polko, Elise. "Ingeborg von Bronsart: biographisches Skizzenblatt." *Neue Musik-Zeitung* 9 (1888): 142–43.

Marie Jaëll

Corre, Christian. "Marie Jaëll (1846–1925): La Virtuosité musicale entre l'art et la science." In *Défense et illustration de la virtuosité*, edited by Anne Penesco. Lyon: Presses universitaires de Lyon, 1997, pp. 141–54.

Schmidt-Rogers, Lea. "Marie Jaëll." In *Women Composers: Music Through the Ages*, vol. 6, edited by Sylvia Glickman and Martha Furman Schleifer. New York: G. K. Hall, 1999.

Johanna Kinkel

Bröcker, Marianne. "Johanna Kinkel's schriftstellerische und musikpädagogische Tätigkeit." *Bonner Geschichtsblätter* 29 (1977): 37–48.

Summerville, Suzanne. "Johanna Kinkel." In *Women Composers: Music Through the Ages*, vol. 7, edited by Sylvia Glickman and Martha Furman Schleifer. New York: G. K. Hall, 2003.

Thalheimer, E. "Johanna Kinkel als Musikerin." Ph.D. diss., University of Bonn, 1922.

Josephine Lang

Krebs, Harald. "Josephine Lang." In *Women Composers: Music Through the Ages*, vol. 7, edited by Sylvia Glickman and Martha Furman Schleifer. New York: G. K. Hall, 2003.

Mendelssohn, Felix. Letter from Munich, October 6, 1831. In Felix Mendelssohn *Letters*, edited by G. Selden-Goth. New York; Pantheon, 1945.

Margaret Ruthven Lang

Cline, Judith. "Margaret Ruthven Lang." In *Women Composers: Music Through the Ages*, vol. 7, edited by Sylvia Glickman and Martha Furman Schleifer. New York: G. K. Hall, 2003.

Luise Adolpha Le Beau

Le Beau, Luise Adolpha. *Lebenserinnerungen einer Komponistin*. Baden-Baden: Emil Sommermeyer, 1910.

Lili'uokalani

The Queen's Songbook: Her Majesty Queen Lili`uokalani. Edited by Dorothy Kahananui Gillett and Barbara Barnard Smith. Honolulu, HI: Hui Hanai, 1999.

Emilie Mayer

Zopff, Hermann. "Compositionen von Emilie Mayer." *Neue Zeitschrift für Musik* 63, no. 21 (May 17, 1867): 181–82.

Sophie Menter

Schleifer, Martha Furman. "Sophie Menter." In *Women Composers: Music Through the Ages*, vol. 6, edited by Sylvia Glickman and Martha Furman Schleifer. New York: G. K. Hall, 1999.

Clara Kathleen Rogers

Radell, Judith, and Delight Malitsky. "Rogers, Clara Kathleen." In *Women Composers: Music Through the Ages*, vol. 6, edited by Sylvia Glickman and Martha Furman Schleifer. New York: G. K. Hall, 1999.
———. "Rogers, Clara Kathleen." In *Women Composers: Music Through the Ages*, vol. 7, edited by Sylvia Glickman and Martha Furman Schleifer. New York: G. K. Hall, 2003.
Rogers, Clara Kathleen. *The Story of Two Lives: Home, Friends, and Travels*. Privately printed by the Plimpton Press, 1932.

Clara Schumann

Burk, John N. *Clara Schumann: A Romantic Biography*. New York: Random House, 1940.
Chissell, Joan. *Clara Schumann, a Dedicated Spirit: A Study of Her Life and Work*. London: H. Hamilton, 1983.
The Complete Correspondence of Clara and Robert Schumann. Edited by Eva Weissweiler; translated by Hildegard Fritsch and Robert L. Crawford. New York: P. Lang, 1994.
Goertzen, Valerie Woodring. "Clara Schumann." In *Women Composers: Music Through the Ages*, vol. 6, edited by Sylvia Glickman and Martha Furman Schleifer. New York: G. K. Hall, 1999.
Litzmann, Berthold. *Clara Schumann: Ein Künstlerleben nach Tagebüchern und Briefen*, 3 vols. Edited and translated by Grace E. Hadow. Leipzig: Breitkopf und Härtel, 1923; New York: Da Capo, 1979.
Reich, Nancy B. *Clara Schumann, the Artist and the Woman* revised edition. Ithaca, NY: Cornell University Press, 2001.
Schumann, Clara.—*dass Gott mir ein Talent geschenkt: Clara Schumann's Briefe an Hermann Härtel und Richard und Helene Schöne*. Zurich: Atlantis, 1997.
Schumann, Clara, and Robert Schumann. *The Complete Marriage Diaries of Robert and Clara Schumann, from their Wedding Day through the Russia Trip*. Edited by Gerd Nauhaus and translated by Peter Ostwald. Boston: Northeastern University Press, 1993.
Schumann, Eugenie. *Memoirs of Eugenie Schumann*, trans. Marie Busch. London, 1927; reprint Westport, CT: Hyperion, 1979.

Ethel Smyth

Smyth, Ethel. *The Memoirs of Ethel Smyth*. Edited by Ronald Crichton. London: Viking, 1987.

Elizabeth Stirling

Owen, Barbara. "Elizabeth Stirling." In *Women Composers: Music Through the Ages*, vol. 6, edited by Sylvia Glickman and Martha Furman Schleifer. New York: G. K. Hall, 1999.

Mary Wurm

Burton, Nigel. "Mary Wurm." In *The Norton/Grove Dictionary of Women Composers*, edited by Julie Anne Sadie and Rhian Samuel. New York and London: W. W. Norton, 1995.

Selected Discography

Amy Beach

Cabildo, Six Short Pieces. New York Concert Singers, Ransom Wilson, conductor. Delos DE 3170 (1995).

Canticle of the Sun. Capitol Hill Choral Society, Betty Buchanan, conductor. Albany Records TROY 295 (1998).

Chamber Music by Women Composers. The Macalester Trio. Vox Box CDX 5029 (1991).

Concerto for Piano and Orchestra, op. 45. Westphalian Symphony Orchestra, Siegfried Landau, conductor; Mary Louise Boehm, pianist. Vox Box 2-5069 (1992).

Deferred Voices: Organ Music by Women. Christa Rakich, organ. AFK 527 (1993).

"Gaelic" Symphony. Detroit Symphony Orchestra, Neeme Järvi, conductor. Chandos Records CHAN 8958 (1991).

"Gaelic" Symphony. Royal Philharmonic Orchestra, Karl Kruger, conductor. Bridge 9086 (1968).

Grand Mass in E Flat for Orchestra and Chorus, op. 5. Stow Festival Chorus and Orchestra, Barbara Jones, conductor. Albany Records TROY 179 (1995).

Music for Violin/Viola and Piano. Laura Klugherz, viola and violin; Jill Timmons, pianist. Centaur CRC 2312 (1997).

Piano Quintet, etc. Ambache Chamber Ensemble. Chandos Records CHAN 9752 (1999).

Piano Works. Virginia Eskin, pianist. Koch 3-7254-2 H1 (1995).

Sacred Music. Choral Society of Southern California, Chancel Choir of Beverly Hills, Nick Strimple, conductor. Music & Arts CD 4921 (1996).

Solo Piano Music. 3 vols. Joanne Polk, pianist. Arabesque Z6693, Z6704, Z6721 (1997–1998).

Sonata in A Minor for Violin and Piano, op. 34. Joseph Silverstein, violin; Gilbert Kalish, pianist. New World Records 80542 (1977).

Songs by Clara Schumann, Poldowski, Amy Beach. Lauralyn Kolb, soprano; Don McMahon, pianist. Albany Records TROY 109 (1994).

Songs, Violin Pieces, and Piano Music. D'Anna Fortunato, mezzo-soprano; Joseph Silverstein, violinist; Virginia Eskin, pianist. Northeastern NR 9004-CD (1988).

Women at an Exposition. Susanne Mentzer, Sunny Joy Langton, Elaine Skorodin, Kimberly Schmidt. Koch International Classics KIC 7240 (1991).

Women Composers for Organ. Music of Beach, Stirling, Hensel, Schumann. Barbara Harbach, organist. Gasparo GSCD 294 (1993).

Teresa Carreño

Chamber Music by French Female Composers. Trio Aperto. Talent Records DOM 291049 (1997).

Chamber Music by Women Composers. The Macalester Trio. Vox Box CDX 5029 (1991).
Piano Works. Alexandra Oehler, pianist. Ars Musici 1258 (1999).

Cécile Chaminade

Chamber Music by Women Composers. The Macalester Trio. Vox Box CDX 5029 (1991).
Klaviernacht—Piano Works by Women Composers. Eva Schieferstein, piano. Bayer BR 100255 (1996).
Music for Piano. Enid Katahn, pianist. Gasparo GSCD 247 (1994).
Piano Music, 3 vols. Peter Jacobs, pianist. Hyperion CDA 66584, CDA 66706, CDA 66846 (1992–1996).
Piano Works. Eric Parkin, pianist. Chandos CHAN 8888 (1991).
Women at an Exposition. Susanne Mentzer, Sunny Joy Langton, Elaine Skorodin, Kimberly Schmidt. Koch International Classics KIC 7240 (1991).

Louise Farrenc

Chamber Music. Ambache Chamber Ensemble. IMP Carlton Classics 6600302 (1996).
Chamber Music by French Female Composers. Trio Aperto. Talent Records DOM 291049 (1997).
Nonet and Sextet. Rheinland-Pfalz State Orchestra soloists. Bayer Records CD 100325 (2000).
Piano Compositions by Women Composers. Monica Pons, pianist. La Ma de Guido DISC 037 (1998).
Piano Quintets, opp. 30 and 31. Linos Ensemble. CPO 999194 (1993).
Symphonies 1 and 3. Hannover Radio Philharmonic Orchestra, Johannes Goritzki, conductor. CPO 999603 (1998).

Fanny Hensel

Chamber Music by Women Composers. The Macalester Trio. Vox Box CDX 5029 (1991).
Chorlieder, Duette-, Terzette. Dortmund, University Chamber Choir, Willi Gundlach, conductor. Thorofon 2299 (1996).
Choruses for A Capella Chorus. Leonarda Ensemble Cologne, Elke Mascha Blankenburg, conductor. CPO 999012 (1988).
Das Jahr. Sarah Rothenberg, pianist. Arabesque Z6666 (1996).
Deferred Voices: Organ Music by Women. Christa Rakich, organ. AFK 527 (1993).
Kantaten von Fanny Hensel und Felix Mendelssohn. Rotterdam Florilegium Musicum, Dortmund University Chamber Choir, Willi Gundlach, conductor. Thorofon 2346 (1997).
Klavierkompositionen aus der Italien-Zeit. Elzbieta Sternlicht, pianist. Ars Musici AM 1180 (1998).
Klaviernacht—Piano Works by Women Composers. Eva Schieferstein, piano. Bayer BR 100255 (1996).
Lieder. Julianne Baird, soprano; Keith Weber, pianist. Newport Classic NPD 85652 (1999).
Lieder. Lauralyn Kolb, soprano; Arlene Shrut, pianist. Centaur 2120 (1992).
Oratorium nach Bildern der Bibel. Cologne Youth Orchestra, Cologne Youth Chorus, Elke Mascha Blankenburg, conductor. CPO 999009 (1984–1986).
Piano Compositions by Women Composers. Monica Pons, pianist. La Ma de Guido DISC 037 (1998).
Piano Music. 2 vols. Liana Serbescu, pianist. CPO 999015 (1987).
String Quartets. Hensel, Fanny Mendelssohn, Emilie Mayer, and Maddalena Sirmen. Erato String Quartet. CPO 999679 (1999).
Vocal Works. Dortmund University Chamber Choir, Willi Gundlach, conductor. Thorofon 2398 (1999).
Women Composers. Music by Schumann, Hensel, Szymanowska. Solveig Funseth, pianist. Swedish Music Society Discofil SCD 1043 (1988).
Women Composers for Organ. Music of Beach, Stirling, Hensel, Schumann. Barbara Harbach, organist. Gasparo GSCD 294 (1993).

Augusta Holmès

Orchestral Music. Rheinland-Pfalz State Orchestra, Patrick Davin, conductor. Marco Polo 8223449 (1994).

Marie Jaëll

Piano Works. Alexandre Sorel, pianist. Solstice Records SOCD 156 (1997).

Johanna Kinkel

Kinkel, Johanna, and Josephine Lang. *Ausgewählte Lieder*. Claudia Taha, soprano; Heidi Kommerell, pianist. Bayer BR 100248 (1995).

Josephine Lang

Lieder von Josephine Lang. Dana McKay, soprano; Therese Lindquist, pianist. Deutsche Schallplatten DS 1016 (1994).

Clara Kathleen Rogers

Women at an Exposition. Susanne Mentzer, Sunny Joy Langton, Elaine Skorodin, Kimberly Schmidt. Koch International Classics KIC 7240 (1991).

Clara Schumann

Chamber Music by Women Composers. The Macalester Trio. Vox Box CDX 5029 (1991).

Choral Songs for A Cappella Mixed Chorus. Heidelberg Madrigal Choir, Gerald Kegelmann, conductor. Bayer BR 100041 (1988).

The Complete Lieder. Isabel Lippitz, soprano; Deborah Richards, pianist. Bayer BR 100206 (1992).

Complete Songs. Gabriele Fontana, soprano; Konstanze Eickhorst, pianist. CPO 999127 (1994).

Complete Works for Piano. 3 vols. Jozef de Beenhouwer, pianist. Partridge 1129-2, 1130-2, 1131-2 (1990–1991).

In Clara Wieck Schumann's Circle. Bichuan Li, pianist. Wa Nui Records WN 49706-2 (1997).

Klaviernacht—Piano Works by Women Composers. Eva Schieferstein, piano. Bayer BR 100255.

Piano Compositions by Women Composers. Monica Pons, pianist. La Ma de Guido DISC 037 (1998).

Piano Concerto, op. 7 and *Piano Trio*, op. 17. Bamberg Symphony Orchestra, Joseph Silverstein, conductor; Veronica Jochum, pianist; C. Carr, cello. Tudor 788 (1988).

Songs by Clara Schumann, Poldowski, Amy Beach. Lauralyn Kolb, soprano; Don McMahon, pianist. Albany Records TROY 109 (1994).

Songs by Robert and Clara Schumann. Barbara Bonney, soprano; Vladimir Ashkenazy, pianist. London 452898-2 (1997).

Women at an Exposition. Susanne Mentzer, Sunny Joy Langton, Elaine Skorodin, Kimberly Schmidt. Koch International Classics KIC 7240 (1991).

Women Composers. Music by Schumann, Hensel, Szymanowska. Solveig Funseth, pianist. Swedish Music Society Discofil SCD 1043 (1988).

Women Composers for Organ. Music of Beach, Stirling, Hensel, Schumann. Barbara Harbach, organist. Gasparo GSCD 294 (1993).

Ethel Smyth

Choral Songs for A Cappella Mixed Chorus. Heidelberg Madrigal Choir, Gerald Kegelmann, conductor. Bayer BR 100041 (1988).

The Complete Lieder. Isabel Lippitz, soprano; Deborah Richards, pianist. Bayer BR 100206 (1992).

Complete Songs. Gabriele Fontana, soprano; Konstanze Eickhorst, pianist. CPO 999127 (1994).

Complete Works for Piano. 3 vols. Jozef de Beenhouwer, pianist. Partridge 1129-2, 1130-2, 1131-2 (1990–1991).

Deferred Voices: Organ Music by Women. Christa Rakich, organ. AFK 527 (1993).

In Clara Wieck Schumann's Circle. Bichuan Li, pianist. Wa Nui Records WN 49706-2 (1997).

Piano Concerto, op. 7, and *Piano Trio*, op. 17. Bamberg Symphony Orchestra, Joseph Silverstein, conductor; Veronica Jochum, pianist; C. Carr, cello. Tudor 788 (1988).

Songs by Robert and Clara Schumann. Barbara Bonney, soprano; Vladimir Ashkenazy, pianist. London 452898-2 (1997).

Elizabeth Stirling

Summershimmer: Women Composers for Organ. Barbara Harbach, organist. Hester Park 7704 (1996).
Women Composers for Organ. Music of Beach, Stirling, Hensel, Schumann. Barbara Harbach, organist. Gasparo GSCD 294 (1993).

Selected Modern Editions

Amy (Mrs. H.H.A.) Beach

Orchestra

Concerto for piano and orchestra in C-sharp minor, op. 45. Bryn Mawr, PA: Hildegard Publishing Company, 1995.
"Gaelic" Symphony, op. 32. In *Three Centuries of American Music,* vol. 10: *American Orchestral Music: Late Nineteenth Century,* edited by Sam Dennison. [Boston]: G. K. Hall, 1992.
"Gaelic" Symphony, op. 32. Boca Raton, FL: Kalmus, 1990.
Symphony in E minor, "Gaelic," op. 32. Boston: Schmidt, 1897; facs., G. K. Hall, 1992.

Chamber

Violin and piano

Barcarolle, op. 28, no. 1. Bryn Mawr, PA: Hildegard Publishing Company, 1994.
Berceuse, op. 40, no. 2. Bryn Mawr, PA: Hildegard Publishing Company, 1994.
Le Captive, op. 40, no. 1. Bryn Mawr, PA: Hildegard Publishing Company, 1994.
Dreaming. Bryn Mawr, PA: Hildegard Publishing Company, 1994.
Invocation for violin and piano, op. 55 (1904). Bryn Mawr PA: Hildegard Publishing Company, 1994.
Lento espressivo, op. 125, for violin and piano. Bryn Mawr, PA: Hildegard Publishing Company, 1994.
Mazurka, op. 40, no. 3. Bryn Mawr, PA: Hildegard Publishing Company, 1994.
Pastorale. Bryn Mawr, PA: Hildegard Publishing Company, 1994.
Romance for violin and piano, op. 23. Bryn Mawr, PA: Hildegard Publishing Company, 1994.
Sonata in A minor for violin and piano, op. 34. Bryn Mawr, PA: Hildegard Publishing Company, 1994.

Cello and piano

Berceuse, op. 40, no. 2. Bryn Mawr, PA: Hildegard Publishing Company, 1994.
Le Captive, op. 40, no. 1. Bryn Mawr, PA: Hildegard Publishing Company, 1994.
Invocation op. 55 (1904). Bryn Mawr PA: Hildegard Publishing Company, 1994.
Mazurka, op. 40, no. 3. Bryn Mawr, PA: Hildegard Publishing Company, 1994.
Romance, op. 23. Bryn Mawr, PA: Hildegard Publishing Company, 1994.

Trio

Trio for violin, cello, and piano, op. 150 Bryn Mawr, PA: Hildegard Publishing Company, 1997.

Quartet

Quartet for Strings in One Movement, op. 89. Edited by Adrienne Fried Block. Recent Researches in American music, vol. 23; Music of the United States of America, vol. 3. Madison, WI: A-R Editions, 1994.

Pastoral for woodwind quintet, op. 151. Bryn Mawr, PA: Hildegard Publishing Company, 1997.

Quintet for Piano and Strings in F-sharp minor, op. 67. Bryn Mawr, PA: Hildegard Publishing Company, 1997.

Quintet in F-sharp Minor, op. 67, for piano and strings. Introduced by Adrienne Fried Block. New York: Da Capo, 1979.

Theme and Variations for flute and string quartet, op. 80. Bryn Mawr, PA: Hildegard Publishing Company, 1996.

Theme and Variations, op. 80, for flute and string quartet. In *Three Centuries of American Music*, vol. 8: American Chamber Music. Edited by John Graziano. [Boston]: G. K. Hall, 1991.

Theme and Variations, op. 80, for flute and string quartet. Huntsville, TX: Recital, 1997.

Keyboard

Ballad, op. 6. Bryn Mawr, PA: Hildegard Publishing Company, 1990.

Barcarolle, from *Trois morceaux caractéristiques*, op. 28. Bryn Mawr, PA: Hildegard Publishing Company, 1990.

By the Still Waters, op. 114. Art, 1925.

Children's Album, op. 36. Bryn Mawr, PA: Hildegard Publishing Company, 1990.

Children's Carnival, op. 25. Bryn Mawr, PA: Hildegard Publishing Company, 1990.

A Cradle Song of the Lonely Mother, op. 108. Cincinnati: Church, 1924; New York: Da Capo Press, 1982, Sylvia Glickman, ed.

Fantasia Fugata, op. 87. Philadelphia: Presser, 1923; New York: Da Capo Press, 1982, Sylvia Glickman, ed.

Five Improvisations, op. 148. Bryn Mawr, PA: Hildegard Publishing Company, 1997.

Five Improvisations for Piano, op. 148. Northbrook, IL: Composers Press, 1982.

Four Sketches, op. 15. Bryn Mawr, PA: Hildegard Publishing Company, 1998.

From Grandmother's Garden, op. 97. Bryn Mawr, PA: Hildegard Publishing Company, 1997.

The Hermit Thrush at Eve and *The Hermit Thrush at Morn*, op. 92. Bryn Mawr, PA: Hildegard Publishing Company, 1997.

A Hermit Thrush at Eve and *A Hermit Thrush at Morn*, op. 92. In *Women Composers: Music Through the Ages*, vol. 6, edited by Sylvia Glickman and Martha Furman Schleifer. New York: G. K. Hall, 1999.

Nocturne, op. 107. Cincinnati: Church, 1924; New York: Da Capo Press, 1982, Sylvia Glickman, ed.

Piano Music. Introduced by Sylvia Glickman. New York: Da Capo Press, 1982.

Prelude and Fugue, op. 81. New York: Schirmer, 1918; New York: Da Capo Press, 1982, Sylvia Glickman, ed.

Les rêves de Colombine, op. 65. Boston: Schmidt, 1907; Bryn Mawr, PA: Hildegard Publishing Company, 1990.

Scottish Legend and Gavotte fantastique, op. 54. Boston: Schmidt, 1903; Bryn Mawr, PA: Hildegard Publishing Company, 1990.

Suite for Two Pianos Founded upon Old Irish Melodies, op. 104. Bryn Mawr, PA: Hildegard Publishing Company, 2001.

Three Movements for Four Hands. Bryn Mawr, PA: Hildegard Publishing Company, 1998.

Three Pianoforte Pieces, op. 128. Philadelphia: Presser, 1928; New York: Da Capo Press, 1982, Sylvia Glickman, ed.

Tyrolean Valse-Fantaisie, op. 116. Boston: Ditson, 1926; New York: Da Capo Press, 1982, Sylvia Glickman, ed.

Valse-Caprice, op. 4. Boston: Schmidt, 1889. Bryn Mawr, PA: Hildegard Publishing Company, 1997.

Variations on Balkan Themes, op. 60. Boston: Schmidt, 1906;. Bryn Mawr, PA: Hildegard Publishing Company, 1997.

Choral

The Chambered Nautilus, op. 66. Bryn Mawr, PA: Hildegard Publishing Company, 1994.

Festival Jubilate, op. 17. Bryn Mawr, PA: Hildegard Publishing Company, 1995.

Festival Jubilate, op. 17. Huntsville, TX: Recital, 1997.

Mass, op. 5. In *Three Centuries of American Music*, vol. 7: *American Sacred Music*, edited by Philip Vandermeer. [Boston]: G. K. Hall, 1991.

Mass, op. 5. Huntsville, TX: Recital Publications, 1996.

Minstrel and the King, op. 16, for male chorus and orchestra. Huntsville, TX: Recital Publications, 1996.

The Rose of Avon-town, op. 30 for women's chorus and soprano solo with piano accompaniment. Huntsville, TX: Recital Publications, 1997.

The Sea-Fairies, op. 59. Edited by Andrew Thomas Kuster. Recent Researches in American Music, vol. 32. Madison, WI: A-R Editions, 1999.

The Sea-Fairies, op. 59. Bryn Mawr, PA: Hildegard Publishing Company, 1996.

Vocal Solo

Elle et moi, op. 21, no. 3. In *Twelve Songs*, Deborah Cook, ed. Bryn Mawr, PA: Hildegard Publishing Company, 1994.

Extase, op. 21, no. 2, in *Twelve Songs*, Deborah Cook, ed. Bryn Mawr, PA: Hildegard Publishing Company, 1994.

Fairy Lullaby, op. 37, no. 3. Boston: Schmidt, 1893; in *Twelve Songs*, Deborah Cook, ed. Bryn Mawr, PA: Hildegard Publishing Company, 1994.

June, in *Three Songs* for voice, violin, cello and piano. Bryn Mawr, PA: Hildegard Publishing Company, 2001 (G. K. Hall reprint).

June, op. 51, no. 3, *A Mirage*, op. 100, no. 1, *Stella viatoris*, op. 100, no. 2; *Rendezvous*, op. 120. In *Women Composers: Music Through the Ages*, vol. 7, edited by Sylvia Glickman and Martha Furman Schleifer. New York: G. K. Hall, 2002.

A Mirage, in *Three Songs* for voice, violin, cello and piano. Bryn Mawr, PA: Hildegard Publishing Company, 2001 (G. K. Hall reprint).

O Mistress Mine, op. 37, no. 1, Boston: Schmidt, 1893; in *Twelve Songs*, Deborah Cook, ed. Bryn Mawr PA: Hildegard Publishing Company, 1994.

Stella Viatoris, in *Three Songs* for voice, violin, cello and piano. Bryn Mawr, PA: Hildegard Publishing Company, 2001 (G. K. Hall reprint).

Take, O Take Those Lips Away, op. 37, no. 2, Boston: Schmidt, 1893; in *Twelve Songs*, Deborah Cook, ed. Bryn Mawr PA: Hildegard Publishing Company, 1994.

Twenty-three Songs. Introduced by Mary Louise Boehm. New York: Da Capo, 1992.

Wouldn't That Be Queer? op. 26, no. 4, Boston: Schmidt, 1893; in *Twelve Songs*, Deborah Cook, ed. Bryn Mawr, PA: Hildegard Publishing Company, 1994.

The Year's at the Spring, op. 44 no. 1. Boston: Schmidt, 1893; in *Twelve Songs*, Deborah Cook, ed. Bryn Mawr, PA: Hildegard Publishing Company, 1994.

Carrie Jacobs-Bond

Vocal

Her Greatest Charm. In *The First Solos: Songs by Women Composers*. Bryn Mawr, PA: Hildegard Publishing Company, 2001.

I Love You Truly. Chicago: Bond and Son, 1901.

Reverie (1902). In *Three Centuries of American Music*, vol. 4: Edited by Sylvia Glickman. [Boston]: G. K. Hall, 1990.

Piano

Reverie (1902). In *American Women Composers: Piano Music from 1865–1915*. Bryn Mawr, PA: Hildegard Publishing Company, 1990.

Ingeborg von Bronsart

Vocal solo

Blumengruss, Frisch auf, zum letzten Kampf und Streit!, Ich stand in dunkeln Träumen, Ik weet en Leed, wat Niemand weet, Letzte Bitte, Verwandlung. In *Women Composers: Music Through the Ages*, vol. 7, edited by Sylvia Glickman and Martha Furman Schleifer. New York: G. K. Hall, 2003.

Six songs, including *Frisch auf, zum letzten kampf und Streit!; Blumengruss; Letzte Bitte; Ik weet en leed, wat Niemand weet; Ich stand in dunkeln Träumen, Verwandlung*. Bryn Mawr, PA: Hildegard Publishing Company, 2001 (G. K. Hall reprint).

Teresa Carreño

Piano

Caprice-Étude, op. 2. Bryn Mawr, PA: Hildegard Publishing Company, 2000 (G. K. Hall reprint).

La Corbeille des fleurs, op. 9. Bryn Mawr, PA: Hildegard Publishing Company, 1996.

Esquisses Italiennes op. 33, no 1. Bryn Mawr, PA: Hildegard Publishing Company, 1996.

Gottschalk Waltz, Caprice Étude, Plaintes au bord d'une tombe (4ème Élégie), op. 20, *Plaintes au bord d'une tombe (5ème Élégie)*, op. 21. In *Women Composers: Music Through the Ages*, vol. 6, edited by Sylvia Glickman and Martha Furman Schleifer. New York: G. K. Hall, 1999.

Highland, Souvenir of Scotland op. 38. Bryn Mawr, PA: Hildegard Publishing Company, 1996.

Kleiner Walzer (Mi Teresita). Bryn Mawr, PA: Hildegard Publishing Company, 1996.

Plainte, op 17. Bryn Mawr, PA: Hildegard Publishing Company, 1996.

Plaintes au bord d'un tombe, op. 20. Bryn Mawr, PA: Hildegard Publishing Company, 2000 (G. K. Hall reprint).

Le Printemps, grande valse, op. 26. Bryn Mawr, PA: Hildegard Publishing Company, 1996.

Une revue à Prague, fantaisie, op. 27. Bryn Mawr, PA: Hildegard Publishing Company, 1996.

Selected Works: Piano Pieces and String Quartet. Edited by Rosario Marciano. New York: Da Capo Press, 1984.

Valse Gottschalk, op. 1. Bryn Mawr, PA: Hildegard Publishing Company, 1996.

Cécile Chaminade

Chamber

Concertino for Flute and Piano, op. 107. In *Flute Music by French Composers*, edited by Louis Moyse. New York: G. Schirmer, 1967.

Piano Trio, op. 11. Bryn Mawr, PA: Hildegard Publishing Company, 1996.

Portrait: valse chantée for soprano, flute, and piano. Translations by Mary Dibbern. New York: Classical Vocal Reprints, 1997.

Piano and orchestra

Concertstück, op. 40, for Piano and Orchestra. Boca Raton, FL: Kalmus, 1997.

Piano

Pierette, op. 41. In *Frauen komponieren: 22 Klavierstücke des 18.–20. Jahrhunderts*, edited by Eva Rieger and Käte Walter. Mainz and New York: Schott, 1985.

Pierette, op. 41 and *L'Ondine*, op. 101. Boca Raton, FL: Masters Music, 1997.

Selected Compositions for the Piano. New York: G. Schirmer, 1927.

Six études de concert for solo piano, op. 35. Boca Raton, FL: Masters Music, [n.d.].

Six romances sans paroles for solo piano, op. 76. Boca Raton, FL: Masters Music, 1996.

Sonata in C minor, op. 21. Bryn Mawr PA: Hildegard Publishing Company, 2001 (G. K. Hall reprint).

Sonata in C minor, op. 21. Boca Raton, FL: Masters Music, 1997.

Sonata in C minor, op. 21. In *Women Composers: Music Through the Ages*, vol. 6, edited by Sylvia Glickman and Martha Furman Schleifer. New York: G. K. Hall, 1999.

Three Piano Works. New York: Da Capo, 1979.

Vocal Solo

Ballade à la lune. Bryn Mawr, PA: Hildegard Publishing Company, 2001.

Plaintes d'amour. Bryn Mawr, PA: Hildegard Publishing Company, 2001.

Louise Farrenc

Orchestra

Ouverture, no. 1, op. 23 (1834). Bryn Mawr, PA: Hildegard Publishing Company, 1997.

Chamber

Allegro deciso, from Trio in E minor for flute or violin, cello, and piano (1857–1862). In *Historical Anthology of Music by Women*, edited by James R. Briscoe. Bloomington and Indianapolis: Indiana University Press, 1987.

Cello Sonata, op. 46. Paris: Farrenc, 1861; Bryn Mawr: Hildegard Publishing Company, 1996.

Nonet in E-flat major for woodwinds and strings, op. 38, arr. by composer for string quintet. Bryn Mawr, PA: Hildegard Publishing Company, 2000.

Nonetto, op. 38. Edited by William Scribner. Richmond, VA: International Opus, 1996.

Piano Quintet, op. 30. Vienna: Hofmeister, 1842; Bryn Mawr, PA: Hildegard Publishing Company, 1995.

Piano Quintet, op. 31. Paris: Farrenc, 1844; Bryn Mawr, PA: Hildegard Publishing Company, 1997.

Piano Trio, no. 1 in E-flat major, op. 33. Paris: Farrenc, 1855; Kassel: Furore, 1993.

Piano Trio no. 2 in D minor, op. 34. Paris: Farrenc, 1855; Bryn Mawr, PA: Hildegard Publishing Company, 1997.

Sextet in C Minor, op. 40 for piano and wind quintet. Edited by Willi Rechsteiner. Kassel: Furore, 1996.

Trio in E-flat Major for clarinet, cello, and piano, op. 44. Edited by John P. Newhill. Wiesbaden: Breitkopf and Härtel, 2000.

Trio for flute/violin, cello, and piano, op. 45. Paris: Farrenc, 1862; Bryn Mawr, PA: Hildegard Publishing Company, 1996.

Trio in E Minor for piano flute (or violin), and Cello, op. 45. Introduced by Miriam Gideon. New York: Da Capo Press, 1979.

Trio, op. 45. Kassel: Furore.

Violin Sonata, no. 1, op. 37. Paris: Leduc, 1848; Bryn Mawr, PA: Hildegard Publishing Company, 1995.

Piano

Air Russe Varié pour le Piano-Forte. In *Women Composers: Music Through the Ages*, vol. 6, edited by Sylvia Glickman and Martha Furman Schleifer. New York: G. K. Hall, 1999; Bryn Mawr, PA: Hildegard Publishing, 2000.

Impromptu. In *Frauen komponieren: 22 Klavierstücke des 18.–20. Jahrhunderts*, edited by Eva Rieger and Käte Walter. Mainz and New York: Schott, 1985.

30 Études, op. 26. Paris: Farrenc, 1839–1840; Bryn Mawr, PA: Hildegard Publishing Company, 2000, Gena Raps, ed.

Eleanor Everest Freer

Summer Night, op. 12, no. 6; *Sweet in Her Green Dell*, op. 17, no. 2. In *Women Composers: Music Through the Ages*, vol. 7, edited by Sylvia Glickman and Martha Furman Schleifer. New York: G. K. Hall, 2003.

Summer Night. Bryn Mawr, PA: Hildegard Publishing Company, 2001 (G. K. Hall reprint).

Sweet in Her Green Dell. Bryn Mawr, PA: Hildegard Publishing Company, 2001 (G. K. Hall reprint).

Fanny Mendelssohn Hensel

Orchestra

Ouverture in C major. Edited by Elke Mascha Blankenburg. Kassel: Furore, 1994.

Chamber

Capriccio in A-flat major for cello and piano. (1829). Wiesbaden: Breitkopf and Härtel, 1994.

Piano Quartet in A-flat major. (1823). Kassel: Furore, 1990.

Piano Trio, op. 11. Leipzig: Breitkopf and Härtel, 1846; Bryn Mawr, PA: Hildegard Publishing Company, 1998.

String Quartet in E-flat major. (1834). Edited by Renate Eggebrecht-Kupsa. Kassel: Furore, 1988.

Piano

Charakterstücke (1846) for piano. Kassel: Furore, 1996.

Das Jahr (1841). Edited by Liana Gavrila Serbescu and Barbara Heller. Kassel: Furore, 1989.

Klavierstücke. 7 vols. Kassel: Furore, 1996.

Mélodie, op. 4, no. 2; *mélodie*, op. 5, no. 4. In *Frauen komponieren: 22 Klavierstücke des 18.—20. Jahrhunderts*, edited by Eva Rieger and Käte Walter. Mainz and New York: Schott, 1985.

Six Pieces from 1824–1827. Bryn Mawr, PA: Hildegard Publishing Company 1994.

Sonata in C minor (1824). Bryn Mawr, PA: Hildegard Publishing Company, 1994.

Sonata in G minor. Bryn Mawr, PA: Hildegard Publishing Company, 1994.

Sonata in G Minor for Piano. Edited by Liana Gavrila Serbescu and Barbara Heller. Kassel: Furore, 1991.

Songs for Pianoforte, 1836–1837. Edited by Camilla Cai. Recent Researchers in the Music of the Nineteenth and Early Twentieth Centuries, vol. 22. Madison, WI: A-R Editions, 1994.

Three Untitled Pieces. In *Women Composers: Music Through the Ages*, vol. 6, edited by Sylvia Glickman and Martha Furman Schleifer. New York: G. K. Hall, 1999.

Three Untitled Pieces for Piano. Bryn Mawr, PA: Hildegard Publishing Company, 2001 (G. K. Hall reprint).

Organ

Farewell from Rome for Solo Organ. Pullman, WA: Vivace Press, 1997.

Organ Works in G Major. Edited by Calvert Johnson. Pullman, WA: Vivace Press, 1996.

Prelude in F Major for Organ. Edited by Barbara Harbach. Pullman, WA: Vivace Press, 1993.

Vocal Solo

Dämmrung senkte sich von oben, Hausgarten, Nähe des Geliebten, Sehnsucht, Wenn ich mir in stiller Seele. In *Von Goethe inspiriert: Lieder von Komponistinnen des 18. und 19. Jahrhunderts*, edited by Ann Willison Lemke. Kassel: Furore, 1999.

Die Ersehnte, Mignon, Neue Liebe, neues Leben. In *Frauen Komponieren: 25 Lieder für Singstimme und Klavier*, edited by Eva Rieger and Käte Walter. Mainz and New York: Schott, 1992.

Im Herbst, from *Gartenlieder*. In *Women Composers: Music Through the Ages*, vol. 7, edited by Sylvia Glickman and Martha Furman Schleifer. New York: G. K. Hall, 2003.

In der stillen Mitternacht, Ist es möglich, Wenn der Frühling kommt, Zauberkreis. In *Women Composers: Music Through the Ages*, vol. 7, edited by Sylvia Glickman and Martha Furman Schleifer. New York: G. K. Hall, 2003.

Is es Möglich. Bryn Mawr, PA: Hildegard Publishing Company, 2001 (G. K. Hall reprint).

Schwanenlied. In *Historical Anthology of Music by Women*, edited by James R. Briscoe. Bloomington and Indianapolis: Indiana University Press, 1987.

Sixteen Songs. Edited by John Glenn Paton. Van Nuys, CA: Alfred, 1995.

Zauberkreis. Bryn Mawr, PA: Hildegard Publishing Company, 2001 (G. K. Hall reprint).

Choral

Duette: Gesamtausgabe. 5 vols. Edited by Willi Gundlach. Kassel: Furore, 1999.
Gartenlieder, op. 3. Kassel: Furore, 1992.
Hiob, cantata for soli, choir, and orchestra. Edited by Conrad Misch. Kassel: Furore, 1992.
Lobgesang, cantata for soli, choir, and orchestra. Edited by Conrad Misch. Kassel: Furore, 1992.
Oratorium nach Bildern der Bibel. Edited by Elke Mascha Blankenburg. Kassel: Furore, 1994.

Augusta Holmès

Piano

Tzigane rêverie. Edited by Christel Nies. Kassel: Furore, 1989.

Solo Vocal

Le Château du rêve. Edited by Christel Nies. Kassel: Furore, 1989.
Les Heures. Edited by Walter Foster. Huntsville, TX: Recital, 1983.
Les Sept Ivresses. Edited by Erin Foster. Huntsville, TX: Recital, 1986.
Selected Songs. Introduction by Marjory Irvin. New York: Da Capo, 1984.

Helen Hood (no modern editions available)

Chamber

Piano Trio.
String Quartet.
Suite for Piano and Violin, op. 6. Boston and Leipzig: Arthur P. Schmidt, 1893.
Suite for Violin and Piano, op. 10.

Keyboard

Novelette in A Major for Piano, op. 20. New York: Schirmer.
Romance for Organ, op. 19. New York: Schirmer.
Suite for Piano, op. 6. Boston: Schmidt.
Three Compositions for Piano, op. 8. Boston: Schmidt.

Vocal Solo

Numerous songs, including:

"Die Bekehrte." Berlin, Ries und Erler, before 1892.
"*The Robin.*"
"Song Etchings," op. 7 Boston: Schmidt, 1893.
"Summer Song."

Helen Hopekirk

Chamber

Piano

Dance. Bryn Mawr, PA: Hildegard Publishing Company, 1990.
Gavotte (1885), *Sundown* (1909). In *Three Centuries of American Music*, vol. 4: *American Keyboard Music 1866 through 1910*, edited by Sylvia Glickman. [Boston]: G. K. Hall, 1990.
Prelude. Bryn Mawr, PA: Hildegard Publishing Company, 1990.
Serenata (Suite). In *Women Composers: Music Through the Ages*, vol. 6, edited by Sylvia Glickman and Martha Furman Schleifer. New York: G. K. Hall, 1999.
Serenata. Bryn Mawr, PA: Hildegard Publishing Company, 2000 (G. K. Hall reprint).

Vocal Solo

Seventy Scottish Songs. New York: Dover, 1992.

Carrie Jacobs-Bond

Piano

Reverie. Bryn Mawr, PA: Hildegard Publishing Company, 1990.

Marie Jaëll

Piano

Aube, Petite pluie fine, Valses pour piano à quatre mains, op. 8. In *Women Composers: Music Through the Ages*, vol. 6, edited by Sylvia Glickman and Martha Furman Schleifer. New York: G. K. Hall, 1999.

French Character Pieces. Bryn Mawr, PA: Hildegard Publishing Company, 1998.

Piano Sonata. Bryn Mawr, PA: Hildegard Publishing Company, 1996.

Valses for piano four hands, op. 8. Bryn Mawr, PA: Hildegard Publishing Company, 1994.

Johanna Kinkel

Choral

Die Vogelkantate, op. 1. Stuttgart: Hänssler, 1966.

Vocal Solo (arranged by opus number)

Sehnsucht nach Griechenland, op. 6, no. 1. (1837). In *Lieder*, vol. 1. Bryn Mawr, PA: Hildegard Publishing Company, 2001.

An Luna, op. 6, no. 4 (1837). In *Lieder*, vol. 1. Bryn Mawr, PA: Hildegard Publishing Company, 2001.

Nachtlied, op. 7, no. 1 (1837. In *Lieder*, vol. 1. Bryn Mawr, PA: Hildegard Publishing Company, 2001.

An den Mond, op. 7, no. 5 (1837. In *Lieder*, vol. 1. Bryn Mawr, PA: Hildegard Publishing Company, 2001.

An den Mond, op. 7, no. 5; *Gegenwart*, op. 16, no. 4. In *Von Goethe inspiriert: Lieder von Komponistinnen des 18. und 19. Jahrhunderts*, edited by Ann Willison Lemke. Kassel: Furore, 1999.

An den Mond, op. 7, no. 5; *Römische Nacht*, op. 15, no. 1; *Wunsch*, op. 7, no. 2. In *Frauen Komponieren: 25 Lieder für Singstimme und Klavier*, edited by Eva Rieger and Käte Walter. Mainz and New York: Schott, 1992.

Die Zigeuner, op. 7, no. 6 (1837). In *Lieder*, vol. 1. Bryn Mawr, PA: Hildegard Publishing Company, 2001.

Der Spanische Zitherknabe, op. 8, no. 1 (1838). In *Lieder*, vol. 1. Bryn Mawr, PA: Hildegard Publishing Company, 2001.

Rheinsage, op. 8, no. 2 (1838). In *Lieder*, vol. 1. Bryn Mawr, PA: Hildegard Publishing Company, 2001.

Gondellied, op. 8, no. 3 (1838). In *Lieder*, vol. 1. Bryn Mawr, PA: Hildegard Publishing Company, 2001.

Abendfeier, op. 8, no. 4 (1838). In *Lieder*, vol. 1. Bryn Mawr, PA: Hildegard Publishing Company, 2001.

Trennung op. 8, no. 5 (1838). In *Lieder*, vol. 1. Bryn Mawr, PA: Hildegard Publishing Company, 2001.

Abreise, op. 8, no. 6 (1838). In *Lieder*, vol. 1. Bryn Mawr, PA: Hildegard Publishing Company, 2001.

Nachgefühl, op. 10, no. 1 (ca. 1839). In *Lieder*, vol. 1. Bryn Mawr, PA: Hildegard Publishing Company, 2001.

Traumdeutung, op. 10, no. 5 (ca. 1839. In *Lieder*, vol. 1. Bryn Mawr, PA: Hildegard Publishing Company, 2001.

Lust und Qual, op. 15, no. 5 (ca. 1841). In *Lieder*, vol. 1. Bryn Mawr, PA: Hildegard Publishing Company, 2001.

Gegenwart, op. 16, no. 4 (ca. 1841). In *Lieder*, vol. 1. Bryn Mawr, PA: Hildegard Publishing Company, 2001.

Wolle Keiner Mich Fragen, op. 18, no. 5 (1843). In *Lieder*, vol. 1. Bryn Mawr, PA: Hildegard Publishing Company, 2001.

Abschied, op. 19, no. 5; *Auf wohlauf, ihr Candioten*, op. 18, no. 3; *Ich will meine Seele tauchen*, op. 10, no. 2; *Nachtgesang*, op. 12, no. 3; *Ritters Abschied, Verlornes Glück*, op. 6, no. 5. In *Women Composers: Music Through the Ages*, vol. 7, edited by Sylvia Glickman and Martha Furman Schleifer. New York: G. K. Hall, 2003.

Josephine Lang

Piano

Zwei Mazurken, op. 49. In *19th Century German Keyboard Music*. Bryn Mawr, PA: Hildegard Publishing Company, 2001.

Solo Song

Ewige Nähe. In *19th Century German Art Songs*. Bryn Mawr, PA: Hildegard Publishing Company, 2001 (G. K. Hall reprint).

Frühzeitiger Frühling; Nur der Abschied schnell genommen, op. 15, no. 1; *Ob ich manchmal Dein gedenke*, op. 27, no. 3. In *Frauen Komponieren: 25 Lieder für Singstimme und Klavier*, edited by Eva Rieger and Käte Walter. Mainz and New York: Schott, 1992.

Frühzeitiger Frühling. In *Historical Anthology of Music by Women*, edited by James R. Briscoe. Bloomington and Indianapolis: Indiana University Press, 1987.

Glückliche Fahrt, op. 5, no. 3; *Lebet wohl, geliebte Bäume; Mignons Klage*. In *Von Goethe inspiriert: Lieder von Komponistinnen des 18. und 19. Jahrhunderts*, edited by Ann Willison Lemke. Kassel: Furore, 1999.

In die Ferne. In *19th Century German Art Songs*. Bryn Mawr, PA: Hildegard Publishing Company, 2001 (G. K. Hall reprint).

Schmetterling, op. 8, no. 1; *In die Ferne*, op. 8, no. 2; *Ewige Nähe*, op. 8, no. 3. In *Women Composers: Music Through the Ages*, vol. 7, edited by Sylvia Glickman and Martha Furman Schleifer. New York: G. K. Hall, 2003.

Schmetterling. In *19th Century German Art Songs*. Bryn Mawr, PA: Hildegard Publishing Company, 2001 (G. K. Hall reprint).

Selected Songs. Introduced by Judith Tick. New York: Da Capo, 1982.

Margaret Ruthven Lang

"Song of the Three Sisters." Boston: Arthur P. Schmidt, 1909.

Choral

The Hawthorn Tree, part song for mixed voices with solos for soprano and tenor. Fort Lauderdale, FL: Walton Music Corporation, 1996.

The Old Man of Dumbree, The Old Lady of France, The Person of Filey for women's chorus. Fort Lauderdale, FL: Walton Music Corporation, 1998.

Piano

Le Chevalier. Bryn Mawr, PA: Hildegard Publishing Company, 2001.

Meditation, op. 26 (1897). In *Three Centuries of American Music*, vol. 4: edited by Sylvia Glickman. [Boston]: G. K. Hall, 1990.

Rhapsody in E minor, op. 21. Bryn Mawr, PA: Hildegard Publishing Company, 1990.

Vocal Solo

An Irish Love Song, op. 22. Bryn Mawr, PA: Hildegard Publishing Company, 2001 (G. K. Hall reprint).

Nonsense Rhymes and Pictures, op. 42. Bryn Mawr, PA: Hildegard Publishing Company, 1996.

Ojala, Spinning Song; op. 9, no. 2; *The Lady of Riga*, op. 9, no. 2; *An Irish Love Song*, op. 42, no. 12; and *Snowflakes*, op. 50, no. 3. In *Women Composers: Music Through the Ages*, vol. 7, edited by Sylvia Glickman and Martha Furman Schleifer. New York: G. K. Hall, 2002.

Ojala. Bryn Mawr, PA: Hildegard Publishing Company, 2001 (G. K. Hall reprint).

Snowflakes. Bryn Mawr, PA: Hildegard Publishing Company, 2001 (G. K. Hall reprint).

Luise Adopha Le Beau

Chamber

Four Pieces for Cello and Piano, op. 24 Leipzig: Rieter-Biedermann, 1882; Bryn Mawr, PA: Hildegard Publishing Company, 1995.

Romanze, op. 35. In *Frauen komponieren: 13 Stücke für Violine und Klavier*, edited by Barbara Heller and Eva Rieger. Mainz and New York: Schott, 1994.

Romanze, op. 24, no. 1. In *Frauen komponieren: 14 Stücke für Violoncello und Klavier*, edited by Barbara Heller and Eva Rieger. Mainz and New York: Schott, 1999.

String Quartet, op. 28. Bryn Mawr, PA: Hildegard Publishing Company, 2001

String Quartet, op. 34 (1885). Edited by Barbara Gabler. Kassel: Furore, 2000.

Violin Sonata, op. 10. Bryn Mawr, PA: Hildegard Publishing Company, 2001.

Vocal

Frühlingsnacht, op. 18, no. 5; *Der Rose Bitte*, op. 39. In *Frauen Komponieren: 25 Lieder für Singstimme und Klavier*, edited by Eva Rieger and Käte Walter. Mainz and New York: Schott, 1992.

Keyboard

Piano Sonata, op. 8: First Movement. In *Frauen komponieren: 22 Klavierstücke des 18.-20. Jahrhunderts*, edited by Eva Rieger and Käte Walter. Mainz and New York: Schott, 1985.

Lili'uokalani

The Queen's Songbook: Her Majesty Queen Lili'uokalani. Honolulu, HI: Hui Hanai, 1999.

Emilie Mayer

Orchestra

Faust-Ouverture, op. 46. Stettin: Paul Witte, [n.d.].

Chamber

Notturno, op. 46. In *Frauen komponieren: 13 Stücke für Violine und Klavier*, edited by Barbara Heller and Eva Rieger. Mainz and New York: Schott, 1994.

Sonata for Cello and Piano, op. 47. Bryn Mawr, PA: Hildegard Publishing Company, 1995.

Violin Sonata in A minor, op. 18. Bryn Mawr, PA: Hildegard Publishing Company, 1997.

Sophie Menter

Piano

Étude en sixtes, op. 8. Bryn Mawr, PA: Hildegard Publishing Company, 2000 (G. K. Hall reprint).

Étude in A-flat Major, op. 9. Bryn Mawr, PA: Hildegard Publishing Company, 2000 (G. K. Hall reprint).

Mazurka, op. 6; *Etude en sixtes*; op. 8, *Etude en la bémol majeur*, op. 9. In *Women Composers: Music Through the Ages*, vol. 6, edited by Sylvia Glickman and Martha Furman Schleifer. New York: G. K. Hall, 1999.

Mazurka, op. 6. Bryn Mawr, PA: Hildegard Publishing Company, 2000 (G. K. Hall reprint).

Clara Kathleen Rogers

Chamber

Chamber Music. Edited by Judith Radell and Dieter Wulfhorst. Recent Researches in American Music, vol. 42. Middleton, WI: A-R Editions, 2001.

Violin Sonata in D minor, op. 25. Bryn Mawr, PA: Hildegard Publishing Company, 1994.

Piano

Romanza, op. 31. In *Women Composers: Music Through the Ages*, vol. 6, edited by Sylvia Glickman and Martha Furman Schleifer. New York: G. K. Hall, 1999.

Romanza, op. 31. Bryn Mawr, PA: Hildegard Publishing Company, 2000 (G. K. Hall reprint).

Scherzo, op. 15. Bryn Mawr, PA: Hildegard Publishing Company, 1990.

Vocal Solo

Apparitions. Bryn Mawr, PA: Hildegard Publishing Company, 2000 (G. K. Hall reprint).

Apparitions, Aubade, Come Not When I Am Dead. In *Women Composers: Music Through the Ages*, vol. 7, edited by Sylvia Glickman and Martha Furman Schleifer. New York: G. K. Hall, 2003.

Come Not When I Am Dead. Bryn Mawr, PA: Hildegard Publishing Company, 2000 (G. K. Hall reprint).

Clara Schumann

Chamber

Romanze, op. 22, no. 1. In *Frauen komponieren: 13 Stücke für Violine und Klavier*, edited by Barbara Heller and Eva Rieger. Mainz and New York: Schott, 1994.

Trio in G minor for piano, violin, and cello, op. 17. Munich: W. Wollenweber, 1989.

Trio in G minor for piano, violin, and cello, op. 17. Edited by Bernhard Päuler. Winterthur, Switzerland: Amadeus, 1989.

Keyboard

Andante con sentimento. In *Frauen komponieren: 22 Klavierstücke des 18.–20. Jahrhunderts*, edited by Eva Rieger and Käte Walter. Mainz and New York: Schott, 1985.

At the Piano with Robert and Clara Schumann. Edited by Maurice Hinson. Van Nuys, CA: Alfred, 1988.

Ausgewählte Klavierwerke. Edited by Janina Klassen. Munich: Henle, 1987.

Caprices en forme de valse, op. 2. Hofheim: F. Hofmeister, 1996.

Drei kleine Klavierstücke. Vienna: Doblinger, 1979.

Drei Romanzen für Klavier, op. 21. Wiesbaden: Breitkopf and Härtel, 1983.

March in E-flat Major for Piano Four Hands. Edited by Gerd Nauhaus. Wiesbaden: Breitkopf and Härtel, 1996.

Piano Sonata in G Minor. Edited by Gerd Nauhaus. Wiesbaden: Breitkopf and Härtel, 1991.

Preludes, Exercises and Fugues. Bryn Mawr, PA: Hildegard Publishing Company, 2000.

Preludes and Fugues for Piano, op. 16. Pullman, WA: Vivace Press 1994.

Quatre pièces caractéristiques, op. 5. Edited by Joachim Draheim and Gerd Nauhaus. Hofheim: F. Hofmeister, 1996.

Quatre pièces fugitives, op. 15. Edited by Joachim Draheim. Wiesbaden: Breitkopf and Härtel, 1994.

Quatre polonaises, op. 1. Edited by Babette Hierholzer. Berlin: Ries and Erler, 1987.

Quatre polonaises, op. 1. Edited by Joachim Draheim and Gerd Nauhaus. Hofheim: F. Hofmeister, 1996.

Romance variée, op. 3. Edited by Joachim Draheim and Gerd Nauhaus. Hofheim: F. Hofmeister, 1996.

Selected Piano Music. Introduced by Pamela Susskind. New York: Da Capo, 1979.

Soirées Musicales, op. 6. Bryn Mawr, PA: Hildegard Publishing Company, 1996.

Soirées musicales, op. 6. Edited by Joachim Draheim and Gerd Nauhaus. Hofheim: F. Hofmeister, 1996.

Three Fugues on Themes of Sebastian Bach (1845), *Praeludium und Fuga in Fis moll* (1845), *Praeludien* (1895). In *Women Composers: Music Through the Ages,* vol. 6, edited by Sylvia Glickman and Martha Furman Schleifer. New York: G. K. Hall, 1999.

Three Preludes and Fugues, op. 16. Bryn Mawr, PA: Hildegard Publishing Company, 1996.

Valses romantiques, op. 4. Edited by Joachim Draheim and Gerd Nauhaus. Hofheim: F. Hofmeister, 1996.

Piano and Orchestra

Concerto, no. 1 in A minor, op. 7. Bryn Mawr, PA: Hildegard Publishing Company, 1992.

Konzertsatz in F Minor for Piano and Orchestra. Edited by Jozef De Beenhouwer. Wiesbaden: Breitkopf and Härtel, 1994.

Piano Concerto in A minor, op. 7. Berlin: Ries and Erler, 1987.

Piano Concerto in A minor, op. 7. Edited by Janina Klassen. Wiesbaden: Breitkopf and Härtel, 1990.

Choral

Drei gemischte Chöre. Edited by Gerd Nauhaus. Leipzig: Breitkopf and Härtel, 1989.

Vocal Solo

Die gute Nacht, Lorelei, Volkslied. In *Women Composers: Music Through the Ages,* vol. 7, edited by Sylvia Glickman and Martha Furman Schleifer. New York: G. K. Hall, 2003.

Sämtliche Lieder für Singstimme und Klavier. 2 vols. Edited by Joachim Draheim and Brigitte Höft. Wiesbaden: Breitkopf and Härtel, 1990–1992.

Seven Lieder. Bryn Mawr, PA: Hildegard Publishing Company, 1992.

Ethel Smyth

Opera

Scene from act 1 of the opera *The Wreckers* (1904). In *Historical Anthology of Music by Women,* edited by James R. Briscoe. Bloomington and Indianapolis: Indiana University Press, 1987.

Chamber

Two Interlinked French Folk Melodies for Flute, Oboe, and Orchestra. Ampleforth, Yorkshire, England: Emerson, 1987.

Orchestra

Concerto in A major for violin, horn, and orchestra. London: Curwen, 1928.

Keyboard

Chorale Preludes for Organ. Edited by Colette Ripley. Pullman, WA: Vivace Press, 1994.

Five Chorale Preludes for Organ (1882–1884); revised 1913. London: Novello, 1913.

Choral

Mass in D for soli, chorus, and orchestra. Introduced by Jane A. Bernstein. New York: Da Capo, 1980.

Elizabeth Stirling

Organ

Romantic Pieces for Organ. Edited by Barbara Harbach. Pullman, WA: Vivace Press, 1995.

Six Fugues for Organ on English Psalm Tunes. Edited by Barbara Harbach. Pullman, WA: Vivace Press, 1995.

Moderato and Maestoso. In *Women Composers: Music Through the Ages,* vol. 6, edited by Sylvia Glickman and Martha Furman Schleifer. New York: G. K. Hall, 1999.

Moderato and *Maestoso*. Bryn Mawr, PA: Hildegard Publishing Company, 2000 (G. K. Hall reprint).

Maria Szymanowska

Keyboard

Caprice sur la romance de Joconde. Bryn Mawr, PA: Hildegard Publishing Company, 1998 (G. K. Hall reprint).

Music for Piano. Bryn Mawr, PA: Hildegard Publishing Company, 1990.

Three Etudes. Bryn Mawr, PA: Hildegard Publishing Company, 1998 (G. K. Hall reprint).

25 Mazurkas. Bryn Mawr, PA: Hildegard Publishing Company, 1992.

Chamber

Divertissement pour le Pianoforte avec Accompagnement de Violon. Bryn Mawr, PA: Hildegard Publishing Company, 1998 (G. K. Hall reprint).

Serenade for cello and piano. Bryn Mawr, PA: Hildegard Publishing Company, 2000 (G. K. Hall reprint).

Vocal Solo

Six Romances: Peine et plaisir, Romance du Saule, Ballade, Romance à la nuit, Le connois-tu, Se Spiegar. Bryn Mawr, PA: Hildegard Publishing Company, 1998 (G. K. Hall reprint).

Mary Wurm (no modern editions available)

Piano

Etude for the Left Hand and Etude for the Right Hand. [N.p.], 1906.

Kag auch heiss das Scheiden brennen, op. 39. Hannover: Louis Oertel, 1907.

Sexten-Etüde in Walzerform, op. 52. Leipzig: Robert Forberg, 1914.

Sexten-Etüden in Walzerform, op. 52 Leipzig: Forberg, 1914.

Studies for the Left Hand, op. 51. Leipzig: Robert Forberg, 1911.

Suite, op. 61. London: Lengnick, 1925.

Vocal Solo

Freudenlied, op. 70 for two voices. Munich: Zachow, 1932.

6

The Twentieth Century

Adeline Mueller

Introduction: The Silent Victory

Setting aside the more obvious advances for women of all professions in the twentieth century, a number of aesthetic and scholarly developments pertaining to art music have coincided with, or enhanced, women's visibility as composers. These include:

- a growing recognition that music is sociohistorically situated
- a break with, and subsequent examination of, tonality
- experiments with new power relationships vis-à-vis sound (e.g., aleatory composition)
- the introduction of alternatives to binary oppositional pairs and hierarchical patterns of structuring and understanding music
- a reevaluation of the circumstances surrounding the canonization of works
- a reconsideration of domestic spheres like the salon as sites of radical music making
- computer and electronics technology and its ability to close the gap between composer and listener
- an expansion of the boundaries of art music to include folk, pop, jazz, and rock traditions; found sound and noise; interactive, installation, and multimedia arts; and music outside Europe and North America
- an increase in written and verbal discourse on music by composers themselves

How do we package the previous 100 years? One could argue for a neat, linear history of women composers' sense of self. With a great deal of trimming and a judicious use of selective memory, the story could be made to follow a plot of thesis, antithesis, and synthesis. One would begin with the exaggerated modesty of Germaine Tailleferre, Alma

Alma Schindler Mahler (sketch by Dolbin).
© Bettmann/CORBIS.

Mahler, and others in the early years of the century. These women appear to modern readers to have internalized the misogynist paranoia of their time, devaluing their efforts in public, perhaps to appease those who warned of "the pink peril" of female achievement. The antithesis to this would be the "just one of the boys" approach, another strategy of integration that involved downplaying any feminist inclinations or feminine elements viewed as threatening to one's acceptance among peers. Its artificially limiting nature is articulated by Ruth Crawford, who in her youth spoke of "[feeling] like composing or loving, one of the two" (Tick 1997). That this was an inevitable, either/or choice was an unchallenged given for many women professionals. The end phase, or synthesis, coincides with the third wave of feminism and involves reclamation of aesthetic and/or political expressions of the feminine—intuitive and collaborative forms of music making, for example. Composers in this category often describe a union of previously gendered and polarized opposites. For instance, Sofia Gubaidulina observes: "Music is developing in two opposite directions: according to the numerical plot and by intuition. And when these two approaches intersect the unanticipated outcome is beautiful" (Tsenova 2001).

The preceding may serve as a thumbnail sketch of women composers in the twentieth century. But it is an oversimplification that ignores much; for one, a number of other factors, such as nationality and class, contribute to an artist's identity and professional stratagems. For another, the three "periods" of thesis, antithesis, and synthesis are, in fact, frequently simultaneous, both in the larger history of the century and within an individual composer's own life. For instance, at the same time that Pauline Oliveros advocated the establishment of libraries of women's music, she railed against the ghettoizing expression "lady composer," which "effectively separates women's efforts from the mainstream....What critic today speaks of a gentleman composer?" (Oliveros 1984).

With apologies to Oliveros, then, and to the many composers profiled here who might object to such a project, this chapter participates in the classification of its subjects first as women, then as composers. Compensatory histories such as these are still needed, and not just for the women who lived and died before this century began. It is true that the perception of women composers as bizarre anomalies worthy of a carnival sideshow has largely faded and that any woman should now expect to be taken as seriously as any man in the field of composition. Yet we cannot afford to abandon the retelling of their stories as the effort to understand their works in the context of their lives as women.

In this chapter, traditional chronology has been deliberately omitted. The entries should read rather like a web, a constellation, or perhaps like Laurie Anderson's *Puppet Motel* CD-ROM. In other words, this selection, grouping, and ordering of certain composers represent one set of paths through the century; the reader may find other connections and possibilities, other causes and effects.

The categories are variable and overlapping. Composers may be discussed or grouped as follows:

CATEGORY EXAMPLES

genre   the opera of Peggy Glanville-Hicks and Judith Weir
          the ragtime of May Aufderheide and Adaline Shepherd
means   the electroacoustic music of Kaija Saariaho
          the computer music of Laurie Spiegel
school   the romantic nationalism of Florence Price and Margaret Bonds
          the serialism of Elisabeth Lutyens, Barbara Pentland, and
          Louise Talma
aesthetic the "listening as practice" of Pauline Oliveros and Lucia
          Dlugoszewski
          the utopian longing of Sofia Gubaidulina

Then, of course, there is that indispensable category, "other," which gains new aptness in a book about an entire group of "others."

Last of the Premoderns: "Her Great Function Is to Praise" (Neuls-Bates 1982)

This epigraph, taken from a 1905 lecture by the art critic and eminent Victorian John Ruskin, is not directed specifically at **Alma (Maria) Mahler [Gropius Werfel] (née Schindler) (b. Vienna, Austria, 1879–d. New York 1964)**. Ruskin is merely repeating a common sentiment of his time regarding women's deficiency in musical composition and their rightful place as muse to the male artist. It is nevertheless an apt introduction to the story of Alma Mahler, for her life represents, in one way, a confirmation of Ruskin's statement. Mahler showed an early skill at composition, but sublimated this gift in favor of a lifelong project of tending male genius. Her wit and bravura endeared her to dozens of great artists, and she fell in and out of love with many of them. Toward the end of her life, she was somewhat derisively nicknamed "the Widow of the Four Arts" due to her romantic affiliations with leading figures in music (Alexander von Zemlinsky [1871–1942] and Gustav Mahler [1860–1911]), architecture (Walter Gropius), poetry (Franz Werfel), and painting (Gustav Klimt and Oskar Kokoschka).

In most cases, Mahler was indifferent to the art produced by these men; indeed, she never warmed to Gustav Mahler's music, thinking it largely "insincere," "dour," and "remote," although she greatly admired his skill as a conductor (Mahler-Werfel 1999). Rather, their talent and intelligence and the unpredictability of their personalities drew her to her husbands and lovers. The unfortunate consequence is that Mahler's small oeuvre is eclipsed by her mythological persona as the greatest muse of fin de siècle Vienna. What little is written about her music is largely speculation about what she might have produced had she not abandoned her own composing career at age thirty-six.

In her youth Mahler studied composition privately with Alexander von Zemlinsky, who would later teach Arnold Schoenberg (1874–1951). Despite Zemlinsky's attentions, Mahler seems to have given little thought to her works or her creative processes; diary entries from this time read merely, "[T]his evening I composed a rhapsody" or "This evening: alone. Composed a little song. Goethe of course!" (Mahler-Werfel 1999) She devoted considerably more ink to describing the concerts she attended—and by far the vast majority of her entries are occupied with her romantic life. From an early age Mahler loved to distraction, and she often found that she could not compose when enamored of her latest suitor. Indeed, Susanne Rode-Breymann, who helped to transcribe and edit Mahler's early diaries, has suggested that perhaps "composition [was] for her primarily an ersatz for emotional life" (Mahler-Werfel 1999).

In 1901, at the age of twenty-one, Alma Mahler fell in love with the forty-one-year-old Gustav Mahler, who had just been appointed the director of the Vienna Opera House. When he proposed to her, he requested an unusual dowry: that Mahler cease to compose. "How do you picture," he wrote in a famous letter, "the married life of a husband and wife who are both composers? Have you any idea how ridiculous and, in time, how degrading for both of us such a peculiarly competitive relationship would inevitably become?" (Giroud 1991). Later in his letter, he challenged her to explain whether she composed "for your own pleasure or in order to enrich humanity's heritage" (Giroud 1991). In the end she accepted his challenge to "renounce all superficiality" and devote herself to his career. To her, abandoning composition was the most powerful symbol of the depth of her fidelity. But to early biographers and music scholars, she became a Romantic martyr, a promising talent fallen victim to internalized misogyny.

Eight years into their marriage, Gustav Mahler learned that his wife was conducting an affair with the young architect Walter Gropius. Soon after, Gustav Mahler "discovered" some songs that Alma Mahler had composed in 1900–1901—he had not heard any of Mahler's works when he wrote the letter quoted above. Perhaps more out of concern for their marriage than for her talent, he recanted his earlier devaluation of her art: "What have I done?…These songs are good–they're excellent. I insist on your working on them and we'll have them published" (Filler 1983).

We do not know how much music Alma Mahler had written by this time—several early instrumental pieces were incomplete, and most were lost in the bombings of Vienna during World War II. But a year before Gustav's death, the *Fünf Lieder* was published, including the five songs that Mahler had composed before their marriage. Gustav insisted she return to composition, and she saw two more collections of songs published during her lifetime, comprising songs from the turn of the century as well as some new ones composed between 1910 and 1915. The early songs, largely settings of symbolist poetry, are often striking in their harmonic inventiveness. One finds in them chromaticism, distant key relationships, unconventional cadences, and even whole-tone scales, as in "Ich Wandle unter Blumen" (I Wander under Flowers) and "Waldseligkeit" (Forest Bliss). The scope and form of her compositions transcend the salon setting for which they were written.

There is no indication that Mahler ever undertook further instruction after 1901, and her later songs do not demonstrate a significant advance in technique. In fact, they are for the most part more tonal and more traditionally Romantic than those of 1900–1901. Recent questions as to what Mahler "might have done" are moot, for they assume resources and priorities, that Mahler simply did not possess. "I want to be a somebody," she wrote at nineteen. "But it's impossible—& why? I don't lack talent, but my attitude is too frivolous for my objectives, for artistic achievement.—Please God, give me some great mission, give me something great to do! Make me happy!" (Mahler-Werfel 1999). Mahler soon found her "mission," only it was not the creative one that modern scholars would perhaps have hoped for her.

Mahler married twice more, to Gropius—who would later found the Bauhaus school of architecture—and then to Franz Werfel, whose poem "Der Erkennende" (The Perceptive One) she had set two years before meeting him. In the latter part of her life, Mahler occupied herself with the cultivation of her legendary status, publishing two candid autobiographies, *And the Bridge Is Love* and *Mein Leben*. She died in New York, having fled Austria for the United States with Werfel in 1938. Remembered more for her life than her music (partly by her own design), she is in several ways the last of the premodern women composers.

Romantic Nationalism: "I, Too, Sing America" (Bonds, *Three Dream Portraits*, vc. 1 pf. 1959)

When Antonin Dvorák (1841–1904) first came to the United States in 1892, he urged composers to build a unique musical movement on the musical traditions of black America. "These are the folk-songs of America," he declared (Southern 1997). A number of composers at the time heeded his call. Among them were longtime friends and musical partners Florence Price and Margaret Bonds. These two participants in the Harlem Renaissance consciously incorporated black folk idioms into the romantic nationalist style popular in American concert music of the early twentieth century. The first black American women whose compositions received wide acclaim, they are pioneers both musically and professionally.

As a child, **Florence Beatrice Price (née Smith) (b. Little Rock, Arkansas, 1887–d. Chicago 1953)** studied piano with her mother, a soprano and concert pianist. She later attended the New England Conservatory of Music, graduating with honors in 1907. Upon returning to her hometown, she became a private teacher of piano and a music educator at local colleges, and in 1912 married Thomas J. Price. Fifteen years later, the couple left Little Rock for Chicago, where Price's career accelerated.

Price began studying composition and orchestration with Carl Busch and others at Chicago Musical College and at the American Conservatory of Music (where Ruth Crawford was on the piano faculty). Having already published some short pieces in her youth, Price submitted her works to the Wanamaker and Holstein competitions, both of which she won. At the World's Fair in 1933, the Chicago Symphony Orchestra performed her *Symphony in E minor* (1931–1932), which had won the Wanamaker Prize. It was the first symphony by a black woman and only the second by an American woman to be performed by a major orchestra.

By this time, Price had befriended Estelle Bonds, a Chicago music teacher whose home was the gathering place of many of the artists and intellectuals associated with the Harlem Renaissance. Price taught composition to Estelle's daughter, **Margaret Allison Jeannette Bonds (née Majors) (b. Chicago 1913–d. Los Angeles 1972)**, who had grown up listening to Will Marion Cook (1869–1944), Langston Hughes, Countee Cullen, and others share ideas in her mother's living room. Bonds was a talented young pianist who had begun composing on her own at age five. In high school, she became a charter member of the National Association of Negro Musicians' junior chapter, receiving a scholarship from the organization. She received bachelor and master of arts degrees from Northwestern University, studying composition with William Dawson. While still a student, she shared the Wanamaker Prize with Price in 1932 for her song "Sea Ghost." In 1934, Bonds premiered her teacher's *Piano Concerto* with the Women's Symphony Orchestra of Chicago.

At twenty, Bonds opened a school of the arts; the project did not survive the Great Depression, but she later formed an eponymous chamber society to promote the music of black American composers. In 1939 she found work as an editor and assistant com-

Florence Price.
University of Arkansas Special Collections.

poser at a New York sheet music publisher. She soon began publishing her own songs, while continuing formal studies in composition with Tobert Storer at Juilliard. Bonds later collaborated with the Works Progress Administration's Negro Theatre Project, and toward the end of her life she lectured at schools, including the Los Angeles Inner City Institute.

Like Price, Bonds wrote in the romantic nationalist style, a relatively programmatic idiom with functional tonality and colorful orchestration. Her virtuosic song accompaniments are somewhat more adventurous than Price's, involving altered and augmented chords gleaned from jazz harmony. As the composers' reputations grew, each began to cite black folk melodies and idioms more explicitly in their music, particularly in their arrangements of spirituals. Price's most famous spiritual is "My Soul's Been Anchored in de Lord" (1937), which has been recorded by Marian Anderson and Leontyne Price. The two also set numerous poems by their close friend, Langston Hughes, for example, Bonds' "The Negro Speaks of Rivers" (1941), "The Ballad of the Brown

Pianist Margaret Bonds in performance, ca. 1950s.
Schomburg Center for Research in Black Culture, The New York Public Library, Astor, Lenox and Tilden Foundations.

King" (1954), and the song cycle "Three Dream Portraits" (1959), from whose last movement this entry takes its epigraph. In Price's Hughes setting, "Songs to the Dark Virgin" (1941), the progressively violent imagery of the poem is contrasted ironically by the tonal calm and strophic consistency of the piano accompaniment.

Postimpressionism: "Dans L'immense Tristesse" (Boulanger, v 1 pf, 1916)

The above, a title of one of the last works of **(Marie-Juliette Olga) Lili Boulanger (b. Paris 1893–d. Mezy 1918)**, fittingly summarizes the grief and loss that marked the life of the Boulanger family. Two babies died, the first born two years before elder sis-

Lili Boulanger.
Fondation Internationale Nadia et Lili Boulanger.

ter **Nadia (Juliette) Boulanger (b. Paris 1887–d. Paris 1979)** and the second dying when Lili was only five. Their father, Ernest, died in 1900. Lili herself was afflicted with debilitating illnesses all her life after contracting bronchial pneumonia in infancy. She eventually succumbed to complications from what is now believed to be Crohn's disease, dying at age twenty-four.

The tragedies that the Boulanger sisters faced shaped their careers in different ways. Ernest's death prompted Lili to compose her first song; her own death initiated Nadia's withdrawal from composing. Nadia has now been canonized by many as the foremost teacher of composition in the twentieth century. However, during her youth, when she struggled to make a name for herself as a composer in the shadow of her more talented sister, she was criticized for her mannish appearance, frank ambition, and tendency to go out unchaperoned. In contrast to this "fearsome" *femme nouvelle* stood her frail and precocious younger sister Lili, the *femme fragile* who won greater accolades with what

Nadia Boulanger.
Fondation Internationale Nadia et Lili Boulanger.

seemed half the effort. Lili's poor health contributed to her romanticization as an oth-erworldly girl-child. Such mythologizations downplay the strength and drive of Lili, the generosity and modesty of Nadia, and the talent of both.

Nadia's first memory of Lili involves an immediate recognition of her responsi-bility for the fragile infant. Ernest, a composer and voice teacher at the Paris Con-servatoire, was seventy-eight when Lili was born, and although his wife, Raïssa, was only thirty-seven, Ernest charged the five-year-old Nadia with Lili's care. Accord-ingly, when Lili turned five, Nadia began to take her along to classes at the Conser-vatoire, where she herself was a student. By age nine, Lili was auditing the composition class taught by Gabriel Fauré (1845–1929) and was studying violin, cello, harp, and piano at home. Meanwhile Nadia, an accomplished organist, was win-ning first prizes at the Conservatoire in numerous subjects, including harmony and fugue. She had begun to concertize and teach privately to support her family, but her ultimate goal was the Prix de Rome in composition. Although some of France's elder composers—such as Claude Debussy (1862–1918)—were opposed to the competition, it was a career imperative for the younger generation, virtually guaranteeing fame and a publishing contract.

In 1906, the year Nadia first competed, the Prix de Rome had been open to women for only three years. While there had already been two women competitors, neither had won the first prize, and Nadia did not even advance past the initial fugue round. On her second attempt, she made it to the final cantata round but won no prize. Her third try, in 1908, was the most successful; submitting a controversial string quartet fugue in place of the required vocal fugue, Nadia nevertheless went on to win the second-place prize, over the objections of Camille Saint-Saëns and others. She became a heroine among the nascent feminist groups in Paris; but there had been too much outcry against the jury's decision. Although it was generally accepted that the second-place composer would be awarded first prize the following year, Nadia took no prize in 1909. It was a humiliating loss, and she never entered the competition again.

While ten years elapsed from the time that Nadia entered the Conservatoire to the time that she was awarded the second prize at the Prix de Rome, Lili won first prize in 1913, only a year after entering the Conservatoire. She was the first woman to win. This achievement is even more striking when one considers that thirty-one of the thirty-six voting members in the final round voted for Lili, an unprecedented landslide.

From age sixteen (the year of Nadia's Prix defeat), Lili was determined to win the Premier Grand Prix. She prepared rigorously with Conservatoire professors Georges Caussade (n.d.) and Paul Vidal (1863–1931), studying previous winning and losing entries for their strengths and weaknesses. Although ill health required her to withdraw from the competition on her first attempt, she reached the final round the next year. There was controversy when Lili brought her mother and a chambermaid along to the required month in isolation at the Palace de Compiègne while she composed her cantata. Some of the male competitors criticized her for bending the rules and hinted that perhaps she was feigning illness for comfort's sake. While it might have exonerated her, Lili and her family did not reveal the extent of her illness.

Lili's eventual success in the competition can be attributed to both musical and personal factors. She was already a more progressive composer than her elder sister, displaying a bolder harmonic motion and freer play with line. Her admiration of Debussy and Richard Wagner (1813–1883) is unmistakable; parallel motion, whole tone scales, and chromaticism are prominent, and she quotes the Tristan chord and the opening of *L'après-midi d'une faune* in several works. Lili's persona was also more appealing to the jury than that of her sister, as Annegret Fauser explains:

> Neither an aggressive socialite nor a "dangerous" *femme nouvelle*, the first female winner of the musical *Prix de Rome* was an artist who skillfully negotiated the concerns over women's emancipation pervading the cultural politics of pre-war

French society through her unthreatening rendition of the child-genius. (Fauser 1998)

The delicate and shy young Lili who hardly ventured a comment during the rehearsals of her cantata, *Faust et Hélène* (1913) and who barely conducted during its performance (her sister Nadia performed the piano part), had a presence that contrasted sharply with that of Nadia, a robust and already commanding conductor four years earlier.

Within one month of being awarded the Premier Grand Prix, Lili signed an exclusive contract with Ricordi, who published her winning cantata—dedicated to her sister—in the winter of 1913. But she could not make the journey to the Villa Medici for the two-year residency granted Prix winners due to illness again sparking controversy among those who saw this as another disregard for the rules and traditions of the Prix. When Lili finally did arrive at the Villa in 1914, she was able to stay only a few months before the outbreak of war forced her to return to Paris. It had been the most productive period of her life, however; she wrote numerous instrumental chamber works there, as well as the song cycle *Clairières dans le ciel* (Clearings in the Sky), set to poetry by the symbolist Francis James.

Lili's health continued to deteriorate over the next four years, and toward the end of her life she turned to sacred texts and sparer textures in her compositions. Her last major work, *Pie Jesu* (1918) for soprano, string quartet, harp, and organ, is perhaps the most striking departure of all her oeuvre. The harmonic vocabulary is avant-garde, beginning with an unusual, undulating, minor-key ground bass and progressing through a labyrinth of ever less familiar key areas before seeming to stumble backward into the parallel major of the home key. The work has a symphonic scope that transcends its short length (around four minutes). It was dictated and dedicated to Nadia, and every year since 1918, it is performed at a memorial Mass in Paris on the day of Lili's death.

Lili had asked her sister to complete her unfinished works after her death, but Nadia did not feel that she was skilled enough. Although she promoted and performed Lili's works tirelessly, after 1919 she never again put forth a composition of her own. Fauré, her Conservatoire professor, tried to dissuade her, but Nadia was adamant: "If there is anything of which I am very sure," she said, "it is that my music is useless" (Campbell 1984).

Nadia began to assist the Conservatoire professors in harmony and organ. She showed a great aptitude for pedagogy and began to teach harmony at the summer course at Fontainebleu. By 1945 she was a professor of composition and *accompagniment du piano* at the Conservatoire. Over the next approximately twenty years she established a reputation as the Conservatoire's most effective, challenging, broad-minded, and beloved composition teacher. Among her students were Aaron Copland (1900–1990), Virgil Thomson (1896–1988/1989), Walter Piston (1894–1976), George Antheil (1900–1959), Peggy Glanville-Hicks (1912–1990), Lennox Berkeley (1903–1989), Thea Musgrave (1928–   ), Quincy Jones (1933–   ), and Philip Glass (1937–   ), to name only a few. Thomson once joked that Nadia was so popular with

American expatriates that every small town in the United States could claim a post office and a Boulanger student.

Nadia was also a distinguished conductor and became the first woman to conduct both the New York Philharmonic and the Philadelphia Orchestra. In her late life, she taught privately at her home on the Rue Ballu in Paris. She commented self-deprecatingly on her legendary fame:

> They [my students] ask me questions as although I was a prophet. I am only a poor teacher travelling hour after hour, trying to do what has to be done, day after day. (Campbell 1984)

One cannot help but hear the weariness in Nadia's words. But both she and her sister made invaluable strides for women composers and conductors and left legacies to all of twentieth-century music.

Post-romanticism: Nightingale

British music of the interwar years has recently begun to receive a great deal more critical and scholarly attention. One of the composers to benefit from this renaissance of interest is **Rebecca (Thacer) Clarke [Friskin] (b. Harrow, England 1886–d. New York 1979)**, in her time a great success both as a violist and as a composer. Her works have something of Lili Boulanger's postimpressionist sensibility, but their bolder use of dissonance and frequent incorporation of English folk tunes make her music an entirely individual departure.

Clarke was born in England to a Bostonian father and a German mother who was an avid amateur musician. She began studying violin at age eight and entered the Royal Academy of Music in London at sixteen. However, her father withdrew her from that institution after only two years when her harmony teacher proposed marriage to her. Perhaps to appease his daughter for the abrupt removal, Clarke's father sent the composer Charles Stanford (1852–1924) some songs that Clarke had set. On seeing them, Stanford immediately invited Clarke to be his first female composition student at the Royal College of Music. From 1907 to 1910 she attended the college, studying composition with Stanford and with Frederick Bridge (1844–1924). She also switched from the violin to the viola at Stanford's suggestion: "[I]n the middle," he told her, "you can tell how it's all done" (Ponder 1983).

The protectiveness displayed by Clarke's father in the Royal Academy incident soon grew into disapproval of his daughter's plan to seek a career in music. As with so many of his generation, he viewed professional music making as an unseemly occupation for a well-bred young woman and he eventually discontinued his daughter's financial support. The director of the college intervened on her behalf, drawing money from an "emergency fund" to enable her to continue her studies. After leaving the Royal College, Clarke became one of the first full-time women members of a professional orchestra: the Queen's Hall Orchestra in London. She also concertized all over the world with such notable performers as Artur Rubinstein, Pablo Casals, and Joseph Szigeti.

Clarke programmed her own works in many of her concerts, often using a male pseudonym as composer. These compositions were, for the most part, miniatures for viola or other stringed instrument and piano. In 1918 she premiered *Morpheus* for viola and piano (1917–1918) at Carnegie Hall to wide acclaim. She twice won second prizes in the Elizabeth Sprague Coolidge Competition, for the *Sonata* for viola and piano in 1919 and for the *Trio* for violin, cello, and piano in 1921. In the 1919 competition the jurors had, in fact, been unable to decide between Clarke's work and a suite for viola and piano by Ernest Bloch (1880–1959), and Mrs. Coolidge herself had cast the tiebreaking vote that awarded Bloch first prize. When the identities of the composers were revealed—the entries were anonymous—it was a great shock to discover that a woman had nearly won the competition. Clarke's achievements prompted Mrs. Coolidge to commission the *Rhapsody* for cello and piano (1923). This, the *Sonata*, and the *Trio* form the core of Clarke's legacy to chamber music and are the most frequently performed and recorded of her works.

In the late 1920s Clarke turned to the composition of works for solo voice, but a fallow creative period followed during which she only performed. At this time she contributed many articles on the viola and string quartet literature to journals, including *Music and Letters*, and to W. W. Cobbett's *Cyclopedic Survey of Chamber Music*. At the outbreak of World War II Clarke was on tour in the United States, where she had to remain for the duration of the conflict. Concertizing and working as a nanny during these years, she returned to composition only briefly and produced a handful of works in the early 1940s. She married pianist James Friskin, a fellow student from her Royal College of Music days, and settled in New York, ceasing to compose after 1954. Not until 1976 did Clarke hear her music performed and discussed when a radio program about her close friend and frequent concert partner Myra Hess brought the two Coolidge Competition works to light again. Since then, a number of recordings have been produced; her famed *Sonata* was published in the 1980s, but several lesser works remain in manuscript.

Clarke's earliest instrumental works, which date from 1909, demonstrate that she had already assimilated the Brahms and Stanford models taught at the Royal College. A sophisticated sense of motivic transformation, vertical-horizontal relationships, and third-related keys is evident. In the works of her mature period (1917–1924), impressionist elements begin to be discernible. This music is more languorous and rhapsodic, with sinewy melodies in the solo instruments (see the violin's opening phrase in *Lullaby* [1918]). Functional harmony is clouded with false relations, major-minor oscillations, modes, and Eastern-influenced scales. Programmatic night themes suitable for the lower registers of her instruments predominate (e.g., *Morpheus, Lullaby, Midsummer Moon*). Although she almost never wrote for large ensembles, works such as the *Rhapsody* for cello and piano display an epic scope and ambitious use of large-scale form. The works of her late period (primarily 1940–1942) represent yet another departure. The tonal language is more chromatic, and a counterpoint of equal voices predominates over the more Romantic melody-plus-accompaniment format of many of her earlier works.

Neo-classicism: "My Little Piano" (Gelfand 1999)

In Jacques-Emil Blanche's 1922 portrait (not available) of the early-twentieth-century French composers known as Les Six, there is a woman at the center of the group. Her blue and white dress draws the eye from the drab and wrinkled suits of the gentlemen who surround her, several of whom seem to be admiring her magnetic beauty. Perched breezily on a chair, she gazes coquettishly, even daringly at the viewer. But she is not **Germaine (Marcelle) Tailleferre (née Taillefesse) (b. near Paris, France 1892–d. Paris 1983)**, the only female member of Les Six. She is the pianist Marcelle Meyer, not an official member of Les Six. Tailleferre kneels in the corner, the lowest figure in the painting. Dressed in a plain black shift, she looks away from both her companions and the viewer. Her hands are clasped in an almost supplicating gesture, complemented by a pleading expression on her face.

History has proven Tailleferre's inclusion in Les Six to be a mixed blessing, for she is often considered one of the lesser members of the group, her presence there more a curiosity than from genuine merit. The situation is not eased by Tailleferre's self-deprecating modesty. She speaks of composition as a way "to amuse myself" at "my little piano." Even when she joined the French Communist Party in 1968, she referred to it as "my little Communist party" (Gelfand 1999). While this attitude was considered eminently ladylike in early-twentieth-century Western society and often was the only way to gain social permission to be an intellectual woman, it often suffers in contemporary translation.

The daughter of an arranged marriage, Tailleferre was already composing an opera by the age of eight. At twelve she entered the Paris Conservatoire, but her father, even more vehement than Rebecca Clarke's, saw a career in music as second only to prostitution in its disrepute for genteel ladies. He soon had her removed from the Conservatoire and sent to a Catholic boarding school. However, the nuns secretly brought Tailleferre back to the Conservatoire daily to continue her training. When her father discovered the ruse, he disavowed financial responsibility of Tailleferre. Although she was only fourteen, she had already won first prizes in harmony, counterpoint, and piano accompaniment at the Conservatoire. From then on, Tailleferre supported herself, primarily by private teaching.

Tailleferre befriended a number of students in the counterpoint class taught by George Caussade at the Conservatoire, including Darius Milhaud (1892–1974), Georges Auric (1892–1983), and Arthur Honegger (1892–1955). When her sister married a sculptor in 1911, Tailleferre's social circle widened to include other young artists and intellectuals. Many nights were spent in conversation at the music halls and cafés along the boulevard Montparnasse, where, in addition to her Conservatoire colleagues, she associated with Apollinaire, Fernand Leger, and, later, Picasso and Modigliani. With the outbreak of World War I, the Conservatoire was emptied of most of its students, and classes all but ceased. Tailleferre—by now notorious for a paralyzing lack of self-confidence—tried a short course of study in art, but her teachers and her own talent drew her back to music.

In 1917, Erik Satie (1866–1925) was casting about for composers who could provide *musique ameublement* ("furniture music") to accompany a friend's art exhibit. He heard Tailleferre playing her *Jeux de plein air* (Outdoor Games) (1917) for two pianos, with Marcelle Meyer. The decorative, playful, and melodious effervescence of the work inspired Satie to declare her his "musical daughter." This was high praise, for Tailleferre and her composer friends revered Satie as the vanguard of an utterly French and modern music. Shortly thereafter, Tailleferre, Milhaud, Honegger, Auric, Francis Poulenc (1899–1963), and Louis Durey (1888–1979) gave a group concert as Les Nouveau Jeunes, with Satie as their acknowledged forefather. The critic Henri Collet soon renamed the group Les Six, a title demonstrating their potential to serve as France's answer to the Russian Five. For the next several years, the group met weekly, programmed works together, and even collaborated on a book of piano music and a theater piece. During this time, Tailleferre was also performing early and Baroque music, as well as participating in performances of her own works.

Tailleferre's music of the Les Six period is quintessentially neo-classical, marked by pianistic bitonality, jazz- and cabaret-style rhythms, an ironic sense of humor, and a deft handling of ensemble. Ostinati and *moto perpetuo* accompaniments support witty, diatonic melodies, and ternary (ABA) form is common. These works frequently draw on the expressive qualities of harmonic motion; for example, in the third movement of the *String Quartet* (1919), an almost feverish density of distantly related key areas gives the development its drama. This is a common device of classical sonata form and one that Tailleferre exploits successfully in a neo-classical idiom.

Tailleferre was poor and in need of a more regular income than her sporadic concerts and private teaching provided, so she traveled to the United States in 1925, hoping to secure a professorship. There, critical response to her works was indifferent at best. At worst, critics would abandon all mention of her music and merely make snide assumptions about her good looks having won her entry into Les Six.

Tailleferre returned to France for good in 1927, by which time Les Six had splintered. This fact, combined with the war and her two failed marriages (to the American caricaturist Ralph Barton, from 1925 to 1929, and to the French lawyer Jean Lageat, from 1932 to 1955), caused Tailleferre's ever-present self-doubt to finally overtake her will to create, and she ceased composing. In the late 1950s, she resumed a light schedule of concertizing and revising earlier works. She received belated honors in the last years of her life—the Legionne d'Honneur in 1973, the formation of an association in her name in 1977, and the Grand Prix Musical de la Ville de Paris in 1978—but had to support herself in her eighties by accompanying children's rhythm classes at an unassuming école around the corner from her house.

Biographers lament Tailleferre's unglamorous last years as a tragic end to what might have been a much happier, more successful life. Likewise, they frequently apologize for her music, comparing it unfavorably to that of her more adventurous Les Six colleagues. But if the original goal of Les Six was a music that did not require treatises and charts to understand, that did not pretend to transcend or freeze time but merely decorated it and then was gone, then Tailleferre might have been its most faithful executant. Perhaps she preferred to be depicted in Blanche's 1922 portrait exactly as she was: just one in a group of artists, a focus of attention neither for her music nor for her looks. Moreover, as for the relative obscurity in which she ended her life, that should not automatically bespeak failure. On the contrary, Germaine Tailleferre had finally located the audience whose joie de vivre Les Six had sought to recapture: children.

A fellow neo-classicist who also studied with Georges Caussade at the Paris Conservatoire, **Claude Arrieu (b. Paris 1903–d. Paris 1990)** won a first prize in composition from that school in 1932. Afterward, she wrote primarily for the stage, film, television, and radio, working in this last capacity as the assistant head of the sound effects department of French radio. She also collaborated with the young Pierre Schaeffer (1910–1995).

Julia Amanda Perry (b. Lexington, Kentucky, 1924–d. Akron, Ohio, 1979, a black American composer, studied with Nadia Boulanger and Luigi Dallapiccola. Her works exhibit a neo-classical focus on counterpoint, syncopation, and extended (yet functional) tonality. She was the recipient of two Guggenheim Fellowships in the 1950s.

Ragtime: "A Totally Different Rag" (Aufderheide, PF, 1910)

Growing out of early black American dance music traditions, the syncopated piano music known as ragtime emerged in the 1890s and soon became popular with both white and black communities. Once ragtime had its international premiere at the 1900 Paris Exposition, it began to be viewed as America's answer to the Romantic character music of European salons. The genre's instrumentation made it a popular art form with American women, for whom pianos were one of the few acceptable instruments on which they could practice. Hired to play rags in sheet music stores to attract customers, women often then tried their hand at writing them. Women represented the majority of ragtime sheet music consumers, and by 1930, over 200 women had published their own rags. Three of the most famous are described here, although even they have left little biographical information beyond their music.

Adaline Shepherd (b. Algona, Iowa, 1883 or 1885–d. Milwaukee, Wisconsin, 1950) was a practitioner of the folk rag, the more informal and spontaneous midwestern counterpart to the classic rag genre epitomized by composers like Scott Joplin (1868–1917). Her most famous rag is *Pickles and Peppers (A Rag Oddity)* (1906), which contains a rather unconventional formal development. Most rags repeat each of their subsections literally, creating an AABBCCDD form. In *Pickles and Peppers*, Shepherd inserts developmental interludes between the iterations of the third theme. These interludes, in turn, transform the theme's basic material, creating a unique formal structure that the ragtime scholars David A. Jasen and Trebor Jay Tichenor (1978) have codified as Intro-AABBC-Interlude-C^{I}Interlude^I-C^I. This rag became so popular that presidential candidate William Jennings Bryan adopted it for his theme song during the 1908 Democratic Convention. It was recorded in 1909, preserved in ten different piano roll versions, and reputedly sold over 200,000 copies.

May Frances Aufderheide (b. Indianapolis, Indiana 1888–d. Pasadena, California, 1972), was active during ragtime's popular era (1906–1912). The daughter of an upper-middle-class family, her youth included such genteel rites of passage as finishing school and a tour of the Continent. She self-published her first rag, *Dusty Rag* (1908), which was enough of a hit that her father, John Henry Aufderheide, started a music publishing company to bring out the rags of his daughter and other composers. Aufderheide's seven published rags, including *A Totally Different Rag*, emphasize chromatic melody, common in the late years of the form. Her fame extended beyond the midwest, as is evident from an article in a 1909 issue of the New York *American Musician and Art Journal*:

> Miss Aufderheide's compositions are invariably written in a popular vein, but, thorough and true artist that she is, there is much in her work that makes a strong appeal to lovers of true music. Her compositions take spontaneously with the public, so delightfully and persistently infectious are they. (Morath 1985)

Aufderheide ceased to compose a few years after her marriage, a move synchronous with ragtime's own wane.

While there are many renowned black male composers of ragtime music, there appear to be no rags traceable to black women, although there are a number of documented black women performers of ragtime. The ragtime pianist Max Morath, in his study of women composers of the genre, wondered how many "initial-bearing composers of ragtime and early popular song (and there were many) were women?" (Morath 1985). One might also wonder how many were black women.

A ragtime revival began in the early 1940s and was solidified with the 1950 publication of the first history of the genre: *They All Played Ragtime* (Blesh and Janis 1966). The resurgence of interest continues to this day; there is a growing body of scholarship concerning ragtime's history, as well as a number of contemporary composers, both male and female, writing rags. The Maple Leaf Club, an organization for ragtime aficionados, was founded in 1967; Shepherd's *Pickles and Peppers* was one of the rags performed at the inaugural meeting.

A friend of May Aufderheide's, **Julia Lee Niebergall (b. Indianapolis 1886–d. Indianapolis 1968)**, was also published by J. H. Aufderheide and Company. Born to a family of amateur musicians, she took the bold step of becoming a professional dance and theater accompanist, a relatively rare occupation for a middle-class woman of her time. An independent woman, she owned her own home for all of her adult life and was one of the first in her town to purchase an automobile. Her recorded rags include *Hoosier Rag, Red Rambler Rag*, and *Horseshoe Rag*.

Jazz: "The Lady Who Swings the Band"

Mary Lou Williams (née Mary Elfreda Winn Scruggs) (b. Atlanta, Georgia, 1910–d. Durham, North Carolina, 1981) is recognized by most jazz musicians and scholars to be the foremost woman composer of jazz and one of its chief pianists. From ragtime to Kansas City swing, to bop and beyond, she was at home in virtually all of the historical subgenres of jazz during her lifetime. She wrote over 350 compositions and arrangements. Duke Ellington (1899–1974) praised her for being "perpetually contemporary...her music retains—and maintains—a standard of quality that is timeless. She is like soul on soul" (Dahl 1999).

Although born in Atlanta, Williams was raised in Pittsburgh. Her mother, Virginia Burley, played the house organ and taught her rags from age three, and her stepfather, Fletcher Burley, bought the young Williams a player piano with rolls by James P. Johnson (1891–1955) and Jelly Roll Morton (1885–1941). Learning entirely by ear, Williams quickly developed such skill at the piano that at age six her stepfather would smuggle her into clubs and gambling joints to show off "the little piano girl." By age eleven, she was well known in town as a regular gigging pianist at parties, dances, and church functions. Soon Williams was offered jobs touring with vaudeville groups; her travels took her to several of the major jazz capitals, where she sat in with such bands as Duke Ellington's Washingtonians, McKinney's Cotton Pickers, and John Williams and his Syncopators. In 1927, when she was sixteen, she married Williams, a saxophonist.

When John went to Kansas City to join another band the year after their marriage, Williams briefly took over for him as leader of the Syncopators. After she joined her husband, the band came under new leadership as Andy Kirk's Twelve Clouds of Joy. Williams, the alternate second pianist, was soon made the principal arranger and composer for the group. However, she did not yet know how to read music. She started out dictating arrangements to Kirk, but as this was too time-consuming, he gave her a fifteen-minute theory lesson, from which, she says, "I memorized what I wanted" (Gottlieb 1996). That was all the training in composition that Williams ever received; she would later be awarded eight honorary degrees in recognition of her achievements.

Sitting in with numerous other bands and participating in marathon jam sessions, Williams made her first recording at age twenty in Chicago. In this year, she also rose within the ranks of the Twelve Clouds to full-time second pianist and finally to the position of the only pianist for the group. Her arrangements and compositions were in high demand not only from Kirk but also from jazz luminaries such as Louis Armstrong (1901–1971), Benny Goodman (1909–1986), Tommy Dorsey (1905–1956), and Earl Hines (1903–1983). Her most famous tunes from this busy time, for example "Froggy Bottom," (1936) and "Little Joe from Chicago" (1938), are stomping "Kaycee" (Kansas City) boogie-woogies. Another tune, this one by Kirk, paid tribute to the rising star of the Twelve Clouds; it is called "The Lady Who Swings the Band."

Eventually, the grueling touring and arranging schedule began to take its toll: "As we were making perhaps 500 miles per night," Williams wrote, "I used to write in the car by flashlight between engagements" (Gottlieb 1996). She finally left the Twelve

Mary Lou Williams at the piano.
© Bettmann/CORBIS.

Clouds in 1942, forming her own combo with another ex-Cloud, the trumpeter Harold "Shorty" Baker. By now divorced from her first husband, she married Baker, and the group toured with Duke Ellington's band. Williams completed fifteen arrangements for the famous bandleader, including "Trumpets No End" (1943), a novel arrangement of the standard "Blue Skies," which became a staple of the band. Their marriage ended when Baker left Williams to join up with Ellington.

New York, her new home, provided a new musical home as well. At that time Thelonious Monk (1917–1982), Dizzy Gillespie (1917–1993), and others were inventing a music that would, they hoped, be impossible to steal (both by rival musicians and by the rather money-hungry producers and promoters of the time). Sitting in with them at clubs and hosting all-night, after-hours jam sessions at her apartment, Williams was the midwife of what would soon come to be known as bop but at the time was jokingly called "zombie music" by its originators. Williams is reported to have taught

Monk the stride piano that she learned as a youth from piano rolls, a technique that Monk would adapt to the new sound (as can be heard in his "Misterioso").

Williams also hosted her own radio show, *The Mary Lou Williams Piano Workshop*, in the mid-1940s; it was a precursor to Marian McPartland's famous *Piano Jazz* show on National Public Radio. (In fact, Williams was McPartland's first guest when *Piano Jazz* premiered in 1979, and the two were longtime friends.) In 1945, Williams premiered her work *The Zodiac Suite*, over the course of twelve weekly installments of her radio show, and three of the movements were subsequently performed at Carnegie Hall with the Carnegie Pops Orchestra in an arrangement for piano and orchestra. *The Zodiac Suite* is a twelve-movement work for chamber-jazz ensemble, in which each movement depicts a different astrological sign—and, frequently, the personalities of musicians and friends whose birthdays fall under that sign.

After extended stays in London and Paris in the mid-1950s, Williams ceased composing altogether for a few years. She converted to Roman Catholicism in 1957, and when she returned to composing, her new works reflected her spiritual interests. Her hymn *Black Christ of the Andes* (1963) is considered one of the first sacred jazz works. She also wrote and performed three full-length Masses; Alvin Ailey choreographed one, *Mary Lou's Mass* (1970), for the American Dance Theater.

In the late 1970s, Williams turned her attention to educating the next generation of jazz musicians, giving lectures and master classes at schools and universities. She was an artist-in-residence at Duke University until her death; her History of Jazz course had to turn away hundreds of interested students. Her method was to begin at the beginning—as she told one interviewer in 1980, the young jazz musicians of the time "need to…go back to the blues, and come up again. Then we'd have that new era that we've missed now for over thirty years, the one that should have followed Bop" (Handy 1980).

At her funeral, luminaries such as Dizzy Gillespie and Marian McPartland remembered Williams in music, and in 1996, the Kennedy Center in Washington, D.C., hosted a festival in which numerous performers paid tribute to the legacy of Williams and other women in jazz. There is now a street in "Kaycee" named Mary Lou Williams Lane in honor of the child prodigy who grew up to become the First Lady of jazz.

The Japanese bandleader and composer **Toshiko Akiyoshi (b. Darien, Manchuria, 1929)** was discovered by Oscar Peterson in Tokyo while performing with her own trio. She came to the United States to study at Berklee College of Music in Boston, and she currently heads her own sixteen-piece band with her husband, reeds-player Lew Tabackin. Her compositions often blend traditional Japanese instruments and timbres and aspects of *Noh* drama with bop style and big band instrumentation.

Carla Bley (née Borg) (b. Oakland, California, 1938) is a cofounder of the Jazz Composers' Orchestra Association. Her jazz opera *Escalator over the Hill* won a Melody Makers Album of the Year award. Her roots are in free jazz, and her work is often influenced by quasi-Dadaist collage and satirically theatrical elements à la Mauricio Kagel. Interpreters of her work include such experimental avant-garde notables as Ursula Oppens and Frederic Rzewski. As with Akiyoshi and Williams, Bley leads her own band, which ranges in size from ten to eighteen members.

Toshiko Akiyoshi.
Courtesy of the Berkeley Agency.

Ultramodernism: "From Stratosphere onto a Solid Well-traveled Highway" (Straus 1995)

Like Alma Mahler, **Ruth (Porter) Crawford (Seeger) (b. East Liverpool, Ohio, 1901–d. Chevy Chase, Maryland, 1953)** gave up composition after she married. But in Crawford's case, a second, different body of work was produced that was at least as influential as her own music. Like Florence Price and Margaret Bonds, Crawford was engaged in the development of what Joseph Straus (1985) calls "a self-consciously independent American music." This led her first to ultramodernism and later in life to the reclamation of ultramodernism's apparent opposite: America's folk music traditions.

Ruth Crawford was the daughter and granddaughter of Methodist ministers. Her mother, Clara, had been forbidden to study piano as a girl so that she would not become trivialized as an "accomplished girl." On Crawford's sixth birthday, Clara took her to her first piano lesson with what Crawford later described as "a mixture of solemnity and triumph" (Tick 1997). Her father, Clark, died in 1913, and although she had hoped to become a poet and novelist, Crawford took a job after high school teaching at the School of Musical Art run by her piano teacher, Bertha Foster, in order to support her family. Writing short pieces for her students provided her introduction to composition. In 1921, she went to Chicago to continue her piano studies at the American Conservatory of Music.

Within a year, Crawford received associate teacher certificates in piano, pedagogy, and harmony but stayed on to continue her studies, supporting herself by working as an usher and hatcheck girl in some of Chicago's theaters. Composition soon overtook piano as her primary musical interest. She studied with Adolf Weidig (n.d.), a faithful disciple of the "old masters" who nevertheless gave Crawford free rein to explore the

Ruth Crawford Seeger.
Courtesy of the Family of Ruth Crawford Seeger.

rather unconventional harmonies that her pieces were already exhibiting. In 1924 she received a bachelor of arts in music, specializing in theory, harmony, and orchestration. She returned once more to the conservatory, receiving a master of arts degree in 1927. This time she sought additional instruction outside the school, beginning piano lessons with Djane Lavoie Herz (1888–1982).

Herz was a passionate Theosophist and disciple of Scriabin, and she warmly drew Crawford into the intellectual circle that would change her life. Among Herz's friends were Henry Cowell (1897–1965) and Dane Rudhyar (1895–1985), men who saw dissonance in music as more than just an aesthetic development; to them, it was no less than a stage in humanity's evolution, "symboliz[ing] the inclusiveness of the theosophical 'Universal Brotherhood'" (Tick 1997). Crawford adopted this philosophy wholeheartedly and developed Rudhyar's dissonance into multiparametric heterophony. Along with Cowell, Rudhyar, and others, she formed the Pan American Association of Composers in 1928, and her *Sonata for Violin and Piano* (1924) was chosen to represent Chicago at the first concert of its newly formed chapter of the International Society for Contemporary Music. The piece won rave reviews; Crawford had arrived.

Soon, Crawford ventured to New York to study with another in Herz's circle of friends: the composer and musicologist Charles Seeger (1886–1979). At first, Seeger doubted that a woman could amount to much of anything in an era of compositional bravado and machismo. By the end of the first lesson, however, the two had found kindred spirits in each other. Seeger began to assign her musical problems that encapsulated his nascent theories of ultramodernist music. The pieces that Crawford produced were anything but exercises; they always contained, as Seeger later observed, "that indefinable extra that really makes the composition" (Wilding-White 1988). In fact, the works—as well as numerous long conversations between the two—influenced the development of Seeger's magnum opus: the treatise *Tradition and Experiment in the New Music*, which was published posthumously in 1994. The early misconception that Crawford's works are only the skillful examples of ideas for which Seeger is the sole author has now been corrected. Correspondence and friends' observations confirm that both Seeger's treatise and Crawford's compositions were truly collaborative efforts.

Ultramodernism's core aesthetic is based on two overlapping principles. The first is "dissonation." This is an active, perhaps even aggressive approach to dissonance—as emphasized by the use of the word as a verb, dissonate—that is to be applied to both melody and rhythm. It is achieved through nonrepetition of pitches, intervals, accents, and meters. Protoserialist retrograde, palindromic, and rotational operations are performed on motivic units in ways more transparent than those of the early Viennese dodecaphonists. An example is the fourth movement of Crawford's *String Quartet 1931*, in which the first violin's phrase development begins with one eighth note, then two, then three, and so on up to ten, while the three other string parts begin with ten-note phrases and decrease to one. The procedure reverses itself in the second half of the movement.

The second major principle of ultramodernism is heterophony, or, as Seeger explains it, "'together-soundingness' in which 'separate-soundingness' predominates" (Seeger 1961). Going beyond polyphony, heterophony advocates the complete independence of lines. Heterophony is at its most stark in the third of Crawford's *Three Songs to Poems by Carl Sandburg*, "Prayers of Steel" (1932), in which the oboe, voice, piano, and percussion each proceeds diligently under wholly independent meters and in unrelated (a)tonalities. This requires that each line be internally consistent as to rhythm, resulting in what Straus (1985) describes as "mechanistic clattering…that is clearly evocative of repetitious manual labor." In "Prayers of Steel," heterophony provides an apt setting for Sandburg's almost futurist text, which begins:

> Lay me on an anvil, O God.
> Beat me and hammer me into a crowbar.
> Let me pry loose old walls.
> Let me lift and loosen old foundations. (Straus 1995) (cited from *The Complete Poems of Carl Sandburg*, New York: Harcourt Brace Jovanovich, 1970)

In the midst of codifying ultramodernism and its implications, Crawford and Seeger were married. The joy of their early years together was soon tempered, however, by the squalor of the Great Depression. Crawford had spent a year in Europe as the first female recipient of a Guggenheim Fellowship in 1930–1931. After her return the couple lived a hand-to-mouth existence, especially after Seeger was fired from his teaching position at the Institute of Musical Art, later the Juilliard School of Music. At the same time, they struggled to discover a means of rendering their work useful to a generation around them that lived in even greater poverty and disfranchisement. They joined the Workers Music League, but the protest songs that this group advocated, modeled after Hanns Eisler (1898–1962) and others in Germany, did not sound to Crawford and Seeger like the voice of the American people (Crawford's deft settings of *Sacco, Vanzetti* and *Chinaman, Laundryman* notwithstanding). Added to this was a growing sense that ultramodernism had lost the battle to be America's premier musical language to neoclassicism (the latter dismissed by Crawford as "sickening sweet inanity" with "nothing to digest" (Tick 1997).

Crawford had already arranged some folk songs for Carl Sandburg's second edition of *The American Songbag* (1927). But when the Seegers befriended Alan Lomax (1915–2002) and discovered his Archives of American Folk Song at the Library of Congress, they found the stimulus that American experimental music needed to move ahead, as well as a rich heritage in its own right. In 1935 Seeger began working for the Resettlement Administration, a government program that sent musicians to the homesteads of the rural South. Crawford was teaching piano and raising a growing family at the time. In 1937, she completed *Twenty-Two American Folk Tunes*, a collection of music arranged for elementary pianists that sought to demonstrate concepts that folk music had in common with the contemporary music of her youth. Two years later, Lomax approached Crawford to assist in the transcription of hundreds of tunes from the Library of Congress archives that would later be published as *Our Singing Country* (1945). Over the next ten years numerous other collections followed, many growing out of Crawford's style and methods of teaching music to children. She wrote at the time that the move to folk music was a refreshing one: "I have descended," she glowed, "from stratosphere onto a solid well-traveled highway, folded my wings and breathed good friendly dust" (Straus 1995).

Although some have interpreted Crawford's abandonment of composition as a kowtow to domesticity, a cursory knowledge of her enlightened partnership with Seeger suggests otherwise. This "second career" was just as challenging to her intellect and demanding of her physical energies as the first, whether or not she was raising five children (Mike, Peggy, Penelope, Barbara, and—most famously—her stepson Pete). It was equally vital to Crawford's experimentalist nationalism. As the preface to her *American Folk Songs for Children* (1948) passionately argues: "This kind of traditional or folk music is thoroughly identified with the kind of people who made America as we know it....Our children have a right to be brought up with it." As it turned out, a joke that she made early in her motherhood years about "composing babies" was apt on two counts. First, her books and teaching raised a generation of musically and socially conscious children. Second, her own children grew up to become central figures in the folk revival movement of the 1960s.

Had it not been for a swift cancer that took her life in 1953, Crawford might have returned to the composition of "art music"; just one year prior to her death, she had composed a *Suite* for woodwind quintet. The music of her youth, however, has not lacked attention. In 1960, George Perle published the first analysis of Crawford's *String Quartet 1931*, launching the work into the public interest. Since then, numerous members of the American postwar avant-garde have acknowledged Crawford's influence: John Cage (1912–1992), Elliott Carter (1908–   ), Christian Wolff (1934–   ), and James Tenney (1934–   ), to name a few. The first retrospective concert of her work took place in New York in 1975, and her music is now a staple of twentieth-century textbooks, anthologies, journals, concerts, and recordings.

The two major phases of Crawford's musical career appear at first glance to be mutually exclusive, yet both embody an experimentalist conviction in music's powerful responsibility to speak to its age. "How does one ever write work," she wondered in her twenties, "without a reminiscence of something that has been written before!" (Tick 1997). That statement encapsulates the central conundrum of modernism, one that, for good or ill, has plagued all of the composers who followed her.

Post-neo-classicism: Rapsodia Polska

Grazyna Bacewicz (b. Lódz, Poland, 1909–d. Warsaw, Poland, 1969) might be called Poland's Ruth Crawford Seeger: the first woman of her country to achieve lasting fame as a truly modernist composer. If Bacewicz's early quasi neo-classicism appears more conservative than Seeger's dissonant counterpoint, it was in fact highly radical for Poland in its espousal of Western European modernism, at a time when the country was only beginning to acknowledge its cultural isolation. Also radical was Bacewicz's determination to continue to write "formalist" concertos and sonatas during the postwar years of Soviet control. Finally, her enthusiasm for the discoveries of a younger generation of Eastern European composers and her experiments with such techniques in her own music of the 1960s set her apart from most of the other Polish composers of her generation.

Bacewicz was born to a family of avid musicians, several of whom performed in a semiprofessional string quartet. By the age of twelve, she was a violinist in the local orchestra, but she had already decided that she would become a composer. After early studies at the Lódz School of Music, she received twin diplomas with distinction in violin and composition from the Warsaw Conservatory, where she studied composition with Kazimierz Sikorski (n.d.). In 1932 and 1933 she studied with Nadia Boulanger at the École Normale de Musique in Paris. While there, Bacewicz's *Wind Quintet* (1932) won first prize in the Aide aux Femmes de Professions Libres Society Competition. After some world travel as a concertizing violinist, she returned to Paris to continue violin studies with the eminent Carl Flesch (1873–1944).

The neo-classical style prevalent in Paris at the time pervaded Bacewicz's compositions for the next twenty-five years. At the same time, she often incorporated overt folk
elements into her work. A good example of these twin strains of her style can be found
in the *String Quartet No. 4* (1951), where the first movement is in a sonata-allegro form
but the second theme is based on a six-note Polish folk mode (D-F-G-A-B-C). Similarly, the last movement applies imitative counterpoint devices such as stretto and
diminution to an *oberek* (a swift, jovial $\frac{6}{8}$ dance form).

By the time that she composed the *String Quartet No. 4*, Bacewicz had spent two years
as the principal violinist with the Polish Radio Orchestra. Like Rebecca Clarke, she
had begun to perform her own compositions in concert to great acclaim. By this time
she was married and had a child. She had suffered through the occupation of Poland
during World War II and was now treading carefully through the increasing state control of art institutions by the Soviet Union. Having joined the Polish Composers Union
in 1945 and begun teaching at the Lódz Conservatory, Bacewicz, like so many others
of her generation, was initially encouraged by the blossoming of organizations devoted
to reevaluating the Polish artist's place in twentieth-century art and society. However,
the debates soon devolved into state-issued denunciations of absolute music. There is
little English-language scholarship on Bacewicz to illuminate how she coped with the
vague and ever-shifting government decrees regarding music. All we know is that she
managed to avoid condemnation, perhaps due to her relatively tonal harmony and frequent use of folk references.

In 1956, the revolution of the Polish working class initiated a new era for Polish
composers, one of greater freedom and exposure to the most experimental music of the
time. The works of the second Viennese school, previously banned in Poland, were made
available, and young composers were able to encounter the music of Olivier Messiaen
(1908–1992), Karlheinz Stockhausen (1928–), Pierre Boulez (1925–), and others of the Western avant-garde. Bacewicz's own musical development reflects this renewed progressive spirit. Beginning with *Music for Strings, Trumpets, and Percussion*
(1958), she broke with traditional forms and began to explore extended techniques,
tone clusters, and athematicism. Her last two string quartets (1960 and 1965), as well
as the evocative *Pensieri Notturni* (Nighttime Thoughts) (1961), trace the evolution of
her new language.

In her lifetime, Bacewicz was honored with the National Prize, the Warsaw Prize
(for her artistic and humanitarian efforts during World War II), First Prize in the International Composers' Competition for the *String Quartet No. 4* in 1951, and Third
Prize in the International Composer's Tribunal of the United Nations Educational, Scientific, and Cultural Organization (UNESCO) for *Music for Strings, Trumpets, and Percussion* in 1960. As for her unique position among the predominantly male group of
midcentury Eastern European composers, she said:

> I have always hated…the same questions repeated by some silly male journal-
> ists which run: Can a woman be a composer? Can a woman be a full-blooded
> composer? Should a woman composer get married? Should a woman composer

Marta Ptaszynska.

have children?...I will tell you: a woman endowed with creative powers can be a composer. She can get married, have children and travel extensively all over the world giving concerts. There is only one little essential needed: "motorek" [short for "*ma motorek w dupie,*" loosely translated, "inexhaustible energy and drive"]—without it don't bother. (Maciejewski 1976)

By the time of her death in 1969, Bacewicz's music had grown from one phase of modernism (the Parisian neo-classical tradition), to the more free-form experiments with sonority of the postwar avant-garde. Her consistently abstract and technically rigorous body of work renders these two worlds, at first glance so disparate, more akin.

Marta Ptaszynska (b. Warsaw, Poland, 1943) is a Polish composer who, like Bacewicz, studied with Nadia Boulanger in Paris. Because Ptaszynska is a professional percussionist, she writes almost exclusively for that instrument group. As with the music of Bacewicz, one finds in Ptaszynska's elements of neo-classicism, and much like

Bacewicz's late pieces, her works are concerned with timbre, particularly the synaesthetic correspondences between tone color and visual colors, as in *Spectri Sonori* (Sonorous Spectra) (1973) for orchestra and *Siderals* (1974) for two percussion quintets and light projection. She is currently a professor at the University of Chicago.

Serialism and Postserialsim: "A Series Is Hardly Necessary Now" (Harries and Harries 1989)

There has never been one kind of serialism. Whether one argues that the twelve-tone works of the second Viennese school or the integral serialism of the postwar era represents the method's ultimate historical moment, there are as many branches, offshoots, and adaptations of each as there are composers. The women composers associated with serialism are no exception. In the quote from which this section takes its epigraph **(Anne) Elisabeth Lutyens (b. London, 1906–d. London 1983)** makes clear that for her serial procedures are, at most tools, for renegotiating one's relationship to sound and to control.

"Twelve-Note Lizzie," as Lutyens was nicknamed, was the daughter of upper-class British intellectuals (her mother was Lady Emily Lytton). In her youth, violin and piano provided Lutyens an outlet for the passionate religious feeling that she experienced as a member of a devoutly Theosophist family. Music also provided her with a way to distinguish herself from her four siblings, including the young boy whom her mother was raising in the belief that he was the next incarnation of the Theosophists' spiritual leader. When the family (and, incidentally, the incarnate himself) became disillusioned with Theosophy in the late 1920s, Lutyens reversed her view on music, declaring it a craft rather than a window to the soul. It is a sentiment that she reiterated throughout her life, most pointedly when she stated that music "is the opposite of self-expression" (Harries and Harries 1989).

Lutyens studied at the Royal Conservatory of Music, whose rather conservative curriculum she balanced with sojourns to the École Normale in Paris. Having married the tenor Ian Glennie in 1933, Lutyens began a love affair three years later with Edward Clark (1888–1962), a conductor and radio programmer who knew many of the composers of the European avant-garde. Clark introduced Lutyens to the music of Schoenberg, and as early as 1939, she was incorporating twelve-tone principles into her own music. Since she was virtually the only British composer to do so, Lutyens liked to claim that she discovered serialism independently of the second Viennese school. In a way she probably did, to the degree that her famous lack of patience with systematic score study meant that she would have comprehended Schoenberg's music on a very intuitive level.

Despite her frequent use of rows with tonal properties, Lutyens' serial works were unpopular in 1940s Britain; her music did not provide enough income to support herself and her four children in the midst of World War II. Consequently, she turned to scoring films, newsreels, and radio programs. In the 1950s, the British avant-garde finally began to acknowledge Lutyens' contribution to serialism in that country. She befriended an admiring generation of new British composers—Peter Maxwell Davies (1934–), Harrison Birtwistle (1934–), and Richard Rodney Bennett (1936–)—and found regular work lecturing and composing. The prevalence of choral commissions made the majority of her output at this time for voices. A most tender example is *Verses of Love* (1970), with a text composed of fragments of Ben Jonson's poetry. With slippery glissandi and gentle retrograde operations, the choir enacts a dialogue between two lovers to a humming accompaniment.

The initial flush of recognition shortly wore off, and Lutyens's stubborn disinterest in integral serialism soon made her appear as much behind the times now as she had been ahead of them in the early 1940s. She voiced disillusionment with much contemporary music, calling it "aural programme note[s]" (Harries and Harries 1989). In 1977 her publisher sought to excise her works from its catalog, and she was obliged to pay the publisher to continue to have her music housed and promoted. The obituaries after her death reinforced a late misconception of her works as "dry" and "crystalline," their evident sensuousness notwithstanding.

Like Lutyens, the Canadian composer **Barbara (Lally) Pentland (b. Winnipeg, Manitoba, 1912–d. Vancouver 2000)** was something of a serialist pioneer in her home country, Canada, which may explain some of the early negative appraisals of her work as "ugly" and even "amoral." When she received the Diplôme d'Honneur in 1977 from the Canadian Conference of the Arts, the citation acknowledged the dual challenge of "ultraconservative attitudes both towards female composers and new means of expression" (Winters and Beckwith 1992).

Pentland's parents tolerated her study of piano as an accomplishment fitting an upper-class girl who would soon be of marriageable age. They discouraged her interest and talent in composition, and not until she went to finishing school in Paris did she finally find the encouragement that she needed. She studied French polyphony and chromaticism with Cecile Gauthiez (n.d.), a professor of harmony at the Schola Cantorum. Pentland then received a tuition fellowship to the Juilliard Graduate School, which she attended from 1936 to 1939. She began composition studies with Frederick Jacobi (1891–1952), whose emphasis on Renaissance polyphony instilled in her an interest in linear counterpoint. Later, she studied with Bernard Wagenaar (1892–1971), who encouraged her to write in a modern, atonal idiom, something that Jacobi had discouraged. Pentland's first published work, the technically accessible *Studies in Line* for piano (1941, published 1949), has been used on the Royal Conservatory of Music in Toronto's piano examinations. Each movement of the work is prefaced by a line drawing reflecting the contour of the movement (e.g., a flat line, a jagged line, intersecting squiggles). The work became Pentland's calling card for the next twenty or so years and is the most often presented and recorded of her entire oeuvre.

Over the next twenty years, Pentland attended three of the most influential summer programs in twentieth-century music: Tanglewood, the MacDowell Colony, and Darmstadt (Germany). At Tanglewood in the summers of 1941 and 1942, Pentland studied with Aaron Copland and attended courses given by Paul Hindemith. At the

MacDowell Colony, where she spent the summers of 1947 and 1948, Pentland met the Schoenberg scholar Dika Newlin, who introduced her to twelve-tone composition. Her 1955 visit to the Darmstadt Summer Festival of New Music exposed her to the economical serialism of Anton von Webern (1883–1945).

Pentland's subsequent compositions incorporated the effects of these three encounters. Her music of the early 1940s emphasizes intervals as structural elements, in the manner of Hindemith, but maintains the neo-classical light textures and dancelike rhythmic motifs popular with Copland and other students of Nadia Boulanger. After adopting serial techniques, Pentland maintained her interest in prominent intervals and an almost diatonic use of tonal centers, although the vocabulary was still atonal. Her rows are often introduced in short motives, rather than in one complete iteration, as in her *String Quartet No. 2* (1953). The works after Darmstadt recall Webern in their spare instrumentation, texture, and length. One of her most highly regarded works from this period is *Symphony for Ten Parts (No. 3)* (1957), which incorporates the retrograde games so often associated with the second Viennese school. In the 1960s Pentland, unlike Lutyens, grew with the times, making use of extended techniques, *sprechtstimme*, aleatory elements, microtonality, and sometimes tape. She also wrote several theater works with political subjects.

Pentland's teaching positions included the Royal Conservatory of Music in Toronto and fourteen years at the University of British Columbia. An early stint in 1943 teaching music to disadvantaged children at the University Settlement Music School reinforced her interest in providing young students with accessible music in a contemporary idiom. Her three-volume *Music of Now* (1969–1970) is a graded piano tutor in modern music, with no regular bar lines appearing until halfway through the first book. By the end of the third book, students have been exposed to tone clusters, irregular meters, retrograde inversions, and other contemporary techniques. The work—which recalls similar projects by her fellow Canadian Violet Archer—can be seen as a continuation of what Pentland started thirty years earlier in *Studies in Line*. As well, it could be considered a sort of Pentland primer, a self-appraisal of the composer's interests and approaches.

Serialist **Louise Talma (b. Arcachon, France, 1906–d. near Saratoga Springs, New York, 1996)**, unique among this group, met with critical success and popular recognition in her lifetime. A typical work, *The Tolling Bell* (1967–1969) for baritone and orchestra, sets passages from the soliloquy of Shakespeare's *Hamlet* among other texts. The tone row that opens the work begins with two rising intervals of a perfect fifth each. She explains, "It seemed to me that the musical equivalent of existence ('to be') was the interval of a fifth without which music is not" (Barkin 1972). Such evocative associations can cause even her instrumental serialist works to appear more accessible than the more abstract works of Lutyens and Pentland.

Talma's parents (Alma Cecile Garrigue and Frederick Talma) were both musicians; after her father died when she was less than two years old, her mother gave up her own career as a singer to train her in piano, *solfège*, and foreign languages. Talma received her formal education at the Institute of Musical Art, New York University, and Columbia University, intending to become a pianist. She went to Fontainebleu in 1926 to study piano with the eminent Isidore Philipp (1863–1958). Upon Philipp's urging, Talma showed some juvenile compositions to Nadia Boulanger, and the renowned pedagogue accepted her as a student for the next eleven years. In 1936 Talma became the first American to teach at Fontainebleu; she would return there to teach and study for over twenty summers throughout her life. During the winters she taught at the Manhattan School of Music and then at Hunter College, the latter for a remarkable fifty-one years.

Talma's works from the 1920s to the mid-1950s are in the neo-classical style favored by Boulanger. However, on hearing the Irving Fine (1914–1962) *String Quartet* in 1952, Talma became fascinated with the possibilities of serial writing. She produced her own serialist *String Quartet* in 1954 and followed it four years later with the extremely successful opera *The Alcestiad* (1955–1958), with a libretto by her friend Thornton Wilder. While her serial and postserial works are atonal, they often incorporate triads and even tonal centers. As she put it, "[To] dismiss the whole lower level of the overtone series…denies the very nature of sound" (Teicher 1984). Programmatic elements in her music include, for example, the four-note blackbird motif that dominates *Thirteen Ways of Looking at a Blackbird* (1979) or the colorful word-painting in *Diadem* (1978–1979), a song cycle on precious gems.

Talma's success can be quantified in a long list of achievements. She was the first woman to be granted two Guggenheim Fellowships (1946 and 1947), to receive a Sibelius Award in composition, and to be elected to the Music Department of the National Institute of Arts and Letters. She is also the first woman to have an opera performed in a major European opera house (*The Alcestiad* in Frankfurt in 1962).

While not exactly a serialist, **Violeta Dinescu (b. Bucharest, Romania, 1953)** uses precompositional models that incorporate mathematical ratios and sequences to determine various parameters. She also incorporates some of the avant-garde elements inherent in Bulgarian and Romanian folk music traditions.

The music of **Betsy Jolas (b. Paris 1926)** is marked by abruptly and idiosyncratically changing timbres within a freely applied serialist control of parameters. Her work reflects the music of Olivier Messiaen, with whom she studied at the Paris Conservatoire and whom she replaced as professor of advanced music analysis when he retired in 1974. It also recalls the early work of Pierre Boulez, who as a conductor was the first to program Jolas' music.

Tui St. George Tucker (b. Fullerton, California, 1924). Microtonality is seen by many as the only logical next step after early serialism's expansion of the octave from eight to twelve tones. Tucker is its foremost female exponent, particularly in her quartertone works for recorder, on which she is also a virtuoso performer.

Alicia Urreta [Urrueta] (Arroyo) (b. Veracruz, Mexico, 1933–d. Mexico City 1987) is known for postserialist music that is highly controlled with regard to parameters such as dynamics and duration (often proportionally notated) and yet at the same time peppered with aleatory passages. She was a piano student of Alfred Brendel (1931–) and Alicia de Larrocha (1923–) and premiered many works of the European avant-garde in Mexico. An instructor of acoustics at the Instituto Politécnico Nacional, she co-founded the Festival Hispano-Mexicano de Música Contemporánea.

Gebrauchmusik: Music for Use

Originating in Germany in the 1920s, the term *gebrauchmusik* ("music for use") was coined by the early music scholar Heinrich Besseler to describe music "access[ed]…not through listening but through participation" (Hinton 2001). Besseler was referring to dance music of the seventeenth century, but soon German composers—most notably Paul Hindemith (1895–1963)—were redefining *gebrauchmusik* as a socially conscious contemporary style, accessible to the lower and middle classes, thousands of whom were amateur musicians. In this respect, *gebrauchmusik* stands along with neo-classicism as one of the first postmodern moments in music. It also represents an early instance of musicology (still a relatively young discipline in the 1920s) influencing the historical development of the object of its research.

A student of Hindemith, **Violet Archer (née Balestreri) (b. Montréal 1913–d. Ottawa 2000)** is frequently labeled a composer of *gebrauchmusik*. Indeed, her works share his concern with lean counterpoint, traditional forms and functional harmony, and technical accessibility. Hers is a distinctly different approach, however, with a freer tonality and a more playful sensibility. Born to Italian parents who were opera aficionados, Archer began to play the piano at age nine. At seventeen she began studies at the McGill Conservatorium, supporting herself as an accompanist and private teacher. After receiving the bachelor of arts degree in 1936, she continued as a composition student of Douglas Clarke (n.d.) and Claude Champagne (1891–1965), while also studying organ. In the summer of 1942, she persuaded Béla Bartók (1881–1945), who rarely taught, to take her on as his student in New York. Her works of the next years showed increasing chromaticism and rhythmic drive.

In the mid-1940s Archer returned to Canada to teach harmony, counterpoint, and fugue at her alma mater and to perform as a percussionist in the Montreal Women's Symphony. A generous combination of scholarships and government grants enabled her to return to the United States in 1947 for graduate study with Hindemith at Yale University. In 1949 she was awarded a master's degree from Yale in composition and won the Woods Chandler Prize for her thesis, the cantata *The Bell* (1949). Faculty positions in Texas and Oklahoma in the 1950s were followed by a long term at the University of Alberta in Edmonton, where she served as chair of the theory and composition department for sixteen years. After retiring from full-time teaching in 1978, Archer maintained a rigorous schedule of composing, lecturing, and adjudicating. She has been recognized with honorary doctorates, festivals of her music, a Festschrift, and a fellowship in her name administered by the University of Alberta.

Violet Archer was a vocal critic of the lack of contemporary music available to young musicians. Her challenge to both composers and teachers to promote student-oriented music in contemporary idioms owes as much to Bartók's *Mikrokosmos* as to Hindemith's

Violet Archer.
Courtesy of the University of Alberta, Canada.

didactic sonatas for underrepresented instruments. It is a challenge that Archer herself accepted. Her later works, the majority of which are for solo instruments or chorus, blend traditional, linear form and regular meters with dissonant modality and clearly discernible motivic development. She also wrote a number of études introducing young pianists to techniques of twentieth-century music; many of these have been selected for inclusion in Canadian graded piano books.

Another student of Hindemith at Yale in the 1940s, **Emma Lou Diemer (b. Kansas City, Missouri, 1927)** utilizes a somewhat more conservative tonality than Archer's, although her stylistic palette is quite broad. She is careful to include in her oeuvre works for amateur and student ensembles, saying, "I have little affinity with the composers who write only for their fellow composers. Some of history's dullest, most ephemeral music has been produced for that reason." (Brown 1992)

After formal training and teaching appointments, a move to a Vermont dairy farm in the 1980s prompted **Gwyneth Van Anden Walker (b. New York 1947)** to begin writing music that addressed the concerns of farming and the small-town life. Often written for specific amateur musicians in her community, the music is mostly diatonic. Performances of her works have taken place in barns and other site-specific locales.

Emma Lou Diemer.

Ascetic Expressionsim:
Dies Irae (Day of Wrath)

We know little of the composer **Galina Ivanovna Ustvolskaya's (b. Petrograd [now St. Petersburg], Russia, 1919)** life, but, more profoundly, her music strikes many as having almost no precedent. It possesses a sound so deeply idiosyncratic and yet so internally consistent for over fifty years that it seems outside time or at least outside the century. It is very difficult to ascribe to a particular school or style. "Spiky," "gaunt," "like a hell-fire sermon," "grinding," "apocalyptic," and "puritanical" are but a few of the searching descriptives with which listeners have attempted to come to terms with her stark work. Ustvolskaya tends to favor tone clusters in the *ffff—ffffff* range, wide pitch leaps, obsessive repetition of clipped motifs, and a willful antivirtuosity, what one might call a "pointed awkwardness." Moments of relative peace are few. Underlying this fire and brimstone is an unrelenting quarter-note pulse—with indivisible regularity, the meter-less beat becomes a beating (one critic dubbed her "the lady with the hammer"). The ponderous weight of this arhythmic plan gives her music its particularly vengeful tone.

Ustvolskaya attended the Music College of the Leningrad Conservatory in the late 1930s and then the conservatory itself, save for two years of compulsory military service during World War II. Dmitri Shostakovich (1906–1975), her teacher at the conservatory, was refreshingly candid about having learned as much from his student as the reverse; scholars are now documenting his musical quotations of Ustvolskaya motives. After graduation, she returned to the college to teach from 1948 to 1977. Beyond that, little is known of her life. She does not accept commissions, nor has she ever sought performances of her music outside Russia. She declined an invitation to attend a performance of her *Symphony No. 4 "Prayer"* at the 1988 Hamburg Festival of Women Composers, citing opposition to being grouped with other composers solely on the basis of gender.

This tantalizing privacy extends to her music, of which Ustvolskaya states: "My works are not religious in a liturgical sense, but they are infused with a religious spirit and to my mind they are best suited to performance in a church, without scholarly introductions and analyses" (Sanin 1992). Indeed, an Ustvolskaya work is more akin to an encounter with a fearsome, incalculable force than to an exercise, experiment, or humanistic dialogue. A prime example is the *Duet* (1964) for violin and piano, which opens with a delicate stasis irregularly interrupted by piercing shrieks from the two instruments' upper registers. Soon after, the piano launches into a frenzied barrage of ffff tone clusters spanning the breadth of the instrument, punctuated by angular, accented pitches in the violin. The effect is quite literally deafening and leaves little room for contemplative response.

Despite this, there is formal construction in Ustvolskaya's music. For example, fugato principles are at work in the *Piano Sonata No. 4* (1957) and in the *Duet*. In other works where "corrupted" triads (with both a major and a minor third) and other tone clusters do not predominate she uses a kind of atonal first species counterpoint.

As a composer living in Moscow under the watchful eye and ever-shifting tastes of the Soviet state, Ustvolskaya found herself in an even more serious position than that of Grazyna Bacewicz in Poland. The production of Mass cantatas and other works of socialist realism was necessary if she was to maintain her teaching position and avoid the party censure to which Shostakovich and others were subjected. Ustvolskaya later excised those works from her catalog, but until the early 1990s they were the only ones that had been recorded. In the last ten years interest in her non-state-approved music has greatly increased in the West, and a multivolume set of albums is under way at Megadisc. However, the continued dearth of English-language scholarship on this composer speaks not only to the difficulty of articulating her place in the canon but also perhaps to an anxiety in the West about what we actually hear in her works.

Experimentalism: Listening as Practice

As final as the "zero degree" reached by John Cage in his silent 4 minutes 33 seconds (1952) may seem, it did not render the creation of new sounds impossible for the American experimental avant-garde. What it did prohibit, rather, were old ways of hearing. In a musical universe where "silence" itself was found to be teeming with sound, a new kind of attentiveness was required. Conceptualism (which emphasized idea over aural result) and minimalism (which emphasized process over aural product) were the aesthetic cousins that reintroduced listening as an aesthetic, even spiritual practice.

The influences, interests, and aesthetics of **Pauline Oliveros (b. Houston, Texas, 1932)** are as webbed and irreducible as those of Cage, to whom she is often compared. However, the sonic awareness that she has trademarked as "deep listening" has been a major thread in her work for over forty years. What makes her music minimalist on its surface is the predominance of drones, whether composed or improvised. What makes it minimalist in the broader sense is the attitude that the listener is a participant in the musical work. To this, Oliveros adds principles drawn from such disparate enterprises as Zen Buddhism, shamanism, and biofeedback.

In recollections of her youth, Oliveros frequently mentions being fascinated by two "peripheral" sounds: the static that she heard on the radio and the combination tones produced on the accordion, her first major instrument. She calls them "negative operant phenomena," and foregrounding them was an early concern. After receiving her bachelor of arts from San Francisco State College in 1957, Oliveros and other students of their composition teacher Robert Erickson (1917–1997) began gathering at the studio of independent radio station KPFA to enact unplanned improvisations using tape. The loose-knit collaborative soon became the San Francisco Tape Music Center, which Oliveros codirected and continued to direct when the center moved to Mills College in Oakland. Her best-known work for tape, *I of IV* (1966), was produced during a summer at the University of Toronto, where Oliveros studied with Hugh Le Caine (1914–1977). In it, Oliveros uses electronics to isolate the accordion combination tones from their fundamentals. The result is a twenty-five minute meditation on ignored sound, the tape heads having been transformed into a magnified pair of ears.

Following the thread of heightened sonic awareness leads beyond Oliveros' absurdist theater works of the early 1960s to the meditation pieces of the late 1960s and later. In a rhetorical prose piece of the time, she asked: "Have I ever become the music, sounds or conversation? Have I identified so completely that I am the sound?" (Oliveros 1984) An interest in bodily and spiritual union with the core of sound led to a group of text scores (traditional notation had long ago proved inadequate for her purposes) that eventually became known as *Sonic Meditations* (1971). These works, some of which resemble Fluxus event actions in the brevity of their instructions, hone various aspects of the twin principles of deep listening: attentiveness (pointed focus) and awareness (broader receptivity). The performers need not be professionals or even musicians in the traditional sense; voice is generally assumed to be the instrument of

Pauline Oliveros.
Photo by Gisela Gamper/Courtesy Pauline Oliveros Foundation.

choice, as many of the meditations emphasize sound arising naturally from breath. There is no conductor, unless one counts Oliveros, who prefers the term "facilitator" when she acts in this capacity; there is no division between performer and listener. Rather, the works are about self-discovery and self-communion: sound production arises naturally from a heightened sensitivity to the sounds in one's environment and those of one's fellow participants.

The *Meditations* grew out of work that Oliveros facilitated as a faculty member at the University of California, San Diego (1967–1981). They have since been adapted for numerous performance contexts, workshops, and retreats. The mid- to late 1970s saw Oliveros producing larger-scale works, influenced by the *Meditations*, which she called "ceremonies" in recognition of their more ritualistic tone. An example is *Crow Two—A Ceremonial Opera* (1974–1975), in which Oliveros' beloved mandala shapes are used to arrange the participants, symbolic figures such as "Crow Godmother" and

"Crow Poet," around the performance space. Significantly, many of these later works incorporate "threats" to the concentration of the meditators. In *Crow Two* for example, the Heyokas (a kind of sacred trickster in Lakota legend) move around the periphery of the mandala, distracting the participants and undermining the sanctity of the meditation. Oliveros continues to create ritual theater works to this day, often incorporating digital media. *Njinga the Queen King* (1993) is one such work whose performances have included satellite uplink, Internet chat, and interactive PictureTel technology to create an interactive performance.

Oliveros retired from teaching in 1981 to have more time for composing but returned to it in 1997 at Mills College and with numerous visiting professorships. In 1985 she began a foundation for the promotion of new music. She performs extensively as both a vocalist and an accordionist in solo concerts and with the Deep Listening Band, a trio of musicians who improvise in spaces with productive acoustics. In their first recording (1989's *Deep Listening*), the band performed in a Port Townsend, Washington, cistern that produces a natural eight-second delay.

One senses in Oliveros' writings and works a keen interest in the reclamation of balances: between active and passive modes of listening, between left and right brains, and between intuitive and analytical forms of creativity. She freely admits that these oppositions have often been gendered in the past, indeed, that listening itself is often misconstrued as a purely receptive and thus feminine state. This only confirms her faith that composers, both male and female, can be rendered whole again through the reclamation of an *actively reactive* mode of listening. "Deep listening," she writes, "involves going below the surface of what is heard and also expanding to the whole field of sound....[it is] essential to the process of unlocking layer after layer of imagination, meaning, and memory down to the cellular level of human experience" (www.deeplistening.org).

A quirky sense of humor, an unabashed reverence for the ritual of music making over a polished musical object, and a body of writing that sometimes contradicts critics' experiences of her music make Oliveros a difficult and often controversial subject in experimental music. This does not seem to bother her. "Music should tune the soul," she has said, "not merely entertain. And I might add that in the tuning process it might fail as an object of admiration[,] which is a risk I'm willing to take" (Von Gunden 1983).

Zen principles inform not only the work of Oliveros but that of another American maverick, **Lucia Dlugoszewski (b. Detroit 1934–d. New York 2000)**. She wrote: "My music is constantly trying to put the mind into a ritual so it never stops listening. You know how people talk about hearing for the first time? That is a religion to me" (Gague 1993).

Dlugoszewski describes something akin to what Zen master Shunryu Suzuki calls *shoshin*, or "beginner's mind": that state of emotionless wonder, before ownership and before understanding, experienced when first apprehending an object, sensation, or moment. Dlugoszewski calls it by other names: the titles to her works include recurring words like "suchness," "quidditas," "swift," "quick," and "flight." Having written most of her works to accompany modern dance, she is acutely aware of the potential for mystery inherent in these two very ephemeral art forms.

A precocious artist, Dlugoszewski exhibited the features of her mature sensibility as early as age fifteen in her *Moving Space Theater Piece* of 1949. The piece employed everyday objects as instruments and hid the musicians and the sources of their sounds behind a curtain. A few years later Dlugoszewski began to experiment with what she later called a "timbre piano"; a cousin to Cage's prepared piano, it involved the placement of objects such as hairpins, thimbles, and jars on or between the strings of the piano. Dlugoszewski also used unusual objects like bows and flexatones to play the strings themselves.

By the early 1950s, Dlugoszewski had studied piano, physics, mathematics, and medicine and was a music analysis student of Felix Salzer (1904–1986) at Mannes College of Music in New York. She also began to study privately with Edgar Varèse (1883–1965), and although she did not absorb his fascination with electroacoustic music, she did appreciate his interest in beautifully strange sounds and novel means to create them. In fact, Dlugoszewski designed numerous (primarily percussion) instruments in the 1960s for use in her work as music director of the Erick Hawkins Dance Company. This was perhaps Dlugoszewski's most rewarding assignment, providing her with a steady income and new dance works of a character similar to her experimental art. She later married Hawkins.

Paradoxically, the work for which this instrument inventor is most known was written for the trumpet. *Space Is a Diamond* (1970) utilizes a number of extended techniques, however, that cause the trumpet to sound like everything from a conch shell, to a theremin, to a violin playing harmonics, to the distant wail of a human voice. The piece consists largely of upward glissandi extending the range of the instrument to a staggering five and a half octaves. Mute changes, trills, tremolos, and other ornaments make up the timbral vocabulary. The work ends with the trumpeter's whistling the final pitch as it is played—by then, the trumpet has been rendered as mysterious and unrecognizable as Dlugoszewski's timbre piano.

Dlugoszewski has not yet received the kind of recognition visited upon Oliveros by the avant-garde elite in America. Although Cage is reputed to have enjoyed a "suchness concert" that she put on while a teenager, the New York School with whom Dlugoszewski shared a home never championed her body of work. In fact, she is generally acknowledged to have more in common with fellow instrument-maker and iconoclast Harry Partch (1901–1974) than with Cage or any of his circles. Her supporters come more from the areas of poetry and painting than from within music (for example, Dlugoszewski won a Tompkins Prize for poetry in 1947). Even as early as 1971, however, Virgil Thomson included her in his volume on twentieth-century composers, praising her "far-out music of great delicacy, originality, and beauty of sound." (Thomson 1971) However she is canonized, it is clear that Dlugoszewski's devotion to the principle of shoshin links her with the otherwise quite different aesthetic goals of Oliveros:

> What strange risk of hearing can bring sound to music—a hearing whose obligation awakens a sensibility so new that it is forever a unique, new-born, antideath surprise, created now and now and now (...) a hearing whose moment in time is always daybreak. (Dlugoszewski 1973)

Barbara Benary (b. Bay Shore, New York, 1946), an ethnomusicologist as well as composer, studied violin in India and cofounded the Gamelan Son-of-Lion (a translation of her Hebrew last name), which performs new and experimental music for Javanese gamelan. In her works for the group, she explores the additive rhythms, phasing techniques, and gradual processes associated with late minimalism. Early in her career, she played in the Philip Glass ensemble, and she wrote a series of works called *System Pieces* (1972/1992) that are somewhat akin to Oliveros' *Sonic Meditations* in their open form (frequently with texted instructions), socially celebratory nature, and use of geometric principles.

Some might call **Johanna Beyer (b. Leipzig, Germany, 1888–d. New York 1944)** a "foremother" of minimalism. Although she was associated with the early twentieth-century American ultramodernists, having studied composition with Rudhyar, Cowell, and the Seegers, her works evince an extreme economy of materials that caused her to be labeled "primitive" in the 1930s and "prescient" in the 1980s. In addition, she is one of the first composers to write extensively for percussion. Her *IV* (1935) for nine unspecified percussion instruments is a rich tapestry of overlapping ostinati consisting of even subdivisions of the beat; the score resembles one by Steve Reich, although it predates him by fifty years. After meeting Cage in the mid-1930s, Beyer dedicated one of her percussion works to him, and he performed it extensively during his Pacific Northwest tours.

Opera: The Last Something Big

Although in the twentieth century the preference was often for new, shorter, and less grandiose genres than opera, two composers, Judith Weir and Peggy Glanville-Hicks, maintain that the genre still has a place in the modern (even postmodern) world. Weir observes:

> I think opera is one of the biggest occasions we have in modern western life, given the decline of religion; it's one of the very few places where everyone gathers with that sense of something big being played out. (Ford 1993)

At the same time, Weir and Glanville-Hicks recognize that any contemporary opera must reappraise its raw materials. For Weir, the use of folktales provides a way to skirt the kind of linear narrative that she believes is no longer viable in today's libretto. Glanville-Hicks, on the other hand, seeks in the music of ancient Greece and the Near East an alternative to Western assumptions about musical structure.

The operas of **Judith Weir (b. Cambridge, England, 1954)** are raw, pared down musical dramas that move in the "prehistoric" realm of the fairytale and folktale. Her libretti—mostly taken from medieval and ancient Chinese stories as well as folktales of the British Isles—are sparse, peculiar, and often brutal. In *Blond Eckbert* (1993), based on a short story by Ludwig Tieck, contemporary of Goethe and Hoffman, the apparently contented life of a mountain-dwelling couple slowly disintegrates as a series of discoveries raises more questions than it answers. The nesting tales-within-tales of the narrative intersect and affect one another in puzzling asymmetry. In another example, *A Night at the Chinese Opera* (1987) incorporates into the action the Yuan Dynasty musical play on which the work is based, allowing it to take up all of act 2 as a play-within-a-play.

Weir appreciates the "flatness" of ancient and folk texts for their ability to "allow space for the music to do what music does, which is usually to complicate things enormously." (Ford 1993) Her abstract harmonic language acts as another level of removed narration; reminiscent of early second Viennese school atonality in its use of developing variation, it also borrows the economical instrumentation of most folk music.

Originally an oboist, Weir was born into a family of dedicated amateur musicians from Aberdeen. She studied composition with Robin Holloway (1943–   ) at King's College, Cambridge, and privately with John Tavener (1944–   ). She received her first commission from Peter Maxwell Davies' ensemble the Fires of London while still an undergraduate. From 1979 to 1982 she taught at the University of Glasgow, and she has had a number of composer residency terms with music schools and ensembles. In recent years she has been the artistic director of the Spitalfields Festival in London, which focuses on early and contemporary music. All three of her full-length operas have been televised.

The use of folk materials is something that Weir shares with **Peggy Glanville-Hicks (b. Melbourne, Australia, 1912–d. Sydney, Australia, 1990)**, although Glanville-Hicks is primarily drawn to traditional musics, rather than traditional narrative models. From early in her career, she was dissatisfied with her perceived limited choice between neo-classicism and atonal serialism. Both, she said, are "reactions against nineteenth-century romantic tonality rather than promising directions for the future." (Hayes 1990) She studied briefly with Nadia Boulanger in Paris (neo-classicism) and with Egon Wellesz (1885–1974) in Vienna (serialism). She soon came to believe that the only way to a truly new music was the "liberation of the ground-bass" (Hayes 1990)—in other words, an alternative to harmony as a structuring principle in music.

This idea was inspired by two of her composition professors—Fritz Hart (1874–1949) at the Albert Street Conservatorium in Melbourne and Ralph Vaughan-Williams (1872–1958) at London's Royal College of Music—both champions of traditional British and Celtic music as the source material for a new music independent of Continental Europe. Glanville-Hicks was also fascinated by orchestral percussion instruments. Once she had been exposed to Indian classical music by her friend Indira Gandhi, whom she met at a summer course at Oxford, she amassed the ingredients of a mature style that was to emphasize the melody-rhythm axis of music of the Near East and antiquity.

Glanville-Hicks married the composer and pianist Stanley Bate (1913–1959) in 1938, and the couple relocated from Britain to the United States in 1942 to escape the war. During the 1940s Glanville-Hicks barely composed and turned instead to writing concert reviews and articles for various newspapers and magazines. Her most fruitful assignment was at the *New York Herald-Tribune*, for which she eventually wrote over

500 reviews. Her work introduced her to a circle of Greenwich Village artists for whom she wrote several vocal chamber works at the end of the decade, for example, *Thomsoniana* (1949) for Virgil Thomson, her editor at the *Herald-Tribune*, and *Letters from Morocco* (1952) for Paul Bowles. These pieces finally gained the composer recognition. She also contributed ninety-eight articles on American composers for the 1954 edition of *Grove's Dictionary of Music and Musicians* and worked as the director of the Composers Forum in New York from 1950 to 1960.

In her articles and reviews, Glanville-Hicks continued to advocate a musical "cross-pollination" between East and West. *The Transposed Heads* (1954), her first commissioned opera, allowed her to put her theories into extended practice. Based on Thomas Mann's retelling of a Hindu folktale, the work translates the *raga-tala* structure of Indian classical music into a modernist melody-rhythm structure. Although some accused her of appropriating the flavor of the East merely for its trendiness, Glanville-Hicks was convinced that she had, in her words, "shed the harmonic dictatorship peculiar to modernists." (Hayes 1990)

Her next major opera was *Nausicaa*, a reinterpretation of the portion of Homer's *Odyssey* dealing with Penelope and her suitors. In preparation for the work, Glanville-Hicks moved to Greece and researched a number of ancient modes, meters, and instruments. The result in her opera is an almost complete absence of vertical harmony beyond an occasional perfect fifth. Instead, the orchestra plays in monodic unison, with Eastern-inflected ornaments decorating the line. The opera was a joint production between Greece and the United States and received eight curtain calls at its premiere at the Acropolis in Greece.

Glanville-Hicks composed relatively few works in the last two decades of her life, returning to the country of her birth to give lectures on Asian music at the Australian Music Centre. Her works were performed frequently during the 1980s: for example, at the Sydney Festival, the Cabrillo Music Festival in California, and the Adelaide Festival. Forty years earlier, she predicted a musical move "Westward to the East" (the title of an article that she wrote for *The New York Times*), in which Australia and Asia would come to occupy a central role in the world's musical development. Glanville-Hicks lived long enough to observe this shift occurring, as the West Coast and Pacific Rim came to the forefront of new music.

The most prolific female opera composer of her time, **Mary (Louise) Carr Moore (b. Memphis, Tennessee, 1873–d. Inglewood, California, 1957)** was part of the first generation of Americans struggling to redefine opera for a young nation and a young century. She also stands out among opera composers as one of the first to delineate a female lead character not primarily through her sexuality but through her works. (*Narcissa*, 1909–1911) Moore's operas were subsidized by and most often performed in the numerous music clubs organized by affluent American women intellectuals in the early twentieth century; later she worked with the Works Progress Administration's Federal Music Project. A staunch fin-de-siècle tonalist, she retained a genteel antipathy to ultramodernism and atonality. Her devotion to the cause of an American—specifically, a West Coast—operatic tradition is, however, indisputable.

In the operas of **Thea Musgrave (b. near Edinburgh, Scotland, 1928)**, great men and women (Mary, Queen of Scots; Harriet Tubman; Simón Bolívar) negotiate difficult external circumstances against their own consciences. Musgrave's uninhibited approach to biographical opera is clear; of her liberties with *Harriet, the Woman Called Moses* (1981–1984), she explains: "I didn't set out to write a historical document. . . . Although it's not literally true, it's true in another way" (Ryder 1992). In a fashion similar to her operas, her self-described "dramatic-abstract" instrumental works—particularly the concerti—concern themselves with the perennial tension between a soloist-hero and the musical communities in which that hero moves.

Song Cycle: Poet to Poet

Adjunct to the medium of opera is the song cycle, which remains a powerful form in the late twentieth century due partly to its economical instrumentation. While virtually every composer of this era has written at least one song cycle, some devote themselves to the medium. **Miriam Gideon (b. Greeley, Colorado, 1906–d. New York 1996)** found that it offered the "challenge of finding an appropriate musical garb" for a poetic or dramatic idea. Although her song cycles were written after World War II, they retain the expressionist atonal aesthetic of the early modernist Arnold Schoenberg. In fact, Gideon used the instrumentation of Schoenberg's revolutionary song cycle *Pierrot Lunaire* (1912) in several of her works, for example, *Voices from Elysium* (1979) and *Böhmischer Krystall* (Bohemian Crystal) (1988), the latter also a setting of a poem about Pierrot.

Gideon showed early promise as a pianist, and her parents—both teachers—allowed her to leave home at age fourteen to live and study with her uncle, the music director of Temple Israel in Boston. She was a choral accompanist there, but her bachelor of arts from Boston University was in French with a minor in math. After graduating, Gideon studied composition at New York University with Marion Bauer (1897–1955) and later privately with Lazare Saminsky (1882–1955). Saminsky introduced her to Roger Sessions (1896–1985), whose group lessons she attended along with Vivian Fine (1913–2000), Milton Babbitt (1916–   ), and Leon Kirchner (1919–   ).

Gideon emerged from this encouraging milieu to return to school for a master of arts degree in composition from Columbia University. While still a student there, Gideon married the scholar and writer Frederick Ewen and began teaching at Brooklyn College. Although the uneasy political climate in the years of the McCarthy hearings led to her dismissal from her post, that was by no means the end of her teaching career. Gideon already had a second position at the City University of New York and would soon add two others that lasted until well into her eighties. The longest term was at the Jewish Theological Seminary, from which she received a doctorate of sacred music in composition in 1970; she taught there for thirty-six years. In 1975, Gideon became the second woman ever to be elected to the American Academy and Institute of Arts and Letters; the first had been her friend Louise Talma, elected to the larger National

Institute the previous year. (They spent their last years living in apartments in the same building near Central Park West in New York City.)

Reluctant to pigeonhole her style, Gideon explained it as "freely atonal." (Interview with Margaret Garwood, Student of Gideon) (Ardit 1996) The "free" applies equally well to the spontaneity and delicacy of her works' unfolding structures and recitative-like text settings. Gideon remarked that she learned the importance of proportion from Roger Sessions, but it could just as likely have stemmed from her youthful interest in languages. In many of her works—*Mixco* (1957) and *The Condemned Playground* (1963), for example—Gideon revisits the same text in its original language and in translation, allowing the music to "react" organically to the characteristics of each language.

Like Gideon, **Tsippi (Zipporah) Fleischer (b. Haifa, Israel, 1946)** pursued degrees in languages (Hebrew and Arabic, in Fleischer's case). As a musicology graduate student at Bar-Ilan University, she published a two-volume anthology of Hebrew song. Her song cycle *Girl-Butterfly-Girl* (1977/1979) sets four Syrian and Lebanese poems that trace the displacement, agony, and eventual resignation of a lonely desert wanderer. The text is in the original Arabic as well as in Hebrew and English translations, and the accompaniment may be played by Western or traditional Arab instruments.

The song cycles (and operas) of **Libby {Elizabeth} (Brown) Larsen (Reece) (b. Wilmington, Delaware, 1950)** deal most often with American historical subjects, and, like the late works of Aaron Copland—an acknowledged influence—they incorporate popular idioms and quotations into a music of vibrant orchestration and rhythms. One of her most popular works, *Songs from Letters* (1989), sets letters purported to be written from Calamity Jane to her daughter Janey; Larsen says that she prefers the first-person female narrative for her librettos due to its honest connection to her own perspective. Unafraid of appearing to cater to a mainstream audience, Larsen actively seeks to engage a wide range of listeners, including children, with a pointedly accessible music.

Electroacoustic Music: The Sound/Noise Spectrum

Coming to prominence just as the overlapping concerns of sonorism, extended technique, graphic notation, and integral serialism all seemed to reach their end limits, electroacoustic music looked to many to be the next phase. For the serialists, using artificial means of sound production meant being able to honor the infinitesimal gradations of time and tone resulting from their mathematical precompositional processes to a greater degree possible than with fallible human beings. To the sonorists, it represented a giant leap beyond extended technique—a means, as Luigi Rossolo proclaimed, of "break[ing] out of this narrow circle of pure musical sounds and conquer[ing] the infinite variety of noise sounds" (Manning 1993).

Libby Larsen.
Photo by Laura Crosby, Minneapolis, MN.

Kaija (Anneli) Saariaho (b. Helsinki 1952), who works primarily with the union of live and electronic instruments, is concerned with demonstrating electroacoustic music's lyrical and expressive potential. Saariaho comes to electronics from a concern for timbre; she has said more than once that her goal is to "enter into" sounds. Paradoxically, such a microscopic focus demands a music in which large-scale, gradual shifts predominate over moment-to-moment dynamism. Metric pulse, therefore, is almost entirely absent in a Saariaho work, and pitch is more often a function of timbre than of melodic plan; subtle nuances of tone quality and texture are impressionistically laid out for the listener.

Saariaho's first major work, *Verblendungen* (Dazzlings) (1984) for orchestra and tape, illustrates these principles. The first seven minutes consist entirely of a single diminuendo in the orchestra from a thick *sforzando* to absolute silence. Saariaho's preliminary sketch for the piece consists of a single stroke of a paintbrush, in which a thick accumulation of paint gives way to light, fading strands. Toward the end of the piece, the orchestral instruments ascend beyond discernible pitch and become noise, while the tape sounds start to resemble string instruments. The two timbres dovetail in a neat illustration of one of Saariaho's abiding concerns: the sound/noise spectrum, which parallels the consonance/dissonance spectrum of functional harmony in its possibility as an organizational tool in atonal music.

Another exploration of the sound/noise spectrum can be found in *Lichtbogen* (Arc of Light) (1985–1986) for nine musicians and live electronics. While the flute oscillates between pure sound and unpitched breath (occasionally even speaking through the instrument), the cello's variations in bow pressure are magnified and manipulated by the live electronics, which are controlled by computer analysis programs. The effect is particularly striking when the cellist bows with force toward the fingerboard, creating a heavy, multiphonic creaking sound that the electronics further "noise-ify."

After graduating in 1981 from the Sibelius Academy, where she had studied composition with Paavo Heininen (1938–), Saariaho received her diploma from the Musikhochschule in Freiburg, where her teachers were Brian Ferneyhough (1943–) and Klaus Huber (1924–). She then took courses at IRCAM (Institut de Recherche et de Coordination Acoustique/Musique) in Paris, where she developed several computer programs for her compositions. Saariaho has worked at electronic studios in Helsinki, Freiburg, Paris, and Stockholm, although her primary residence (with her husband, the composer Jean-Baptiste Barrière [1958–] and their son) is currently Paris. She is the recipient of numerous prizes, including the Kranichsteiner Prize, the Prix Italia, the Ars Electronica Prize, and the Nordic Council's Music Prize. Her first opera, *L'amour de loin* (Love from Afar) (2000), won the 2003 Grawemeyer Award for Music Composition, making Saariaho the second woman to win that award.

An interest in meeting the practical needs of independent composers began in Helsinki, where Saariaho was a member of a group called Korvat auki, or The Ears Open Association. It continues to this day at the Web site "Petals" (www.petals.org), where she produces and markets her own multimedia artworks with three other musicians.

With her husband, Louis, **Bebe Barron (b. Minneapolis 1927)** established one of the first electronic music studios in the United States in 1949. The couple is known primarily for the score to the science fiction film *Forbidden Planet* (1956), the first to be made exclusively of electronic sounds. The circuitry that they designed for it was inspired by their knowledge of cybernetics and approximates the human central nervous system. In 1997, the Barrons were recipients of a lifetime achievement award from the Society for Electro-Acoustic Music in the United States, an organization of which Bebe Barron was the only female founding member in 1984.

Daria Semegen (b. Bamberg, Germany, 1946) worked at the Columbia-Princeton Electronic Music Center under Vladimir Ussachevsky from 1971 to 1975; her works from this time period typify the classical electronics studio sound: tape splicing and the use of wave form oscillators create a *musique concrète*-like atonal collage.

In the 1970s, **Alicia Terzian (b. Córdoba, Argentina, 1934)** wrote a number of multimedia works incorporating tape, slides, and other visual media as well as strategic placement of sound sources. Today, she writes primarily for traditional instruments and devotes her energies to promoting new music in Argentina as the conductor of Grupo Encuentros, an ensemble that she founded in 1979.

Computer Music: *Voyager*

The computer has been likened to a pencil, "a tool for working out ideas," in the words of Kaija Saariaho (Roads 1986). For other composers, it may be more akin to a musical instrument, a piece of scientific equipment, an assistant, or a collaborator. For **Laurie Spiegel (b. Chicago 1945)**, the computer is a catalyst in a vast transformation of recent socioeconomic circumstances surrounding the production and consumption of art. In 1981, she wrote that with the aid of technology advances in the late twentieth century

> [t]he economics of the arts of the future may well be founded on the intrinsic worth of the composed information itself, what Marxists might call "use" value as opposed to "exchange" value. That is, the image the artist creates will not derive its value…from its status as a material object…nor from the idea that only one instance of a work fully or properly embodies the creator's intent. It will derive its value, [*sic*] from its informational content, from people's wanting to look at it or hear it. (Spiegel 1982)

More than twenty years later, some of the shifts that Spiegel predicted have come about with the proliferation of digital means of direct communication between artists and audiences such as the Internet. At the same time, however, computers and software have become more and more commercialized, a fact noted by Spiegel in an essay written fourteen years after the preceding remarks (Spiegel 1996). She observed that standardization, sprawl, and indifference had largely supplanted the craft and efficiency of early code and the sense of wonder among its early programmers.

Regardless of the ultimate outcome of the "information revolution," Spiegel has certainly seen it through its formative age. From working with mainframe computers at Bell Labs in the 1970s, to creating one of the first composition software programs in the 1980s, to maintaining her own Web site from which she is able to independently control the dissemination of her works, Spiegel is a seminal figure in computer music.

Spiegel's most prominent legacy will probably be the software program that she designed in 1986: *Music Mouse—An Intelligent Instrument*. With an easily navigable, yet extremely sophisticated, program, the user can control a vast number of parameters of sound using only the mouse and keyboard of a personal computer. It received rave reviews when it first appeared, most notably for its accessibility (even to those with no musical training) and for the almost infinite variety of sounds that it could produce. It boasts user groups ranging from rock musicians, to music therapists, to film scorers. The difficulty of classifying *Music Mouse*—it has been variously called a musical composition, a program, and an interactive artwork, depending on the user—raises valuable questions regarding intellectual property and "combined authorship," issues that Spiegel has addressed in several of her writings.

Spiegel began her career as a guitarist and lutenist, instruments that she studied while pursuing a bachelor of arts in social sciences at Shimer College in Illinois. While she wrote songs for her own enjoyment, she did not intend to pursue composition as a profession until a stint at Juilliard studying composition with Jacob Druckman (1928–1996) and Vincent Persichetti (1915–1987) introduced her to electronic and computer music. She was soon composing for the Kitchen in New York and experimenting with Morton Subotnick's (1933–) Buchla synthesizer at the New York University Composers Workshop. When she submitted these works in fulfillment of composition assignments, Juilliard initially rejected them due to their lack of a score.

After graduating, Spiegel worked at Bell Telephone Laboratories' Department of Acoustic and Behavioral Research, where she encountered a hospitable and collaborative atmosphere, despite being one of a very few women in an overwhelmingly male-dominated field. At home among mavericks, Spiegel began at the beginning, carrying punch cards from one end of a room-sized computer to the other. Later she worked primarily with GROOVE (Generated Real-time Output Operations on Voltage-controlled Equipment), the first hybrid digital-analogue system. Spiegel and a colleague developed a program that used GROOVE technology to integrate real-time audio and video productions and improvisations. They dubbed the program VAMPIRE (Video and Music Program for Interactive Real-time Exploration).

In the early 1980s, Spiegel became involved with the early personal computer movement, which appealed to her desire to eliminate the barriers, both artistic and economic, that traditional Western musical practice placed between composer and listener. With *Music Mouse*, Spiegel sought to provide a means of personal, domestic music-making a latter-day counterpart to the piano, which once was a staple of almost every household.

In her album *Unseen Worlds*, Spiegel uses *Music Mouse* to facilitate nine real-time compositions (realized between 1989 and 1990). While many of the *"études"* have programmatic titles, their material is richly multivalent, with some implying tonal centers and others consisting primarily of pitchless atmospheric sounds. Spiegel's background in guitar is evident in the prevalence of plucked attacks and metallic timbres in her melodic material. Above all, she seems to prefer to set in motion an organically self-generating process rather than to impose an artificial form on the material. An example of this aesthetic is *A Harmonic Algorithm* (1980), an autoreproductive program that proposes to answer the question, "[W]hat music would an Apple II computer make to entertain itself when it is alone?" In another work, *A Strand of Life ("Viroid")* (1990), the melodic material consists solely of the genetic code of a potato tuber viroid. The pitches A, E, G, and C (the first letters of the four enzymes that constitute the viroid's RNA sequence) merrily play themselves out in a poignant, minute-long declaration of self.

While Spiegel has received virtually no official recognition of her contribution to music in the form of awards or grants to date, she has in fact been given another, far greater honor. A work of hers made at Bell Labs in 1977, *Harmony of the Planets*, is the opening track of the gold record *Sounds of Earth* aboard the National Aeronautics and Space Administration (NASA) spacecraft *Voyager*. It seems entirely appropriate that a composer committed to technology as a means of distilling communication to its essence and ushering it into the future should be an ambassador of humanity into space.

As with Laurie Spiegel's works, those of **Ruth Anderson (b. Kalispell, Montana, 1928)** tend toward interactive play and playful research. One of her pieces, *Centering* (1979), uses a double biofeedback process between a dancer and four observers; galvanic skin resistance oscillators attached to the observers generate sounds to which the dancer responds. In another, *Points* (date unknown), meditative sine tones produce what Anderson calls "a kind of sonic acupressure" (Rosen). She designed and directed the electronic music studio at Hunter College in New York, where she was a professor from 1966 to 1988.

Daphne Oram (b. Devizes, Wiltshire, England, 1925–d. 2003) is the cofounder and later director of the BBC Radiophonic Workshop. She left that position in 1959 to found her own studio where she invented a computer-like composition tool called *Oramics*. The system originates from the early experiments in drawing directly onto the sound track of 35mm film. *Oramics* consists of ten sprocketed clear filmstrips that, when drawn over an array of photocells, govern a vast number of parameters of sound. It was more affordable than most electroacoustic equipment of the time and had greater subtlety as to attack, decay, and vibrato. Oram, like Spiegel, sees computers and digital technology as important tools by which artists—women in particular, according to Oram—can "reclaim" a medium in which they have been traditionally underrepresented and underprivileged.

A former student of the Institute of Sonology at Utrecht, **Cecilie Ore (b. Oslo, Norway, 1954)** uses the computer to arrive at a geometric, prismlike sense of time in music. Her goal, as she puts it, is to represent "a manifold of realities…exist[ing] simultaneously" (Billing 1992), a philosophy exemplified in her string quartet of 1989, appropriately titled *Praesens subitus* (Abrupt Present).

In 1973, **Diane Thome (b. Pearl River, New York, 1942)** became the first woman to receive a Ph.D. in music from Princeton University. For her, as for Kaija Saariaho, the timbral and spectral processes made possible by the computer's sensitivity are ushering in a redefinition of harmony. Her multimedia works often explore the relationships between sound makers, whether it be instruments and tape, composers and computers, or music and the other arts.

Sound Installation: "It Starts with a Place"

If electroacoustic and computer music, by doing away with the need for scores and performer/interpreters, had not already generated enough questions about what constitutes "music," sound art certainly does. A slippery category that can encompass sound sculptures and installations, radio art, and even *musique concrète*, sound art challenges the notion of a fixed "work" taking place in a unique location and time. As well, the traditional roles of the composer and listener are no longer givens. In sound art, the form of the work is determined by the sounds of the environment and their source and location in space. Composition is less an act of shaping than of framing, and "listening" may be quite participatory.

Sound art focuses the ear on the ambient sounds that occupy one's aural environment, aestheticizing "found" sound in a similar fashion to *arte povera*'s and land art's aestheticization of "found" spaces. In the works of the following sound artists, place is primary; Christina Kubisch's artworks deal with places that listen, while Hildegard Westerkamp's deal with places that speak. The latter's description of her process is applicable to both: "It starts with a place, then it creates a new place inside the composition." (website:www.emf.org/artists/mccartney/studio.html)

Christina Kubisch's (b. Bremen, Germany, 1948) early musical training was in flute and music education and occurred at various schools in Germany from 1967 to 1974. As a composition student of Franco Donatoni (1927–2000) at the Milan Conservatory, she also began to study electronic music with Angelo Paccagnini (1930–   ). In the late 1970s, she concentrated mainly on video art, but after studying electrical engineering for a year, she began creating sound installations.

Kubisch describes her work as "ethno-electronics": a study in the mutual influence of natural and technological phenomena. An existing space is rigged to respond to changes in light and shadow via photoelectric panels, translating the visual patterns into sound patterns. The sounds produced are intrinsic and meaningful to the place; for example, in *Dreaming of a Major Third* (date unknown), an installation at the Boston Museum of Contemporary Art, bell sounds were projected according to the movement of the sun across the museum's clock tower. In another installation, *Sechs Spiegel* (Six Mirrors) (date unknown), mirrors treated with a light-sensitive pigment were placed around a church. The mirrors sonically "reacted" not only to the sun but also to each other's reflections.

Kubisch teaches sound installation at the Kunstakademie in Münster and experimental art at Saar College of Visual Arts. Her work has been exhibited at the Venice Biennale, among many other locations, and she is the recipient of numerous grants and awards.

The compositions of **Hildegard Westerkamp (b. Osnabrück, Germany, 1946)** are more constrained than those of Kubisch, taking shape largely in "traditional" media such as tape, compact disc (CD), radio, and even as scores. Although Westerkamp maintains a significant role as composer in the formation of her works, she is still interested in the sounds that places make on their own. "I compose," she says, "with any sound that the environment offers to the microphone, just as a writer works with all the words that a language provides....I like to use the microphone the way photographers often use the camera" (website:www.sfu.ca/westerka/reviews/transformations.html). In Westerkamp's works—often referred to as "sound documents" or "soundscapes"—an environment is recorded in its natural state and only minimally manipulated electronically. A work that typifies the soundscape aesthetic is *Soundwalking* (1978–1979, produced for Vancouver Co-operative Radio), in which Westerkamp recorded the sonic environments of various sites around the city and broadcast them back to their original locations in what has been called a "sonic-mirroring."

"Soundscape" is a term borrowed from the World Soundscape Project (WSP), a research group founded by the Canadian composer R. Murray Schafer (1933–   ) in 1969 and devoted to acoustic ecology (the study and improvement of the relationship between humans and their sound environment). Westerkamp, who emigrated to Canada in 1968, met Schafer while studying for a master of arts degree in communication at Simon Fraser University in Vancouver, where the WSP was based. She soon joined the fledgling organization and in the early 1990s edited its newsletter. In 1993 Westerkamp helped found the WSP's successor, the World Forum for Acoustic Ecology. Currently on the editorial committee of *Soundscape—The Journal of Acoustic Ecology*, she continues to produce sound documents and installations and travels all over the world conducting acoustic ecology workshops. She is married to the poet and playwright Norbert Ruebsaat, with whom she has collaborated on several works.

As an acoustic ecologist, Westerkamp is acutely aware of imposed and unwanted sound such as noise pollution and Muzak; several of her works on these subjects have a protest or satirical element to them. She has said more than once that she wishes to cultivate a critical intelligence on the part of listeners, a discerning taste for the sounds in one's environment that does not simply accept all noise as inevitable and benign. This is a different approach from that of John Cage; although both he and Westerkamp are concerned with heightening aural awareness, Cage perceived virtually all noise, even stuck car sirens, as natural and potentially beautiful. However, the two shared an abiding interest in silence. From 1985 to 1986 Westerkamp and eleven other artists camped in a unique region of New Mexico known as the Zone of Silence in order to make art that addressed or incorporated the quiet of the desert. And in a 1998 installation that took place in New Delhi called *NADA—An Experience in Sound*, Westerkamp explored concepts of silence in the secular and sacred traditions of numerous cultures around the world.

Like Kubisch, **Liz [Elizabeth] Phillips (b. Jersey City, New Jersey, 1951)** frequently uses light, wind, and other natural phenomena to "play" her sound sculptures as a musician would an instrument. Phillips is probably even better known for spaces that sense and interact with human movement. Her primary work in this genre is *Sunspots* (1979), an installation that took place at the San Francisco Museum of Modern Art. For this, Phillips used a synthesizer that she designed and constructed herself to generate invisible radio frequency "capacitance fields" in a room. When participants moved through the space, copper sculptures responded sonically to their movements, transmitting information to a pair of speakers. Pitch, rhythm, volume, and timbre were all "performed" by the people moving through the space.

Annea [Anna] (Ferguson) Lockwood (b. Christchurch, New Zealand, 1939) is the historical link between the conceptualists and the sound artists. In the late 1960s she performed *The Glass Concert*, in which she explored the acoustic properties of different glass objects—rods, goblets, water gongs, and lightbulbs, to name a few—to often controversial critical response. "For me," she said, "every sound has its own minute form...lives out its own structure." (Lockwood, *The Glass World* [recording], 1997) Later, her *Piano Transplants* (1972–1982)—event actions in which a piano is set on fire, buried in a garden, and drowned in a body of water—evoked Fluxus in their destructive attitude toward one of the preeminent icons of Romanticism.

Performance Art 1: "The Dancing Voice" (Jowitt 1997)

An old woman with white hair, a white shift, and white pants crisscrossed with rope below the knee sits on a small stool. She adjusts her rimless glasses and begins to breathe. Her breath evolves into movement; she rises from her stool and is soon traveling/dancing along a "road" of white muslin. Shedding glasses and wig and unrolling her long, dark hair, the woman has by the end of the dance, moved backward through her life to become her youthful self.

This is act 2 of the dance theater piece *Education of the Girlchild*. The dancer is **Meredith (Jane) Monk (b. New York 1942)** (Some reference works cite Monk's place of birth as Lima, Peru; this is an error stemming from a playful white lie that Monk initiated in an early interview), and the time could either be 1973, when she choreographed the work at thirty-one and only intuitively grasped the complexities of old age, or 1993, when she revived the work as a fifty-year-old and found herself in the ironic position of having to affect the spontaneity and bodily grace of a youth. In this autobiographical artwork, the artist herself experiences the multidirectionality of time as it is warped and rewritten first by anticipation and later by memory.

As with most artists who work in "performance" (a disappointingly vague, catchall label), Meredith Monk is something of a polymath; she is a composer, singer, and filmmaker in addition to being a choreographer and dancer, but all her interests are branches of a tree at whose roots are movement and gesture. She calls herself a "choreographer" even when referring to her compositions and film works. She also refers to some of her works as "operas," but even that label is incomplete. If anything, her works recall the seventeenth-century French operas of Lully in their use of dance as an integral element in a triangle with music and drama.

Whatever their label, Monk's works all incorporate "ordinary" events and materials, whether props and costumes or actual locations. Many of her early works, such as *Juice* (1969) and *Vessel* (1971), are site-specific, in which the audience travels along with the performers through a familiar urban environment. These familiar elements are transformed by her gestural dance, in which the performer slows down, speeds up, repeats, or decontextualizes a movement so as to render it surreal. The dance critic Susan Foster (1985) has written, "The sequence of events...never manifests causal relations or temporal continuity." If ritual is evident in her dances, it is not the participatory, freeform ritual of an Oliveros work but is rather more akin to the abstracted, spare, displayed ritual of a medieval mystery play. It is not multicultural so much as transcultural;

Meredith Monk.
© Massimo Agus.

a piece about war, for instance, does not exhibit the trappings of any particular war but rather the emotional qualities common to all wars.

If dance is at the root of Monk's intermedia performances, music is the seed. Born into a family of singers (her mother sang for radio and early television commercials, and her great-grandfather was a cantor), she received a performing arts degree from Sarah Lawrence College, where she added classical vocal training and opera experience to her dance studies. After graduating, Monk was creating dance/theater pieces when, in a self-described epiphany, she realized that "the voice could have the same kind of flexibility and range that the body has, and that you could find a language for the voice that had the same individuality as a dancer's movement" (Strickland 1991).

Whether written to accompany her theatrical and filmed works or purely for concertizing or recording, her vocal pieces reflect this bodily concern in a number of ways. First, they usually begin with diatonic motivic cells (gestures) out of which patterns and alterations grow organically. Second, breath is foregrounded, reminding the listener of the physical source of the sound. Third, while the music is often virtuosic in its use of extended techniques such as isolated overtones and controlled glottal stops, it remains idiomatic to Monk's vocal range, just as her dances accommodate her own body's strengths and limitations. Finally, the phonemes that she uses hint at language but never fully break into recognizable text, in much the same way that the motions of her dancers may evoke, but do not represent, everyday tasks.

Each piece is thus an intimate, yet open, sketch whose details the listener is invited to fill in. The result, especially when Monk accompanies herself with triadic ostinati on the piano, has often been called minimalist, but Monk resents the term as she is less interested in structural permutations than in the voice as messenger, mirror, and vehicle for a dramatic catharsis.

Monk has been a prominent member of the "downtown" arts scene in TriBeCa (New York City) since her first works appeared in the late 1960s. In the early days, Monk led a dance theater company called the House, many of whose original members have gone on to form their own troupes. In 1978, she formed Meredith Monk and Vocal Ensemble, for which she wrote a number of works. Her process for generating works for ensembles has not changed much over forty years: she creates collaboratively, working with and within her performers' ranges and limits, as well as their personal interests. (Act 1 of *Girlchild*, she says, grew out of her fellow House members' curiosities about ancestry and heritage.) She uses notation, if at all, to jog her memory rather than to enable another group of performers to reproduce her work. Showing and telling are her preferred means of passing on a work, as they are for most dancers.

Monk has won much critical and popular acclaim as is evident from the following partial list of achievements: a summer at the MacDowell Colony; a MacArthur Foundation "Genius" Grant; honorary doctorates from five colleges, including Bard and Juilliard; a screening of her film *Book of Days* at the Whitney Museum Biennial; a retrospective art exhibition at Lincoln Center; a record contract (with the independent label ECM Records); a performance for the Dalai Lama (at the 1999 World Festival of Sacred Music in Los Angeles); and a commission from the New World Symphony to create her first orchestral work.

In many of Monk's theater works, a heroic quest or rite of passage is witnessed and even assisted by a benevolent community of fellow travelers. As her manifesto proclaims, she has great faith in the power of this kind of empathetic theater to affirm "the world of feeling in a time and society where feelings are in danger of being eliminated." (Jowitt 1997) While such convictions may appear naive, Monk's is a willful innocence that acknowledges the debt owed to experience. In *Jade (Old Woman's Song)* from her album *Songs from the Hill* (1976–1977), a mournful melody that may at one time have been a dance tune is remembered by the singer in a breathless whisper. The halting cadence of her voice could just as easily be that of a child or of an elderly woman. The simultaneity of the woman's two possible selves is as clearly audible here as it is visible in *Education of the Girlchild*.

The dance critic Rob Baker has observed that "Monk's works are all journeys...back to a kind of collective childhood of shared images, shared traditions" (Monk, *Songs from the Hill/Tablet* [recording], 1989). Monk agrees, adding that she perceives her own music as an infinite series of manifestations of the lullaby archetype. It is a fitting image, for the lullaby is the essence of old meeting young, of the continuity of generations, and of healing.

While Monk's belief that art can be a tool for truth telling is shared by **Diamanda (Dimitria Angeliki Elena) Galás (b. San Diego 1955)**, the latter's performance art is most vehemently not about catharsis. Her "Schrei-Oper" (or shriek operas) combine vocal howls, moans, and wails; bald texts of self-immolation, homicide, and crucifixion; and piano accompaniments that reference the rawness of rock or a distorted and facile waltz. She is devoted to the outcast, whether modern (as with the HIV-positive community) or biblical (both Jesus and Satan fall into this category). Although classically trained in piano and voice, Galás has more in common with Antonin Artaud and his "theatre of cruelty" than with anyone who has come before (or, indeed, since) in the classical world.

Unlike her fellow vocal virtuosa Monk, **Joan (Linda Lotz) La Barbara (Subotnick) (b. Philadelphia 1947)**, has devoted most of her professional life to exploring the interaction of her dynamic voice with electronic equipment. The wife of Morton Subotnick and a fellow explorer of the Buchla synthesizers at California Institute for the Arts, La Barbara has developed a signature repertoire of multiphonics and other extended techniques to which she adds the layering effects enabled by multitracking technology. She often produces what she calls "sound paintings"; in one, *Time(d) Trials and Unscheduled Events* (written for the 1984 Olympic Games), sounds of La Barbara panting and swallowing are looped into an ostinato on top of which coughing, grunting, and other sounds of physical effort are projected in playful rhythmic patterns.

Performance Art 2 "This Is Your Captain. And We Are Going Down." (Anderson, *Big Science* [Recording], 1982)

"From the Air," the first song from the epic performance piece *United States I–IV* (1983) by **Laurie Anderson (b. Chicago 1947)**, begins with a simple minor-key ostinato pattern of even eighth notes outlined by a synthesizer and drums. Saxophones and a clarinet soon join in with their own pattern. Eventually a voice enters:

> Good evening. This is your Captain.
> We are about to attempt a crash landing.
> Please extinguish all cigarettes.

This is the "voice of authority," Anderson's term for that bland, androgynous voice that one hears in malls and train stations and on automated telephone answering services. It is a voice at once ominous and comforting, and in this case, it is explaining an impending disaster. In slow, measured locution, the voice turns a set of safety instructions into a menacing game of Simon Says: "Captain says: Put your head in your hands./ Put your hands on your hips. Heh heh."

"From the Air" is an example of the primacy of persona (as mediated through language) in Anderson's performance art. For all of *United States I–IV*, she stands alone at the center of the stage dressed in neutral black. Transforming her body into a blank screen, she turns her voice into a microphone, using digital technology to alter and thus "hide" her natural voice. Once she virtually disappears, she makes room for the

Joan La Barbara.
© Jack Mitchell.

nameless strangers whose stories she tells. "I don't really consider myself an artist," Anderson has explained. "I think I'm more of a spy. That's really what I do. I look at the stuff in other people's lives" (Hodgkinson 2001).

Anderson was raised in a midwestern Protestant family, but her grandmother, to whom she was very close, was a Southern Baptist. Exposure to such disparate realizations of faith—a mild, benevolent Jesus, on the one hand, and a formidable, vengeful Jehovah, on the other—laid the foundation for an abiding interest in the mediation of sociocultural extremes and binary pairs. More specifically, Anderson admired the intriguingly spare stories and the ritual pomp of organized religion; explicit biblical imagery can be found in much of her work. *United States I–IV*, for instance, begins with the story of the Flood, while "Langue d'amour" (Language of Love), a song from *Mister Heartbreak* (1984), addresses the possible interior worlds of Eve.

An early aspiration of Anderson's was to become a librarian. Her youthful mixed-media artworks as a student at Mills and Barnard Colleges accordingly dealt with systems of information processing—newspapers woven together to obscure their text, for instance, as in *New York Times, Horizontal/China Times, Vertical* (1971–1979)—and with the physical experience of reading, as in *Handbook* (1972). Her later multimedia performances give the viewer/listener an impression of browsing through a vast catalog of signs and symbols. A screen often looms behind her, onto which are projected clocks, maps, and directional arrows, all removed from the contexts in which they transmit information so that their inherent ambiguity and exoticism are laid bare for the viewer. A student of American Sign Language and a trained visual artist, Anderson frequently dwells in the zones where gesture, picture, and word overlap.

Anderson's performance art developed out of her work teaching community college while pursuing a master of fine arts in sculpture from Columbia University in the early 1970s. In particular, *United States I–IV* originated from questions that she was asked about America while on tour in Europe. She retains a classic, educational stance in her mature works, "lecturing"—frequently using the "voice of authority"—to a largely passive, silent audience. The slide shows and podium that are common elements of her stage design add to the educational atmosphere. Finally, the songs themselves are often about "learning the rules of the game," be it a linguistic or technological game.

Oddly, the two works that most vividly illustrate this concept are those that depart most from the live performance medium. The first, the CD-ROM *Puppet Motel* (1998), was designed by Anderson and programmer Hsin-Chien Huang. It consists of a series of rooms, each of which contains elements from other Anderson works and interactive games such as editing a short film or rewriting a Dostoyevsky novel. There are no instructions for how the user is to navigate the motel, nor is there a single "solution" or fixed path. Some hidden treasures appear only once; others shift location, frustrating the user's efforts to "learn." A playful elusiveness of information can also be found in Anderson's on-line artwork *Here* (1996), which takes as its raw material the 258 most frequently used words in the English language (accounting for 55 percent of written English). These words can be arranged, organized, and eliminated according to their rhymes, definitions, component letters, and so on. However, each page of the artwork contains only the game without rules; it falls to the user to uncover the operation being performed on the words (which are also often accompanied by aural effects).

Anderson has taught herself the rules of another game, generating some controversy within the avant-garde. In 1981, she signed a major record contract with the commercial house Warner Brothers. Her first recording for them, the song "O Superman" from *United States I–IV*, was a major hit upon its release, rising to a number two position on the British pop charts. This was a move for which Anderson received much criticism, as have subsequent collaborations with big business (*Puppet Motel* with Voyager, a commercial for American Express). Calling it "adaptive resistance," she maintains that success in mainstream institutions does not disqualify an artist from membership in a still viable avant-garde: "There are plenty of rules and taboos yet to be broken," she observes. "I'll do my part" (Dery 1991).

At press time, Anderson's most recent large-scale multimedia work was *Songs and Stories from Moby Dick* (1999). It is no surprise that Herman Melville's novel should provide the raw material for an Anderson piece, given its kaleidoscope of zoological tangents, historical and literary epigrams, and overt biblical symbolism. However, in a recent interview Anderson revealed that what appealed to her most about the work was the constantly morphing identity of the narrator. From the opening sentence, the reader is asked to manufacture what may be an entirely false narrative persona. This kind of narrative is something in which Anderson has been participating for years; it occurs in "From the Air" when, halfway through the Captain's monologue, the narrator suddenly turns into a fellow traveler ("And I said: Uh oh. This is gonna be some day"), and it is something that Anderson practices in each of her performances, where she may take on as many different personas as does Melville's hero.

To facilitate this fluidity, Anderson uses vocoders and synthesizers to digitally manipulate her voice, often lowering its register to achieve the disconcerting androgyny of the "voice of authority." She also digitally modifies the violin she studied in her youth, incorporating it into most of her performances. Her most famous such instrument is the tape bow violin (1977), whose bowhair is replaced by a length of magnetic tape that is "played" by drawing it across a tape head affixed to the strings of the violin. *Moby Dick* makes frequent use of a "talking stick," an instrument that processes and replicates other sounds. These ventriloquist technologies act as aural masks, assisting Anderson in calling forth the "No Bodies. I've written many songs and stories for these 'people.' They have no names, no histories. They're outside of time and place and they are the ones who truly speak for me" (Anderson 1994).

A cellist, **(Madeline) Charlotte Moorman (b. Little Rock, Arkansas, 1933–d. New York 1991)** collaborated with the avant-garde composer Nam June Paik on his works for "prepared" cello, in which, as with Laurie Anderson, digital technology is explicitly incorporated into the very body of the instrument. For example, in *TV Cello* (1971), Moorman plays a cello made of three appropriately sized television sets. Her own physical body is also an integral component—some might say a kind of canvas— in works such as *TV Bra for Living Sculpture* (1969) and the infamous *Opera Sextronique* (1967), a performance of which landed Moorman in jail for indecent exposure. For her own part, Moorman never claimed even partial authorship of Paik's works, declaring herself to be "an art work of his" (Decker Phillips 1998). She was, however, the founder and impresario of fifteen installments of the site-specific New York Avant Garde Festival. It has been said that, in lieu of a published oeuvre, the festivals "are Miss Moorman's pieces, and everyone [performers and audience alike] is her willing, anonymous collaborator" (Bourdon 2000).

By reading this book, you have already performed *Spatial Poem* #5 (ca. 1965–1975) by **Mieko [Chieko] Shiomi (b. Okayama, Japan, 1938)**, which consists solely of the instruction, "Open something which is closed." Along with Alison Knowles and Yoko Ono, Shiomi is one of several female artists associated with the loose collective of conceptualist performance artists known as Fluxus. She came to Fluxus from Group-Ongaku, a similarly experimental performance ensemble that she cofounded in Japan. Her more recent pieces, while emphasizing the aural dimension, retain the deconstructionist play of her early work.

Neo-romanticism, Neo-impressionism: *Millefoglie*

The vague prefix "neo," when applied to music history, is vulnerable to misuse. Joan Tower's label as a "neo-Romantic" composer tends to exaggerate what is often no more than a lack of abhorrence of the triad and an interest in intuitive means and expressive ends. Barbara Kolb's supposed "neo-impressionism" mislabels a movement that was already mislabeled to begin with. Both composers confront and collect from numerous musical eras. As Kolb has said, "The more an individual develops a sense of consciousness of what he is, of himself, the more he's able to transform what comes to him and integrate it into some substance or energy which is also creative" (*Music of Barbara Kolb* [recording] 1990).

Joan Tower (b. New Rochelle, New York, 1938) is forthright about her influences, which include Olivier Messiaen's *Quartet for the End of Time* (1940) Igor Stravinsky's (1882–1971) *Rite of Spring* (1911–1913) and the symphonies and piano sonatas of Ludwig van Beethoven (1770–1827). In *Black Topaz* (1976) one can hear Beethovenian altered-note transitions, piano/percussion duels reminiscent of Stravinsky, and aspects of Pierre Boulez and Claude Debussy. Tower shares with these predecessors not just a keen ear for forward, driving rhythms and appropriately harnessed fury but also a concern for the balance between the singular event and the host of implications that result from its development and transformation.

Tower's father, George Tower, was a mining engineer and amateur violinist; her mother, Anna Robinson, was a music teacher. Her father's preoccupation with gems is an acknowledged influence on many of Tower's works: Several "mineral" pieces depict in music the properties of different stones. But even her other works display geological properties; an extended solo or single tone can attract surrounding material like a magnet or, like a crystal, organically reproduce itself in three dimensions. A dense and busy texture may suddenly give way to an aural "clearing," in which a single tall chord is built up triad by triad as though a bright light were shined on it for detailed observation. Unsurprisingly, one frequently finds gemological words such as "clarity" and "brilliance" in literature about Tower.

These processes and characteristics apply mostly to works that Tower composed after 1975, when she abandoned the serialism of her early student years in favor of a more eclectic approach. After receiving her bachelor of arts from Bennington College, she went to Columbia University for a master of arts and doctor of musical arts. While there Tower studied composition with eight different teachers, including Chou Wenchung (1923–), Otto Luening (1900–1996), Ralph Shapey (1921–2002), and Charles Wuorinen (1938–). In 1969 she founded the Da Capo Players, a chamber ensemble dedicated to new music of which she is the pianist. This gave Tower the unique opportunity to hear her works performed on a regular and immediate basis. The group won a Naumberg Award for Chamber Music in 1973.

In 1979, Tower was encouraged by the music director of the Hudson Valley Philharmonic to rewrite *Amazon* (1977), a chamber ensemble piece, for chamber orchestra.

The result, *Amazon II*, gained much critical acclaim and led to her first original orchestral commission, the equally successful *Sequoia* (1981), another nature-oriented tone poem. Tower has focused largely on works for orchestra since then and has received numerous commissions, awards, and composer residencies—for example, with the St. Louis Symphony and the Orchestra of St. Luke's. In 1998 Tower was inducted into the American Academy of Arts and Letters (joining her colleagues Louise Talma and Miriam Gideon). She is currently the Asher B. Edelman professor of music at Bard College.

Like Tower, **Barbara Kolb (b. Hartford, Connecticut, 1939)** confines herself almost exclusively to instrumental works and prefers spatial over linear forms. Kolb calls her approach "positive staticism" and achieves it by operating on confined materials with a sophisticated polyphony that often involves numerous different meters occurring simultaneously. Her polymetric sensibility comes from film, particularly that of Michelangelo Antonioni and Luis Buñuel. Indeed, their use of montage is akin to much of Kolb's work, which may draw on anything from medieval rondeaus, to eighth-century Chinese poetry, to Satie's aphoristic piano miniatures, to Boulez's *Structures 1* (1952). Besides film, Kolb has mentioned an affinity in her music with mobiles and microscopes; appropriately, all are tools for observing an object from numerous perspectives.

Kolb, initially encouraged by her family to pursue a career in music began as a clarinetist. Her father, Harold Judson Kolb, was a musician, a big band conductor, and the music director of a Connecticut radio station. However, once she received a bachelor of arts degree from the Hartt College of Music and wished to go on for a master's degree, Kolb's father disapproved and withdrew financial support (a move that recalls the obstacles faced by Germaine Tailleferre and Rebecca Clarke a half century earlier). Undaunted, Kolb studied composition with Arnold Franchetti (1904–1993) at Hartt while supporting herself by playing for the Hartford Summer Band and Hartford Symphony Orchestra. She attended summer festivals at Tanglewood in 1964 and 1968, studying with Gunther Schuller (1925–) and Lukas Foss (1922–). In 1969, Kolb made history: she was the first American woman to win the Prix de Rome for music composition. This immediately garnered her attention from numerous renowned American orchestras, and she was inundated with commissions. Since then, she has received four MacDowell Colony fellowships, two Guggenheims, a National Endowment for the Arts grant, and a Fulbright scholarship. Her teaching positions include Brooklyn College and Eastman School of Music, and from 1979 to 1982 she was the director of the contemporary music concert series *Music New to New York*.

Several of Kolb's orchestral works include tape, which acts as a mirror to the instruments, permitting a quasi-spatial multiplicity of perspectives on the material, as in Tower's works. Sometimes, the tape is merely prerecorded instruments, as in *Soundings* (1971–1972). This work can be performed either by three orchestras (playing in three different tempi for much of the piece) or by chamber ensemble and tape, with the tape filling out the parts not present. At other times, the tape is computer-generated, as with *Millefoglie* (1985/1987) for chamber orchestra and tape. This work, which won the Friedheim Award in 1987, was commissioned and realized during a term that Kolb spent at IRCAM in Paris on the invitation of Boulez. The tape does not appear until five minutes into the piece and remains an outsider to the music of the ensemble, while at the same time triggering shifts in the ensemble's texture that in turn alter the computer's own timbre.

Calling and listening are elements in Kolb's music that link perception to a wider category of message transmission and receipt (e.g., *Looking for Claudio* (1975) for solo guitar and tape). Also of interest is the musical homage, another kind of response, as for example *Homage to Keith Jarrett and Gary Burton* (1976/1977) for flute and vibraphone and *Toccata* (1971) for harpsichord and tape. In the latter, a toccata by Domenico Scarlatti (1685–1757), is manipulated, refracted, and superimposed on itself until the listener can barely grasp recognizable motives from an atonal cacophony of sound.

Kolb's conviction that "one doesn't have to write…in specifically one style, to represent something valid" (Gague and Cavas 1982) applies equally well to both composers. Their eclectic styles represent not only one possible response to a postmodern world of infinite access, musicohistorical simultaneity, and complicated aesthetic agendas; they also reflect a renewed sense that there is more to a work than its genealogy.

Another composer who focuses almost exclusively on instrumental works, **Ellen Taaffe Zwilich (b. Miami 1939)** is concerned primarily with large-scale orchestral forms such as the symphony and concerto. With her *Symphony No. 1* (1982), she became the first woman to be awarded the Pulitzer Prize in music. All three movements of the symphony develop their pitch material out of the rising minor third interval that opens the piece. "My aim," writes Zwilich in her preface to the work, "was to create a rich harmonic palette and a wide variety of melodic gestures, all emanating from a simple source." Her more recent works, though frequently more diatonic and programmatic, maintain the focus on developing variation and transparent structure. Zwilich was the first woman to receive a doctorate in composition from Juilliard, where her teachers included Roger Sessions and Elliott Carter. After many years in the rare position of being able to make her living solely through commissions, performance fees, and royalties, Zwilich recently took a position as Francis Eppes Professor of Music at her alma mater, Florida State University.

Of the so-called Neo-Romantics, **Nancy (Jean Hayes) Van de Vate (Smith)** (she has also used the pseudonyms Helen Huntley and William Huntley) **(b. Plainfield, New Jersey, 1930)** leans more toward the lyrical chromaticism of Johannes Brahms, (1833–1897) Bela Bartók (1881–1945) and the postwar Polish school. Van de Vate outlines her aesthetic thus: "I make no effort to eliminate those elements which have marked Western music during most of its history—melody, coherent rhythm, structure, vertical sonority, tension-resolution relationships…and the intention of being expressive" (Ellis 1992). An outspoken critic of the lack of opportunities and resources for women composers, she has written numerous articles on the subject and in 1975 founded the International League of Women Composers.

Judith Lang Zaimont (b. Memphis, Tennessee, 1945), a composer of programmatic instrumental works and vocal and choral music, shares with the mature Copland a rhythmic sensibility that marries French neo-classical and American popular idioms. One hears this particularly in her *Calendar Collection* (1976), a set of twelve piano minia-

Ellen Taaffe Zwilich.
© Cori Wells Braun.

tures that explicitly reference popular associations with the months of the year. A lecturer (and, later, professor) of music since she was twenty-four, Zaimont shares with Van de Vate a concern for the status of women in the composition profession. She is the editor in chief of the book series *The Musical Woman: An International Perspective*, of which three volumes have been published since the mid-1980s, and a coeditor of *Contemporary Concert Music by Women* (1981).

Free Atonality: The Cerebral Soul

In **Shulamit Ran's (b. Tel Aviv, Israel, 1949)** *Private Game* (1979) for clarinet and cello, blocks of disparate material are placed side by side: an atonal rush of progressively shorter note values, next to a relatively static cadential figure marked by three

Judith Zaimont.

rising semitones, next to a weary waltz fragment marked "Schubertian." These motivic snapshots reappear throughout the brief piece, sometimes in literal repetition and sometimes with their intervallic structure altered. The work was commissioned by Joan Tower's Da Capo Players in honor of their tenth anniversary and it is, in fact, a meditation on the formal principle from which the ensemble took its name. As the clarinet and cello chase each other in a playfully aggressive dance, so the mind chases down the salient elements of the work, comparing, identifying, and cataloging moment by moment. It is, for each of its listeners, a most private game.

Ran showed a remarkable gift for music at a very early age. By the age of nine she was already studying composition, having won a radio competition in Israel the year before when her piano teacher submitted some of her works without Ran's knowledge. Her first composition teachers were Alexander Boskovic (1907–1964) and Paul Ben-Haim (1897–1984). At the age of fourteen, a scholarship enabled her to attend Mannes

Shulamit Ran.

College of Music in New York City while simultaneously completing her high school degree. She studied composition there with Norman Dello Joio (1913–   ), and won a competition to perform her own piano concerto, *Capriccio* (1963), on Leonard Bernstein's (1918–1990) *Young People's Concerts* program. Touring as a concert pianist after her graduation from Mannes, Ran wrote what she calls "not unconsciously derivative" works at this early stage in her career (Guzzo 1996). She began teaching at the University of Chicago at age twenty-four, after the composer Ralph Shapey heard a recording of one of her works. Ran has taught at the university ever since and studied briefly with Shapey while the two were colleagues. In 1986 she married the otolaryngologist Abraham Lotan, with whom she has two children.

Among Ran's numerous awards, the most notable is the Pulitzer Prize that she won in 1991 for her *Symphony* (1989–1990). The work also won first prize in the Kennedy Center's Friedheim Awards the following year—the same year that Ran was elected to the American Academy of Arts and Sciences. From 1990 to 1997, she was composer-in-residence of the Chicago Symphony Orchestra. In this capacity, she not only wrote music but also conducted interviews with other living composers whose works were on upcoming orchestra concerts; the interviews were broadcast on the evening of the performance. From 1994 to 1997, Ran was also the composer-in-residence of the Lyric Opera of Chicago, for which she wrote the opera *Between Two Worlds (The Dybbuk)* (1997).

Ran, like Miriam Gideon, prefers not to label the music of her mature period any more specifically than "free atonal." In fact, while her works tend to be marked by chromatic saturation, they do call upon certain pitches to hierarchically organize the music by acting as magnets or, as Ran calls them, "centers of gravity." (Guzzo 1996) In recent years, her tonal vocabulary has begun to reference Middle Eastern modes, a development that parallels her increasing interest in subject matter drawn from Israel and Judaism. But across her oeuvre and no matter what the tonality, Ran has been lauded by critics for an organic balance between the spontaneous and the inevitable, intuition and discipline, as *Private Game* demonstrates. She feels strongly about her role as an educator in this regard:

> I…want to debunk the myth that something that has a certain complexity to it can't at the same time be emotional and passionate and touching and moving, that it therefore means that it is cerebral.…In fact, there is nothing wrong with the word cerebral because anything and everything that we are comes first from the brain. The brain…experiences all sensations, including happiness and grief, and everything else. (Guzzo 1996)

A former student of Ran's, **Melinda Wagner (b. Philadelphia 1957)** joined her and Ellen Taaffe Zwilich as the third woman ever to receive a Pulitzer Prize in music, for her *Concerto for Flute, Strings, and Percussion* (1998). She shares her teacher's predilection for energetic chromaticism, lively rhythms, and evocative, even droll, score markings ("Rapid; conspiratorial" and "Heroic; self-important" are two examples from the *Concerto*). Holding degrees from Hamilton College, the University of Chicago, and the University of Pennsylvania, Wagner studied not only with Ran but with George Crumb, Ralph Shapey, and others. With the *Concerto*, commissioned by the conductor and flutist Paul Lustig Dunkel for the Westchester Philharmonic, Wagner sought to replace the "heroic" role generally assigned to concerto soloists with one more akin to, as she put it, "an artistic beacon, or navigator."

Integrating Traditional *Ts'ao Shu*

Chou Wen-chung (1923–   ), **Chen Yi's (b. Guangzhou, China, 1953)** mentor and occasional teacher, has remarked on the affinity between various arts practiced in China and the art of *ts'ao shu*, or cursive script calligraphy. What he observes in *ts'ao shu*—"the fluidity in its movement, so rich with unpredictable twists and turns; the play between deliberateness and swiftness" (Ryker 1991)—could be equally true of the music of Chen Yi, in which delicacy and robustness, exuberance and rigor coexist. Chen

Melinda Wagner.
Steve Singer.

has even based a composition, *The Points* (1991) for solo *pipa*, on the eight standard brush strokes in the Zhengkai style of calligraphy.

Chen grew up in the Guangzhou Province of China, born to a family of doctors. From age three, she studied piano, violin, and Chinese traditional instruments, as well as Western and Chinese music theory. With the Cultural Revolution of the late 1960s, Chen, along with thousands of teenagers, was sent to work in the countryside for several years. She recalls playing violin for herself and her fellow farmers, although Western instruments and music were forbidden at this time. After her service, Chen returned to her hometown to become the concertmaster and a composer for the local Beijing Opera Troupe.

By 1978, the political climate in China had thawed somewhat, and after the school system was reinstated, the Central Conservatory at Beijing reopened its doors to students. Although there were only 100 available spots, over 17,000 applied. Chen Yi was one of those accepted. This first generation of students soon moved away from the so-

Chen Yi and percussionist Evelyn Glennie rehearse Chen Yi's Percussion Concerto *for the world premiere performance in Singapore March 1999. The piece was commissioned and performed by the Singapore Symphony and was recorded in August 2001.*
Photo by Zhou Long.

cialist realist cantatas and watered-down "folk" music that it had been their duty to compose just years before and began to rediscover both traditional and abstract music.

One important influence on Chen and others was the composer Alexander Goehr (1932–), who upon his arrival at the Central Conservatory in 1980 became the first Westerner in decades to teach Western music in China. Goehr introduced Chen and her classmates to the music of Stravinsky, Boulez, Messiaen, and the second Viennese school. In 1986, Chen became the first woman to receive a master's degree from the conservatory, after studying with Goehr and Wu Zu-qiang (1927–). Around this time, many Chinese composers were moving to the west. The respected composer Chou Wen-chung had come to New York to teach at Columbia University. Chen and her husband, fellow conservatory student and composer Zhou Long (1953–), followed Chou to Columbia, where Chen received a Ph.D. with distinction in 1993 under Chou and Mario Davidovsky (1934–).

Since then, Chen has taught composition at the Peabody Conservatory and is currently a professor of composition at the Conservatory of the University of Missouri, Kansas City. She has received numerous awards, fellowships, and commissions, including the Guggenheim, the Lili Boulanger Award, a National Endowment for the Arts Fellowship, a Grammy award, and an Ives Living Award (2001–2004) from the Academy of Arts and Letters, and the ASCAP 2001 Concert Music Award. She serves on the board of the International Alliance for Women in Music and continues to act as new music adviser to the Women's Philharmonic and to the acclaimed vocal ensemble Chanticleer. She is also active as a violinist and ethnomusicologist.

Chen's *Ge Xu (Antiphony)* (1994) for chamber orchestra demonstrates her sensitivity in handling elements from both Western and Eastern musical traditions. The piece is inspired by the antiphonal singing of the Zhuang people of Southern China in their celebrations of the lunar New Year. An ornamented and rhapsodic pentatonic melody, first heard in the high strings, becomes the primary theme of the work. In contrast to this theme's melodic emphasis, the second theme is dominated by rhythm, with the strings articulating an arpeggiated major triad in syncopated eighth notes. The two themes appear together in the vigorous high point of the work, but it is not an unwelcome clash; rather, the contrasting elements complement each other. *Ge Xu* ends with a final iteration of the primary theme in the bassoon—one can only assume this to be an homage to the opening of Stravinsky's *Rite of Spring*, which is recalled in other moments in the work.

Chen and others of her generation face a difficult reconciliation between a vast and ancient musical heritage, itself a conglomerate of numerous cultures, and a painful recent past, including technological and cultural encroachment by the West. The question of how to balance "global village" postmodernism, on the one hand, and more localized identity politics, on the other, can be maddening. However, this is a welcome challenge for Chen Yi:

> Modern society is a great network of complex latitudes and attitudes...every experience encountered can become both a source and medium of creativity....I want to try my best to get the essence of both Eastern and Western cultures and write more compositions that embody my temperament and the spirit of this brave epoch. (Zhou 1992)

In contrast to Chen's early experience, **Frangiz Ali-zade [also spelled Franghiz Ali-zadeh] (b. Baku, Azerbaijan, 1947)** found only Western models promoted at the Baku Conservatory where she studied and later taught music. None of the native musical traditions of Islamic Azerbaijan were included in the curriculum. In the process of teaching herself about these traditions, Ali-zade began to observe their kinship with those of the Western avant-garde. Since emigrating to Turkey after the breakup of the Soviet Union, Ali-zade has devoted herself to the music of her land and her state. *Mugam Sayagi* (1993), for example, uses a mixed ensemble of string quartet, harmonium, and gong to update *Mugamat*, a medieval Azerbaijani song cycle. Through the coded musical language of a Mugam, says Ali-zadeh "the ecstatic longing of a man for a woman could be [secretly] expressed as the love of God" (Night Prayers [recording], 1994).

Raised in the Australian outback, **Anne (Elizabeth) Boyd (b. Sydney, Australia, 1946)** studied at the University of Sydney and worked on Australia's first contemporary music journal, premiering many avant-garde works in the country (including Cage's *4933O*). Australia's proximity to, and cultural affinities with, the Pacific Rim have only recently begun to be acknowledged, and they are a frequent concern of Boyd's. She explores these connections in works incorporating aspects of *gagaku* (ancient Japanese court music) and *gamelan* (Indonesian orchestral music), as well as in her collabo-

Tania León.
© Marbeth Schnare.

rations with the Korean expatriate writer Don'o Kim. For nine years she was the head of the Music Department at the University of Hong Kong.

    Tania Justina León (b. Havana, Cuba, 1943) describes her work as the "express[ion of] the dichotomy between the folk-music traditions of my native Cuba and the Classical European training I received at the Havana Conservatory. (León, *A La Par* [recording], 1999)" Having come to New York to become a pianist, León was engaged in 1968 as the accompanist for Arthur Mitchell's newly formed Dance Theatre of Harlem. Soon, she was writing music for the company, acting as its music director and thereafter as the director, composer-in-residence, and orchestra conductor of the adjacent Music School. León's music is well suited to the needs of contemporary dance, ingeniously marrying a driving polyrhythmic pulse with pointillist lines that swing from atonality to pentatonicism. León is also a successful conductor, having appeared with the Gewandhausorchester Leipzig, the Brooklyn Philharmonic, and other orchestras.

The magnum opus of **Gillian Whitehead (b. Whangarei, New Zealand, 1941)** may be her *Babel* (1969–1970), which confronts cultural misinterpretation via a text of over fifty languages. Its apparently critical stance is understandable, given that the one-eighth-Maori composer's own works have occasionally been "Orientalized" by reviewers (one praised her *Pakuru* [1967] for voice and chamber ensemble for its "sultry and exotic" setting of a "mystically erotic" text [Le Page 1988]). Like Boyd, Whitehead attended the University of Sydney, after which she studied privately with Peter Maxwell Davies in London, making use of a version of his "magic square" as a compositional tool. Since the mid-1980s, Whitehead has eschewed certain elements that she describes as "European" in her music. She now prefers to apply other techniques—such as those drawn from Maori weaving traditions—to her works' internal structures, and to focus on the natural landscape of New Zealand for much of her subject matter. These reflect a concern for the country's compositional voice, but it is nonetheless a personal journey: "You have a duty," she maintains, "to write the kind of music that only you can write" (Thomson 1990).

Fragmentation: After the Collapse

> On Fragmentation. This is indispensable if one does not want to fall into REPRESENTATION. See beings and things in separate parts. Render them independent in order to give them a new dependence.—Robert Bresson (as quoted by Olga Neuwirth at www.olganewirth.com)

Almost all of the following four composers have yet to gain wide recognition outside Germany, the country in which they make their home; and two are under forty. However, in their steadfast disavowal of the grand narrative and their allegiance to disintegration as the only honest musical mode, they represent a significant trend in contemporary European art music. Even their large-scale works are marked by fragmentation, silence, the strangled gesture, and the sound of effort. The positing of an unbroken whole is no longer an option for these musical poststructuralists.

Originally a violinist, **Rebecca Saunders (b. London 1967)** received her bachelor of arts and Ph.D. from Edinburgh University. She studied with Wolfgang Rihm (1952–) at the Musikhochschule in Karlsruhe and currently makes her home in Berlin. She has received commissions from German radio and grants from the Berlin Academy of Arts and the Siemens Foundation. Saunders' works are deliberate and detached, she speaks of holding and weighing sounds and then setting them "next to, above, beneath and against each other," as a curator or collector might (Adlington 1999).

Saunders' most characteristic work may be her series based on Molly Bloom's monologue from the end of James Joyce's *Ulysses*. In *CRIMSON—Molly's Song 1* (1996) for twelve soloists, metronome, whistles, music boxes, and conductor, Saunders uses unconventional instruments and extended techniques to "set" the implied text abstractly. Only the "Yes!" that ecstatically concludes Molly's monologue is spoken, whispered by the musicians in the final bars of the piece. The rest of the work is characterized by a constricted tonal background confined largely to the interval of a half step over which are sprinkled growls, ratchets, and other inconclusive outbursts. When the music boxes are wound up at the beginning of the final movement, their plucky persistence sounds feebly optimistic next to the rest of the ensemble's abortive gestures.

For **Younghi Pagh-Paan (b. Cheong-ju, South Korea, 1945)**, disassociation is manifested not in individual lines themselves but between the parts. Rhythmic and timbral heterophony is prominent, although in works like *U-MUL* (Wellspring) (1991–1992) and *Nim* (Beloved) (1987) there are subtle shifts toward a group ethic. Such moments are brief, however, and prone to disintegration. Also prominent is a focus on a freely rhythmic microtonal elaboration of a single tone as opposed to a linear melody. This relative stasis is common to much traditional music of Pagh-Paan's native Korea and is frequently exploited in the conclusions of her works.

Pagh-Paan studied at Seoul National University and then at Freiburg College of Music, where her teachers included Klaus Huber (1924–) and Brian Ferneyhough (1943–). Her works have been presented at the festivals of Donaueschingen and the International Society for Contemporary Music, and *Man-Nam* (Rendezvous) (1977) for clarinet and string trio was awarded First Prize from the 1979 UNESCO International Rostrum of Composers. She currently teaches composition at the Hochschule fur Künste in Bremen and is a guest professor of composition and analysis at the Music Academy Karlsruhe.

Adriana Hölszky (b. Bucharest, Romania, 1953) currently teaches at the Stuttgart Musikhochschule, her alma mater, as well as at the Musikhochschule in Rostock and the Mozarteum in Salzburg. Her own teachers included Stefan Niculescu (n.d.) at the Bucharest Music Conservatory and Franco Donatoni (1927–2000), among others. She is the recipient of numerous prizes from international music competitions, most often for chamber music that veers toward theater. Particularly in her works for voices, Hölszky evokes a chillingly trembling atmosphere in which stuttering gestures echo obsessively. For instance, *Vampirabile* (Failing Light) (1988) engages its singers and percussionists in sensual extended techniques that inhabit a no-man's-land somewhere between identifiable pitch and glottal vibration. Hölszky's gothic humor often manifests amid gruesome effects.

Olga Neuwirth (b. Graz, Austria, 1968) has cited Hölszky as a major influence, and critics have noted their similar taste for the grotesque and anxious, while at the same time exploring delicate, almost celestial sounds. For Neuwirth, meeting Hölszky was a welcome change from the relatively staid atmosphere at the Vienna Academy of Musical and Dramatic Art, where she first studied. One can hear Hölszky's influence particularly in Neuwirth's fondness for noise; she often has her violins draw the bow violently across the strings to produce an unpitched, gritty rubbing sound, as in Kaija Saariaho's *Lichtbogen* (1985–1986). She is particularly attached to the bass clarinet, from which she coaxes multiphonic groans that resemble some kind of electrified didgeridoo. Terms that she spent at IRCAM (Institut de Recherche et de Coordination Acoustique/Musique) and the Institute for Electro-Acoustics may be the inspiration for some of these spectral experiments.

All of this is secondary, however, to a music that, while abstract, is quite intricate in its plot and even melodramatic in its vacillations between humor and horror. *Five Daily Miniatures* (1994) for countertenor, violin, cello, and prepared piano is one example. In it, Neuwirth sets five absurdist aphorisms by Gertrude Stein, each describing a particular day in pithy nonsense, for example, "August the fourth then I would like to like to very much" or "The eighteenth of May yesterday. A disappointment." The already cavernous gap between Stein's bland words and their estranging, "incorrect" placement is exaggerated in Neuwirth's setting. The singer stretches out the words, articulating not only separate phonemes but also even separate consonants ("th," "n") until English is rendered unrecognizable, foreign. The instruments burp and cluck in a similarly unfathomable manner yet still maintain a consistency of ensemble.

Toward the end of the last *Miniature*, a perverse mockery of a Purcell-ian aria suddenly emerges, complete with Dido-like leaps in the countertenor and mordents in the piano. But it is a prepared piano, not a harpsichord, and the voice makes anachronistic "errors," such as glissandi, that draw attention to the inappropriateness of the time warp. Almost as soon as it is identifiable, the aria dissolves back into the former texture, and after the last words are spoken in a didactic, flat tone, the strings give a final, meager, pitiful groan.

Post-postmodernism: "Most Holy, Most Necessary" (Lukomsky 1998a)

Composers living under Soviet rule had three options: to write state-approved music, to write state-approved music that secretly mocked or criticized the state, or to write music not approved by the state. The last and riskiest of the three was the alternative pursued by **Sofia (Asgatovna) Gubaidulina (b. Chistopol', Republic of Tatar, 1931)**. Her works exhibit a profound and unmistakable religious mysticism that flies in the face of socialist realism. In this way she continues a Russian tradition at times shared by her predecessors Dmitri Shostakovich and Alexander Skryabin (1872–1915). Like Shostakovich, she suffered for her noncompliance, receiving an official condemnation from the Composers Union in 1980. To hear her describe it, there never was a choice; she goes so far as to declare, "I've never written any non-religious pieces" (Lukomsky 1998a).

Gubaidulina's Russian mother was a teacher; her Tatar father, a surveying engineer. The family lived in fear of arrest for much of Gubaidulina's childhood, for her father was the son of a Muslim *mullah*, or religious leader. As a student at the Kazan Conservatory, Gubaidulina and her fellow students obtained contraband scores of Hindemith, Cage, and that most reviled of "Western" decadents, Stravinsky, despite periodic raids of the dormitories. After graduating in 1954, Gubaidulina went on to the Moscow Conservatory, where she studied with Nikolai Peiko (n.d.), himself a pupil of Shostakovich. Soon after arriving, she and some other student composers were subjected to official cri-

tique by the senior staff at the conservatory for their indifference towards socialist realism. Gubaidulina remarked that Shostakovich, who was then the chair of the State
Examination Committee, defended her work when the criticisms arose again at her
graduation. He told her personally, "Everybody thinks that you are moving in the
wrong direction. I wish you to continue on your 'mistaken' path" (Lukomsky 1998b).

After graduation, Gubaidulina made her living primarily through composing film
scores. Her concert music of the time, when not boldly sacred in subject matter, was
consciously, even daringly abstract. A lifelong interest in the implications of a single,
magnetic, dronelike pitch was evident as early as the *String Quartet #1* (1971). In 1975
she founded Astraea, a trio of musician-composers that met to improvise, partly because
there was so little published music with which they could identify. Tellingly, the group
is named after the last Greco-Roman goddess to leave Earth. Around the same time,
her music began to garner attention in the West; she won second prize in the Rome International Composition Competition in 1974. Commissions began to increase, and
by 1989, a recording of her violin concerto entitled *Offertorium* (1980) had won the
Koussevitzky International Record Award.

Such recognition was not, however, as immediate as was Gubaidulina's censure by
the Composers Union, along with that of Edison Denisov (1929–1996) and others. This
official opprobrium was due to the supposedly abstract nature of their music, although
perhaps in Gubaidulina's case it was her increasing focus on religious subject matter
that made it so offensively "impractical."

Perhaps her most profoundly mystical work from this period is *The Seven Last Words*
(1982) for cello, *bayan* (a Russian relative of the accordion), and string orchestra. The
piece, over thirty minutes long, is a meditation on the last words of Christ on the cross
as told in the Gospels. Gubaidulina has remarked on some of the more salient references
in the work. For example, at one point in the seventh movement ("Father, into Thy
hands I commend my spirit") form a crosslike shape in the score. Gubaidulina also dis-
cusses the notion of the cello itself as a "crucified deity," with the bow crossing the
bridge of the instrument at the end of the work. On a more general level, the *bayan* and
cello spend each movement of the piece hovering around a particular pitch, usually on
an open string of the cello. The soloists "crucify" the pitch by means of glissandi reach-
ing a semitone above and below it.

Other allusions abound: the fifth movement's ("I thirst") recurring quote of Heinrich Schutz's (1585–1672) own *Die Sieben Wortte* (1657). Or the opening of the sixth
movement ("It is finished"), in which the bellows of the *bayan* are opened without de-
pressing the keys, resulting in the sound of a labored and quite human inhalation. Or
the overall harmonic progression of the work, which—beginning on A and ending on
E—forms a massive plagal cadence. The manner in which these explorations play themselves out—the rhapsodic and often aleatory solo parts set against the progressive chromaticism of the strings' murmuring, choralelike refrain—that grants the work its
expressive power.

In the climactic chaos of the fourth movement ("My God, my God, why hast Thou
forsaken me?"), one recognizes Gubaidulina's distinction from her countrywoman

Galina Ustvolskaya, for if Ustvolskaya's religion takes place in the punishment of Apoc-
alypse, Gubaidulina's—particularly in this moment of the piece—inhabits the ecstasy
of the Eucharist. As she puts it:

> In the moment [of Transubstantiation] the congregation is prepared to die to-
> gether with Christ; the congregation is not just receiving grace, it really dies
> calling for the Holy Spirit: it is a fearful moment....For me it is most holy, most
> necessary in my life. In each of my works I experience the Eucharist in my fan-
> tasy. (Lukomsky 1998a)

Not until the years just before perestroika did Russia begin to admit that
Gubaidulina's critical acclaim in the West had some legitimacy. In 1989 she was made
a Meritorious Artist of the Russian Soviet Republic. But as with Chen Yi in China and
her colleagues after the years of the Chinese Cultural Revolution, most of Gubaidulina's
peers in the Soviet avant-garde left their homes after the fall of the Union. She eventually did the same, moving to Germany in 1992. In a belated gesture she was given a
Russian State Prize the same year.

Since that time, Gubaidulina has become almost exclusively devoted to a mystical
numerology in her works, employing the Fibonacci series to structure their forms. As
the series progresses, it approximates ever more closely the true ratio of the golden
mean, long explored by composers from Debussy to Stockhausen as a structuring principle in music. For Gubaidulina, however, the golden mean is more than just a path to
aesthetic beauty. As she describes it, it is a way to "heal the material" (Lukomsky 1999)
to a perfect rhythmic consonance. To attempt such a project at the close of the twentieth century will likely strike many as hopelessly anachronistic. But Gubaidulina has
never been one to shrink from anachronism; she writes numerous concertos, despite (or
because of) the fact that "the soloist is no longer a hero...[and] nobody knows what
the truth is" (Lukomsky 1998a). Nor is she concerned with appearing behind the times.
For her, the term avant-garde is irrelevant: "[C]omposers should think about depth, not
about innovations" (Lukomsky 1998b). The *Novum* in her music is just what that other
social idealist, the philosopher Ernst Bloch, defined as not new but beyond. Bloch held
that it was art's sacred duty to create a haven for *Vor-Schein*, the anticipatory illumina-
tion that looks with clear eyes at the present and posits an at once ideal and conceiv-
able future:

> Nothing is more human than venturing beyond what is. The fact that dreams of
> blossoming rarely blossom has long been known. Hope that has been tested
> knows this best of all; and even here, it does not attain the status of confidence.
> Above all, hope knows—by its own definition, so to speak—not only that dan-
> ger implies salvation, but that wherever salvation exists, danger increases.
> (Bloch 1998)

For Gubaidulina, as for Bloch, the very fragility of hope is what makes it so powerful
and so worthy. Her *Seven Last Words*, then, represents a plea, an abandonment, a reconciliation—and a welcoming.

Timeline for the Twentieth and Twenty-first Centuries

Date	History/Politics	Science/Education	The Arts/Literature	Music
1900				Andrée Rochat George Antheil (1900–1959) **Elinor Warren (1900–1991)** Aaron Copland (1900–1990) Ernst Krenek (1900–1991) Otto Luening (1900–1996) Kurt Weill (1900–1950)
1901	Edward VII succeeds Queen Victoria Theodore Roosevelt president First Nobel Prizes awarded	Margaret Mead, anthropologist (1901–1978) Instant coffee, hearing aid, and safety razor invented	Marlene Dietrich, actor (1901–1992) Zora Neale Hurston, writer (1901–1960) Enrico Fermi (1901–1954)	**Ruth Crawford Seeger (1901–1953)** **Lotte Backes (1901–1990)** **Suzanne Daneau (1901–1971)** Henri Sauguet (1901–1989) Harry Partch (1901–1974)
1902		Alva Reimer Myrdal, sociologist (1902–1986)	John Steinbeck, author (1902–1968) Langston Hughes, poet (1902–1968) Marian Anderson, singer (1902–1993)	Helvi Leiviskä (1902–1982) Maurice Duruflé (1902–1986) Stefan Wolpe (1902–1972)
1903	Clare Boothe Luce, writer and politician (1903–1987) Wright brothers fly airplane successfully First World Series (baseball)		First silent movie, *The Great Train Robbery* Lillian Hellman, writer (1903–1984) Tallulah Bankhead, actor (1903–1968) Anaïs Nin, writer (1903–1977) Mark Rothko, painter (1903–1970)	**Priaulx Rainier (1903–1986)** **Claude Arrieu (1903–1990)** **Radie Britain (1903–1994)** Boris Blacher (1903–1975) Lennox Berkeley (1903–1989) Aram Khatchaturian (1903–1978)
1904	Russo-Japanese War begins New York City Subway opens Trans-Siberian Railway completed	Mary Steichen Calderone, physician, sex educator, and feminist (1904–1998)	Nancy Mitford, writer (1904–1973) Willem de Kooning, painter (1904–1997) Isaac Bashevis Singer, writer (1904–1991)	**Mathilde McKinney** Luigi Dallapiccolo (1904–1975) Dmitri Kabalevsky (1904–1987) Goffredo Petrassi Felix Salzer (1904–1986)
1905	Russian Revolution	Albert Einstein formulates theory of relativity Sigmund Freud founds psychoanalysis and publishes his Theory of Sexuality	Ayn Rand, writer (1905–1982) Agnes de Mille, choreographer, dancer, and writer (1905–1993) Jean-Paul Sartre, writer (1905–1980)	**Undine Smith Moore (1905–1989)** **Ulric Cole (1905–1992)** Marc Blitzstein (1905–1964) Michael Tippitt (1905–1998)

Date	History/Politics	Science/Education	The Arts/Literature	Music
1906	Margaret Bourke-White, photographer and war correspondent (1906–1971) Hannah Arendt, philosopher and historian (1906–1975) San Francisco earthquake Finland is first European country to give women the right to vote		Greta Garbo, actor (1906–1990) Samuel Becket, writer (1906–1989) Anne Morrow Lindbergh, writer and aviator (1906–2000)	Miriam Gideon (1906–1996) Louise Talma (1906–1996) Grace Williams (1906–1977) Paul Creston (1906–1985) Elisabeth Lutyens (1906–1983) Dmitri Shostakovich (1906–1975)
1907		Rachel Carson, environmentalist (1907–1964)	Picasso introduces cubism Lillian Helman (1907–1984)	Elizabeth Maconchy (b. 1907–1994) Yvonne Desportes (1907–1993) Henk Badings (1907–1987)
1908	Three-year-old Pu Yi becomes emperor of China	Ford introduces Model-T automobile	Simone de Beauvoir, feminist writer (1908–1986) Sylvia Ashton-Warner, teacher and writer (1908–1984) Bette Davis, actor (1908–1989)	Elliott Carter Alice Samter Nina Makarova (1908–1976) Jean Coulthard (1908–2000) Wen-Ying Hsu (b. 1908) Olivier Messiaen (1908–1992) Verdina Shlonsky (1908–1990)
1909	National Association for Advancement of Colored People (NAACP) founded		Katharine Hepburn, actor Eudora Welty, writer (1909–2001)	Isabel Aretz Grazyna Bacewicz (1909–1969) Ljubica Maric
1910	The Boy and Girl Scouts are introduced in America Millicent Fenwick, congresswoman and editor (1910–1992) Mother Teresa (1910–1997)	Halley's comet	Frida Kahlo, painter (1910–1954)	Elsa Barraine Mary Lou Williams (1910–1981) Samuel Barber (1910–1981) William Schuman (1910–1992)
1911		Greenwich Mean Time adopted Invention of the refrigerator	Lucille Ball, comedian and TV producer (1911–1989) Hortense Calisher, educator and novelist	Phyllis Tate Kikuko Kanai (1911–1981) Dana Duesse (1911–1987) Jeanne Behrend (1911–1989) Julia Smith (1911–1988) Alan Hovhaness

Date	History/Politics	Science/Education	The Arts/Literature	Music
1911			Mahalia Jackson, gospel singer (1911–1972)	Gian Carlo Menotti Nino Rota (1911–1979) Vladimir Ussachevsky (1911–1990)
1912	The U.S. government establishes a Children's Bureau within the Department of Labor to improve and regulate child labor *Titanic* sinks Lady Bird Johnson, First Lady and environmentalist Pat Nixon, First Lady (1912–1993)		May Sarton, writer (1912–1995) Jackson Pollock, painter (1912–1956) Barbara Tuchman, historian (1912–1989)	**Peggy Glanville-Hicks (1912–1990)** **Matilde Capuis** **Barbara Pentland (1912–2000)** John Cage (1912–1992) Jean Françaix (1912–1997) Conlon Nancarrow (1912–1997)
1913	Rosa Parks, freedom fighter	Mary Leakey (1913–1996)	Muriel Rukeyser, poet (1913–1980) Albert Camus, writer (1913–1960)	**Margaret Bonds (1913–1973)** **Vivian Fine (1913–2000)** **Violet Archer (1913–2000)** **Netty Simons** **Dulcie Holland** **Miriam Hyde** Henry Brant Benjamin Britten (1913–1976) Norman Dello Joio Morton Gould (1913–1996) Witold Lutoslawski (1913–1994)
1914	The assassination of Archduke Francis Ferdinand, heir to the throne of Austria, sets off World War I World War I (1914–1918) Opening of the Panama Canal	First traffic lights (only red and green) in the United States	Charlie Chaplin's first appearance as the Little Tramp Dylan Thomas, writer (1914–1953) Ralph Ellison, writer (1914–1994)	Felicitas Kukuck Gail Kubik (1914–1984) Andrzej Panufnik (1914–1991)
1915	Jane Addams and Carrie Chapman Catt, two women's rights activists, organize the Woman's Peace Party		Helen Yglesias, writer Saul Bellow, author	**Esther Williamson Ballou (1915–1973)** **Eunice Katunda** David Diamond George Perle Vincent Persichetti (1915–1987) Carlos Surinach (1915–1997)
1916	Easter Rising in Ireland			**Ruth Shaw Wylie (1916–1989)**

Date	History/Politics	Science/Education	The Arts/Literature	Music
1916	Jane Jacobs, architectural writer and social critic			Milton Babbitt Henri Dutilleux Alberto Ginastera (1916–1983)
1917	The Russian Revolution ends the reign of the czars First Pulitzer Prizes awarded Katharine Graham, newspaper publisher and editor (1917–2001) Helen Suzman, South African politician Indira Gandhi, Indian political leader (1917–1984)	Sigmund Freud: *Introduction to Psychoanalysis*	Carson McCullers, writer (1917–1967) Ella Fitzgerald, singer (1917–1996) Lena Horne, singer and actress	**Maj Sonstevold (1917–)** Robert Ward
1918	Czar Nicholas II and family are killed Betty Ford, First Lady	Worldwide influenza epidemic kills 22 million people	Ann Landers, columnist	Leonard Bernstein (1918–1990) George Rochberg
1919	Treaty of Versailles marks the official end of World War I		Uta Hagen, actor Pauline Kael, film critic (1919–2001) Doris Lessing, writer Iris Murdoch, writer (1919–1999)	**Galina Ustvolskaya** **Dorothy Freed** Leon Kirchner
1920	League of Nations established in Geneva August 18, Women win the right to vote with the ratification of the Nineteenth Amendment Bella Abzug, lawyer and feminist politician (1920–1998)	Rosalind Franklin (1920–1958)	P. D. James, mystery writer	Bruno Maderna (1920–1973) Earl Kim (1920–1998)
1921	Betty Friedan, feminist Nancy Reagan, First Lady	Rosalyn Yalow, biologist		**Adrienne Clostre** **Jeanne Demessieux (1921–1968)** Karel Husa Ralph Shapey (1921–2002) Andrew Imbrie

Date	History/Politics	Science/Education	The Arts/Literature	Music
1922	King Tut's tomb found		Judy Garland, actress and singer (1922–1969)	Lukas Foss Iannis Xenakis Iain Hamilton
1923			Bessie Smith records her first jazz album Diane Arbus (1923–1971) Nadine Gordimer, writer and lecturer Denise Levertov, poet (1923–1997) Sarah Caldwell, opera/orchestra conductor	**Dika Newlin** **Ruth Watson Henderson** Gyorgy Ligeti Ned Rorem Chou Wen-chung Peter Mennin (1923–1983) **William Kraft** **Jean Eichelberger Ivey**
1924	Shirley Chisholm, politician, author, and educator			**Krystine Moszumanska-Nazar** **Ruth Schonthal** **Erzsébet Szöny** **Julia Perry (1924–1979)** **Ida Presti (1924–1967)** **Denise Rogers** **Tatiana Nikolayeva (1924–1993)** **Ruth Gipps (1924–2000)** **Jeanne Singer** **Yvonne Loriod** **Tui St. George Tucker** Ezra Laderman
1925	Margaret Thatcher, prime minister Barbara Bush, First Lady		Julie Harris, actor Flannery O'Connor (1925–1964)	**Cathy Berberian (1925–1983)** **Daphne Oram (1925–2003)** **Ruth White** Pierre Boulez **Edith Boroff** **Alice Parker** **Yolanda Uyttenhove** **Hilda Dianda** Luciano Berio William Mayer
1926	Queen Elizabeth II, English queen	Elizabeth Kübler-Ross, psychiatrist and author Carolyn Heilbrun, social critic and educator	Marilyn Monroe, actress (1926–1962) Joan Sutherland, opera singer	**Betsy Jolas** **Marga Richter** **Ruth Zechlin** **Kazuko Osawa** Morton Feldman (1926–1987) Hans Werner Henze Milton Babbitt Lee Hoiby

Date	History/Politics	Science/Education	The Arts/ Literature	Music
1927	Gertrude Ederle becomes the first woman to swim across the English Channel Babe Ruth makes home run record Charles Lindbergh flies the Atlantic Althea Gibson, athlete (tennis and golf)		Ruth Prawer Jhabvala, writer Günter Grass, author Leontyne Price, opera singer	**Eva Schorr** **Bebe Barron** **Margrit Zimmermann** **Emma Lou Diemer** **Mary Jeanne van Appledorn** Dominick Argento **Margaret Garwood** Donald Erb
1928		Discovery of penicillin Sliced bread invented	Sound added to motion pictures Walt Disney makes his first Mickey Mouse cartoon Maya Angelou, writer and actor Jeanne Moreau, actor Ruth Westheimer, writer Gabriel García Márquez, writer	**Beth Anderson** **Thea Musgrave** **Ursula Mamlok** **Ruth Anderson** **Beverly Grigsby** **Betty Jackson King** Jacob Druckman (1928–1996) Karlheinz Stockhausen
1929	In October the stock market crashes		Ursula Le Guin, writer Beverly Sills, opera singer	**Siegrid Ernot** **Elena Petrova** **Toshiko Akiyoshi** **Lena Johnson McLin** George Crumb
1930	Sandra Day O'Connor, Supreme Court justice	Pluto discovered		**Nancy Van de Vate** **Yardena Alotin** **Ann L. Silsbee** **Jacqueline Fontyn** **Judith Dvorkin** **Ruth Loman** Stephen Sondheim Toru Takemitsu
1931	Empire State Building opens in New York Barbara Walters, television interviewer		Toni Morrison, writer	**Sofia Gubaidulena** **Myriam Marbe** **Joyce Mekeel** **Nancy Laird Chance** Mauricio Kagel
1932	Franklin Delano Roosevelt wins U.S. presidential election		Sylvia Plath, poet (1932–1963)	**Tera de Marez-Oyens** (1932–1997) **Pauline Oliveros**

Date	History/Politics	Science/Education	The Arts/ Literature	Music
1932	Amelia Earhart is first woman to fly solo across the Atlantic Ocean			**Philippa Duke Schuyler (1932–1967)** **Elaine Barkin** **Sylvia Glickman** **Betty Beath** Henri Lazarof
1933	Frances Perkins becomes first woman to hold a cabinet post (secretary of labor) Corazón Aquino, Philippine political leader Ruth Bader Ginsberg, Supreme Court justice and lawyer Adolf Hitler becomes chancellor of Germany; first Nazi concentration camp established		Susan Sontag, writer	**Alicia Urreta (1933–1987)** Henryk Górecki Krzysztof Penderecki Morton Subotnick Quincy Jones **Charlotte Moorman (1933–1991)**
1934	Gloria Steinem, feminist writer and editor Winnie Madikizela Mandela, South African leader		Sophia Loren, actress Kate Millett, writer	**Teresa Procaccini** **Norma Beecroft** **Lucia Dlugoszewski (1934–2000)** **Mary Mageau** **Alicia Terzian** Mario Davidovsky **Rocia Sanz** Peter Maxwell Davies Alfred Schnittke (1934–1998) Richard Wernick
1935	Social Security enacted in United States Mary Bethune founds the National Council of Negro Women Geraldine Ferraro, politician and congresswoman		Anne Roiphe, writer	**Kazuko Hara** **Mirjana Zivkovic** **Valerie Capers** Arvo Pärt Peter Schickele
1936	Spanish civil war begins Barbara Jordan, politician and educator (1936–1996)	Carol Gilligan, psychologist and writer	First TV broadcast	**Barbara Heller** **Lucie Robert** **Brunhilde Sonntag** **Sieglind Ahrens** Elliott Schwartz

Date	History/Politics	Science/Education	The Arts/ Literature	Music
1937	Japan invades China			Ann Souther
				Janet Beat
				Katherine Hoover
				Persis Vehar
				David Del Tredici
				Philip Glass
1938	Kristallnacht, November Janet Reno, lawyer		Joyce Carol Oates, writer	Gloria Coates
				Tona Scherchen
				Ann Carr-Boyd
				Mieko Shiomi
				Micheline Saint-Marcou (1938–1985)
				Joan Tower
				Carla Bley
				Elizabeth Scheidel-Austin
				William Bolcom
				Patsy Rogers
				John Corigliano
				John Harbison
				Charles Wuorinen
1939	World War II (1939–1945)		Jane Alexander, actress Margaret Atwood, essayist and novelist Judy Chicago, artist, painter, and lecturer Margaret Drabble, writer	Annea Lockwood
				Elinor Armer
				Barbara Kolb
				Jennifer Fowler
				Ellen Taaffe Zwilich
				Mable Bailey
				Margaret Lucy Wilkins
				Wendy Carlos
1940	Patricia Schroeder, politician		Maxine Hong Kingston, writer	Dorothy Rudd Moore
				Joan Baez
1941	December 7, Pearl Harbor attack on United States by Japan		Twyla Tharp, dancer Barbara Ehrenreich, author	Doris Hays
				Viera Janárceková
				Gillian Whitehead
				Ivana Loudova
				Elizabeth Vercoe
				Judith Bailey
				John Melby
1942	May 15, women are allowed to serve in the military	Enrico Fermi splits the atom		Diane Thome
				Priscilla McLean
				Ewa Synowiec
				Tyoko Yamashita
				Meredith Monk
1943	Warsaw ghetto uprising Billie Jean King, athlete (tennis) and feminist		Judith Jamison, dancer and choreographer	Joanna Bruzdowicz
				Elizabeth Sikora
				Etsuko Hori
				Maryanne Amacher
				Marta Ptaszynska
				Pril Smiley
				Tania León

Date	History/Politics	Science/Education	The Arts/ Literature	Music
1944	D-Day invasion of France FDR wins an unprecedented fourth term as president		Alice Walker, writer	**Denise Hulford** **Alison Bauld** Larry Nelson
1945	May 8, "V.E. Day" ends war in Europe June 26, the United Nations established August 6, the United States drops 1st atomic bomb on Hiroshima, Japan Women's suffrage becomes law in France	First computer built		**Younghi Pagh-Paan** **Elzbieta Sikora** **Judith Lang Zaimont** **Laurie Spiegel** **Victoria Bond** **Joelle Wallach** **Nagako Konishi**
1946		Dr. Spock, *The Common Book of Baby and Child Care*		**Renate Birnstein** **Tsippi Fleischer** **Dorothy Buchanan** **Barbara Benary** **Anne (Elizabeth) Boyd** **Daria Semegen** **Jane Strong O'Leary** **Marilyn Shrude** **Sheila Silver** **Suzanne Ciani** **Janice Giteck** **Hildegard Westerkamp** Peter Lieberson
1947	Jackie Robinson becomes first African American to play baseball for the Major Leagues			**Liana Alexandra** **Frangiz Ali-zade** **Laurie Anderson** **Ada Gentile** **Mayako Kubo** **Gwyneth Walker** **Nicola LeFanu** **Joan La Barbara** **Hilary Tann** **Janice Hamer** John Adams
1948	Mahatma Gandhi assassinated Establishment of State of Israel		Catherine Drinker Bowen: *Women and Music* published	**Christina Kubisch** **Bernadette Speach** **Diana Burrell** **Carol Ann Weaver**
1949				**Alexina Louie** **Shulamit Ran** **Jane Brockman** **Judith Shatin Allen** Christopher Rouse

Date	History/Politics	Science/Education	The Arts/Literature	Music
1950	Korean War begins	Einstein develops his general field theory First organ transplant	Wendy Wasserstein, playwright	Song-On Cho Elena Firsova Ornella Guidi Anna Rubin Beth Anderson Libby Larsen Elizabeth Swados Vivienne Olive Nancy Telfer
1951		Color television introduced in the United States		Patricia Jünger Anneli Arho Karolina Eiriksdottir Lois Vierk Marcela Rodriguez LaDonna Smith Liz Phillips Gerald Levinson
1952	Dwight D. Eisenhower elected Queen Elizabeth II crowned	Polio vaccine created		Jana Haimsohn Kaija Saariaho Mia Schmidt Megan Roberts Barbara Bennett Bunita Marcus
1953				Violeta Dinescu Adriana Hölszky Chen Yi Eibhlis Farrell Anne Le Baron Daniel Asia
1954				Lam Bun-Ching Elisabetta Brusa Cecilie Ore Olga Magidenko Judith Weir Susan Frykberg Elizabeth Pizer
1955	December 1, Rosa Parks refuses to give her seat to a white man on a bus in Montgomery, Alabama	Salk serum for polio developed		Susane Erding Swiridoff Diamanda Galas
1956	Hungarian Revolution Suez Crisis	September 25, the first transatlantic telephone cable begins operation		Babette Koblenz Stefania de Kenessey Caroline Szeto Iris Szeghyova Eve de Castro Robinson Melinda Wagner James Primosch Linda Dusman Richard Danielpour Iris Szeghyora Daniel Dorff

Date	History/Politics	Science/Education	The Arts/ Literature	Music
1957		*Sputnik* launches space age		**Karin Rehnquist** **Linda Bouchard** **Carmen Maria Carneci** **Karen Griebling**
1958				**Augusta Read Thomas**
1959	Alaska becomes a state			**Carola Bauckhold** **Silvia Astuni** Ronald Caltabiano
1960	John F. Kennedy elected president	The first laser device is developed by U.S. scientists		Aaron Jay Kernis
1961	Berlin Wall built Soviets launch first man in space	Peace Corps founded		**Cindy Cox** Daron Hagen
1962		U.S. astronaut John Glenn orbits the earth in a spacecraft		**Florentine Mulsant** **Heva Chan** **Brigitte Robindoré**
1963	November 22, John F. Kennedy assassinated		Betty Friedan writes *The Feminine Mystique*	**Isabel Mundry** **Calliope Tsoupaki**
1964	Congress ratifies Civil Rights Act		The Beatles debut	**Annette Schlünz** **Jennifer Higdon** Robert Maggio
1965	First walk in space			
1966	Indira Gandhi elected prime minister of India Mao Zedong launches the Cultural Revolution			
1967	Six-Day War in Middle East		First heart transplant	**Rebecca Saunders**
1968				**Olga Neuwirth**
1969	July, the United States becomes the first nation to land astronauts on the moon			
1970		Computer floppy disks introduced		
1971				**Birgitte Alsted**
1972	The Equal Rights Amendment passed by Congress, to be ratified by the states Terrorist attack at Olympic Games in Munich			
1973		Abortion legalized in United States		
1974				**Dalit Warshaw**

Date	History/Politics	Science/Education	The Arts/ Literature	Music
1975	Arthur Ashe, first black to win Wimbledon	The Soviet *Soyuz* and U.S. *Apollo* link up in space		Gudruyn Lund
1978		First test-tube baby born		
1979	Margaret Thatcher, first woman prime minister, Great Britain Mother Teresa awarded Nobel Peace Prize			
1981	Sandra Day woman appointed to U.S. Supreme Court	AIDS first identified by scientists		
1982	The Equal Rights Amendment fails to be ratified by Congress			
1983		Sally Ride becomes the first American woman to travel in space on the space shuttle *Challenger*		
1984	Geraldine Ferraro, Democrat, becomes the first woman to run for the vice presidency	The Macintosh computer with a mouse is launched		
1987	World stock market crash occurs			
1989	Berlin Wall falls			
1991	Collapse of the Soviet Union			
1992	Carol Mosely Braun becomes the first black woman elected to the U.S. Senate			
1993	World Trade Center bombed (first time)			
1997		Scientists clone sheep		
2001	World Trade Center bombed; both towers fall; ca. 4,000 killed			

Bibliography

Toshiko Akiyoshi

McManus, Jill. "Women Jazz Composers and Arrangers." In *The Musical Woman: An International Perspective—1983*, editor in chief Judith Lang Zaimont. Westport, CT: Greenwood Press, 1984, pp. 197–208.

Robinson, J. Bradford. "Toshiko Akiyoshi." In *The New Grove Dictionary of Jazz*, vol. 1, edited by Barry Kernfeld. New York: St. Martin's Press, 1994, p. 9.

Frangiz Ali-zade

See general reference works, e.g. *Norton/Grove.*

Laurie Anderson

Anderson, Laurie. *Stories from the Nerve Bible: A Retrospective, 1972–1992*. New York: HarperPerennial, 1994.

————. *United States*. New York: Harper and Row, 1984.

Celant, Germano. *Laurie Anderson: Dal Vivo*. Milan: Fondazione Prada, 1998.

Dery, Mark. "Signposts on the Road to Nowhere: Laurie Anderson's Crisis of Meaning." *The South Atlantic Quarterly* 90, no. 4 (1991): 785–801.

Edwards, J. Michele. "North America since 1920." In *Women and Music: A History*, 2d ed., edited by Karin Pendle. Bloomington: Indiana University Press, 2001, pp. 314–385.

Gann, Kyle. *American Music in the Twentieth Century*. New York: Schirmer Books, 1997.

Hodgkinson, Will. "Home Entertainment [interview with Laurie Anderson]." *The Guardian* 7/20/01. Accessed on line (www.guardian.co.uk) 1/1/03

Kardon, Janet. Laurie Anderson, works from 1969 to 1983 [exhibition]. Philadelphia: The Institute of Contemporary Art, University of Pennsylvania, 1983.

McClary, Susan. *Feminine Endings: Music, Gender, and Sexuality*. Minneapolis: University of Minnesota Press, 1991.

McKenzie, Jon. "Laurie Anderson for Dummies." *The Drama Review* 41, no. 2 (1997): 30–50.

Smith, Geoff, and Nicola Walker Smith. *American Originals: Interviews with 25 Contemporary Composers*. London: Faber and Faber, 1994.

Sumner, Melody, Kathleen Burch, and Michael Sumner, eds. *The Guests Go In to Supper*. Oakland, CA: Burning Books, 1986.

On-line and other resources

www.laurieanderson.com. Anderson's official Web site. Includes biography; interviews; audio and video downloads; and information on current and upcoming projects, tours, and recordings. Features extensive information and photos on *Songs and Stories from Moby Dick*. N.d.; accessed November 12, 2001.

www.cc.gatech.edu/jimmyd/laurie-anderson/. Called "Homepage of the Brave" in honor of Anderson's 1986 album *Home of the Brave*, this is reported to be the first and most extensive Anderson fan site and was created in 1994. Includes biographies of various lengths; a discography, videography, and list of works; lyrics and artwork by Anderson; photos; the full performance text of *Stories from the Nerve Bible*; a frequently asked-questions list; and links to interviews, reviews, articles, dissertations, on-line clubs and chat rooms. Last updated August 2001.

www.stedelijk.nl/capricorn/anderson/index.html. Web page of Anderson's Net-artwork *Here*, composed for the exhibition *Under Capricorn/The World Over*, hosted by the Stedelijk Museum in Amsterdam in 1996. N.d.; accessed November 12, 2001.

Collected Videos (video). Warner Reprise Video 38180-3, 1990.

Home of the Brave (video). Warner Reprise Video 38157-3, 1986.

The Puppet Motel (CD-ROM). Voyager Company 1-58125-039-8, 1998.

Ruth Anderson

Barkin, Elaine, ed. "In Response." *Perspectives of New Music* 20 (1981/1982): 288–329.

Mead, Rita H. "Report from Hunter College: The Electronic Music Studio." *Current Musicology* 15 (1973): 18–20.

Rosen, Judith. "Composers Speaking for Themselves: An Electronic Music Panel Discussion." In *The Musical Woman: An International Perspective—volume 2: 1984–1985*, editor in chief Judith Lang Zaimont. New York: Greenwood Press, 1987, pp. 280–312.

Violet Archer

Canadian Broadcasting Corporation International Service. *Thirty-Four Biographies of Canadian Composers*. St. Clair Shores, MI: Scholarly Press, 1972.

Dalen, Brenda. "The Composer's Voice 'What Women Can Do.'" *Canadian University Music Review: Voices of Women: Essays in Honour of Violet Archer* 16, no. 1 (1991): 14–40.

Edwards, J. Michele. "North America since 1920." In *Women and Music: A History*, 2d ed., edited by Karin Pendle. Bloomington: Indiana University Press, 2001, pp. 314–385.

Harbach, Barbara. "Violet Archer: A Life Long Learner." *Women of Note Quarterly* 6, no. 1 (1998): 1–14.

Hartig, Linda. *Violet Archer: A Bio-Bibliography*. New York: Greenwood Press, 1991.

Hinton, Stephen. "Gebrauchmusik." In The *New Grove Dictionary of Music and Musicians*, Stanley Sadie, ed. 2d ed. 2001: v.9: 619–621.

Keillor, Elaine, and Helmut Kallmann. "Violet Archer (Balestreri)." In *Encyclopedia of Music in Canada*, 2d ed., edited by Helmut Kallmann, Gilles Potvin, and Kenneth Winters. Toronto: University of Toronto Press, 1992, pp. 35–37.

Matthews, Michael. "Violet Archer." In *Contemporary Composers*, edited by Brian Morton and Pamela Collins. Chicago: St. James Press, 1992, pp. 21–26.

Proctor, George A. "Notes on Violet Archer." *Musical Canada: Words and Music Honouring Helmut Kallman*. Toronto: University of Toronto Press, 1988, pp. 188–202.

Claude Arrieu

Pendle, Karin, and Robert Zierolf. "Composers of Modern Europe, Israel, Australia, and New Zealand." In *Women and Music: A History*, 2d ed., edited by Karin Pendle. Bloomington: Indiana University Press, 2001, pp. 252–313.

May Aufderheide

Blesh, Rudi, and Harriet Janis. *They All Played Ragtime*. 2d ed. New York: Oak Publications, 1966.

Jasen, David A., and Trebor Jay Tichenor. *Rags and Ragtime: A Musical History*. New York: Seabury Press, 1978.

Jasen, David A., and Gene Jones. *That American Rag—The Story of Ragtime from Coast to Coast*. New York: Schirmer Books, 2000.

Lindeman, Carolyn A. *Women Composers of Ragtime*. Bryn Mawr, PA: Theodore Presser, 1985.

Morath, Max. "May Aufderheide and the Ragtime Women." In *Ragtime: Its History, Composers, and Music*, edited by John Edward Hasse. New York: Schirmer Books, 1985.

Grazyna Bacewicz

LePage, Jane Werner. "Grazyna Bacewicz: Composer, Virtuoso Violinist, Pianist." In *Women Composers, Conductors, and Musicians of the Twentieth Century: Selected Biographies—volume 3*. Metuchen, NJ: Scarecrow Press, 1988, pp. 1–17.

McNamee, Ann K. "Grazyna Bacewicz's Second Piano Sonata (1953): Octave Expansion and Sonata Form." In *Music Theory Online* 0/4 (1993). Available at http://boethius.music.ucsb.edu/mto/issues/mto.93.0.4/mto.93.0.4.mcnamee.art. Accessed July 13, 2001.

Maciejewski, Boguslaw M. *Twelve Polish Composers*. London: Allegro Press, 1976.

Pendle, Karin, and Robert Zierolf. "Composers of Modern Europe, Israel, Australia, and New Zealand." In *Women and Music: A History*, 2d ed., edited by Karin Pendle. Bloomington: Indiana University Press, 2001, pp. 252–313.

Rosen, Judith. "Grazyna Bacewicz: Evolution of a Composer." In *The Musical Woman: An International Perspective—1983*, editor in chief Judith Lang Zaimont. Westport, CT: Greenwood Press, 1984, pp. 105–117.

———. *Grazyna Bacewicz: Her Life and Works*. Polish Music History Series, vol. 2. Los Angeles: Friends of Polish Music, 1984.

Shafer, Sharon Guertin. *The Contribution of Grazyna Bacewicz (1909–1969) to Polish Music*. Lewiston, NY: Edwin Mellen Press, 1992.

Thomas, Adrian. *Grazyna Bacewicz—Chamber and Orchestral Music*. Polish Music History Series 3. Los Angeles: Friends of Polish Music, 1985.

Wood, Elizabeth. "Grazyna Bacewicz: Form, Syntax, Style." In *The Musical Woman: An International Perspective—1983*, editor in chief Judith Lang Zaimont. Westport, CT: Greenwood Press, 1984, pp. 118–127.

Selected on-line resources

www.usc.edu/dept/polish_music/composer/bacewicz.html. Bacewicz's page on the Polish Music Reference Center's Online Encyclopedia of Polish Music. Includes biographical sketch, extensive bibliography, discography, list of works, selected quotations, and links of interest. Last updated December 2000.

www.pwm.com.pl. From the Web site of Polskie Wydawnictwo Muzyczne (PWM) Edition, one can reach a page on Bacewicz including a biographical sketch and list of works published by PWM. N.d.

Bebe Barron

Brown, Royal S. *Overtones and Undertones: Reading Film Music*. Berkeley: University of California Press, 1994.

Edwards, J. Michele. "North America since 1920." In *Women and Music: A History*, 2d ed., edited by Karin Pendle. Bloomington: Indiana University Press, 2001, pp. 314–385.

Barbara Benary

Gann, Kyle. *American Music in the Twentieth Century*. New York: Schirmer Books, 1997.

Goode, Daniel. "Braiding Hot Rolled Steel: The Music of Barbara Benary." *Musicworks* 56 (1993): 14–23.

Johanna Beyer

Gann, Kyle. *American Music in the Twentieth Century*. New York: Schirmer Books, 1997.

Kennedy, John, and Larry Polansky. "'Total Eclipse': The Music of Johanna Magdalena Beyer." *Musical Quarterly* 80, no. 4 (1996): 719–778.

Carla Bley

McManus, Jill. "Women Jazz Composers and Arrangers." In *The Musical Woman: An International Perspective—1983*, editor in chief Judith Lang Zaimont. Westport, CT: Greenwood Press, 1984, pp. 197–208.

Robinson, J. Bradford. "Carla Bley." In *The New Grove Dictionary of Jazz*, vol. 1, edited by Barry Kernfeld. New York: St. Martin's Press, 1994, p. 118.

Margaret Bonds

Ammer, Christine. *Unsung: A History of Women in American Music*. Westport, CT: Greenwood Press, 1980.

Brown, Rae L. "Florence B. Price and Margaret Bonds: The Chicago Years." *Black Music Research Bulletin* 12, no. 2 (1990): 11–14.

Edwards, J. Michele. "North America since 1920." In *Women and Music: A History*, 2d ed., edited by Karin Pendle. Bloomington: Indiana University Press, 2001, pp. 314–385.

Green, Mildred Denby. *Black Women Composers: A Genesis*. Boston: Twayne, 1983.

Peters, Penelope. "Deep Rivers: Selected Songs of Florence Price and Margaret Bonds." *Canadian University Music Review* 16, no. 1 (1991): 74–95.

Simpson, Anne Key. "Two Outstanding Afro-American Women Composers: Florence Price and Margaret Bonds." *New Journal for Music* 1, no. 2 (1990): 57–75.

Southern, Eileen. *The Music of Black Americans—A History*. 3d ed. New York: W. W. Norton, 1997.

Selected on-line resource

www.uni.edu/taylord/composers.html. From the Web site of the African-American Art Song Alliance, links to pages with excerpted biographical sketches of Bonds. Last updated December 6, 2000.

Lili Boulanger

Citron, Marcia J. "European Composers and Musicians, 1880–1918." In *Women and Music: A History*, 2d ed., edited by Karin Pendle. Bloomington: Indiana University Press, 2001, pp. 175–192.

Dopp, Bonnie Jo. "Numerology and Cryptology in the Music of Lili Boulanger: The Hidden Program in *Clairières dans le ciel*." *Musical Quarterly* 78, no. 3 (1994): 557–583.

Fauser, Annegret. "*La Guerre en dentelles*: Women and the *Prix de Rome* in French Cultural Politics." *Journal of the American Musicological Society* 51, no. 1 (1998): 83–129.

———. "Lili Boulanger's *La princesse Maleine*: A Composer and Her Heroine as Literary Icons." *Journal of the Royal Musical Association* 122, no. 1 (1997): 68–108.

Jezic, Diane Peacock. *Women Composers: The Lost Tradition Found*. 2d ed. New York: Feminist Press at City University of New York, 1988.

Landormy, Paul. "Lili Boulanger (1893–1918)." *Musical Quarterly* 16 (1930): 510–515.

Potter, Caroline. "Nadia and Lili Boulanger: Sister Composers." *Musical Quarterly* 83, no. 4 (1999): 536–556.

Rosenstiel, Léonie. *The Life and Works of Lili Boulanger*. Rutherford, NJ: Fairleigh Dickinson University Press, 1978.

Nadia Boulanger

Campbell, Don G. *Master Teacher: Nadia Boulanger*. Washington, DC: Pastoral Press, 1984.

Fauser, Annegret. "*La Guerre en dentelles*: Women and the *Prix de Rome* in French Cultural Politics." *Journal of the American Musicological Society* 51, no. 1 (1998): 83–129.

Kendall, Alan. *The Tender Tyrant, Nadia Boulanger: A life devoted to music*. London: Macdonald and Jane's, 1976.

Pendle, Karin, and Robert Zierolf. "Composers of Modern Europe, Israel, Australia, and New Zealand." In *Women and Music: A History*, 2d ed., edited by Karin Pendle. Bloomington: Indiana University Press, 2001, pp. 252–313.

Potter, Caroline. "Nadia and Lili Boulanger: Sister Composers." *Musical Quarterly* 83, no. 4 (1999): 536–556.

Rosenstiel, Léonie. *Nadia Boulanger: A Life in Music*. New York: W. W. Norton, 1982.

Anne Elizabeth Boyd

Boyd, Anne. "A Solitary Female Phoenix Reflects on Women in Music." *Contemporary Music Review* 11, nos. 1–2 (1994): 39–43.

LePage, Jane Werner. "Anne Elizabeth Boyd." In *Women Composers, Conductors, and Musicians of the Twentieth Century: Selected Biographies—volume 3*. Metuchen, NJ: Scarecrow Press, 1988, pp. 37–55.

Tokita, Alison. "Japanese Influence on Contemporary Australian Composers." In *Tradition and Its Future in Music: Report of SIMS {Symposium of the International Musicological Society} 1990 Osaka*. Tokyo: Mita Press, 1991, pp. 465–473.

Chen Yi

Edwards, J. Michele. "North America since 1920." In *Women and Music: A History*, 2d ed., edited by Karin Pendle. Bloomington: Indiana University Press, 2001, pp. 314–385.

Kouwenhoven, Frank. "A Global Musical Culture [review of Ryker's *New Music in the Orient*]." *CHIME Journal* 4 (Autumn 1991): 96–100.

———. "Mainland China's New Music (1): Out of the Desert." *CHIME Newsletter* 2 (Autumn 1990): 58–93.

———. "Mainland China's New Music (2): Madly Singing in the Mountains." *CHIME Newsletter* 3 (Spring 1991): 42–75.

———. "Mainland China's New Music (3): The Age of Pluralism." *CHIME Journal* 5 (Spring 1992): 76–134.

Ryker, Harrison. *New Music in the Orient: Essays on Composition in Asia since World War II*. Buren, the Netherlands: Frits Knuf, 1991.

Zhou Long. "Chen Yi." In *Contemporary Composers*, edited by Brian Morton and Pamela Collins. Chicago: St. James Press, 1992, pp. 175–176. [Chen, in turn, wrote the entry on her husband in this volume; see pp. 993–995.]

Selected on-line and other multimedia resources

www.presser.com/chen/html. Chen's Web page at her publisher, Theodore Presser. Includes long and short biographical sketches, list of works published by Presser, reviews, discography and other resources, and links to related Web sites. Last updated July 2001.

www.umkc.edu/mpact/people.html. Chen's Web page at the University of Missouri-Kansas City. Includes biographical sketch and lists of awards and commissions. N.d.

www.musicfromchina.org. Web site of the New York-based traditional ensemble Music From China, founded in 1984. Chen's husband, Zhou Long, is its music director, and Chen helped produce their annual festivals in the 1990s. The group also sponsored a newsletter, which was coedited by Chen. Issues of the newsletter are reproduced on-line; the winter 1991 issue includes a review of Chen's *The Points*. N.d.

www.newmusicnow.org. From the Web site of the American Symphony Orchestra League's "Music for a New Millennium" initiative, a link to a page on Chen's *Symphony No. 2* (1993). Includes composer biography, critical introduction, Chen's notes on the piece, audio excerpts, and an interview with conductor JoAnn Falletta of the Women's Philharmonic, who premiered the work in 1994. N.d.

Sound and Silence: Chen Yi and Her Music [film]. International Society for Contemporary Music, Adamov Films and Polish TV, Paris: 1989.

Rebecca Clarke

Curtis, Liane. "Rebecca Clarke and Sonata Form: Questions of Gender and Genre." *Musical Quarterly* 81, no. 3 (1997): 393–429.

Jezic, Diane Peacock. *Women Composers: The Lost Tradition Found*, 2d ed. New York: Feminist Press at City University of New York, 1988.

Kielian-Gilbert, Marianne. "On Rebecca Clarke's *Sonata for Viola and Piano*—Feminine Spaces and Metaphors of Reading." In *Audible Traces: Gender, Identity, and Music*, edited by Elaine Barkin and Lydia Hamessley. Zurich: Carciofoli, 1999.

MacDonald, Calum. "Rebecca Clarke's Chamber Music (I)." *Tempo* 160 (1986): 15–26.

Ponder, Michael. "Rebecca Clarke." *Journal of the British Music Society* 5 (1983): 82–88.

Roma, Catherine. "Contemporary British Composers." In *Women and Music: A History*, 2d ed., edited by Karin Pendle. Bloomington: Indiana University Press, 2001, pp. 227–251.

Selected on-line resources

www.rebeccaclarke.org. Web site of the Rebecca Clarke Society. Includes biographical sketch, timeline, and works list, as well as a description of the society and announcements of upcoming performances of Clarke's music. Last updated October 7, 2001.

Ruth Crawford [Seeger]

Ammer, Christine. *Unsung: A History of Women in American Music*. Westport, CT: Greenwood Press, 1980.

Edwards, J. Michele. "North America since 1920." In *Women and Music: A History*, 2d ed., edited by Karin Pendle. Bloomington: Indiana University Press, 2001, pp. 314–385.

Gann, Kyle. *American Music in the Twentieth Century*. New York: Schirmer Books, 1997.

Gaume, Matilda. *Ruth Crawford Seeger: Memoirs, Memories, Music*. Metuchen, NJ: Scarecrow Press, 1986.

Gilbert, Steven E. "'The Ultra-Modern Idiom': A Survey of *New Music*." *Perspectives of New Music* 12 (1973–1974): 282–314.

Nelson, Mark D. "In Pursuit of Charles Seeger's Heterphonic Ideal: Three Palindromic Works by Ruth Crawford." *Musical Quarterly* 72, no. 4 (1986): 458–475.

Nicholls, David. *American Experimental Music, 1890–1940*. Cambridge: Cambridge University Press, 1990.

Ro, Nancy Yunhwa. "Partnership in Modern Music: Charles Seeger and Ruth Crawford, 1929–31." *American Music* 15, no. 3 (1997): 352–380.

Seeger, Charles. "On Dissonant Counterpoint." *Modern Music* 7, no. 4 (1930): 25–31.

———. "Ruth Crawford." In *American Composers on American Music*, edited by Henry Cowell. New York: Frederick Ungar, 1933 (copyright renewed 1961), pp. 110–118.

———. *Studies in Musicology II—1929–1979*. Edited and with an introduction by Ann M. Pescatello. Berkeley: University of California Press, 1994.

Straus, Joseph N. *The Music of Ruth Crawford Seeger*. Cambridge: Cambridge University Press, 1995.

Tick, Judith. *Ruth Crawford Seeger—A Composer's Search for American Music*. New York: Oxford University Press, 1997.

———. "Ruth Crawford's 'Spritiual Concept': The Sound-Ideals of an Early American Modernist, 1924–30." *Journal of the American Musicological Society* 44, no. 2 (1991): 221–261.

Wilding-White, Ray. "Remembering Ruth Crawford Seeger: An Interview with Charles and Peggy Seeger." *American Music* 6, no. 4 (1988): 442–454.

Emma Lou Diemer

Ammer, Christine. *Unsung: A History of Women in American Music*. Westport, CT: Greenwood Press, 1980.

Barkin, Elaine, ed. "In Response." *Perspectives of New Music* 20 (1981/1982): 288–329.

Brown, Cynthia Clark. "Emma Lou Diemer." In *Contemporary Composers*, edited by Brian Morton and Pamela Collins. Chicago: St. James Press, 1992, pp. 227–231.

LePage, Jane Werner. "Emma Lou Diemer." In *Women Composers, Conductors, and Musicians of the Twentieth Century: Selected Biographies*. Metuchen, NJ: Scarecrow Press, 1980, pp. 54–70.

Violeta Dinescu

Maarten, Henk. "Violeta Dinescu." In *Contemporary Composers*, edited by Brian Morton and Pamela Collins. Chicago: St. James Press, 1992, pp. 232–235.

Pendle, Karin, and Robert Zierolf. "Composers of Modern Europe, Israel, Australia, and New Zealand." In *Women and Music: A History*, 2d ed., edited by Karin Pendle. Bloomington: Indiana University Press, 2001, pp. 252–313.

Sperber, Roswitha. "From Ritual to Abstraction: Women Composers from Romania." In *Women Composers in Germany*, edited by Roswitha Sperber and translated by Timothy Nevill. Bonn, Germany: Inter Nationes, 1996, pp. 106–111.

Lucia Dlugoszewski

Ammer, Christine. *Unsung: A History of Women in American Music*. Westport, CT: Greenwood Press, 1980.

Collins, Pamela. "Lucia Dlugoszewski." In *Contemporary Composers*, edited by Brian Morton and Pamela Collins. Chicago: St. James Press, 1992, pp. 235–237.

Conrad, Daniel, dir. *Accident by Design: Creating and Discovering Beauty* [film]. National Film Board of Canada/Rhodopsin Productions Ltd., 1998. [Dlugoszewski is one of the artists featured in this documentary on the myriad ways that artists and scientists understand and respond to beauty.]

Dlugoszewski, Lucia. "What Is Sound to Music?" *Main Currents in Modern Thought* 30, no. 1 (1973): 8.

Edwards, J. Michele. "North America since 1920." In *Women and Music: A History*, 2d ed., edited by Karin Pendle. Bloomington: Indiana University Press, 2001, pp. 314–385.

Gagne, Cole. *Soundpieces 2: Interviews with American Composers*. Metuchen, NJ: Scarecrow Press, 1993.

Montano, Linda M. *Performance Artists Talking in the Eighties*. Berkeley: University of California Press, 2000.

Silverton, Mike. "A Tribute to Lucia Dlugoszewski." *21st Century Music* 7, no. 7 (2000): 17.

Thomson, Virgil. *Twentieth Century Composers—vol. 1: American Music since 1910*. London: Weidenfeld and Nicolson, 1971.

Tsippi Fleischer

Fleisher, Robert Jay. *Twenty Israeli Composers*. Detroit: Wayne State University Press, 1997.

Lauer, Elizabeth. "Tsippi Fleischer—Vocal Music." *ILWC Journal* (June 1994): 38–39.

Pendle, Karin, and Robert Zierolf. "Composers of Modern Europe, Israel, Australia, and New Zealand." In *Women and Music: A History*, 2d ed., edited by Karin Pendle. Bloomington: Indiana University Press, 2001, pp. 252–313.

Diamanda Galás

Edwards, J. Michele. "North America since 1920." In *Women and Music: A History*, 2d ed., edited by Karin Pendle. Bloomington: Indiana University Press, 2001, pp. 314–385.

Galás, Diamanda. "Intravenal Song." *Perspectives of New Music* 20 (1981–1982): 59–62.

Gann, Kyle. *American Music in the Twentieth Century*. New York: Schirmer Books, 1997.

Miriam Gideon

Ammer, Christine. *Unsung: A History of Women in American Music*. Westport, CT: Greenwood Press, 1980.

Ardito, Linda. "Miriam Gideon: A Memorial Tribute." *Perspectives of New Music* 34, no. 2 (1996): 202–214.

Barkin, Elaine, ed. "In Response." *Perspectives of New Music* 20 (1981/1982): 288–329.

Brown, Emily Freeman. "Jewish Liturgical Music by American Women since 1945." *Women of Note Quarterly* 3, no. 1 (1995): 8–11.

Edwards, J. Michele. "North America since 1920." In *Women and Music: A History*, 2d ed., edited by Karin Pendle. Bloomington: Indiana University Press, 2001, pp. 314–385.

Ewen, David. *American Composers: A Biographical Dictionary*. New York: G. P. Putnam, 1982.

Gray, Anne. "Miriam Gideon (1906–1996): A Jewish Pioneer." *IAWM Journal* 3, no. 1 (1997): 20.

Hans, Nathan. "United States of America." In *A History of Song*, edited by Denis Stevens. New York: W. W. Norton, 1960 (Norton Library, 1970), pp. 408–460.

LePage, Jane Werner. "Miriam Gideon." In *Women Composers, Conductors, and Musicians of the Twentieth Century: Selected Biographies—volume 2*. Metuchen, NJ: Scarecrow Press, 1983, pp. 118–162.

Perle, George. "The Music of Miriam Gideon." *American Composers Alliance Bulletin* 7, no. 4 (1958): 2–6.

Petersen, Barbara A. "The Vocal Chamber Music of Miriam Gideon." In *The Musical Woman: An International Perspective—volume 2: 1984–1985*, editor in chief Judith Lang Zaimont. New York: Greenwood Press, 1987, pp. 222–255.

Peggy Glanville-Hicks

Ammer, Christine. *Unsung: A History of Women in American Music*. Westport, CT: Greenwood Press, 1980.

Beckett, Wendy. *Peggy Glanville-Hicks*. New South Wales: Angus and Robertson (HarperCollins), 1992.

Ewen, David. *Composers since 1900: A Biographical and Critical Guide*. New York: H. W. Wilson, 1969.

Hayes, Deborah. "Peggy Glanville-Hicks: A Voice from the Inner World." In *The Musical Woman: An International Perspective—volume 3: 1986–1990*, editor in chief Judith Lang Zaimont. New York: Greenwood Press, 1991, pp. 371–409.

———. *Peggy Glanville-Hicks: A Bio-Bibliography*. New York: Greenwood Press, 1990.

Pendle, Karin, and Robert Zierolf. "Composers of Modern Europe, Israel, Australia, and New Zealand." In *Women and Music: A History*, 2d ed., edited by Karin Pendle. Bloomington: Indiana University Press, 2001, pp. 252–313.

Selected on-line resources

www.amcoz.com.au/comp/g/pghicks.htm. Glanville-Hicks' page on the Australian Music Centre Web site. Includes biographical sketch and list of works and recordings. N.d.

Bloch, Ernst. *Literary Essays*. Transl. Andrew Joron and others. Stanford: Stanford University Press, 1998.

Sofia Gubaidulina

Ford, Andrew. *Composer to Composer: Conversations about Contemporary Music*. London: Quartet Books, 1993.

Lukomsky, Vera. (1998a) "'The Eucharist in My Fantasy': Interview with Sofia Gubaidulina [part 1]." *Tempo* 206 (1998): 29–35.

———. "'Hearing the Subconscious': Interview with Sofia Gubaidulina [part 2]." *Tempo* 209 (1999): 27–31.

———. (1998b) "Sofia Gubaidulina: 'My Desire Is Always to Rebel, to Swim against the Stream!'" *Perspectives of New Music* 36, no. 1 (1998): 5–41.

Pendle, Karin, and Robert Zierolf. "Composers of Modern Europe, Israel, Australia, and New Zealand." In *Women and Music: A History*, 2d ed., edited by Karin Pendle. Bloomington: Indiana University Press, 2001, pp. 252–313.

Redepenning, Dorothea. "Staccato Existence: Russian Women Composers in Germany." In *Women*

Composers in Germany, edited by Roswitha Sperber and translated by Timothy Nevill. Bonn, Germany: Inter Nationes, 1996, pp. 100–105.

Tsenova, Valeria. "Number and Proportion in the Music of Sofia Gubaidulina." *Mitteilungen der Paul Sacher Stiftung* 14 (2001): 23–28.

Selected on-line resources

www.boosey.com/publishing/pages/Composer/composer_main_page.asp. From the Web site of Boosey and Hawkes, a link to a page on Gubaidulina; includes an introduction, biography, and lists of works and upcoming performances. N.d.

www.schirmer.com/composers/gubaidulina_bio.html. Gubaidulina's North American publisher, G. Schirmer, provides this page with a brief biography, work list, and links to other articles and reviews. Updated August 9, 2001.

www.siue.edu/aho/musov/discrev/gubchron.html. A limited chronology of works by, and significant events in the life of, Gubaidulina, from the Web site Music under Soviet Rule. N.d.

Adriana Hölszky

Pendle, Karin, and Robert Zierolf. "Composers of Modern Europe, Israel, Australia, and New Zealand." In *Women and Music: A History*, 2d ed., edited by Karin Pendle. Bloomington: Indiana University Press, 2001, pp. 252–313.

Sperber, Roswitha. "From Ritual to Abstraction: Women Composers from Romania." In *Women Composers in Germany*, edited by Roswitha Sperber and translated by Timothy Nevill. Bonn, Germany: Inter Nationes, 1996, pp. 106–111.

Selected on-line resources

www.breitkopf.de. Link to Hölszky includes biographical sketch, upcoming performances, critical essay, bibliography (including writings by and about the composer), and list of works including those carried by other publishers or still in manuscript form. Last updated September 12, 2001.

Betsy Jolas

LePage, Jane Werner. "Betsy Jolas." In *Women Composers, Conductors, and Musicians of the Twentieth Century: Selected Biographies*. Metuchen, NJ: Scarecrow Press, 1980, pp. 103–115.

Pendle, Karin, and Robert Zierolf. "Composers of Modern Europe, Israel, Australia, and New Zealand." In *Women and Music: A History*, 2d ed., edited by Karin Pendle. Bloomington: Indiana University Press, 2001, pp. 252–313.

Barbara Kolb

Ammer, Christine. *Unsung: A History of Women in American Music*. Westport, CT: Greenwood Press, 1980.

Edwards, J. Michele. "North America since 1920." In *Women and Music: A History*, 2d ed., edited by Karin Pendle. Bloomington: Indiana University Press, 2001, pp. 314–385.

Gagne, Cole, and Tracy Caras. *Soundpieces—Interviews with American Composers*. Metuchen, NJ: Scarecrow Press, 1982.

Jezic, Diane Peacock. *Women Composers: The Lost Tradition Found*. 2d ed. New York: Feminist Press at the City University of New York, 1988.

LePage, Jane Werner. "Barbara Anne Kolb." In *Women Composers, Conductors, and Musicians of the Twentieth Century: Selected Biographies*. Metuchen, NJ: Scarecrow Press, 1980, pp. 116–132.

Weir, Bea. "Barbara Kolb." In *Contemporary Composers*, edited by Brian Morton and Pamela Collins. Chicago: St. James Press, 1992, pp. 501–502.

Selected on-line resources

www.boosey.com/publishing/pages/Composer/composer_main_page.asp. Web page of Boosey and

Hawkes, with a link to a page on Kolb. Includes biographical and critical sketches, a works list, and a downloadable sound file of an excerpt from *Millefoglie*. N.d.

Christina Kubisch

Christina Kubisch: Cross-Examination (Sound 1 Light) [exhibition catalog]: Philadelphia: Galleries at Moore, 1996.

Davies, Hugh. "Sound Sculpture." In *New Grove Dictionary of Music and Musicians*, edited by Stanley Sadie. 2nd ed. New York: Grove's Dictionaries, 2001. vol. 23, pp. 785–791.

Helmig, Martina. "Of Space and Sound: Music and New Media." In *Women Composers in Germany*, edited by Roswitha Sperber and translated by Timothy Nevill. Bonn, Germany: Inter Nationes, 1996, pp. 112–117.

Kubisch, Christina. "About My Compositions." In *Sound by Artists*, edited by Dan Lander and Micah Lexier. Toronto: Art Metropole, 1990, pp. 68–72.

Selected on-line resources

www.ampersound.com/kubisch.htm. From the record label Ampersound, a description of Kubisch's collaborative work with Fabrizio Plessi entitled *Two and Two*, an interactive performance piece recorded in 1977. N.d.

Joan La Barbara

Edwards, J. Michele. "North America since 1920." In *Women and Music: A History*, 2d ed., edited by Karin Pendle. Bloomington: Indiana University Press, 2001, pp. 314–385.

Gann, Kyle. *American Music in the Twentieth Century*. New York: Schirmer Books, 1997.

Grigsby, Beverly. "Women Composers of Electronic Music in the United States." In *The Musical Woman: An International Perspective—1983*, editor in chief Judith Lang Zaimont. Westport, CT: Greenwood Press, 1984, pp. 151–196.

Zimmerman, Walter. *Desert Plants: Conversations with 23 American Musicians*. Vancouver: ARC, 1976.

Libby Larsen

Bezerra, Jeanenne Gray Barton. "The Relationship between Text and Music in the Works of Libby Larsen." M.M. thesis, Baylor University, 1999.

Edwards, J. Michele. "North America since 1920." In *Women and Music: A History*, 2d ed., edited by Karin Pendle. Bloomington: Indiana University Press, 2001, pp. 314–385.

Killam, Rosemary N. "Calamity Jane: Strength, Uncertainty, and Affirmation." *Women of Note Quarterly* 1, no. 3 (1993): 17–25.

Tania León

Edwards, J. Michele. "North America since 1920." In *Women and Music: A History*, 2d ed., edited by Karin Pendle. Bloomington: Indiana University Press, 2001, pp. 314–385.

Annea Lockwood

Barkin, Elaine, ed. "In Response." *Perspectives of New Music* 20 (1981/1982): 288–329.

Edwards, J. Michele. "North America since 1920." In *Women and Music: A History*, 2d ed., edited by Karin Pendle. Bloomington: Indiana University Press, 2001, pp. 314–385.

Gann, Kyle. *American Music in the Twentieth Century*. New York: Schirmer Books, 1997.

Thomson, John Mansfield. *A Biographical Dictionary of New Zealand Composers*. Wellington: Victoria University Press, 1990.

Elisabeth Lutyens

Bradshaw, Susan. "The Music of Elisabeth Lutyens." *Musical Times* 112, no. 1541 (1971): 653–656.

Doctor, Jennifer. "Intersecting Circles: The Early Careers of Elizabeth Maconchy, Elisabeth Lutyens, and Grace Williams." *Women and Music* 2 (1998): 90–109.

Harries, Meirion, and Susie. *A Pilgrim Soul—The Life and Work of Elisabeth Lutyens*. London: Faber and Faber, 1989.

Henderson, Robert. "Elisabeth Lutyens." *Musical Times* 104, no. 1446 (1963): 551–554.

Lutyens, Elisabeth. *A Goldfish Bowl*. London: Cassell, 1972.

Roma, Catherine. "Contemporary British Composers." In *Women and Music: A History*, 2d ed., edited by Karin Pendle. Bloomington: Indiana University Press, 2001, pp. 227–251.

Alma Mahler

Citron, Marcia J. "European Composers and Musicians, 1880–1918." In *Women and Music: A History*, 2d ed., edited by Karin Pendle. Bloomington: Indiana University Press, 2001, pp. 147–174.

Filler, Susan M. "A Composer's Wife as Composer: The Songs of Alma Mahler." *Journal of Musicological Research* 4 (1983): 427–441.

———. *Gustav and Alma Mahler: A Guide to Research*. New York: Garland, 1989.

Giroud, Francoise. *Alma Mahler, or The Art of Being Loved*. Translated by R. M. Stock. Oxford: Oxford University Press, 1991.

Keegan, Susanne. *The Bride of the Wind: The Life and Times of Alma Mahler-Werfel*. New York: Viking, 1992.

Kravitt, Edward F. "The *Lieder* of Alma Maria Schindler-Mahler." *Music Review* 49, no. 3 (1988): 190–204.

Mahler-Werfel, Alma. *Diaries 1898–1902*. Selected and translated by Antony Beaumont. Ithaca, NY: Cornell University Press, 1999. From the German edition, transcribed and edited by Antony Beaumont and Susanne Rode-Breymann.

———. *Mein Leben*. Frankfurt-am-Main: Fischer, 1960.

Mahler-Werfel, Alma, and E. B. Ashton. *And the Bridge Is Love*. London: Hutchinson, 1959.

Monson, Karen. *Alma Mahler, Muse to Genius: From Fin-de-Siècle Vienna to Hollywood's Heyday*. Boston: Houghton Mifflin, 1983.

Meredith Monk

Baker, Rob. "Material Worlds." *Parabola* 16, no. 3 (1991): 88–92.

Balk, H. Wesley, with Meredith Monk and Andrew Foldi. *The Radiant Performer: The Spiral Path to Performing Power*. Minneapolis: University of Minnesota Press, 1991.

Cunningham, Merce, ed. *Art Performs Life: Merce Cunningham, Meredith Monk, Bill T. Jones*. Minneapolis: Walker Art Center. Reprinted by Distributed Art, New York, 1998.

Edwards, J. Michele. "North America since 1920." In *Women and Music: A History*, 2d ed., edited by Karin Pendle. Bloomington: Indiana University Press, 2001, pp. 314–385.

Foster, Susan. "The Signifying Body: Reaction and Resistance in Post-Modern Dance." *Theatre Journal* 37, no. 1 (1985): 45–64.

Gann, Kyle. *American Music in the Twentieth Century*. New York: Schirmer Books, 1997.

Jowitt, Deborah, ed. *Meredith Monk*. Baltimore: Johns Hopkins University Press, 1997.

Montano, Linda M. *Performance Artists Talking in the Eighties*. Berkeley: University of California Press, 2000.

Morton, Brian. "Meredith Monk." In *Contemporary Composers*, edited by Brian Morton and Pamela Collins. Chicago: St. James Press, 1992, pp. 663–664.

Sandow, Gregory. "Invisible Theater: The Music of Meredith Monk." In *The Musical Woman: An International Perspective—1983*, editor in chief Judith Lang Zaimont. Westport, CT: Greenwood Press, 1984, pp. 147–150.

Smith, Geoff, and Nicola Walker Smith. *American Originals: Interviews with 25 Contemporary Composers*. London: Faber and Faber, 1994.

Strickland, Edward. *American Composers: Dialogues on Contemporary Music*. Bloomington: Indiana University Press, 1991.

Selected on-line and other multimedia resources

www.meredithmonk.org. The composer's own Web site, which contains a biography and an extensive bibliography; lists of works, awards, fellowships, and recordings; a calendar of upcoming performances; biographies of the members of her vocal ensemble; and answers to "Frequently Asked Questions." N.d.

www.ecmrecords.com/ecm/artists/148.html. Monk's Web page at ECM Records. Includes a brief biography and information on all of her ECM recordings, including sound files. N.d.

www.boosey.com/publishing/pages/Composer/composer_main_page.asp. From the Web site of Boosey and Hawkes, a link to a page on Monk, which includes a brief biographical introduction, list of works published by Boosey, and related news items. N.d.

Greenaway, Peter, director. *Four American Composers: Meredith Monk* [video]. New York: Mystic Fire Video, 1991.

Monk, Meredith, director. *Book of Days* [film]. The Stutz Company, 1988.

Mary Carr Moore

Ammer, Christine. *Unsung: A History of Women in American Music*. Westport, CT: Greenwood Press, 1980.

Edwards, J. Michele. "North America since 1920." In *Women and Music: A History*, 2d ed., edited by Karin Pendle. Bloomington: Indiana University Press, 2001, pp. 314–385.

Johnson, H. Earle. *Operas on American Subjects*. New York: Coleman-Ross, 1964.

Smith, Catherine Parsons. "Athena at the Manuscript Club: John Cage and Mary Carr Moore." *Musical Quarterly* 79, no. 2 (1995): 351–367.

Smith, Catherine Parsons, and Cynthia S. Richardson. *Mary Carr Moore, American Composer*. Ann Arbor: University of Michigan Press, 1987.

Charlotte Moorman

Bourdon, David. "A Letter to Charlotte Moorman." *Art in America* (June 2000): 80–85, 135–137.

Decker-Phillips, Edith. *Paik Video*. Barrytown, NY: Barrytown, 1998.

On-line and other multimedia resources

Barzyk, Fred, dir. *Strange Music of Nam June Paik—with Charlotte Moorman* [video]. Kent, CT: Creative Arts Television, 1975.

Thea Musgrave

Hamer, Janice. "Thea Musgrave—An Appreciation." *Contemporary Music Review* 11, nos. 1–2 (1994): 219–220.

LePage, Jane Werner. "Thea Musgrave." In *Women Composers, Conductors, and Musicians of the Twentieth Century: Selected Biographies*. Metuchen, NJ: Scarecrow Press, 1980, pp. 145–164.

Roma, Catherine. "Contemporary British Composers." In *Women and Music: A History*, 2d ed., edited by Karin Pendle. Bloomington: Indiana University Press, 2001, pp. 227–251.

Ryder, Georgia A. "Thea Musgrave and the Production of 'Harriet, the Woman Called Moses': An Interview with the Composer." In *New Perspectives on Music: Essays in Honor of Eileen Southern*, edited by Josephine Wright. Warren, MI: Harmonie Park Press, 1992.

Olga Neuwirth

Selected on-line resources

www.olganeuwirth.com. The composer's own Web site. Includes biography, bibliography, and discography; lists of works, upcoming concerts, and projects; writings and photos by the composer; and links to her publishers and other sites (in German) on her work. N.d.

http://www.ricordi.de/. Website of Ricordi, Neuwirth link includes brief chronology, critical appraisals, and list of works. N.d.

Julia Niebergall

Jasen, David A., and Gene Jones. *That American Rag—The Story of Ragtime from Coast to Coast*. New York: Schirmer Books, 2000.

Jasen, David A., and Trebor Jay Tichenor. *Rags and Ragtime: A Musical History*. New York: Seabury Press, 1978.

Lindeman, Carolyn A. *Women Composers of Ragtime*. Bryn Mawr, PA: Theodore Presser, 1985.

Morath, Max. "May Aufderheide and the Ragtime Women." In *Ragtime: Its History, Composers, and Music*, edited by John Edward Hasse. New York: Schirmer Books, 1985.

Pauline Oliveros

Ammer, Christine. *Unsung: A History of Women in American Music*. Westport, CT: Greenwood Press, 1980.

Barkin, Elaine. "Four Texts." In *Perspectives on Musical Aesthetics*, edited by John Rahn. New York: W. W. Norton, 1994.

Edwards, J. Michele. "North America since 1920." In *Women and Music: A History*, 2d ed., edited by Karin Pendle. Bloomington: Indiana University Press, 2001, pp. 314–385.

Gagne, Cole. *Soundpieces 2: Interviews with American Composers*. Metuchen, NJ: Scarecrow Press, 1993.

Gann, Kyle. *American Music in the Twentieth Century*. New York: Schirmer Books, 1997.

Montano, Linda M. *Performance Artists Talking in the Eighties*. Berkeley: University of California Press, 2000.

Oliveros, Pauline. "Cues." *Musical Quarterly* 77, no. 3 (1993): 373–382.

———. *The Roots of the Moment*. New York: Drogue Press, 1998.

———. *Software for People*. Baltimore: Smith, 1984.

Pasler, Jann. "Postmodernism, Narrativity, and the Art of Memory." *Contemporary Music Review* 7, no. 2 (1993): 3–32.

Revill, David. "Pauline Oliveros." In *Contemporary Composers*, edited by Brian Morton and Pamela Collins. Chicago: St. James Press, 1992, pp. 708–710.

Simoni, Mary. "Profiles in Determination." *Computer Music Journal* 22, no. 4 (1998): 19–28.

Smith, Geoff, and Nicola Walker Smith. *American Originals: Interviews with 25 Contemporary Composers*. London: Faber and Faber, 1994.

Subotnick, Morton. "Pauline Oliveros: Trio." *Perspectives of New Music* 2 (1963): 77–82.

Taylor, Timothy. "The Gendered Construction of the Musical Self: The Music of Pauline Oliveros." *Musical Quarterly* 77, no. 3 (1993): 385–395.

Von Gunden, Heidi. *The Music of Pauline Oliveros*. Metuchen, NJ: Scarecrow Press, 1983.

Weidenbaum, Marc. "Deep Listening." *Music Now* (November 1996). Reprinted on www.disquiet.com/oliveros.html. Copyright 1997. Accessed August 8, 2001.

Zimmerman, Walter. *Desert Plants: Conversations with 23 American Musicians*. Vancouver: ARC, 1976.

Selected on-line and other multimedia resources

www.pofinc.org and www.deeplistening.org. Web sites, respectively, of the Pauline Oliveros Foundation and its trademarked program, Deep Listening. These linked sites include a biography and curriculum vitae; selected writings, press clippings, and interviews; lists of works, awards, teaching positions, affiliations, recordings, and archives; selected, downloadable scores; interactive Web pages on current projects; roster of artists connected to the Deep Listening Band and Deep Listening Foundation; Deep Listening retreats, workshops, and newsletters; and an introduction to Oliveros' Expanded Instrument System. N.d.

Daphne Oram

Davies, Hugh, "Oramics." In *The Norton/Grove Dictionary of Musical Instruments*, vol. 2, edited by Stanley Sadie. London: Macmillan, 1984, p. 823.

Oram, Daphne. "Looking Back…to See Ahead." *Contemporary Music Review* 11, nos. 1–2 (1994): 225–228.

Cecilie Ore

Billing, Björn. "Cecile Ore." in *Contemporary Composers*. Edited by Brian Morton and Pamela Collins. Chicago. St. James Press, 1992, pp. 712–713.]

Pendle, Karin, and Robert Zierolf. "Composers of Modern Europe, Israel, Australia, and New Zealand." In *Women and Music: A History*, 2d ed., edited by Karin Pendle. Bloomington: Indiana University Press, 2001, pp. 252–313.

Younghi Pagh-Paan

Howard, Keith. "Different Spheres: Perceptions of Traditional Music and Western Music in Korea." *The World of Music* 39, no. 2 (1997): 61–67.

Sperber, Roswitha. "Concordance of Many Cultures: Germany as Refuge for Women Composers?" In *Women Composers in Germany*, edited by Roswitha Sperber and translated by Timothy Nevill. Bonn, Germany: Inter Nationes, 1996, pp. 87–99.

Selected on-line resource

http://www.ricordi.de/. Ricordi's website; Pagh-Paan link includes brief chronology and critical appraisals, lists of works, German-language discography and bibliography. N.d.

Barbara Pentland

Dixon, Gail. "The String Quartets of Barbara Pentland." *Canadian University Music Review*, 11 no. 2 (1991): 94–121.

Eastman, Sheila, and Timothy J. McGee. *Barbara Pentland*. Toronto: University of Toronto Press, 1983.

Edwards, J. Michele. "North America since 1920." In *Women and Music: A History*, 2d ed., edited by Karin Pendle. Bloomington: Indiana University Press, 2001, pp. 314–385.

Winters, Kenneth, and John Beckwith. "Barbara Pentland." In *Encyclopedia of Music in Canada*, 2d ed., edited by Helmut Kallmann, Gilles Potvin, and Kenneth Winters. Toronto: University of Toronto Press, 1992, pp. 1032–1034.

Julia Perry

Ammer, Christine. *Unsung: A History of Women in American Music*. Westport, CT: Greenwood Press, 1980.

Edwards, J. Michele. "North America since 1920." In *Women and Music: A History*, 2d ed., edited by Karin Pendle. Bloomington: Indiana University Press, 2001, pp. 314–385.

Liz Phillips

Ahlstrom, David. "Liz Phillips: Sunspots [review]." *Computer Music Journal* 6, no. 3 (1982): 83–85.

Florence Price

Ammer, Christine. *Unsung: A History of Women in American Music*. Westport, CT: Greenwood Press, 1980.

Brown, Rae L. "Florence B. Price and Margaret Bonds: The Chicago Years." *Black Music Research Bulletin* 12, no. 2 (1990): 11–14.

———. "William Grant Still, Florence Price, and William Dawson: Echoes of the Harlem Renaissance." In *Black Music in the Harlem Renaissance*, edited by Samuel A. Floyd Jr. New York: Greenwood Press, 1990, pp. 71–86.

———. "The Woman's Symphony Orchestra of Chicago and Florence B. Price's Piano Concerto in One Movement." *American Music* 11, no. 2 (1993): 185–205.

Edwards, J. Michele. "North America since 1920." In *Women and Music: A History*, 2d ed., edited by karin Pendle. Bloomington: Indiana University Press, 2001, pp. 314–385.

Green, Mildred Denby. *Black Women Composers: A Genesis*. Boston: Twayne, 1983.

Johnson, Calvert. "Florence B. Price: Chicago Renaissance Woman." *American Organist Magazine* 34, no. 1 (2000): 68–75.

Peters, Penelope. "Deep Rivers: Selected Songs of Florence Price and Margaret Bonds." *Canadian University Music Review* 16, no. 1 (1991): 74–95.

Simpson, Anne Key. "Two Outstanding Afro-American Women Composers: Florence Price and Margaret Bonds." *New Journal for Music* 1, no. 2 (1990): 57–75.

Southern, Eileen. *The Music of Black Americans—A History*, 3d ed. New York: W. W. Norton, 1997.

Wilson, Pamela. "Conserving, Performing, and Recording the Music of Florence Price." *Women's Philharmonic Newsletter* (Summer 1999). Available on-line at www.womensphil.org/newsletters/summer1999/Price.html. Accessed October 11, 2001.

Selected on-line resources

www.uni.edu/taylord/composers.html. From the Web site of the African-American Art Song Alliance, links to pages with excerpted biographical sketches of Price. Last updated December 6, 2000.

Marta Ptaszynska

LePage, Jane Werner. "Marta Ptaszynska." In *Women Composers, Conductors, and Musicians of the Twentieth Century: Selected Biographies—volume 2*. Metuchen, NJ: Scarecrow Press, 1983, pp. 221–239.

M., T. "Composer's Workshop: Marta Ptaszynska *Siderals*." *Polish Music* 10, no. 2 (1975): 20–23.

Pendle, Karin, and Robert Zierolf. "Composers of Modern Europe, Israel, Australia, and New Zealand." In *Women and Music: A History*, 2d ed., edited by Karin Pendle. Bloomington: Indiana University Press, 2001, pp. 252–313.

Shulamit Ran

Ammer, Christine. *Unsung: A History of Women in American Music*. Westport, CT: Greenwood Press, 1980.

Barkin, Elaine, ed. "In Response." *Perspectives of New Music* 20 (1981/1982): 288–329.

Guzzo, Anne. "Shulamit Ran: Her Music and Life." M.A. thesis, University of California, Santa Cruz, 1996.

Pendle, Karin, and Robert Zierolf. "Composers of Modern Europe, Israel, Australia, and New Zealand." In *Women and Music: A History*, 2d ed., edited by Karin Pendle. Bloomington: Indiana University Press, 2001, pp. 252–313.

White, C. B. "Equilibria: Shulamit Ran Balances." *ILWC Journal* (October 1994): 1–4.

Selected on-line resource

www.presser.com/ran.html. Ran's Web page at Theodore Presser, including a biographical sketch and discography, list of works published by Presser, and excerpted reviews. Last updated November 1999.

Kaija Saariaho

Anderson, Julian. "Seductive Solitary." *The Musical Times* (December 1992): 616–619.

Beyer, Anders. "Till Death Do Us Part: A Portrait of the Finnish Composer Kaija Saariaho." *Nordic Sounds* 1 (2000): 3–9.

Ford, Andrew. *Composer to Composer: Conversations about Contemporary Music*. London: Quartet Books, 1993.

Manning, Peter. *Electronic and Computer Music*. Oxford: Clarendon Press, 1993. 2d ed.

Morton, Brian, "Kaija (Anneli) Saariaho." In *Contemporary Composers*, edited by Brian Morton and Pamela Collins. Chicago: St. James Press, 1992, pp. 797–798.

Pendle, Karin, and Robert Zierolf. "Composers of Modern Europe, Israel, Australia, and New Zealand." In *Women and Music: A History*, 2d ed., edited by Karin Pendle. Bloomington: Indiana University Press, 2001, pp. 252–313.

Richmond, Eero. "Finnish Women Composers." In *The Musical Woman: An International Perspective— volume 3: 1986–1990*, editor in chief Judith Lang Zaimont. New York: Greenwood Press, 1991, pp. 439–455.

Roads, Curtis. "Symposium on Computer Music Composition." *Computer Music Journal* 10, no. 1 (1986): 40–63.

Saariaho, Kaija. "Timbre and Harmony: Interpolations of Timbral Structures." *Contemporary Music Review* 2, no. 1 (1987): 93–133.

Selected on-line resources

www.saariaho.org. The composer's own Web site, with a biographical sketch in three languages, list of works, discography, and links to related Web sites. Last updated October 9, 2001.

www.petals.org. Founded in 1998 by Saariaho, her husband, Jean-Baptiste Barrière, and two other musicians, Petals is a nonprofit association that disseminates independently produced CDs, CD-ROMs, and other multimedia created by the four. It contains a list of works, discography, and links to other Web sites on Saariaho. Last updated October 9, 2001.

www.schirmer.com/composers/saariaho/bio.html. Saariaho's page at G. Schirmer, including a biographical sketch and links to other articles, reviews, and Web sites. Last updated May 3, 2001.

Prisma: Discovering Contemporary Music through the Works of Kaija Saariaho [CD-ROM]. Finnish Music Information Center, IRCAM, and Chester Music, n.d. [includes original texts, sound recordings, documentary footage, and an interactive musical game designed by Saariaho.]

Rebecca Saunders

Adlington, Robert. "Into the Sensuous World: The Music of Rebecca Saunders." *The Musical Times* 140, no. 1868 (1999): 48–56.

Sperber, Roswitha. "Concordance of Many Cultures: Germany as Refuge for Women Composers?" In *Women Composers in Germany*, edited by Roswitha Sperber. Translated by Timothy Nevill. Bonn, Germany: Inter Nationes, 1996, pp. 87–99.

Selected on-line resources

www.edition-peters.de/saunders/index_engl.html. Saunders' page at Peters Edition. Includes biographical sketch and list of works published by Peters. Last updated 1997.

Daria Semegen

Hinkle-Turner, Anna Elizabeth. "Daria Semegen: Her Life, Work, and Music." D.M.A. thesis, University of Illinois at Champaign-Urbana, 1991.

Adaline Shepherd

Jasen, David A., and Gene Jones. *That American Rag—The Story of Ragtime from Coast to Coast*. New York: Schirmer Books, 2000.

Jasen, David A., and Trebor Jay Tichenor. *Rags and Ragtime: A Musical History*. New York: Seabury Press, 1978.

Lindeman, Carolyn A. *Women Composers of Ragtime*. Bryn Mawr, PA: Theodore Presser, 1985.

Morath, Max. "May Aufderheide and the Ragtime Women." In *Ragtime: Its History, Composers, and Music*, edited by John Edward Hasse. New York: Schirmer Books, 1985.

Mieko Shiomi

Hendricks, Jon. *Fluxus Codex*. Detroit: Gilbert and Lila Silverman Fluxus Collection in association with H. N. Abrams, New York, 1988.

Laurie Spiegel

Ammer, Christine. *Unsung: A History of Women in American Music*. Westport, CT: Greenwood Press, 1980.

Barkin, Elaine, ed. "In Response." *Perspectives of New Music* 20 (1981/1982): 288–329.

Gagne, Cole. *Soundpieces 2: Interviews with American Composers*. Metuchen, N.J.: Scarecrow Press, 1993.

Gann, Kyle. *American Music in the Twentieth Century*. New York: Schirmer Books, 1997.

Grigsby, Beverly. "Women Composers of Electronic Music in the United States." In *The Musical Woman: An International Perspective—1983*, editor in chief Judith Lang Zaimont. Westport, CT: Greenwood Press, 1984, pp. 151–196.

Rosen, Judith. "Composers Speaking for Themselves: An Electronic Music Panel Discussion." In *The Musical Woman: An International Perspective—volume 2: 1984–1985*, editor in chief Judith Lang Zaimont. New York: Greenwood Press, 1987, pp. 280–312.

Simoni, Mary. "Profiles in Determination." *Computer Music Journal* 22, no. 4 (1998): 19–28.

Spiegel, Laurie. "Music and Media." *Ear Magazine East* 7, no. 2 (1982): 9. Accessed on line at www.retiary.org/ls, 1/1/03.

———. "That Was Then—This Is Now." *Computer Music Journal* 20, no. 1 (1996): 42–45.

Selected on-line and other multimedia resources

www.retiary.org/ls. Maintained by Spiegel, this Web site includes compositions, software, and CDs (with downloadable samples of each); a number of published writings, most reprinted on-line introductions to, and narrative histories of, GROOVE, VAMPIRE, and *Music Mouse*; photos and memoirs from Spiegel's years at Bell Labs; visual art by the composer, and an unconventional twist on the traditional composer autobiographical sketch. The host Web site, www.retiary.org, also tended by Spiegel, contains links on some of her other interests, including tea and animal welfare. Last updated July 7, 2001.

Murmurs of Earth: The Voyager Interstellar Record. *Harmony of the Planets* [excerpt]. Warner New Media (CDROM) 1402, 1992.

Germaine Tailleferre

Gelfand, Janelle Magnuson. "Germaine Tailleferre (1892–1983): Piano and Chamber Works." Ph.D. diss., University of Cincinnati College-Conservatory of Music, 1999.

Mitgang, Laura. "Germaine Tailleferre: Before, during and after *Les Six*." In *The Musical Woman: An International Perspective—volume 2: 1984–1985*, editor in chief Judith Lang Zaimont. New York: Greenwood Press, 1987, pp. 176–221.

Pendle, Karin, and Robert Zierolf. "Composers of Modern Europe, Israel, Australia, and New Zealand." In *Women and Music: A History*, 2d ed., edited by Karin Pendle. Bloomington: Indiana University Press, 2001, pp. 252–313.

Shapiro, Robert. *Germaine Tailleferre: A Bio-Bibliography*. Westport, CT: Greenwood Press, 1994.

Louise Talma

Ammer, Christine. *Unsung: A History of Women in American Music*. Westport, CT: Greenwood Press, 1980.

Barkin, Elaine. "Louise Talma: *The Tolling Bell*." *Perspectives of New Music* 10, no. 2 (1972): 142–152.

Edwards, J. Michele. "North America since 1920." In *Women and Music: A History*, 2d ed., edited by Karin Pendle. Bloomington: Indiana University Press, 2001, pp. 314–385.

Goss, Madeleine. *Modern Music Makers—Contemporary American Composers*. New York: E. P. Dutton, 1952.

Teicher, Susan. "Louise Talma: Essentials of Her Style As Seen through the Piano Works." In *The Musical Woman: An International Perspective—1983*, editor in chief Judith Lang Zaimont. Westport, CT: Greenwood Press, 1984, pp. 128–146.

Selected on-line resources

www.omnidisc.com/Talma/html. Web site of the Louise Talma Society. Includes a biography, list of works, discography, bibliography, sound files, and interview with the composer. N.d.

Alicia Terzian

Lifchitz, Max. "New Music in Latin America." *Living Music* 7, no. 1 (1989): 1–2.

Diane Thome

Barkin, Elaine, ed. "In Response." *Perspectives of New Music* 20 (1981/1982): 288–329.

Simoni, Mary. "Profiles in Determination." *Computer Music Journal* 22, no. 4 (1998): 19–28.

Straughn, Greg. "Composer Profile: Diane Thome." *ILWC Journal* (June 1993): 23.

Thome, Diane. "Reflections on Collaborative Process and Compositional Revolution." *Leonardo Music Journal* 5 (1995): 29–32.

Joan Tower

Ammer, Christine. *Unsung: A History of Women in American Music*. Westport, CT: Greenwood Press, 1980.

Edwards, J. Michele. "North America since 1920." In *Women and Music: A History*, 2d ed., edited by Karin Pendle. Bloomington: Indiana University Press, 2001, pp. 314–385.

Gann, Kyle. *American Music in the Twentieth Century*. New York: Schirmer Books, 1997.

Johnson, Rosemary. "Joan Tower." In *Contemporary Composers*, edited by Brian Morton and Pamela Collins. Chicago: St. James Press, 1992, pp. 930–931.

LePage, Jane Werner. "Joan Tower." In *Women Composers, Conductors, and Musicians of the Twentieth Century: Selected Biographies—volume 3*. Metuchen, NJ: Scarecrow Press, 1988, pp. 264–280.

Lochhead, Judy. "Joan Tower's *Wings* and *Breakfast Rhythms I and II*: Some Thoughts on Form and Repetition." *Perspectives of New Music* 30, no. 1 (1992): 132–156.

Selected on-line resources

www.schirmer.com/composers/tower bio.html. Tower's Web page at G. Schirmer. Includes a biographical sketch; list of works published by Schirmer; and links to related articles, reviews, and other Web sites. Last updated June 3, 2001.

www.newmusicnow.org. From the Web site of the American Symphony Orchestra League's "Music for a New Millennium" initiative, a link to a page on Tower's *Fanfare for the Uncommon Woman* series. Includes a composer biography, critical introduction, audio excerpts, and interviews with Tower and conductor Marin Alsop, who has recorded the work with the Colorado Symphony. N.d.

Tui St. George Tucker

Ammer, Christine. *Unsung: A History of Women in American Music*. Westport, CT: Greenwood Press, 1980.

Alicia Urreta

Edwards, J. Michele. "North America since 1920." In *Women and Music: A History*, 2d ed., edited by Karin Pendle. Bloomington: Indiana University Press, 2001, pp. 314–385.

Pulido, Esperanza. "Mexico's Women Musicians." In *The Musical Woman: An International Perspective—volume 2: 1984–1985*, editor in chief Judith Lang Zaimont. New York: Greenwood Press, 1987, pp. 313–334.

Galina Ustvolskaya

Blois, Louis. "Shostakovich and the Ustvolskaya Connection: A Textual Investigation." *The Music Review* 52, no. 3 (1991): 218–224.

Pendle, Karin, and Robert Zierolf. "Composers of Modern Europe, Israel, Australia, and New Zealand." In *Women and Music: A History*, 2d ed., edited by Karin Pendle. Bloomington: Indiana University Press, 2001, pp. 252–313.

Sanin, A. "Galina Ustvolskaya." In *Contemporary Composers*, edited by Brian Morton and Pamela Collins. Chicago: St. James Press, 1992, pp. 936–937.

Selected on-line resources

www.sikorski.de/_english/index.html. From the Web site of Sikorski Music Publishers, a link to a biographical sketch of Ustvolskaya, list of works, and discography (with Ustvolskaya's preferred recordings marked). N.d.

www.siue.edu/aho/musov/ust/ust.html. From the Web site "Music under Soviet Rule," a critical-biographical sketch of Ustvolskaya, including chronology and discography. N.d.

http://ovar.myweb.nl/ustvol.htm. From a Web site on twentieth-century Soviet composers, a catalog of Ustvolskaya's works with links to reprinted reviews of several performances and recordings. Last updated April 16, 2001.

Nancy Van de Vate

Ammer, Christine. *Unsung: A History of Women in American Music*. Westport, CT: Greenwood Press, 1980.

Edwards, J. Michele. "North America since 1920." In *Women and Music: A History*, 2d ed., edited by Karin Pendle. Bloomington: Indiana University Press, 2001, pp. 314–385.

Ellis, Stephen W. "Nancy Van de Vate." In *Contemporary Composers*. Edited by Brian Morton and Pamela Collins. Chicago: St. James Press, 1992, pp. 939–941.

Gann, Kyle. *American Music in the Twentieth Century*. New York: Schirmer Books, 1997.

LePage, Jane Werner. "Nancy Van de Vate." In *Women Composers, Conductors, and Musicians of the Twentieth Century: Selected Biographies*. Metuchen, NJ: Scarecrow Press, 1980, pp. 256–275.

Melinda Wagner

Harbach, Barbara. [Profile of Melinda Wagner.] *Women of Note Quarterly*, vol. 7, issue 3 (1999): 1–6.

Online and Other Resources

www.presser.com/composers/wagner.html. Wagner's Web page at Theodore Presser includes a biographical sketch and list of works.

Gwyneth Walker

[see general reference works like the *Norton/Grove*]

Judith Weir

Dreyer, Martin. "Judith Weir, Composer: A Talent to Amuse." *Musical Times* 122, no. 1663 (1981): 593–596.

Ford, Andrew. *Composer to Composer: Conversations about Contemporary Music*. London: Quartet Books, 1993.

Maddocks, Fiona. "Highland Wedding [interview with Weir]." *Opera Now* (October 1990): 32–35.

Roma, Catherine. "Contemporary British Composers." In *Women and Music: A History*, 2d ed., edited by Karin Pendle. Bloomington: Indiana University Press, 2001, pp. 227–251.

Weir, Judith. "A Note on a Chinese Opera." *Musical Times* 128, no. 1733 (1987): 373–375.

————. "The Vanishing Bridegroom." *Contemporary Music Review* 11, nos. 1–2 (1994): 297–299.

Wright, David. "Weir to Now?" *Musical Times* 134, no. 1806 (1993): 432–437.

Selected on-line resource

www.schirmer.com/composers/weir/bio.html. Weir's page at G. Schirmer. Includes biographical sketch and links to notes by the composer, reviews, and articles. Last updated May 25, 2001.

Hildegard Westerkamp

LaBelle, Brandon. "The Sound of Music: Contemporary Sound-Art and the Phenomenal World." *Art Papers* 23, no. 2 (1999): 36–39.

Westerkamp, Hildegard. "Cool Drool." In *Sound by Artists*, edited by Dan Lander and Micah Lexier. Toronto: Art Metropole, 1990, pp. 223–226.

————. "Listening and Soundmaking." In *Sound by Artists*, edited by Dan Lander and Micah Lexier. Toronto: Art Metropole, 1990, pp. 227–234.

Selected on-line resources

www.sfu.ca/~westerka. Westerkamp's own home page. Includes a biography; an extensive list of compositions, installations, "sound documents," and other projects, many with notes by the composer; selected writings and lectures; workshops offered; and reviews, news, and updates. The Web site is designed by the composer's daughter. N.d.

http://interact.uoregon.edu/MediaLit/WFAE/home. Home page for the World Forum for Acoustic Ecology. Includes several articles and papers by Westerkamp. N.d.

www.emf.org/artists/mccartney00/index.html. Web site devoted to the works of Westerkamp. Maintained by the composer Andra McCartney, whose Ph.D. dissertation on Westerkamp is included in the site, as are excerpts from interviews with, and pieces by, Westerkamp (score excerpts play in real time along with sound files). N.d.

Gillian Whitehead

Kerr, Elizabeth. "Gillian Whitehead in Conversation with Elizabeth Kerr." *Contemporary Music Review* 11, nos. 1–2 (1994): 305–314.

LePage, Jane Werner. "Gillian Whitehead." In *Women Composers, Conductors, and Musicians of the Twentieth Century: Selected Biographies—volume 3*. Metuchen, NJ: Scarecrow Press, 1988, pp. 281–294.

Pendle, Karin, and Robert Zierolf. "Composers of Modern Europe, Israel, Australia, and New Zealand." In *Women and Music: A History*, 2d ed., edited by Karin Pendle. Bloomington: Indiana University Press, 2001, pp. 252–313.

Thomson, John Mansfield. *Biographical Dictionary of New Zealand Composers*. Wellington: Victoria University Press, 1990.

Mary Lou Williams

Budds, Michael J. "American Women in Blues and Jazz." In *Women and Music: A History*, 2d ed., edited by Karin Pendle. Bloomington: Indiana University Press, 2001, pp. 460–478.

Dahl, Linda. *Morning Glory: A Biography of Mary Lou Williams*. New York: Pantheon Books, 1999.

Ellington, Duke. *Music Is My Mistress*. New York: Da Capo Press, 1976.

Gottlieb, Robert, ed. *Reading Jazz*. NY: Vintage Books, 1996.

Gourse, Leslie. *Madame Jazz: Contemporary Women Instrumentalists*. New York: Oxford University Press, 1995.

Handy, D. Antoinette. "Conversation with…Mary Lou Williams: First Lady of the Jazz Keyboard." *The Black Perspective in Music* 8, no. 2 (1980): 194–214.

Kernodle, Tammy L. "'Anything You Are Shows Up in Your Music': Mary Lou Williams and the Sanctification of Jazz." Ph.D. diss., Ohio State University, 1997.

McManus, Jill. "Women Jazz Composers and Arrangers." In *The Musical Woman: An International Perspective—1983*, editor in chief Judith Lang Zaimont. Westport, CT: Greenwood Press, 1984, pp. 197–208.

McPartland, Marian. *All in Good Time*. New York: Oxford University Press, 1987.

Southern, Eileen. *The Music of Black Americans—A History*. 3d ed. New York: W. W. Norton, 1997.

Torff, Brian Q. *Mary Lou Williams: A Woman's Life in Jazz*. New York: Garland, 1999.

Unterbrink, Mary. *Jazz Women at the Keyboard*. Jefferson, NC: McFarland, 1983.

Williams, Mary Lou. "My Friends the Kings of Jazz." Reprinted in *Reading Jazz*, edited by Robert Gottlieb. New York, Vintage Books, 1999, pp. 87–116.

Selected on-line resources

http://mlw.stuaff.duke.edu. Web site of the Mary Lou Williams Center for Black Culture at Duke University. Includes biographical sketch, text of *Mary Lou's Mass*, and information on the Center. N.d.

www.umkc.edu/orgs/kcjazz/jazzfolk/wilm_00.htm. From the Web site "Club Kaycee," hosted by the Miller Nichols Library of Duke University, a brief biography of Williams and four complete tracks, including *Froggy Bottom*, in on-line sound-file format. Last updated July 1, 2000.

www.duke.edu/lmr/. Web page out of Duke University, maintained by Luke Roush. Includes biographical essay on Williams and list of institutions who have recognized her work. N.d.

www.harlem.org. Web site devoted to Art Kane's famous 1958 photograph of 57 jazz artists in Harlem, in which Williams can be seen flanked by Thelonious Monk and Marian McPartland. Includes Williams discussion boards and links. N.d.

Judith Lang Zaimont

Ammer, Christine. *Unsung: A History of Women in American Music*. Westport, CT: Greenwood Press, 1980.

Brown, Emily Freeman. "Jewish Liturgical Music by American Women since 1945." *Women of Note Quarterly*, no. 1 (1995): 8–11.

Jezic, Diane Peacock. *Women Composers: The Lost Tradition Found*. 2d ed. New York: Feminist Press at City University of New York, 1988.

Ellen Taaffe Zwilich

Baker's *Biographical Dictionary of Musicians*. 8th ed. S.v. Zwillich.

Duncan, Scott. "Ellen Taaffe Zwilich: Emerging From the Mythos." In *The Musical Woman: An International Perspective—volume 3: 1986–1990*. Judith Lang Zaimont, ed.-in-chief. New York: Greenwood Press, 1991. pp. 410–438.

Ford, Andrew. *Composer to Composer: Conversations About Contemporary Music*. London: Quartet Books Ltd., 1993.

Schnepel, Julie. "Ellen Taaffe Zwilich's Symphony No. 1: Developing Variation in the 1980s." *Indiana Theory Review* vol. 10 (1989): 1–20.

Online and Other Resources

www.presser.com/composers/zwilich.html. Zwilich's Web page at Theodore Presser includes a biographical sketch, selected list of recordings, and selected reviews. Last updated May 2002.

Selected on-line resources

www.presser.com. Publisher of works by Zwillich.

Discography

Introduction

Solo Piano Works by 20th Century Women Composers. Coronet (LP) 3206, n.d.

Women in Electronic Music. Composers Recordings Incorporated 728, 1997. [reissue of 1977 Arch LP: New Music for Electronic and Recorded Media.]

Toshiko Akiyoshi

Finesse. Various works. Concord Jazz (LP) 4069, 1978.

Land Yellow Road. Various works. RCA Victor AFL 1-1350, 1975.

Frangiz Ali-zade

Crossings...Music by Fragiz Ali-zade. Crossing II; Dilogie I; From Japanese Poetry; Music for Piano; Three Watercolors. BIS 827, 1996.

Night Prayers. Mugam Sayagi. Elektra Nonesuch 9 79346-2, 1994.

Laurie Anderson

Big Science. Warner Brothers 9 23674-2, 1982.

Bright Red. Warner Brothers 9 45534-2, 1994.

Home of the Brave. Warner Brothers 9 25400-2, 1986.

Life on a String. Nonesuch Records, 2001.

Mister Heartbreak. Warner Brothers 9 25077-2, 1984.

Strange Angels. Warner Brothers 9 25900-2, 1989.

The Ugly One with the Jewels and Other Stories. Warner Brothers 9-45847-2, 1995.

United States Live. Warner Brothers 9 25192-2, 1984.

You're the Guy I Want to Share My Money With. East Side Digital 8072, 1981.

Ruth Anderson

Lesbian American Composers. SUM (State of the Union Message). CRI 780, 1998.

New Music for Electronic and Recorded Media (Women in Electronic Music 1977). Points. CRI 728, 1997.

Violet Archer

Frivolités canadiennes. Sinfonietta. Canadian Broadcasting SM 226, n.d.

Quatrains. Northern Landscape. Centrediscs (LP) 1083, 1983.

Sonata for Alto Saxophone and Piano. Aca Digital 20036, n.d.

Sonata for Alto Saxophone and Piano; Sonata for Clarinet and Piano; Sonata for Horn and Piano. Radio Canada International (LP) 412, n.d.

Violet Archer (Anthology of Canadian Music volume 17). Various works. Radio Canada International (LP) 4472, ACM 17 (7 discs), 1983. [includes interview with Archer.]

Claude Arrieu

Musique Francaise pour trio d'anches. Suite en Trio; Trio en Ut. REM Editions 311251, 1994.

Summer Music. Quintet in C. Discover International 920322, 1995.

May Aufderheide

Fluffly Ruffle Girls: Women of Ragtime. A Totally Different Rag; Buzzer Rag; Dusty Rag; Novelty Rag; The Richmond Rag; The Thriller. Northeastern Records 9003, 1992.

Rags and Riches: Ragtime and Classical Piano Music by Women. A Totally Different Rag. Dorchester
    Classic 1004, 1993.
The Ragtime Women. The Thriller. Vanguard 79402-2, n.d.

Grazyna Bacewicz

Concerto for String Orchestra; Piano Sonata No. 2; Sonata No. 4 for Violin and Piano; Violin Concerto No. 7.
    Olympia 392, 1993.
*Concerto for Symphony Orchestra; Concerto for Two Pianos and Orchestra; Concerto for Viola and Orchestra;
    Divertimento for Strings; Pensieri Notturni.* Olympia 311, 1988.
*Four Capriccios; Lullaby; Oberek No. 1; Polish Capriccio; Sonata No. 2 for Violin Solo; Sonata No. 4 for Vi-
    olin and Piano.* Chamber Sound 95011, n.d.
Piano Quintet No. 1; String Quartets Nos. 4 and 7. Olympia 310, 1988.
Piano Quintet No. 2; String Quartets Nos. 3 and 5. Olympia 387, 1993.
Music for Violin and Piano. Partita for Violin and Piano; Sonatas for Violin and Piano Nos. 3–5. Cambria
    90717, 1995.

Bebe Barron

Forbidden Planet Electronic Music. Forbidden Planet [film score; with Louis Barron]. Small Planet
    Records PR-D-001, 1989 [from the 1956 recording].

Barbara Benary

New Gamelan/New York. Mostly Slendro Passacaglia. Gamelan Son of Lion CD-1, 1995.

Johanna Beyer

New Music for Electronic and Recorded Media (Women in Electronic Music 1977). Music of the Spheres. CRI
    728, 1997.

Carla Bley

Escalator over the Hill: A chrono-transduction by Carla Bley. Jazz Composers' Orchestra Records 2641802,
    1971.

Margaret Bonds

Black Diamonds: Althea Waites Plays Piano Music by African-American Composers. Troubled Water. Cam-
    bria 1097, 1993.
Kaleidoscope: Music by African-American Women. Troubled Water. Leonarda 339, 1995.
Watch and Pray: Spirituals and Art Songs by African-American Women Composers. Various spirituals by
    Bonds. Koch International Classics 3-7247-2 H1, 1994.

Lili Boulanger

*Clairières dans le ciel. Clairières dans le ciel; Hymne au soleil; Les Sirènes; Pour les funerailles d'un soldat; Re-
    nouveau; Soir sur la plaine.* Hyperion 66726, 1994.
D'un matin de printemps; D'un soir triste; Faust et Hélène; Psaumes 24 and 130 (Du fond de l'abîme). Chan-
    dos 9745, 1999.
*D'un matin de printemps; D'un soir triste; Pour les funerailles d'un soldat; Psaumes 24, 129, and 130 (Du
    fond de l'abîme); Vieille prière bouddhique.* Timpani 1C1046, 1998.
*In Memoriam Lili Boulanger. Clairières dans le ciel; Cortège; Dans l'immense tristesse; D'un jardin clair; D'un
    matin de printemps; D'un vieux jardin; Le Retour; Nocturne; Pie Jesu; Thème et Variations.* Marco Polo
    8.223636, 1993.
*Pie Jesu; Psaumes 24, 129, and 130 (Du fond de l'abîme); Trois pièces pour violon et piano (Nocturne, Cortège,
    and D'un matin de printemps); Vieille prière bouddhique.* EMI Classics 7 64281 2, 1992.

Songs—selections. Lili Boulanger: various songs. Signum X39-00, 1993.

Nadia Boulanger

In Memoriam Lili Boulanger. Le Couteau; Lux aeterna; Pieces for Cello and Piano; Vers la vie nouvelle. Marco
 Polo 8.223636, 1993.

Lieder und Kammermusik. Nadia Boulanger: various works. Troubadisc 01407, 1993.

Anne Elizabeth Boyd

Contemporary Australian Piano Music. Angklung. RCA (LP) VRLI-0083, 1974.

Chen Yi

Colors of Love. Tang Poems [excerpt]. Teldec 3984-24570-2, 1999.

The Music of Chen Yi. Chinese Myths Cantata; Duo Ye No. 2; Ge Xu (Antiphony); Symphony No. 2. New
 Albion 090, 1997.

Sparkle. As in a Dream; Duo Ye; Near Distance; Qi; Shuo; Song in Winter; Sparkle. CRI 804, 1999.

Rebecca Clarke

Komponistinnen des 20. Jahrhunderts: Werke für Violoncello. Sonata for Cello and Piano. Bayer Records
 100200, 1994.

Lullaby; Midsummer Moon; Trio for Violin, Cello, and Piano. Chandos 9844, n.d.

Midsummer Moon. Various works. Epoch 7105, 2000.

*Music for Viola—Rebecca Clarke. Passacaglia on an Old English Tune; Prelude, Allegro, and Pastorale; Sonata
 for Viola and Piano; Two Pieces for Viola and Cello.* Northeastern 212, 1989.

Sonates pour alto et piano. Sonata for Viola and Piano. Calliope 9285, 2000.

Songs for Voice and Piano, Voice and Violin with Works for Violin and Piano. Various works. Gamut Classics 534, 1992.

Ruth Crawford [Seeger]

American Folk Songs for Children. Performed by Pete Seeger. Smithsonian Folkways SF-45020, 1990
 [CD reissue of 1953 LP].

American Visionary Ruth Crawford Seeger. Various works. Musical Heritage Society 513493M, 1993.

Animal Folk Songs for Children. Performed by Mike and Peggy Seeger. Rounder 8001, n.d. [CD reissue of 1977 LP.]

Arditti. String Quartet 1931. Gramavision R 215 79440, 1989.

*Music of Marion Bauer and Ruth Crawford Seeger. Kaleidoscopic Changes on an Original Theme Ending with
 a Fugue; Nineteen American Folk Songs* [selections]; *Suite No. 2.* Albany TROY 297, 1998.

Music of Ruth Crawford. Various works. CRI (American Masters Series) 658, 1993.

Music by Ruth Crawford Seeger. Various works. Musical Heritage (LP) 91229Z, 1986.

Ruth Crawford Seeger: Portrait. Various works [Also includes Charles Seeger's *John Hardy* (1940)].
 Deutsche Gramaphon 449 925-2, 1997.

Emma Lou Diemer

The West Texas State University Chorale Sings Compositions of Emma Lou Diemer. Various works. Golden
 Crest (LP) ATH-5063, 1979.

Violeta Dinescu

Tautropfen. Aretusa; Echoes I; Lichwellen; Ostrov II; Satya IV; Tautropfen; Wenn der Freude Tränen Fliessen.
 Gedok 5235, 1994.

Lucia Dlugoszewski

Duende Quidditas [timbre piano part performed by the composer]. David Taylor, bass trombone. New World Records 80494-2, 1996.

Disparate Stairway Radical Other. Disparate Stairway Radical Other; Exacerbated Subtlety Concert: Why Does a Woman Love a Man?; Space Is a Diamond; Tender Theater Flight Nageire. CRI 859, 2000.

Fire Fragile Flight. Music of Schoenberg, Dallapiccola, Crumb, Boulez, others. Vox Box CDX 5144, 1995.

Tsippi Fleischer

Israel at 50: A Celebration with Music of Tsippi Fleischer. As a Diamond; Girl Butterfly Girl; Hexaptychon; Resuscitation: Five Miniatures for Cello Solo; Spielmobil; Ten Fragments for Oboe, Clarinet, and Bassoon. Opus One 175, 1999.

Vocal Music. The Clock Wants to Sleep; Girl Butterfly Girl; The Gown of Night; In the Mountains of Armenia; Lamentation; Scenes of Israel: Six Madrigals. Opus One 158, 1990.

Diamanda Galás

Malediction and Prayer. Asphodel 0984-2, 1998.

Plague Mass. Mute Records 9 61043-2, 1991.

Miriam Gideon

American-Jewish Art Songs. Psalm 128. Centaur 2108, 1992.

A Miriam Gideon Retrospective. Various works. New World Records 80393-2, 1990.

Music for Voice and Ensemble. The Hound of Heaven; Nocturnes; The Resounding Lyre; Rhymes from the Hill; Sonnets from Shakespeare; Spirit above the Dust; Wing'd Hour. CRI 782, 1998.

Voices from Elysium. Voices from Elysium. New World Records 80543-2, 1998.

Peggy Glanville-Hicks

Nausicaa—Scenes from the Opera. CRI 695, 1995.

The Transposed Heads. Louisville (LP) 545-6, 1955.

Sofia Gubaidulina

Concerto No. 2 for Cello and Orchestra ("And: The Feast Is in Full Progress"); Ten Preludes. col legno WWE 31881, 1995.

Concordanza; Märchenbild; Pro et Contra. CPO 999 164-2, 1994.

Concordanza; Meditation on the Bach Chorale "Vor deinen Thron tret ich hiermit"; Sieben Worte. Berlin Classics 0011132BC, 1994.

Hommage à T. S. Eliot; Offertorium. Deutsche Grammophon 427 336-2, 1989.

Jetzt immer Schnee; Perception. Philips 442 531-2, 1995.

Live at the 1995 Lockenhaus Festival. Dancer on a Tightrope (Der Seiltänzer); Ein Engel...; Meditation on the Bach Chorale "Vor deinen Thron tret ich hiermit"; Silenzio [also includes free improvisation by Gubaidulina with Astraea]. BIS CD-810, 1996.

String Quartets 1–3; String Trio. CPO 999 064-2, 1994.

Stufen; Symphony in Twelve Movements ("Stimmen...Verstummen"). Chandos 9183, 1993.

Adriana Hölszky

...es kamen schwarze Vögel; Kommentar für Lauren; Monolog; Vampirabile. Aulos 66013, 1998.

Floten des Lichts; Gemalde Eines Erschlagenen;...Gertraumt; Immer Schweigender; Message. CPO 999290, n.d.

Hängebrücken—Streichquartetten an Schubert: I, II, Doppelquartett; Hörfenster für Franz Liszt; Jagt die Wölfe zurück! CPO 999 112-2, 1993.

Betsy Jolas

D'un Opera de Voyage; J.D.E.; Points d'Aube; Stances. Adès 14.087-2, 1986.

Barbara Kolb

Barbara Kolb. Chromatic Fantasy; Extremes; Millefoglie; Solitaire. New World Records 8042-2, 1992.

Music of Barbara Kolb. Appello; Looking for Claudio; Soundings; Spring River Flowers Moon Night; Toccata. CRI 576, 1990.

Twentieth-Century Voices in America. The Sentences. Vox Box 5145, 1995.

Women Write Music: Orchestral Music by 20th Century Women Composers. All in Good Time. ATMA 2 2199, 1999.

Christina Kubisch

Dreaming of a Major Third. Edition RZ 10006, n.d.

Sechs Spiegel. Edition RZ 10003, n.d.

Two and Two [with Fabrizio Plessi]. Ampersound 9, n.d.

Vier Stücke. Edition RZ 10011, n.d.

Joan La Barbara

ShamanSong. Calligraphy II/Shadows; Rothko; ShamanSong. New World Records 80545-2, 1998.

Sound Paintings. Berliner Traüme; Erin; Klee Alee; ShadowSong; Time(d) Trials and Unscheduled Events; Urban Tropics. Lovely Music 3001, 1990.

Libby Larsen

In a Winter Garden: A Choral Work for Advent. Pro Arte (LP) 151, 1983.

Songs from Letters; Songs of Light and Love; String Symphony. Koch International Classics 3-7481-2141, 2000.

Tania León

Batá; Carabalí. Louisville 010, 1995.

Indigéna. *A La Par; Batéy; Indigéna; Parajota delaté.* CRI 662, 1994.

Annea Lockwood

The Glass World. What Next Recordings 0021, 1997.

Thousand Year Dreaming. What Next Recordings 0010, 1992-3.

Elisabeth Lutyens

British Chamber Music for Oboe and Strings. Driving Out the Death. Redcliffe 6, 1991.

Twentieth Century British Choral Music. Verses of Love. Usk 1216, 1992.

Alma Mahler

Lieder: Alma and Gustav Mahler. Fünf Lieder. Adda 581 208, 1990.

Lieder. Fünf Gesänge, Fünf Lieder, Vier Lieder. Classic Produktion Osnabrück 999 018-2, 1987.

Mahler, Mahler and Friends: Songs by Alma Mahler, Gustav Mahler, Alexander Zemlinsky and Hans Pfitzner. Fünf Lieder. Victoria 19069, 1995.

Meredith Monk

Atlas: An Opera in Three Parts. ECM New Series 289437773-2, 1993.

Book of Days. ECM New Series 839624-2, 1990.

Dolmen Music. ECM New Series 825459-2, 1981.

Facing North. ECM New Series 437439-2, 1992.
Our Lady of Late. Wergo Spectrum SM 1058, 1986.
Songs from the Hill/Tablet. Wergo Spectrum SM 1022-50, 1979/1989.

Mary Carr Moore

The Songs of Mary Carr Moore. Various works. Cambria (LP) 1022, 1985.

Charlotte Moorman

No recordings apparently available.

Thea Musgrave

Autumn Sonata (Concerto for Bass Clarinet and Orchestra); Concerto for Clarinet and Orchestra; The Seasons.
    Cala 1023, 1997.
The Making of a Medium. (The Verdehr Trio, vol. 2). *Pierrot.* Crystal Records 742, 1991.
Mary Queen of Scots. Novello 108, 1989.

Julia Neibergall

Fluffly Ruffle Girls: Women of Ragtime. Hoosier Rag, Horseshoe Rag, Red Rambler Rag. Northeastern
    Records 9003, 1992.

Olga Neuwirth

!? dialogues suffisants !?; Five Daily Miniatures; Lonicera Caprifolium; Spleen; Vexierbilder. Accord
    205232, 1995.
Donaueschinger Musiktage 1995. Vampyrotheone. col legno WWE 31898, 1995.
Todesraten [incidental music for a radio play by Elfriede Jelinek]. col legno WWE 20033, 1999.

Pauline Oliveros

Deep Listening. Ione; Lear; Nike; Suiren. New Albion NA 022, 1989.
Electronic Works 1965 + 1966. I of IV, Big Mother Is Watching You, Bye Bye Butterfly. Paradigm Discs
    04, 1997.
In Memoriam Mr. Whitney; St. George and the Dragon. Mode 40, 1994.
The Roots of the Moment. Oliveros: [improvisation]. Hat Hut 6009, 1988.

Daphne Oram

From One to Another for Viola and Prepared Tape [with Thea Musgrave; cassette for rehearsal purposes
    only]. Novello, 1986.

Cecilie Ore

Cikada. Praesens Subitus. Aurora 4961, 1990.

Younghi Pagh-Paan

75 Jahre Donaueschinger Musiktage 1921–1996. Nim. col legno WWE 31899, 1996.
Aa-Ga I; Dreisam-Nore; Man-Nam I; No-Ul; Pyon-Kyong; U-Mul. Montaigne MO 782026, 1994.
Ensemble Belcanto: Pagh-Paan/Nono/Brass/Spahlinger. Flammenzeichen; Hin-Nun. Aulos 66034, 1990.
Wittener Tage fur neue Kammermusik 1996. WOMON/Wunsch I. WDR WD96, 1996.

Barbara Pentland

Barbara Pentland. (Anthology of Canadian Music volume 25). Various works. Radio Canada Inter-
    national (LP) ACM 25 (6 discs), 1986. [includes interview with Pentland.]
Pentland Piano Works. Suite Borealis; Vincula; Vita Brevis. Centrediscs 1985, 1985.

THE TWENTIETH CENTURY 331

Julia Amanda Perry

Homunculus c.f. CRI (LP) 252, 1970.
Kaleidoscope: Music by African-American Women. Prelude for Piano. Leonarda 339, 1995.

Liz Phillips

No recordings apparently available.

Florence Price

Althea Waites Performs the Music of Florence Price. Cotton Dance; Dances in the Canebrakes; The Old Boatman; Sonata in e Minor. Cambria (LP) C1027, 1987.
Black Diamonds: Althea Waites Plays Piano Music by African-American Composers. Dances in the Canebrakes; Sonata in e Minor. Cambria 1097, 1993.
Kaleidoscope: Music by African-American Women. Fantasie Negre. Leonarda 339, 1995.
Lucille Field Sings Songs by American Women Composers. Four Songs (Travel's End, To My Little Son, Night, To the Dark Virgin). Cambria 1037, 1990.
Mississippi River Suite; The Oak; Symphony No. 3 in C Minor. Koch International Classics 7518, 2000.
Music of Afro-American Composers. Three Negro Dances. Northern Arizona University 003, n.d.
Watch and Pray: Spirituals and Art Songs by African-American Women Composers. Various spirituals by Price. Koch International Classics 3-7247-2 H1, 1994.

Marta Ptaszynska

Epigrams; Moon Flowers; Space Model. Pro Viva 152, 1988.
Polish Percusson Music. Jeu-pari for Vibraphone and Harp. Olympia 324, 1989.

Shulamit Ran

Concerto da Camera II; East Wind; Hatzvi Israel Eulogy; Mirage; O, the Chimneys; Sonatina for Two Flutes. Erato Disques 0630-1278702, n.d.
Curtis Macomber: Songs of Solitude. Inscriptions. CRI 706, 1996.
Music by Shulamit Ran. Concerto da Camera II; East Wind; Inscriptions; Mirage; For an Actor: Monologue for Clarinet; Private Game. Bridge 9052, 1995.
Music of Shulamit Ran. Apprehensions; Concerto da Camera II; Hyperbolae; Private Game. CRI 609, 1991.
Three Fantasy Movements. String Quartet No. 1; Three Fantasy Movements. Koch International Classics 3-7269-2 H1, 1995.

Kaija Saariaho

...à la fumée; Du Cristal; Nymphéa. Ondine 804-2, 1993.
Amers; Château de l'âme; Graal Théatre. Sony Classical 60187, n.d.
Cloud Music; La Dame à la Licorne. Petals 003, 1998.
Electro-Acoustic Music 1. Petals. Neuma 450-73, 1990.
From the Grammar of Dreams. Ondine 958-2, 2000.
Io; Lichtbogen; Stilleben; Verblendungen. Finlandia 374, 1989.
Maa: Ballet Music in Seven Scenes. Ondine 791-2, n.d.
Private Gardens. Lonh; NoaNoa; Près; Six Japanese Gardens. Ondine 906-2, 1997.

Rebecca Saunders

Wittener Tage fur neue Kammermusik 1996. CRIMSON—Molly's Song 1. WDR WD96, 1996.
Wittener Tage fur neue Kammermusik 1998. Quartet. WDR WD98, 1998.

Daria Semegen

Columbia-Princeton Electronic Music Center 1961–1973. Electronic Composition No. 1. New World Records 80521-2, 1998.

Soundbridge. Rhapsody for Midi-Grand Piano. Opus One 152, n.d.

Adaline Shepherd

Fluffly Ruffle Girls: Women of Ragtime. Pickles and Peppers (A Rag Oddity). Northeastern Records 9003, 1992.

Rags and Riches: Ragtime and Classical Piano Music by Women. Pickles and Peppers (A Rag Oddity). Dorchester Classic 1004, 1993.

The Ragtime Women. Pickles and Peppers (A Rag Oddity). Vanguard 79402-2, n.d.

Mieko Shiomi

Japanese Composers. If We Were a Pentagonal Memory Device. Japan Federation of Composers (LP) R8102, 1981.

Laurie Spiegel

The Expanding Universe. Philo Records (LP) 9003, 1980. Out of print.

Obsolete Systems. EMF 119, n.d.

Unseen Worlds. Aesthetic Engineering 11001-2, n.d.

The Virtuoso in the Computer Age III. Cavis Muris. Centaur 2166, 1993.

Germaine Tailleferre

Kammermusik fur Streicher, Blaser und Klavier. Various works. Trouba Disc 01406, 1993.

Musique de Chambre. Various works. Cambria 1085, 1994.

La Musique de Germaine Tailleferre volume II. Various works. Helicon 1048, 1999.

Music for Two Pianos and Piano Four-Hands. Various works. Élan 82278, 1997.

The Music of Germaine Tailleferre. Various works. Helicon Music 1008, 1996.

Songs by Le Groupe des Six. Six Chansons Françaises. Cambridge (LP) 2777, 1980.

Louise Talma

Music by American Women. Sonata for Violin and Piano. Gasparo 300, 1995.

Music of Louise Talma. Alleluia in Form of a Toccata; Piano Sonatas Nos. 1 and 2; Seven Episodes for Flute, Viola, and Piano; Six Etudes; Three Duologues for Clarinet and Piano. CRI 833, 1999.

Voices from Elysium. Diadem. New World Records 80543-2, 1998.

Alicia Terzian

Terzian: Concierto para Violin y Orquesta. Instituto Lucchelli Bonadeo (LP) 3001, 1972.

Diane Thome

Composers in the Computer Age. The Ruins of the Heart. Centaur 2144, 1992.

Joan Tower

Amazon; Breakfast Rhythms I and II; Hexachords; Noon Dance; Petroushskates; Platinum Spirals; Wings. CRI 582, 1985.

Black Topaz. Black Topaz; Night Fields; Snow Dreams; Stepping Stones; Très Lent: In Memoriam Olivier Messiaen. New World Records 80470-2, 1995.

Fanfares for the Uncommon Woman. Concerto for Orchestra; Duets for Orchestra; Fanfares for the Uncommon Woman Nos. 1–5. Koch International Classics 3-7469-2 H1, 1999.

Island Prelude; Music for Violoncello and Orchestra; Sequoia; Silver Ladders. Elektra Nonesuch (Meet the Composer) 9-79245-2, 1990.

Joan Tower Concertos. Clarinet Concerto; Flute Concerto; Piano Concerto; Violin Concerto. D'Note 1016, 1997.

Tui St. George Tucker

Soundbridge. My Melancholy Baby—Fantasy on Ernie Burnett's Theme for Quartertone Piano; Second Piano Sonata ("The Peyote"). Opus One 152, n.d.

Alicia Urreta

No recordings apparently available.

Galina Ustvolskaya

Compositions No. 1, 2, and 3. Phillips 442 532-2, 1995.

Galina Ustvolskaya—The Complete Piano Sonatas. Piano Sonatas Nos. 1–6. Conifer Classics 75605 51262 2, 1995.

Galina Ustvolskaya [complete works]. Megadisc 7854, 7858, 7863, 7865, 7867, and 7876, various dates.

Galina Ustvolskaya #1. Trio for Violin, Clarinet, and Piano; Sonata No. 5 in Ten Movements; Duet for Violin and Piano. HatART 6115, 1993.

Gorecki: Solo Piano Works. Preludes (12) for piano. by Ustvolskaya. David Arden, piano. Koch International Classics 7301, 1995.

Grand Duet for Cello and Piano; Piano Sonata No. 5; Symphony No. 4 "Prayer"; Trio for Violin, Clarinet, and Piano. Etcetera 1170, 1993.

Unveiled: Music from Russia's Women Composers. Piano Sonatas Nos. 2 and 6. Black Box 1039, n.d.

Wittener Tage fur neue Kammermusik 1993. Composition No. 1: Dona Nobis Pacem. Westdeutschen Rundfunk WD04, 1993.

Nancy Van de Vate

Journeys: Orchestral Works by American Women. Journeys. Leonarda 327, 1987.

Lucille Field Sings Songs by American Women Composers. Songs for the Four Parts of the Night. Cambria 1037, 1990.

Melinda Wagner

Concerto for Flute, Strings, and Percussion. Bridge 9098, 2000.

Gwyneth Walker

Ah! Love but a Day—Songs and Spirituals by Women Composers. Maggie and Millie and Mollie and May; Still. Albany Records/Videmus TROY385, 2000.

Judith Weir

Blond Eckbert. Collins Classics 14612, 1995.

A Night at the Chinese Opera. NMC D060, 2000.

3 Operas. The Consolations of Scholarship; King Harald's Saga; Missa del Cid. Novello 109, 1989.

Hildegard Westerkamp

Electro Clips. Breathing Room. Empreintes DIGITALes IMED 9604, 1996.

Harangue II. Gently Penetrating. Earsay 98005, 1998.

Transformations. Beneath the Forest Floor; Cricket Voice; Fantasie for Horns II; Kits Beach Soundwalk; A Walk through the City. Empreintes DIGITALes IMED 9631, 1996.

Gillian Whitehead

Café Concertino. Manutaki. Tall Poppies 002, 1991.
New Zealand Composers. Resurgences. Continuum NZ 1073, 1995.

Mary Lou Williams

The Best of Mary Lou Williams. Pablo (LP) 2310-856, 1980.
Excerpts from *Mary Lou's Mass.* Helicon (LP) 9, 1985.
History of Jazz [compiled, performed, and narrated by Williams]. Folkway (LP) 2680, 1978.
The King and Queen: Art Tatum and Mary Lou Williams. Jazztone (LP) 1280, 1958.
The Lady Who Swings the Band {Andy Kirk and His Twelve Clouds of Joy}. MCA (LP) 1343, 1982.
Marian McPartland Plays the Music of Mary Lou Williams. Concord Jazz 4605, 1994.
Marian McPartland's Piano Jazz with Guest Mary Lou Williams. Jazz Alliance 12019, 1995.
Mary Lou Williams, 1927–1940. Classics 630, 1992.
Mary Lou Williams— The Asch Recordings 1944–1947. Folkways (LP) 2966, 1977.
The Zodiac Suite. Vintage Jazz Classics 1035, 1991.
Zodiac Suite. Smithsonian Folkways 40810, 1995.

Judith Lang Zaimont

Summer Melodies: A Piano Album. Evening; From "Calendar Collection" (June, July, August, September); Nocturne: La Fin de Siècle; Snazzy Sonata: An Entertainment for Two; Suite Impressions. 4-Tay 4001, 1996.

Ellen Taaffe Zwilich

Celebration; Prologue and Variations; Symphony No. 1. New World Records, 1986.
Concerto for Bass Trombone, Strings, Timpani and Cymbals; Concerto for Horn and String Orchestra; Symphony No. 4 ("The Gardens"). Koch International Classics, 3-7487-2 H1, 2000.
Concerto for Oboe and Orchestra; Concerto Grosso; Symphony No. 3. Koch International Classics, 3-7278-2 H1, 1995.
Concerto for Piano and Orchestra; Concerto for Violin and Orchestra; Concerto for Violin, Cello and Orchestra. Koch International Classics, KIC CD-7537, 2002.
Symphony No. 2. First Edition Recordings, LCD002, n.d.

Selected List of Works

Laurie Anderson

"Americans on the Move." Performance Piece. 1979.
"Empty Places." Performance Piece. 1989.
"Halcion Days: Stories for the Nerve Bible." Performance Piece. 1992.
"Mister Heartbreak." Performance Piece. 1984.
"Moby Dick." Performance Piece. 1999.
"Talk Normal." Performance Piece. 1987.
"United States, I–IV." Performance Piece. 1983.

Violet Archer

The Bell. Text by John Donne. Toronto, Ontario: Canadian Music Centre, 1949.
Eleven Short Pieces, for piano. Toronto, Ontario: Canadian Music Centre, n.d.
Scherzo Sinfonico. Score. 1940.
Shorter Pieces for Shorter Fingers, piano. Toronto, Ontario: Canadian Music Centre, n.d.

Sonata, for alto saxophone and piano. Toronto, Ontario: Canadian Music Centre, n.d.

May Aufderheide

Buzzer Rag. Score. 1909.
Dusty Rag. Northport, NY: Arcadian Press, 1908.
The Richmond Rag. Northport, NY: Arcadian Press, 1909.
Three Rags. Bryn Mawr, PA: Hildegard Publishing Company, 2000.
(The) Thriller! Score. 1909.
(A) Totally Different Rag. Northport, NY: Arcadian Press, 1910.

Grazyna Bacewicz

Concerto, for string orchestra. Krakow, Poland: PWM, 1948.
Concerto, for piano and orchestra. Krakow, Poland: PWM, 1949.
Musik for Strings, Trumpets and Percussion. Krakow, Poland: PWM, 1958.
Pensieri Notturni, for chamber orchestra. Krakow, Poland: PWM, 1961.
Quintet, for flute, oboe, clarinet, bassoon, and horn. Krakow, Poland: PWM, 1933.
String Quartet No. 1. Krakow, Poland: PWM, 1938.
String Quartet No. 4. Krakow, Poland: PWM, 1951.
String Quartet No. 6. Krakow, Poland: PWM, 1960.

Margaret Bonds

(The) Ballad of the Brown King, Christmas Cantata. Text by Langston Hughes. New York: Sam Fox, 1961.
Credo, for baritone, chorus, and orchestra. Text by W.E.B. Du Bois. 1972.
(The) Negro Speaks of Rivers, for voice and piano. Text by Langston Hughes. New York: Handy Bros., 1941.
Sea Ghost, for voice and piano. Score. 1932.
Shakespeare in Harlem, incidental music for a play. Text by Langston Hughes. Score. 1959.
Spring Will Be So Sad When She Comes This Year, for voice and piano. Text by Margaret Bonds and Harold Dickinson. New York: Mutual Music, 1941.
Three Dream Portraits for voice and piano. Text by Langston Hughes from the Dream Keeper. New York: Ricordi, 1959; Bryn Mawr, PA: Hildegard Publishing Company, 1995.

Lili Boulanger

Clairières dans le ciel (cycle of 13 songs), for tenor and piano. Text by F. Jammes. 1914.
Cortège, for violin or flute and piano. 1914.
Dans l'immense tristesse, for solo voice and piano. Text by B. Galéron de Calone. 1918.
D'un matin de printemps, for violin or flute and piano or orchestra. London: United Music, 1918.
D'un soir triste, for string trio or cello and piano or orchestra. London: United Music, 1918.
Faust et Hélène, for mezzo-soprano, tenor, baritone, and orchestra. Winning composition of the Prix de Rome. Text by E. Adenis after J. S. von Goethe. Score. 1913.
Nocturne, for flute or violin and piano or orchestra. Feldkirchen, Germany: Ricordi, 1911.
Piè Jesu, for soprano, string quartet, harp, and organ. 1918.
Pour les funérailles d'un soldat, for baritone, chorus, and orchestra. Text by A. de Musset. 1913.
Psalm cxxx "Du fond de l'aböme," for alto, tenor, chorus, organ, and orchestra. 1917.
Vieille prière bouddhique (Buddhist prayer from Visuddhimagga), for tenor, chorus, and orchestra. Translation by S. Karpéles. 1917.

Nadia Boulanger

La siréne, for 3 voices and orchestra. Text by E. Adenis/Desveaux. 1908.

La ville morte, opera with Raoul Pugno. Libretto by D. d'Annunzio. 1913.

Le couteau, for voice and piano. Text by C. Mauclair. 1922.

Lux Aeterna (adaptation of Hymne à l'amour, 1910) for soprano, violin, cello, and harp. N.d.

Rhapsodie variée, for piano and orchestra. 1912?

Three Pieces for Cello and Piano. Paris, France: Huegel (Alphonse Leduc), 1915.

Chen Yi

Chinese Myths cantata, for male choir and orchestra. Bryn Mawr, PA: Theodore Presser, 1996.

Duo Ye. Bryn Mawr, PA: Theodore Presser, 1985.

Duo Ye No. 2. Bryn Mawr, PA: Theodore Presser, 1987.

Ge Xu. Bryn Mawr, PA: Theodore Presser, 1994.

(The) Points. Bryn Mawr, PA: Theodore Presser, 1991.

Qi, for flute, cello, piano, and percussion. Bryn Mawr, PA: Theodore Presser, 1997.

Sparkle, octet. Bryn Mawr, PA: Theodore Presser, 1992.

Tang Poems, cantata for chorus and chamber orchestra. Text from four poems by Li Po, Li Shang-yin, Bai Ju-yi, and Chen Zi-ang. Bryn Mawr, PA: Theodore Presser, 1995.

Rebecca Clarke

Cortège, for piano. Score. 1930s. Rebecca Clarke Estate.

Lullaby, for violin and piano. Score. 1918. Rebecca Clarke Estate.

Midsummer Moon, for violin and piano. London: Oxford University Press, 1926.

Morpheus, for Viola and Piano. 1917. New York: Oxford University Press, 2002.

Passacaglia on an Old English Tune (for viola or cello and piano). Bryn Mawr, PA: Hildegard Publishing Company, 2000.

Prelude, Allegro, and Pastorale. London: Oxford University Press, 1942, 2000.

Rhapsody, for cello and piano. Score. 1923.

Sonata for viola, or cello, and Piano. London/Genf: J. & W. Chester, 1921; New York: DaCapo, 1986; Bryn Mawr: PA: Hildegard Publishing Company, 1999.

Trio, for violin, cello, and piano. London: Winthrop Rogers, 1928; New York: DaCapo, 1981; London: Boosey and Hawkes, 1994.

Two Pieces for viola, or violin, and cello. 1. *Lullaby*; 2. *Grotesque*. London: Oxford University Press, 1930.

Ruth Crawford (Crawford-Seeger)

American Folk Songs for children, piano arrangements. Garden City, NJ: Doubleday, 1948.

American Songbag, piano accompaniments. New York: Harcourt Brace, 1927.

Diaphonic Suite No. 1, for unaccompanied flute or oboe. Bryn Mawr, PA: New Music Edition, 1954; New York: Continuo Music Press, 1972.

Our Singing Country, transcriptions. New York: Macmillan, 1941.

Piano Study in Mixed Accents. Bryn Mawr, PA: New Music Editions, 1932; Bryn Mawr, PA: Theodore Presser, 1984.

Preludes 1–5. Bryn Mawr, PA: Hildegard Publishing Company, 1992.

Sonata for violin and piano. Bryn Mawr, PA: Theodore Presser, 1926, 1985.

String Quartet. Bryn Mawr, PA: New Music Editions, 1931. Bryn Mawr, PA: Merion Music, 1941.

Suite for Wind Quintet. New York: Alexander Broude, 1952.

Three Songs to Poems of Carl Sandburg, for contralto, oboe, piano, and percussion. Bryn Mawr, PA: New Music Editions, 1933.

Twenty-two American Folk Tunes, arranged for piano. New York: Alexander Broude, 1938.

Two Songs, poems of H. T. Tsiang. Santa Fe, NM: Soundings Press, 1973; Bryn Mawr, PA: Merion Music, 1973.

Lucia Dlugoszewski

Abyss and Caress. New York: G. Schirmer: Margun Music, 1975.

Balance Naked Flung, for clarinet, trumpet, bass trombone, violin, and percussion. Newton Centre, MA: Margun Music, 1966.

Disparate Stairway Radical Other, for string quartet. Newton Centre, MA: Margun Music, 1995.

Fire Fragile Flight, for 17 instruments. Newton Centre, MA: Margun Music, 1974.

Moving Space Theatre Piece. Newton Centre, MA: Margun Music, 1949.

Radical Suchness Concert, for flute, clarinet, trumpet, trombone, violin, and double bass. Newton Centre, MA: Margun Music, 1991.

Space Is a Diamond, for solo trumpet. Newton Centre, MA: Margun Music, 1970.

Tender Theater Flight Nageire, for brass ensemble and percussion. New York: G. Schirmer: Margun Music, 1971, rev. 1978.

Miriam Gideon

Boehmischer Krystall, for flute clarinet, piano, voice, violin, and cello. Text by Otto Erich Hartleben. New York: American Composers Alliance, 1988.

The Condemned Playground, for Soprano, Tenor, Flute, Bassoon, and String Quartet. 1963. Hillsdale, NY: Mobart Music, 1978.

(The) Hound of Heaven. 1945.

Mixco, for Voice and Piano. New York: American Composers Alliance, 1957.

(The) Resounding Lyre. 1979.

Rhymes from the Hill, for clarinet, marimba, voice, and cello, arranged for solo clarinet and voice in 1968. English translation by Max Knight. New York: American Composers Alliance, 1966.

Sacred Service for Sabbath Morning, for Cantor, Soprano, Alto, Tenor, Bass, Mixed Chorus, and Chamber Ensemble. 1970. New York: American Composers Alliance, 1971.

Voices from Elysium, for flute, clarinet, piano, voice, violin, and cello. New York: American Composers Alliance, 1979.

Peggy Glanville-Hicks

Caedmon, opera for soloist, chorus, and orchestra. Libretto by P. Glanville-Hicks. Score. 1933.

(The) Glittering Gate: An Opera in One Act. Play by Lord Dunsany. Sydney: Australian Music Centre, 1958.

Letters from Morocco, for tenor and chamber orchestra. Text by Paul Bowles. New York: C. F. Peters, 1953.

Nausicaa, an opera in 3 acts, with prologue and interludes. Libretto by R. Graves and A. Ried. Sydney: Australian Music Centre, 1961.

Sappho, an opera in 3 acts. Libretto by Lawrence Durrell. Sydney: Australian Music Centre, 1963.

Thomsoniana, for soprano, flute, horn, piano, and string quartet. Text by Virgil Thomson. Sydney: Australian Music Centre, 1949.

(The) Transposed Heads, a legend of India in six scenes after the novel by Thomas Mann. English libretto based on H. T. Lowe Porters translation by the composer. New York: Associated Music, 1958.

Sofia Asgatovna Gubaidulina

Alleluja, for large orchestra, organ, mixed chorus and boy's voice. New York: G. Schirmer, 1990.

De Profundis, for bayan solo. New York: G. Schirmer, 1978.

Galgenlieder (à 3), 15 pieces for mezzo-soprano, double bass, and percussion. Poems by Christian Morgenstern. New York: G. Schirmer, 1996.

In Croce, for cello and organ. New York: G. Schirmer, 1979.

Meditation on the Bach Chorale Vor di enem Thron thet ich hiermit, for harpsichord and string quintet. New York: G. Schirmer, 1993.

Offertorium, concerto for violin and orchestra. New York: G. Schirmer, 1986.

St. John Passion (Johannes-Passion), for chamber chorus and large chorus. Text from biblical texts. New York: G. Schirmer, 2000.

Seven Words (Sieben Worte), for cello, bayan, and strings. New York: G. Schirmer, 1982.

Stimmen Verstummern, symphony in 12 movements. New York: G. Schirmer, 1986.

String Quartet No. 1. New York: G. Schirmer, 1971.

Adriana Hölszky

Es kamen schwarze Vögel, for Five Female Voices and Percussion. 1978.

Hangebrucken: Streichquartette/Doppelquartett an Schubert. Berlin, Germany: Astoria Verlag, 1991.

Jagt die Wölfe zurück!, for six timpani. 1989–90. Wiesbaden: Breitkopf and Härtel, 1990.

Monolog: fur Frauenstimme mit Pauke, for womans voice and timpani. Berlin, Germany: Astoria Verlag, 1989.

Vampirabile: Lichtverfall fur funf Frauenstimmen mit Percussion, for 5 female singers, each playing percussion. Berlin, Germany: Astoria Verlag, 1990.

Barbara Kolb

Chromatic Fantasy, for narrator and ensemble. London: Boosey and Hawkes, 1979.

Grisaille, for full orchestra. London: Boosey and Hawkes, 1979.

Homage to Keith Jarrett and Gary Burton, for mixed ensemble. London: Boosey and Hawkes, 1976.

Looking for Claudio, for Guitar and Tape. 1975. Oceanside, NY: Boosey and Hawkes, 1978.

Millefoglie, for mixed ensemble. London: Boosey and Hawkes, 1985.

Soundings, for full orchestra. London: Boosey and Hawkes, 1978.

Soundings, for mixed ensemble. London: Boosey and Hawkes, 1972.

Toccata, for Harpsichord and Tape. 1971. New York: C. F. Peters, 1976.

Trobar Clus, for mixed ensemble. London: Boosey and Hawkes, 1970.

Christina Kubisch

Dreaming of a Major Third. N.d.

Iter magneticum. Berlin, Germany. 1986.

Klanginstallationene. Bremen, Germany. 1985.

Kubisch und Plessi. Aachen, Germany; Antwerp, Belgium. 1978.

Sechs Spiegel. N.d.

Vier Stucke. N.d.

Elisabeth Lutyens

Catena, for soprano, tenor, and 21 instruments. Score. 1962.

De Amore, cantata. Score. 1957.

Motet "Excerpta Tractatus logico-philosophici," op. 27, for chorus. 1953. London: Schott, 1965.

0 Saisons, 0 Châteaux, cantata for soprano, mandolin, guitar, harp, and strings. Score. 1946.

Quincunx. 1960.

6 Chamber Concerti, some with solo instruments. Score. 1948.

Three Symphonic Preludes. Score. 1942.

Time Off? Not a Ghost of a Chance. Op. 68, a charade. Libretto by E. Lutyens. London: University of York Press, 1968.

Verses of Love, for Chorus. 1970. London: Novello, 1971.

Alma Mahler [Schindler]

Fünf Gesange. London: Josef Weinberger, 1924.

Sämtliche Lieder fur mittlere Stimme und Klavier. Wien: Universal Edition, 1984.

Two Lieder, first publication. Bryn Mawr, PA: Hildegard Publishing Company, 2000.

Vier Lieder. Bryn Mawr, PA: Hildegard Publishing Company, 2000, G. K. Hall reprint.

Meredith Monk

Atlas: An Opera in Three Parts, for 18 voices, 2 keyboards, clarinet, bass clarinet, sheng, bamboo sax, 2 violins, viola, 2 celli, French horn, percussion, and shawm. Score. 1991.

Book of Days, for 10 voices, cello, shawm, synthesizer, hammered dulcimer, bagpipe, and hurdy-gurdy. Score. 1988.

Boys 1; Boys 2; Boys 3, for 4 voices (overdubbed tape piece). Score. 2001.

Do You Be, for 10 voices, 2 pianos, synthesizer, violin, and bagpipes. Score. 1987.

Dolmen Music, for 6 voices, cello, and percussion. Score. 1979.

Education of the Girlchild: An Opera, for 6 voices, electric organ, and piano. Score. 1973.

Juice: A Theater Cantata, for 85 voices, Jew's harp, and 2 violins. Score. 1969.

Our Lady of Late, for solo voice and win glass. Score. 1973.

Quarry: An Opera, for 38 voices, 2 pump organs, 2 soprano recorders, and tape. Score. 1976.

Songs from the Hill/Tablet, for 4 voices, piano, and 2 soprano recorders. Score. 1979.

Vessel: An Opera Epic, for 75 voices, electric organ, dulcimer, and accordion. Score. 1971.

Olga Neuwirth

!?dialogues suffisants!?, for cello, percussion, tape, and video. Feldkirchen, Germany: Ricordi, 1992.

Five Daily Miniatures, for countertenor, bass clarinet, piano, violin, and cello. Text by Gertrude Stein. Feldkirchen, Germany: Ricordi, 1994.

Lonicera Caprifolium, for ensemble with tape. Feldkirchen, Germany: Ricordi, 1993.

Spleen, for bass clarinet. Feldkirchen, Germany: Ricordi, 1994.

Vampyrotheone, for 3 soloists and 3 ensemble sections. Feldkirchen, Germany: Ricordi, 1995.

Vexierbilder, for flute, clarinet, soprano saxophone, trombone, and live electronics. Feldkirchen, Germany: Ricordi, 1994.

Pauline Oliveros

Bonn Feier, a verbally notated theater piece. Akron, OH: Smith Publications, 1971.

Bye Bye Butterfly, for Oscillators, Amplifiers, and Tape. 1965. Tape piece.

Crow Two: A Ceremonial Opera. 1974. Akron, OH: Smith, n.d.

Duo, for Accordion and Bandoneon with Optional Mynah Bird Obbligato. 1964. Performance piece.

Njinga the Queen King. Score. 1993. Deep Listening Archives.

I of IV, for tape. 1966. Tape piece.

(The) Single Stroke Roll Meditation, for solo snare drum. Akron, OH: Smith, 1973.

Sonic Meditations I Ò XXV, a collection of verbally notated meditations. Akron, OH: Smith, 1971.

To Valerie Solanas and Marilyn Monroe in Recognition of Their Desperation, for any instruments or voices (6 Ò large orchestra). Akron, OH: Smith, 1970.

Younghi Pagh-Paan

Dreisam-Nore, for flute. Feldkirchen, Germany: Ricordi, 1975.

Man-Nam I, for clarinet, violin, viola, and cello. Feldkirchen, Germany: Ricordi, 1977.

Man-Nam II, for alto flute, violin, viola, and cello. Feldkirchen, Germany: Ricordi, 1977.

Nim, for large orchestra. Feldkirchen, Germany: Ricordi, 1987.

Pyon-Kyong, for piano and percussion. Feldkirchen, Germany: Ricordi, 1982.

U-Mul/The Well, for alto flute, clarinet, percussion, violin, viola, cello, and double bass. Feldkirchen, Germany: Ricordi, 1992.

Barbara Pentland

Music for Now, Book I, for piano. Waterloo, Ontario: Waterloo Music, 1970.
Music for Now, Book II, for piano. Waterloo, Ontario: Waterloo Music, 1970.
Music for Now, Book III, for piano. Waterloo, Ontario: Waterloo Music, 1970.
Octet for Winds. Score. 1948.
String Quartet No. 2. Score. 1953.
Studies in Line, for piano. Winnipeg, Canada: BMI Canada, 1941.
Symphony for Ten Parts: Symphony No. 3. Toronto: Berandol, 1961.
Variations for Piano, for piano. Score. 1942.

Florence Beatrice Price

Dances in the Canebrakes, for piano. Score. 1953.
Mississippi River, for symphony. Score. 1934.
My Soul's Been Anchored in de Lord, for Voice and Piano. Chicago: Gamble Hinged Music, 1935.
Piano Concerto. Score. 1934.
Sonata, for piano. Score. 1932.
Songs to the Dark Virgin. Text by Langston Hughes. Score. 1941; Bryn Mawr, PA: Hildegard Publishing Company, 1995.
Symphony No. 1. Score. 1932.

Shulamit Ran

Apprehensions, for voice, clarinet, and piano. Bryn Mawr, PA: Theodore Presser, 1979.
Between Two Worlds (The Dybbuk). Libretto by Charles Kondekd. Score. 1997.
Capriccio, for Piano and Orchestra. 1963.
Concerto de Camera II, for clarinet, string quartet, and piano. Bryn Mawr, PA: Theodore Presser, 1987.
Ensembles for 17, for soprano and instrumental ensemble. Bryn Mawr, PA: Theodore Presser, 1975.
For an Actor: Monologue for Clarinet. Bryn Mawr, PA: Theodore Presser, 1978.
Hatzvi Israel Eulogy. Bryn Mawr, PA: Theodore Presser, 1969.
Hyperbolae, for piano. Israel Music Institute, Bryn Mawr, PA: Theodore Presser, 1976.
O, The Chimneys. Bryn Mawr, PA: Theodore Presser, 1969.
Private Game, for clarinet and cello. Bryn Mawr, PA: Theodore Presser, 1979.
Symphony. Bryn Mawr, PA: Theodore Presser, 1990.

Kaija Saariaho

…à la fumée, for string ensemble. Copenhagen, Denmark: Edition Wilhelm Hansen, 1990.
Io, for bass, tape, and electronics. Copenhagen, Denmark: Edition Wilhelm Hansen, 1987.
L'amour de loin (Love from Afar), opera. Score. 2000.
Lichtbogen, for flute, percussion, piano, harp, 2 violins, viola, cello, double bass, and electronics. Copenhagen, Denmark: Edition Wilhelm Hansen, 1986.
Lonh, for soprano and electronics. London: Chester Music, 1996.
Maa, music for dance in seven parts: 1. Journey, 2. Gates, 3. Door (de la terre in the concert version), 4. Forest, 5. Windows, 6. Fall, 7. Phoenix (Aer in the concert version. Copenhagen, Denmark: Edition Wilhelm Hansen, 1991.
Nymphea (Jardin secret III), for 2 violins, viola, cello, and electronics. Copenhagen, Denmark: Edition Wilhelm Hansen, 1987.
Près, for cello and electronics. London: Chester Music, 1992.
Six Japanese Gardens, for percussion and electronics. London: Chester Music, 1993.

Stilleben, for solo tape. Text is a collage. Score. 1988.

Verblendungen, for orchestra. Copenhagen, Denmark: Edition Wilhelm Hansen, 1984.

Rebecca Saunders

Cinnabar, double concerto for violin and trumpet, ensemble, music boxes, and conductor. Score. N.d.

Crimson, Mollys Song 1, for 12 solotists, metronomes, whistles, and 3 music boxes. London: Edition Peters, 1995.

String Quartet. Score. 1997.

Adaline Shepherd

Pickles and Peppers Rag. Wiscasset, ME: Artcraft Music Rolls, 1909.

Powder Rag, for piano. Score. N.d.

Laurie Spiegel

Appalachian Grove, GROOVE system (computer controlled analog synthesis). New York: Laurie Spiegel, 1974.

Cavis Muris, Music Mouse, MIDI, FM synthesis, and digital signal processing. New York: Laurie Spiegel, 1986.

(The) Expanding Universe, GROOVE system (computer controlled analog synthesis). New York: Laurie Spiegel, 1975.

(A) Harmonic Algorithm, Apple II with Mountain Hardware boards. New York: Laurie Spiegel, 1981.

Keplers Harmony of the Planets, computer realization of Kepler treatise. New York: Laurie Spiegel, 1977.

A Living Painting, VAMPIRE system, silent visual study, and videotape. New York: Laurie Spiegel, 1979.

Music Mouse: An Intelligent Instrument, interactive generative musical process for Apple Macintosh, Commodore Amiga, Atari ST personal computers. New York: Laurie Spiegel, 1986.

Music Mouse Demonstration Music, 12 computer-assisted improvisations. New York: Laurie Spiegel, 1986.

Two Intellectual Interludes (Data and Process): A Strand of Life (Viroid), and From a Harmonic Algorithm, C language, Macintosh, MIDI, and FM sythesis. New York: Laurie Spiegel, 1990.

Germaine Tailleferre

Cantate de Narcissus, for voice, chorus, and orchestra. Score. 1937.

Concerto pour Piano et Orchestre. Paris, France: Huegel and Cie, 1924.

Enfantines, piano pieces for children. Paris, France: Les Editions Henry Lemoine, 1981.

Jeux de plein air, for 2 pianos. France: Durand Music, 1918.

Le marchand doiseaux, ballet with orchestra. Score. 1923.

Le Sacré du printemps, reduction for 2 pianos. Arranged by G. Tailleferre. Score. 1924.

Quatuor à cordes, for string quartet. France: Durand Music, 1921; Bryn Mawr, PA: Hildegard Publishing Company, 2002.

Seule dans la Forêt, for piano. Paris, France: Les Editions Henry Lemoine, 1958.

Six Chansons françaises, for voice and piano. Paris, France: Huegel and Cie, 1929.

Louise Talma

(The) Alcestiad, opera. Text by Thornton Wilder. Score. 1958.

Alleluia in Form of Toccata, for piano. New York: Carl Fischer, 1947.

Diadem, for tenor and Pierrot ensemble. Text by Confucius. Score. 1980.

Soundshots, for piano. Bryn Mawr, PA: Hildegard Publishing Company 2000.

String Quartet. Score. 1954.

Thirteen Ways of Looking at a Blackbird. New York: Carl Fischer, 1984.

(The) Tolling Bell, for baritone and orchestra. Score. 1969.

Joan Tower

Amazon I. New York: Associated Music, 1977.
Amazon II, arranged by the composer from the original quintet. New York: Associated Music, 1979.
Black Topaz, for piano and 6 instruments. New York: Associated Music, 1976.
Breakfast Rhythms I and II, for clarinet and 5 instruments. New York: Associated Music, 1975.
Concerto for Clarinet. New York: Associated Music, 1988.
Fanfare for the Uncommon Woman. New York: Associated Music, 1986.
Island Rhythms. New York: Associated Music, 1985.
Petroushskates. New York: Associated Music, 1980.
Sequoia. New York: Associated Music, 1981.
Silver Ladders. New York: Associated Music, 1986.

Galina Ivanovna Ustvolskaya

Composition No. 1, Dona Nobis Pacem, for piccolo, tuba, and piano. Score. 1971.
Duet, for violin and piano. Score. 1964.
Grand Duet, for cello and piano. Score. 1959.
Piano Sonata No. 1. Score. 1947.
Piano Sonata No. 4. Score. 1957.
Symphony No. 4, Prayer. Score. 1987.
Trio, for clarinet, violin, and piano. Score. 1949.
Concerto for Flute, Strings, and Percussion: Solo part and piano reduction. Theodore Presser Company, 1998.
Falling Angels. Theodore Presser Company, 1992.

Judith Weir

Blond Eckbert. Score. 1994.
(The) Consolations of Scholarship, for soprano and 9 players. Score. 1985.
Hans the Hedgehog, for speaker, 2 oboes, bassoon, and harpsichord. Score. 1978.
King Haralds Saga, for soprano. Score. 1979.
Missa del Cid, for chorus and speaker. Score. 1988.
(A) Night at the Chinese Opera. Score. 1987.
Scotch Minstrelsy, for tenor, or soprano, and piano. Score. 1982.
Serbian Cabaret. Score. 1984.
(The) Vanishing Bridegroom. Score, 1990.

Hildegard Westerkamp

Breathing Room, for 2-channel tape. Score. 1990.
Cool Drool, for spoken voice and 2-channel tape. Score. 1983.
Cricket Voice, for 2-channel tape. Score. 1987.
From the India Sound Journal, work in progress, for spoken voice and 2-channel tape. 1993.
Gently Penetrating beneath the Sounding Surfaces of Another Place, for 2-channel tape. Score. 1997.
Harbour Symphony, for over 100 boat horns in Vancouver Harbour. Score. 1986.
Kits Beach Soundwalk, for spoken voice and 2-channel tape. Score. 1989.
Nada: An Experience in Sound, a sound installation about listening at the Mati Ghar. Score. 1998.
Soundwalking. 1978–1979.
(A) Walk through the City, for 2-channel tape. Poem and reading by Norbert Ruebsaat.
(B) Score. 1981.
Zone of Silence Story, an acoustic environment for a group exhibition of the Zone of Silence Project. Score. 1985.

Mary Lou Williams

Black Christ of the Andes. 1963.

The Colonel's in Love with Nancy. 1954.

Froggy Bottom. 1936.

Five Piano Solos as Played and Written by Mary Lou Williams. London: Peter Maurice Music, 1941.

The Genius of the Jazz Giants: Piano Solos. Miami, FL: Columbia Pictures, 1980.

Little Joe from Chicago. 1938.

Mary Lou's Mass. New York: Cecilia Music, 1970.

Nite Life. Bryn Mawr, PA: Hildegard Publishing Company, 1992.

Six Original Boogie-Woogie Piano Solos [Special freight—Deuces wild—Twinklin'—Bob and Doodles—The duke and the count—Chili sauce]. New York: Robbins Music, 1944.

Trumpets No End (arrangement of Blue Skies). 1943.

What's Your Story, Morning Glory? 1938.

Zodiac Suite. 1945.

Ellen Taaffe Zwilich

Concerto for Piano and Orchestra. Theodore Presser, 1986.

Symphony No. 1 (Three Movements for Orchestra). Margun Music Inc., 1982.

Symphony No. 2 (Cello Symphony). Theodore Presser, 1985.

Symphony No. 4 ("The Gardens"). Theodore Presser, 1999.

Appendix 1
A Chronological List of Women Composers

800

Kassia   (ca. 810–before 867) Greece

1000

Hildegard von Bingen   (1098–1179)
   Germany

1100

Dia, Comtessa Beatriz(?) de   (fl. late 1100s)
   France
Herrad of Landsperg   (fl. 1167–1195) Alsace
Garsenda   (b. ca. 1170?) Provence
Maria de Ventadorn   (b. ca. 1165–?), Limousin
Tibors   (n.d.) Provence.
Azalais de Porcairagues   (n.d.) Montpellier

1200

Mechtild von Magdeburg   (1212–1282)
   Saxony
Hadewijch of Brabant   (fl. 1230–1260/1265)
   Saxony
Gertrude the Great   (1256–1302) Saxony
Dame Maroie de Dregnau de Lille   (fl. 1200's)
   France
Blanche of Castille   (?–1252) France

1300

Adelheid of Landeau   (?1300's) Germany
Saint Birgitta of Sweden   (ca. 1303–1373)

1400

Suster Bertken   (1426/1427–1514) Utrecht,
   Holland
Margaret of Austria   (1480–1530) Austria

1500

Anne Boleyn   (?1502/1507–1536) England
Casulana, Madalena   (ca. 1540–ca. 1590)
   Italy
Isabella de'Medici Orsini   (1542–1576) Italy
Baptista, Gracia   (fl. 1557) Spain
Orsini, Leonora   (?1560–1634) Italy
Ricci, Cesarina   (ca. 1573–   ), Italy
Aleotti, Vittoria/Aleotta Raphaela   (ca.
   1574?–1646?) Italy
Cesis, Sulpitia Lodovica   (1577–after 1619)
   Italy
Massarenghi, Paola   (1565–?) Italy
Caccini, Francesca   (1587–1645) Italy
Vizzana, Lucrezia Orsina   (1590–1662) Italy
Trissina Alba [Trissini]   (ca. 1590–after 1638)
   Italy
Assandra, Caterina   (early 1590s–1620) Italy
Caccini, Settimia   (1591–ca. 1660) Italy
Sessa, Claudia   (ca. 1597–1615) Italy

1600

Cozzolani, Chiara Margarita   (1602–ca. 1677)
   Italy
Campana, Francesca   (ca. 1605/1610–1665)
   Italy
Quinciani, Lucia   (fl. 1611) Italy
Sophie Elisabeth Duchess of Brunswick and
   Lüneburg   (1613–1676) Brunswick,
   Germany
Strozzi, Barbara   (ca. 1619–ca. 1664) Italy
Leonarda, Isabella   (1620–1704) Italy
Orsina, Lucrezia   (1623–?) Italy
Antonia Bembo   (ca. 1643–ca. 1715) Italy

Peruchona, Maria Xaveria (ca. 1652–after 1709) Italy

Nascinbeni, Maria Francesca (1658–?) Italy

Badalla, Rosa Giacinta (ca. 1660–ca. 1715) Italy

la Guerre, Elizabeth-Claude Jacquet de (1665–1729) France

Meda, Bianca Maria (ca. 1665–after 1700) Italy

Gratianini, Caterina Bendicta (fl. early 18th century) Italy

Raschenau, Marianne von (fl. 1690s–1703) Vienna

1700

Rossi, Camilla de (fl. 1708–12) Italy

Wilhelmina, Margravine of Bayreuth (1709–1785)

Eicher, Maria (1710–1784) America

Grimani, Maria Margherita (fl. 1713–1718) Italy

Agnesi, Maria Teresa (1720–1795) Italy

Anna Amalia, Princess of Prussia (1723–1787) Germany

Walpurgis, Maria Antonia (1724–1780) Germany

Gambarini, Elisabetta de (1731–1765) England

Anna Amalia, Duchesss of Saxe-Weimar (1739–1807) Germany

Bon, Anna (1739/40–after 1767) Italy

Hunter, Anne Home (1742–1821) England

Brillon de Jouy, Anne-Louise d'Hardancourt (1744–1824) France

Martines, Marianna (1744–1812) Austria

Lombardini Sirmen, Maddelena (1745–1818) Italy

Bayon Louis, Marie-Emmanuelle (1746–1825) France

Beausmenil, Henriette Adélaïde Villard de (1748–1813) France

Mara, Gertrude Schmeling (1749–1833) Germany

Barthélemon, Maria Young (1749–1799) England

Hagen, Elizabeth von (1750–1809/10) Holland

Pownall, Mary Ann Wrighten (1751–1796) England

Schröter, Corona (1751–1802) Austria

Reichardt, Juliane Benda (1752–1783) Germany

Krumpholtz, Anne-Marie Steckler (ca. 1755–1813) Germany

Lebrun, Franziska Danzi (1756–1791) Germany

Cavendish, Georgiana (1757–1806) England

Auernhammer, Josepha Barbara von (1758–1820) Austria

Abrams, Henriette (ca. 1758–ca. 1822) England

Paradis, Maria Theresia von (1759–1824) Austria

Coccia, Maria Rosa (1759–1833) Italy

Westenholz, Sophia Maria Fritscher (1759–1838) Germany

Cosway, Maria (1759/60–1838) England

Savage, Jane (ca. 1760–ca. 1830) England

Park, Maria Hester Reynolds (1760–1813) England

Valentine, Ann (1762–1842) England

Montgeroult, Hélène de Nervo (1764–1836) France

Miles, Jane Mary Guest (ca. 1765–ca. 1830) England

Candeille, Amélie-Julie (1767–1834) France

Danzi, Maria Margarethe Marchand (1768–1800) Germany

Cianchettini, Veronika Rosalia Dussek (1769–1833) Bohemia

Barthélemon, Cecilia Maria (1769/70–after 1840) England

Parke, Maria F. (1772/73–1822) England

Dussek, Sophia Giustina Corri (1775–ca. 1847) Scotland

Reichardt, Louise (1779–1826) Germany

Dülcken, Sophie Lebrun (1781–1813) Germany

Krumpholtz, Fanny Pittar (ca. 1785–after 1815) Germany

Arnim, Bettine Brentano von (1785–1859) Germany

Auenbrugger, Marianna von (d. 1786) Austria

Bigot, Marie Kiené (1786–1820) France

Szymanowska, Maria Agate Wolowska (1789–1831) Poland

Dussek, Olivia (1791–1847) England

Essex, Margaret (fl. 1795–1802) England

Liebmann, Hélène   (1796–1819) Germany

Zumsteeg, Emilie   (1796–1857) Germany

1800

Farrenc, Louise   (1804–1875) France

Hensel, Fanny Mendelssohn   (1805–1847) Germany

Malibran, Maria Felicia   (1808–1836) France

Kinkel, Johanna   (1810–1858) Germany

Blahetka, Leopoldine   (1811–1875) Austria

Lang, Josephine   (1815–1880) Germany

Schumann, Clara Wieck   (1819–1896) Germany

Stirling, Elizabeth   (1819–1895) England

Viardot, Pauline Garcia   (1821–1910) France

Hodges, Faustina   (1822–1895) United States

Mayer, Emilie   (1821–1883) Germany

Sloman, Jane   (1824–?) United States

Pittman, Evelyn La Rue   (1827–1903) United States

Grandval, Maria   (1830–1907) France

Wieck, Marie   (1832–1916) Germany

Lina Ramann   (1833–1912) Germany

Peterson, Clara Gottschalk   (1837–?) United States

Bardazewska-Baronowska, Thekla   (1838–1861) Poland

Lili'uokalani, Queen   (1838–1917) Hawai'i

Bronsart, Ingeborg von   (1840–1913) Germany

Héritee-Viardot, Louise   (1841–1917) France

Rogers, Clara Kathleen   (1844–1931) England

Jaëll, Marie Trautmann   (1846–1925) France

Menter, Sophie   (1846–1918) Germany

Holmès, Augusta   (1847–1903) France

Backer-Grøndahl, Agathe   (1847–1907) Norway

Le Beau, Luise Adolpha   (1850–1927) Germany

Carreño, Maria Teresa   (1853–1917) Venezuela

Rivé-King, Julie   (1855–1937) United States

Hoperkirk, Helen   (1856–1945) United States

Chaminade, Cécile   (1857–1944) France

Smyth, Dame Ethel Mary   (1858–1944) England

Bonis, Mel   (1858–1937) France

Wurm, Mary (Marie)   (1860–1938) Germany

Jacobs-Bond, Carrie   (1862–1946) United States

Hood, Helen   (1863–1949) United States

Gilchrist, Anne   (1863–1954) England

Freer, Eleanor Everest   (1864–1942) United States

Beach, Amy Marcy Cheney   (1867–1944) United States

Lang, Margaret Ruthven   (1867–1972) United States

Beaton, Isabella   (1870–1929) United States

Moore, Mary Carr   (1873–1957) United States

Daniels, Mabel Wheeler   (1878–1971) United States

Mahler, Alma Schindler (Werfel)   (1879–1964) Austria

Landowska, Wanda   (1879–1959) Poland

Wieniawska, Irene Regine (Poldowski)   (1880–1932) Belgium

Dillon, Fannie Charles   (1881–1947) United States

Branscombe, Gena   (1881–1977) United States

Howe, Mary   (1882–1964) United States

Shepherd, Adaline   (1883–1950) United States

Pejačević, Dora   (1885–1923) Hungary

Leginska, Ethel   (1886–1970) England

Clarke, Rebecca   (1886–1979) England

Niebergall, Julia   (1886–1968) United States

Bauer, Marion   (1887–1955) United States

Price, Florence   (1887–1953) United States

Strickland, Lily   (1887–1958) United States

Boulanger, Nadia Juliette   (1887–1979) France

Beyer, Johanna   (1888–1944) Germany

Aufderheide, May   (1888–1972) United States

Fromm-Michaels, Ilse   (1888–1986) Germany

Bordewijk-Roepman, Johanna   (1892–1971) Holland

Tailleferre, Germaine   (1892–1983) France

Boulanger, Lili   (1893–1918) France

Prieto, Maria Teresa   (1895–1982) Mexico

Vellère, Lucie   (1896–1966) France
Bach, Maria   (1896–1978) Germany
Gyring, Elizabeth   (1896–1970) Austria
Sutherland, Margaret   (1897–1984)
  Australia
Zubeldia, Emiliana   (1898–1987) Mexico
Eckhardt-Gramatté, Sophie   (1899–1974)
  Canada
Manziarly, Marcelle de   (1899–1989) France

1900

Warren, Elinor Remick   (1900–1991) United
  States
Backes, Lotte   (1901–1989) Germany
Daneau, Suzanne   (1901–1971) Belgium
Seeger, Ruth Crawford   (1901–1953) United
  States
Ranier, Priaulx   (1903–1986) South Africa
Arrieu, Claude   (1903–1990) France
Britain, Radie   (1903–1994) United States
Cole, Ulric   (1905–1992) United States
Moore, Undine Smith   (1905–1989) United
  States
Gideon, Miriam   (1906–1996) United States
Talma, Louise   (1906–1996) United States
Lutyens, Elisabeth   (1906–1983) England
Williams, Grace   (1906–1977) Wales
Maconchy, Elizabeth   (1907–1994) England
Desportes, Yvonne   (1907–1993) France
Coulthard, Jean   (1908–2000) Canada
Makarova, Nina   (1908–1976) USSR
Samter, Alice   (1908–   ) Germany
Hsu, Wen-Ying   (1908–   ) United States
Shlonsky, Verdina   (1908–1990) Israel
Bacewicz, Grazyna   (1909–1969) Poland
Maric, Ljubica   (1909–   ) Yugoslavia
Barraine, Elsa   (1910–   ) Canada
Williams, Mary Lou   (1910–1981) United
  States
Behrend, Jeanne   (1911–1989) United States
Kanai, Kikuko   (1911–1986) Japan
Smith, Julia   (1911–1988) United States
Tate, Phyllis   (1911–1981) England
Pentland, Barbara   (1912–2000) Canada
Glanville-Hicks, Peggy   (1912–1990)
  Australia
Archer, Violet   (1913–2000) Canada
Fine, Vivian   (1913–2000) United States
Holland, Dulcie   (1913–   ) Australia
Hyde, Miriam   (1913–   ) Australia

Simons, Netty   (1913–   ) United States
Bonds, Margaret   (1913–1972) United States
Kessler, Minuetta   (1914–   ) United States
di Vito-Delvaux, Berthe   (1915–   ) Belgium
Ballou, Esther   (1915–1973) United States
Nunlist, Juli   (1916–   ) United States
Wylie, Ruth Shaw   (1916–1989) United
  States
Sonstevold, Maj   (1917–   ) Norway
Woll, Ema   (1917–   ) Germany
Freed, Dorothy   (1919–2000) New Zealand
Ustvolskaya, Galina   (1919–   ) USSR
Clostre, Adrienne   (1921–   ) France
Demessieux, Jeanne   (1921–1968) France
Gilbert, Pia   (1921–   ) United States
Gartenlaub, Odette   (1922–   ) France
Henderson, Ruth Watson   (1923–   ) United
  States
Ivey, Jean Eichelberger   (1923–   ) United
  States
Newlin, Dika   (1923–   ) United States
Gipps, Ruth   (1924–2000) England
Loriod, Yvonne   (1924–   ) France
Perry, Julia Amanda   (1924–1979) United
  States
Presti, Ida   (1924–1967) France
Schonthal, Ruth   (1924–   ) Germany
Singer, Jeanne   (1924–   ) United States
Szöny, Erzsébet   (1924–   ) Hungary
Tucker, Tui St. George   (1924–   ) United
  States
Berberian, Cathy   (1925–1983) United States
Boroff, Edith   (1925–   ) United States
Oram, Daphne   (1925–2003) England
Parker, Alice   (1925–   ) United States
Uyttenhove, Yolande   (1925–2000) Belgium
Osawa, Kazuko   (1926–   ) Japan
Zechlin, Ruth   (1926–   ) Germany
Jolas, Betsy   (1926–   ) France
Richter, Marga   (1926–   ) United States
Polin, Claire   (1926–1997) United States
Diemer, Emma Lou   (1927–   ) United States
Barron, Bebe   (1927–   ) United States
Van Appledorn, Mary Jeanne   (1927–   )
  United States
Garwood, Margaret   (1927–   ) United States
Feigen, Sarah   (1928–   ) Israel
Grigsby, Beverly   (1928–   ) United States
Musgrave, Thea   (1928–   ) Scotland
Mamlok, Ursula   (1928–   ) Germany

King, Betty Jackson (1928–) United States

Anderson Ruth (1928–) United States

McLin, Lena Johnson (1929–) United States

Akiyoshi, Toshiko (1929–) Japan

Dvorkin, Judith (1930–) United States

Fontyn, Jacqueline (1930–) Belgium

Van de Vate, Nancy (1930–) United States

Alotin, Yardena (1930–) Israel

Loman, Ruth (1930–) United States

Chance, Nancy Laird (1931–) United States

Gubaidulina, Sofia (1931–) Russia

Marbe, Myriam (1931–1998) Romania

Oliveros, Pauline (1932–) United States

Oyens, Tera de Marez (1932–1997) Netherlands

Barkin, Elaine (1932–) United States

Bearer, Elaine (1932–) United States

Beath, Betty (1932–) Australia

Glickman, Sylvia (1932–) United States

Schuyler, Philippa Duke (1932–1967) United States

Moorman, Charlotte (1933–1991) United States

Urreta, Alicia (1933–1987) Mexico

Beecroft, Norma (1934–) Canada

Dlugoszewski, Lucia (1934–2000) United States

Mageau, Mary (1934–) Australia

Sanz, Rocia (1934–) Costa Rica

Procaccini, Teresa (1934–) Italy

Terzian, Alicia (1934–) Argentina

Hara, Kazuko (1935–) Japan

Zivkovic, Mirjana (1935–) Yugoslavia

Capers, Valerie (1935–) United States

Ahrens, Sieglind (1936–) Germany

Hoover, Katherine (1937–) United States

Souther, Ann (1937–) Canada

Vehar, Persis (1937–) United States

Carr-Boyd, Ann (1938–) Australia

St. Marcoux, Micheline Coulombe (1938–1985) Canada

Shiomi, Mieko [Chicko] (1938–) Japan

Bley, Carla (1938–) United States

Rogers, Patsy (1938–) United States

Scheidel-Austin, Elizabeth (1938–) United States

Tower, Joan (1938–) United States

Armer, Elinor (1939–) United States

Fowler, Jennifer (1939–) England

Kolb, Barbara (1939–) United States

Wilkins, Margaret Lucy (1939–) England

Zwilich, Ellen Taaffe (1939–) United States

Carlos, Wendy (1939–) United States

Bailey, Mable (1939–) United States

Lockwood, Annea (1939–) New Zealand

Moore, Dorothy Rudd (1940–) United States

Bailey, Judith (1941–) England

Loudova, Ivana (1941–) Czechoslovakia

Vercoe, Elizabeth (1941–) United States

Whitehead, Gillian (1941–) New Zealand

Monk, Meredith (1942–) United States

Yamashita, Tyoko (1942–) Japan

Thome, Diane (1942–) United States

McLean, Priscilla (1942–) United States

Hori, Etsuko (1943–) Japan

León, Tania (1943–) Cuba

Ptaszynska, Marta (1943–) Poland

Smiley, Pril (1943–) United States

Bauld, Alison (1944–) Australia

Hulford, Denise (1944–) New Zealand

Konishi, Nagako (1945–) Japan

Spiegel, Laurie (1945–) United States

Bond, Victoria (1945–) United States

Sikora, Elzbieta (1945–) United States

Pagh-Paan, Younghi (1945–) Korea

Wallach, Joelle (1945–) United States

Zaimont, Judith Lang (1945–) United States

Benary, Barbara (1946–) United States

Boyd, Anne Elizabeth (1946–) Australia

Buchanan, Dorothy (1946–) New Zealand

Ciani, Suzanne (1946–) United States

Giteck, Janice (1946–) United States

Semegen, Daria (1946–) Germany

O'Leary, Jane Strong (1946–) United States

Fleischer, Tsippi (1946–) Israel

Shrude, Marilyn (1946–) United States

Silver, Sheila (1946–) United States

Westerkamp, Hildegard (1946–) Canada

LeFanu, Nicola (1947–) England

Hamer, Janice (1947–) United States

Ali-zade, Frangiz (1947–) Azerbaijan

Anderson, Laurie (1947–) United States

La Barbara, Joan (1947–) United States

Alexandra, Liana   (1947–   ) Romania
Walker, Gwyneth   (1947) United States
Tann, Hilary   (1947–   ) Wales
Burrell, Diana   (1948–   ) England
Kubisch, Christina   (1948–   ) Germany
Weaver, Carol Ann   (1948–   ) Canada
Brockman, Jane   (1949–   ) United States
Ran, Shulamit   (1949–   ) Israel
Louie, Alexina   (1949–   ) Canada
Shatin, Judith   (1949–   ) United States
Anderson, Beth   (1950–   ) United States
Firsova, Elena   (1950–   ) United States
Larsen, Libby   (1950–   ) United States
Swados, Elizabeth   (1950–   ) United States
Telfer, Nancy   (1950–   ) Canada
Arho, Anneli   (1951–   ) Finland
Phillips, Liz [Elizabeth]   (1951–   ) United
    States
Smith, LaDonna   (1951–   ) United States
Eiriksdottir, Karolina   (1951–   ) Iceland
Rodriguez, Marcela   (1951–   ) Mexico
Vierk, Lois   (1951–   ) United States
Bennett, Barbara   (1952–   ) United States
Marcus, Bunita   (1952–   ) United States
Saariaho, Kaija   (1952–   ) Finland
Hölszky, Adriana   (1953–   ) Romania
Dinescu, Violeta   (1953–   ) Romania
Farrell, Eibhlis   (1953–   ) Ireland

Le Baron, Anne   (1953–   ) United States
Chen Yi,   (1953–   ) China
Brusa, Elisabetta   (1954–   ) Italy
Ore, Cecilie   (1954–   ) Norway
Pizer, Elizabeth   (1954–   ) United States
Weir, Judith   (1954–   ) England
Galás, Diamanda   (1955–   ) United States
de Castro Robinson, Eve   (1956–   ) New
    Zealand
Dusman, Linda   (1956–   ) United States
Szeghyova, Iris   (1956–   ) Czechoslovakia
de Kenessey, Stefania   (1956–   ) Hungary
Szeto, Caroline   (1956–   ) Australia
Thomas, Karen P.   (1957–   ) United States
Bouchard, Linda   (1957–   ) Canada
Wagner, Melinda   (1957–   ) United States
Thomas, Augusta Read   (1958–   ) United
    States
Astuni, Silvia   (1959–   ) Argentina
Cox, Cindy   (1961–   ) United States
Chan, Heva   (1962–   ) Austria
Robindoré, Brigitte   (1962–   ) France
Higdon, Jennifer   (1964–   ) United States
Saunders, Rebecca   (1967–   ) England
Neuwirth, Olga   (1968–   ) Austria
Alsted, Birgitte   (1971–   ) Denmark
Warshaw, Dalit   (1974–   ) Israel
Lund, Gudruyn   (1976–   ) Denmark

Appendix 2
A Geographical List of Women Composers

ARGENTINA

Astuni, Silvia   (1959–   ) Argentina
Terzian, Alicia   (1934–   ) Argentina

AUSTRALIA

Bauld, Alison (1944–   ) Australia
Beath, Betty   (1932–   ) Australia
Boyd, Anne Elizabeth   (1946–   ) Australia
Carr-Boyd, Ann   (1938–   ) Australia
Glanville-Hicks, Peggy   (1912–1990) Australia
Holland, Dulcie   (1913–   ) Australia
Hyde, Miriam   (1913–   ) Australia
Mageau, Mary   (1934–   ) Australia
Sutherland, Margaret   (1897–1984) Australia
Szeto, Caroline   (1956–   ) Australia

AUSTRIA

Auernhammer, Josepha Barbara von
   (1758–1820) Austria
Auenbrugger, Marianna von   (d. 1786)
   Austria
Blahetka, Leopoldine   (1811–1875) Austria
Chan, Heva   (1962–   ) Austria
Gyring, Elizabeth   (1896–1970) Austria
Mahler, Alma Schindler (Werfel)
   (1879–1964) Austria
Margaret of Austria   (1480–1530) Austria
Martines, Marianna   (1744–1812) Austria
Neuwirth, Olga   (1968–   ) Austria
Paradis, Maria Theresia von   (1759–1824)
   Austria
Raschenau, Marianne von   (flourished
   1690s–1703) Vienna
Schröter, Corona   (1751–1802) Austria

AZERBAIJAN

Ali-zade, Frangiz   (1947–   ) Azerbaijan

BELGIUM

Daneau, Suzanne   (1901–1971) Belgium
di Vito-Delvaux, Berthe   (1915–   )
   Belgium
Fontyn, Jacqueline   (1930–   ) Belgium
Uyttenhove, Yolande   (1925–2000)
   Belgium
Wieniawska, Irene Regine (Poldowski)
   (1880–1932) Belgium

BOHEMIA

Cianchettini, Veronika Rosalia Dussek
   (1769–1833)

CANADA

Archer, Violet   (1913–2000)
Barraine, Elsa   (1910–   ) Canada
Beecroft, Norma   (1934–   ) Canada
Bouchard, Linda   (1957–   ) Canada
Coulthard, Jean   (1908–2000) Canada
Eckhardt-Gramatté, Sophie   (1899–1974)
   Canada
Louie, Alexina   (1949–   ) Canada
Pentland, Barbara   (1912–2000) Canada
Souther, Ann   (1937–   ) Canada
St. Marcoux, Micheline Coulombe
   (1938–1985) Canada
Telfer, Nancy   (1950–   ) Canada
Weaver, Carol Ann   (1948–   ) Canada
Westerkamp, Hildegard   (1946–   )
   Canada

CHINA

Chen Yi   (1953–   ) China

COSTA RICA

Sanz, Rocia   (1934–   ) Costa Rica

CUBA

León, Tania   (1943–   ) Cuba

CZECHOSLOVAKIA

Loudova, Ivana   (1941–   ) Czechoslovakia

DENMARK

Alsted, Birgitte   (1971–   ) Denmark
Lund, Gudruyn   (1976–   ) Denmark

ENGLAND, SCOTLAND, IRELAND, WALES

Abrams, Henriette   (ca. 1758–ca. 1822)
   England
Bailey, Judith   (1941–   )
Barthélemon, Cecilia Maria (1769/70–after
   1840) England
Barthélemon, Maria Young   (1749–1799)
   England
Boleyn, Anne   (?1502/1507–1536) England
Burrell, Diana   (1948–   ) UK
Cavendish, Georgiana   (1757–1806)
   England
Clarke, Rebecca   (1886–1979) UK
Cosway, Maria   (1759/60–1838) England
Dussek, Olivia   (1791–1847) England
Dussek, Sophia Giustina Corri   (1775–ca.
   1847) Scotland
Essex, Margaret   (fl. 1795–1802) England
Farrell, Eibhlis   (1953–   ) Ireland
Fowler, Jennifer   (1939–   ) UK
Gambarini, Elisabetta de   (1731–1765)
   England
Gilchrist, Anne   (1863–1954) England
Gipps, Ruth   (1924–2000) UK
Hunter, Anne Home   (1742–1821) England
LeFanu, Nicola   (1947–   ) England
Leginska, Ethel   (1886–1970) England
Lutyens, Elisabeth   (1906–1983) England
Maconchy, Elizabeth   (1907–1994) England
Miles, Jane Mary Guest   (ca. 1765–ca. 1830)
   England
Musgrave, Thea   (1928–   ) Scotland
Oram, Daphne   (1925–2003) England

Park, Maria Hester Reynolds   (1760–1813)
   England
Parke, Maria F.   (1772/73–1822) England
Pownall, Mary Ann Wrighten   (1751–1796)
   England
Rogers, Clara Kathleen   (1844–1931)
   England
Savage, Jane   (c. 1760–c. 1830) England
Saunders, Rebecca   (1967–   ) England
Smyth, Dame Ethel   (1858–1944) England
Stirling, Elizabeth   (1819–1895) England
Tann, Hilary   (1947–   ) Wales
Tate, Phyllis   (1911–1981) England
Valentine, Ann   (1762–1842) England
Weir, Judith   (1954–   ) England
Wilkins, Margaret Lucy   (1939–   ) England
Williams, Grace   (1906–1977) Wales

FINLAND

Arho, Anneli   (1951–   ) Finland
Saariaho, Kaija   (1952–   ) Finland

FRANCE

Arrieu, Claude   (1903–1990) France
Bayon Louis, Marie-Emmanuelle
   (1746–1825) France
Beausmenil, Henriette Adélaïde Villard de
   (1748–1813) France
Bigot, Marie Kiené   (1786–1820) France
Bonis, Mel   (1858–1937)
Blanche of Castille   (?–1252) France
Boulanger, Lili   (1893–1918) France
Boulanger, Nadia Juliette   (1887–1979)
   France
Brillon de Jouy, Anne-Louise d'Hardancourt
   (1744–1824) France
Candeille, Amélie-Julie   (1767–1834) France
Chaminade, Cécile   (1857–1944) France
Clostre, Adrienne   (1921–   ) France
Dame Maroie de Dregnua de Lille   (fl. 1200's)
   France
Demessieux, Jeanne   (1921–1968) France
Desportes, Yvonne   (1907–1993) France
Dia, Comtessa Beatriz de   (fl. late 1100's)
   France
Farrenc, Louise   (1804–1875) France
Garsenda   (ca. 1170–?)
Gartenlaub, Odette   (1922–   ) France
Grandval, Maria   (1830–1907) France
Héritte-Viardot, Louise   (1841–1917) France

Holmès, Augusta   (1847–1903)

Jaëll, Marie Trautmann   (1846–1925) France

Jolas, Betsy   (1926–   ) France

la Guerre, Elizabeth-Claude Jacquet de   (1665–1729) France

Loriod, Yvonne   (1924–   ) France

Malibran, Maria Felicia   (1808–1836) France

Manziarly, Marcelle de   (1899–1989) France

Montgeroult, Hélène de Nervo de   (1764–1836) France

Presti, Ida   (1924–1967) France

Porcairagues, 'Azalais de   (n.d.) Montpellier

Robindoré, Brigitte   (1962–   ) France

Tailleferre, Germaine   (1892–1983)

Tibors   (n.d.) Provence

Vellère, Lucie   (1896–1966) France

Ventadorn, Maria de   (b. ca. 1165–?)

Viardot, Pauline Garcia   (1821–1910) France

GERMANY

Adelheid von Landeau   (?1300's)

Ahrens, Sieglind   (1936–   ) Germany

Anna Amalia, Duchesss of Saxe-Weimar   (1739–1807) Germany

Anna Amalia, Princess of Prussia   (1723–1787) Germany

Arnim, Bettine Brentano von   (1785–1859) Germany

Bach, Maria   (1896–1978) Germany

Backes, Lotte   (1901–1989) Germany

Beyer, Johanna   (1888–1944)

Bronsart, Ingeborg von   (1840–1913) Germany

Danzi, Maria Margarethe Marchand   (1768–1800) Germany

Dulcken, Sophie Lebrun   (1781–1863) Germany

Fromm-Michaels, Ilse   (1888–1986) Germany

Gertrude the Great   (1256–1302) Saxony

Hadewijch of Brabant   (fl. 1230–1260/65) Saxony

Hensel, Fanny Mendelssohn   (1805–1847) Germany

Herrad of Landsperg   (fl. 1167–1195) Alsace

Hildegard von Bingen   (1098–1179) Germany

Kinkel, Johanna   (1810–1858) Germany

Krumpholtz, Anne-Marie Steckler   (ca. 1755–1813) Germany

Kubisch, Christina   (1948–   )

Lang, Josephine   (1815–1880) Germany

Le Beau, Luise Adolpha   (1850–1927) Germany

Lebrun, Franziska Danzi   (1756–1791) Germany

Liebmann, Hélène   (1796–1819) Germany

Mamlok, Ursula   (1928–   ) Germany

Mara, Gertrude Schmeling   (1749–1833) Germany

Mayer, Emilie   (1821–1883) Germany

Mechtild von Magdeburg   (1212–1282) Saxony

Menter, Sophie   (1846–1918) Germany

Lina Ramann   (1833–1912)

Reichardt, Juliane Benda   (1752–1783) Germany

Reichardt, Louise   (1779–1826) Germany

Samter, Alice   (1908–   ) Germany

Schonthal, Ruth   (1924–   ) Germany

Schumann, Clara Wieck   (1819–1896) Germany

Sophie Elisabeth Duchess of Brunswick and   Luneburg (1613–1676)

Semegen, Daria   (1946–   )

Walpurgis, Maria Antonia   (1724–1780) Germany

Westenholz, Sophia Maria Fritscher   (1759–1838) Germany

Wieck, Marie   (1832–1916) Germany

Wilhelmina, Margravine of Bayreuth   (1709–1785)

Woll, Ema   (1917–   ) Germany

Wurm, Mary (Marie)   (1860–1938) Germany

Zechlin, Ruth   (1926–   ) Germany

Zumsteeg, Emilie   (1796–1857) Germany

GREECE

Kassia   (ca. 810–before 867) Greece

HUNGARY

de Kenessey, Stefania   (1956–   ) Hungary

Pejačević, Dora   (1885–1923) Hungary

Szöny, Erzsébet   (1924–   ) Hungary

ICELAND

Eiriksdottir, Karolina   (1951–   ) Iceland

ISRAEL

Alotin, Yardena   (1930–   ) Israel

Feigen, Sarah   (1928–   ) Israel
Fleischer, Tsippi   (1946–   ) Israel
Ran, Shulamit   (1949–   ) Israel
Shlonsky, Verdina   (1908–1990) Israel
Warshaw, Dalit   (1974–   ) Israel

ITALY

Agnesi, Maria Teresa   (1720–1795) Italy
Aleotti, Vittoria/Aleotta, Raffaela   (ca.
   1574?–1646?) Italy
Assandra, Caterina   (early 1590's–1620) Italy
Badalla, Rosa Giacinta   (c. 1660–ca. 1715)
   Italy
Bembo, Antonia   (ca. 1643–ca. 1715)
Bon, Anna   (1739/40–after 1767) Italy
Brusa, Elisabetta   (1954–   ) Italy
Caccini, Francesca   (1587–1645) Italy
Caccini, Settimia   (1591–ca. 1660) Italy
Campana, Francesca   (ca. 1605/1610–1665)
   Italy
Casulana, Maddalena   (ca. 1540–ca. 1590)
   Italy
Cesis, Sulpitia Lodovica   (1577–after 1619)
   Italy
Coccia, Maria Rosa   (1759–1833) Italy
Cozzolani, Chiara Margarita   (1602–ca. 1677)
   Italy
Gratianini, Caterina Benedicta   (fl. early 18th
   century) Italy
Grimani, Maria Margherita   (fl. 1713–18)
   Italy
Leonarda, Isabella   (1620–1704) Italy
Lombardini Sirmen, Maddalena
   (1745–1818) Italy
Massarenghi, Paola   (1565–?) Italy
Meda, Bianca Maria   (ca. 1665–after 1700)
   Italy
Nascinbeni, Maria Francesca   (1658–?) Italy
Orsina, Lucrezia   (1623–?) Italy
Orsini, Isabella de'Medici   (1542–1576) Italy
Orsini, Leonora de'Medici Orsini
   (?1560–1634) Italy
Peruchona, Maria Xaveria   (ca. 1652–after
   1709) Italy
Procaccini, Teresa   (1934–   ) Italy
Quinciani, Lucia   (fl. 1611) Italy
Ricci, Cesarina (ca. 1573)
Rossi, Camilla de   (fl. 1708–12) Italy
Sessa, Claudia   (ca. 1597–1615) Italy
Strozzi, Barbara   (ca. 1619–ca. 1664) Italy

Trissina Alba [Trissini]   (ca. 1590–after 1638)
   Italy
Vizzana, Lucrezia Orsina   (1590–1662) Italy

JAPAN

Akiyoshi, Toshiko   (1929–   ) Japan
Hara, Kazuko   (1935–   ) Japan
Kanai, Kikuko   (1911–1986) Japan
Shiomi, Mieko [Chicko]   (1938–   )
Konishi, Nagako   (1945–   ) Japan
Osawa, Kazuko   (1926–   ) Japan
Shiomi, Mieko [Chieko]   (1938–   ) Japan
Yamashita, Tyoko   (1942–   ) Japan

KOREA

Pagh-Paan, Younghi   (1945–   ) Korea

MEXICO

Prieto, Maria Teresa   (1895–1982) Mexico
Rodriguez, Marcela   (1951–   ) Mexico
Urreta, Alicia   (1935–1987) Mexico
Zubeldia, Emiliana   (1898–1987) Mexico

NETHERLANDS

Bertken, Suster   (1426/27–1514) Utrecht
Bordewijk-Roepman, Johanna   (1892–1971)
   Holland
Hagen, Elizabeth von   (1750–1809/10)
   Holland
Oyens, Tera de Marez   (1932–1997)
   Netherlands

NEW ZEALAND

Buchanan, Dorothy   (1946–   ) New Zealand
Castro Robinson, Eve de   (1956–   ) New
   Zealand
Freed, Dorothy   (1919–2000) New Zealand
Hulford, Denise   (1944–   ) New Zealand
Lockwood, Annea   (1939–   ) New Zealand
Whitehead, Gillian   (1941–   ) New Zealand

NORWAY

Backer-Grondahl, Agathe   (1847–1907) Norway
Ore, Cecilie   (1954–   )
Sonstevold, Maj   (1917–   ) Norway

POLAND

Bacewicz, Grazyna   (1909–1969) Poland
Bardazewska-Baronowska, Thekla
   (1838–1861) Poland

Landowska, Wanda   (1879–1959) Poland
Ptaszynska, Marta   (1943–   ) Poland
Szymanowska, Maria Agate Wolowska
   (1789–1831) Poland

ROMANIA

Alexandra, Liana   (1947–   ) Rumania
Dinescu, Violeta   (1953–   ) Rumania
Hölszky, Adriana   (1953–   ) Rumania
Marbe, Myriam   (1931–1998) Rumania

RUSSIA (USSR)

Gubaidulina, Sofia   (1931–   ) Russia
Makarova, Nina   (1908–1976) USSR
Ustvolskaya, Galina   (1919–   ) USSR

SOUTH AFRICA

Ranier, Priaulx   (1903–1986) South Africa

SPAIN

Baptista, Gracia   (fl. 1557) Spain

SWEDEN

Saint Birgitta of Sweden   (ca. 1303–1373)

UNITED STATES/AMERICA

Anderson, Beth   (1950–   ) USA
Anderson, Laurie   (1947–   ) USA
Anderson Ruth   (1928–   ) USA
Armer, Elinor   (1939–   ) USA
Aufderheide, May   (1888–1972) USA
Bailey, Mable   (1939–   ) USA
Ballou, Esther   (1915–1973) USA
Barkin, Elaine   (1932–   ) USA
Barron, Bebe   (1927–   ) USA
Beach, Amy Marcy Cheney   (1867–1944)
   USA
Bearer, Elaine   (1932–   ) USA
Beaton, Isabella   (1870–1929) USA
Behrend, Jeanne   (1911–1989) USA
Benary, Barbara   (1946–   ) USA
Bennett, Barbara   (1952–   ) USA
Berberian, Cathy   (1925–1983) USA
Bley, Carla   (1938–   ) USA
Bond, Victoria   (1945–   ) USA
Bonds, Margaret   (1913–1972) USA
Boroff, Edith   (1925–   ) USA
Branscombe, Gena   (1881–1977) USA
Britain, Radie   (1903–1994) USA

Brockman, Jane   (1949–   ) USA
Capers, Valerie   (1935–   ) USA
Carlos, Wendy   (1939–   ) USA
Chance, Nancy Laird   (1931–   ) USA
Ciani, Suzanne   (1946–   ) USA
Cole, Ulric   (1905–1992) USA
Cox, Cindy   (1961–   ) USA
Daniels, Mabel Wheeler   (1878–1971) USA
Diemer, Emma Lou   (1927–   ) USA
Dillon, Fannie Charles   (1881–1947) USA
Dlugoszewski, Lucia   (1934–2000) USA
Dusman, Linda   (1956–   ) USA
Dvorkin, Judith   (1930–   ) USA
Eicher, Maria   (1710–1784) (America)
Fine, Vivian   (1913–2000) USA
Firsova, Elena   (1950–   ) USA
Freer, Eleanor Everest   (1864–1942) USA
Galás, Diamanda   (1955–   ) USA
Garwood, Margaret   (1927–   ) USA
Gideon, Miriam   (1906–1996) USA
Gilbert, Pia   (1921–   ) USA
Giteck, Janice   (1946–   ) USA
Glickman, Sylvia   (1932–   ) USA
Grigsby, Beverly   (1928–   ) USA
Hamer, Janice   (1947–   ) USA
Henderson, Ruth Watson   (1923–   ) USA
Higdon, Jennifer   (1964–   ) USA
Hodges, Faustina   (1822–1895) USA
Hood, Helen   (1863–1949) USA
Hoover, Katherine   (1937–   ) USA
Hopekirk, Helen   (1856–1945) USA
Howe, Mary   (1882–1964) USA
Hsu, Wen-Ying   (1908–   ) USA
Ivey, Jean Eichelberger   (1923–   ) USA
Jacobs-Bond, Carrie   (1862–1946) USA
Kessler, Minuetta   (1914–   ) USA
King, Betty Jackson   (1928–   ) USA
Kolb, Barbara   (1939–   ) USA
La Barbara, Joan   (1947–   ) USA
Lang, Margaret Ruthven   (1867–1972) USA
Larsen, Libby   (1950–   ) USA
Le Baron, Anne   (1953–   ) USA
Lili'uokalani, Queen   (1838–1917) Hawai'i
Loman, Ruth   (1930–   ) USA
Marcus, Bunita   (1952–   ) USA
McLean, Priscilla   (1942–   ) USA
McLin, Lena Johnson (1929–   ) USA
Monk, Meredith   (1942–   ) USA
Moore, Dorothy Rudd   (1940–   ) USA

Moore, Mary Carr   (1873–1957)
Moore, Undine Smith   (1905–1989) USA
Moorman, Charlotte   (1933–1991) USA
Niebergall, Julia   (1886–1968) USA
Newlin, Dika   (1923–   ) USA
Nunlist, Juli   (1916–   ) USA
O'Leary, Jane Strong   (1946–   ) USA
Oliveros, Pauline   (1932–   ) USA
Parker, Alice   (1925–   ) USA
Perry, Julia Amanda   (1924–1979) USA
Peterson, Clara Gottschalk   (1837–?) USA
Phillips, Liz [Elizabeth](1951–   )
Pittman, Evelyn La Rue   (?1827–1903) USA
Pizer, Elizabeth   (1954–   ) USA
Polin, Claire   (1926–1997) USA
Price, Florence   (1887–1953) USA
Richter, Marga   (1926–   ) USA
Rivé-King, Julie   (1855–1937) USA
Rogers, Patsy   (1938–   ) USA
Samegen, Daria   (1946–   ) USA
Scheidel-Austin, Elizabeth   (1938–   ) USA
Schuyler, Philippa Duke   (1932–1967) USA
Seeger, Ruth Crawford   (1901–1953) USA
Shatin, Judith   (1949–   ) USA
Shepherd, Adaline   (1883–1950) USA
Shrude, Marilyn   (1946–   ) USA
Sikora, Elzbieta   (1945–   ) USA
Silver, Sheila   (1946–   ) USA
Simons, Netty   (1913–   ) USA
Singer, Jeanne   (1924–   ) USA
Sloman, Jane   (1824–?) USA
Smiley, Pril   (1943–   ) USA
Smith, Julia   (1911–1988) USA
Smith, LaDonna   (1951–   ) USA

Spiegel, Laurie   (1945–   ) USA
Strickland, Lily   (1887–1958) USA
Swados, Elizabeth   (1950–   ) USA
Talma, Louise   (1906–1996) USA
Thomas, Augusta Read   (1958–   ) USA
Thomas, Karen P.   (1957–   ) USA
Thome, Diane   (1942–   ) USA
Tower, Joan   (1938–   ) USA
Tucker, Tui St. George   (1924–   ) USA
Van Appledorn, Mary Jeanne   (1927–   )
   USA
Van de Vate, Nancy   (1930–   ) USA
Vehar, Persis   (1937–   ) USA
Vercoe, Elizabeth   (1941–   ) USA
Vierk, Lois   (1951–   ) USA
Wagner, Melinda   (1957–   )
Walker, Gwyneth   (1947–   )
Wallach, Joelle   (1945–   ) USA
Warren, Elinor Remick   (1900–1991)
   USA
Williams, Mary Lou   (1910–1981) USA
Wylie, Ruth Shaw   (1916–1989) USA
Zaimont, Judith Lang   (1945–   ) USA
Zwilich, Ellen Taaffe   (1939–   ) USA

VENEZUELA

Carreño, Maria Teresa   (1853–1917)
   Venezuela

YUGOSLAVIA

Maric, Ljubica   (1909–   ) Yugoslavia
Zivkovic, Mirjana   (1935–   ) Yugoslovia

Appendix 3
Suggested Syllabus for a Fifteen-Week Semester with Three Class Hours per Week

This "great women/great works" outline presents important composers in chronological order and uses this book and included discographies to illustrate the development of musical styles and genres for an introductory class.

Week 1 Introduction (Chapter 1) and Early Composers (Chapter 2)
  Background: introduction to Women Composers.
  Accustoming audiences to listening to "new," unfamiliar music today.
  General information to follow through the semester:
      Life, education, and support
      Styles and genres of the music
      Performance opportunities and venues
  The Middle Ages: Kassia (chant), Dia (trobairitz), others.

Week 2 (Chapter 2, cont.)
  Hildegard: the antiphons; the *Ordo Virtutum*; authoring words and music.

Week 3
  The Renaissance: Italian nuns Aleotti/Aleotta, Vizzana, Orsini, Assandra,
      Orsini, Cesis, Caccini, Sessa and motets.
  Secular composers Aleotti/Aleotta, Casulana, Massarenghi and madrigals.

Week 4 Seventeenth Century (Chapter 3)
  Sacred music in Italy: Isabella Leonarda, Trissini, Cozzolani, Peruchona,
      Nascinbeni, Badalla, Meda.
  The German lands: von Raschenau, Grazianini, de Rossi, and Grimani.
  Motets, sacred dialogues, oratorios.

Week 5
  Secular music in Italy: F. Caccini, Strozzi, Bembo, S. Caccini, Campana,

France: Jacquet de la Guerre.

Madrigals; the rise of opera; cantatas.

Instrumental music: Suites and sonatas.

Week 6 Eighteenth Century (Chapter 4)

An overview of the growth of public music, private and public music education for women, new styles and genres.

Professional performer/composers in Italy: Lombardini-Sirmen, Bon, and Agnesi.

Opera singer/composers in France: Brillon de Jouy, Bayon Louis, Candeille. Salons.

Week 7

Austria: Martines, Paradis, Auernhammer, and their supporters.

German lands: Schröter, La Mara, Lebrun, Danzi, Krumpholtz, L. Reichardt, J. Reichardt, von Arnim, Zumsteeg.

Poland; Szymanowska.

Week 8

English and American composers: Gambarini, Park, Dussek, Bulckley, Cianchettini, Guest, Pownall, Van Hagen.

Week 9 Nineteenth Century (Chapter 5)

Progress in technology and music, the growth of conservatories and education for women.

Activism for women's rights; the rise of the virtuoso performer: Hensel and Schumann.

Week 10

Other German women: Kinkel, Lang, Mayer, von Bronsart, Le Beau.

France: Farrenc, Holmès, Chaminade.

Week 11

Virtuoso performer/composers: Rogers, Jaëll, Menter, Carreño, Hopekirk, Wurm and Beach.

Songwriters: Liliʻuokalani, Jacobs-Bond; Hood, Freer.

Weeks 12–15 Twentieth century (Chapter 6)

Choose from among the composers and styles.

(Numbers below correspond to the sections of Chapter 6).

(12)   1. Last of the Premoderns—Mahler; 2. Romantic Nationalism—Price, Bonds; 4. Postromanticism—Clarke; 21. Neoromanticism, Neoimpressionism—Tower, Kolb, Van de Vate, Zwilich, Zaimont;

12. Ascetic Expressionism—Ustvolskaya; 25. Postpostmodernism—Gubaidulina

(13) 3. Postimpressionism—Boulanger: Lili and Nadia; 5. Neoclassicism—Tailleferre, Arrieu, Perry; 9. Postneoclassicism—Bacewicz, Ptaszynska; 14. Opera—Glanville-Hicks, Moore, Musgrave, Weir; 15. Song Cycle—Gideon, Fleisher, Larsen; 11. *Gebrauchmusik*—Archer, Diemer, Walker

(14) 6. Ragtime—Aufderheide, Shepherd, Neibergall; 7. Jazz—Williams, Akiyoshi, Bley 8. Ultramodernism—Seeger; 23. Integrating Traditional—Chen Ali-Zad; Boyd, Whitehead, Leòn; 19. Performance Art 1.—Monk, La Barbara Galás; 20. Performance Art 2.—Anderson, L., Moorman, Shiomi

(15) 10. Serialism and Postserialism—Lutyens, Jolas, Talma, Pentland, Dinescu, Tucker, Urreta; 13. Experimentalism—Dlugoszewski, Oliveros, Beyer, Benary, 16. Electroacoustic Music—Saariaho, Barron, Semegen, Terzian; 17. Computer Music—Spiegel, Anderson, R., Oram, Ore, Thome; 18. Sound Installation—Kubisch, Westerkamp, Phillips, Lockwood; 22. Free Atonality—Ran, Wagner; 24. Fragmentation—Hölszky, Neuwirth, Pagh-Paan, Saunders.

Glossary

a cappella. Unaccompanied choral music.

absolute music. Instrumental music with no extramusical connotations. *See* program music.

Accademia (Academy). In the seventeenth century, a society of scholars, musicians, and/or literary persons who met to explore their common interests. Such groups were quite widespread in Italy and later in France. In France the term **Académie** was used for various specialized groups.

affects. According to seventeenth- and eighteenth-century theorists and composers, the emotions or passions that music could excite and the specific musical means by which they could be aroused.

agréments. French ornament formulas indicated by special signs placed over a note.

aleatory. Music in which a significant element or elements are determined by chance operations (from the Latin "alea," or dice).

alto. The voice range below the soprano range.

antiphon. Short text set to monophonic music in a syllabic, neumatic or melismatic, style sung before and after a psalm.

appoggiatura. An ornamental dissonant note that falls on the beat and resolves by step on a weaker beat.

aria. An independent song or duet within an opera, oratorio, or other large work.

aria. An extended melodic piece, usually for accompanied solo voice, in an opera, oratorio, or cantata or sometimes as an independent piece. The **da capo aria** is a special type in which the music and text begin with a section (A), which then appears again after a contrasting section (B), forming an ABA pattern.

arpeggio. A broken chord.

articulation. The way in which tones are attacked and allowed to decay.

atonality. Music that contains no functional tonality or tonal center and that generally eschews tonal chords such as major and minor triads.

augmented sixth chord. A harmony containing the interval of an augmented sixth (ten half steps) above the lowest pitch; these chords often resolve to a dominant chord.

ballad opera. A genre of English-language opera that features spoken dialogue in alternation with songs, often to the tunes of traditional ballads. Popular in England, Ireland, and the American colonies in the eighteenth century.

ballet. Theatrical dance work or the music for such a work.

Baroque. The period of Western music history extending from approximately 1600 to 1750.

bass. The lowest range of the male human voice; the low part of a musical texture.

basso continuo (continuo). A part notated as a bass line with chord symbols that is played continuously under the melody.

bassoon. A double reed woodwind instrument with a bass range.

benefit concert. In the eighteenth and nineteenth centuries, a public concert where the proceeds went to the performer-organizer.

binary form. Consisting of two parts, each of which is usually repeated; the first section normally modulates to the dominant or relative major key, and the second section, back to the tonic.

boogie-woogie. A twelve-bar piano blues characterized by a heavy, syncopated ostinato in the left hand.

bop. A rhythmically and harmonically complex style of jazz whose revolutionary effect paralleled that of early atonality in classical music (also called bebop).

bravura. Characterized by display of a performer's technical abilities.

Buchla synthesizer. One of the earliest voltage-controlled synthesizers; a keyboardless studio system that enables control over the tone quality of the sounds generated; developed by Donald Buchla in 1966.

cadence. The ending notes or chords of a piece of music.

canonical hours (Divine Office). In the Roman Catholic Church the daily services celebrated eight times a day, distinct from the Mass.

canso (canzo). Type of troubadour song usually in AAB form.

cantata. In the early seventeenth century this term was one of many used for solo accompanied song. Later in the century it became more sectional in its structure, eventually alternating arias and recitatives. It was most often for a solo singer, although there could be more than one. The singer or singers were accompanied by continuo or by a larger group of instruments. Italian cantatas were usually secular; when a sacred subject was used, the language was Latin. The cantata spread from Italy to France and ultimately to Germany; there it was often written for soloists and choir with instruments.

canzonetta. A term sometimes used for light solo accompanied songs in early seventeenth-century Italian music. A strophic solo song.

castrato (pl. castrati). A male singer surgically altered in boyhood to keep his voice from changing. The practice dates from the sixteenth through the nineteenth centuries. They sang Catholic Church music and became the stars of Italian opera seria.

cello (violoncello). The bass instrument of the violin family. Also called **bassetto.**

cembalo. Usually harpsichord but sometimes used in reference to the piano in the eighteenth century.

chalumeau (pl. chalumeaux). A single-reed woodwind instrument that was a predecessor of the clarinet; also the lower register of the clarinet

chanson. French word for song; counterpart of German lied.

chansonnier. A medieval manuscript containing songs of *troubadours* and *trouvères*.

character piece. Short, lyrical composition for solo piano, often with programmatic connotations. Typical examples from the nineteenth century include nocturnes, impromptus, intermezzi, songs without words, and capriccios.

chorale, Lutheran. A song or hymn sung by the congregation in Lutheran churches from the seventeenth century onward. The term refers either to the tune or to the tune with its text. Lutheran chorales were sung in the vernacular language, German. They normally had several stanzas.

chromatic scale. The twelve pitches within an octave.

chromaticism. Using all or many notes of the chromatic scale. A middle ground between diatonicism and atonality, in which nonchord tones (e.g., sixths, sevenths, and ninths) and enharmonic relationships (e.g., D-sharp/E-flat) "color" the chords, obscuring their diatonic functions.

clausura. The strict enclosure of nuns within a convent with no contact with the outside world except to a limited degree by family members.

clavichord. A keyboard instrument in which strings are hit by a tangent when a key is depressed. The instrument has a soft sound but a fairly wide dynamic range.

combination tone. A pitch that emerges when two different pitches are sounded simultaneously and whose frequency is either the sum of, or the difference between, the frequencies of the two original pitches.

commedia. Comedy, especially a comic dramatic-musical work.

concenti. A term used for some sacred pieces.

concertato. Contrast of small number of singers (or instrumentalists) with full chorus or larger instrumental group. A term used for the style in the early seventeenth century in which vocal and instrumental performers were combined and contrasted.

concertmaster. The first violinist, responsible for leadership of an ensemble.

concerto. A group of performers. In the seventeenth century musical works for a combined group of voices and instruments. The term was especially used for sacred works. From the late seventeenth century to the present, a work for a soloist or group of soloists and orchestra, usually in several movements.

conservatory (Ospedale). An institution for teaching music; originally, a charitable institution in Venice that cared for orphaned or abandoned children and educated them in various skills. A school for training in music.

consonance. Intervals or chords that sound free of tension or instability. Opposite of dissonance.

continuo. *See* basso continuo.

contrapuntal. Having a texture in which the different instrumental or vocal lines move independently of one another.

cross-stringing. Technological innovation that improves the volume and tone quality of the grand piano by crossing the lower strings over the midrange strings.

da capo aria. An aria in which the first section is sung again (ABA) with additional improvised ornamentation.

damper pedal. The sustaining pedal on the piano; it causes the dampers to be lifted, allowing the strings to vibrate after the key is released.

developing variation. A formal principle first identified by Arnold Schoenberg in the music of Johannes Brahms and later employed by Schoenberg himself in which a small motivic or intervallic cell is altered in a myriad of ways over the course of a piece.

dialogue. A form of motet that often has two or more voices or groups of voices, with texts in question and answer form.

diminished seventh chord. Chord consisting of four notes spaced a minor third apart.

dissonance. Intervals or chords that sound tense or unstable. Opposite of consonance.

divertimento (pl. divertimenti). A secular work for chamber ensemble, sometimes light and informal in character.

dominant. The fifth scale degree; the chord or key built on that scale degree.

dominant seventh chord. The major triad built on the fifth scale degree with an added minor third above.

double-escapement action. Technological innovation introduced by Sébastien Erard in 1821 that allows a piano key to be struck again without raising it completely.

dynamics. Degrees of volume (loudness or softness).

dynamophone. One of the earliest electrical musical instruments; a kind of protosynthesizer invented by the American Thaddeus Cahill in 1902 (also called the telharmonium).

electroacoustic music. Music in which electronics generate, reproduce, or change the sound.

empfindsamer Stil. Delicate and highly ornamented expressive, almost proto-Romantic music that flourished in the late Baroque. Popular in north Germany in the mid-eighteenth century.

étude. A study or exercise.

Eucharist. Those portions of the Mass in which the bread and wine are offered. The Sanctus and Agnus Dei are the Ordinary sections of the Eucharist.

expressionism. A term borrowed from the visual arts to describe a music marked by emotional agitation and anxiety, in which the subconscious of the composer is laid bare in a kind of quasi-autobiographical catharsis.

extended techniques. Musical techniques that go beyond the traditional effects produced by an instrument, for example, bowing behind the bridge of a violin, isolating glottal stops with the voice, clicking the keys of a flute without blowing through the instrument, or striking the strings of a piano with a mallet.

falsetto. The male voice using a special type of voice production to sing above the normal male range. It may be used to extend the tenor range or to sing in the range of female voices.

fantaisie, fantasia. An imaginative, sometimes improvisatory piece displaying the ingenuity of a performer or composer.

figured bass. A system of figures (numerals) used to notate continuo chords.

finale. The final movement or section of a composition.

first species counterpoint. The most pure of the five species established by Johann Joseph Fux in the eighteenth century, in which two voices move in a homophonic counterpoint of whole notes, or *nota contra nota*.

fortepiano. One of the early forms of the piano.

Fluxus. The wry, post-Dada art movement that flourished in New York and Germany in the 1950's and '60s, and influences many contemporary artists.

frottola. A type of Italian secular song that preceded the madrigal, in three or four parts with the melody and text in the upper part.

galant style. Early Classical style characterized by light, homophonic (chordal) textures, periodic phrase structures, simple and clear harmonies, and restrained expression.

glass harmonica. An instrument invented by Benjamin Franklin, played by rubbing the rims of spinning glass bowls either with the fingers or by means of a mechanism attached to a keyboard.

golden mean. A mathematical ratio in which an unequal division of a line results in the ratio of the smaller section to the larger equaling the ratio of the larger to the whole; believed to have harmonious properties when used in architecture, design, and music (also called golden section).

graphic notation. Musical notation in which the traditional staff, clefs, bar lines, and notes may be partially or wholly abandoned in favor of pictorial signs and symbols.

harmony. The chordal or vertical structure of music.

harpsichord. A keyboard instrument in which the strings are plucked by plectra; it is capable of only limited gradations in dynamic level.

homophonic. A musical texture with one melody of primary importance accompanied by chords.

hymn. A simple religious song in several stanzas.

idiomatic. Particularly suited to a specific instrument or voice.

imitation. The playing or singing of a melodic figure in two or more parts in succession.

improvise. Perform music spontaneously without written music.

indeterminacy. Music in which a significant element or elements are left to the choice of the performer(s).

integral serialism. An extension of twelve-tone that applies the principle of an ordered row to other parameters such as instrumentation, duration, tempo, dynamics, and so on (also called total serialism).

les goûts reunis (the reunited tastes). A French term used by François Couperin for music in which both Italian and French styles were merged.

librettist. The author of the text, or libretto, of an opera or oratorio.

libretto. The written text of an opera or oratorio, set to music by the librettist.

lied (pl. lieder). Late-eighteenth- and nineteenth-century solo German art song accompanied by keyboard, guitar, or harp.

liturgy. The prescribed texts and formal arrangement services for public worship. In the Christian church particularly the Mass and the Divine Office, a series of services of prayer and praise scheduled throughout the day. **Liturgical music** is the music written for such services.

madrigal. The most important secular polyphonic vocal music of the Renaissance. In the seventeenth century the same term was used for some accompanied Italian solo songs and madrigals that use Italian devotional or religious texts called spiritual madrigals.

maestra (f.), maestro (m.). Teacher or director, literally, "master." The director of a musical establishment (as in a court or church) was called a *maestro di cappella; chormesterin* is German feminine.

Magnificat. The song of the Virgin Mary from Luke 1:42–55, whose text begins "Magnificat anima mea Dominum" (My soul doth magnify the Lord), used in the Vespers liturgy (an evening service of the Divine Office); may be sung with a simple chanted formula. In the Renaissance it was set polyphonically, and elaborate musical settings were made in the seventeenth and eighteenth centuries.

Mass. The most important service in the Roman Catholic Church, which celebrates the distribution of bread and wine by Christ to the disciples at the Last Supper. The liturgy consists of many sections. The parts that always have the same text is called the Ordinary of the Mass, and parts in which the text changes according to what is appropriate for the day, season, or occasion for which the Mass is celebrated is called the Proper. It became the custom in the Renaissance for composers to set the sections of the Ordinary beginning with the words Kyrie, Gloria, Credo, Sanctus, and Agnus Dei as a unified musical whole, and this practice has continued.

Matins. The first of the canonical hours.

mazurka. Dance piece in triple meter modeled on a Polish folk dance; a stress placed on beat two or three of the measure is a characteristic feature.

melisma. Many notes sung on a single syllable of text.

melismatic. A passage in which many notes are sung to a single syllable of text.

mélodie. French art song with piano accompaniment, typically for solo voice.

melody. A succession of musical notes played or sung in a particular rhythm; the horizontal element of music.

microtonality. Music in which the scale is divided into more than twelve pitches.

minimalism. A term adopted from the plastic arts to describe music of reduced melodic, rhythmic, and/or harmonic materials, whose form may be wholly static (as in one note sounded for an entire piece) or may consist of a regular pulse and short repeated patterns in the manner of some African and Indonesian traditional music.

minuet and trio. A pair of dances in triple meter, moderate tempo, and binary form that often serves as the third movement of a symphony, sonata, string quartet, or other multimovement work. (The minuet is usually repeated after the trio.)

Miserere. Psalm text sung in the days preceding Easter; multivoiced settings of it were composed from the Renaissance onward.

mixed chorus. A choral group in which both male and female voices sing together, normally arranged sopranos and altos, tenors and basses.

modal. A kind of tonality in which folk or ancient modes are used, as opposed to diatonic scales.

mode. An arrangement of tones in a scale.

modulation. Change of key within a piece.

monody. An early seventeenth-century Italian type of solo song with a recitative-like voice part accompanied by continuo with figured bass.

monophonic. A musical texture with a single melodic line.

motet. In church music of the Renaissance, a sacred polyphonic choral composition. Later often replaced by the **solo motet**, in which one solo singer (often a treble voice) was accompanied by a continuo part. Sometimes motets in this style used two, three, or four solo singers.

motif, motive. Melodic or rhythmic idea used as a basis for composition.

moto perpetuo. A piece of music in which a pattern of short-valued notes is repeated throughout (also called *perpetuum mobile*).

multiphonics. An extended technique in which a singer or instrumentalist who normally can produce only one pitch at a time produces multiple pitches simultaneously, either by emphasizing overtones or mechanical means.

musicology. The scholarly study of music.

musique concrète. An early electroacoustic music in which recorded acoustic sounds, rather than abstract pitches, are the primary material.

Muzak. Instrumental music (often reorchestrated popular tunes) that is piped into public buildings such as shopping malls, grocery stores, and factories in order to stimulate productivity and calm; invented by the American George Owen Squier in 1922 (from a combination of the words "music" and "Kodak").

neoclassicism. A musical movement that, in reaction to Romanticism and chromaticism, emphasizes a clarity, delicacy, and (relative) emotional detachment that its proponents identified primarily with the late Baroque and early Classical eras.

neoimpressionism. A term applied to a broad range of postwar music that exhibits any of the characteristics associated with impressionism, for example, a focus on timbre; tall, jazzlike chords; and "exotic" (read: non-Western) harmonies.

neoromanticism. A musical movement that seeks to recapture the lush orchestration; extended, yet functional, tonality; and evocative programs of the Romantic era.

neumes. Notational signs of the Middle Ages used for writing music.

nocturne. Genre of solo piano piece first used by John Field in 1812 and made famous by Frédéric Chopin. Often features a lyrical right-hand melody over widely spaced left-hand accompaniment patterns sustained by the damper pedal.

opera. A staged dramatic work that is sung throughout. The earliest operas were performed in Florence at the beginning of the seventeenth century.

opera buffa. Italian comic opera of the eighteenth and nineteenth centuries.

opéra-comique. French eighteenth- and nineteenth-century opera with spoken dialogue; plots may be either lighthearted or tragic.

opera seria. Eighteenth-century Italian opera consisting of recitatives, da capo arias, and other musical numbers. These works, based on plots from history or mythology, were primarily vehicles for solo singing.

oratorio. A dramatic musical work, usually unstaged. The form originated in Italy and was well developed by the mid-seventeenth century. The subject matter was religious, but the language was usually Italian. Oratorios served as a form of spiritual recreation, mediating on sacred stories during times like Lent when the opera houses were closed.

organ. A keyboard instrument operated by the player's hands and feet consisting of a series of pipes of different pitches through which air is passed.

Ospedale. *See* conservatory.

ostinato. A short and repeating pattern of notes.

parallel major, parallel minor. Major and minor keys having the same tonic or keynote.

parallelism. A technique in which harmonic interval relationships between notes are kept the same in relation to the melodic line. Also called "planing."

partbooks. Books containing music for an individual voice (e.g., soprano, alto, tenor, bass).

pentatonic. A mode that consists of five notes to the octave (representing scale degrees 1, 2, 4, 5, and 6); often used for coloristic effect due to its association with the Orient, although it also appears in the folk traditions of the United States and the British Isles.

piano quartet. Composition for piano and three string instruments, typically violin, viola, and cello.

piano trio. Composition for piano, violin, and cello.

pièce. The French term for a short movement or piece, often grouped together to form a suite.

plainchant (plainsong, Gregorian chant). Unaccompanied monophonic music without fixed rhythm or meter used in the services of the Catholic Church.

planing. *See* parallelism.

pleasure gardens. English venues for music and other entertainments during the summer months, either outdoors or in rotundas. The most prominent were Vauxhall Gardens, Ranelagh Gardens, Marylebone Gardens, and Sadler's Wells.

polyphonic. A musical texture with two or more melodic lines played or sung simultaneously.

polyphony. Music that combines more than one musical line into a whole.

portamento. In vocal and string music, the sliding from one pitch to another through all the intervening pitches.

postimpressionism. Term sometimes used to describe late impressionist works in which a more robust and even violent emotional palette is introduced and in which the harmonies are more adventurous.

prepared piano. A piano, with various objects (e.g., combs, bolts, pieces of rubber) placed between or on the strings, to alter the tone quality and pitch of certain notes (originated by John Cage).

prime row. A unique and fixed sequence, in original transposition, of the twelve semi-tones that constitute the primary tonal material in a twelve-tone or serial work (also called set or series).

program music. Music that depicts extramusical images or ideas through imitation of sounds, quotation of familiar tunes or musical styles, or literary allusion. *See* absolute music.

Psalm. One of the poems found in the biblical Book of Psalms, often sung in religious services.

raga. Used in Indian classical music. The Western equivalent might fall somewhere between a scale, a melody, and a twelve-tone row; there are hundreds of ragas, and each has a unique history, affect, and method of unfolding.

razo. A commentary in which troubadours are mentioned.

realize. To play a figured bass (continuo) part.

recitative. A style of text setting used in operas, oratorios, and other vocal works in which the single line of the singer reflects the rhythms and inflections of speech accompanied by a bass line and chords (continuo); invented in early-seventeenth-century Italy. In the latter seventeenth century **secco recitative** (dry recitative) was sparsely accompanied by chords and presented the text rapidly and clearly. In French music a special style, **récitatif**, used the carefully notated rhythm of the text.

relative major, relative minor. Major and minor keys having the same key signature; the relative minor keynote is a minor third below its relative major keynote.

responsory. A type of chant sung mostly at Matins.

retrograde. A particular kind of operation performed on a row in serialist music, in which the intervals of the row appear in reverse order.

rhythm. Having to do with the time aspect of music; the duration of notes.

ritornello form. The typical form of the first movement (and sometimes the final movement) of a Baroque concerto, in which versions of a refrain played by the orchestra alternate with other material played by the soloist(s).

rococo. Elegantly ornamented, decorative.

romance. A lyrical strophic song, often a love song.

rondo form. Sectional form in which a recurring refrain in the tonic alternates with subsidiary sections. In the Classical period, it was often used for the final movement of a multimovement instrumental work.

rounded binary form. Two-part form in which material from the first section returns to close out the second section; often both sections are marked to be repeated.

second Viennese school. The triumvirate of early-twentieth-century atonalist-serialists, consisting of Arnold Schoenberg and his two most famous students, Alban Berg and Anton von Webern.

secondary dominant. Dominants (major chord built a fifth above) of any degree of the scale other than the tonic; often used to accomplish modulations.

sequence. In the Middle Ages long poems in free style usually in A,BB,CC,DD...form; the first and last lines are not repeated; the music is parallel to the text. Later, a restatement of a melodic figure or phrase at different pitch levels within a single voice of the texture. Later, a motive or phrase repeated at a different pitch.

serenade. A work in several movements for instrumental ensemble, often written for specific occasions.

serialism. A method of composition in which the structure of a particular parameter or parameters is determined by an ordered series of instances of that parameter; may be either twelve-tone or integral serialism.

sine tone. The simplest of the four electronically generated waveforms (the others being sawtooth, square, and triangle); because it consists of only one frequency and has no harmonics, it can be produced only artificially.

sinfonia. An instrumental piece often in one or more movements that precede an act of an opera or oratorio. Instrumental overture or prelude to a large work.

singspiel (pl. singspiele). Eighteenth- or early-nineteenth-century German opera with spoken dialogue.

sonata. A work in several movements for keyboard or other instrument(s). In the seventeenth century commonly a work in several movements for one or more solo instruments and continuo. The term always implies instrumental music as opposed to vocal.

sonata da camera. Baroque chamber sonata for one or more treble instruments with basso continuo; the sonata da camera usually consisted of a series of dance movements.

sonorism. A musical aesthetic that emphasizes the acoustic properties of sounds—their tone color or timbre—as the guiding formál principle.

soprano. The highest range of the human voice, normally a woman's highest voice range or the range of a boy's voice.

spinning out. The construction of an extended melodic line by elaborating upon a brief figure; the technique was typical of Baroque rather than Classical compositions.

sprechtstimme. A vocal technique common in atonal works in which the declamation of the text is somewhere between speech and pitched song (from the German "speaking part").

staccato. Detached.

sticheron. In the Byzantine Church music sung between verses of the Psalms.

string quartet. An ensemble consisting of two violins, viola, and cello; also a composition for this ensemble.

strophic. Consisting of two or more verses of text sung to the same music.

Sturm und Drang. "Storm and Stress." A compositional approach of the 1760s–1770s characterized by strong, turbulent emotion and frequent use of minor keys.

syllabic. One note sung to one syllable.

symphonic poem. Single-movement orchestral work whose form is determined by programmatic content rather than traditional formal structures.

tala. The rhythmic parameter of Indian classical music, which often consists of intricate and extended polyrhythmic patterns.

Te Deum. A long liturgical text beginning with the words Te Deum (Thee, oh God, we praise). It is often set to music for occasions of thanksgiving and celebration.

tenso. A dialogue or debate (song) in which lovers disagree or argue, often written by two troubadours.

ternary form. Three-part form.

text-painting (word-painting). Melodic, harmonic, or rhythmic patterns that graphically depict the words of the text being sung, for example, descending lines to refer to "falling" or a rising line to set a word like "heaven."

texture. The combination of individual vocal or instrumental voices within a composition.

theorbo. A large bass lute especially suitable for continuo playing.

theremin. One of the first electronic instruments, in which the movement of the performer's hand next to one of two sine oscillators produces an audible combination tone; invented by the Russian Leon Termenin (Thérémin) in 1919 and still in use.

through-composed. A song in which new music is provided for each verse, as opposed to a strophic song.

toccata. A virtuosic piece for keyboard employing full chords and running passages.

tone cluster. A group of dissonant notes (usually semitones) sounded together; first utilized in American experimentalist music of the early twentieth century.

tonic. Home pitch or key.

tragédie-lyrique. Serious French opera of the seventeenth and eighteenth centuries, usually based on mythological or historical topics.

transpose, transposition. To move a passage or piece of music to another key.

treble. The high part of a musical texture, either played by an instrument or sung.

trio texture. A characteristic texture of Baroque music featuring two treble instruments or voices plus basso continuo.

trio-sonata. The most important type of Baroque chamber music, usually in four movements, scored for two melodic instruments (usually treble) and continuo.

trombone. A brass instrument in tenor-bass range that produces its pitches by sliding a section of tubing in and out to raise or lower the basic pitch. It is capable of playing all the notes of the chromatic scale.

twelve-tone. The first historical form of serialism, in which the twelve semitones of the Western octave are arranged in a specific order that is not to be changed, though it may be reversed and/or inverted (also called twelve-note or dodecaphony).

ultramodernism. A term used by its practitioners and contemporaries to describe much early American experimental music and to emphasize its distance from neoclassicism.

una corda pedal. Causes the hammers to strike only one or two strings for each pitch on the piano, producing a softer sound.

Vespers. The evening service of the Divine Office for which special musical settings were often composed.

vida. A biography.

viola da gamba (viol). A bowed stringed instrument with frets tied around the neck marking the half steps. It normally has six strings and is made in several sizes, each with a different range. Whether large or small, viols are held between the legs to play. They were in widespread use from the sixteenth through the eighteenth century. The bass viola da gamba has the same range as the cello and is used today by early music groups for continuo playing.

violone. The double bass member of the viol family.

virtuoso (f. virtuosa) (pl. virtuosi, f. virtuose). A performer with great technical skill on his or her instrument or voice.

vocoder. An electronic device for analyzing and resynthesizing sounds, developed in 1936 by the American Homer Dudley of Bell Labs and first used by musicians in the 1960s (from the words "voice" and "coder").

wave form oscillator. A machine that generates sound waves via the oscillation of electronic circuits.

word-painting. *See* "text-painting."

General Bibliography

Ammer, Christine. *Unsung: A History of Women in American Music.* Contributions in Women's Studies 14. Westport, CT, and London: Greenwood Press, 1980.

———. *Unsung, a History of Women in American Music.* Portland, OR: Amadeus Press 2001.

Anderson, Bonnie S., and Judith P. Zinsser. *A History of Their Own, Women in Europe.* 2 vols. New York: Harper and Row, 1988.

Armstrong, William. "New Gems in the Old Classics." *Étude* 22, no. 2 (1904): 51–52

Austern, Linda Phyllis. "Music and the English Renaissance." In *Cecilia Reclaimed: Feminist Perspectives on Gender and Music*, edited by Susan C. Cook and Judy S. Tsou. Urbana and Chicago: University of Illinois Press, 1994.

Baldauf-Berdes, Jane L. *Women Musicians of Venice: Musical Foundations 1525–1855.* Rev. ed. Oxford: Clarendon Press, 1993.

Barkin, Elaine. "[Questionnaire.]" *Perspectives of New Music* 19 (1981): 460–462.

———, ed. "In Response." *Perspectives of New Music* 20 (1981/1982): 288–329.

Barzun, Jacques. *From Dawn to Decadence, 500 Years of Western Cultural Life.* New York: Perennial, an imprint of HarperCollins, 2001.

Beyond Their Sex: Learned Women of the European Past. Edited by Patricia H. Labalme. New York and London: New York University Press, 1980.

Bible, The. Revised Standard Version. Camden, NJ: Thomas Nelson and Sons, 1952.

Block, Adrienne Fried, and Carol Neuls-Bates. *Women in American Music: A Bibliography of Music and Literature.* Westport, CT: Greenwood Press, 1979.

Boenke, Heidi M. *Flute Music by Women Composers: An Annotated Catalog.* New York: Greenwood Press, 1988.

Bomberger, E. Douglas. "A. B. Marx on Composition Training for Women." *Journal of Musicological Research* 17 (1998): 211–26.

Bowers, Jane. "The Emergence of Women Composers in Italy, 1566–1700." In *Women Making Music: The Western Art Tradition 1150–1950*, edited by Jane Bowers and Judith Tick. Urbana and Chicago: University of Illinois Press, 1986.

Bowers, Jane, and Judith Tick, eds. *Women Making Music: The Western Art Tradition, 1150–1950.* Urbana and Chicago: University of Illinois Press, 1986.

Briscoe, James R., ed. *Historical Anthology of Music by Women.* Bloomington and Indianapolis: Indiana University Press, 1987.

———, comp. *Contemporary Anthology of Music by Women.* [Includes 3 compact discs.] Bloomington: Indiana University Press, 1999.

Brower, Edith. "Is the Musical Idea Masculine?" *Atlantic Monthly* 73 (March 1894): 332–39.

Burney, Charles. *The Present State of Music in Germany, the Netherlands, and the United Provinces.* 2d ed. 2 vols. London: T. Becket, 1775.

Bury, John B. *A History of the Eastern Roman Empire.* London: Macmillan, 1912.

Citron, Marcia J. *Gender and the Musical Canon.* Cambridge: Cambridge University Press, 1994.

————. *Gender & the Musical Canon.* Chicago: University of Illinois Press, 2000.

————. "Women and the Lied 1775–1850." In *Women Making Music*: The Western Art Tradition, 1150–1950 edited by Jane Bowers and Judith Tick. Urbana and Chicago: University of Illinois Press, 1986.

Clarke, Helen J. "The Nature of Music and Its Relation to the Question of Women in Music." *Music* 7 (March 1895): 459–61.

Cohen, Aaron I. *International Encyclopedia of Women Composers.* 2d ed. New York and London: Books and Music (USA), 1987.

Cook, Susan C., and Judith S. Tsou. *Cecilia Reclaimed: Feminist Perspectives on Gender and Music.* Urbana: University of Illinois Press, 1994.

Cusick, Suzanne G. "Eve…Blowing in Our Ears?…Toward a History of Music Scholarship on Women in the Twentieth Century." *Women & Music* 5 (2001): 125–39.

Downs, Philip G. *Classical Music: The Era of Haydn, Mozart, and Beethoven.* New York: W. W. Norton, 1992.

Drinker, Sophie. *Music and Women, the Story of Women in Their Relation to Music.* 1948. Reprint New York: Feminist Press at the City University of New York, 1995.

Ebel, Otto. *Women Composers: A Biographical Handbook of Woman's Work in Music.* Brooklyn, NY: Chandler-Ebel Music, 1902.

Edwards, J. Michelle. "Women in Music to ca. 1450." In *Women in Music: A History*, 2d ed., edited by Karin Pendle. Bloomington and Indianapolis: Indiana University Press, 2001.

Einstein, Alfred. *The Italian Madrigal.* Translated by Alexander H. Krappe, Roger Sessions, and Oliver Strunk. Princeton, NJ: Princeton University Press, 1949.

Elson, Arthur. *Women's Work in Music.* 1903. Reprint Portland, ME: Longwood Press, 1974.

Elson, Louis C[harles]. *The History of American Music.* New York: Macmillan, 1904.

Elson, Louis Charles. *Woman in Music.* New York, 1918; reprint New York: Gordon Press, 1976.

Erickson, Mary. *Women and Music: A Selective Bibliography on Women and Gender Issues in Music, 1987–1992.* New York: G. K. Hall, 1995.

Fétis, François-Joseph. *Biographie universelle des musiciens et bibliographie générale de la musique.* Rev. ed. 8 vols. Paris: Firmin-Didot et Cie, 1881–1884.

————. *Biographie universelle des musiciens et bibliographie générale de la musique.* 2d ed. 8 vols. Paris, Firmin-Didot of Cie, 1873–1878. Supplément et complément. Ed. Arthur Pougin. 2 vols., 1878–1880. Reprint Brussels: Culture et Civilisation, 1963.

Frank, Paul, and Wilhelm Altmann. *Kurzgefasstes Tonkünstler-Lexikon.* 14th ed. Regensburg: Gustav Bosse, 1936.

Friedan, Betty. *Life So Far, a Memoir.* New York: Simon and Schuster, 2000.

Fuller, Sophie. *The Pandora Guide to Women Composers, Britain and the United States 1629–Present.* London: Pandora, an Imprint of HarperCollins, 1994.

Gann, Kyle. *American Music in the 20th Century.* New York: Schirmer Books, 1997.

Gies, Frances, and Joseph. *Women in the Middle Ages.* New York: Thomas Y. Crowell.

Gill, Katherine. "Open Monasteries for Women in Late Medieval and Early Modern Italy: Two Roman Examples." In *The Crannied Wall: Women, Religion, and the Arts in Early Modern Europe*, edited by Craig A. Monson. Ann Arbor: University of Michigan Press, 1992.

Gillett, Paula. "Encroaching on All Man's Privileges." In *Musical Women in England, 1870–1914.* New York: St. Martin's Press, 2000.

Glickman, Sylvia. "Women's Performance in Music Competitions, 1967–1988." In *The Musical Woman*, vol. 3. New York and Westport, CT: Greenwood Press, 1991.

Glickman, Sylvia, and Martha Furman Schleifer. *Women Composers: Music Through the Ages*. Vols. 1–7. Michigan: Gale Group, G. K. Hall Reference Imprint, 1996–2003.

Gorrell, Lorraine. *The Nineteenth-Century German Lied*. Portland, OR: Amadeus, 1993.

Green, Lucy. *Music, Gender, Education*. New York: Cambridge University Press, 1997.

Grun, Bernard. *The Timetables of History*. 3d, rev. ed. New York: Simon and Schuster, 1991.

Halstead, Jill. *The Woman Composer: Creativity and the Gendered Politics of Musical Composition*. Aldershot, England: Ashgate Publishing Ltd., 1997.

Hayes, Deborah. "Some Neglected Women Composers of the Eighteenth Century and Their Music." *Current Musicology* 39 (1985): 42–65.

Heinrich, Adel. *Organ and Harpsichord Music by Women Composers: An Annotated Catalogue*. Music Reference Collection 30. Westport, CT: Greenwood Press, 1991.

Higgins, Paula. "The 'Other Minervas': Creative Women at the Court of Margaret of Scotland." In *Rediscovering the Muses: Women's Musical Traditions*, edited by Kimberly Marshall. Boston: Northeastern University Press, 1993.

———. "Parisian Nobles, a Scottish Princess, and The Woman's Voice in Late Medieval Song," *Early Music History* 10 (1991): 169.

Hitchcock, H. Wiley. *Music in the United States: A Historical Introduction*. 3d ed. Englewood Cliffs, NJ: Prentice-Hall, 2000.

Hixon, Don I., and Don A. Hennessee. *Women in Music*. 2d ed. Metuchen, NJ: Scarecrow Press, 1993.

Howard, John Tasker. *Our American Music: Three Hundred Years of It*. New York: Thomas (Crowell, 1931)

Hughes, Rupert. "Women Composers." *The Century Magazine* 40 (1898): 768–79.

———. "The Women Composers." In *Contemporary American Composers*. Boston: Page, 1900, pp. 432–41.

Jackson, Barbara Garvey. "Musical Women of the Seventeenth and Eighteenth Centuries." In *Women & Music: A History*, 2d ed, edited by Karin Pendle. Bloomington: Indiana University Press, 2001.

———. *"Say Can You Deny Me": A Guide to Surviving Music by Women from the 16th through the 18th Centuries*. Fayetteville: University of Arkansas Press. 1994.

Jezic, Diane Peacock. *Women Composers, the Lost Tradition Found*. New York: The Feminist Press, 1988.

Jezic, Diane Peacock, and Daniel Binder. "A Survey of College Music Textbooks: Benign Neglect of Women Composers?" In *The Musical Woman*, vol. 2. New York and Westport, CT: Greenwood Press, 1987.

Johnson, Rose-Marie. *Violin Music by Women Composers: A Bio-Bibliographical Guide*. New York: Greenwood Press, 1989.

Kelly, Joan. *Women, History & Theory: The Essays of Joan Kelly*. Chicago and London: University of Chicago Press, 1984.

Kelso, Ruth. *Doctrine for the Lady of the Renaissance*. Urbana: University of Illinois Press, 1956.

Kolb, Barbara. "A Matter of Art Not Sex." *The New York Times Magazine*, 10 November 1975.

LaBelle, Brandon. "The Sound of Music: Contemporary Sound-Art and the Phenomenal World." *Art Papers* 23, no. 2 (1999): 36–39.

Ledebuhr, Carl. *Tonkünstler-Lexicon Berlins von den ältesten Zeiten bis auf die Gegenwart*. Berlin, 1861; reprint Tutzing: Schneider, 1965.

Leppert, Richard. *Music and Image: Domesticity, Ideology, and Socio-cultural Formation in Eighteenth-Century England*. Cambridge: Cambridge University Press, 1988.

Lewis, Bernard. *What Went Wrong?* New York: Oxford University Press, 2002.

Loesser, Arthur. *Men, Women, and Pianos: A Social History*. New York: Simon and Schuster, 1954.

Macy, Laura W. "Women's History and Early Music." In *Companion to Medieval and Renaissance*

Music, edited by Tess Knighton and David Fallows. Berkeley and Los Angeles: University of California Press, 1997.

Marshall, Kimberly, ed. *Rediscovering the Muses: Women's Musical Traditions. Boston:* Northeastern University Press, 1993.

Matter, Ann, and John Coakley, eds. *Creative Women in Medieval and Early Modern Italy: A Religious and Artistic Renaissance.* Philadelphia: University of Pennsylvania Press, 1994.

McClary, Susan. *Feminine Endings: Music, Gender, and Sexuality.* Minneapolis: University of Minnesota Press, 1991.

————. "Narrative Agendas in 'Absolute' Music: Identity and Difference in Brahms's Third Symphony." In *Musicology and Difference*, edited by Ruth A. Solie. Berkeley: University of California Press, 1993.

McDonnell, Ernest W. *The Beguines and Beghards in Medieval Culture.* New Brunswick, NJ: Rutgers University Press, 1954.

Meggett, Joan M. *Keyboard Music by Women Composers: A Catalog and Bibliography.* Westport, CT: Greenwood Press, 1981.

Michaelis, A[lfred]. *Frauenals Schaffen de Tonkünstlersein biographisches* Lexicon-Leipzige A Michaelis, 1888.

Midgette, Anne. "Closing the Gender Gap without Much Conviction." *The New York Times*, 26 February 2002, sec. E1.

Miles, Rosalind. *Who Cooked the Last Supper? The Women's History of the World.* New York: Three Rivers Press, 2001.

Monson, Craig. *Disembodied Voices: Music and Culture in an Early Modern Italian Convent.* Berkeley, Los Angeles, and London: University of California Press, 1995.

————, ed. *The Crannied Wall: Women, Religion, and the Arts in Early Modern Europe.* Ann Arbor: University of Michigan Press, 1992.

Die Musik in Geschichte und Gegenwart. Personenteil. 2d ed. 12 vols. Edited by Ludwig Finscher. Kassel: Bärenreiter, 1999– .

Neuls-Bates, Carol, ed. *Women in Music: An Anthology of Source Readings from the Middle Ages to the Present.* New York: Harper and Row, 1982.

————. *Women in Music.* Rev. ed. Boston: Northeastern University Press, 1996.

Newcomb, Anthony. *The Madrigal at Ferrara, 1579–1597.* Princeton, NJ: Princeton University Press, 1980.

Newman, William S. *The Sonata in the Baroque Era.* 3d ed. New York: W. W. Norton, 1972.

————. *The Sonata in the Classic Era.* 3d ed. New York: W. W. Norton, 1983.

Nochlin, Linda. *Women, Art, and Power and Other Essays.* New York: Harper and Row, 1988.

Olsen, Tillie. *Silences.* New York: Delacorte Press, 1979.

Osborne, William. "Art is Just an Excuse." In *Journal of the International Alliance of Women in Music*, October 1996.

Partnow, Elaine T. *The Quotable Woman, the First 5,000 Years.* New York: Checkmark Books, 2001.

Peeples, Georgia, and Jennifer Holz. "Where Are We Now? The Inclusion of Women, 1750–1900 in Music History Textbooks." *Journal of the International Alliance for Women in Music* 7, no. 3 (2001). 33–35.

Pendle, Karin, ed. *Women and Music: A History.* Bloomington and Indianapolis: Indiana University Press, 1991; 2d ed., 2001.

Raff, Helene. *Joachim Raff, eín Lebenshild.* Reqenburg: Bosse, 1925.

Rediscovering the Muses: Women's Musical Traditions. Edited by Kimberly Marshall. Boston: Northeastern University Press, 1993.

Reich, Nancy. *Clara Schumann, the Artist and the Woman.* Ithaca, NY: Cornell University Press, 1985; Rev. ed. 2001.

————. "Women as Musicians: A Question of Class." In *Musicology and Difference: Gender and Sexuality in Music Scholarship*, edited by Ruth Solie. Berkeley: University of California Press, 1993.

Roche, Jerome. *Northern Italian Church Music in the Age of Monteverdi*. Oxford: Clarendon Press, 1984.

Sadie, Julie Anne, and Rhian Samuel, eds. *The New Grove Dictionary of Women Composers*. London: Macmillan Press Limited, 1994.

————. *The Norton/Grove Dictionary of Women Composers*. New York and London: W. W. Norton, 1995.

Sadie, Stanley, ed. *New Grove Dictionary of Music and Musicians*. 2d ed. New York: Grove's Dictionaries, 2001.

Schoenberg, Harold C. *The Great Pianists from Mozart to the Present*. Rev. ed. New York: Simon and Schuster, 1987.

Skronowski, JoAnn. *Women in American Music: A Bibliography*. Metuchen, NJ: Scarecrow Press, 1978.

Slonimsky, Nicolas. *Baker's Biographical Dictionary of Musicians*, 7th edition. New York and London; Schirmer Books, 1984.

Sperber, Roswitha, ed. *Women Composers in Germany*. Translated by Timothy Nevill. Bonn: Inter Nationes, 1996.

Stewart-Green, Miriam. *Women Composers: A Checklist of Works for the Solo Voice*. Boston: G. K. Hall, 1980.

Sutro, Florence. *Women in Music and Law*. New York: Authors' Publishing Company, 1895.

Tick, Judith. *American Women Composers before 1870*. Ann Arbor: UMI Research Press, 1983.

Timbrell, Charles. *French Pianism: A Historical Perspective*. 2d ed. Portland, OR: Amadeus, 1999.

Upton, George. *Women in Music*. Boston: Osgood, 1880.

Vester, Frans. *Flute Music of the 18th Century: An Annotated Bibliography*. Monteux, France: Musica Rara, 1985.

Weissweiler, Eva. *Komponistinnen aus 500 Jahren: Eine Kultur-und Wirkungsgeschichte in Biographien und Werkbeispielen*. Frankfurt: Fischer, 1981.

Wilhartitz, Adolph. *Some Facts about Women in Music*. Los Angeles: Press of Out West, 1902.

Zaimont, Judith Lang, ed. *Contemporary Concert Music by Women: A Directory of the Composers and Their Works*. Westport, CT: Greenwood Press, 1981.

————. *The Musical Woman: An International Perspective*. 3 vols. New York: Greenwood Press, 1984–1991.

Zaslaw, Neal, ed. *The Classical Era: From the 1740s to the End of the 18th Century*. Englewood Cliffs, NJ: Prentice-Hall, 1989.

Selected On-line Resources

http://music.acu.edu/www/iawm/. Web site of the International Alliance for Women in Music. Includes articles, discographies, audio and image files, syllabi, and other educational resources; notices of upcoming conferences and other special events; and many related links. Last updated September 27, 2001.

http://eamusic.dartmouth.edu/;wowem/. Web site of Women on the Web/ElectronMedia. Intended primarily for young women interested in the media arts. Includes histories of electroacoustic music and multimedia digital arts; essays on the contributions of women to the digital arts; information on hardware, software, and the World Wide Web; professional advice to aspiring artists from professionals in the field; links to schools, professional organizations, and publishers; and teacher resources. Last updated February 25, 2001.

www.womensphil.org. Web site of the Women's Philharmonic, an orchestra formed in 1981 that is composed entirely of women and conducted by women and that performs music by women (very often living composers). Web site contains a history of the Philharmonic, profiles of some of its members, and notices of special events, programs, competitions, and initiatives N.d.

www.ibiblio.org/nywc. Web site of New York Women Composers, Inc., a member-controlled organization dedicated to promoting the music of living women composers of the greater New York area. Includes a catalog cross-referenced by genre, composer, and publisher; short biographies of the composers; and links to many home pages and E-mail addresses. Last updated February 20, 2000.

Index

About the Editors and Contributors

Sylvia Glickman was among the first group awarded a Solo Recitalist Grant from the National Endowment for the Arts in 1981. She was honored by Women's Way of Philadelphia in May 1986 for her "exceptional talent as a musician and teacher and for her unique contributions to women's music history" and received the New York Women Composers annual award in 1995 for "Distinguished Service in support of concert music composed by women." She has performed to critical acclaim throughout the United States and in Europe, Israel, and Africa. She recorded the *Four Piano Sonatas of Alexander Reinagle*, the first keyboard sonatas written in America (1982) and was the pianist on the first American recording of Bartók's *Piano Quintet* (1904) with the Alard String Quartet (1982). A teacher and researcher, Glickman has held positions at the New England Conservatory of Music, at the Rubin Academy of Music in Jerusalem, Israel, at Haverford College, and at Franklin and Marshall College. She was, for nineteen years, director of chamber music activities and pianist-in-residence at Haverford.

Glickman founded the Hildegard Publishing Company, a press devoted to furthering the music of women composers, past and present, in 1988. She is the president of the Hildegard Institute, devoted to research and performance of this music, and serves as artistic director of the Hildegard Chamber Players, a group devoted to playing this repertoire. Her publications include *Amy Beach: Virtuoso Piano Music* (1982) and *Anthology of American Piano Music from 1865–1909* (in *Three Centuries of American Music*, vol. 4, 1990). Currently coeditor of *Women Composers: Music Through the Ages* (1996–2002), she has also contributed articles to *The New Grove Dictionary of Women Composers* (1995) and *Grove's Dictionary of Music and Musicians* (2001). A reviewer for *Choice: Books for College Libraries*, she edited the keyboard section of the annual *Books for College Libraries* in 1987. She has served on the Music Panel of the Pennsylvania Council on the Arts (1989–1991) and on the board and as editor of the *Journal* of the International Alliance for Women in Music (1995–1996) and was elected to the Board of Directors of the Musical Fund Society of Philadelphia in 1998.

Three commissioned works include *The Walls Are Quiet Now* for chamber orchestra, *Am I a Murderer?* for basso and eight instruments, and *Carved in Courage* for orchestra. Albany Records recently released a CD of these works entitled *The Walls Are Quiet Now—A Holocaust Remembrance.*

Martha Furman Schleifer is a member of the music history faculty at Temple University and is senior editor of Hildegard Publishing Company. She coedited *Three Centuries of American Music* (1986–1992), a twelve-volume anthology of music by American composers. She is a series editor for *Composers of North America* and was the author of *William Wallace Gilchrist (1846–1916)*, the first book in the series. She is coeditor of *Latin American Classical Composers: A Biographical Dictionary* (1996 2nd edition 2002), author of *American Opera and Music for the Stage: Eighteenth and Nineteenth Centuries* and *American Opera and Music for the Stage: Early Twentieth Century* (vol. 5 and 6 of *Three Centuries of American Music*), and coauthor of the Cumulative Index for *Three Centuries of American Music* (included in vol. 12). She is currently coeditor of *Women Composers: Music Through the Ages* (1996–2002). Author of numerous articles and papers on music and musicians in Philadelphia, she has also made contributions to *The New Grove Dictionary of Women Composers* (1995), the *New Grove Dictionary of American Music* (1986), and the 2001 edition of *Grove's Dictionary of Music and Musicians*. She was the review editor for the *Journal of the International Alliance for Women in Music* in 1995–1998.

Contributors

E. Douglas Bomberger is Professor of music at the University of Hawaii at Manoa, where he teaches courses in music history and serves as chair of musicology. He is the editor of *Brainard's Biographies of American Musicians* (Greenwood Press, 1999) and author of *A Tidal Wave of Encouragement: American Composers' Concerts in the Gilded Age* (Praeger, 2002). His articles have appeared in numerous books and periodicals, including *Opera in Context: Essays on Historical Staging* (1998), *Piano Roles: 300 Years with the Piano* (1999), and *Women Composers: Music through the Ages*, vol. 6 (1999).

Valerie Woodring Goertzen is Adjunct Professor and coordinator of graduate studies in the School of Music at the University of Southern Mississippi. She has studied the piano transcriptions of Johannes Brahms and is currently editing a volume of these works for the Johannes Brahms Gesamtausgabe. She has written and lectured on a variety of topics relating to issues of performance, practice and musical life in eighteenth- and nineteenth-century Europe and the United States. Among her publications are "By Way of Introduction: Preluding by 18th- and Early 19th-Century Pianists" in *The Journal of Musicology* (Summer 1996) and "Setting the Stage: Clara Schumann's Preludes" in the *Course of Performance: Studies in the World of Musical Improvisation*, edited by Bruno Nettl. She has edited keyboard works of Clara Schumann for vol. 6 of *Women Composers: Music through the Ages* and prepared *Clara Schumann: Exer-*

cises, Preludes, and Fugues (2001). She has taught at Wesleyan University, the University of North Carolina at Greensboro, and Kenyon College.

Barbara Garvey Jackson is Professor Emerita from the University of Arkansas at Fayetteville. She is founder, publisher, and editor of ClarNan Editions, a desktop publishing company specializing in historic music by women, which has over forty volumes in print. She has taught music in the Los Angeles public schools, at Arkansas Technological University in Russellville, and at the University of Arkansas for thirty-two years. Her research on women composers includes journal articles on Florence Price and Camilla de Rossi, entries for anthologies of music by women, the chapter on seventeenth- and eighteenth-century women in music for *Women in Music: A History*, and entries on women composers in *The New Grove Dictionary of American Music, Notable American Women, New Grove Dictionary of Women Composers*, and the second edition of *The New Grove Dictionary of Music and Musicians*. She coauthored a music theory text, two books on the minnesingers, and a string-bowing dictionary and has edited Baroque violin music. Her major reference work is *"Say Can You Deny Me": A Guide to Surviving Music by Women from the 16th through the 18th Centuries* (1994).

Adeline Mueller earned a master's degree in twentieth-century music analysis and aesthetics from the University of Sussex in Brighton, England. Her thesis was a multimedia analysis of the composer Mauricio Kagel's experimental film "Antithese." Her paper analyzing remixes of the Björk song "Hyperballad" was presented at the Conference on Popular Music and American Culture at the University of Texas, Austin. A version of that paper is in preparation for a book of essays on Björk. Ms. Mueller lives in Los Angeles.